EGYPT ESSAYS ON ANCIENT KEMET

FREDERICK MONDERSON

SUMON PUBLISHERS

EGYPT ESSAYS ON ANCIENT KEMET

SuMon Publishers
PO Box 160586
Brooklyn, New York 11216

fredsegypt.com@fredsegypt.com
sumonpublishers.com@sumonpublishers.com
blackfolksbooks.com@blackfolksbooks.com
blackegyptbooks.com@blackegyptbooks.com

Copyright Frederick Monderson/SuMon Publishers, 2014. All Rights Reserved. No part of this book may be reproduced, stored in a retrieval system, or transmitted by any means without written permission of the author.

ISBN – 9781610230230
LCCN – 2011939177

In the Tribute to Professor George Simmonds, "Unsung Hero," Dr. Fred Monderson sat at the feet of his heroes, Brother X, Michael Carter, Dr. Leonard Jeffries, El Hombe Brath, Dr. Lewis, Prof. George Simmonds, Dr. ben-Jochannan, Sister Camille Yarbrough, among others.

FREDERICK MONDERSON

ABOUT THE AUTHOR

Dr. Frederick Monderson is a retired *college* professor and school teacher who taught African History in the City University of New York and American History and Government in the NY public schools. He has written more than 1000 articles in the NY Black Press, *Daily Challenge*, *Afro Times* and *New American* newspapers. Very active in community service he has also written several books on Egypt including *Who were the Ancient Egyptians?*; *The Awesome Egyptian Temple*; *Eternal House: The Egyptian Tomb*; *Grassroots View of Ancient Egypt*; *Celebrating Dr. Ben Jochannan*; *Michael Jackson: The Last Dance*; as well as *Barack Obama: Ready, Fit to Lead*; *Barack Obama: Master of Washington, DC*; and *Obama: Master and Commander*; *Where are the Kamite Kings?*; *Medinet Habu: Mortuary Temple of Rameses III*; *Temple of Karnak: The Majestic Architecture of Ancient Egypt*; *An Egyptian Resurrection*; *Intrigue Through Time* (*a novel on Ancient Egypt*); *Egypt: The Holy Land*; *The Majesty of Egyptian Gods and Temples* (a book of Egyptian Poems); *The Ramesseum: Mortuary Temple of Rameses II*; *Hatshepsut's Temple at Deir el Bahari*; *Research Essays on Ancient Egypt*; *The Colonnade: Then and Now*; *Reflections on Ancient Kemet*; *Seven Letters to Mike Tyson on Egyptian Temples*; *10 Poems Praising Great Blacks for Mike Tyson*; also *Sonny Carson: The Final Triumph* (*5* Volumes); *and Glory of the Ancestors: 19 Letters to O.J. Simpson on Ancient African History.* A student of the esteemed Dr. Yosef ben-Jochannan, Dr. Monderson conducts tours to Egypt annually. Next Tour is scheduled for July 12-26, 2014.

For tour information, please contact Orleane Brooks-Williams at Nostrand Travel, 726 Nostrand Avenue, Brooklyn, New York 11216. Phone Number 718-756-5300.

EGYPT ESSAYS ON ANCIENT KEMET

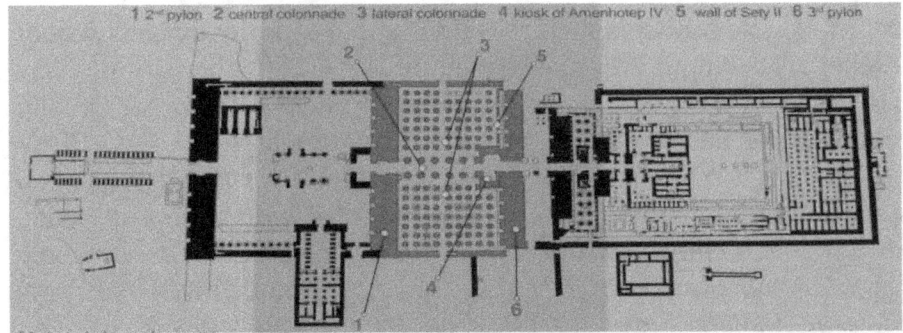

Plan view of Karnak temple emphasizing various features of the Hypostyle Hall.

In Karnak's Hypostyle Hall, Seti I kneels to present two ointment jars to Amon as Min. Notice how Min's creative organ, from his navel not scrotum, is defaced.

FREDERICK MONDERSON

The Middle Kingdom "White Chapel," reconstructed and on view in the "Open Air Museum" at Karnak Temple.

INTRODUCTION

While Egypt continues to remain a subject of fascinating interest to students, professional academics and tourists alike; new revealing research and new analysis of "ancient data" continues to challenge accepted notions and beliefs established in 19th and 20th Century times devoid of critical and constructive intellectual scrutiny. Nevertheless, the falsity of a "white Egypt," propagated in the "white supremacy mold" has begun to crack under the weight of its untenable structure revealing what it really is, a construct not supported by the pillars of logic. The structural foundations upon which modern understanding of the history, culture and ethnicity of the ancient inhabitants of Egypt were laid in the 19th Century by foreign experts in an era of political colonialism and intellectual imperialism devoid of constructive indigenous Egyptian involvement and critique. Hence, many false notions fabricated in the "Penny Press" age of "rapid publication" quickly became ossified in the historical record upon which many of these contemporary views are based.

EGYPT ESSAYS ON ANCIENT KEMET

It was Mr. Zahi Hawass, Chairman of the Egyptian Antiquities Council, who, after the recent study to determine the heritage, identity and ethnicity of King Tutankhamon, declared "King Tut is the only pharaoh whose identity we know with certainty because we found him in a sealed tomb." Subsequently, Queen Hatshepsut was identified. That is not to say the other kings and queens are not who we think they are, but not with King Tut's certainty. In all historical inquiry, the yardstick should be akin to the American jurisprudential insistence of "beyond a reasonable doubt." Whereas, the "King Tut Yardstick" applies to the identities of the various kings, it should also apply to all aspects of the cultural, physical and scientific history of the ancient Egyptian experience. The recent Nubian Conference in October 2012 showed new research challenging some ancient accepted norms. This supports the view all aspects of the culture's interpretation are suspect; and, until we painstakingly re-examine every iota of evidence, we would not know for sure if what we have always believed is actually correct. In essence, we must extricate ourselves from ossified interpretations handed us from the German intellectual tradition and the citadels of Oxford and Cambridge as well as the discussion rooms of the Museums and societies of Europe and America.

One of my most cogent observations at the Temple of Mut was, despite the great archaeological effort expended to unearth the principal regions of the temple, many statues and who knows what lies shoulder-deep in the sand. Thus, we cannot conclusively detail the temple. As such, using Dr. Hawass' "King Tut Yardstick" we must be careful about the modern interpretation of ancient Egyptian history because of the potential "rifts between the lutes" propounded by more than two centuries of falsity to justify a false sense of racial superiority. What is surprising, a great many scholars and even local Egyptians had bought into unquestioned acceptance of a belief system that has begun to come apart.

FREDERICK MONDERSON

That is, there are many inconsistencies in presentation of the history of the beloved ancient Egypt. Here, as an example, are just a few.

1. The Ancient Egyptians were Caucasians.

2. The Ancient Egyptians were a race of "red men," that is "red Caucasians;" yet, this is actually due to the red color in image representations.

3. The Ancient Egyptians originated in South-west Asia and migrated to Egypt, entering by way of the Isthmus of Suez and migrating up the Nile; by way of the Wady Hammamat, crossing the desert and arriving at Koptos, home of God Min; entering the Nile Valley from the South-west desert by Caucasians who had crossed the Mediterranean and settled in North Africa, migrated to the Sahara then into the Nile Valley.

4. The Ancient Egyptians were "pastoralists."

5. The Ancient Egyptians were "boat people."

Still, there are many more such ridiculous propositions, in the process of establishing Egyptology and Egyptian archaeology on a firm foundation. They became solidified in that process that included no indigenous Egyptian experts in the field of analysis as the colonial administration channeled lucrative archaeological concessions to "favorite sons" who did wonderful work untangling the temples and tombs but were allowed to set the intellectual standards and offered choice pick of the very best artifacts recovered. Today, the great museums of the world particularly in Europe and America proudly boast of the splendors of their collections on Egypt acquired in an age before the Egyptian people could effectively regulate who got what; all, enriched in the process

Brian Fagan's labeled *The Rape of the Nile*. Now, in ongoing and balanced research using modern technology and more evolved methods of examination and analysis of extant knowledge are

EGYPT ESSAYS ON ANCIENT KEMET

increasing, many "archaeological findings" are proving to be falsely interpreted, but as "old ideas die hard," they linger rather than be consigned to the basement of outdated and useless information. Case in point!

An American scholar John David Wortham from his "pulpit of absolute wisdom" in *The Genesis of British Egyptology: 1549-1906* (University of Oklahoma Press, Norman, Oklahoma, 1971: 93) has written: "Great progress was made during the nineteenth century in the study of Egyptian mummification. Augustus Bozzi Granville, a physician and a student of Coptic, undertook the earliest nineteenth-century dissection of a mummy at his London home in 1825. From his detailed dissection he correctly concluded that the ancient Egyptians were Caucasians. He also succeeded in clearing up many erroneous ideas about the embalming process. Among other things, he proved the correctness of Herodotus' assertion that the ancient Egyptians had, when preparing a cadaver for burial, extracted the pituitary through the nostrils." He accepts this view of Herodotus who in all likelihood never visited a mummy factory, certainly not the "Mummification Museum in Luxor," ha, ha; but discounted Herodotus' statement that the "Ethiopians, Egyptians, and Colchians had thick lips, broad noses, wooly hair and were burnt of skin!" Let us not forget, as Diop says regarding the Negro character of the Egyptians, that" It is certain that the natives of the country are black with the heat." Equally, that "the Egyptians, Ethiopians, and Colchians belong to the same race....." Even further, "Herodotus, after relating his eyewitness account informing us that the Egyptians were Blacks, then demonstrated, with rare honesty (for a Greek), that Greece borrowed from Egypt all the elements of her civilization. Moreover, archaeological discoveries continually justify Herodotus against his detractors. Thus, Christiane Desroches-Noblecourt writes about recent excavations in Tanis: 'Herodotus had seen the outer buildings of these sepulchers and had described them.... Pierre Montet has proved once again 'The Father of History did not lie.'"

FREDERICK MONDERSON

Now, in an interesting article entitled "Egyptian Mummy" among Antiquarian and Philosophical Studies in *The Gentleman's Magazine* of October 1820, pp. 349-350, in describing a mummy donated by Mr. Joshua Heywood to the Hunterian Museum at Glasgow, the writer states: "The body, shrouded in from fifty to sixty folds of coarse pale brick-red colored linen, is deposited in a strong wooden coffin, fashioned so as to bear a rude resemblance to the human shape. At the upper extremity is carved a face, the features of which (as in the case with all Egyptian sculpture) are very much of the Negro cast." We know the Egyptians loved the color red because they associated it with the sun, a solar and special phenomenon. They considered themselves special! Dr. Cheikh Anta Diop said the "Egyptians painted themselves red to be distinguished from other Africans." Even Dr. ben-Jochannan has often said, "The Egyptians painted themselves red with the Henna plant. Even young brides, particularly Nubians, were painted red with henna." Going back to the most ancient African "Bushman Art" and even art among the "Tassili Frescoes" of the Sahara, red was the favorite color; again like gold, it was considered to be of a divine nature!

The article continued, "Though the features were very much collapsed, the face was nowhere divested of skin. The skin itself was of a chestnut-brown color. The brow was well shaped, though, if any way defective, narrow; and to some it may be interesting to learn, the organ of music was prominent. The nose, though slightly compressed, retained enough of its original shape to be recognized as Roman." Might I also add; the original color of the mummy of Rameses II when first unwrapped in the 1880s was of similar "brown splashed with black!" Dr. Van Sertima, however, recounted Cheikh Anta Diop's observations that "the mummy of Rameses II was exposed to so much radiation when it was being repaired in Paris, it turned white." So, if in the future people of interest are told the mummy is white understand how it got so.

EGYPT ESSAYS ON ANCIENT KEMET

Even further, the gentleman of the article continued, "One circumstance must have struck all who had an opportunity of seeing the above interesting examination; namely, *the dissimilarity of the features to what we are taught to believe were those of the inhabitants of Egypt* [This writer's emphasis], at the remote period at which the custom of embalming existed in that country. A moment's reflection will suffice to convince us that this circumstance can in no way throw discredit on the antiquity of the genuine character of the mummy."

The writer goes on to say, "Mr. Millar, portrait painter in Glasgow, is at present finishing a likeness in oil of the face and surrounding parts. As they appeared immediately after they were exposed; and was completely successful in the accuracy of the likeness before the exposure to the air had converted the face from a brown to a sable hue, which it did in the short period of three hours."

Scant if any attempt has been made to force the retraction of Wortham's arrogant statement. The article of 1820, five years before Granville's dissection, gets no credit; yet, young scholars, particularly from Europe and some from Egypt under the tutelage of professors at the "American University in Cairo" know of Wortham but not the *Gentleman Magazine* article. So, returning to my annotated list.

1.   The Ancient Egyptians were Caucasians! Suppose that I acknowledge such. In 1857, an advocate for American Negro (Nubian) slavery, Samuel Cartwright argued: "The monumental record shows the Negro as nothing but slaves in Egypt from time immemorial." As a defender of slavery, Cartwright used hardly if any referents or references in his book *Slavery and Ethnology* (1857). At least he admits the Negro's existence in Egypt from time immemorial as opposed to Herman Junker (in 1924) who argued

FREDERICK MONDERSON

they only got there "yesterday!" He probably had not heard of Champollion, who, in a letter to his brother discussed the classification of the races of man he witnessed in the Biban el Moluk. At Oxford University, England, they never tear down any building built more than a thousand years ago but simply build upon these older ones. So too, in the misguided interpretation of the archaic views new edifices of falsity have assumed a prominent role in the propagation of the history of Egypt making what many contemporary young and old scholars know and profess pillars cemented on a veneer of papyrus laid upon a bed of quicksand!

2. The Ancient Egyptians were a race of red men - Caucasians. While the Ancient Egyptians were painted many colors, red, black, blue, green, etc., they were never painted white to have any significance. That is, with the exception of Champollion's Biban Moluk image, as Dr. Diop pointed out, whites were below the Egyptian, African, Asiatic, on the "lowest round of the human ladder," "a virtual savage!"

Henri Lhote's "Tassili Frescoes;" Mary Leakey's "Bushman Art;" all show ancient man's fascination with "The predominant Red" as choice of color in their art. Dr. Diop in *The African Origin of Civilization: Myth or Reality* stated ancient Egyptians painted themselves red to be distinguished from other Africans," viz., Libyans, Nubians, etc.

Gay Robbins in *Art of Egypt* noted, in the Egyptian view, "gold and red" were associated with the sun, the gods; and as a special people they painted themselves red. In preparation for the afterlife journey those Egyptians who could not afford the luxury of lavish gold wealth in their tombs, if they had one, simply painted their coffin's

EGYPT ESSAYS ON ANCIENT KEMET

image gold to symbolically represent the real thing, unfortunately for tomb robbers looking for "Ancient treasure." When the wealthy Egyptian painted trees and bunches of grapes on the ceiling of their tombs, this was to symbolically represent the fruit at their arms reach. Thus, symbolism and symbolic logic were hallmarks of ancient Egyptian thinking in the Nile Valley experience.

Everyone has acknowledged the 25th Dynasty was Nubian and Black! Yet, in their tombs these kings are pictured red! The *New York Times* of October, 2012 printed an article on the discovery of a "paint factory" found in South Africa dated to 107,000 (105,000 B.P) years ago, where evidence of the "predominant red" indicated how these ancient painters mixed their colors. The article further noted there was evidence of art material elsewhere in Africa dated at 150,000 but this was the first time actual paint, red, was discovered. Even more revolutionary, the article revealed this discovery pushed modern understanding of "complex thinking among the ancients," much further back in time. Are we to believe these "South Africans" were Egyptian or White?

Dr. Diop speaks of the "absurd conclusion" that "Africans are Caucasians" which would support the contention that ancient peoples throughout Africa who painted themselves red were Egyptians and by extension Caucasians.

3. The Ancient Egyptians were Caucasians who originated in Southwest Asia and migrated to Egypt. Either there were three waves of migration, each contradicting the other or the myth cannot be made tangible in fact. This argument of migration of the Egyptians was first stated by Von Luschan in 1896 and upheld since supported by William Flinders Petrie's "Migration" emphasis in 1911 and even Walter Emery, then David Wortham.

FREDERICK MONDERSON

First, the entry via the Isthmus of Suez means upon arrival the cultural influence ascended the Nile to impact Thebes and then Aswan, if they got that far. Moret posed the view, the Delta influenced the South and Diop demolished this argument.

Second that they entered Africa by way of the Horn, passing through Ethiopia, perhaps northward along the coast and through the Wady Hammamat arriving at Koptos, then sailing down the Nile. We're not sure if they first sailed southward to confer their blessing on Thebes. Suffering from sun stroke in the desert they either split some going downstream and others going upstream to Aswan then making their way again north to Memphis and points further into the Delta. Unfortunately, this migrating Caucasian "man of cultural goodwill" did not seem to have created and left any evidence in his place of origin of the cultural ideas he so graciously blest the Africans with upon his arrival. Von Luschan had argued, "For some unknown reason" he left his place of origin to migrate to Africa. We know people seldom leave their place of origin while experiencing comfort but because they are fleeing sufferable or inhospitable conditions or seeking a better way of life elsewhere; case in Point, those Englishmen who settled Australia or the Englishmen and other Europeans who settled America all seeking opportunities for a better way of life. Importantly, they retained knowledge of their roots and practiced their culture in the new land. None of this applies to Egyptian consciousness.

In the *Gentleman's Magazine* mentioned above and elsewhere, writers with an unbiased agenda speak of the "African mold" upon which Egyptian portraiture is molded despite later intermingling of peoples after the Hyksos occupation and imperialist adventures of the pharaohs who brought untold numbers of whites to settle in their land as captives and given as endowments to the temples; the mold still showed the African imprint as late as Roman times. However,

EGYPT ESSAYS ON ANCIENT KEMET

still none of the cultural traits migrating Caucasians "blest the Africans with" have been found in place of origin - that is, no imprint of pyramid concept, Hieroglyphics, no colonnade which was invented at Sakkara by Imhotep c. 2680 B.C.; neither the Egyptian concept of the Nile boat upon which the gods first sailed across the wonderful Egyptian sky then method of Nile River travel. Thus, Caucasians, not having invented the prototype, nor possess such, nor bring it with them or bequeath same to the Egyptians.

As a caveat to this segment two powerful ideas are raised. In the "for some unknown reason" argument, it is stated these Caucasian migrants brought no cultural artifactual evidence but "a superior mental faculty" that "provided a great stimulus to the existing culture." Pressed for a time of this happening a date given in the Old Kingdom is all that was possible. Upon an analysis of the arrogance of the "superior mental faculty" argument in the Old Kingdom, molded in white supremacy myth, all this occurred hundreds of years after Narmer (Mena, Aha) the Theban, had mobilized an armada with all the attendant logistical ramifications of a military expedition, sailed north to conquer then establish the foundations of pharaonic rule, monarchical system of government with a multi-tiered social order supporting the status quo; a bureaucratic administrative hierarchy that maintained all the cultural trappings of trade, education, agriculture, medicine, building, endowment, mortuary practice, boat-building, mastering river navigation, quarrying and transportation of large stone over great distances, irrigation exploiting the wonders of the bountiful Nile Inundation, establishment of religious practice with the metaphysical implications of the ritualizing of the gods, astronomical observation of the heavens, the development of mathematics and invention of all the social amenities that made life enjoyable. That is, after all this, these peoples, possessing a "superior mental attitude," upon arrival began re-inventing Narmer's wheel! How arrogant!

FREDERICK MONDERSON

During the emergence of the 11th Dynasty consolidation Intef organized a force and coming out of the pass at Thebes to challenge Mentuhotep II, he encountered Mentuhotep with a superior military force, ready and waiting on the field of battle. He paused and said, purportedly, "Wait a minute, brother!" Thereupon he called upon his mother to intercede with Mentuhotep's mother Queen Aam to broker a peace treaty, consolidating their forces and set about bringing the Middle Kingdom into reality. Conceptually speaking, the same thing happened to the migrating Caucasians, who upon arriving at Koptos realized God Min, the alter-ego of Amon-Ra. Some as Arthur Weigall have argued Min was a Southwest Asian; viz., Sumerian, Mesopotamian; god, brought to Koptos by the migrants. What does this mean?

Flinders Petrie discovered huge wooden statues of Min painted black at Koptos, which he dated to prehistoric times placing him among the foundation gods. Again, "new research" has argued, the statues were actually Old Kingdom; perhaps this is to coincide with the migrant's arrival. Coinciding is another strategy employed to make SWA culture complex contemporary with or superior to Egyptian. For example, the "Long Chronology" is dated more than a thousand years before the "Short Chronology," variously given between 3200-3000 (3050) B.C. Some critical scholars see the reality of Mesopotamian history in the Egyptian short chronological history.

All this notwithstanding, even if the Caucasians did bring Min from SWA, why is he painted black? Was he painted black in Mesopotamia? Is he painted black for some form of symbolism? If he is painted black as a form of symbolism, are the Egyptians painted red as a form of symbolism? Are the Nubians painted red a form of symbolism? Interesting, at this conference on the 25th Nubian Dynasty, I did not see any Nubians at the Conference? However, their images were painted red like the Egyptians.

EGYPT ESSAYS ON ANCIENT KEMET

Imagine; noblemen of the "only black dynasty" were painted red in their representation! Nevertheless, Min being black means the Caucasians were worshipping black gods! Therefore, we must believe, "when God Amon instructed his public relations people" of his intent to incorporate Min into his esoteric being, he meant the black god should become the poster child of the new reality of divine worship and rule!

Gaston Maspero insisted the origins of the ancient Egyptians, must be sought not from the east but the west. This is interesting because for a people who have had a historical record of one (26,000); two (52,000); three (78,000); possibly a fourth (104,000) years of precession star-gazing have no record of their "ancestors" who arrived in the Old Kingdom when their records were very accurate. However, Maspero's argument is that they entered from the western desert but they were a Caucasian people who migrated from Southern Europe to North Africa, into the Sahara and then the Nile Valley. Keep in mind, this is an extraordinary Egyptological scholar who made the Cairo Museum place-cards and described the New Kingdom Nobleman Mahepra as "Negroid but not Negro" (Nubian). Conversely, the biographers of the musical great Beethoven, a contemporary of Maspero, described the musical genius as "Swarthy;" "Black;" "Negro;" "Negroid," etc.

Maspero's western origins bring us to the people of Nabta Playa whom Bauval and Brophy described as "Black Africans" but from misguided indigenous Egyptian "field experience" were Caucasians! As is generally known, the question of dating is somewhat problematic. The four methods of dating are thermoluminesence, Potassium Argon, C-14 and Dendo-chronology. The first three are used in Egypt, the last in Southwest America. Nevertheless, all dates before 1750 B.C. are uncertain.

FREDERICK MONDERSON

Bauval and Brophy authors of *Black Genesis: Black African Predecessors of the Pharaohs* date these Africans of this region to 8,000-3500 B.C. "Egyptian experts" give 8500-3500 when they migrated to the Aswan area when their habitat could no longer sustain the culture mix developed there. We must be careful to unintentionally label these people, Aswan Nubians, as Caucasians and if Caucasians then the Thebans with whom these early Africans share a heritage may also be considered Caucasians and thus, as we descend the Nile, the whole Valley becomes Caucasian. We must be careful of the insidious attempts to displace Africans throughout the continent. Otherwise, we come full circle to Diop's "absurd conclusion" that "African blacks are essentially Caucasians."

In *Genesis of the Pharaohs* (2003) Toby Wilkinson identifies Min as "the earliest image of a god" discovered among Petroglyphs in the Eastern Desert of Upper Egypt. Yet, Armour identifies Min as a "black god related to the Negroes of Nubia." Those Petroglyphs discovered in the Eastern Desert, Wilkinson wrote, were "1,000 years before Winkler's Mesopotamians."

We must remember, in the slavery experience, whether the Arab Slave Trade that lasted a thousand years or the European Slave Trade that lasted four hundred years, the African was enslaved because he was "different," less than a man; not created by God; in all respects victimized by the avaricious nature of capitalist accumulation and religious bigotry. Nevertheless, there is one unmistakable fact: Even if we concede the ancient Egyptians were Caucasian, given all that was stated above, and that the whites were enslaving blacks, a la, Samuel Cartwright, "The Egyptian monuments show blacks (Negro, Nubians) as slaves from time immemorial" - the whites were painting their principal gods BLACK! viz., Amon-Min, Koptos and the Luxor Museum and at Karnak beside the Sanctuary; Ptah - "a bald-headed pygmy;" Osiris - the "Great Black" (Hapi).

EGYPT ESSAYS ON ANCIENT KEMET

In the *Papyrus of Hunefer* the nobleman states: "We came from the headwaters of the Nile at the foothills of the mountains of the moon where the God Hapi dwells." This is as clear as ever, not some mythical "unknown reason." Hunefer actually gives us the place of Osiris' origin in Central Africa which means his wife Isis was African and also his son Horus who went north with the blacksmiths, "followers of Horus." Budge states, the great goddess Hathor, known for her "many moods" and for carrying the mummy, "was of Sudani origin." Even further, not to belabor the example, when Ra the great creator had finished making the world, "he first made the Nubian people!" The gods liked to travel and "holiday" in Nubia or Central Africa called "God's Land." Now, all of this notwithstanding, antedating the Egyptian civilization by millennia as the Leakeys, Johansson, etc., etc., have shown - *Zinjanthropus Boisie*, *Australopithecus African*, some 107,000 years ago South Africans had established a paint factory, were mixing red paint to a set and regular pattern and blazing an artistic trail of culture indicating development and expression of "complex thought patterns." This pushed modern man's understanding of the ancient revolutionary thought process millennia before such abstract processes began in places like Europe at some 40,000 years (38,000 Before Present).

One last example. Arnett in *Evidence for the Development of Hieroglyphics in Upper Egypt* states, "Diop was right in proving the Egyptians were not Caucasians but did not prove they were Negroes." He argued archaeology cannot prove the race of a people especially that they were Black! Of course, the "Bones of Hen Nekht" argued they were Negroid. Certainly David O'Connor has argued, "The Egyptians were not white!" nevertheless, Diop did provide evidence in "Totemism," "Circumcision," "Kingship," "Cosmogony," "Social Organization," "Matriarchy," "Kingship of the Meroitic Sudan and Egypt," "Cradles of Civilization located in the Heart of Negro Lands,' and "Languages."

FREDERICK MONDERSON

Thus, to rest my case and to say no more! Critical African scholarship crying in the wilderness is becoming more vocal!

Ps. Dr. Diop has written: "While the branches of the tree of my argument could use some pruning, the trunk stands firmly planted beside the river of truth" to be watered perennially and bear fruit as part of the tremendous effort in praise of "mother Africa" and the incorporation of Egypt into the monumental effort taking place in African Historical Reconstruction.

Mural in the lobby of the Oberoi Hotel at Aswan as Rameses II offers flowers to enthroned Hathor while Nefertari raises the sistrum at his rear

EGYPT ESSAYS ON ANCIENT KEMET

In the Hypostyle Hall at Karnak Temple, Seti I gestures towards "Traveling Amon" with Mut in Double crown at his rear.

Poles with heads of divinities Ram as Amon, Ra-Horakhty, Anubis, Hathor etc., show great diversity with a Hathor sistrum to the left.

EGYPT ESSAYS ON ANCIENT KEMET

TABLE OF CONTENTS

1. Africa — 54
2. Cheikh Anta Diop — 66
3. Culture for Liberation — 91
4. The Fascination of Egyptian Archaeology — 102
5. The Egyptian Tomb — 123
6. The Nile Valley in World Antiquity/History — 156
7. The Priesthood — 193
8. Sakkara — 273
9. Upper Egypt/Kemet — 287
10. Temple of Isis at Philae — 305
11. Thebes — 329
12. Temple of Karnak: The Majestic Architecture of Ancient Kemet — 423
13. The Temple of Luxor — 484
14. Abydos — 505
15. The Dance, Music and Musical Instruments — 526
16. African Art — 558

FREDERICK MONDERSON

17. North Africa: Egypt, Kush — 598
18. Time Measurement — 606
19. Pharaonic Crowns, Names and Regalia — 611
20. The Nile River — 623
21. Kemetic Technology/ Sciences — 632
22. Warfare — 669
23. Egyptian Medicine and — 677
24. The Conspiracy Against Ancient Egypt — 713
25. Egypt as Black History — 735
26. Great African Philosophers Teach — 739
27. Senmut, Architect of Queen Hatshepsut — 743
28. Egyptology — 755
29. Black Egypt and the StruggleFor Incluion — 751
30. Who Was Mentuhotep II — 757
31. Queen of Sheba in Racial Portrait as Historical Distortion — 761
32. The Wisdom of the Ancient — 772

EGYPT ESSAYS ON ANCIENT KEMET

Egyptians

33. **The Pyramids** — 772
34. **The Clerestory** — 774
35. **Walls in Ancient Egyptian Temples and Tombs** — 776
36. **The Blessing** — 779
38. **References** — 783
39. **Index** — 787

Egypt Essays Illustration 1. Bust of Nefertiti, wife of Amenhotep IV, Akhnaton, the XVIIIth Dynasty religious reformer.

FREDERICK MONDERSON

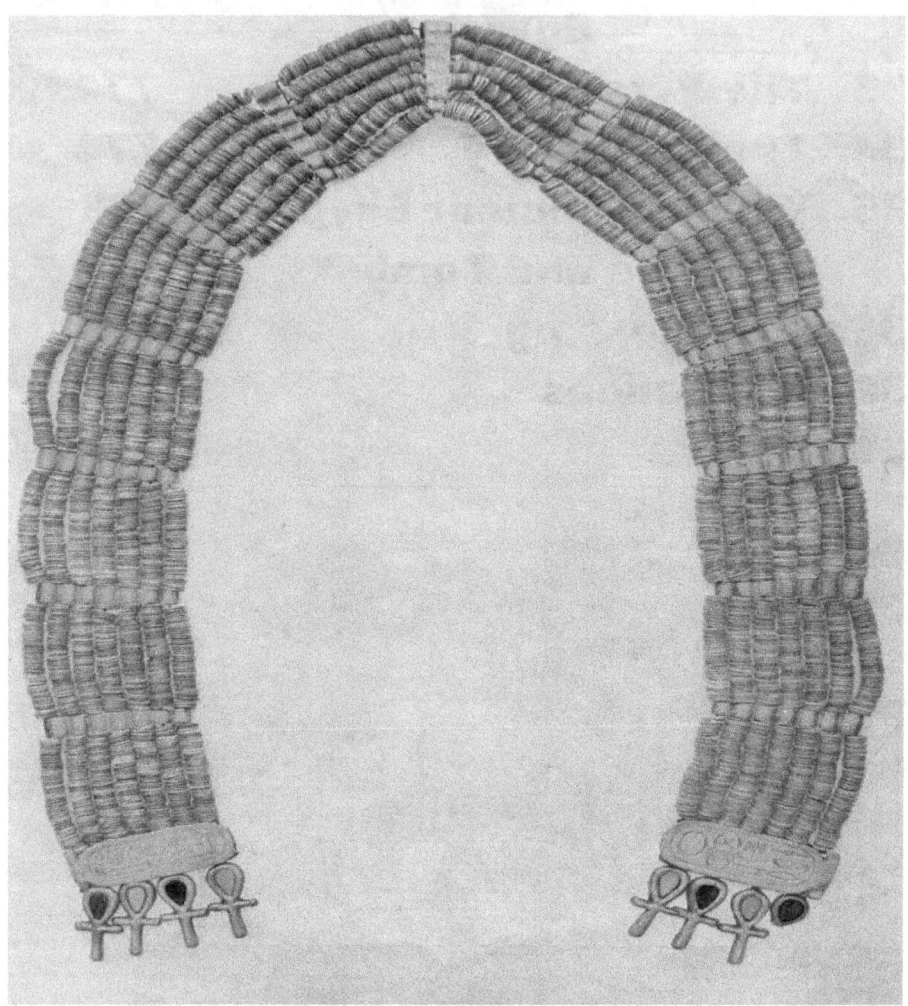

Egypt Essays Illustration 1a. Necklace sash bounded by gold cartouches of King Tut with fringes of the sacred symbol of life, the ankh.

EGYPT ESSAYS ON ANCIENT KEMET

Egypt Essays Photographs

Egypt Essays Photo 1. Plan of the Imhotep Museum Complex.

Egypt Essays Photo 1a. Abu Simbel Temple of Rameses II. As visitors mill around, four seated colossi line the temple's entrance with image of Ra-Horakhty above the door and baboons on the cornice.

Egypt Essays Photo 1b. Abu Simbel Temple of Rameses II. Plaque dedicated to its first President Gamal Abdul-Nasser who built the High Dam at Aswan creating Lake Nasser.

Egypt Essays Photo 2. Abu Simbel Temple of Rameses II. Close-up of the two right side seated colossal statues of the Pharaoh on the façade of his Temple.

Egypt Essays Photo 2a. Abu Simbel Temple of Rameses II. Rameses offers to the titulary deity of the temple, his name as Ma'at on the cornice between the seated colossal statues.

Egypt Essays Photo 3. Abu Simbel Temple of Rameses II. Close-up of the two left side seated colossal statues of the Pharaoh on the façade of his Temple.

Egypt Essays Photo 3a. Abu Simbel Temple of Rameses II. At the base of a seated statue images of "prisoners" subdued by the king. The other side has other such persons sharing the same fate.

Egypt Essays Photo 4. Abu Simbel Temple of Rameses II. Entrance Hall view of the 8 standing colossal Osiride statues of the monarch.

Egypt Essays Photo 4a. Abu Simbel Temple of Rameses II. Baboons and cartouches line the cornice of the temple.

Egypt Essays Photo 5. Abu Simbel Temple of Rameses II. Into the Sanctuary with divinities, from the right (left as the gods look out), Ra-Horakhty, Rameses II, Amon-Ra and Ptah.

Egypt Essays Photo 5a. Abu Simbel Temple of Rameses II. Two rightmost seated statues of the king with miniature statues of queens at his feet.

FREDERICK MONDERSON

Egypt Essays Photo 5b. Abu Simbel Temple of Rameses II. Two Nile gods uniting the land beneath Rameses *Usr-Maat-Ra* Cartouche on the (left most) seated statue of Rameses and just to the right, a small statue of his Queen.

Egypt Essays Photo 5c. Abu Simbel Temple of Rameses II. Two Nile gods uniting the land beneath Rameses *Usr-Maat-Ra* Cartouche on the (right most) seated statue of Rameses and just to the left, a small statue of his Queen.

Egypt Essays Photo 6. Abu Simbel Temple of Rameses II. The Queen offers a sistrum and flowers to Hathor, deity of the Temple.

Egypt Essays Photo 6a. Abu Simbel Temple of Rameses II. The left two seated statues, one damage and whose head lies on the ground, also with miniature statues of the king's queens.

Egypt Essays Photo 6b. Abu Simbel Temple of Rameses II. Rameses gestures with an open right hand and holds an incenser in his left as Osiris sits enthroned on a pedestal throne.

Egypt Essays Photo 6c. Abu Simbel Temple of Rameses II. In double image, Rameses slays a prisoner before Amon Ra and he kneels left); and again slays a prisoner before Amon Ra but this time stoops before the God.

Egypt Essays Photo 7. Abu Simbel Temple of Rameses II. Hathor, Ptah and Ra-Horakhty on the pillars.

Egypt Essays Photo 7a. Abu Simbel Temple of Rameses II. Statues of the King and Hathor front the nearby Queen's temple.

Egypt Essays Photo 8. Abu Simbel Temple of Rameses II. Rameses offers two bouquets to Hathor while Nefertari stands behind him with sistrum and flowers.

Egypt Essays Photo 8a. Abu Simbel Temple of Rameses II. Two standing statues sandwich the king's cartouches.

Egypt Essays Photo 8b. Abu Simbel Temple of Rameses II. Two statues of the king sandwich one of a defaced Hathor whose face may be truly Nubian like Rameses.

Egypt Essays Photo 9. Philae Temple of Isis. The Mammisi with its fronting columns as seen from the river approach with two

EGYPT ESSAYS ON ANCIENT KEMET

sets of "First Pylon." The center opening is the river's entrance to the temple.

Egypt Essays Photo 9a. Philae Temple of Isis. Native Egyptian Guide Showgi Abd Rady, "the Black," stands at the Pier with his equipment ready to work.

Egypt Essays Photo 10. Philae Temple of Isis. The Dromos to the temple's First Pylon with the Eastern (right) and Western (left) Colonnades. Two altars remain *in situ*.

Egypt Essays Photo 10a. Philae Temple of Isis. The Eastern Colonnade with its 17 columns, with different capitals, undecorated.

Egypt Essays Photo 10b. Philae Temple of Isis. The Western Colonnade with its 32 columns with their varied capitals and water mark from the time when the temple was flooded by the river's Inundation.

Egypt Essays Photo 11. Philae Temple of Isis. From the Dromos and northern end of the Eastern Colonnade to the right, the decorated Entrance Pylon with Isis' First Pylon visible through the opening at top.

Egypt Essays Photo 11a. Philae Temple of Isis. The "Kiosk of Trajan," architecture in its majestic form with varied capitals.

Egypt Essays Photo 11b. Philae Temple of Isis. One of the many varied capitals atop columns in the "Kiosk of Trajan's" architecture repository.

Egypt Essays Photo 12. Philae Temple of Isis. The "Second Eastern Colonnade" to the left and inner face to the Entrance Pylon enclosing the Open Court of Isis's Temple.

Egypt Essays Photo 12a. Philae Temple of Isis. More of the varied capitals atop columns in this wonderful repository of architecture.

Egypt Essays Photo 12b. Philae Temple of Isis. Enthroned Osiris atop the crocodile with Isis at the left, all within a shrine depicted by the sun, stars and moon.

Egypt Essays Photo 13. Philae Temple of Isis. Short columns with different capitals and elevated die supporting the overhead architrave all atop screened walls.

FREDERICK MONDERSON

Egypt Essays Photo 13a. Philae Temple of Isis. As Thoth stands to the left, Amon-Ra sits enthroned between two goddesses, Isis and Nephthys, as Seshat writes and Ptah sits to the right with another deity to his rear.

Egypt Essays Photo 13b. Philae Temple of Isis. Varied capitals beneath the raised Hathor Head abacus with illustrated underside of the architrave.

Egypt Essays Photo 13c. Philae Temple of Isis. Another, broader, view of varied capitals with raised Hathor Head abacus.

Egypt Essays Photo 14. Philae Temple of Isis. While Isis sits nursing Horus and Nephthys sits beside her, Khnum makes man on his "potters' wheel" as Thoth stands at his rear doing his job of recording.

Egypt Essays Photo 15. Philae Temple of Isis. King makes a Presentation of 2 ointment jars to enthroned Hathor as Isis, while Horus as a babe with his hands to his mouth, sits behind the goddess.

Egypt Essays Photo 15a. Philae Temple of Isis. Sharp and crispy Hieroglyphic inscriptions with only the face seeming erased.

Egypt Essays Photo 16. Kalabsha Temple of Mendulese. Columns at the entrance, each with a varied capital and with winged disk overhead.

Egypt Essays Photo 16a. Kalabsha Temple of Mendulese Vicinity. Ruins from the Temple of Beit Wali.

Egypt Essays Photo 16b. "The Register" introduced order into Hieroglyphic writing enabling the beauty of the art to be emphasized.

Egypt Essays Photo 17. Kalabsha Temple of Mendulese Vicinity. Entrance to Kalabsha with the giant stele.

Egypt Essays Photo 17a. Kalabsha Temple of Mendulese. Columns at the entrance, each with a varied capital and with winged disk overhead.

Egypt Essays Photo 18. Beit Wali Temple of Rameses II. Columned Court and Entrance.

Egypt Essays Photo 18a. Kalabsha Temple of Mendulese. Ruins that speak to architectural and cultural splendor.

EGYPT ESSAYS ON ANCIENT KEMET

Egypt Essays Photo 19. Beit Wali Temple of Rameses II. Rameses offers his name as Ma'at to the enthroned Amon-Ra.

Egypt Essays Photo 19a. The Temple of Kalabsha moved from Nubia and relocated to this area under circumstances similar to the nearby Beit Wali Temple of Rameses II.

Egypt Essays Photo 20. Kom Ombo Temple of Haroeis and Sobek. Wall, Columns of the right-side Court Colonnade and more columns of the magnificent entrance Hypostyle Hall with its twin uraeus and entrance to twin aisles, signifying the "double nature" of the Temple.

Egypt Essays Photo 20a. Kom Ombo Temple of Haroeis and Sobek. In the Entrance Court, left side part of the Peristyle Colonnade.

Egypt Essays Photo 20b. Kom Ombo Temple of Haroeis and Sobek. In the Entrance Court, right side part of the Peristyle Colonnade.

Egypt Essays Photo 21a. The individual image at top right generally means "Prince of the Land" is often shown defaced, which is perhaps because he is in the "Negro mold!"

Egypt Essays Photo 21b. Kom Ombo Temple of Haroeis and Sobek. The king offers pellets of incense to Haroeis, the "Elder Horus," twin deity of this Kom Ombo temple.

Egypt Essays Photo 22. Kom Ombo Temple of Haroeis and Sobek. Twenty-three uraei on the cornice.

Egypt Essays Photo 22a. Kom Ombo Temple of Haroeis and Sobek. Various forms of the Vulture wearing the Osiris Crown and the Red Crown on a ceiling decoration.

Egypt Essays Photo 22b. Kom Ombo Temple of Haroeis and Sobek. *Suten Bat*, King of Upper and Lower Egypt, title of Pharaoh.

Egypt Essays Photo 23. Kom Ombo Temple of Haroeis and Sobek. View of the Sanctuary of Sobek, on the left from the entrance but from the right, looking out, as the God stands to view his creation.

FREDERICK MONDERSON

Egypt Essays Photo 23a. Kom Ombo Temple of Haroeis and Sobek. The Vulture goddess Mut, meaning "mother," stands before her shrine with a goddess at rear indicating femininity and divinity.

Egypt Essays Photo 24. Kom Ombo Temple of Haroeis and Sobek. View from the rear of the Sanctuary of Sobek, on the right from the entrance but from the left, looking out, as the God sees it.

Egypt Essays Photo 24a. Kom Ombo Temple of Haroeis and Sobek. The "Two Ladies" title stands behind to protect the king.

Egypt Essays Photo 25. Kom Ombo Temple of Haroeis and Sobek. View from the rear of the twin Sanctuary with some evidence of how the Temple was divided and structured. Dr. ben-Jochannan always instructed his students to never enter the Sanctuary area.

Egypt Essays Photo 25a. Kom Ombo Temple of Haroeis and Sobek. Ptah behind the symbol for millions of years for the Red Crown.

Egypt Essays Photo 25b. Kom Ombo Temple of Haroeis and Sobek. Hathor stands behind and pats Horus (Haroeis) on a column that still retains some color.

Egypt Essays Photo 26. Kom Ombo Temple of Haroeis and Sobek. View from the rear corridor, the outer back of the temple wall roper, with depiction of colossal figure and hieroglyphics beside him. Notice the ten crocodiles.

Egypt Essays Photo 26a. Kom Ombo Temple of Haroeis and Sobek. Sobek, enthroned with solar disk, and all!

Egypt Essays Photo 26b. Kom Ombo Temple of Haroeis and Sobek. On a column, in White Crown and sporting "tail," the king presents a pyramid to Horus, partly hidden.

Egypt Essays Photo 27. Temple of Horus at Edfu. Entrance Pylon of the Temple of Horus with double colossal depiction of the king slaughtering Egypt's enemies before Horus and Hathor; the upper representations depict the king before various gods and goddesses; while on the cornice, an orb with double uraei protects the Temple. Two stone hawks greet the visitor while beyond, entrance columns of the Hypostyle Hall or Pronaos.

EGYPT ESSAYS ON ANCIENT KEMET

Egypt Essays Photo 27a. Temple of Horus at Edfu. From within the Great Court, columns along the roofed ambulatory with the inner face of the Pylon left and right as visitors mill about.

Egypt Essays Photo 27b. Temple of Horus at Edfu. Osiris (left) and Horus (right), both victims of vandalized defacement.

Egypt Essays Photo 28. Edfu Temple of Horus. In the rear "Corridor of Victor," the King and his Queen make a presentation before Horus and the symbol plan of his Temple.

Egypt Essays Photo 28a. Edfu Temple of Horus. In the rear "Corridor of Victory," wearing the White Crown, the king leads three Anubii figures as he prepares to incense the Goddess also in White Crown.

Egypt Essays Photo 28b. Edfu Temple of Horus. Also in the rear "Corridor of Victory," God Horus in Red and White Double Crown is hoisted by Anubii figures.

Egypt Essays Photo 29. Edfu Temple of Horus. In the "Corridor of Victory," a scene from the war with Seth. The evil Seth is captured disguised as a hippopotamus and held by a spear as Isis as Hathor and other Gods participate.

Egypt Essays Photo 30. Edfu Temple of Horus. In the rear "Corridor of Victory," the King and his Queen make a Presentation to the God before another emblem of his Temple.

Egypt Essays Photo 30a. Edfu Temple of Horus. Two images of Khepre, the Beetle, sits atop an emblem before the Red Crown and a defaced face that signifies a prince of the area.

Egypt Essays Photo 31. Edfu Temple of Horus. Khnum hard at work making man on his "Potter's Wheel" before the Red Crown and entrance to a structure while a squatting figure looks on.

Egypt Essays Photo 31a. Broken granite body of statue showing a well-proportioned body, a "belt" and dagger within and to the right a "White Crown."

Egypt Essays Photo 31b. Part of the Nekhbet and Wadjit duo and to the right broken cartouche with image of Thoth's head.

Egypt Essays Photo 32. Edfu Temple of Horus. In the rear "Corridor of Victory," the God Thoth defaced!

FREDERICK MONDERSON

Egypt Essays Photo 32a. Edfu Temple of Horus. In the rear "Corridor of Victory," the God Amun as Min, defaced!

Egypt Essays Photo 32b. Edfu Temple of Horus. Wearing horns and feathers, the king makes a presentation of "millions of years" to Horus in Double Crown.

Egypt Essays Photo 33. Edfu Temple of Horus. In Double Crown, the king makes a double handed Presentation.

Egypt Essays Photo 33a. Edfu Temple of Horus. The beneficiary of the previous Presentation, Horus stands in "Traveling" gear.

Egypt Essays Photo 34. Edfu Temple of Horus. The God Thoth, inventor of writing and all forms of intellectual activities, in the right rear corridor.

Egypt Essays Photo 34a. Edfu Temple of Horus. Oh, to be entertained by three, nevertheless, defaced playing the tambourine!

Egypt Essays Photo 34b. Edfu Temple of Horus. Even more joyful, to be entertained some more by still more ladies paying the tambourine.

Egypt Essays Photo 34c. Edfu Temple of Horus. An Ad for evening entertainment.

Egypt Essays Photo 34d. Edfu Temple of Horus. The "Sphinx of Edfu!"

Egypt Essays Photo 34e. Karnak Temple of Amon. Beauty of Hieroglyphics, "Life, Health, Dominion, Stability."

Egypt Essays Photo 35. Karnak Temple of Amon. Entrance to the Temple of the Theban deity Amon, later Amon-Ra. Notice the Sphinxes of the Avenue leading to the entrance. These were placed here by Rameses II. Look carefully at the little figures between the sphinxes paws and beyond the entrance pylon, statues and the Second Pylon.

Egypt Essays Photo 35a. Karnak Temple of Amon. Plan of the temple with its principal features comprising the Central Group.

Egypt Essays Photo 35b. Karnak Temple of Amon. Plan of the Temple of Montu, and the principal features of the "Northern Group" of the Karnak Temples.

EGYPT ESSAYS ON ANCIENT KEMET

Egypt Essays Photo 35c. Karnak Temple of Amon. Plan of the Temple of Mut with its Sacred Lake, comprising the "Southern Group" of the Karnak Temples.

Egypt Essays Photo 35d. Karnak Temple of Amon. The "Gatekeepers." Mr. Showgi Abd el Rady (left), Chief of Security (right) and a friend (center).

Egypt Essays Photo 36. Karnak Temple of Amon. Plan of the Temple of Amon-Ra at Karnak, with the ten Pylons (heavily indicated) and subsidiary structures within the Enclosure Wall.

Egypt Essays Photo 36a. Karnak Temple of Amon. The "Kiosk of Seti II" dedicated to the Theban Triad, Amon (center); Mut (left) and Khonsu (right).

Egypt Essays Photo 36b. Karnak Temple of Amon. Northern end of the "Southern Colonnade" in the "Great Court."

Egypt Essays Photo 37. Karnak Temple of Amon. In the First or "Great Court," sphinxes and the rear of the right half of the First Pylon. Notice the first or end column is incomplete, giving evidence of how these were first erected as squares then pounded into the finished and polished round columns.

Egypt Essays Photo 37a. Karnak Temple of Amon. Eastern end of the "Northern Colonnade" in the "Great Court," abutting the First Pylon.

Egypt Essays Photo 37b. Karnak Temple of Amon. Remains of an altar in situ in the Great Court with columns of the "Northern Colonnade" further on.

Egypt Essays Photo 37c. Karnak Temple of Amon. "The Gatekeepers." Chief of Karnak Temple Security (center) and two of his assistants.

Egypt Essays Photo 38. Karnak Temple of Amon. In the First or "Great Court," the eastern sphinxes fronting the east side columns of the "Southern Colonnade." Notice the first or end column is incomplete, giving evidence of how these were first erected as squares then pounded into the finished round columns.

Egypt Essays Photo 38a. Karnak Temple of Amon. A surviving Sphinx of Tutankhamon in the "Great Court."

FREDERICK MONDERSON

Egypt Essays Photo 38b. Karnak Temple of Amon. Columns of the "Southern Colonnade" in the "Great Court" with the inner face of the "First Pylon." Notice the last column, square blocks, that were pounded round in decoration.

Egypt Essays Photo 39. Karnak Temple of Amon. Obliquely opposite from the previous picture in the Great Court, another line of columns in a colonnade, the bases of columns of the Taharka Kiosk, a statue of Rameses II and the "Second Pylon" in the right rear.

Egypt Essays Photo 39a. Karnak Temple of Amon. A base and the one remaining complete "Taharka Column" in the "Great Court."

Egypt Essays Photo 39b. Karnak Temple of Amon. An artist rendition of the Temple of Karnak from the rear.

Egypt Essays Photo 40. Karnak Temple of Amon. View of the "Second Pylon" and the "Processional Colonnade" further on.

Egypt Essays Photo 40a. Karnak Temple of Amon. Visitors mill about in the "Great Forecourt" as a guest snaps a photo of the Sphinx of Tutankhamon.

Egypt Essays Photo 40b. Karnak Temple of Amon. This individual is certainly in a hurry to deliver his birds and flowers. Notice his sandals and imagery on his apron.

Egypt Essays Photo 41. Karnak Temple of Amon. On a broken stone, two images, one of an enthroned King holding an ankh and the other of a standing figure wearing an illustrated apron.

Egypt Essays Photo 41a. Karnak Temple of Amon. Plan of the Hypostyle Hall with the names of kings who did work there.

Egypt Essays Photo 41b. Karnak Temple of Amon. Mr. Showgi (right) and his assistant Mr. Sayeed (left) stand before twin-statues of Amon and Rameses II in the Hypostyle Hall.

Egypt Essays Photo 42. Karnak Temple of Amon. The Author, Dr. Fred Monderson, stands between "The pillars of truth!"

Egypt Essays Photo 42a. Karnak Temple of Amon. Plan of the temple showing the Hypostyle Hall accentuated with its many features, Processional Colonnade, Wall of Seti I, etc.

EGYPT ESSAYS ON ANCIENT KEMET

Egypt Essays Photo 42b. Karnak Temple of Amon. Seti presents a "Table of Offerings" to Amon-Ra with Mut at his rear wearing the Red Crown. Both the king and gods are on the same plane.

Egypt Essays Photo 43. Karnak Temple of Amon. View of columns of the "Processional Colonnade" with remains of opening for the "Clerestory" which let light into the Hypostyle Hall.

Egypt Essays Photo 43a. Karnak Temple of Amon. With the Bull running alongside him and the protective vulture flying overhead, Seti dances before Amon as Min.

Egypt Essays Photo 43b. Karnak Temple of Amon. Barque of the God at rest in the Shrine, evidence some forty-odd uraei overhead.

Egypt Essays Photo 43c. Karnak Temple of Amon. From the feet displacement, the king seems in close embrace between gods such as Amon and Khonsu.

Egypt Essays Photo 43d. Karnak Temple of Amon. Seti kneels to present two vessels to "Traveling Amon."

Egypt Essays Photo 44. Karnak Temple of Amon. Another view of the columns with their open umbel columns comprising the "Processional Colonnade" in the Hypostyle Hall.

Egypt Essays Photo 44a. Karnak Temple of Amon. The beauty of "Sunk Relief."

Egypt Essays Photo 44b. Karnak Temple of Amon. Seti kneels to present two ointment jars to Amon as Min, balancing, not holding the flagellum. Notice the god's food, lettuce in rear.

Egypt Essays Photo 44c. Karnak Temple of Amon. While Seti kneels to have his name written in the "Tree of Life" (left); Sekhmet introduces him kneeling to Ra Horakhty in his shrine.

Egypt Essays Photo 45. Karnak Temple of Amon. "Son of Ra" cartouche of Rameses II on the underside of an architrave in the Hypostyle Hall.

Egypt Essays Photo 45a. Karnak Temple of Amon. More "Sunk Relief" indicating the feathers of Amon and "Health" and "Life."

FREDERICK MONDERSON

Egypt Essays Photo 45b. Karnak Temple of Amon. Seti kneels to present a plant to "Traveling" Amon-Ra.

Egypt Essays Photo 45c. Karnak Temple of Amon. In Red Crown, Seti kneels to present a plant to "Traveling" Amon-Ra.

Egypt Essays Photo 46. Karnak Temple of Amon. Another cartouche on the underside of an architrave in the Hypostyle Hall.

Egypt Essays Photo 46a. Karnak Temple of Amon. Seti gestures toward Amon-Ra with Mut at his rear.

Egypt Essays Photo 46b. Karnak Temple of Amon. While Thoth writes his name in the "Tree of Life," Rameses II kneels before the Theban Triad of Amon-Ra (enthroned), with Mut and Khonsu at her rear.

Egypt Essays Photo 47. Karnak Temple of Amon. From the east of the "Third Pylon," view of the "Processional Colonnade" with widows of the "Clerestory" to the right and on to the "First Pylon" in the rear, as visitors walk through.

Egypt Essays Photo 47a. Karnak Temple of Amon. Brother Nasser, son of Brother Abdul "Master of Karnak."

Egypt Essays Photo 47b. Karnak Temple of Amon. Chief of Temple Security (right) and an assistant.

Egypt Essays Photo 47c. Karnak Temple of Amon. View of the Hypostyle Hall from the northern half, beyond the wall depicting the "Wars of Seti I."

Egypt Essays Photo 48. Karnak Temple of Amon. Seti I in his chariot trampling some of his enemies as indicated on a wall north of the Hypostyle Hall.

Egypt Essays Photo 48a. Karnak Temple of Amon. Description of the Hypostyle Hall.

Egypt Essays Photo 48b. Karnak Temple of Amon. The gods lay hands on Rameses II in the Hypostyle Hall.

Egypt Essays Photo 49. Karnak Temple of Amon. King Amenhotep offers a vessel in this broken stone image.

Egypt Essays Photo 49a. Karnak Temple of Amon. Broken stone with hieroglyphic inscription.

EGYPT ESSAYS ON ANCIENT KEMET

Egypt Essays Photo 49b. Luxor temple of Amenhotep III. Native Egyptian Guide in the "Ramessean Front beside an image of Nefertari enthroned.

Egypt Essays Photo 50. Karnak Temple of Amon. View of the Heraldic symbol of Egyptian unification, the lotus and papyrus, placed here by Thutmose III of the 18th Dynasty.

Egypt Essays Photo 50a. Karnak Temple of Amon. Plan of the Temple showing the "Third Pylon" and work of Thutmose I and IV.

Egypt Essays Photo 50b. Karnak Temple of Amon. Plan of the Temple showing the "Barque Sanctuary" area.

Egypt Essays Photo 50c. Temple of Mut. Under the shelter, colossal face of Goddess Mut.

Egypt Essays Photo 50d. Temple of Mut. Within the temple gate, ruins of the entranceway.

Egypt Essays Photo 50e. Temple of Mut. Looking back through the broken Sphinxes of the Avenue towards Karnak with the Tenth Pylon in foreground and further on a crane at the Ninth Pylon.

Egypt Essays Photo 50f. Temple of Mut. Some of the broken statues of Goddess Sekhmet placed here by Amenhotep III.

Egypt Essays Photo 50g. Temple of Mut. Panoramic view of part of the temple with some columns still visible.

Egypt Essays Photo 50h. Temple of Mut. Another view of the grounds with the worker shed in rear.

Egypt Essays Photo 50i. Temple of Mut. The Sacred Lake, after much labor was expended in repairing it, but unlike Karnak's it is not square but horse-shoe like.

Egypt Essays Photo 50j. Temple of Mut. Another view of the landscape with sphinxes and statues of Goddess Sekhment lie scattered.

Egypt Essays Photo 50k. Temple of Mut. More statues of Goddess Sekhmet before the Sacred Lake.

Egypt Essays Photo 50l. Temple of Mut. Some statues of Goddess Sekhmet still lie in the sand to be excavated.

FREDERICK MONDERSON

Egypt Essays Photo 50m. "The most beautiful tableau ever found in Egypt;" the back panel of Tutankhamon's throne, covered with sheet gold and richly inlaid, representing the king and his queen.

Egypt Essays Photo 50n. Temple of Amon-Ra at Karnak. Wonderful view of Hatshepsut's obelisk against a blue sky.

Egypt Essays Photo 51. Karnak Temple of Amon. Frontal view of the *Akh Menu*, "Festival Temple" of Thutmose III, beyond the "Sanctuary" and "Middle Kingdom Court." This perpendicular temple is the last major structure on the East-West Axis.

Egypt Essays Photo 51a. Karnak Temple of Amon. View from the Great Court through the Taharka Column, Second Pylon, Processional Colonnade, and towards the Sanctuary at evening time as the sunlight casts its ebbing shadow back towards the Sanctuary.

Egypt Essays Photo 52. Karnak Temple of Amon-Ra. Column (left) and pillar (right) in the *Akh Menu*, "Festival Temple" of Thutmose III.

Egypt Essays Photo 52a. Karnak Temple of Amon-Ra. "Suten Bat" title of Pharaoh as "King of Upper and Lower Egypt/Kemet."

Egypt Essays Photo 53. Karnak Temple of Amon-Ra. On his "Girdle Wall," Rameses offers two sistra (sistrum) to Mut as Hathor.

Egypt Essays Photo 53a. Karnak Temple of Amon-Ra. The majestic ibis is a manifestation among the many attributes of God Thoth, but the grace of the bird is in itself a major asset.

Egypt Essays Photo 53b. Temple of Mut. Another view of some of the buried seated statues of Goddess Sekhmet, showing more work to be done at the temple.

Egypt Essays Photo 54. Karnak Temple of Amon-Ra. View of Thutmose I (left) and Hatshepsut's (right) obelisks among the ruins from southeast of the "Sanctuary."

Egypt Essays Photo 54a. Karnak Temple of Amon-Ra. From east of the "Sacred Lake," the "Seventh" and "Eighth Pylons" along the East/West Axis.

EGYPT ESSAYS ON ANCIENT KEMET

Egypt Essays Photo 54b. Karnak Temple of Amon-Ra. A vulture with out-stretched wings, hold a Shen ring above Horus image wearing the Double Crown with uraei sporting other rings.

Egypt Essays Photo 54c. Karnak Temple of Amon-Ra. From south-east of the Sacred Lake the two obelisks and ruins of the Hypostyle Hall.

Egypt Essays Photo 55. Karnak Temple of Amon-Ra. Looking past Thutmose I's obelisk, through the "Processional Colonnade" and on to some of the throngs of people who visit daily.

Egypt Essays Photo 56. Karnak Temple of Amon-Ra. Ruins of the "Ninth Pylon" and a crane for heavy lifting. The "Tenth Pylon" (right) is further on.

Egypt Essays Photo 57. Karnak Temple of Amon-Ra. Statues along the North/South Axis in the "Cachette Court" and before the "Seventh Pylon." These statues do not face the Axis but face parallel to it. Conversely, on the main East/West Axis, the statues face the Axis which is the path of the Sun God!

Egypt Essays Photo 57a. Karnak Temple of Amon-Ra. The Temple of Amenhotep II placed perpendicular to the north/south axis.

Egypt Essays Photo 57b. A native Egyptian Guide stands before the south side of the Eighth Pylon with its statues placed here by Thutmose III.

Egypt Essays Photo 58. Karnak Temple of Amen-Ra. From the south along the North/South axis, view of the southern face of the "Ninth Pylon" constructed by Horemhab.

Egypt Essays Photo 58b. Karnak Temple of Amen-Ra. Figure with a head of two birds holds a knife.

Egypt Essays Photo 59. Luxor Temple of Amenhotep III. Sphinxes line the Dromos or "Avenue of Sphinxes" give access to two seated statues, one of two remaining obelisks, and one of four remaining standing statues entrancing the temple. Look closely, beyond the entrance opening another seated statue and beginning of the columns of the "Processional Colonnade."

FREDERICK MONDERSON

Egypt Essays Photo 59a. Luxor Temple of Amenhotep III. A broken head from a seated statue of Rameses II.

Egypt Essays Photo 60. Luxor Temple of Amenhotep III. This gentleman claims to be the "Keeper of the Temple."

Egypt Essays Photo 60a. Luxor Temple of Amenhotep III. A close-up of one of the surviving sphinxes of the Dromos.

Egypt Essays Photo 60b. Luxor Temple of Amenhotep III. Seated statues wearing the "White Crown" of Rameses II outside and a seated statue beyond the "Pylon" beside the "Processional Colonnade."

Egypt Essays Photo 61. Luxor Temple. Cartouche of Rameses II *Usr-Maat-Ra* beside his seated statue before the "Pylon."

Egypt Essays Photo 61a. Luxor Temple of Amenhotep III. The last of four standing statues of Rameses II outside the "Pylon."

Egypt Essays Photo 61b. Luxor Temple of Amenhotep III. Beyond the First Pylon, an ancient survival refurbished with mud-bricks in structure and columns.

Egypt Essays Photo 61c. Luxor Temple of Amenhotep III. View of the area east of the Great Pylon.

Egypt Essays Photo 61d. Luxor Temple of Amenhotep III. From the west, late period structures and the various colonnades.

Egypt Essays Photo 62. Luxor Temple of Amenhotep III. "Ramessean Front." On the southeast wall of the "Great Court," sons of Rameses II in Procession to the Temple of Luxor illustrated to the far left.

Egypt Essays Photo 62a. Luxor Temple of Amenhotep III. "Ramessean Front." One of the fat cows led by priests in the procession of the sons of Rameses II.

Egypt Essays Photo 62b. Luxor Temple of Amenhotep III. "Ramessean Front." Rameses II sits enthroned within a shrine with flags being flown above him.

Egypt Essays Photo 63. Luxor Temple of Amenhotep III. The "Kiosk of Hatshepsut" dedicated to the Theban Triad and usurped by Thutmose and later Rameses II stands in the "Ramessean Front."

EGYPT ESSAYS ON ANCIENT KEMET

Egypt Essays Photo 63a. Luxor Temple of Amenhotep III. "Ramessean Front." Alignment of column bases.

Egypt Essays Photo 63b. Luxor Temple of Amenhotep III. "Ramessean Front." Statues seemingly coming out from between the columns. White Crown heads lie on the ground.

Egypt Essays Photo 64. Luxor Temple of Amenhotep III. More bases of the columns of the Peristyle Colonnade in the "Ramessean Front."

Egypt Essays Photo 64a. Luxor Temple of Amenhotep III. Another view of the columns featured in the previous image, in the northwest corner of the "Ramessean Front" "Peristyle Court."

Egypt Essays Photo 64b. Luxor Temple. From the southwest, view of the magnificent "Processional Colonnade" with its 14-open calyx columns enclosed by two short walls whose inner face depict the journey to and from Luxor to celebrate the "Opet Festival," the purpose for the Temple of Luxor.

Egypt Essays Photo 65. Luxor Temple of Amenhotep III. Ascent into the "Peristyle Court of Amenhotep III" with its closed bud calyx capitals, an attractive magnet for photographers captivated by the "play of sun and light" reflected in the waning evening sun.

Egypt Essays Photo 65a. Luxor Temple of Amenhotep III. Columns of the Hypostyle Hall beyond the "Court of Amenhotep III."

Egypt Essays Photo 65b. Luxor Temple of Amenhotep III. From the southwest, view of the closed-bud with two bands colonnades in the "Court of Amenhotep III."

Egypt Essays Photo 66. Deir el Bahari Temple of Queen Hatshepsut. From the northeast, the "Birds' Eye View," of the Temple with its colonnades.

Egypt Essays Photo 66a. Deir el Bahari Temple of Queen Hatshepsut. Coming down the Mountain, view of the "First Ramp" and the "Fishes and Birds" and the "Obelisk" Colonnades.

Egypt Essays Photo 66b. Deir el Bahari Temple of Queen Hatshepsut. A better view of the principal features of the temple. The opening below leads to the Tomb of Senmut, Queen's architect.

FREDERICK MONDERSON

Egypt Essays Photo 67. Deir el Bahari Temple of Queen Hatshepsut. The Tomb of Vizier Nespakashuty (664-610 B.C.) on the slope of the mountain.

Egypt Essays Photo 67a. Deir el Bahari Temple of Queen Hatshepsut. From the "Birds' Eye View," the "Second Court," "Second Ramp" and "Middle" and "Upper Colonnades."

Egypt Essays Photo 68. Deir el Bahari Temple of Queen Hatshepsut. Two surviving Hathor Head columns in the Hathor Shrine.

Egypt Essays Photo 68a. Deir el Bahari Temple of Queen Hatshepsut. View of the Ramesseum from the mountain above Deir el Bahari.

Egypt Essays Photo 68b. Deir el Bahari Temple of Queen Hatshepsut. Untold numbers of visitors come to Deir el Bahari to view and appreciate this wonderful architectural experiment of the Queen and her architect Senmut. The opening leads to the Tomb of Senmut.

Egypt Essays Photo 69. Deir el Bahari Temple of Queen Hatshepsut. A crowd has gathered to view events of the "Virgin Birth" at the "Birth Colonnade," to the left; while to the right, a visitor leaves the "Anubis Shrine."

Egypt Essays Photo 69a. Deir el Bahari Temple of Queen Hatshepsut. An "Old Photograph" depicts the "Upper Court Hypostyle Hall" and "Portico" to the "Sanctuary."

Egypt Essays Photo 69b. Deir el Bahari Temple of Queen Hatshepsut. Shrine of Hathor. Close-up image of the goddess sporting a female face, cows ears, big wig and surmounted by a capital with cows wearing horns at its front.

Egypt Essays Photo 70. Deir el Bahari Temple of Queen Hatshepsut. On the north wall of the "Birth Colonnade," Thutmose III makes a presentation to "Sokar, Theban God of the Dead."

Egypt Essays Photo 70b. Deir el Bahari Temple of Queen Hatshepsut. The Queen's soldiers who came out to greet the two obelisks returning from Aswan to be erected at Karnak.

EGYPT ESSAYS ON ANCIENT KEMET

Egypt Essays Photo 71. Deir el Bahari Temple of Queen Hatshepsut. An attentive Guard on duty on the "Upper Terrace" before the Colonnade with a few surviving Osiride statues of the Queen.

Egypt Essays Photo 71a. Deir el Bahari Temple of Queen Hatshepsut. "Portico" entrance to the "Sanctuary" in the "Upper Court" with the mountain as a backdrop.

Egypt Essays Photo 71b. Deir el Bahari Temple of Queen Hatshepsut. While pillars and columns alternate in this temple's Colonnades, the "Middle Colonnade" boasts columns.

Egypt Essays Photo 71c. Deir el Bahari Temple of Queen. Previously people could climb the mountains to get a "Bird's Eye" view of the temple but now that is no longer allowed.

Egypt Essays Photo 72. Ramesseum, Mortuary Temple of Rameses II. Remains of a seated statue, four Osiride statues of the King, a broken head on the ground and stairs to the vestibule before the "Hypostyle Hall."

Egypt Essays Photo 72a. Ramesseum, Mortuary Temple of Rameses II. Looking past the massive columns into the "Hypostyle Hall," centerpiece of this testament to a great pharaoh.

Egypt Essays Photo 72b. Ramesseum, Mortuary Temple of Rameses II. Looking out from within the "Hypostyle Hall" at the columns that reflected the grandeur of its builder.

Egypt Essays Photo 73. Ramesseum, Mortuary Temple of Rameses II. The Colonnade is the majesty of this masterpiece of the Pharaoh.

Egypt Essays Photo 73a. Ramesseum, Mortuary Temple of Rameses II. The temple in its essentials with Osiride figure before the "Portico" and "Clerestory" above the "Hypostyle Hall."

Egypt Essays Photo 73b. Ramesseum, Mortuary Temple of Rameses II. Column bases in the "Hypostyle Hall."

Egypt Essays Photo 74. The Tomb of Sen-nefer. Thoth and Ra-Horakhty sail in their boat, with others while to the left, Sen-Nefer stands in another frame.

FREDERICK MONDERSON

Egypt Essays Photo 74a. The Tomb of Sen-Nefer. Sen-Nefer and his wife before the gods.

Egypt Essays Photo 74b. The Tomb of Sen-Nefer. Thoth introduces Sen-Nefer to enthroned Osiris colored green, which is actually a form of black.

Egypt Essays Photo 75. The Tomb of Sen-Nefer. Sen-Nefer and his wife pay respects to the Gods.

Egypt Essays Photo 75a. The Tomb of Sen-Nefer. Sen Nefer sails the heavens with the principal gods led by Isis and Thoth.

Egypt Essays Photo 75b. The Tomb of Sen-Nefer. Ra-Horakhty in his boat with baboons at fore and aft.

Egypt Essays Photo 77. Medinet Habu, Mortuary Temple of Rameses III. Alignment into the Temple, while above the entrance, the King smites Egypt's enemies.

Egypt Essays Photo 77a. Medinet Habu, Mortuary Temple of Rameses III. The "First Pylon" to the Temple of Rameses III, 20th Dynasty.

Egypt Essays Photo 77b. Medinet Habu, Mortuary Temple of Rameses III. Colored black, Amon-Ra sits enthroned with his consort "watching his back."

Egypt Essays Photo 77c. Medinet Habu, Mortuary Temple of Rameses III. Osiride statues decorated this "Second Court" of the temple.

Egypt Essays Photo 77d. Medinet Habu, Mortuary Temple of Rameses III. A small "Ramp" elevates to the next level, this time the "Hypostyle Hall" area of the temple.

Egypt Essays Photo 78. Medinet Habu, Mortuary Temple of Rameses III. Disfigured Osiride statues of the King in the "First Court." Notice the elevated steps to the "Second Court."

Egypt Essays Photo 78a. Medinet Habu, Mortuary Temple of Rameses III. One side of this "Court" with "Osiride Figures" and Columns.

Egypt Essays Photo 78b. Medinet Habu, Mortuary Temple of Rameses III. The other side of this "Court" with "Osiride Figures" and Columns.

EGYPT ESSAYS ON ANCIENT KEMET

Egypt Essays Photo 79. Medinet Habu, Mortuary Temple of Rameses III. Decorated columns behind pillars. Notice the base for each is different: column bases are round; pillar bases are square.

Egypt Essays Photo 79a. Medinet Habu, Mortuary Temple of Rameses III. Amon-Ra, painted Black, sits among the gods and goddesses.

Egypt Essays Photo 79b. Medinet Habu, Mortuary Temple of Rameses III. Rameses makes a presentation to enthroned Osiris who sits alongside Isis and Hathor.

Egypt Essays Photo 80. Medinet Habu, Mortuary Temple of Rameses III. Amon-Ra enthroned smells his flowers in his Shrine, while a defaced Mut stands to his rear.

Egypt Essays Photo 80a. Medinet Habu, Mortuary Temple of Rameses III. Fat cows in procession and above cows being slaughtered.

Egypt Essays Photo 81. Medinet Habu, Mortuary Temple of Rameses III. Rameses offers a platter to an enthroned Black Amon-Ra.

Egypt Essays Photo 81a. Medinet Habu, Mortuary Temple of Rameses III. Rameses prepares to pour a libation and incense enthroned Amon-Ra with Mut at the god's back.

Egypt Essays Photo 82. Hathor's Temple at Dendera. The classic columned hall entrance to the Temple. Each column sports a different capital, with the outer ones sporting Hathor Heads.

Egypt Essays Photo 82a. Hathor's Temple at Dendera. An image from the "Crypt," showing some secrets of the temple.

Egypt Essays Photo 82b. Hathor's Temple at Dendera. Horus, in size and beauty, evident a major player in this temple.

Egypt Essays Photo 83. Hathor's Temple at Dendera. Ceiling of a chapel to Goddess Nuit, depicting the divinity giving birth to the sun in the morning and swallowing it in the evening.

Egypt Essays Photo 83a. Hathor's Temple at Dendera. A Thoth ape with knives in the "Setting up the Tet" Osiris ritual.

Egypt Essays Photo 84. Osiris Temple at Abydos. The view from a distance shows six openings between the columns on each side of the middle or principal entrance. There were altogether seven entrances before Rameses closed all but the center one.

Egypt Essays Photo 84a. Osiris Temple at Abydos. Columns of the "Second Hypostyle Hall" showing the rise to the platform housing the shrines of the seven deities.

Egypt Essays Photo 84b. Osiris Temple at Abydos. Isis and Seti I set up the Tet or backbone of Osiris. Notice the kneeling figure. Four versions of the "Pillar" are indicated.

Egypt Essays Photo 84c. Osiris Temple at Abydos. An enthroned goddess from the nearby temple of Rameses II at Abydos.

Egypt Essays Photo 85. Osiris Temple at Abydos. Another view before shrines provides a look at an interior of great mystery and symbolism.

Egypt Essays Photo 85a. Osiris Temple at Abydos. An enthroned goddess from the nearby temple of Rameses II at Abydos.

Egypt Essays Photo 86. Osiris Temple at Abydos. Inner chambers depict more formalism and mystery.

Egypt Essays Photo 86a. Osiris Temple at Abydos. Part of the "Osireion" in the temple's rear. This mysterious region was always surrounded by water fed by underground springs connected to the Nile.

Egypt Essays Photo 86b. Osiris Temple at Abydos. Another enthroned goddess from the nearby temple of Rameses II at Abydos.

Egypt Essays Photo 87. Osiris Temple at Abydos. Wearing the leopard skin, the King, assisted by Hathor as Isis, presents a plant to Osiris, in full "Traveling Regalia."

Egypt Essays Photo 87a. Osiris Temple at Abydos. Seti kneels between enthroned gods as Amon-Ra gives him an instrument of power and Ra-Horakhty pats him on the back.

Egypt Essays Photo 87b. Osiris Temple at Abydos. Seti offers an instrument to enthroned Amon-Ra, painted Black!

Egypt Essays Photo 88. Osiris Temple at Abydos. Seti presents a platter to enthroned Isis.

Egypt Essays Photo 88a. Osiris Temple at Abydos. Seti makes a presentation of Ma'at to enthroned Ra-Horakhty.

EGYPT ESSAYS ON ANCIENT KEMET

Egypt Essays Photo 88b. Osiris Temple at Abydos. Ra-Horakhty gives life to the nostrils of Rameses II, from his nearby temple at Abydos.

Egypt Essays Photo 89. Osiris Temple at Abydos. Enthroned Isis offers ankh or life to Seti's nostrils.

Egypt Essays Photo 89a. Osiris Temple at Abydos. Carrying three vessels in each hand, Rameses II dances in an image from his nearby temple at Abydos.

Egypt Essays Photo 90. Osiris Temple at Abydos. Thoth restores life to Osiris.

Egypt Essays Photo 90a. Osiris Temple at Abydos. Isis gets intimate with Seti who smells her garment.

Egypt Essays Photo 90b. Osiris Temple at Abydos. Three Horus images carry vessels, from the nearby Rameses II temple at Abydos.

Egypt Essays Photo 91. Osiris Temple at Abydos. Anubis greets Seti I.

Egypt Essays Photo 91a. Osiris Temple at Abydos. Another part of the "Osireion" set-up some believe since the time of the Old Kingdom.

Egypt Essays Photo 91b. Osiris Temple at Abydos. The immediate entrance to the temple's central opening.

Egypt Essays Photo 92. Memphis Museum. The fallen colossus of Rameses II lies majestically as visitors mill around regularly at the Museum built around this statue.

Egypt Essays Photo 92a. Memphis Museum. Part of the nearby landscape at Memphis.

Egypt Essays Photo 92b. Memphis Museum. Bruised and battered statue, a survival of an age of greatness at Memphis.

Egypt Essays Photo 92c. Memphis Museum. Side view of the "Sphinx at Memphis."

Egypt Essays Photo 92d. Memphis Museum. *Suten Bat* title with Ma'at, more than likely Rameses II's cartouche.

FREDERICK MONDERSON

Egypt Essays Photo 92e. Memphis Museum. In the "Memphis Garden," a visitor pauses to take a photo of a colossal statue of Rameses II.

Egypt Essays Photo 93. Memphis Museum. Colossal standing statue wearing the White Crown.

Egypt Essays Photo 93a. Memphis Museum. Sign indicating a Sarcophagus of Amenhotep of the 19th Dynasty.

Egypt Essays Photo 93b. Memphis Museum. One of the souvenir vending stalls on the Museum grounds.

Egypt Essays Photo 94. Memphis Museum. Anubis atop the sarcophagus with that "thousand yard stare."

Egypt Essays Photo 95. Memphis Museum. Horus on the Sarcophagus.

Egypt Essays Photo 96. Sakkara. Home of the Step-Pyramid. Classic picture of the Step-Pyramid at Sakkara, built by Imhotep for Pharaoh Zoser of the Third Dynasty.

Egypt Essays Photo 96a. King Tutankhamon and his wife in an intimate mood.

Egypt Essays Photo 97. Sakkara. Home of the Step-Pyramid. Classis view of the world's first colonnade, enduring for 3000 years.

Egypt Essays Photo 98. Karnak Temple of Amen-Ra. Figure with a head of two birds holds a knife.

Egypt Essays Photo 98a. His wife presents King Tut with a bouquet of flowers.

Egypt Essays Photo 98b. Hathor and Mut on Papyrus.

Egypt Essays Photo 98c. Memphis Museum. Sign indicating more of the glory of the ancients.

Egypt Essays Photo 98d. A stone boat at rest on the grounds of the Cairo Museum of Egyptian Antiquities.

Egypt Essays Photo 99. Sakkara. Home of the Step-Pyramid. Another view of the wall enclosing the "Great Court" with uraei on the cornice.

Egypt Essays Photo 99a. Sakkara. Home of the Step-Pyramid. Image of the Step-Pyramid under construction.

EGYPT ESSAYS ON ANCIENT KEMET

Egypt Essays Photo 99b. Sakkara. Home of the Step-Pyramid. Ptah (center) flanked by two other divinities. The one on the right may be an image of Ptah for he seems to hold the emblems.

Egypt Essays Photo 100. Sakkara. Home of the Step-Pyramid. Colossal painting of Ptah-Hotep as he does his rounds.

Egypt Essays Photo 100a. Sakkara. Home of the Step-Pyramid. In the religious belief system, the deceased needed a statue for the spirit to return to. Several statues made this more likely.

Egypt Essays Photo 100b. Sakkara. Home of the Step-Pyramid. Laborers at work doing their many chores.

Egypt Essays Photo 100c. Sakkara. Home of the Step-Pyramid. Another view of the entranceway, providing shelter for workmen.

Egypt Essays Photo 101. Ghizeh. View of the Sphinx, the Great Pyramid of Khufu, and some of the throngs of people who visit this site on a daily basis.

Egypt Essays Photo 101a. Ghizeh. Not only camels but horses are another way to get around.

Egypt Essays Photo 101b. Ghizeh. Naturally, motor vehicles are essential. The guys in white are Tourist Police who make an extraordinary effort to provide security for tourists.

Egypt Essays Photo 102. Ghizeh. The "Great Pyramid of Khafra" viewed from the desert.

Egypt Essays Photo 102a. Ghizeh. Two of the Great Pyramids, Khufu (left) and Khafra (right) viewed from a local street near the Mena House Garden Hotel.

Egypt Essays Photo 102b. Ghizeh. Still another look at the "Great Pyramid of Khafra" from a local street and near the hotel.

Egypt Essays Photo 103. Ghizeh. View of the Mena House Garden Hotel as seen from the street.

Egypt Essays Photo 104. Cairo Museum of Egyptian Antiquities. Kashida Maloney of Brooklyn, beside a "Hathor Head" figure.

FREDERICK MONDERSON

Egypt Essays Photo 104a. Cairo Museum of Egyptian Antiquities. Broken stone showing the king in adoration and offering Ma'at.

Egypt Essays Photo 105. Cairo Museum of Egyptian Antiquities. The first of two statues of King Tutankhamon, painted black, to reflect his color.

Egypt Essays Photo 105a. Cairo Museum of Egyptian Antiquities. Tutankhamon as a bronze sphinx attacking Nubians painted black!

Egypt Essays Photo 105b. Cairo Museum of Egyptian Antiquities. Bronze plaque of the boy king attacking a lion.

Egypt Essays Photo 106. Cairo Museum of Egyptian Antiquities. The second statue of the King painted Black!

Egypt Essays Photo 106a. Cairo Museum of Egyptian Antiquities. Statues of the young king painted gold.

Egypt Essays Photo 106b. Cairo Museum of Egyptian Antiquities. Hathor as a calf, among King Tut's possessions.

Egypt Essays Photo 107. Cairo Museum of Egyptian Antiquities. Part of the ushabti collection that accompanied Tutankhamon into the afterlife.

Egypt Essays Photo 107a. Cairo Museum of Egyptian Antiquities. A beautiful piece of furniture for the king's personal effects.

Egypt Essays Photo 108. Cairo Museum of Egyptian Antiquities. Seated figure of the Goddess Sekhmet.

Egypt Essays Photo 108a. Cairo Museum of Egyptian Antiquities. More jewel and other personal boxes of the king.

Egypt Essays Photo 108b. Cairo Museum of Egyptian Antiquities. A duck or goose painted black to represent its color.

Egypt Essays Photo 109. Cairo Museum of Egyptian Antiquities. Kings and gods of early Egypt.

Egypt Essays Photo 109a. Cairo Museum of Egyptian Antiquities. Old and Middle Kingdom Kings of Egypt.

EGYPT ESSAYS ON ANCIENT KEMET

Egypt Essays Photo 110. Cairo Museum of Egyptian Antiquities.   Mainly New Kingdom Pharaohs.

Egypt Essays Photo 110a. Cairo Museum of Egyptian Antiquities. Late Period Pharaohs.

Egypt Essays Photo 111. Cairo Museum of Egyptian Antiquities. Graeco-Roman Pharaohs.

Egypt Essays Photo 111a. Cairo Museum of Egyptian Antiquities. Commentators on Egypt.

Egypt Essays Photo 112. Cairo Museum of Egyptian Antiquities. 19th Century scholars who worked to make Hieroglyphics a sound language and advance the discipline of Egyptology.

Egypt Essays Photo 112a. Cairo Museum of Egyptian Antiquities. The lintel above the doorway entrance to the Museum.

Egypt Essays Photo 113. Cairo Museum of Egyptian Antiquities. The Goddess Hathor personified atop the entrance to the Museum.

Egypt Essays Photo 113a. Cairo Museum of Egyptian Antiquities. An Egyptian manifestation of the beautiful decorating the entrance.

Egypt Essays Photo 113b. Cairo Museum of Egyptian Antiquities. M. Dourgnon, architect, who had the vision to build such a structure.

Egypt Essays Photo 114. Cairo Museum of Egyptian Antiquities. Rosellini, the Italian linguist and archaeologist who worked alongside Champollion to lay the foundation for the discipline.

Egypt Essays Photo 114a. Cairo Museum of Egyptian Antiquities. Champollion, the master who cracked the Hieroglyphic Code in 1822, but died in 1832.

Egypt Essays Photo 115. Cairo Museum of Egyptian Antiquities. Samuel Birch, master Egyptologist whose efforts were instrumental in guiding the young science.

FREDERICK MONDERSON

Egypt Essays Photo 115a. Cairo Museum of Egyptian Antiquities. Classic case of "Stand by Your Man" in the Museum Gardens.

Egypt Essays Photo 115b. Cairo Museum of Egyptian Antiquities. A facade view of this magnificent structure, repository to a glorious past.

Egypt Essays Photo 116. Cairo Museum of Egyptian Antiquities. The Mariette Memorial that pays tribute to the greatest Egyptological minds.

Egypt Essays Photo 116a. Cairo Museum of Egyptian Antiquities.

Egypt Essays Photo 116b. Cairo Museum of Egyptian Antiquities.

Egypt Essays Photo 116c. Cairo Museum of Egyptian Antiquities.

Egypt Essays Photo 116d. Cairo Museum of Egyptian Antiquities.

Egypt Essays Photo 116e. Cairo Museum of Egyptian Antiquities.

Egypt Essays Photo 116f. Cairo Museum of Egyptian Antiquities.

Egypt Essays Photo 116g. Cairo Museum of Egyptian Antiquities.

Egypt Essays Photo 116h. Cairo Museum of Egyptian Antiquities.

Egypt Essays Photo 116i. Cairo Museum of Egyptian Antiquities.

Egypt Essays Photo 116j. Cairo Museum of Egyptian Antiquities.

Egypt Essays Photo 116k. Cairo Museum of Egyptian Antiquities.

Egypt Essays Photo 116l. Cairo Museum of Egyptian Antiquities.

EGYPT ESSAYS ON ANCIENT KEMET

Egypt Essays Photo 116m. Cairo Museum of Egyptian Antiquities.

Egypt Essays Photo 116n. Cairo Museum of Egyptian Antiquities. Hippolito Rosellini.

Egypt Essays Photo 116o. Cairo Museum of Egyptian Antiquities.

Egypt Essays Photo 116p. Cairo Museum of Egyptian Antiquities.

Egypt Essays Photo 116q. Cairo Museum of Egyptian Antiquities.

Egypt Essays Photo 116r. Cairo Museum of Egyptian Antiquities.

Egypt Essays Photo 116s. Cairo Museum of Egyptian Antiquities.

Egypt Essays Photo 116t. Cairo Museum of Egyptian Antiquities. Jean Francois Champollion.

Egypt Essays Photo 116u. Cairo Museum of Egyptian Antiquities.

Egypt Essays Photo 116v. Cairo Museum of Egyptian Antiquities. Pleyte

Egypt Essays Photo 116w. Cairo Museum of Egyptian Antiquities. Dr. Gaston Maspero

Egypt Essays Photo 116x. Cairo Museum of Egyptian Antiquities.

Egypt Essays Photo 117. Imhotep Museum at Sakkara. This building houses artifacts relative to the world's first multi-genius.

Egypt Essays Photo 118. Sakkara, Home of the Step-Pyramid. From between the Colonnade looking out into the Great Court.

Egypt Essays Photo 118a. Sakkara, Home of the Step-Pyramid. From the Great Court looking toward the Colonnade.

Egypt Essays Photo 119. Since the deceased needed an extra head or body as an insurance in the afterlife, several increased the chances of survival.

FREDERICK MONDERSON

Egypt Essays Photo 119a. Sakkara, Home of the Step-Pyramid. Reserve statues, to ensure survival of the deceased in a private tomb. Again, several statues gave the deceased several chances of survival.

Egypt Essays Photo 120. Sakkara, Home of the Step-Pyramid. A great man sits before a "Table of Offerings" still showing good color.

Egypt Essays Photo 120a. Sakkara, Home of the Step-Pyramid. Part of the entourage bringing goods to the same great man.

Egypt Essays Photo 121. Sakkara, Home of the Step-Pyramid. From beyond some ruins looking at the roof of the Colonnade and towards the Step Pyramid in the rear.

Egypt Essays Photo 121a. Sakkara, Home of the Step-Pyramid. Part of the sand-covered ruins of the surrounding area.

Egypt Essays Photo 122. Sakkara, Home of the Step-Pyramid. An area filled with debris (left); and a cleared area descending to a tomb (right).

Egypt Essays Photo 123. Sakkara, Home of the Step-Pyramid. Entrance to the Akhnaton Carpet School where wonderful rugs are made.

Egypt Essays Photo 124. Cairo Museum of Egyptian Antiquities. A defaced Sphinx stands before the entrance as throngs of people prepare to enter (left); and an enclosed pair of statues in the garden area where photography is permitted though "banned" inside (right).

Egypt Essays Photo 125. Karnak Temple of Amon-Ra. From the north, view of a crane atop the Ninth Pylon on the North/South Axis; Hatshepsut (left) and her father Thutmose I's Obelisk (right); and ruins of the Hypostyle Hall further right.

Egypt Essays Photo 126. Karnak Temple of Amon-Ra. From the north, view of a crane atop the Ninth Pylon on the North/South Axis; Hatshepsut (left) and her father Thutmose I's Obelisk (right); and ruins of the Hypostyle Hall further right.

EGYPT ESSAYS ON ANCIENT KEMET

Egypt Essays Photo 127. Karnak Temple of Amon-Ra. The "Red Chapel" of Hatshepsut. A kneeling Hatshepsut offers a vessel to enthroned Amon-Ra (top left); and (top right) her image is defaced doing the same; while below she offers two plants to members of the enthroned Theban Ennead.

Egypt Essays Photo 128. Karnak Temple of Amon-Ra. The "Red Chapel" of Hatshepsut. Whether kneeling or standing before the enthroned Ennead, Hatshepsut's image is erased.

Egypt Essays Photo 129. Karnak Temple of Amon-Ra. The "Red Chapel" of Hatshepsut. In this instance, while the Ennead's image has been destroyed, Hatshepsut's has escaped the destructor's hands and she presents two vessels and a "Table of Offerings." Egypt Essays Photo 129a. Karnak Temple of Amon-Ra. The "Red Chapel" of Hatshepsut. With nutrients placed before the Gods of the Theban Ennead, Hatshepsut's image stands erased.

Egypt Essays Photo 130. Karnak Temple of Amon-Ra. The "Red Chapel" of Hatshepsut. To the left, Hatshepsut (Cartouche *Ma'at-Ka-Ra* above) offers two plants to Amon-Ra, while (right); the now defaced Queen offers flowers to Min version of Amon.

Egypt Essays Photo 130a. Karnak Temple of Amon-Ra. The "Red Chapel" of Hatshepsut. While the Queen offers food with both hands to Min as Amon-Ra (left); she offers flowers with one hand (right) to Min balancing, not holding, the flagellum.

Egypt Essays Photo 131. Karnak Temple of Amon-Ra. The "Red Chapel" of Hatshepsut. The ark at rest with victuals and unguents nearby.

Egypt Essays Photo 131a. Karnak Temple of Amon-Ra. The "Red Chapel" of Hatshepsut. Symbols - "Life, Stability, Dominion."

Egypt Essays Photo 132. Karnak Temple of Amon-Ra. The "Red Chapel" of Hatshepsut. While Mut in Red Crown embraces Hatshepsut, image of Hatshepsut, having escaped the destroyer, presents two plants to enthroned Amon-Ra.

Egypt Essays Photo 132a. Karnak Temple of Amon-Ra. The "Red Chapel" of Hatshepsut. Saluting and looking back at Amon, Min, and Amon again.

FREDERICK MONDERSON

Egypt Essays Photo 133. Memphis Museum. Defaced bust of an unknown, possibly Rameses II. Interesting, however, that such hard stone could be easily defaced.

Egypt Essays Photo 133a. Memphis Museum. The Memphis colossal lying in the prone position.

Egypt Essays Photo 134. Memphis Museum. The statue of Rameses II, again in the prone position, from the left side.

Egypt Essays Photo 135. Memphis Museum. An offering table with the depression for blood to run out.

Egypt Essays Photo 136. Luxor Temple of Amenhotep III. Baboons in erection at base of remaining Luxor Obelisk. On the other in Paris, the French severed the penis.

Egypt Essays Photo 137. Native Guide "Showgi" Abd el-Rady (center) and friends outside the Tomb of Inherkha.

Egypt Essays Photo 138. Native Guide "Showgi" and friends in a startled mood.

Egypt Essays Photo 139. Showgi Abd el Rady with more friends.

Egypt Essay Photo 140. While conducting his tour, Native Guide Hasan Elian signals to his friend, the author and photographer.

Egypt Essays Photo 141. Sakkara, Home of the Step-Pyramid. An area filled with debris (left); and a cleared area descending to a tomb (right).

Egypt Essays Photo 142. Sakkara, Home of the Step-Pyramid. Entrance to the Akhnaton Carpet School where wonderful rugs are made.

Egypt Essays Photo 143. Cairo Museum of Egyptian Antiquities. A defaced Sphinx stands before the entrance as throngs of people prepare to enter at rear.

Egypt Essays Photo 144. Karnak Temple of Amon-Ra. From the north, view of a crane atop the Ninth Pylon on the North/South Axis; Hatshepsut (left) and her father Thutmose I's Obelisk (right) and ruins of the Hypostyle Hall further right.

EGYPT ESSAYS ON ANCIENT KEMET

Egypt Essays Photo 145. An Egyptian Guide to the Tomb of Userhat in the South Assasif.

Egypt Essays Photo 146. Karnak Temple of Amon-Ra. The "Red Chapel" of Hatshepsut. A kneeling Hatshepsut offers a vessel to enthroned Amon-Ra (top left); and (top right) her image is defaced doing the same; while below she offers two plants to the enthroned Ennead.

Egypt Essays Photo 147. Karnak Temple of Amon-Ra. The "Red Chapel" of Hatshepsut. Whether kneeling or standing before the enthroned Ennead, Hatshepsut's image is erased.

Egypt Essays Photo 148. Guide "Showgi" Abd el-Rady stands with friends before the First Pylon at Medinet Habu Temple of Rameses III.

Egypt Essays Photo 149. Karnak Temple of Amon-Ra. The "Red Chapel" of Hatshepsut. In this instance, while the Ennead's image has been destroyed, Hatshepsut's has escaped the destructor's hands and she presents two vessels and a "Table of Offerings."

Egypt Essays Photo 150. Karnak Temple of Amon-Ra. The "Red Chapel" of Hatshepsut. To the left, Hatshepsut (Cartouche *Ma'at-Ka-Ra* above) offers two plants to Amon-Ra, while to the right, now the now defaced Queen offers flowers to Amon as Min.

Egypt Essays Photo 150a. Karnak Temple of Amon-Ra. The "Red Chapel" of Hatshepsut. While the Queen offers food with both hands to Amon as Min (left); she offers flowers with one hand (right) to Min balancing, not holding the flagellum.

Egypt Essays Photo 151. Karnak Temple of Amon-Ra. The "Red Chapel" of Hatshepsut. The ark at rest with victuals and unguents nearby.

Egypt Essays Photo 152. Karnak Temple of Amon-Ra. The "Red Chapel" of Hatshepsut. While Mut in Red Crown embraces Hatshepsut (left); an image of Hatshepsut, having escaped the destroyer, presents two plants to enthroned Amon-Ra (right).

Egypt Essays Photo 152a. Karnak Temple of Amon-Ra. "Red Chapel" of Hatshepsut. Saluting Amon, Min and Amon again.

FREDERICK MONDERSON

Egypt Essays Photo 153. Memphis Museum. The Memphis colossal lying in the prone position.

Egypt Essays Photo 154. Memphis Museum. An offering table with the depression for blood to run out.

Egypt Essays Photo 155. Native Guide "Showgi" Abd el-Rady and a friend in embrace while he does work on the cell-phone.

Egypt Essays Photo 155a. Classic view of the Great Pyramid, devoid of its facings.

Egypt Essays Photo 156. Partial view of greenery and the Cairo Skyline from the Mena House Garden Hotel.

Egypt Essays Illustrations

Egypt Essays Illustration 1. Bust of Nefertiti, wife of Amenhotep IV, Akhnaton, the XVIIIth Dynasty religious reformer.

Egypt Essays Illustration 1a. Necklace sash bounded by gold cartouches of King Tut with fringes of the sacred symbol of life, the ankh.

Egypt Essays Illustration 1c. Wreath of real flowers placed around the neck of Tutankhamon's inner coffin, with the inlaid eyes disintegrated by the composition caused by the consecration unguents, and a napkin tucked between the head and the sides of the second coffin.

Egypt Essays Illustration 1d. The Egyptian Zodiac, different from later Graeco-Roman examples.

Egypt Essays Illustration 1e. Shu, the Air God, separates Nut, the Sky Goddess, from Seb, the Earth God. Thoth and Horus or Ra-Horakhty were there as witnesses at that phenomenal happening.

Egypt Essays Illustration 2. Sahu (Orion) and the cow Sothis sailing the heavens but separated by the Sparrow-Hawk wearing the Double Crown.

Egypt Essays Illustration 2a. Close-up image of an Old Kingdom boat pit, showing bricks separating sections of the structure.

EGYPT ESSAYS ON ANCIENT KEMET

Egypt Essays Illustration 3. Flint knife of the Predynastic Age.

Egypt Essays Illustration 4. Flinders Petrie's Decorated Vase of the Gerzean Period.

Egypt Essays Illustration 5. An incident in the wars of Harmachis and Sit or Set, found in the "Corridor of Victory" at Horus Temple at Edfu.

Egypt Essays Illustration 5a. Head of a seated figure of a XVIIth Dynasty priestess wearing a full-plaited wig, bandlet, etc., now in the British Museum.

Egypt Essays Illustration 6. Prehistoric images of boats plying the Nile River with one and two deckhouses and various Nome signs.

Egypt Essays Illustration 7. A close-up of boats and birds on the waterside.

Egypt Essays Illustration 8. Corpus of Badarian Pottery: Assortment of copper and ivory pieces, etc. (left); and Black Topped Brown (right).

Egypt Essays Illustration 9. Prehistoric Ivory Figures (left); and Female Figurines (right).

Egypt Essays Illustration 10. Corpus of Badarian Pottery: Black Topped, Brown (left); and Black Topped, Red (right).

Egypt Essays Illustration 10a. Corpus of Badarian Pottery: All Black (left); and Mummified Ibises (right).

Egypt Essays Illustration 11. Prehistoric bone harpoons and clay and wood model weapons (left); and slate figures and spacers (right).

Egypt Essays Illustration 11a. Corpus of Badarian Pottery: Black Topped Red and Polished Red.

Egypt Essays Illustration 12. View of sphinxes and statues (left); and house timbers, bed frame and arrows from Tarkhan (right).

Egypt Essays Illustration 12a. Base of a limestone statue of the Third Dynasty Pharaoh Zoser, builder of the Step Pyramid at Sakkara; and front view of the base.

FREDERICK MONDERSON

Egypt Essays Illustration 13. Tarkhan burials and pottery of different shapes.

Egypt Essays Illustration 13a. Tarkhan House Timbers, Bed Frames and Arrows (left); and Tarkhan Alabaster – Handled and Pear Vases (right).

Egypt Essays Illustration 14. Tarkhan coffins (left); and sealings, armlets, coffins, etc (right).

Egypt Essays Illustration 14a. Tarkhan view, and vessels of stone and copper (left); and Ptah Bowl, Sa Case, Scarabs, Flint Armlets, and Zebra drawings (right).

Egypt Essays Illustration 15. Tarkhan ivory and beads (left); and pottery (right).

Egypt Essays Illustration 15a. Tarkhan Pottery Inscriptions and marks (left); and Tarkhan Mastaba 1060, Clay Sealings and Pottery Marks (right).

Egypt Essays Illustration 16. Tarkhan pottery, bowl, wall (left); worked flings and copper bowls (right).

Egypt Essays Illustration 16a. Intricate details of engraved solid gold and precious stones of King Tut's third innermost coffin showing the mid-section of his arms grasping the symbols of power.

Egypt Essays Illustration 17. Tarkhan. Plan of small mastabas, with surface stacks of offerings (left); and tomb from different views with deceased in contracted position with goods of the grave nearby (right).

Egypt Essays Illustration 17a. Tarkhan Curves of Dimensions of Skulls (left); and Tarkhan Plans of Small Mastabas with Surface Stacks for Offerings (right).

Egypt Essays Illustration 18. Foreign pottery of the First Dynasty and Fifteenth Dynasty pottery (left); as well as cones from the early period (right).

Egypt Essays Illustration 18a. Abydos Bracelets from the Tomb of King Zer (left); and Inscriptions of Kings Ka, Narmer and Sam (right).

Egypt Essays Illustration 19. Abydos. Sealings of King Aha-Men (left); and of Kings Ka and Narmer (right).

EGYPT ESSAYS ON ANCIENT KEMET

Egypt Essays Illustration 19a. Ivories from the Tomb of King Zer-Ta (left); and Tomb of King Khasekhemui (right).

Egypt Essays Illustration 20. Tombs of Qa-Sen and Sekhemab-Perabsen (left); and Seth-Ath and of Den-Setui (right).

Egypt Essays Illustration 20a. Steles around the Tomb of Zer-Ta (left); and Steles around the Tomb of Sen-Setui (left).

Egypt Essays Illustration 21. Prostration in presence of the deified King.

Egypt Essays Illustration 21a. Tomb of King Zer-Ta, Ivories; Seal of Ka, Narmer alabaster, ebony and ivory, etc.

Egypt Essays Illustration 21b. Ebony Tablet of King Mena of the Ist Dynasty (left); and Ist Dynasty Tomb of King Zer showing brick partitions to contain offerings.

Egypt Essays Illustration 22. Amenhotep III of the 18th Dynasty gives audience to one of his ministers.

Egypt Essays Illustration 23. Steles around Tomb of Zer-Ta and Steles around Tomb of Den-Setui.

Egypt Essays Illustration 23a. Statues of Hor (left); and Pakhouroi (right). One with Inscription (left) the other with Hathor head (right).

Egypt Essays Illustration 24. "Stele of Choi" (left); and "Stele of the Mireacle of Aahmes I" at Abydos (right).

Egypt Essays Illustration 25. Stele of Tehuti, a royal kinsman of the King's throne and Ka-priest of the King. XIIth Dynasty (left); and Limestone sepulchral stele of Nbekht-Anher dated in the 7th year of the reign of Khakauri Usertesen (Senusert III) III. XIIth Dynasty (right).

Egypt Essays Illustration 26. Herdsmen giving accounts of cattle.

Egypt Essays Illustration 27. The weighing of the Heart of Ani, the scribe, in the Great scales in the Judgment Hall of Osiris (From the Papyrus of Ani (left); and Horus, the son of Isis, introducing the Scribe Ani, who has been declared to be a "Speaker of Truth" by Thoth, into the presence of Osiris; the Scribe Ani kneeling before Osiris, from the Papyrus of Ani (left).

FREDERICK MONDERSON

Egypt Essays Illustration 28. Cast in bronze of the head of a portrait-statue of Tutankhamon in the Egyptian Museum in Berlin (left); and seated figures of Khamuast and his wife, XVIIIth Dynasty (right).

Egypt Essays Illustration 29. Painted wooden sepulchral chest in the form of a pylon, with figures of the amulets of Isis and Osiris, XXVIth Dynasty or later (left); and rectangular painted limestone shrine with pyramid roof, of Ani, a gardener of Amarna. On each side, in relief, is a figure of the deceased holding a tablet inscribed with a hymn to Ra, XVIIIth Dynasty (right).

Egypt Essays Illustration 30. Fishing for statues in Karnak Temple's "Cachette Court" under the direction of Legrain.

Egypt Essays Illustration 31. Further fishing for statues in the "Cachette Court" with the 7th Pylon in background to the rear (left); and finding a statue of Merenptah of the XIXth Dynasty (right). In this "Cachette Court, in foreground to the 7th Pylon, Legrain discovered some eight thousand statues in golden bronze, and more than five hundred in granite, basalt, beryl, limestone, petrified, and other materials. Almost all the discoveries bear historical inscriptions. This find is said to be the most important since Mariette's famous discovery of the Serapeum at Memphis. Important that these statues last handled by the ancient Egyptian and discovered under the cloud of fanfare do not have their noses broken!

Egypt Essays Illustration 32. Craftsmanship ancient and modern: Ancient Greek and Egyptian Art discovered in Egypt: The Treasure of Touk-El-Garmous.

Egypt Essays Illustration 33. A group of carved ivory wands, all found in one burial shaft, near the pyramid of Amenemhat I at Lisht, described as "Amuletic in character. Made to protect their owner from the fearsome creatures he expected to encounter in the Under-world."

Egypt Essays Illustration 34. Copper implements found at Lisht during the time of the XIIth Dynasty, including "Nails, tweezers, fish-hooks, and harpoons, lance and arrow heads, rasps, needles, and Axe-Head."

EGYPT ESSAYS ON ANCIENT KEMET

Egypt Essays Illustration 35. An Egyptian village that existed from about 1700 B.C., showing a group of houses at Lisht built against the side of the Pyramid of Amenemhat I, after it had been plundered and reduced to ruin.

Egypt Essays Illustration 36. At Tell El-Amarna, a stone table for offerings sits in front of a doorway, made of stone and painted red (left); and a Besom and paint-brushes, wickerwork stand, and fiber-ring for balancing the tray on the head (right).

Egypt Essays Illustration 37. A Baboon-God Shrine revealed, showing a recessed image of Thoth as a Baboon-Headed God (Cynocephalus) with a light-shaft (left) to illumine it. An underground chapel at Hermopolis whose walls contained a mummy.

Egypt Essays Illustration 38. An Open-Air chapel at one of the entrances to the subterranean galleries at Hermopolis. A view showing the desolate site of the City where baboons and ibis were held sacred, and part of the excavations (left); mud-brick building beyond the balustrade of sandstone pillars containing an embalmer's workshop and a chamber where pilgrims paid fees for the mummification of baboons and ibis brought as offering.

Egypt Essays Illustration 39. Egyptian ships in full decorated sail.

Egypt Essays Illustration 39a. A beautiful Ptolemaic chalice in light-blue faience: One of several vessels of fine workmanship found in the subterranean tombs at Hermopolis (left); and a faience bowl in deep rich blue from the sacred city of Hermopolis: An under-side view showing the curious pattern of the decoration.

Egypt Essays Illustration 40. Vulture in flight with outspread wings and clutching an ankh in its talons as shown in the restored "White Chapel" of Senusert I at Karnak (left); and the reconstructed "White Chapel" of Senusert I of the XIIth Dynasty and now in Karnak Temple's Open Air Museum.

Egypt Essays Illustration 41. The earliest stone building ever found: Two third dynasty chapels excavated from the Step Pyramid at Sakkara, with fluted columns 2500 years older than the earliest one known of Greek construction (left); A bowman-

FREDERICK MONDERSON

charioteer illustrated showing the king, Rameses II, in blue crown with reins attached to his waist as he fires his arrow (right).

Egypt Essays Illustration 42. A kneeling statue of Hatshepsut with its face damaged and missing parts of both arms, while another kneeling statues stands nearby.

Egypt Essays Illustration 43. A splendid alabaster offering plate found near the grave of Ti-Mery, "Chief of the king's linen chamber" at Sakkara (described as one of the best single finds) (left); and fragments of broken statues of Queen Hatshepsut, buried at her death (right).

Egypt Essays Illustration 44. Early indication of wrestling as part of military training.

Egypt Essays Illustration 45. Tutankhamon's canopic chest, a gem of Egyptian sculpture showing the gold dada and guardian goddesses.

Egypt Essays Illustration 46. Released from its Sarcophagus, the coffin containing Tutankhamon's mummy rests in quiet solitude.

Egypt Essays Illustration 47. Gable-topped coffin containing the earliest known mummified horse, found near the pyramids and dated to c. 1200 B.C.

Egypt Essays Illustration 47a. The remains of the horse wrapped in "mummy cloth" (left); and the remains of the horse with the "mummy cloth" removed.

Egypt Essays Illustration 48. The First Cataract on the Nile at Aswan (Syene).

Egypt Essays Illustration 48a. Wreath of real flowers placed around the neck of Tutankhamon's inner coffin, with the inlaid eyes disintegrated by the composition caused by the consecration unguents, and a napkin tucked between the head and the sides of the second coffin.

Egypt Essays Illustration 49. A sculpture never meant to be seen; part of the roof of the Sarcophagus room, showing the Goddess Nuit swallowing the sun at evening time.

EGYPT ESSAYS ON ANCIENT KEMET

Egypt Essays Illustration 50. View of the Central hall of the "Osireion," recognized as the Cenotaph of Seti I (left); and in the foreground two steps leading down to the "Primeval Waters" and behind them two holes to take the shrines into where the tomb of Osiris was found (right).

Egypt Essays Illustration 50b. "An exquisitely worked vulture" shown in flight with outspread wings, and clutching in its talons an ankh (the sign of life) Part of a mural relief in the restored temple of Senusert I at Karnak in the "Open Air Museum."

Egypt Essays Illustration 50c. A gold pectoral depicting the Ba-bird that was the king's spirit with a diadem similar to that actually found on King Tut's head.

Egypt Essays Illustration 51. In the foreground, steps leading down to the "Primeval Waters" and behind them, the place for a shrine of Seti as Osiris, ruler of the other-world; a corner of the Island representing the "Primeval Hill" (left); and in the background, one of the cells for the "Guardian Spirits;" on the right, the ledge of the Island, the "Primeval Hill," the "Primeval Waters" of the Cenotaph (right).

Egypt Essays Illustration 52. Men's dresses and a shirt from the work of Professor Rosellini.

Egypt Essays Illustration 52a. Causeway of Khafra, from the Mortuary Shrine at the Pyramid to the Valley Temple (the so-called Temple of the sphinx) – A threefold way, finely paved with limestone.

Egypt Essays Illustration 52b. Aerial photographs of the Subterranean Cenotaph of Seti I in the foreground, with its pillared hall representing the "Primeval Hill" rising out of the "Primeval Waters"; and, one of the earliest arches in architecture: The five course arch of bricks, which was closed after the ritual of the burial of the dead, had been performed.

Egypt Essays Illustration 53. Dresses of priests and sacred scribes (Thebes).

Egypt Essays Illustration 53a. Tutankhamon's gold diadem showing gold uraei on the side appendages (left); and from

FREDERICK MONDERSON

behind, the symbolic bow at the back, the ribbons and side appendages (right).

Egypt Essays Illustration 54. An important milestone in the development of civilization: one of the two Tutankhamon daggers, with an iron blade resembling steel and in perfect condition (left); and, with a blade of gold and richly ornamented haft, one of two magnificent daggers found on Tutankhamon's mummy (right).

Egypt Essays Illustration 55. In their sheaths: The same two daggers shown above unsheathed, that on the right having a rock-crystal knob on the shaft (left); and the other side of the left hand sheath beautifully embossed with wild animals (right).

Egypt Essays Illustration 56. A fine Egyptian Balsamary inscribed Green Duck-Egg (left); and Black Balsalt head of King Amasis II (right).

Egypt Essays Illustration 57. Composed of 255 separate gold plaques, finely inlaid, and threaded together by means of tiny eyelets: "The Collar" is a wonderfully flexible pectoral-showing (top center) the Gold wire by which it hung from the king.

Egypt Essays Illustration 58. A side view of the right profile of the sphinx undergoing repairs after the paws were uncovered in excavation (left) and a back view of the famous monument under scaffolding (right).

Egypt Essays Illustration 59. A parallel to "The contents of a modern corner-stone," saucers of fruit for her "Eternal provision" showing part of a foundation deposit from Hatshepsut's temple (left); and scraps of pleated linen from the tomb of the eleventh-dynasty Queen Neferu, showing "Still retaining the folds ironed into them from four thousand years ago" (right).

Egypt Essays Illustration 60. The entrance to Neferu's tomb showing "The ancient tourists' entrance" dated to 3500 B.C. when the tomb was blocked up (left); and scraps of sculpture and a wall torn down by ancient robbers that bears "The names of Tourists who had scribbled on the walls 35 centuries ago.

Egypt Essays Illustration 61. The first step in the discovery of the tomb of Meryet Amun beside the temple of

EGYPT ESSAYS ON ANCIENT KEMET

Hatshepsut (left) and Plan of the tomb of Meryet-Amun (below) the ground plan and (above) the sectional plan.

Egypt Essays Illustration 62. Top of the brickwork blocking the entrance of the tomb, and the rubbish filling the pit: straw basket-lids and bits of a coffin (left); and corridor of the tomb from the entrance: *Shawabti Boxes* and (beyond) Baskets of the 18th Dynasty (right).

Egypt Essays Illustrations 63. Plan of Thebes showing both sides of the river with principal monuments.

Egypt Essays Illustration 63a. The inner coffin and mummy of Princess Entiu-Ny, a later burial (1000 B.C.), found in the corridor of the above tomb of Queen Meryet-Amun (left); and the empty coffin of Entiu-Ny on the brink of the well (right).

Egypt Essays Illustration 64. A shattered head of Hatshepsut belonging to a headless statue now in Berlin showing the Queen without the conventional Royal Beard.

Egypt Essays Illustration 64a. Close-up of Tutankhamon's death mask showing the king with his scepter and flagella or whip.

Egypt Essays Illustration 65. Anubis tending the Mummy while the Ba Bird hovers overhead.

Egypt Essays Illustration 65a. A bowman-charioteer firing his arrow in stride in an Abu Simbel illustration

Egypt Essays Illustration 65b. The mummy of Queen Meryet-Amun in its place inside the coffin, in her newly found tomb (left); and stripped of its gold casing by ancient tomb-robbers: The lid of Meryet-Smun's inner coffin (right).

Egypt Essays Illustration 66. Examples of how the Ancient Egyptians applied principles to irrigation, fowling, agriculture and harvest.

Egypt Essays Illustration 67. Illustrations depicting the Ancient Egyptians method of agricultural tools and effort.

Egypt Essays Illustration 68. Before excavation of the Great Tomb at Meydum, lying at the northeast side of the pyramid (left); after excavation, the north end of the Great Mastaba: a unique

FREDERICK MONDERSON

stepped type, showing the high brick retaining wall foreground, and rubble core beyond built in three stages (right).

Egypt Essays Illustration 69. The Great North Wall of the Mastaba (here 56 ft. high): A view showing the depth of the foundations (left); and ancient leveling marks on the Mastaba: "6 cubits" – The level shown by a horizontal line.

Egypt Essays Illustration 70. Made to mislead tomb-robbers: A stairway in the west side of the Mastaba, leading down to a "blind" tunnel beneath it (left); and a Diagram of the Construction of the mastaba with the position of the "6 Cubits" level mark (in No. 5) indicated just above the words "stage" (right).

Egypt Essays Illustration 71. Another part of the structure designed to mislead tomb-robbers: The mouth of the "Blind" tunnel (left); and originally walled and roofed: A chapel or offering niche, on the east side of the Mastaba (right).

Egypt Essays Illustration 72. Beautiful Queen Hatshepsut dressed as a man in head-dress and kilt, but with a distinctly female face (left); as it appeared before restoration, the beautiful marble statue of Hatshepsut, with the head and other fragments found and rejoined to the seated body from Berlin (right). Notice the statue on the left has both hands while the right one has the hands missing.

Egypt Essays Illustration 73. Profile of Queen Hatshepsut without her beard (left); and full face view of the Queen. Notice her nose is not broken. As in other frames where the body is broken.

Egypt Essays Illustration 74. A clothes-basket belonging to Queen Meryet-Amun, sister and wife of Amenhotep II and daughter of Thutmose III (left); and a little basket of Queen Meryet-Amun decorated with ostriches, some 3500 years old (right).

Egypt Essays Illustration 75. Sandal footwear, 3000 years old, a man, child's and wooden pattern used for cutting out soles in the center.

Egypt Essays Illustration 76. A painted clay pot found in a 14th Century B.C. workmen's village at Tell El-Amarna (left); and another painted clay pot also found at Amarna.

EGYPT ESSAYS ON ANCIENT KEMET

Egypt Essay Illustration 77. Colonnade at Sakkara perpendicular to the passage that entrances the Great Court (top right) during early excavation and without the shelter later added.

Egypt Essays Illustration 78. A statue of King Amenhotep IV, Akhenaten, found at Karnak Temple.

Egypt Essays Illustration 1b. In that familiar pose Goddess Isis kneels with outstretched arms exposing her winged prowess.

Egypt Essays Illustration 1c. Wreath of real flowers placed around the neck of Tutankhamon's inner coffin, with the inlaid eyes disintegrated by the composition caused by the consecration unguents, and a napkin tucked between the head and the sides of the second coffin.

FREDERICK MONDERSON

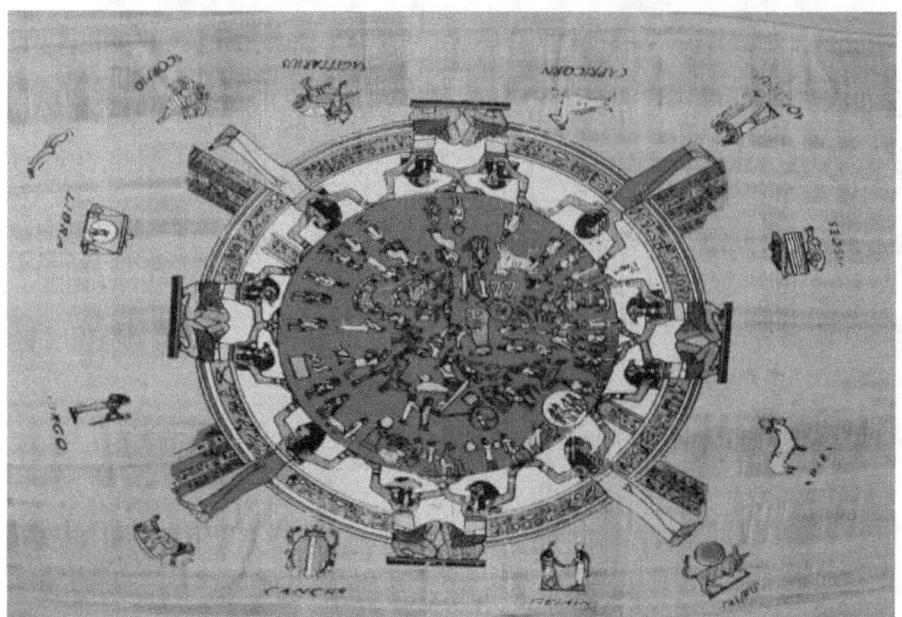

Egypt Essays Illustration 1d. The Egyptian Zodiac, different from later Graeco-Roman examples.

Plans

Egypt Essays Plan of the Temples of Rameses II and his Queen Nefertari Abu Simbel in Nubia.
Egypt Essays Plan of the Temple of Isis of Philae now on Agilka Island.
Egypt Essays Plan of the Double Temple at Kom Ombo.
Egypt Essays Plan of the Temple of Horus at Edfu.
Egypt Essays Plan of the Temple of Esneh.
Egypt Essays General Plan of the Temples of Karnak.
Egypt Essays Plan of Karnak Temple.
Egypt Essays Plan of the Temple of Karnak during the reigns of Thutmose I and Hatshepsut.

EGYPT ESSAYS ON ANCIENT KEMET

Egypt Essays Plan of Karnak Temple during the reign of Thutmose III.
Egypt Essays Plan of Karnak Temple during the reign of Amenhotep III.
Egypt Essays Plan of Karnak Temple under Rameses II.
Egypt Essays Plan of Karnak Under the Ptolemies.
Egypt Essays Plan of Hatshepsut's Temple at Deir el Bahari.
Egypt Essays Plan of Seti I's Temple to Osiris at Abydos.
Egypt Essays Plan of the Temple of Rameses II at Abydos.
Egypt Essays Plan of the Ramesseum, Mortuary Temple Rameses II.

Egypt Essays Photo 1. Plan of the Imhotep Museum Complex

FREDERICK MONDERSON

Egypt Essays Illustration 1e. Shu, the Air God, separates Nut, the Sky Goddess, from Seb, the Earth God. Thoth and Horus or Ra-Horakhty were there as witnesses at that phenomenal happening.

Egypt Essays Illustration 2. Sahu (Orion) and the cow Sothis sailing the heavens but separated by the Sparrow-Hawk wearing the Double Crown.

EGYPT ESSAYS ON ANCIENT KEMET

Egypt Essays Illustration 2a. Close-up image of an Old Kingdom boat pit, showing bricks separating sections of the structure.

FREDERICK MONDERSON

1. Africa

Today, only the most knowledgeable and culturally aware African-Americans know the accurate story about Egypt/ancient Kemet/Tawi and the rest of Africa. Young people, in particular those with parents who were civil rights activists, Black scholars, and whose teachers know the truth, have a better understanding of Egypt and Africa. This is further underscored as unfolding scholarship details the Black substructure, structure and superstructure of ancient Egypt, without question, and this has caused the racist pseudo-scientists who distorted history, to be in retreat.

Egypt Essays Photo 1a. Abu Simbel Temple of Rameses II. As visitors mill around, four seated colossi line the temple's entrance with image of Ra-Horakhty above the door and baboons on the cornice.

Without question, the history of Africa has been distorted to exclude the contributions of Egypt as the "Voice of the Mother Continent," Africa. Academic and cultural imperialists created a mythical area

EGYPT ESSAYS ON ANCIENT KEMET

called the "Middle East," then postulated and preached a false history of this ancient African civilization. They projected Egypt as being a part of that area, part of the "Fertile Crescent," at the expense of Africa. The fact is, from time immemorial, Egypt/Sinai has been and still is a state in Africa and the Egyptians were and still are Africans. For that matter, some years ago, Egypt was the host and it's President Mubarak, Chairman of the Organization of African Unity (OAU). This clearly shows Egypt is in Africa, not the Middle East!

Egypt Essays Photo 1b. Abu Simbel Temple of Rameses II. Plaque dedicated to its first President Gamal Abdul-Nasser who built the High Dam at Aswan creating Lake Nasser.

The great writers of antiquity including Herodotus, Strabo and Diodorus among many others, all held that the Egyptians/Kamites were Black people and this was based on their physical observations. Such a view was held at a time when Egyptian civilization had been thousands of years old and been through its many incursions and conquests by foreigners. Nevertheless, this belief was accepted until interest in Egypt/Kemet was developed by c. 1800 of our era. Because Africans were enslaved and had been downtrodden in the West, at that time, pseudo-Scientists felt it necessary and natural to exclude Egypt from Africa to justify that condition as being a perpetual one. As such, Africa's true role in Egypt was omitted and the history falsified to show the superiority of Europeans and their culture. Why not, since White-men subjugated Black-men in an institution of slave trade and slavery in the west. And so, successive generations accepted the false belief and systematically shaped history to justify their story, or as the man said, "His-Story."

Egypt Essays Photo 2. Abu Simbel Temple of Rameses II. Close-up of the two right side seated colossal statues of the Pharaoh on the façade of his Temple.

EGYPT ESSAYS ON ANCIENT KEMET

As the Science of Egyptology, aided by the disciplines of Anthropology and Archaeology, developed the strategy was to elevate Europe and derogate Africa. This outlook was achieved by falsifying the historical record. The falsity was accepted and perpetuated by innocent and ignorant scholars and writers who dared not challenge the prevailing myths about Africa, and so, timidity and ignorance reigned. Professor John H. Clarke has consistently advocated, "The people who preached racism colonized the writing and teaching of history."

Modern European scholars including Volney, *Ruins of Empire*, 1791; Denon, *Travels in Egypt and Assyria*, 1793; and Sir Godfrey Higgins, *Anacalypsis* in 2 Vols. (1836) took an iconoclastic view. They shattered the myths surrounding Africa, Africans and especially Egypt/Kemet. They too, had read Herodotus, "the Father of History," and understood his eye-witness accounts and descriptions of Egyptians/Kamites, as having "thick lips, broad nose, wooly hair and being burnt of skin." Diodorus Siculus had said the Ethiopians claimed to have found Egypt/Kemet as a colony. And so, a new school of thought arose, but these iconoclasts paid the price in ostracism.

Egypt Essays Photo 2a. Abu Simbel Temple of Rameses II. Rameses offers to the titulary deity of the temple, his name as Ma'at on the cornice between the seated colossal statues.

FREDERICK MONDERSON

Egypt Essays Photo 3. Abu Simbel Temple of Rameses II. Close-up of the two left side seated colossal statues of the Pharaoh on the façade of his Temple.

In as much as Murray's *Guide to Egypt* (1888) described the land beyond Aswan, Abu Simbel area in particular as, "The land of the Ethiopians." These people and the area are consistent with the Black Genesis view, the people of Nabta Playa settled there no later than 3500 B.C. Bruce Williams' revelation that the earliest monarchy existed at Qustol centuries before the First Egyptian Dynasty and Toby Wilkinson's finds and their ramifications in Upper Egypt's Eastern Desert that dates "1000 years before Winkler's

EGYPT ESSAYS ON ANCIENT KEMET

Mesopotamians" certainly crushes the straw-man current misconception regarding the people of ancient Kemet/Egypt.

Egypt Essays Photo 3a. Abu Simbel Temple of Rameses II. At the base of a seated statue images of "prisoners" subdued by the king. The other side has other such persons sharing the same fate.

Nevertheless, European writers such as Volney had written: "Africans now enslaved had once founded the arts and sciences that now govern the universe." Godfrey Higgins also wrote that Jesus, the Virgin Mary, and many other ancient "Holy Men" and races including the Sumerians, Buddha and Hercules were also Black! To these may be added the works of Gerald Massey, Raymond Dart and Albert Churchward that also challenged European distortion and omission. Their works were only published in limited editions! Western society ostracized them! Naturally, their works were excluded and publishers refused to print their research. Such iconoclastic European scholars and their scholarship suffered for attacking the false myths about Africans and the misinterpretation about Europeans! Nonetheless, these iconoclasts paved the way for Africans such as Duse Mohammed, Caseley Hayford, Dantes

FREDERICK MONDERSON

Bellgrade and Marcus Garvey, founder of the Universal Negro Improvement Association in 1916, to take pride in the blackness of the Egyptians/Kamites. Then in 1922, Howard Carter discovered the tomb of Tutankhamon of the XVIIIth Dynasty. To that time, his was the greatest find of any ancient cultural remains. The wealth of his tomb, found in the Valley of the Kings at Thebes, is reflected in the jewelry, furniture and ushabti figures, musical instruments and other untold wealth. However, the most astonishing but overlooked discovery relative to this issue of Egyptian ethnicity were the two boy-like replica statues of the young king standing guard in front of the burial chamber. Dressed in regal attire including head-dress, the replicas were to accompany, protect, present and represent the king in the after-life. They were painted black to physically describe how the king actually looked. Since they accompanied him into eternity he could not misrepresent how he or they looked.

This find then aided other critical historians such as W. E. B Du Bois, *The Negro*, 1915; and Carter G. Woodson, the "Father of Black History," who founded the *Journal of Negro History* and wrote *The Mis-Education of the Negro* followed by a sequel *The Education of the Negro* to look more closely at Tutankhamon's roots and it helped them trace the blackness of the XVIIIth Dynasty. Then, J. A. Rogers in his *Sex and Race* Vol. I and *World's Great Men of Color* Vol. I took up the mantle. He showed how great Africans had been in the past. These scholars began to expose the distortions and to include the omissions of African history and culture systematically implanted by racist pseudo-scientists, theologians, writers, dramatists, publicists, publishers, teachers, ET. Al. Following these great African-American writers, the baton was passed to John Jackson, Dr. Clarke and Dr. Yosef ben-Jochannan, who continued the assault on the bastions of mis-information about the indigenous quality of Africa in Egypt.

Dr. John H. Clarke wrote and lectured. Dr. ben-Jochannan too, lectured and wrote *African Origins of the Major "Western Religions," 1970*; *Africa*: *Mother of Western Civilization, 1971*;

EGYPT ESSAYS ON ANCIENT KEMET

Black Man of the Nile and His Family, 1972; and, *Cultural Genocide in the Black and African Studies Curriculum, 1972.* Then Dr. Cheikh Anta Diop published his *The African Origins of Civilization: Myth or Reality? (1955) 1974*; *The Cultural Unity of Black Africa, (1959) 1978*; *Pre-colonial Black Africa, (1960) 1987;* and *Civilization or Barbarism*, 1981, now released in English translation.

Egypt Essays Photo 4. Abu Simbel Temple of Rameses II. Entrance Hall view of the 8 standing colossal Osiride statues of the monarch.

FREDERICK MONDERSON

Dr. Ivan Van Sertima founded the *Journal of African Civilizations*, April 1979, with focus on Africa and that great ancient culture, Egypt. Lastly, he published *Nile Valley Civilizations* in 1984, *Black Women in Antiquity* in 1986, *Blacks in Science* 1987, *and Great African Thinkers*: *Cheikh Anta Diop* in 1986. He followed this up with *Egypt Revisited* in 1988 as well as *Egypt*: *Child of Africa* in 1995. In addition, the University of Chicago scholar Dr. Bruce Williams published his findings of "Ancient Nubian Artifacts Yield Evidence of Earliest Monarchy," as reported in *The New York Times*, March 1, 1979. This scholar showed, the symbols of power and authority generally associated with Dynastic Egypt at 3200 B.C., viz., White Crown, enthroned Pharaoh, crook and flail, incense burner, palace façade, etc., were dated to at least 3400 B.C. from Qustol, Nubia. This is the land south of Egypt/Kemet called Ta-Seti that predated Egypt and remained consistently contemporary with her neighbor to the north. Here Mr. Williams struck a major blow for the anteriority of Nubian/Ethiopian cultural origins that gave further credence to Diodorus' statement that the Ethiopians founded Egypt as a colony.

Egypt Essays Photo 4a. Abu Simbel Temple of Rameses II. Baboons and cartouches line the cornice of the temple.

EGYPT ESSAYS ON ANCIENT KEMET

Between these last five African-American writers, more than 60 books were written. They documented the greatness of Africa, Africans, and their cultural heritage. They exposed the myths, attacked the false information and introduced new approaches and methods of studying and understanding the African past. Meanwhile, they taught the African-American youth to be proud and be able to achieve for the ancestors and their posterity.

The new African scholars, mirroring the efforts of teachers like Dr. Leonard Jeffries, Dr. Leonard James, Regent Adelaide Sanford, Dr. Donald H. Smith, Marimba Ani, Prof. George Simmonds, the unsung hero in our community, aided by the 'complimentarity of the African male-female principle,' have continued to forge ahead, research, write and teach steadfastly, asserting that Egypt is African! Those who understand what is at stake must waste no time! Young and old Black-manhood are at stake! More importantly, Black cultural heritage is at stake! We must defend Egypt as African and teach the attitude of critical humanism while challenging the dehumanizing Euro-centric perspective that Africans and their descendants in Diaspora have made no significant contributions to human culture and/or civilization. We must also continue to provide for our constituency the cognitive tools of critical analysis and synthesis, which will better enable them to apply their own intellect and psyche to a more systematic, rigorous and objective search for truth in all areas of study.

The history and culture of Africans and their descendants at home and abroad, will then become a valid corrective to the omissions and distortions of that history and culture, which are characteristic of Euro-centric education, which in turn wreaked such psycho/socio/cultural havoc in Western European/American societies.

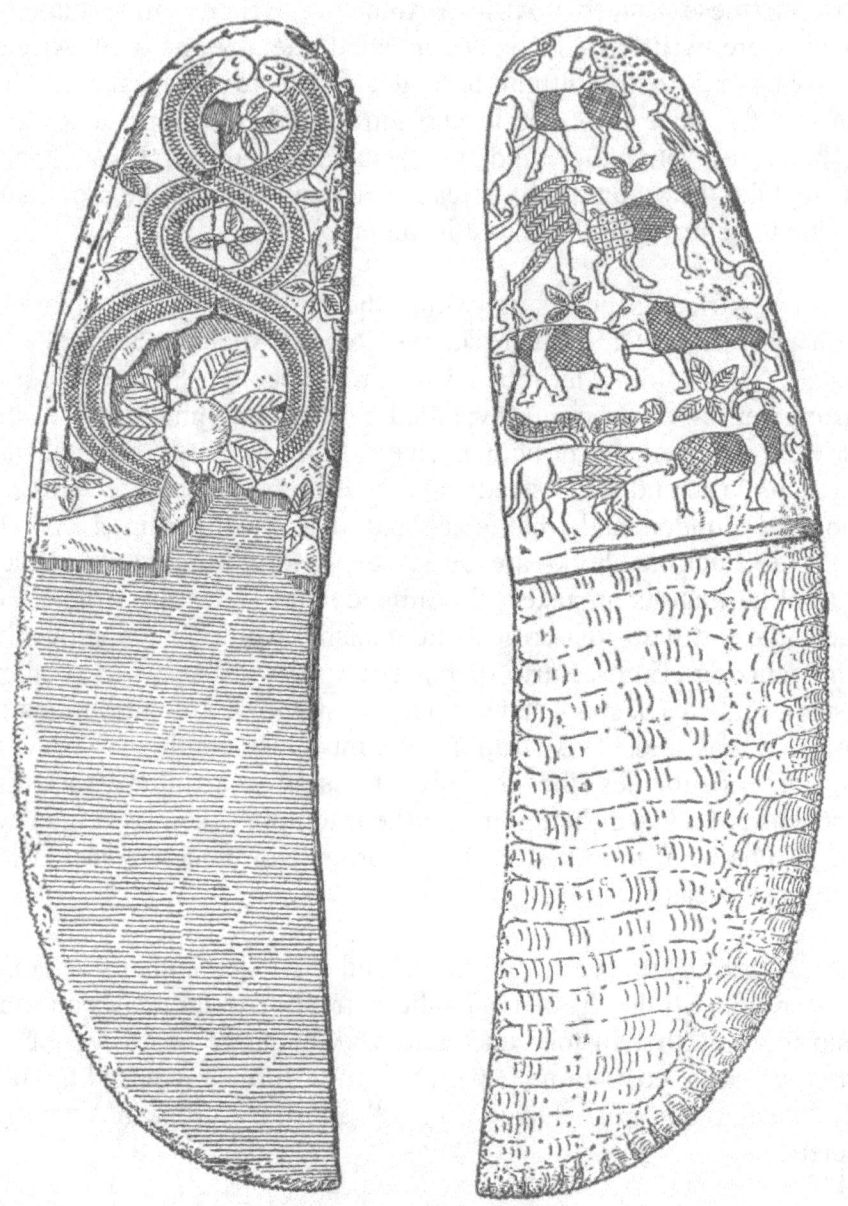

Egypt Essays Illustration 3. Flint knife of the Predynastic Age.

EGYPT ESSAYS ON ANCIENT KEMET

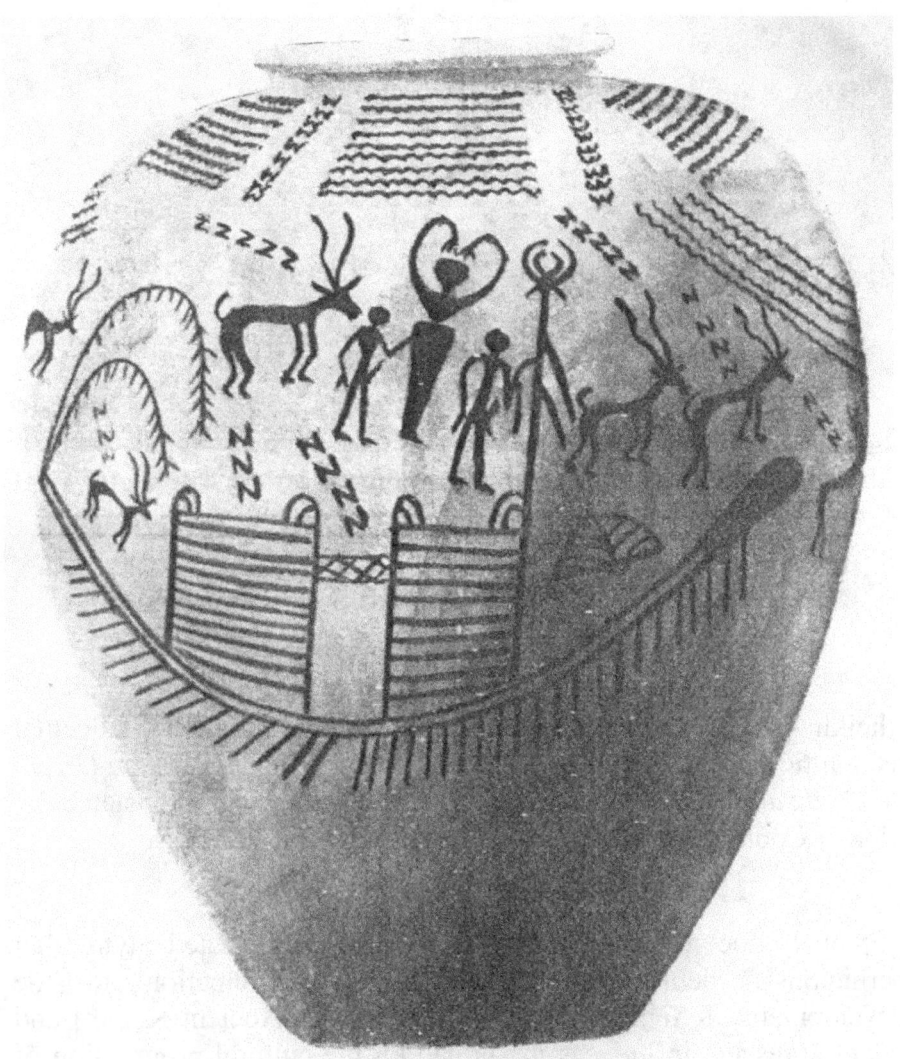

Egypt Essays Illustration 4. Flinders Petrie's Decorated Vase of the Gerzean Period.

FREDERICK MONDERSON

Egypt Essays Illustration 5. An incident in the wars of Harmachis and Sit or Set, found in the "Corridor of Victory" at Horus Temple at Edfu.

2. CHEIKH ANTA DIOP

Cheikh Anta Diop, a Senegalese scholar of the highest intellectual recognition has masterfully posed the question of *The African Origin of Civilization: Myth or Reality* (1955), Edited and translated by Mercer Cook, New York: Lawrence Hill and Co., 1974.

Copiously documented, this scholarly work has refuted myths that perniciously denied the Black race's participation in the development of Ancient Egyptian civilization [Ancient Kemet] and the effervescent influences it has had on the cultural progression of the ancient world. Diop has skillfully articulated a most profound tour de force analysis utilizing anthropological, archaeological, craniological, historical, demographic, and linguistic disciplines to examine Egypt and Africa's history and human contributions to the development of science, language, art, etc., human intellectual progress.

EGYPT ESSAYS ON ANCIENT KEMET

The African Origin of Civilization: *Myth or Reality* is indeed a seminal treatise written by an African on the history of the continent's relations with ancient Egypt. He rightfully takes his place among the great critical scholars who faced tumultuous forces while arguing their cases in defense of Africa and truth in scholarship. In so doing, he attacked the structural foundations on which myths of white supremacy and anteriority of European cultural emergence rests.

Such a mind-set, born in the cauldron of a colonialist and imperialist machinations, has relegated Africans to a secondary place on the human cultural ladder; and thus; this book seeks to undergird the historical record with a more proper and balanced perspective.

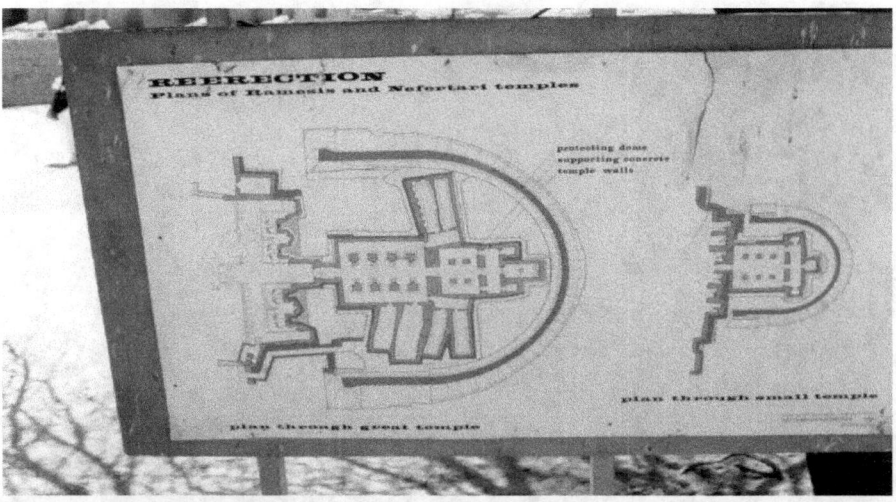

Egypt Essays Plans 1. Plan of the Temples of Rameses II and his Queen Nefertari at Abu Simbel in Nubia.

The Table of Contents is impressive and reads as follows: The Meaning of Our Work; What Were the Egyptians; Birth of the Negro Myth; Modern Falsifications of History; Could Egyptian Civilization be of Asian Origin; The Egyptian Race as Seen by Egyptologists;

FREDERICK MONDERSON

Arguments Supporting a Negro [Black] Origin; Arguments Opposing a Negro [Black] Origin, Etc.

This work has a main and supporting thesis; the principal thesis is that historical, archaeological and anthropological evidence supports the theory that the civilization of ancient Egypt, the first that history has recorded, was actually Negroid [Black] in character. Its implications are that Blacks originated civilization and had a profound impact on the Mediterranean world, which provided the proto-cultural basis for classical and western civilization. This is indeed a serious contention and thus the book generated extreme criticism such as that offered by Raymond Mauny, published in the Bulletin de L'Ifan (*Bulletin of the Fundamental Institute of Black Africa*) in 1960.

Egypt Essays Photo 5. Abu Simbel Temple of Rameses II. Into the Sanctuary with divinities, from the right (left as the gods look out), Ra-Horakhty, Rameses II, Amon-Ra and Ptah.

EGYPT ESSAYS ON ANCIENT KEMET

Egypt Essays Photo 5a. Abu Simbel Temple of Rameses II. Two rightmost seated statues of the king with miniature statues of queens at his feet.

Egypt Essays Photo 5b. Abu Simbel Temple of Rameses II. Two Nile gods uniting the land beneath Rameses *Usr-Ma'at-Ra* Cartouche on the (left most) seated statue of Rameses and just to the right, a small statue of his Queen.

FREDERICK MONDERSON

Egypt Essays Photo 5c. Abu Simbel Temple of Rameses II. Two Nile gods uniting the land beneath Rameses *Usr-Ma'at-Ra* Cartouche on the (right most) seated statue of Rameses and just to the left, a small statue of his Queen.

By arguing that all Greek science was inherited from the ancient Egyptians, and that Egyptians, Ethiopians and Nubians were Black, Cheikh Anta Diop provided the launch pad for an objective reappraisal of the writing of history that is demonstrably distorted, vis-à-vis, Africa. Another of Diop's theses is that summarized by Immanuel Wallenstein, in his book *Africa: The Politics of Independence*. Wallenstein writes "the world," in Cheikh Anta Diop's view, "is divided between northerners and southerners," Negro-Africans and Aryans. He holds that the: "Northerners have developed patriarchy, and patrilineal succession characterized by the suppression of women and a propensity for war. Also, associated with such societies are materialist religion, sin and guilt, xenophobia, the tragic drama, the city-state, individualism, and pessimism. Southerners, on the other hand, are matriarchal. The women are free and the people peaceful; there is a Dionysian approach to life; religious idealism, and no concept of sin. With a matriarchal society come xenophilia, the tale as a literary form, the territorial state, social collectivism, and optimism."

Egypt Essays Illustration 5a. Head of a seated figure of a XVIIth Dynasty priestess wearing a full-plaited wig, bandlet, etc., now in the British Museum.

In his Preface, "The Meaning of Our Work," Diop provides evidence of the motivation that led to his study bent on "restoring the collective African personality," that has been systematically debased and dehumanized by centuries of slave trade, colonialism and their resulting rampage. Commensurate, he identifies "three factors" that

FREDERICK MONDERSON

"compete to form the collective personality of a people: a psychic factor, susceptible to a literary approach; this is the factor that would elsewhere be called a national temperament and that the Negritude poets have over-stressed. In addition there are the historical factor and the linguistic factor, both susceptible to being approached scientifically." To accomplish this task he establishes such positions:

1. "Ancient Egypt was a Negro [Black] civilization and the Ancient Egyptians were Negroes." [Blacks]
2. "Anthropologically and culturally speaking the Semitic world was a fusion of White-skinned and Black-skinned peoples."
3. The "monogenetic thesis" demonstrates that "all races descended from the Black race."
4. He seeks to write African History objectively and to "define laws governing African socio-political structures."
5. To assist Africa in preparing for its future!
6. To "retrace the history of the African nation" and thus help to clarify the history of humanity.
7. He asked: "Why no Negro [Black] African author or artist has posed the problem of man's fate."
8. He affirms that "African languages could express philosophic and scientific thought."
9. He reaffirmed the "possibilities of pre-Columbian relations between Africa and America."
10. Diop did argue that though the branches of his tree could use some pruning, the trunk was fundamentally sound!

EGYPT ESSAYS ON ANCIENT KEMET

Egypt Essays Photo 6. Abu Simbel Temple of Rameses II. The Queen offers a sistrum and flowers to Hathor, deity of the Temple.

FREDERICK MONDERSON

Egypt Essays Photo 6a. Abu Simbel Temple of Rameses II. The left two seated statues, one damage and whose head lies on the ground, also with miniature statues of the king's queens.

With these premises established, the author appeals to young American scholars, Black and White, to work in teams and further explore scientifically the issues he raises. The hope is they would be unbiased enough to delve deeper and correct injustices history has heaped on Africa and Africans.

The chapter on the "Modern Falsification of History" is an excellent analysis of various positions.

Moderns such as Volney, Champollion the Younger, Amelineau, Cailliaud, and Fontanes made early and objective observations about the ancient Egyptian/Kamite/Tawi culture. Their positions were in accord with classical scholars such as Diodorus Siculus, who claimed the Ethiopians founded Egypt as a colony, and Herodotus who said the Egyptians, Ethiopians, and Colchians were Black skinned and had thick lips, broad noses and frizzy hair. These are predominantly Negroid/Black characteristics!

EGYPT ESSAYS ON ANCIENT KEMET

Pseudo-scientists, including Champollion Figeac (Black skin and woolly hair "do not suffice to characterize the Negro [Black] race"); Cherubini (Blacks, "a race on the lowest rung of the human ladder"); Maspero (Egyptian civilization had come from the south of Europe and had "slipped into the valley via the west or south-west"), have, in spite of their contributions to Egyptology, written with a predisposed subjectivity bent on distorting facts, portraying Africans as less civil and glorifying Europe's role in the development of the Egyptian culture. Whereas in that early time, Europe had not even reached the lowest rung of the civilization ladder!

Egypt Essays Illustration 6. Prehistoric images of boats plying the Nile River with one and two deckhouses and various Nome signs.

FREDERICK MONDERSON

Egypt Essays Illustration 7. A close-up of boats and birds on the waterside.

Diop cites a most persuasive source to support the validity of his beliefs: the bas-reliefs in the Tomb of Sesostris where the Caucasian was not shown differently, but culturally inferior.

Such and other evidence notwithstanding, biased Egyptologists have sought to negate the cultural, political, military, religious, economic and physiological contributions inner Africa made to Egypt and the world. These apologists sought to twist linguistic, physical and artifactual evidence to present meanings that are, in Diop's view, not what the Egyptians and ancients meant when perchance they gave ethnological descriptions of fellow Africans' roles in shaping their material civilization and cultural world view.

Moret's book *The Nile and Egyptian Civilization* poses an interesting question: "By whom was Upper Egypt influenced if not by Lower Egypt?" It led to a chapter by Diop entitled "Could Egyptian civilization have originated in the Delta?"

Using the *Book of the Dead* as the earliest literature, the Texts of the Pyramids and archaeological evidence, Cheikh Anta Diop affirms

EGYPT ESSAYS ON ANCIENT KEMET

the paucity of early monuments and artifacts that would attest to the anteriority of the Delta over the south. He then dismisses this region as antedating Upper Egypt in cultural civilization evolution.

Such written documents as the *Palermo Stone*, the *Royal Papyrus of Turin*, the *Tablet of Abydos*, the *Second Abydos Tablet*, *Tablet of Karnak*, and the *Tablet of Sakkara*, Manetho's *Chronicle*, Strabo as well as such moderns as Dieulafoy, Dr. Contenau, Lenormant and Bertholon provide the basis for Diop's rejection of an Asiatic origin. They further buttress his formulated view of the predominance of Blacks in such cultures as Chaldea, Phoenicia, Babylonia and Sumeria.

An interesting but short chapter the "Egyptian Race as seen by Anthropologists" includes works of the authorities Massoulard, Thompson, and Randall-McIver, Falkenburger and Petrie. These writers significantly attest to the Negro/Black basis of Egyptian demography. Equally, no authority has established any evidence for a White Egyptian race! This is important! Based on the strength of Diop's arguments for a Negro/Black Egypt and in the interest of objectivity to argue the Egyptians were White is not scientifically tenable. It swings the pendulum too far back!

In "Arguments supporting a Negro [Black] Origin," Diop adduces Africa's cultural contributions to Egypt through Totemism, Circumcision, Kingship, Cosmogony, Social Organization, Matriarchy, and Linguistic evidence.

FREDERICK MONDERSON

Egypt Essays Photo 7. Abu Simbel Temple of Rameses II. Hathor, Ptah and Ra-Horakhty on the pillars.

EGYPT ESSAYS ON ANCIENT KEMET

Egypt Essays Photo 7a. Abu Simbel Temple of Rameses II. Statues of the King and Hathor front the nearby Queen's temple.

A supporting thesis and one of his strong arguments is the role of matriarchy in lineage descent among the Egyptians. Evidence abounds of how the Egyptians revered womanhood and even practiced sister/brother marriages. Europeans, who, in their own right, practiced patriarchy, have consistently criticized this practice as barbaric. In the Old Kingdom Queen Hetepheres, for example, married every potential pharaoh of her time, because she transmitted divine right to rule! Diop holds that early Europe could not have practiced matriarchy but patriarchy. This he bases on the absence of Queens in Greek, Roman and Persian history. However, the practice of matriarchy could be found in ancient Egypt as well as all of Black Africa. This is certainly evidence of continental cultural continuity.

The chapter on the "Peopling of Africa from the Nile Valley" primarily compares the cultural and linguistic transmissions found among Western African peoples such as the Senegalese, Yoruba, Loto, Kara, Laobe, Peul, Toucoleur, Serer, Agni, etc., with that of their Eastern origin. That is, according to some legends these people migrated from the Nile region.

In an erudite survey of the political and social forces in the development of ancient Egypt, Diop reconstructs the historical rise of the culture from the earliest times to the Greco-Roman conquest. Contributions of Ethiopia, Nubia and Egypt, to the early world, are very interesting. Here are enumerated some of the many classical minds who drank at the Egyptian fountain of wisdom. Among these were Thales, Pythagoras, Empedocles, Solon, Plato, Socrates, Aristotle, Lycurgus, Archimedes, Eratosthenes, etc.

Diop's method of approach is objectively scientific. He provides an argument, compares it with pro and con evidence, then supplies analyses that allow the reader to grasp the facts and make judgments. Critics aside; this work is serious, panoramic and resists pernicious detraction.

Other chapters are a "Reply to the critic Raymond Mauny," "An Early History of Humanity" and the "Evolution of the Black World," plus a conclusion. The work is profusely documented, provides notes on archaeological terms used in the text, brief biographical notes, a selected bibliography, and an index.

Raymond Mauny's critique of Diop's *The African Origin of Civilization: Myth or Reality* is a typical reactionary invective against a work that, while not a pioneer African treatise, is a major synthesis of its kind. This critic dismisses the in-depth scholarship involved, because he takes to task a subject long taboo regarding Europe's dominance pertaining to intellectualism and half-truths about the growth of early civilization culture. Mauny feels the book and its writer are not the caliber of a Doctor of Letters. Yet, to this day, Diop's work has withstood the onslaught of critical destructive commentary and more and more new evidence keeps bolstering his contentions.

This writer views Mauny's position as quite understandable owing to the cultural, political and intellectual ramifications Diop's work

EGYPT ESSAYS ON ANCIENT KEMET

poses. That is, Diop exposes European scholarship and its likeminded American counterpart of not simply distortion and omission but also racial and cultural oppression. Thus, in an effort to withstand the tide of new truths, as a result, Mauny's criticism, while striving for objectivity, contradicts itself. As an example, he adds that there are "two Negro races existing on earth; the straight haired Dravidian and the wooly haired Negro," [Black] whatever that means! It should be add here, a Dravidian doctor came to Harlem, USA, to a Dinner honoring Dr. Yosef ben-Jochannan in 1992. There he complained of the racism they faced in India because of their blackness, but that we all suffer the same racial oppression of white supremacy! The good Indian doctor, who made the complaint, insisted that Blacks in the West not forget them for "We all look alike!"

Another of Diop's contentions concerns the "skin of the mummies." He states, the "epidermis appears pigmented exactly like that of all other African blacks." Further he adds, "Invariably from prehistory to the Ptolemaic epoch, the Egyptian mummy has remained Negro/Black. In other words, throughout Egyptian history the skin as well as the bone structure of all Egyptian social classes (from Pharaoh to Fellah) has remained that of authentic Negroes. [Blacks]." Yet still, such a statement as "I see nowhere mentioned the fact that the Egyptians were blacks," is typical of the antonymous nature of his criticism. However, and significantly, the ancients never mentioned that the Egyptians were white! Only moderns have sought to interpolate that contention.

FREDERICK MONDERSON

Egypt Essays Photo 8. Abu Simbel Temple of Rameses II. Rameses offers two bouquets to Hathor while Nefertari stands behind him with sistrum and flowers.

EGYPT ESSAYS ON ANCIENT KEMET

Egypt Essays Photo 8a. Abu Simbel Temple of Rameses II. Two standing statues sandwich the king's cartouches.

Egypt Essays Photo 8b. Abu Simbel Temple of Rameses II. Two statues of the king sandwich one of a defaced Hathor whose face may be truly Nubian like Rameses.

Again, good old Mauny wrote, "… archaeology proves super-abundantly that Egypt was the civilizing factor on Ethiopia, and not the reverse." However, an article in *The New York Times* of March

FREDERICK MONDERSON

I, 1982 entitled "Oldest Monarchy found in Nubia," proves the contrary. The symbols of power and authority, the white crown, scepter, enthroned Pharaoh, flail, incense burner, temple façade, etc., which we see as characteristic of kingship and pharaonic rule at 3200 B.C. are evident in Nubia approximately 3400 B.C. That is, some 200 years before such appears in Egypt. This finding gives credence to statements such as that by Diodorus, Strabo, and Stephanus of Byzantium, Homer, Herodotus, etc. al. that Ethiopia was an imperial power before Egypt. What is disturbing concerns the exorbitant portion of funding spent to prove the "whiteness" of Egypt. If such sums were dedicated to proving otherwise then much more "lost information" would be more readily available. This, however, in no way obscures the fact that many Europeans have written objectively and truthfully about Africa.

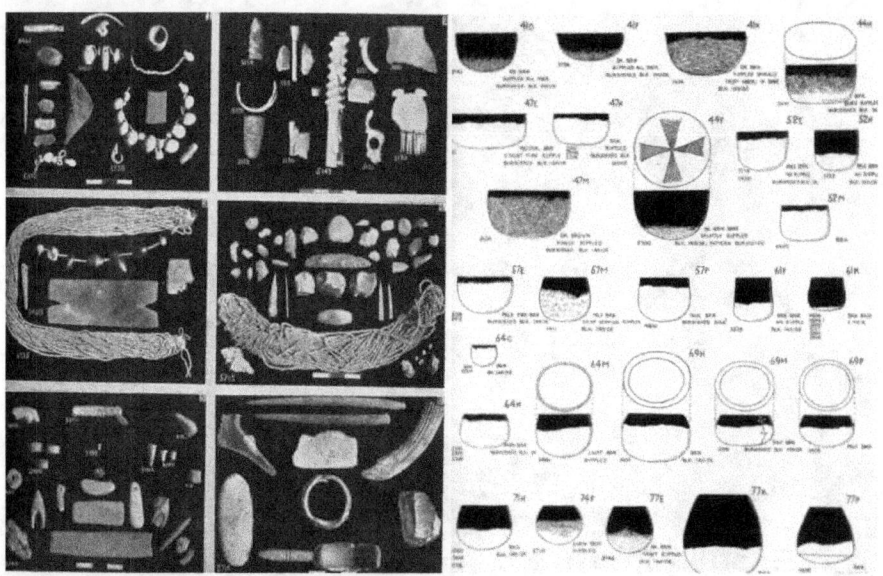

Egypt Essays Illustration 8. Corpus of Badarian Pottery: Assortment of copper and ivory pieces, etc. (left); and Black Topped Brown (right).

EGYPT ESSAYS ON ANCIENT KEMET

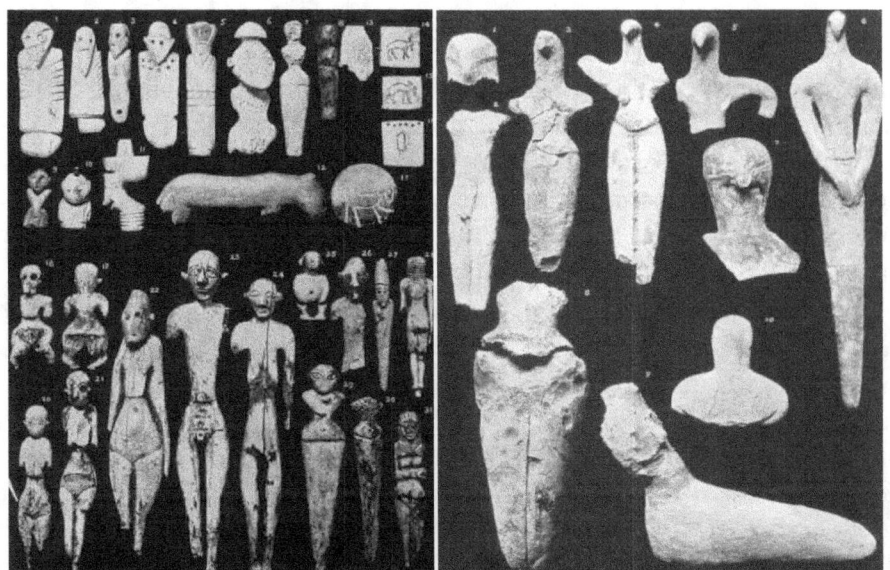

Egypt Essays Illustration 9. Prehistoric Ivory Figures (left); and Female Figurines (right).

Another of Mauny's contentions argues: "If West African blacks are descendants of the Egyptians, why have they become 'decivilized' between 500 B.C. when Diop says they left Egypt, and 900 A.D., after which we have texts depicting them as being rather 'retarded.'"

Poor Mauny, he is manifestly ignorant of the dynamic forces in history. While there is historical progression in evolution, there is also historical regression. Demographical, environmental, as well as politico-socio-economic factors impact on and influence a nation's place on the historical horizon. This is a given fact! History has shown that Cicero claimed the British were not fit to be slaves, and in 1800 years they ruled the world. Also, the Greeks who gave the western world classical greatness, by 1900 A.D. were scoring less on aptitude tests than African Americans who were less than four decades out of slavery.

To continue an examination of Mauny is an exercise in futility. He clearly has an axe to grind! The position he defends is understandable. When Egyptological studies began in the 19th Century, Blacks were enslaved and colonized. Thus, few serious attempts were made to give them appropriate credit or to interpret the evidence in a manner that praised their contributions. European writers, including Volney, Higgins, Vail, Graves, Reade, Massey, Dart, Churchward, etc., who pointed out the hypocrisy of western scholarship, vis-à-vis, Africa, were ostracized and disparaged. It should be added that the significant work in archaeology, anthropology, etc, on reclamation of Egyptian knowledge was done from 1822 to 1870 and more scientifically from 1870 to 1930, when interest escalated dramatically. During this period, to argue as Diop did meant loss of funding and facility of publishing.

The strengths of Mauny's criticism have been dismissed and consigned to the junk heap of history! Many scholars, Africans as well as Europeans have come to view Diop's contribution as timely scientific erudition, swinging the pendulum about the role of Blacks in Ancient Egypt.

Egypt Essays Photo 9. Philae Temple of Isis. The Mammisi with its fronting columns as seen from the river approach with two sets of "First Pylon." The center opening is the entrance to the river.

EGYPT ESSAYS ON ANCIENT KEMET

Egypt Essays Photo 9a. Philae Temple of Isis. Native Egyptian Guide Showgi Abd Rady stands at the Pier with his equipment ready to work.

CONCLUSIONS

A bold and scholarly Egyptologist, Cheikh Anta Diop has dissected, exposed and destroyed much of the deliberate distortions of the historical record pertaining to the demographic formation and dispersion of the Nile Valley's culture and its influences on all subsequent civilizations.

FREDERICK MONDERSON

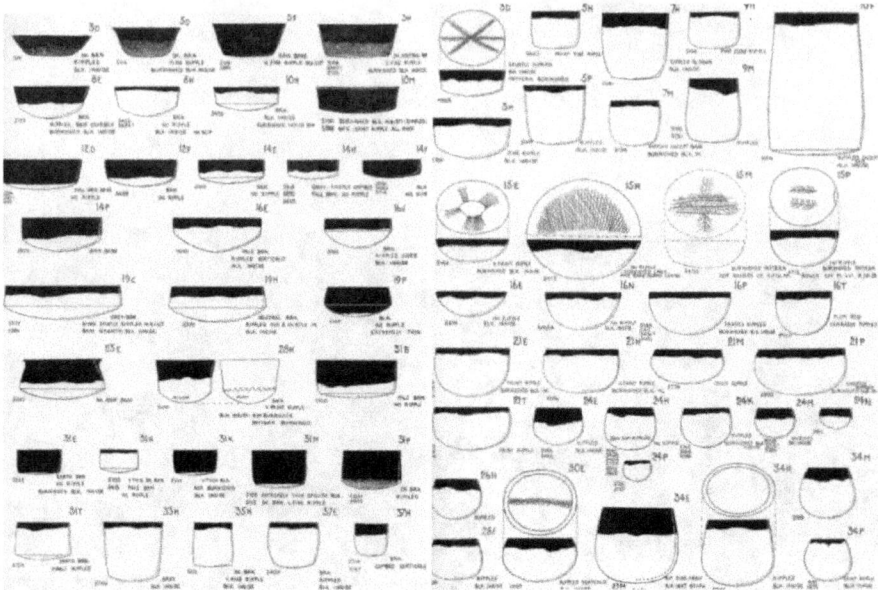

Egypt Essays Illustration 10. Corpus of Badarian Pottery: Black Topped, Brown (left); and Black Topped, Red (right).

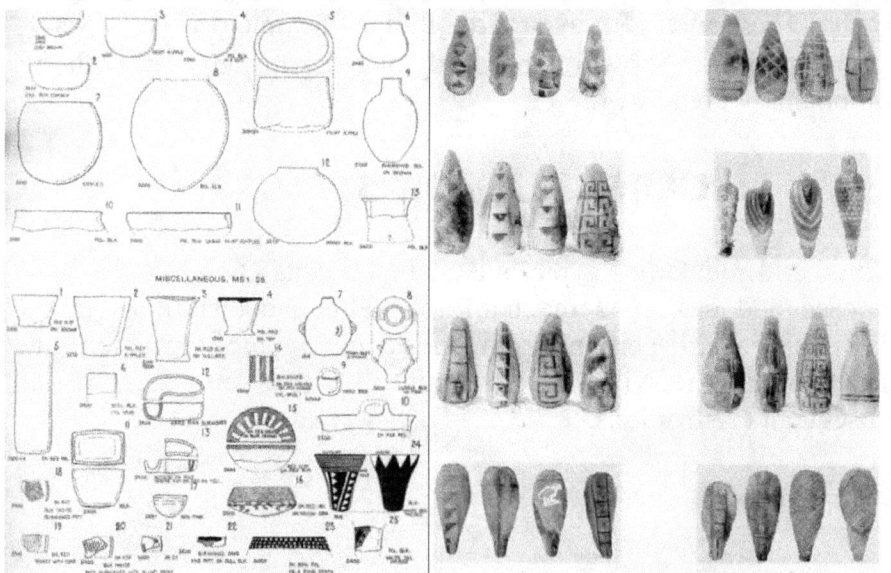

Egypt Essays Illustration 10a. Corpus of Badarian Pottery: All Black (left); and Mummified Ibises (right).

EGYPT ESSAYS ON ANCIENT KEMET

What's significant about this research is the masterful use of sources dating to early exploration of the ancient world that are extremely important for a proper understanding of how history can be systematically falsified. Equally too, it provides the basis upon which younger scholars, less biased and prejudiced, could put various aspects of Diop's arguments in proper scientific perspective. He displays integrity of scholarship and states that while branches of the tree he has elaborated may be faulty, the trunk or fundamental premise of the blackness of ancient Egypt is certain and sound! Cheikh Anta Diop argues that on a scientific plane, his work could honestly stand criticism.

Today, when cultural identification is so important, this book is a welcome watershed. It calls for a total reconsideration of the role that African people have played in history and their impact on the development of early societies, science and institutions. It represents one of the great legacies that an African mind could bequeath his race, shattering the myths that have retarded Africa's cultural cohesiveness as a prerequisite to its advancement in the modern world.

In an address to African intellectuals, Cheikh Anta Diop has written: "The black man must become able to restore the continuity of his national historic past, to draw from it the moral advantage needed to reconquer his place in the modern world without falling into excesses of a Nazism in reverse for, insofar as one can speak of a race, the civilization that is his might have been created by any other human race placed in so favorable and unique a setting."

His belief is, the "history of Africa would remain suspended in air and cannot be written correctly until African historians connect it with the history of Egypt." Dr. John H. Clarke has argued, "African history must be written by African scholars/historians." In this vein Diop indicts the "African historian who evades the problem of Egypt" as by Africanists, Black and White, but also by all people of good will.

FREDERICK MONDERSON

To seek the truth one sometimes is confronted with a reality that detracts from the accepted status quo and can be self-destructive or tremendously enlightening.

Egypt Essays Photo 10. Philae Temple of Isis. The Dromos to the temple's First Pylon with the Eastern (right) and Western (left) Colonnades Two altars remain in situ.

Egypt Essays Photo 10a. Philae Temple of Isis. The Eastern Colonnade with its 17 columns, with different capitals, undecorated.

EGYPT ESSAYS ON ANCIENT KEMET

Egypt Essays Photo 10b. Philae Temple of Isis. The Western Colonnade with its 32 columns with their varied capitals and water mark from the time when the temple was flooded by the Inundation.

3. CULTURE FOR LIBERATION

Increasingly, and across the spectrum of African-American discussion, most speakers emphasize history and culture as a potent aspect of liberation. Today, when we contemplate Black Solidarity, and in keeping with this state of affairs, Egypt/ancient Kemet/Tawi looms even larger in the scheme of things because of its significant legacy in the evolution of ideas, methodology, achievements and influence. This notwithstanding, we ought to be mindful of the transposition of ideas and their potential damages particularly when their origination is based on a distorted perception.

On October 16, 1995, while on the bus to the Million Man March we viewed a tape in which a young brother, articulate, sincere, revolutionary and committed, kept referring to the cliché' "Tell Pharaoh to let my people go." He was certainly not aware he parroted someone-else's history and that Pharaoh was "our people." Herein lies the need for solidarity in the methodology of liberation where we become more versed in our history and culture as this relates to the Nile Valley experience as fundamental to our spiritual, psychological, intellectual and physical freedom.

Prof George Simmonds, our "Unsung Hero" once uttered the following: "I don't write about Martin Luther King or Malcolm X, there are enough people who do that! I speak and instruct about ancient Egypt, a subject our people do not know about but should know a great deal about!"

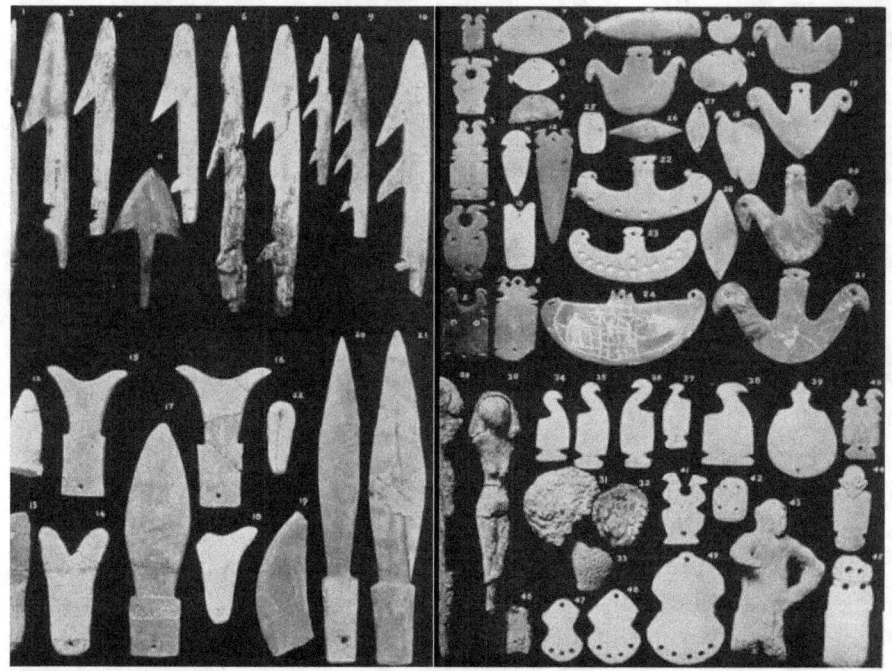

Egypt Essays Illustration 11. Prehistoric bone harpoons and clay and wood model weapons (left); and slate figures and spacers (right).

Therefore, and after an intellectually and spiritually uplifting pilgrimage to the ancient "Holy Land" of Kemet now Egypt, it is only appropriate that I seek "permission to speak" from the ancestors and elders on whose shoulders I stand. I can therefore praise their wonderfully creative spirit, that on the banks of the Nile where that night some of us stood in a place which engineered the fundamentals of science, medicine, architecture, art-sculpture, painting, writing, astronomy, metallurgy, agriculture, philosophy, and mathematics." "Ma'atian principles" or equality, balance, order, propriety or goodness, undergirded these accomplishments that so influenced later civilizations. Today, our people simply need only let these shining examples of early African genesis of faith, and perseverance help assist their path toward self-awareness, self-actualization, and intellectual and spiritual empowerment.

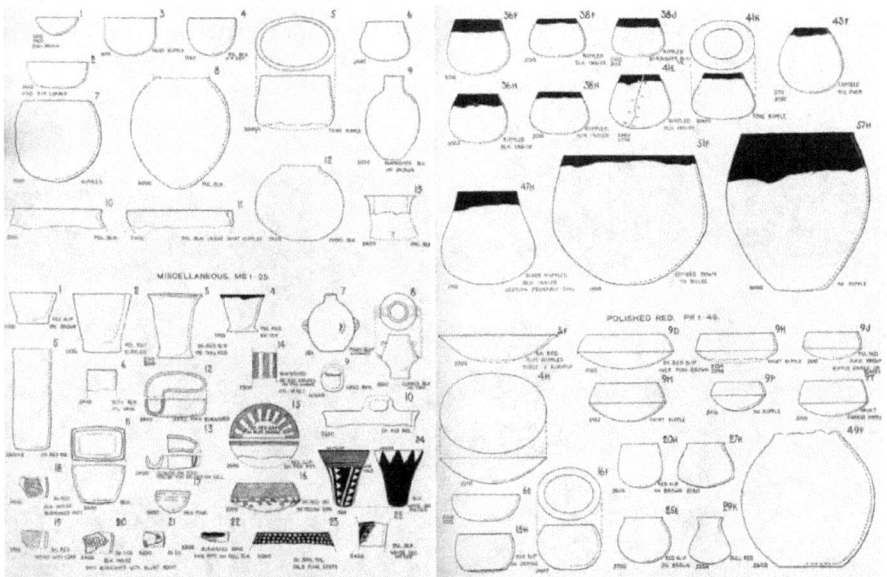

Egypt Essays Illustration 11a. Corpus of Badarian Pottery: Black Topped Red and Polished Red.

Luxor Temple, the "Grand Lodge" of Masonic beliefs, was built by Amenhotep III of the Eighteenth Dynasty, and added to by Rameses II of the Nineteenth Dynasty. Today as one entrances the temple, from the north, pass the standing obelisk and seated statues of Rameses II, through the First Pylon, there is a small chapel in the northwest corner of the Great Court of Rameses II. On a wall in the southwestern corner of this court an interesting relief is depicted.

FREDERICK MONDERSON

Here Rameses II is seated in front of his sons along with cattle and priests in preparation for the offering.

No women are represented, that is to say there are none of his daughters present. In a way it could be argued this procession to greet the great king by his sons and priests mirrors in genesis the "Million Man March," where the brothers stood firm and the sisters understood. Thus, there is some precedence in African historiography in pledge to work for the betterment of such a gathering of strong black men, millennia later.

Egypt Essays Photo 11. Philae Temple of Isis. From the Dromos and northern end of the Eastern Colonnade to the right, the decorated entrance pylon with Isis' First Pylon visible through the opening at top.

EGYPT ESSAYS ON ANCIENT KEMET

Egypt Essays Photo 11a. Philae Temple of Isis. The Kiosk of Trajan, architecture in its most majestic form with varied capitals.

Egypt Essays Photo 11b. Philae Temple of Isis. One of the many varied capitals atop columns in the repository of architecture.

This notwithstanding, on any travel expedition designed to be educational, the crafters of the trip envision a general purpose as to

FREDERICK MONDERSON

what the trip hopes to accomplish. There are individual purposes for the many travelers. On my trip one summer, some fathers brought their sons and grandsons. Nuclear families, singles and families complete with grandfather and grandmother intact, were able to physically and collectively experience the ancient monuments and seek to learn some of the wisdom of their memories these monuments speak to.

My principal and personal reason for going on that trip, had been to take my sister Cherise on that wonderful experience I have so often partook along the banks of the Nile at Aswan, Luxor and in Cairo, Egypt, where the ancestral heritage reigns supreme. Dr. ben-Jochannan's book *From Abu Simbel to Ghizeh: A Guidebook and Manual* included Abydos, "where it all began." In that journey was encompassed the need for love of self, love of one's woman, and love for god. At the completion of the experience was reinforced love of self, love for thy neighbor, then we come to appreciate love for god.

Egypt Essays Photo 12. Philae Temple of Isis. The Second Eastern Colonnade to the left and inner face to the Entrance Pylon enclosing the Open Court.

EGYPT ESSAYS ON ANCIENT KEMET

Egypt Essays Photo 12a. Philae Temple of Isis. More of the varied capitals atop columns in this wonderful repository of architecture.

Egypt Essays Photo 12b. Philae Temple of Isis. Enthroned Osiris atop the crocodile with Isis at the left, all within a shrine depicted by the sun, stars and moon.

Except for Abydos, Luxor, the Ramesseum, Medinet Habu and Hatshepsut's temple at Deir el-Bahari; the others at Philae,

FREDERICK MONDERSON

Kalabsha, Kom Ombo, Edfu and Esna, were all constructed at the twilight in the history of the ancient land of Kemet, today's Egypt. More importantly, these temples were built on much older foundations, sites chosen for their ancient sacredness, dating back in most cases to the beginnings of dynastic Egypt.

The greater vision would be to imagine a "High Holy Day" with temples lit at the cardinal centers of divinity worship, religious practice and theological learning, home of Ptah at Memphis, Ra at Heliopolis, Osiris at Abydos and Amun-Ra at Karnak and Luxor. Then there's Abu Simbel. Such abounding religiosity! Imagine, the first great Egyptian/African nation, at pray!

Now to picture Abydos with its splendid and magnificent artistic depictions, wonderful collection of 3,000-year old paintings, housed in a wonderful architectural structure where the power of Osiris manifested itself amidst the 7-deities to whom the temple was dedicated. These, right to left, consist of Horus, Isis, Osiris, Amon, Ra-Horakhti, Ptah and the builder and King, Seti I, deified. What is also significant about the sister-city of Abydos, in addition to the Tomb of Osiris or Osireion, it houses First and Second Dynasty Royal Tombs and remains of an old fortress. In addition, Petrie identified the strata of 10 successive levels of temples at Abydos, dating back to 3200 Before Christ. Therefore, evidence shows, in the architectural evolution of their religiosity and spirituality, the ancient African temple building practices evolved from leaves, mud and daub, then to bricks, and finally stone construction. Those perishable materials cannot tell us how long our ancestors were "making joyful sounds unto the lord," "having sweet communion with deity" and "crafting moral and ethical standards for their children." We were children and our children will have children of their own, and they should know all this. Albert Churchward gives a time period of 300,000 years in which Africans have been experiencing the wonderful relationship with god force.

In this experience, the ancestors carefully created conventions of wisdom, science and learning that benefited their society and all subsequent societies. Today our children must enmesh themselves

EGYPT ESSAYS ON ANCIENT KEMET

in the study of ancient African history with a methodological approach, through the development of its architecture which tells of worship and ritualizing of the gods; festivals, frolics and flowers; the management of estates' wealth; imperial wars, conquest and endowments; advances in observational and instrumental astronomy; music and instruments; and the most fabulous raised, incised and painted reliefs of art together with other wonderful architectural accomplishments.

This brings me to the statement: "The Fool says there is no God." In 1989, Dr. ben-Jochannan held a Panel Discussion, one of a kind, with the members including a practicing minister, a former minister, a twelve-year-old lad, an assertive sister and a young couple. To begin the discussion persons were asked to answer two simple questions. "What has coming to Egypt done for you?" And "Now that you have accumulated this much knowledge, 'What are you going to do with it?'"

The assertive sister on the panel during the "Question and Answer" period said to the minister, "Rev. Dr. McNair," from Philadelphia, "How can you go back to your congregation and teach in like manner after what you have witnessed?" The astute Rev. McNair simply responded by saying: "I cannot teach my people there is no God. I can only show them where God comes from." I thought that was the most revolutionary profound, yet sincere response, one could have expressed relative to religious experience.

To understand something about "sweet African communion with Deity" one needs examine the temple. In this respect, the essential elements of ancient Kemetic temples, generally built along the river's banks, included a Quay where on a visit by the king, the royal boat would dock. Generally, but not always, a canal led from the Dock towards an Avenue of Sphinxes entrancing the Temple. Oftentimes, as at, say, Deir el Bahari, there is a Valley Temple at the Quay and from this building, instead of the Canal, an Avenue of Sphinxes leads directly to the entrance Pylon or Gate. As at Luxor, two Obelisks and four standing statues stood before the pylon. Generally there is a court. The Hypostyle Hall has a varied arrangement of columns. There may be a second, though smaller Hypostyle and this leads to the Sanctuary that now stands atop a gradual incline upwards as one approached this sacred spot, the "Holy of Holies." This incline represents a sort of "hillock," a high ground, out of which legend has it, the God first emerged from the waters of chaos and sat upon his mound.

In front of the Sanctuary, juxtaposing a generally east/west axis could be found sphinxes, kneeling and seated statues, obelisks, and inscriptional depictions somehow connected with the central worship. Some temples had an assortment of buildings nearby where a number of supportive functions were performed. There was generally a Sacred Lake fed through some underground spring. In the Graeco-Roman period, a Mammisi or Birth House of the god was added.

Egypt Essays Photo 13. Philae Temple of Isis. Short columns with different capitals and elevated die supporting the overhead architrave all atop screened walls.

EGYPT ESSAYS ON ANCIENT KEMET

Egypt Essays Photo 13a. Philae Temple of Isis. As Thoth stands to the left, Amon-Ra sits enthroned by two goddesses, Isis and Nephthys as Seshat writes and Ptah sits to the right with

As such, understanding these achievements in religious theory and practice, architectural and artistic constructions and their influence and the fortitude and originality of their creators allows both young and old to take pride in African genius. This awareness provides a significant beacon for knowledge of self and is a powerful source of inspiration and strength.

Egypt Essays Photo 13b. Philae Temple of Isis. Varied capitals beneath the raised Hathor Head abacus with illustrated underside of the architrave.

FREDERICK MONDERSON

Egypt Essays Photo 13c. Philae Temple of Isis. Another broader view of varied capitals with raised Hathor Head abacus.

4. FACINATION OF EGYPTIAN ARCHAEOLOGY

Ancient Egyptian/Kemetic archaeology has proved to be one of the most fascinating subjects in the modern world. It has masterfully unearthed and pieced together the artistic, architectural, craftsmanship, industry and religious beliefs of ancient man of the Nile Valley in Northeast Africa. Today, the phenomenal development of early civilization still casts a long beam of light. This fascination and resultant utility helps to illuminate and explain modern man's quest to utilize, understand and accept the promises of those long established principles, sciences and beliefs that today govern the world. This foundation, shaped by ethical principles is the ancient Egyptian, African, legacy to humankind.

In a world of tourists, collectors, thieves, merchants of genuine and faked artifacts, attaches,' a new science struggled to establish a systematic method of retrieving and chronicling mortuary, artistic and architectural data for study of Nile Valley culture. Archaeology, principally under pioneering and widespread excavation undertaking established the discipline on a firm footing. That particular age, 1870-1930, experienced an unprecedented amount of exploration,

EGYPT ESSAYS ON ANCIENT KEMET

excavation, discussion, and publishing of "interpretation" of the evidence. However, if the great African and African American scholars of the last century alone, DuBois, Woodson, Huggins, Jackson, Rogers, ben-Jochannan, John H. Clarke, Van Sertima, Karenga, Carruthers, Diop, Obenga, who, after lengthy years of scholarship, research, lectures, publications, study of history and historical phenomenon, have determined that the record has been falsified, we must believe them! Therefore, we are forced to concede that despite the wonders of its revelation, archaeology's practitioners may have erred in their interpretations of the "Who" and "What" of ancient Nile Valley culture in its formation and the wherewithal of its permanent influence. Hence, there is the need to more fully analyze and reevaluate the evidence, to show and educate African peoples especially about this fact and elicit their support in the efforts of correcting history.

If we argue from a philosophic perspective, ancient Kemetic Architecture can be perceived as living manifestations of cosmic experience. Sculpture became wood, stone and metal expressions of physical and metaphysical features, and official and social portraits of the society. Surviving paintings were mainly found on walls of tombs and some temples for which the people of ancient Kemet, today's Egyptians, generally used four colors, viz., red, blue, green and yellow to express their thematic concepts. They used black color for significant representations. In the Cairo Museum, a displays show Osiris, "the Great Black" God, Mentuhotep II and others painted black. We know Queen Aahmes-Nefertari is painted black and Tutankhamon specifically, revealed his blackness. However, these "survivals" in their limited numbers still evoke ethnographic discussions, yet begging the question as to why so few! In this it points to the destructive nature of time and man.

FREDERICK MONDERSON

Egypt Essays Photo 14. Philae Temple of Isis. While Isis sits nursing Horus and Nephthys sits beside, Khnum makes man on his potters' wheel as Thoth stands at his rear doing his job of recording.

Tomb depiction represented history, literature, theology, ritual and medicine. Architecture, horticulture, clothing, feasting at banquets, farming, fishing, and hunting as well as religious practices were represented as art in tombs. Literature was very extensive throughout dynastic history. The "Wise Sayings" of Imhotep were quoted for centuries. He was the Grand Vizier of King Zoser of the Third Dynasty. Imhotep built his Pharaoh Zoser's mortuary temple called the Step-Pyramid at Sakkara. The artistic and architectural conventions he introduced provided the experimental basis of the Step and Great Pyramids at Giza that represented the great flowering of ancient Kemet's mortuary and religious structures, beliefs and practices, as well as in science, medicine, agriculture, quarrying, navigation, etc., which so characterized the Old Kingdom of dynasties 3, 4, 5, and 6.

The *Tale of Sinuhe* told of an official under King Amenemhet, 2000 B.C. Perhaps after some intrigue, he fled to Palestine and later longed for his native land. Finally he was welcomed home just before he died. The *Prophecies of Nefert* and the *Miracles* during the reign of Khufu are interesting pieces also. So too were *The Tale of the Two Brothers*, *The Eloquent Peasant*, and *The Shipwrecked Sailor*. These are all wonderful specimens of the literary genius of

EGYPT ESSAYS ON ANCIENT KEMET

ancient African man. The *Book of Surgery* is dated to the Old Kingdom and *Ebers* and *Edwin Smith* Papyri to the 18th Dynasty. These were copies of much older medical works and were copied by students for centuries. The *Pyramid Texts* were found in tombs of kings of the 5th and 6th Dynasties. The *Coffin Texts* are the same religious teachings and inscriptions that were written on the outside and inside of coffins that dates to the Middle and New Kingdoms. The famous *Book of the Dead* became a compilation of religious beliefs and very illustratively and graphic representations of what was to be expected in the next world. These Africans of the Nile Valley were original in their intellectual adventures in sciences, arts and metaphysics. Their creative genius pioneered in establishing the parameters of today's scientific disciplines. All of this was revealed through the discipline and science of archaeology.

The Englishman W.M. Flinders Petrie spent some 50-years digging in Egypt and was dubbed "The father of Egyptian Archaeology" because he introduced and modeled a systematic method to conduct and study excavations. This approach was especially needed due to the wanton efforts to secure Egyptian artifacts during the years after decipherment in 1822; an age Brian Fagan described that permitted "The Rape of Nile."

This notwithstanding, Kemetic/Egyptian archaeology has also taught us that modern man is not unique in disturbing the resting-place of the revered ancestors. The only difference today, man's search is clouded in the dubious term "science." We have learnt that most of the royal and wealthy burials were desecrated from the earliest times, especially in the twentieth through twenty-second dynasties. Celebrated investigations were conducted to focus attention on this vile practice. During the late ages of the nineteenth century, Maspero had found many in the modern village Abu el Gurneh were tomb robbing despoilers who were equally aided and abetted by European travelers, tourists, bureaucrats, consuls, all bent on creating and expanding "collections" in museums, academic institutions, government buildings and in private hands or private collections. Yet, despite all the acquisitions bolstering museums and other displays "abroad," Egypt/Kemet still remains a cultural beacon that reinforces the genius of ancient African Nile Valley ancestral heritage as it attracts visitors to enjoy the culture "in situ."

Egypt Essays Photo 15. Philae Temple of Isis. King makes a Presentation of 2 jars to enthroned Hathor as Isis, while Horus as a babe with his hands to his mouth sits behind the goddess.

Egypt Essays Photo 15a. Philae Temple of Isis. Sharp and crispy Hieroglyphic inscriptions with only the face seeming erased.

EGYPT ESSAYS ON ANCIENT KEMET

Dr. ben-Jochannan, whom the writer has known for more than thirty-five years, and traveled with to the "Holy-Land" on several occasions, has always insisted that in the temples we should not enter the sanctuary or "Holy of Holies." To "bathe" in that philosophic, metaphysical and mystical splendor these "temple nucleuses" possess, we see this admonition being contravened by visitors and many natives don't fully respect the ancient culture either. This is why critical scholars, our children, families and whomsoever we convert, must move tenaciously and boldly to reclaim the revered African past. To ensure the deserved respect, therefore, we must defend the culture's sanctity with vehemence inclandestine whether in teaching or researching and writing about that glorious ancestral heritage. If we don't, no one else will!

To have a clear picture of the state of affairs, we must understand that modern interest in Egypt began around 1800 A.D., when Napoleon, the French Emperor, visited Egypt with an army and a coterie of scholars who made the first systematic study of the culture of the ancient Africans. Their efforts produced a work entitled *Description of Egypt*. At a place called Rosetta in 1798, engineers unearthed the Rosetta Stone. This important document is a trilingual inscription in Hieroglyphic, Demotic and Greek. It became the key to decipherment of the ancient language allowing scholars to establish a scientific discipline called Egyptology. Flinders Petrie has described Egyptology as a discipline requiring knowledge of a combination of Egyptian geography, history and language, Hieroglyphics.

The language was deciphered by Champollion in 1822 and simultaneously inaugurated antiquarian interest in Egypt. Prior to the Rosetta Stone's discovery, Count Volney had visited Egypt and in his book *Ruins of Empires*, wrote on the science and ethnicity question, that black or people of sable skin, "then enslaved in the modern world, founded thousands of years ago, the principles and sciences that today govern the universe." Another distinguished French visitor, Baron Denon, was the first modern visitor to draw a picture of the Sphinx of Giza. Some scholars claimed Napoleon's

FREDERICK MONDERSON

artillery shot off the Sphinx's nose for Denon's drawing shows this part of the anatomy intact.

In 1836 Sir Godfrey Higgins wrote *Anacalypsis* in two volumes. This book became a veritable reference reservoir on 'Black Who's Who' of the ancient world. It indicated that Osiris, Jesus, Buddha, Hercules, etc., were all black personalities. These pioneering works were done in the period from 1800-1875 when great scholars were engrossed in establishing the linguistic system and structures that came to characterize Egyptology. Concomitantly, archaeology and related sciences emerged and were coming of age.

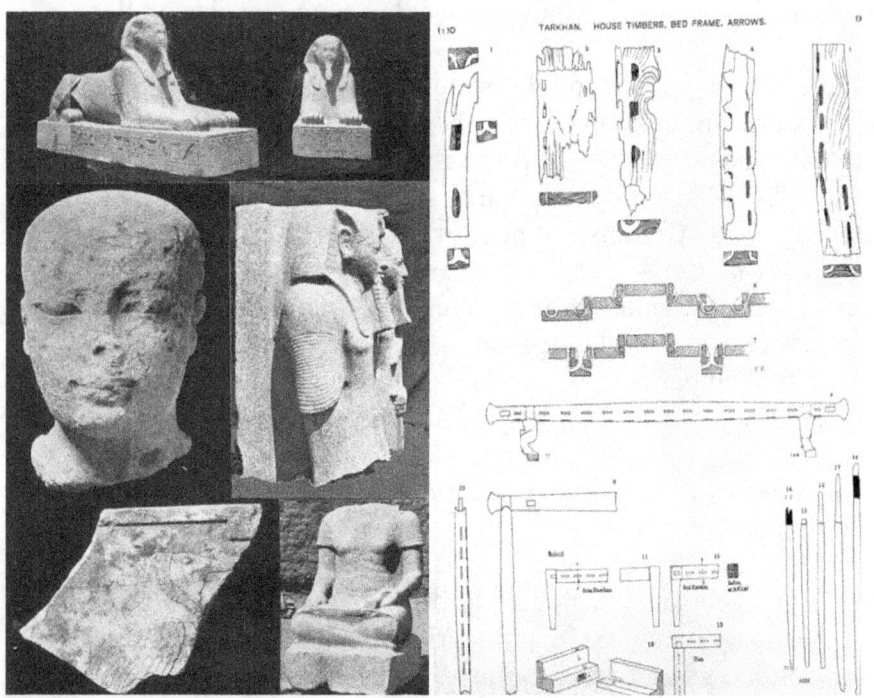

Egypt Essays Illustration 12. View of sphinxes and statues (left); and house timbers, bed frame and arrows from Tarkhan (right).

Garner Wilkinson's *Manners and Customs of the Ancient Egyptians*, Samuel Birch's edited *Records of the Past* and Bunsen's *Egypt's*

EGYPT ESSAYS ON ANCIENT KEMET

Place in Universal History were all outstanding works, still regarded as classics today. From mid-19th Century, imperialism and colonialism emerged across the globe and especially in Africa. This brutal system launched a physical assault against the psychic nature as well as the personality and intellectual integrity of Africa and Africans. To a great degree it was successful. While some may claim these are harsh charges, we cannot forget the horrors of the slave trade and institution of slavery perpetuated by people originating in Europe. On the other hand, the Arab Slave Trade was no different and it lasted much longer!

Samuel Cartwright, the "banana skin physician," in his classic *Slavery and Ethnology* represented a significant culture of pro-slavery advocates. He wrote in 1857 the "Nilotic monuments record Negroes were nothing but slaves in Egypt from time immemorial." Clearly, this "defense of slavery" treatise was not factually or referenced based.

Anton's *Dictionary of Classical Antiquity* in 1863 noted, the "red color is evidently intended to represent the complexion of the people, and is not put on in the want of a lighter paint or flesh color for when the limbs or bodies are represented as seen through a thin veil, the tint used resembles the complexion of Europeans." How interesting that Europeans extolled the "red man of Egypt" and denigrated the "red man of America!" In 1864, Dr Hunt wrote an article entitled "The Negro is a Beast." This type of psychological assaults amidst physical emasculation and degradation of slavery, were typical of the backdrop of 19th Century racist scholarship regarding Africans and this skewed the pendulum far to the right. In the umbrella of this "denigrating the Negro" strategy, imperialists studied, excavated, controlled and molded the presentation of a distorted version of Africa and history. In regard Ancient Egypt, many European scholars including De Rouge, as late as 1897, in laying a false foundation, argued for the Asiatic origin of the Ancient Egyptians that has been coming apart a century later.

FREDERICK MONDERSON

Egypt Essays Photo 16. Kalabsha Temple of Mendulese. Columns at the entrance, each with a varied capital and with winged disk overhead.

The period from 1875-1900 represents the birth and classical period of Egyptian Archaeology when European academic, governmental and private organizations sponsored scholars, adventurers and archaeological expeditions to unearth and study this ancient African culture. Herein then lay the ossification and concretization of the falsity of a "White Egypt." However, and ostensibly, in the interest of science, they were particularly interested in acquiring artifacts for private collections and museums. These scientists and pillagers swarmed all over the ancient land. Of particular interest were the numerous magazines and journals that came into being as a result and helped to record their excavations. Such institutions as the Smithsonian Institution, the Metropolitan Museum of Art, are today considered "reservoirs of information" as well that molded and ossified the man in the street view of the Ancient Egyptians. These and the British and Manchester Museums, the Philadelphia Museum *Journal, Bulletin of the Museum of Fine Arts, University of California Publications of Egyptian Archaeology*, among others, all published Journals. Academic and scholarly publications in the forefront of the new information and the interpretation and presentation that posed today's questions of reinterpretation included, *Ancient Egypt*, the *Journal of Egyptian Archaeology, Society of Biblical Archaeology Journal, Biblia, American Philological Society Journal*, the *Journal of the Asiatic Society*,

EGYPT ESSAYS ON ANCIENT KEMET

Antiquity, American Antiquity, Annals of Archaeology and Anthropology, Art and Architecture, Harvard African Studies, Modern Quarterly, Journal of Biblical Literature, Nation, Memnon, Good News, Open Court, Academy, Dublin University Magazine, and *Annals of Medical History,* to name some sources of important documentation that are "Treasure troves of information."

Egypt Essays Photo 16a. Kalabsha Temple of Mendulese Vicinity. Ruins from the Temple of Beit Wali.

Egypt Essays Photo 16b. "The Register" introduced order into Hieroglyphic writing enabling the beauty of the art to be emphasized.

FREDERICK MONDERSON

Egypt Essays Photo 16a. Kalabsha Temple of Mendulese Vicinity. Standing remains of statue of Rameses II at Beit Wali.

EGYPT ESSAYS ON ANCIENT KEMET

We know historical sources come in primary and secondary categories. Additional references of source material containing recovered information of critical historical value include *Biblical World, Journal of the Royal Anthropological Institute, Man, Biometrika, Journal of Semitic Languages* and the *American Anthropologist, American Journal of Archaeology, Isis, Journal of Near Eastern Studies*, and numerous other publications of archaeological, anthropological and other scientific data that in themselves are extremely significant reservoirs of ancient knowledge. These represent "primary sources of the primary sources." All these entities published briefs, extracts and reports of archaeological finds. Africans wrote none and none had a black editor! None were systematically taken to tasks for any and all disparagement, discrepancies or distortions of the Egyptian historical past Africans were so significant in molding. With present knowledge of the fields, much of the foundation conclusions are being reevaluated and revised!

Egypt Essays Illustration 12a. Base of a limestone statue of the Third Dynasty Pharaoh Zoser, builder of the Step Pyramid at Sakkara; and front view of the base.

FREDERICK MONDERSON

Several individuals excavated at the various pyramids from Giza (Ghizeh) through Meydum, Hawara and Lahun. These structures were large and inviting. They yielded interesting mathematical and technological information as well as shedding much light on religious beliefs and practices. The pyramids of Egypt are immortal. These gigantic monoliths came to characterize a period and a culture in Egypt, Northeast Africa. The pyramids were not a new idea to Africa for several places along the Nile could be found naturally hewn stone pyramids that were shaped by wind, sand and other forces of nature, over thousands of years. These portray the picture of a permanent abode with an elevated peak reaching skyward. The ancient burial lands to the south of Egypt are strewn with such pyramids. Several can be viewed in the Aswan area. Perhaps these natural monoliths influenced the evolution of the pyramid idea in the minds of these ancient Africans of the Nile Valley.

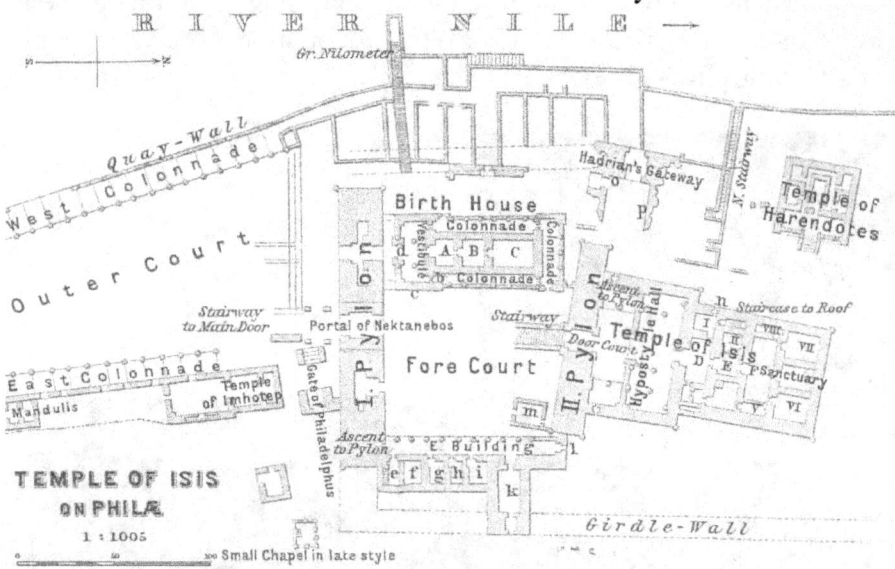

Egypt Essays Plan of the Temple of Isis of Philae now on Agilka Island.

In an effort to bolster extra-African origins and because of the great body of knowledge unearthed in archaeological excavations during the late 19th and early 20th Centuries, a concept called the "Hamitic Hypothesis" was born. It argued, essentially, "Any evidence of

EGYPT ESSAYS ON ANCIENT KEMET

civilization and high culture found in Africa was brought there by a migrating people of white morphology." While this is one example, since the existence of the natural pyramids, absence the remains of pyramids as burial structures of people alien to Africa, we must conclude Africa and African people are the source and inspiration of the wonderful man-made mountains we call the pyramids. The genius of their construction owes nothing, if anything to Europeans and other foreigners. In fact, they represent mountains of hope, intellect and steadfastness, yet resilient nature and aspirations of Africans, those at home and in the Americas. Again, by the time of Narmer's unification their mathematical attainment, counting in the millions, can give evidence of other "Scientific advances." Let us remember Nabta Playa residents were mapping the sky, breaking ground in astronomy and astrology and practicing agriculture and pastoralism, while mapping routes of migration to "water their cattle."

The idea of the pyramids grew out of the Old Kingdom's need to preserve the remains of a dead king who journeyed into immortality in the next world. At first kings were buried in elaborate structures underground that were covered with a superstructure called mastabas. The "Step-pyramid" was a development of seven such mastabas in decreasing size from the bottom up. The "True-pyramid" emerged from the trial and error of the "Bent-pyramid" until the building techniques had been mastered.

FREDERICK MONDERSON

Egypt Essays Photo 17. Kalabsha Temple of Mendulese. Columns at the entrance, each with a varied capital and with winged disk overhead.

Egypt Essays Photo 17a. Kalabsha Temple of Mendulese Vicinity. Entrance to Kalabsha with the giant stele.

When it came to the specific argument of the origin of the Egyptians there were many discrepancies. In 1897, 3 theories existed as to

EGYPT ESSAYS ON ANCIENT KEMET

origin of the Egyptians. 1. They came from Asia via the Suez Isthmus. 2. Another version noted they came from Asia, entered along the Horn of Africa and through Ethiopia, and then journeyed down the Nile. 3. That the majority of the Egyptian population, it is held, had its origin in Europe and passed into Egypt by the West and Southwest. Maspero seemed to argue that they came from southern Europe, crossed the Mediterranean and slipped into the valley from the west.

That same year, 1897 Frenchman Gaston Maspero in one of his archaeological excavations discovered a *Table of Offerings* that was a replica found in Memphite tombs. The best examples are two Old Kingdom tombs of Ti and Pepi II. They listed thousands of loaves of bread, cakes, game, meat, cloths, perfumes and so on be given to the deceased. A set of rites was listed on the table to be performed in five parts. These were:

1. Two purifications, by water and incense.
2. A ceremony of Opening the Mouth with purification and a summary meal.
3. The dressing of the deceased.
4. The anointing of the deceased.
5. Two additional purifications by incense and water.

This notion of cleanliness significantly characterized the ancient Egyptian/Kemet culture. The image of a "flea-infested Arab" scratching himself is itself alien to Africa! These excavations were made in the classical Victorian period. Dr. ben-Jochannan equally got a lot of mileage from a book of the time called *Dirt*. It noted Queen Elizabeth I's castigations of the women of Europe. She boasted of being the cleanest woman in all of Europe because she had taken "one bath that year." Thousands of years ago, the people of Kemet had constructed baths with provisions for the water to be brought and to also exit the contraption. The Temple of Rameses III at Medinet Habu had four such bathrooms.

FREDERICK MONDERSON

Abydos and Thebes were the most extensively excavated archaeological sites in Egypt. Abydos gained fame very early in Egyptian history for a vast number of reasons. It was the cemetery of the Thinite kings of the First and Second Dynasties. In this vicinity forts were constructed. Most of their remains have disappeared. There were temples dating back to the First Dynasty. There was a great Hypostyle Hall located here as well as monuments of kings Khasekhemwy and Perabsen. From this site we have a Stela of King Zet and a Great Stella of Ahmose. Strabo the Greek Geographer (63 B.C. to 24 A.D.) recorded seeing a well here when he visited Abydos. In addition, among the temples were those of Ahmose I, Khentiamenti, Rameses II and his father Seti I. Most importantly, at Abydos the "ladder to heaven" was located.

Thebes was the capital of Egypt during the Middle and New Kingdoms. The twin temples of *Warit* and *Waset*, Karnak and Luxor, were located here. Archaeology revealed the city boasts the richest architectural and religious remains anywhere on earth. The site is endowed with art, architecture, religious beliefs and preparations for the otherworld. Archaeological excavations exposed records of military engagements and other historical developments and provide geologic and botanical evidence of ancient man along the Nile River in Northeast Africa.

EGYPT ESSAYS ON ANCIENT KEMET

Egypt Essays Photo 18. Beit Wali Temple of Rameses II. Columned Court and Entrance.

Egypt Essays Photo 18a. Kalabsha Temple of Mendulese. Ruins that speak to architectural and cultural splendor.

FREDERICK MONDERSON

Generally, worship temples were located on the east bank and mortuary temples on the west bank of the Nile River. The Colossi of Memnon are two gigantic seated statues of Amenhotep III that stood outside a large temple on the West Bank that has now disappeared. Interesting, but these tow colossi are not unique. There were others. In the vicinity of Merenptah's temple the remains of at least one lies broken in a depression.

The Temple of Luxor, dedicated to Amon-Ra, was built by Amenhotep III of the 18th Dynasty and extended by Rameses II of the 19th Dynasty.

The Great Temple of Karnak was begun about 2000 B.C., in the Middle Kingdom, and successive pharaohs built here for 2000 years. The architect Senmut built Deir el-Bahari temple for Queen Hatshepsut who ruled as pharaoh. He also began a temple to Goddess Mut. Both Queen Hatshepsut and later Pharaoh Amenhotep III claimed to have had "divine births" and these were recorded in their temples. Pharaoh Rameses II, the great statesman of the 19th Dynasty, and builder, military strategist, who also erected the twin temples of Abu Simbel, built the Ramesseum, his mortuary temple. Then there is Medinet Habu a great mortuary structure, built by Rameses III, of the Twentieth Dynasty.

The Valley of the Kings, first chosen by Thutmose I, became the final resting-place for the greatest pharaohs of the New Kingdom. In 1881, 36 royal mummies were discovered in a "cache" at Deir el-Bahari, hidden by 22nd Dynasty priests, who sought to foil the tomb-robbing agents and invading forces of their time. The Egyptians/people of ancient Kemet believed the entrance, a subterranean passage, into the underworld, lay at Deir El Bahari. In 1898, Loret found another cache of 13 mummies in the tomb of Amenhotep II. The illustrious Dr. Cheikh Anta Diop in his *Civilization or Barbarism* has pointed out, from his observations, that many of the mummy remains in Egypt have had their skins stripped from the flesh. The skin was the surest way to tell the race of their owners. Still, he was able to detect significant amounts of melanin in the bodies. Many of the mummies seemed like "peeled

EGYPT ESSAYS ON ANCIENT KEMET

potatoes," he wrote. This means, these preserved remains were tampered with!

The Valley of the Queens, Valley of the Nobles and Valley of the Artisans are all outstanding examples of creative Egyptian, African, and genius in theology, art, mummification practice, science, and building with other contributions to the pageantry of human and civilization drama.

This is all said to reinforce Drs. Diop, ben-Jochannan and Ivan Van Sertima's convincing arguments for the blackness of ancient Egypt/Kemet and the significant role of Africans in that culture! This powerful legacy without question belongs to people of African descent. We must teach others especially our young, particularly during Black History Month and Women's History Month; African people have a proud and illustrious heritage. We possess a determined and resilient spirit that helps us to survive and grow. The twenty-first century must not find African people wanting knowledge of their past. These Africans must possess the tenacity to conduct research and engage in meaningful African historiographic reconstruction. We must set the record straight. Ancient Kemet archaeology holds the key. We must study archaeology, correct misunderstandings and mold the future for our youth.

FREDERICK MONDERSON

Egypt Essays Photo 19. Beit Wali Temple of Rameses II. Rameses offers his name as Ma'at to the enthroned Amon-Ra.

Egypt Essays Photo 19a. The temple of Kalabsha moved from Nubia and relocated to this area under circumstances similar to the nearby Beit Wali Temple of Rameses II.

EGYPT ESSAYS ON ANCIENT KEMET

Egypt Essays Photo 20. Kom Ombo Temple of Haroeis and Sobek. Wall, Columns of the right-side Court Colonnade and more columns of the magnificent entrance Hypostyle Hall with its twin uraeus and entrance to twin aisles, signifying the "double nature" of the Temple.

5. THE EGYPTIAN TOMB

The Egyptian tomb has held a significant place in the religious, psychic and socio-ethical experiences of ancient Kemetic Nile Valley culture called the civilization of Egypt. While such beginnings are clouded in the prehistoric past, one African man first posed the question of life's existence and how to account for it after death. In quest for this heavenly realization, elaborate pomp and fanfare surrounded disposal and preservation of bodies in order to

FREDERICK MONDERSON

gain immortality associated with various Egyptian deities, whether Ptah worshipped at Memphis, Ra at Heliopolis, and Amun-Ra at Thebes and Osiris at Abydos. It was Professor John Clarke, who, when asked about African and African American funerary efforts on behalf of loved ones, responded. "We put them away nicely!"

In this early progression of the Egyptian, similarly African mind, the motivations, challenges and ostentatious architectural displays remain a source of wonder and testimony of scientific and associated achievements of these ancestors. From the simple internment in shallow graves, efforts were made to preserve the human body in hopes of returning the elements of the person to continue its otherworldly existence. The King, that ethereal substance of the nation and people, was considered an earthly manifestation of the deity on earth, whose body had to be protected to mend with the eternal spirit. This idea became enshrined in monumental architectural works as the pyramids atop the Giza plateau extending through the entire region of pharaonic internment, whether toward Sakkara or Abusir. However, while not as ostentatious above ground, subterranean tombs of the Valley of the Kings, Valley of the Queens, Valley of the Nobles and place of internment of the artisans who build those resplendent structures, have helped preserve a bonanza of cultural history.

EGYPT ESSAYS ON ANCIENT KEMET

Egypt Essays Photo 20a. Kom Ombo Temple of Haroeis and Sobek. In the Entrance Court, left side part of the Peristyle Colonnade.

FREDERICK MONDERSON

Egypt Essays Photo 20b. Kom Ombo Temple of Haroeis and Sobek. In the Entrance Court, right side part of the Peristyle Colonnade.

To this end, ancient Egyptian (Kemetic) burial structures grew out of simple holes in the ground to complex mastaba tombs. Regarding the mastaba tombs, Watson (1987: 9) notes in *Egyptian Pyramids and Mastaba Tombs*: "Their massive forms can be divided into three major sections, the excavated substructure, the mud-brick superstructure and various ancillary structures." Emphasizing size, Watson further gives the example the magazines of tomb 3035, many of which were completely empty when excavated, yet still held the "remains of 901 pottery vessels, 362 stone vessels, 493 arrows, 305 flint tools, 60 wooden tools, 45 spindle whorls and other miscellaneous items including ivory and textile fragments. In tomb 3504 the robbers had left behind 2500 pottery vessels and 1500 stone jars. The magazines had false floors of clean sand and were roofed with timber." Thus, this idea of "taking it with you" remained a principal feature of burial practices down through dynastic rule becoming particularly extravagant during the New Kingdom.

Pyramids were executed, developed through a process of trial and error, finally culminating in the finely executed monoliths. Finally, there were elaborately decorated tombs hollowed out of the hills. The simple pits of the prehistoric period yielded a mass of information about early customs, and levels of cultural attainment of these ancient Africans. Their earliest graves were simple pits where the dead were placed on a mat. Here were added weapons, food, pottery, ornaments, jewelry, body paint and possibly a slate palette. Sometimes replicas of the opposite sex were also interred. Forces of nature and sheer luck preserved these resting-places.

Egypt Essays Illustration 13. Tarkhan burials and pottery of different shapes.

FREDERICK MONDERSON

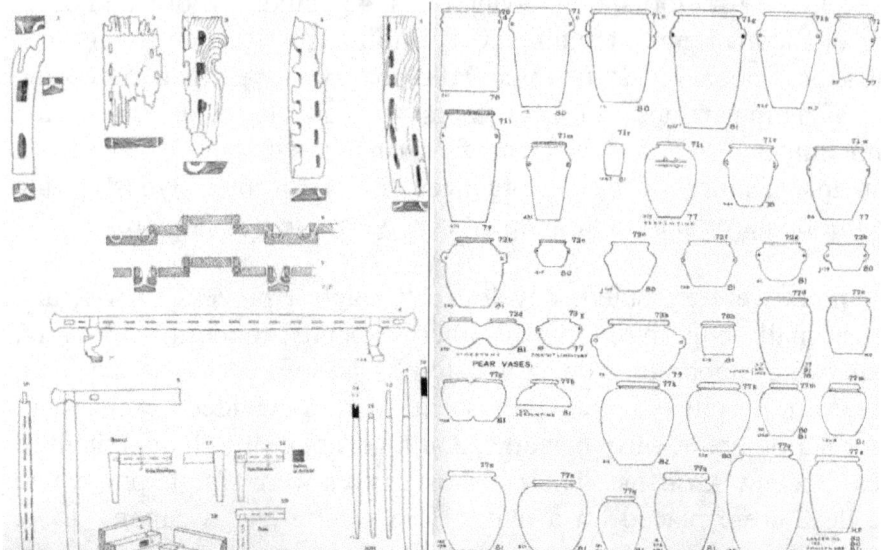

Egypt Essays Illustration 13a. Tarkhan House Timbers, Bed Frames and Arrows (left); and Tarkhan Alabaster – Handled and Pear Vases (right).

By the time of dynastic rule, 1090 *Nile Year* (N.Y.) 3150 B.C. conceptions of religious belief became clearly defined. At that time and earlier, it was believed man had certain entities that made up his personality. According to Maspero's *Manual of Egyptian Archaeology* (1926), "there was a visible form, the body to which the *ka* or double attached during life. The *Ka* was a replica of the body, of a substance less dense, a colored but ethereal projection of the individual; the *Ka* of a child would reproduce the child, that of a woman the woman, that of a man the man, each of them feature for feature. Next there was the *Khu* or *Luminous*, and one or more other entities perhaps of less importance." These elements were, wrote Maspero wrote, "not imperishable, and if left to themselves they would gradually cease to exist, and the man would die a second time-that is to say, he would become non-existent." The existence of the *Ka* depended on the body, and to save that from destruction was the object of the survivors. Even further he continued:

EGYPT ESSAYS ON ANCIENT KEMET

"By the process of drying and embalming the body they could prolong its existence for ages, while by means of prayers and offerings they saved the double, the soul, and the luminous from the second death, and procured for them all that was necessary for prolonged existence. The double scarcely quitted the place where the mummy dwelt; the soul and the luminous left it to follow the gods, but they always returned to it as a traveler returns home."

Egypt Essays Photo 21. Kom Ombo Temple of Haroeis and Sobek. Close-up of the double entrance cornice with Haroeis (left) and Sobek right).

FREDERICK MONDERSON

Egypt Essays Photo 21a. Kom Ombo Temple of Haroeis and Sobek. Band, stalk of the flowers and five expanding levels of the leaves of the flowers of the composite capital.

Egypt Essays Photo 21a. The individual image at top right generally means "Prince of the Land" is often shown defaced, which is perhaps because he is in the "Negro mold!"

EGYPT ESSAYS ON ANCIENT KEMET

Egypt Essays Photo 21b. Kom Ombo Temple of Haroeis and Sobek. The king offers pellets of incense to Haroeis, the "Elder Horus," twin deity of this Kom Ombo temple.

Through the process of continuity and change, and certainly by the New Kingdom, the tombs of the kings and some nobles were constructed to reflect an understanding of this belief system. To them, the tomb was a "dwelling-house," an "eternal house." In contrast, the earthly houses were but inns for temporary sojourn. Importantly, the "arrangement of these eternal houses corresponded faithfully to the conception held regarding the future life. They contained private apartments for the soul, where after the day of the funeral no living creature would enter without committing sacrilege." Dodson's Egyptian *Rock Cut Tombs* (1991) offered the following comment on the method by which some of these final resting places were built. She wrote:

"Fundamental to construction was the establishment of a center line; cutting proceeded from the center out, and from the ceiling down; numerous examples exist of tombs where central axis at roof level is finished, but whose wings are incomplete and rise in steps to the ceiling at the extremities. These steps are the result of the method of quarrying, which removed blocks of limestone in layers; tools used were stone and metal (copper, later bronze), the latter used for the finer work."

Further, in the tombs, space was provided for the double where priests, friends and families came to give prayers and make offerings. In reflecting such a picture, tomb scenes from daily life show crafts, recreation, and other aesthetic and religious representations. The tomb was a sacred place intended to insure the well-being of the owner. Dodson again expressed the view: "However they were constructed, Egyptian tombs were visualized as the eternal homes of the dead, to preserve the body and its effects intact, and to allow the spirit to obtain nourishment."

The kings of the First and Second Dynasties were buried in Mastaba tombs. A number of these were found at Abydos. These kings also built second tombs or cenotaphs at Memphis, which came to symbolize their dual nature as kings of Upper and Lower Kemet/Egypt. It has finally been agreed, the cenotaphs, were dummy tombs while those at Abydos contained the body. These tombs helped provide names of these kings of the Archaic Period. Many other mastaba tombs were found at Sakkara. Larger tombs of this earlier Memphite period have been found at Memphis, Meydum, and between Abu Roash and Dashur.

EGYPT ESSAYS ON ANCIENT KEMET

The larger tombs stood 30 to 40 feet high, 150 feet in length and 40 feet in width. They were built of brick and stone. The bricks were sun-dried and of two kinds. The first, used until the Sixth Dynasty, were according to Maspero, "small (8 3/4 X 5 3/4 inches), yellowish, and made of sand mixed with a little clay and gravel. The other is black, compact, well molded, and made of mud mixed with straw and fairly large (15 X 7 X 5 1/2 inches)."

Generally speaking, the mastaba was oriented with the four cardinal points. The doors into the tombs and even the false doors inside faced east, south, north, but never west. An unpaved platform served as the flooring. It was covered with fine sifted sand. The structure had a forecourt opening to the north. It was sometimes square or irregular and this sometimes depended on the size of the tomb and the court. Some of these tombs were large enough to accommodate more than one person. Many times wives and other family members were buried with husbands and fathers.

Egypt Essays Photo 22. Kom Ombo Temple of Haroeis and Sobek. Twenty-three uraei on the cornice.

FREDERICK MONDERSON

Egypt Essays Photo 22a. Kom Ombo Temple of Haroeis and Sobek. Various forms of the Vulture wearing the Osiris Crown and the Red Crown on a ceiling decoration.

EGYPT ESSAYS ON ANCIENT KEMET

Egypt Essays Photo 22b. Kom Ombo Temple of Haroeis and Sobek. *Suten Bat*, King of Upper and Lower Egypt, title of Pharaoh.

There was a chapel for prayers that also served as a reception room for the double. In the tomb there was also a concealed passage called a serdab. In these, doubles of the deceased were hidden. Regarding these doubles, the following belief prevailed. "A single body gave him one chance of prolonged existence, whereas twenty bodies gave him twenty chances." Among the "furniture" of the tomb was a stele with the message of the deceased and a "Table of Offerings."

At the "Table of Offerings" in the chapel, funerary sacrifices were made on the days prescribed by law. Lichtheim gives a good example of this below. Maspero located the "Table of Offerings" where "offerings were deposited in the principal hall at the foot of the west wall at the precise spot where the entrance to the eternal house was indicated."

The name of the tomb's owner was inscribed in hieroglyphic and he shown reaching for the offerings. The individual soon realized no matter how great his endowments for future offerings, they could not continue indefinitely. Therefore, relying on the power of prayer and magic, he decorated his tomb with the "food and drink he would require, with an invocation to the gods of the dead, Osiris or Anubis, to supply him with all good things necessary." He went so far as to depict the entire process of preparation of the feast animals, whether ox or gazelle, by the butcher. He also depicted farming, sowing, and harvest: "beating out the grain, storing it in the granary, and kneading the dough. Clothing, ornaments, and furniture offered a pretext for introducing spinning and weaving, gold-working and joiner's tools." Also added on the walls of his tombs were dancing girls, musicians, or his favorite gaming board, all for his personal entertainment. Further, believing in the power of the spoken word, he felt that "any chance stranger in time to come could simply repeat the magic formula of the stelae aloud, which would instantly activate the feast he had prepared. Added to this, his name, rank and civil status were inscribed in the tomb so he could enjoy the same in the next life."

The "mastaba concept" expanded upwards into the "Step-Pyramid," the "Bent Pyramid" and finally the "True Pyramid." For their builders, the pomp and elaborateness of these tombs gained for them immortality in the eyes of man. Pyramids attracted satellite or subsidiary pyramids as well as fields of mastaba tombs of nobles in surrounding areas that were dwarfed by the great pyramidal structures. All this entailed an enormous bureaucratic and administrative network for construction and management. Yet, in all their majesty, they were vulnerable to tomb-robbers that plundered the tomb, desecrated the mummy and its resting-place and stole buried treasure. This notwithstanding, artistic changes were taking place. So much so, by the time of the Fifth and Sixth Dynasties, the

EGYPT ESSAYS ON ANCIENT KEMET

large mastabas of the nobles and pyramids of the kings were elaborately decorated with religious and other social aesthetic reliefs. In *Ancient Egyptian Literature*, Vol. I: *The Old and Middle Kingdoms*, Miriam Lichtheim mentions an interesting set of prayers found on the architrave of the entrance of the pillared hall of Princess Ni-Sedjer-Kai.

In her depicted horizontal line request for good reception in the west, she asked, and this emphasized that social and religious practice of perennial bonding with deity in glorious adoration and expectation:

"May offerings be given her on the New Year's feast, the Thoth feast, the First-of-the-Year feast, the *waq*-feast, the Sokar feast, the Great Flame feast, the Brazier feast, the Procession-of-Min feast, the monthly *sadj*-feast, the Beginning-of-the-Month feast, the Beginning-of-the Half-Month feast, every feast, every day, to the royal daughter, the royal ornament, Ni-sedjer-kai."

This clear delineation points out some of the more important feasts celebrated as far back as the Old Kingdom. On the other hand, very early evidence showed the ravages and desecration some of the tombs were subjected to. This led to more elaborate plans to protect the tombs and bodies while the deceased journeyed into the west or land of the dead.

Naguib Kanawati's Prism Archaeological Series Number 3: *The Tomb and its Significance in Ancient Egypt* raised the question of protection of the dead man's final resting-place. "The wealthy employed guards to keep watch over their tombs. This, however, had its limitations. Nevertheless, there was: 'little that he could do other than leave an inscription in his tomb' that recounted his life on earth and appealed for help from the living."

One important individual, Khentika, a vizier in Dynasty 6, emphasizing ethical behavior and responsible social conduct, offered a reminder to "the living on earth that he exercised justice, and never used force against any man because he wanted his name to be good before the god and his reputation to be good before all men. He also rescued the wretched, gave bread to the hungry and clothing to the naked, and brought the stranded to land, he buried him who had no son and never said any evil thing about any man. Furthermore, he feared his father and was gracious to his mother and brought up their children properly, etc."

Nevertheless, he also threatened the impure and those intent on desecration that entered his tomb. Evidently the belief system had some impact on the tomb robbers who became famous throughout Kemetic history. Robbers attacked the body of the deceased, for fear of being hurt in retaliation. They sometimes mutilated or set the bodies afire. This was a permanent way of ensuring the final death. Evidence indicates some bodies were unwrapped for their precious jewels and then re-wrapped, sometimes out of fear or respect for the body.

Egypt Essays Photo 23. Kom Ombo Temple of Haroeis and Sobek. View of the Sanctuary of Sobek, on the left from the entrance but from the right, looking out, as the God sees it.

EGYPT ESSAYS ON ANCIENT KEMET

Egypt Essays Photo 23a. Kom Ombo Temple of Haroeis and Sobek. The Vulture goddess Mut, meaning "mother," stands before her shrine with a goddess at rear indicating femininity and divinity.

Tombs were also desecrated by usurpation because many people reused abandoned or desecrated tombs for themselves. However, some people went to great lengths to ensure that the tombs they built were made of new material and were constructed on virgin soil. Two particular bits of advice from the First Intermediate Period by King Merikare's father and a Governor of Moalla in Upper Kemet respectively show this concern. This admonition is as follows: "Do not despoil the monument of another, but quarry stone in Tura. Do not build your tomb out of ruins using what had been made for what is to be made." Again: "I have indeed acquired this sarcophagus and all parts of this tomb by my own means; for there is no usurped door, or usurped column in this tomb.

FREDERICK MONDERSON

During the later Old Kingdom, in the fifth and sixth dynasties, pharaohs began to decorate their tombs with "Pyramid Texts," rituals for the afterlife.

In the Middle Kingdom pharaohs were still buried in the mastaba and a number of pyramids were still being built. The magical formulae of the "Pyramid Texts" were now written on coffins. In the cultural explosion of this magnificent period, Old Kingdom ideas were synthesized and syncretized. The "Coffin Texts" were born in aid of the wealthy as a continuation of the "Pyramid Texts."

Taylor, in *Egyptian Coffins* (1989) notes: "The coffin was primarily a container for the corpse, to protect it from destruction by scavenging animals or tomb robbers, but already in very early times it had a religious role to fulfill, the aim of which was the protection of the deceased and the ensuring of his well-being in the afterlife. The coffin was given the means to do this in two ways: by the symbolic power inherent in its shape and by painting and inscribing on it specific religious scenes and texts, the magical presence of which around the mummy would achieve the desired effects. Much of this was then bequeathed to the New Kingdom, where that process of democratization of immortality now assured the poor a place among the rich in heaven. Osiris particularly had a popular appeal to the people, for his life was more easily comprehended. As a king, his conception, birth, death, rebirth and triumph to judge the other world had been a reality for nearly 10,000 years." In all this, his wife, and sister, Isis, and their son Horus, represented the epitome of the black family. Strong, persevering, resolute, kind and just. Among the masses, simple burials persisted but a significant Nubian group called the 'C-Group' or for the style with which they were buried, 'Pan Grave' people entered Kemet. Coming from the south, they were part of a large population shift during the Middle Kingdom. They joined the army and helped to expel the Hyksos invaders who occupied the land for a century. The New Kingdom was founded as a result. This militarism set in motion a period of great imperialist undertaking by warrior pharaohs. This movement ushered in a "golden age" in Egypt/Kemet unparalleled in its history.

EGYPT ESSAYS ON ANCIENT KEMET

The new wealth impacted on the splendor of style and type of burials.

The pharaohs stopped building the large and vulnerable mastaba and pyramids. Sakkara and Giza were not the only burial sites. There were burials throughout the ancient land. Amelineau had found the "Tomb of Osiris" at Abydos, the earliest "Shrine of Pilgrimage," before the Third Dynasty, where rested "Osiris the Good God," the "Great Black," with his nearby, "Stairway to Heaven." The tombs of many Middle Kingdom pharaohs remain unknown, either preserved or destroyed. Tombs were also found at Beni Hasan and at Thebes. The Intefs chose to be buried at el-Taria, while Mentuhotep chose Deir el-Bahari.

In 1881 the "Deir el Bahari Cache" was unearthed by Mariette and found to contain the mummies of most of the New Kingdom pharaohs. Seventeen years later, in 1898 M. Loret discovered the tomb of the New Kingdom Pharaoh, Amenhotep II, containing the mummy and sarcophagus of the King. "Nine other royal mummies were also found, according to *American Journal of Archaeology III*, 1899, p. 58. In addition to the Mummy of Amenhotep II, nine others were found and identified from inscriptions as those of Thutmose IV, Amenhotep II, Seti II, Setnakht and Rameses V, VI, VIII. The eight mummy was thought by Loret to be Amenhotep IV (Akh-en-Aten); but Mr. Grobb has shown that is it really the mummy of Merenptah (sometimes identified with the Pharaoh who in the Biblical account was drowned in the Red Sea.)"

FREDERICK MONDERSON

Egypt Essays Photo 24. Kom Ombo Temple of Haroeis and Sobek. View from the rear of the Sanctuary of Sobek, on the right from the entrance but from the left, looking out, as the God sees it.

Egypt Essays Photo 24a. Kom Ombo Temple of Haroeis and Sobek. The "Two Ladies" title stand behind to protect the king.

EGYPT ESSAYS ON ANCIENT KEMET

As the archaeology movement got into high gear during the last decades of the 19th Century, *American Journal of Archaeology* VII, 1899, p. 597 reported, "tombs discovered by Flinders Petrie at Ballas and Neggadeh, Amelineau at Abydos, and De Morgan at Neggadeh holds keys to the heritage and legacy of dynastic Egyptian religion, culture and history." This geographic area is therefore important in African historiographic reconstruction! Even further was noted: "The presence of two boats and of two women (representing domain) is explained by the supposition that two forms of beliefs survive side by side, an earlier form according to which the deceased resided in the tomb, and a later form which sends him on a voyage in the other world."

During the early New Kingdom, kings as well as nobles began to build or rather hide their tombs in the hills surrounding Thebes. The Valley of the Kings and the Valley of the Queens were burial sites for royalty. Thutmose I was the first king to build his tomb in the Valley of the Kings. This King's internment was defiled. His mummy was unwrapped, robbed of its valuables, and then re-wrapped. In his tomb, accordingly, workmen discovered a papyrus containing texts from the *Book of the Dead* with colored pictures finely executed; a draught-board, with a full set of draughtsmen; some garlands; thirteen large earthen beer jars, with a large number of other vessels; weapons, two beautiful armchairs; and remains of food. The most remarkable piece of all was a large and beautifully preserved couch, consisting of a quadrangular wooden frame, overspread with a thick rush mat, over which were stretched three layers of linen with a life size figure of the god of death, Osiris, drawn upon the outer layer. The material was smeared with some liquid to make the under layer waterproof. Over this, mingled with some adhesive substance, soil had been spread, in which barley was planted.

FREDERICK MONDERSON

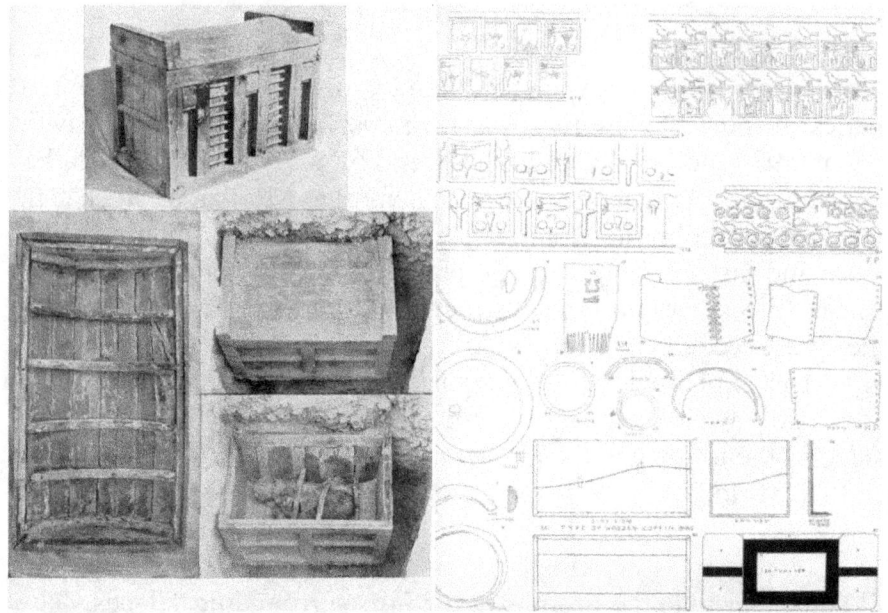

Egypt Essays Illustration 14. Tarkhan coffins (left); and sealings, armlets, coffins, etc (right).

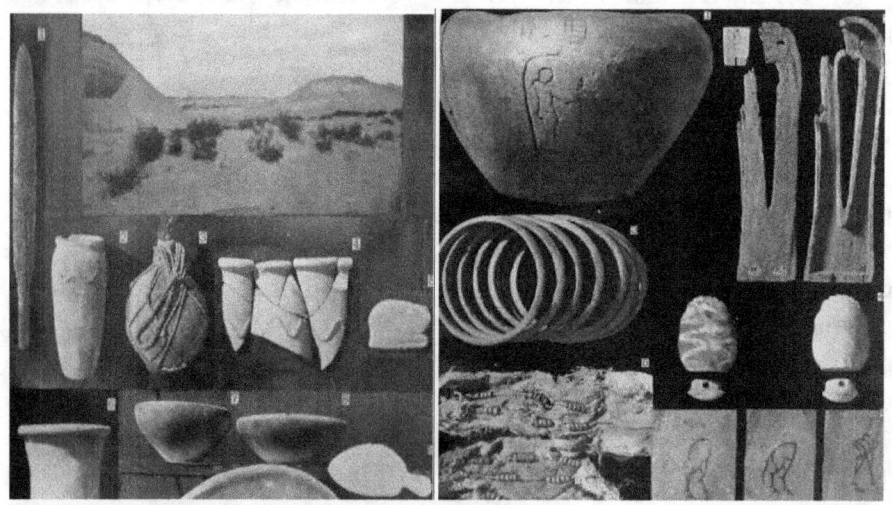

Egypt Essays Illustration 14a. Tarkhan view, and vessels of stone and copper (left); and Ptah Bowl, Sa Case, Scarabs, Flint Armlets, and Zebra drawings (right).

EGYPT ESSAYS ON ANCIENT KEMET

Tombs were worked by Newberry at Abd el-Qurneh; Garstang at Beit Khallaf; Davis at Thebes; Leonard Woolley at Anibeh; Newberry discovered "twenty seven tombs of Ekhmin, the city of the thunderbolt god, Min;" Quibell at Memphis; Blackman at Meir; the Tomb of Petosiris at Hermopolis; and at Thebes, the Tomb of Queen Tiy, wife of Amenhotep III; are all significant. *Nation* of February 14, 1907 informed, buried with the queen were solid gold plates and jewelry. On her head was the royal gold crown, representing a vulture with a signet ring in each talon. Of special beauty and interest are several portrait busts of the queen in alabaster set with obsidian and lapis lazuli.

Whereas, in the Eighteenth Dynasty, important officials built their tombs at Sheikh Abd-el-Qurna in the upper slopes and the lesser officials used the lower slopes. Minor officials were buried at Dra Abu-el-Naga. Now, during the Ramesside period of the nineteenth and twentieth dynasties, important officials cut their tombs at Dra Abu-el-Naga south and in the lower level of Sheikh Abd-el-Qurna. The poorer tombs were located at Deir el- Median. Throughout this period, tombs all took on a whole new outlook. They began to be more elaborately decorated, more complex structurally and much later provided posterity with a wealth of information of ancient African/Egyptian culture, social practice, ethical behavior and religious, philosophic and spiritual concepts, so important today!

Interestingly enough, two sons of Rameses II were found buried in the Valley of the Queens! In addition, KV 5 is a tomb Kent Weeks discovered in the Valley of the Kings that contained the remains of 35 sons of Rameses II. This mausoleum was discovered earlier and then lost then finally re-discovered by Weeks who subsequently began work to map and rehabilitate it.

FREDERICK MONDERSON

Egypt Essays Photo 25. Kom Ombo Temple of Haroeis and Sobek. View from the rear of the twin Sanctuary with some evidence of how the Temple was divided and structured. Dr. ben-Jochannan always instructed his students to never enter the Sanctuary area.

Egypt Essays Photo 25a. Kom Ombo Temple of Haroeis and Sobek. Ptah behind the symbol for millions of years for the Red Crown.

EGYPT ESSAYS ON ANCIENT KEMET

Egypt Essays Photo 25a. Kom Ombo Temple of Haroeis and Sobek. Hathor stands behind and pats Horus (Haroeis) on a column that still retains some color.

Regular and irregular themes were painted on walls and ceilings of tombs along the Nile River in Northeast Africa. Regular scenes included the tomb owner and his family, at a banquet or at an offering table supplied with various foods. Rural scenes of agriculture and animal husbandry are depicted. Workers in the field ploughing, farming and harvesting the crops are shown. Their work include dropping seeds, pulling flax, cutting barley and wheat by the stalks. They hold sickles and other tools. Animals are shown in a

FREDERICK MONDERSON

repertoire of themes. Some, such as donkeys and oxen are shown on the threshing floors. Kanawati writes: "Animal breeding features prominently in tomb scenes. 'Herdsmen are shown leading their animals, tending them, if sick, force-feeding them, milking cows, etc. Scenes of mating and of cows giving birth, often helped by a herdsman, are also frequent.' Bulls are sometimes shown fighting, as well as the famous 'cattle crossing a river preceded by the herdsmen in a papyrus boat or by one of them carrying a calf on his shoulders to entice the mother and the herd to follow.' Other animals such as dogs, donkeys, sheep, goats and even pigs, as well as gazelles, oryx, and hyenas are shown. Duck, geese and cranes provide beautiful models. Other themes include fishing, fowling and the desert hunt. The professions and industries reflect a variety of specializations. They indicate levels of technical sophistication in craftsmanship and diversity of metals and minerals used in various trades. Carpentry tools and wooden products are shown. These include saws, adzes, axes, chisels and mallets. Such furniture as chairs, headrests, chests, draughtboards, scribal-palettes, arrows, frames for chariots, doors, etc., make-up the wooden repertoire. Leather working is shown along with sandals, military equipment, shields, arrow quivers, and such crafts as bee-keeping, weaving and rope making are only some of the tomb decorations.

Sports and recreation, funerary rites and the afterlife are all represented. There are children games of jumping, spinning and wrestling. Also board games, music and musical instruments including flutes, harps, trumpets, clappers or cymbals, lutes, lyres, tambourines, and drums all attest to cultural and musical flowering and the prodigious scientific and other contributions of these ancient Africans are shown depicted on tomb walls.

Funerary rites show the coffins being carried, and people crying and dancing. The deceased is "usually accompanied by a lector-priest, an embalmer, rites and mourners, both men and women, who demonstrate their grief by beating their heads and faces which they perhaps smear with mud."

EGYPT ESSAYS ON ANCIENT KEMET

Egypt Essays Photo 26. Kom Ombo Temple of Haroeis and Sobek. View from the rear corridor, the outer back of the temple wall roper, with depiction of colossal figure and hieroglyphics beside him. Notice the ten crocodiles.

FREDERICK MONDERSON

Egypt Essays Photo 26a. Kom Ombo Temple of Haroeis and Sobek. Sobek, enthroned with solar disk, and all!

EGYPT ESSAYS ON ANCIENT KEMET

Egypt Essays Photo 26b. Kom Ombo Temple of Haroeis and Sobek. ON a column, in White Crown and sporting "tail," the king presents a pyramid to Horus, partly hidden.

The judgment scene in the Afterlife is shown. The principal Gods Osiris, Isis, Nephthys, Thoth, the devourer Am-Mit, and the deceased as well as the company of judges, forerunner of the jury system, are all shown. The 42 Judges of the dead, who also hear the 42 Negative Confessions, addressed respectively, were representative of the 42 Nomes of Upper and Lower Kemet/Egypt. "Heaven" or the "Elysian Fields," or "Fields of Reeds," are Egyptian/African conceptions that show wonders of bountiful wheat, very large bunches of grapes and the splendid serenity for which a life of goodness and justice was worth working for, all in praise of an almighty deity who loved his people. This is why throughout the various temples, the Pharaoh or High Priest is always shown in humble adoration, kneeling, offering prayers, incense and other gifts to deity who so bountifully and majestically subscribed to ancient Nile Valley Africans' ethical behaviors.

Some of the irregular themes shown in tombs include battle scenes of chariots and other forms of siege warfare. The tomb of Seti I, the largest and most profusely decorated in the Valley of the Kings, with theological and theosophical representations, is here given: "The total horizontal length of this catacomb is 320 ft., without the inclined descent below the sarcophagus, and its perpendicular depth 90. But, including that part, it measures 470, and in depth about 180 ft. to the spot where it is closed by fallen rock." Hall after hall of wonderful sculptures abounds in this majestic and sacred place!

Astronomical representations are shown in the tombs of Rameses VI and Senmut, the architect of Queen Hatshepsut. This queen, who gave her architect more than 40 noble titles, intended a tunnel to connect her august mortuary temple at Deir el-Bahari, with a tomb she built in the Valley of the Kings. This followed a more modest tomb in the Valley of the Queens. Similarly, in passage through the world's first tunnel at Sakkara, after her mortuary ceremony, Hatshepsut hoped to be carried directly to her place of final internment. Such was unheard of! For this boldness, along with the fact that as a woman she dared to become the "Son of Ra," Rameses II left her cartouche blank on the *Abydos Tablet* in the temple of his father Seti I. The opulence of the tomb's representation was to have those social and spiritual/religious necessities represented at the deceased's reach, when needed. The religious magical spells and precautions were also designed to accord him or her pleasing and successful reception as he or she passed through the Gates of the Underworld, to the Hall of Judgment, and if deserved a peaceful existence in the new life.

EGYPT ESSAYS ON ANCIENT KEMET

In this quest, skillful designs and other attempts were made to deter desecrators of the tomb and those individuals who disturbed the deceased' remains! It is this heritage that African-Americans must celebrate in the new millennium and particularly during Black History Month celebrations. They must know that their ancestors, the people named Egyptians for three thousand years through the Graeco-Roman experience, in the land of ancient *k m t*, the "black land," created the foundations of the sciences, viz., astronomy, medicine, mathematics, chemistry and physics, quarrying and transportation of large stone to erect immortal testaments of ingenuity to their gods. In turn, the gods endowed them with the wonders of mental faculty to create as well as enjoy earthly peace, happiness and the promised bliss of eternity. For this we see they created that blessed and ever potent social ethic - '*Ma'at*,' - meaning balance, harmony, justice; if you will, the forerunners of Kawaida and the Nguzo Saba, 7 Principles of Kwanza, etc., to enable this firmness to blossom and help create pillars in support of their community.

It was Malcolm X who reminded in his *Autobiography* that when he wanted to become a lawyer, his teacher dissuaded him! Recently, a karate instructor, another teacher, reminiscing on his boyhood in Harlem, recounted his father; as he said, "When I told my father I wanted to become a tailor..." the father, looking with that majestic and strong African fatherly figure, with sphinx-like wisdom, whispered softly, "You can do more!"

Yes! Let us teach the children, "You can do more!" Let those among us strive to do more to make young Black men and women live to create, share and contribute to their communities. Let us look, towards Black History month celebrations in 2027, as the Afrocentrists would say, at that time Blacks in America should be living Dr. King's dream!

Now, Dr. King would say if Churchill had the right words then quote him! For it was Churchill, who when faced with the threat to his beloved nation, eloquently responded: "We will fight them in the air, at sea, and on land." Yes! But we must fight them in the urban areas, too! We must also fight them in the classroom, in the churches, in the homes, in the family, in the community boards, in those committees and in the banks and credit unions. We must fight them at the supermarket, stores and in every form of business. We must fight to control our community, for a better education and to save our children! We must fight them at the ballot box and in the proper allocation of power. We must fight them in the hospitals where Black surgeons must work. We must fight them in the board rooms. Then, we must fight against prejudice, but the dream can become a reality if we teach the children "You can do more!"

Egypt Essays Photo 27. Temple of Horus at Edfu. Entrance Pylon of the Temple of Horus with double colossal depiction of the king slaughtering Egypt's enemies before Horus and Hathor; the upper representations depict the king before various gods and goddesses; while on the cornice, an orb with double uraei protects the Temple. Two stone hawks greet the visitor while beyond, entrance columns of the Hypostyle Hall or Pronaos.

EGYPT ESSAYS ON ANCIENT KEMET

Egypt Essays Photo 27a. Temple of Horus at Edfu. From within the Great Court, columns along the roofed ambulatory with the inner face of the Pylon left and right as visitors mill about.

Egypt Essays Photo 27b. Temple of Horus at Edfu. Osiris (left) and Horus (right), both victims of vandalized defacement.

FREDERICK MONDERSON

6. THE NILE VALLEY IN WORLD ANTIQUITY/HISTORY

The ancient Nile Valley civilization of Kemet, modern Egypt, was an African and by today's standards, black culture, first of its kind to become conscious of its intellectual, philosophical and spiritual creativity. The Black people of Ancient Kemet along the Nile enlightened the world! So argued the great African intellect Cheikh Anta Diop in systematic, inter-disciplinary, erudite, irrefutable and well thought-out scholarship described in *The African Origin of Civilization*: *Myth or Reality*. A number of dedicated writers including Martin Delaney, W.E.B. Du Bois, Carter G. Woodson, George G.M. James, John Jackson, Yosef ben-Jochannan, Ben Carruthers, John H. Clarke, Theophile Obenga, Molefi Asante, and Ivan Van Sertima, after many years of research, publishing and teaching, have asserted the exact idea. This then, is the idea to advocate! For, if our scholars and heroes tell us after their long years of research, teaching, lectures, writings, intellectual disappointments, etc., that the historical record has been falsified to show prominence of Europe and degradation of Africa, who are we to believe? Equally however, if we carefully examine the series of arguments Diop makes in his book, the crime of willful distortion for racial gain is a charge that many European scholars are guilty of. Think of the influence these people have had on modern learning and scholarship and the argument can easily be made based on the question: "Did these scholars purposely mislead or were these experts guilty of unknowingly misleading?"

The great achievement and gift of this Northeast African culture was its theosophical, religious, architectural and moral genius embodied in the ancient Egyptian or Kemetic temple. This creation, unlike the Jewish synagogue, Greek or Roman Temple, Muslim Mosque, or Christian Cathedral, was unique and still evokes and exudes profound theological and cosmological spiritualism, posing thoughtful questions for scholars still seeking to define it. Here, in the temple, no public worship was performed, the faithful did not congregate for public prayer, and no one was admitted inside the

EGYPT ESSAYS ON ANCIENT KEMET

inner portals of the temple except the priests. Still, wrote Maspero, the "temple was built as an image of the world, as the Egyptians imagined it to be."

Egypt Essays Photo 28. Edfu Temple of Horus. In the rear Corridor, the King and his Queen make a presentation before Horus and the symbol plan of his Temple.

Egypt Essays Photo 28a. Edfu Temple of Horus. In the rear "Corridor of Victory," wearing the White Crown, the king leads three Anubii figures as he prepares to incense the Goddess also in White Crown.

FREDERICK MONDERSON

Egypt Essays Photo 28b. Edfu Temple of Horus. Also in the rear "Corridor of Victory," God Horus in Red and White Double Crown is hoisted by Anubii figures.

The stupendous architecture in all its dimensions of great glory was certainly divinely inspired; and with space for the principal gods, the buildings became complex with small rooms for secondary gods, statues, dim lights, maze of halls, and arrangement of trick doors; even as well as stairs to the roof. There were also side rooms for keeping garments, jewelry, and cult objects for the religious ceremonies on altars. Libraries were an essential part of any temple, for scholars congregated in temples that were considered "Colleges." There were stairs that led to the roof where Kiosks or chapels were located so the god of that temple could be bathed in the sun at regular times. Some temples had a well, Nilometer, while others had a well, even a sacred lake. All had granaries and dwellings for the temple staff. To meet needs of the daily rituals, gardens provided fresh flowers for the temple service and food for the staff. Granaries and storehouses were filled with staff produce, looked-over by large contingents of scribes, overseers and managers in charge of administration. Temples were frequently provided with allocations of prisoners-of-wars for work on its lands. They were also recipients of kingly and noble endowments for mortuary cults, building construction, and these enjoyed tax-free status. The library was also an essential part of every temple for the daily ritual, as well as functioning as universities for training other priests, government bureaucrats, nobles and physicians. Thus, it's easier to speak about the ancient Tawi/Kemet/Egyptian temple, rather than say what it really is, since it meant many things. Oftentimes the temples served as a clearing-house for civic matters providing literary functions, letters, wills, documents for its public citizens.

Egypt Essays Photo 29. Edfu Temple of Horus. In the "Corridor of Victory," a scene from the war with Seth. The evil Seth is captured disguised as a hippopotamus and held by a spear as Isis as Hathor and other Gods participate.

FREDERICK MONDERSON

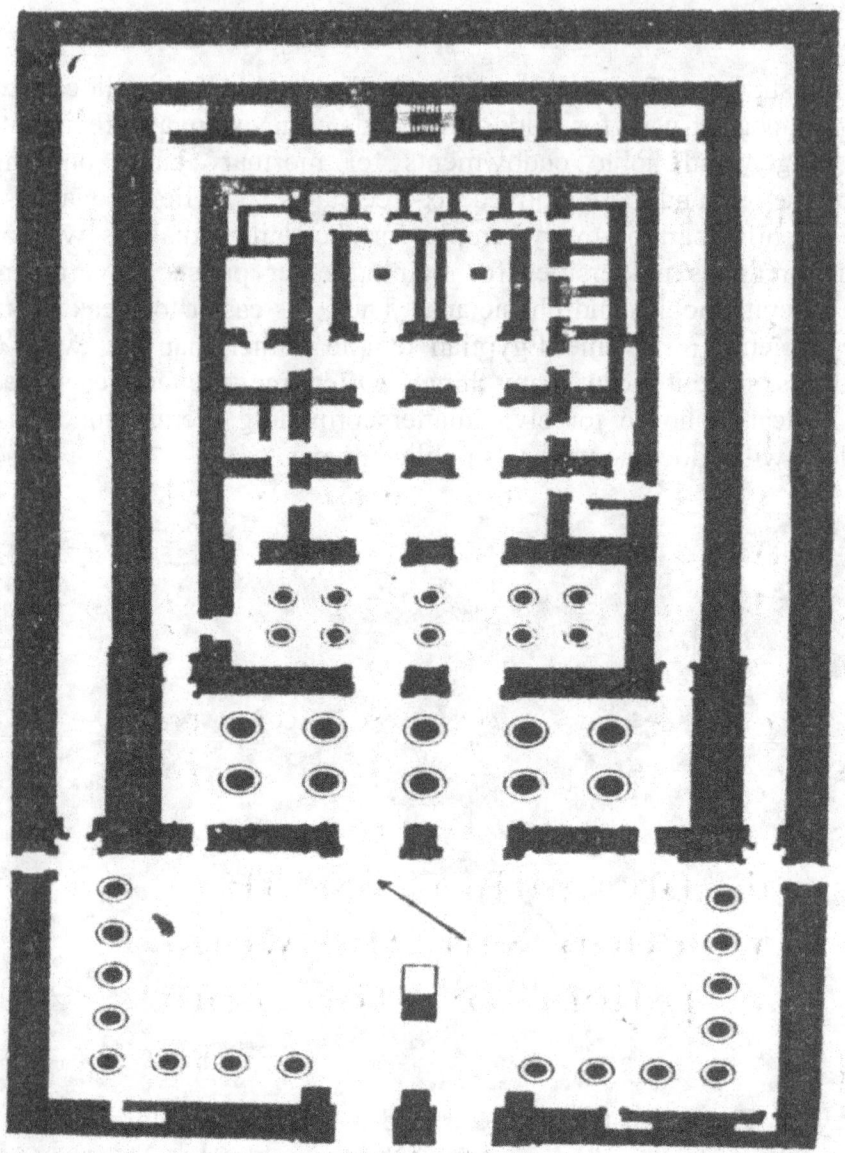

Egypt Essays Plan of the Double Temple at Kom Ombo.

Nevertheless, within the philosophic construct and principally, however, in regards is physical and spiritual embodiment, Marriet-Bey explained: "Egyptian temples are always dedicated to three gods. It is what Champollion calls the triad. The first is the male principle, the second is the female principle, and the third is the offspring of the other two. But these three deities are blended into one. The father engenders himself in the womb of the mother and thus become at once his own father and his own son. Thereby are expressed the un-created-ness and the eternity of the being who has had no beginning and who shall have no end."

So, to understand more fully the nature of the, we can look to the principle of sculptural decoration. In this, images are arranged symmetrically side by side. Several series of pictures are disposed in tiers one above the other and cover the walls of chambers from top to bottom. The role of the king is shown as important for he, "presents an offering (a table laden with victuals, flowers, fruits, and emblems) and solicits a favor from the god. In his answer the god grants the gift that is prayed for." Thus, decoration of the temple consists of nothing more than an act of adoration from the king. As such, a temple can be viewed as a primordial hill, or, the "exclusive personal monument of the king by whom it was founded or decorated." Even more is gleaned, for in foundation deposits, founders' emblems, tools, food and blood from sacrificial animals were deposited to ensure blessings to the temple.

The king is generally shown in the pictures on one side and one or more divinities on the other.

The worship consists of prayers, recited within the temple in the name of the king, and above all, of processions. In these processions which the king is supposed to head, are carried the insignia of the gods, the coffers in which their statues are enclosed, and also the sacred barks which later are generally deposited in the temple, to be brought out on fete days. In the middle, concealed under a veil, stands the coffer within which lies the emblem that none must see. The processions are commonly held within the temple. They generally ascend the terraces and sometimes spread themselves inside the enclosure away from the profane gaze. On rare occasions, the processions may be seen leaving the city and winding their way, either along the Nile or along a canal called the "Sacred Canal," toward some other city more or less distant. There are times, when, as at Karnak, the God and his procession cross the river to view the mortuary temples of deceased kings. This is called the "Feast of the Valley." Close to every temple is a lake. In all probability the lake played an important part in the processions and the sacred barks were deposited there, at least while the fete lasted. This "Sacred Lake," fed by underground streams from the Nile, is also where the priests washed themselves, sometimes two or three times per day.

These ancient Africans of Egypt were the genesis of their own genius who thought out the fundamental principles of religion and its significance for salvation of their people. Their "houses of life," for whom were crafted the cosmological creation of the particular cult, grew from simple beginnings into huge and complex structures of stone. As such then, the temple can be seen, as Maspero says, as a "royal proscynem, or ex voto that is a token of piety from the king who erected it in order to deserve the favor of the gods. It is a kind of royal oratory and nothing more."

Some two hundred years ago in the aftermath of the American and French Revolutions, Napoleon invaded Egypt in "carrying the war to Britain." Whatever the intent, he helped to unleash intensive European scholarship interests when his men found the Rosetta Stone. Dispersed throughout the land his savants or scholars, studied temples as Kom Ombo, Edfu, Dendera, Karnak, Luxor, Abu Simbel, Esneh, and a host of other wonderfully enlightening religious, artistic and educational sites. Their efforts culminated in academic revivals in ancient studies, a groundbreaking work entitled *The Description of Egypt*, and with Champollion's decipherment of Hieroglyphics, began the discipline of Egyptology. A century later, anthropology and archaeology in the Nile Valley, capitalized on opportunities presented in the dynamics of European imperial intrigue and designs of the Berlin Congress of 1884. Thus, the recovery of ancient Egypt ensured.

EGYPT ESSAYS ON ANCIENT KEMET

Egypt Essays Photo 30. Edfu Temple of Horus. In the rear corridor, the King and his Queen make a Presentation to the God before the emblem of his Temple.

Egypt Essays Photo 30a. Edfu Temple of Horus. Two images of Khepre, the Beetle, sits atop an emblem before the Red Crown and a defaced face that signifies a prince of the area.

FREDERICK MONDERSON

Egypt Essays Photo 31. Edfu Temple of Horus. Khnum hard at work making man on his "Potter's Wheel" before the Red Crown and entrance to a structure while a squatting figure looks on.

Egypt Essays Photo 31a. Broken granite body of statue showing a well-proportioned body, a "belt" and dagger within and to the right a "White Crown."

EGYPT ESSAYS ON ANCIENT KEMET

By 1900, the British and French, still in Egypt since the days of Napoleon, were joined by the Germans, Americans, Swiss, Belgians and Italians. Together they unleashed extensive and systematic expeditions to excavate and map the ancient land. They unearthed much buried treasure, while the Cairo Museum of Egyptian Antiquities got its share, much of artifactual value were later dispersed in all forms of *Quid Pro Quo* agreements to adorn museums throughout Europe and America. Nevertheless, a derivative benefit was the unearthing, clearance and reconstruction of Egyptian/Kemetic architectural history enabling scholars to trace the evolution and growth of the temple.

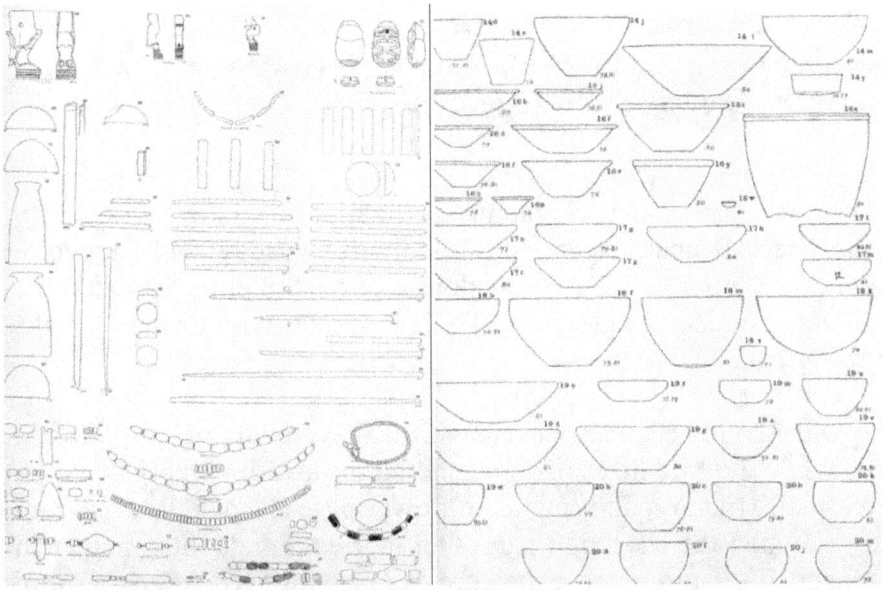

Egypt Essays Illustration 15. Tarkhan ivory and beads (left); and pottery (right).

FREDERICK MONDERSON

Egypt Essays Illustration 15a. Tarkhan Pottery Inscriptions and marks (left); and Tarkhan Mastaba 1060, Clay Sealings and Pottery Marks (right).

Briefly, it's agreed that pharaonic civilization from the first dynasty to the Greco-Roman experience was divided into the Old Kingdom, Middle Kingdom and New Kingdom. The late Period included the Ethiopian conquest, and that of the Persians, Assyrians, then Greeks and later Romans.

The Old Kingdom is associated with achievements of the Pyramid Age, while the Middle Kingdom ushered in salvation, reorganization and artistic, literary, and linguistic flowering. The Middle Kingdom also provided the transition from Old to New Kingdom, whether in language, literature or architecture. The New Kingdom in turn, represented great flowering of culture due to imperial expansion, reformulation of religious beliefs, democratization of the afterlife, new forms of art, techniques in quarrying and transportation of stone, and construction of monumental architectural projects.

EGYPT ESSAYS ON ANCIENT KEMET

After the decline of the New Kingdom, the Ethiopian conquerors of Kemet/Egypt founded the Twenty-Fifth Dynasty. Headed by Piankhy, Shabaka, Shabataka and Taharka, they restored some of the old greatness to a culture exposed to the changing geo-political dynamics of a world now awake and aroused to the possibilities of the human spirit, but having scores to settle with Egypt and Africa, the Persians, Assyrians and Greeks and Romans all invaded and sacked Egypt. However, while the former two more visibly destroyed, the latter two nations sought to imitate, placate and inculcate the culture. In this process they initiated great rebuilding efforts helping to preserve much that we know today. Greek and Roman culture at this time set western tradition in vogue. These conquerors built extensively, using Kamite/Egyptian technology, craftsmanship and knowledge. They erected many temples that are today called "Graeco-Roman," such as Edfu, Kom Ombo, Isis at Philae and Esneh. However, and importantly, though these later temples are called "Graeco-Roman," they were built by Egyptian and Nubian craftsmen, along the ancient patterns, though under the patronage and tutelage the "Graeco-Roman" conquerors.

In this new method and pattern, the walls, columns, and ceilings of these structures, were inundated with sculptures, illustrations and inscriptions. Important also, these later temples were modeled after more ancient ones and built on sites already consecrated as holy, dating to the earliest times of Egyptian history.

Just as King Zoser's Step Pyramid of the third dynasty was, according to John Lundquest in *The Temple*, an "architectural realization of the primordial hill," that was later modified into depicting "some aspects of the origins, growth, and construction," of ancient Egyptian or ancient Kemetic temples; subsequent buildings either served as a spiritual worship, living or mortuary temple with a divine function.

In the Pre-Dynastic Period before 3100 B.C., there were 42 mini states later called Nomes and headed by Nomarchs or minor kings. These can be equated with our governors. This number 42 was also symbolical of the 42 "Negative Confessions" and 42 "Books of Thoth." The entrance to the 19th Dynasty Temple of Seti I at

FREDERICK MONDERSON

Abydos had a famed 42-step ascent to the temple. Wars of religious animosity, competition for trade and early geo-political dynamics before the emergence of a strong Nile Valley leadership made life unsafe. Still, as the local deity emerged to prominence in the nomes, their temples became the center of the community. Here pilgrims came, feasts were held and the finest art could be found. Still, because of prevailing conditions, the enclosure wall emerged as an essential feature of the temple, particularly for purposes of safety for the god, priest and their ritual. These "enclosure walls" were huge, surrounding the temple so that what transpired within was not seen or heard from the outside.

Petrie's *Religious Life in Ancient Egypt* states, in the earliest times, the "great wall which surrounded each temple formed a fortress, which was the last refuge in case of invasion." Even so, temple origins in pre-dynastic times were patterned after the simplest huts made of reeds or maize stalks. Such early temple buildings had projecting roofs for shade as well as rope in front to keep out stray cattle.

Egypt Essays Photo 31b. Part of the Nekhbet and Wadjit duo and to the right broken cartouche with image of Thoth's head.

EGYPT ESSAYS ON ANCIENT KEMET

Egypt Essays Photo 32. Edfu Temple of Horus. In the rear Corridor, the God Thoth defaced!

FREDERICK MONDERSON

Egypt Essays Photo 32a. Edfu Temple of Horus. In the rear Corridor, the God Amun as Min, defaced!

EGYPT ESSAYS ON ANCIENT KEMET

Egypt Essays Photo 32b. Edfu Temple of Horus. Wearing horns and feathers, the king makes a presentation of millions of years to Horus in Double crown.

Admittedly a product of the Pyramid Age, and located at Giza, the Temple of the Sphinx is an early surviving religious building. Constructed of blocks of red granite transported from Aswan, it also had blocks of beautiful alabaster. Consisting of a descending passage, leading to an open area, it's divided into three aisles by columns and lintels. A short passage leads to a second transept where were found statues of Khafra, builder of the second largest pyramid on the Giza plateau. Also found in this spot were cynocephali apes in hard green stone. In this chamber granite blocks measure 18 feet in length and 7 feet in height. In the Southwest corner of the transept was a mortuary chamber with six niches for statues. This temple is connected with the temple of the second pyramid by a causeway cut in the rock, about a quarter of a mile in length. The upper temple is also constructed of massive blocks of granite and alabaster.

Petrie's chronological sequence explains, "First, the pyramid of Khafra; secondly, the temple built symmetrically in front of that pyramid; third, the causeway, leading askew from that temple down a ridge of rock; fourth, the granite temple at the foot of the causeway." This puts the Temple of the Sphinx in great company and served as prototype of the physical structure with its theological and philosophical implications.

During the First and Second Dynasties (Archaic Period 3100 B.C. - 2780 B.C.), the earliest temple shrine had three chambers as at Abydos. In the Pyramid temples of the IVth and Vth Dynasties the temple chambers were increased to five. While the three and five chambers appear in temples of the XIXth and XXth Dynasties, the XIXth Dynasty Temple of Seti I at Abydos was increased to seven chambers, each dedicated to a separate deity. Here, from right to left, these deities in their respective chapels were Horus, Isis, Osiris "Gods of the Osirian Cycle;" Amun, Re-Horakhty, Ptah "Gods of the New Kingdom;" and Seti I, deified.

With site plans plotted, archaeologists further informed of differences between temples, whether mortuary, worship or prayer and processional. The first of these was the Mortuary Temple dating to the Pyramid Age; Mentuhotep's, of the 11th Dynasty, Middle Kingdom; Hatshepsut's and Thutmose's at Deir el Bahari of the 18th Dynasty, New Kingdom; Rameses II's Ramesseum, 19th Dynasty; and Rameses III's Medinet Habu of the 20th Dynasty. In fact, Carpiceci (1994: 88) has shown in a three mile area, the Theban Necropolis housed New Kingdom structures or, "Mortuary Temples of the kings Seti I, Mentuhotep, Thutmose III, Hatshepsut, Rameses VI, Mentuhotep II, Amenhotep II, Ramses II, Thutmose IV,

EGYPT ESSAYS ON ANCIENT KEMET

Merenptah, Ptolemaic, that of Amenhotep III with the nearby 'Colossi of Memnon,' Rameses III, Thutmose I, Amenhotep and Thutmose II." Baines and Malek (1980: 95) wrote regarding these mortuary temples: "Their main function was to maintain the cult of the deceased kings buried in their tombs cut in the cliffs further to the west, though gods also were worshiped there, particularly Amun and Re'-Horakhty. The most important of these temples are those of Deir-el-Bahari, the Ramesseum and Medinet Habu. The mortuary temple of Sethos I stands at Qurna (Qurneh, Kurneh), while only huge seated statues, the 'Memnon Colossi,' and other fragmentary sculptures mark the site of the temple of Amenhotep III. Several of the temples of the West Bank were not mortuary, such as the temples of Hathor (Deir-el-Medina), Thoth (Qasr el-'Aguz) and Isis (Deir el-Sheltwt), all of the Greco-Roman Period."

All were generally constructed on the West Bank, the "land of the dead." Worship temples as Luxor, Karnak, Esneh, Edfu, Dendera, Kom Ombo and Abu Simbel were generally on the east bank, "land of the living." The third type was the processional temple, a sort of halfway house, a kiosk, where the Ark with image of the god, was housed, when being transported from one temple to another on festivals or other solemn occasions. These were generally on the east bank.

It's further recognized that the Pyramid Age (Dynasties III-VI 2780-2240 B.C.) came to an end when Pepi II became old and weak after a reign of 94 years. During his later years, nobles increased their power and influence. Thus, with the collapse of strong centralized government, the social order broke down and ushered in the First Intermediate Period, Dynasties VII-X (2240-2100 B.C.).

FREDERICK MONDERSON

Egypt Essays Photo 33. Edfu Temple of Horus. In Double Crown, the king makes a double handed Presentation.

EGYPT ESSAYS ON ANCIENT KEMET

Egypt Essays Photo 33a. Edfu Temple of Horus. The beneficiary of the previous Presentation, Horus stands in "Traveling" gear.

FREDERICK MONDERSON

The XIth Dynasty under the Intefs and Mentuhoteps reunited the states, first, of Upper and then Lower Egypt/Kemet, and founded the Middle Kingdom. They conquered the warring Nomarchs, curtailed their power, restored centralization and reorganized the society. These kings ushered in a period of prosperity, heralded by artistic, literary, religious, linguistic and architectural flowering that in turn set standards for the greater legacy in the New Kingdom.

The Middle Kingdom became tremendously significant providing a transition from the Old to New Kingdom building practices. Modern archaeology enables identification of Mentuhotep's XIth Dynasty Mortuary Temple at Deir el Bahari as an important bridge in transition from 2240 to 1600 B.C.

Mentuhotep's temple was a profound architectural, artistic and philosophical construction. Mentuhotep's temple was accurately aligned with the Karnak vicinity across the river attesting to surveying techniques. It served as inspiring prototype and model for Hatshepsut, female ruler, 500 years later. Juxtaposed at Deir el Bahari, the architect Senmut built an enlarged mortuary temple, for his beloved Pharaoh Hatshepsut. She hoped to connect it by tunnel to her tomb in the Valley of the Kings, an unheard of yet revolutionary proposition for a woman, in ancient times.

The next famous ruler to build extensively was Thutmose III. He erected several buildings in the religious complex at Karnak. His fabulous Festival Hall or Jubilee Temple, the *Akh Menu*, consisting of columns and pillars is an exceptional creation. Seems it contained the earliest clerestory, an important architectural innovation. In addition, he added a smaller temple at Deir el Bahari, against the cliffs and between the earlier Mentuhotep and Hatshepsut temples.

Amenhotep III was a prolific builder as his great-grandfather, Thutmose III. He began the central part of the Hypostyle Hall at Karnak Temple, with a dozen center columns called the *Processional Colonnade*, as part of the 134 columns of this hall, made famous by Seti I and Rameses II. In fact, this Processional Colonnade gave Horemheb the idea of adding the two wings of the

EGYPT ESSAYS ON ANCIENT KEMET

hall that Rameses I began to build, Seti I finished and partly decorated and Rameses II finished decorating. Amenhotep built his renowned Luxor Temple, at which time Egypt/Kemet reached a "golden age." However, while the Processional Colonnade at Karnak had a double row of six for twelve columns, at Luxor it's a double row of seven for fourteen columns. With successive Pharaohs doing repair work here, the names of Tutankhamen, Smenkare, Seti I, Rameses II and even Alexander the Great are credited with adding restoration to this temple. At a smaller temple at Luxor, Hatshepsut built an early shrine to three Theban deities that Amenhotep tore down to build his magnificent structure. During the 19th Dynasty this Luxor Temple was enlarged by adding what became the later Court of Rameses, the "Ramessean Front." Thutmose III usurped Hatshepsut's Kiosk, erased hers and inscribed his name, like he did in so many also places where she had built. Still, evidence links her work here. Rameses II also did restoration to the Kiosk and placed his name on it. Hatshepsut's cartouche was also found at Edfu temple of Horus and is now in the Cairo Museum. Because of the valuable nature of this piece found at such a later location, it had to be removed to the museum for safekeeping.

The Temple of Seti I at Abydos is a masterpiece of temple architecture. Strabo mistakenly called this building the Memnonium but also mentions a well here. The temple's foundations belong to one of ten successive temples Petrie discovered at Abydos, that date back to the first dynasty. The plan is irregular. Sculptures show Rameses receiving blessings from Thoth, Anubis, Osiris, and Horus. An interesting fact regarding temple building is that Seti I began building his temple her at Gurneh and the Karnak Hypostyle Hall that his son Rameses II completed. Many critics have compared and classed Seti's decoration as superior to those of his son.

FREDERICK MONDERSON

Egypt Essays Photo 34. Edfu Temple of Horus. The God Thoth, inventor of writing and all forms of intellectual activities, in the right rear corridor.

EGYPT ESSAYS ON ANCIENT KEMET

Egypt Essays Photo 34a. Edfu Temple of Horus. Oh, to be entertained by three nevertheless, defaced playing the tambourine!

Egypt Essays Photo 34b. Edfu Temple of Horus. Even more joyful, to be entertained some more by still more ladies paying the tambourine.

FREDERICK MONDERSON

Egypt Essays Photo 34c. Edfu Temple of Horus. An Ad for evening entertainment.

EGYPT ESSAYS ON ANCIENT KEMET

Significantly, the opposite west wall is divided into four scenes similar to the one on the left. The famous *Tablet of Abydos* is here with Seti I and Rameses II offering homage to 76 predecessor kings. The list of kings begins with Menes, the founder of the First Dynasty and ends with Seti I, father of Rameses II. Five ovals are left without names. These belong to the heretic Akhnaton, Tutankhamen, Aye, and Smenkare all associated with the Amarna heresy. Hatshepsut cartouche is also excluded because she ruled as King, constructed a tomb in the Valley of the Kings, wore a beard, and built the Deir el Bahari structure greater than her predecessor Mentuhotep II and even entertained building a tunnel from her temple to her Valley of the Kings tomb. Midway through construction the ground proved soft and so the project was abandoned. Beyond the Temple of Seti I, is the Temple of Osiris, where Amelineau is thought to have found the divinity's body lying on his bed.

The *Tablet of Abydos*, discovered by Mariette in 1865, was conjectured to be the original of the fragmentary one found in a Temple of Rameses II, off to the side, at Abydos. This latter document, the *Second Abydos List*, is now in the British Museum. This *Abydos Tablet* is similar in substance to a king list engraved by Thutmose III, the *Karnak Tablet*, in what is called the "Hall of Ancestors" of Karnak, which was robbed by Prisse de Avenges, who took it to Paris. Inscribed are names of kings who particularly benefited Thebes. A king list, the *Sakkara Tablet* was found in the tomb of a noble named Tjunney who lived during the reign of Rameses II. The *Palermo Stone* is a similar, though earlier, king list, from the First through Sixth Dynasty while the *Turin Canon* rounds out the list of similar early historical documents."

Rameses II was a builder of exceptional note, who added a Court at Luxor, completed the Hypostyle Hall at Karnak, and also built a magnificent rock temple at Abu Simbel, in Nubia. Juxtaposed to this Abu Simbel temple for worship, he built a second temple for his Nubian wife, Queen Nefertari. This Pharaoh also built the splendid Ramesseum, his mortuary temple.

FREDERICK MONDERSON

The Temple of Rameses III at Medinet Habu is considered the last major New Kingdom building project. The classical writer Diodorus Siculus is thought to have mentioned Medinet Habu as one of four temples he wrote about. The others were Karnak, Luxor and the Ramesseum.

The Temple of Philae is dedicated to the Goddess Isis. In ancient Egyptian the island was called Pilak or Ailak, and Ma-ne-lek "the place of the Frontier." The Arabs call it *Anas el Wogood*, or more generally *Gezeeret el-Beerbeh*. The earliest ruins date to about mid-fourth century B.C., yet, there is a cartouche of Taharka in the Court of the Temple of Isis. This means the temple was in use in Taharka's reign and this may have been preceded by still earlier structures of which no evidence remains.

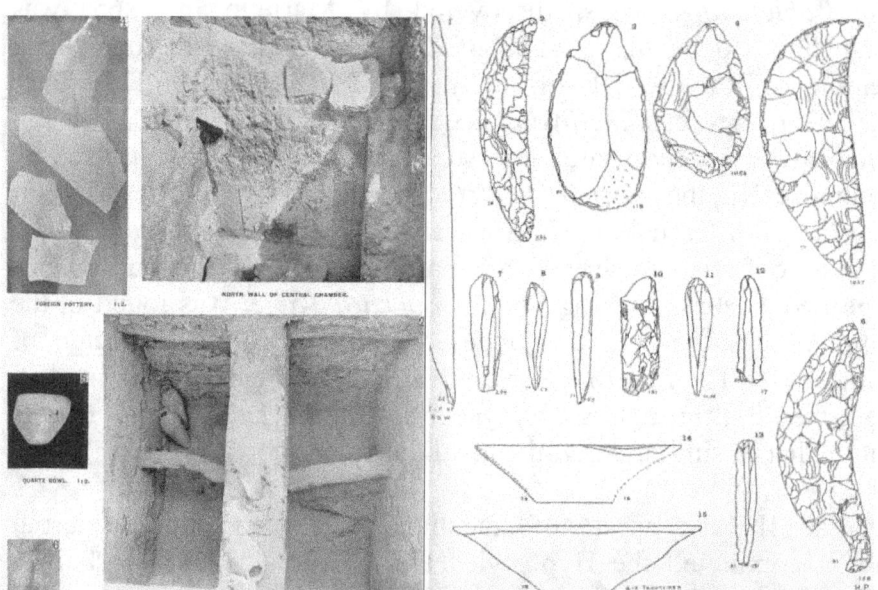

Egypt Essays Illustration 16. Tarkhan pottery, bowl, wall (left); worked flings and copper bowls (right).

EGYPT ESSAYS ON ANCIENT KEMET

Egypt Essays Photo 34d. Edfu Temple of Horus. The "Sphinx of Edfu!"

This Temple of Isis is the principal building in its new home, the Island of *Agilquiyyah* or *Agilka*. Ptolemy II Philadelphus and Arsinoe commenced it. Succeeding monarchs built here including

FREDERICK MONDERSON

Euergetes I, Philometer, his brother, Euergetes II, the two Cleopatras, and Ptolemy the elder son of Auletes, whose name is found in the area and on the pylon. Many sculptures on the exterior are of the later epoch of Roman emperors, Augustus Tiberius, Claudius, Domitian, Nerva, and Trajan.

Interesting that, nowhere has the mania of the Egyptians for irregularity been carried to such an extent as here. J. Ferguson, the 19th Century authority on architecture is quoted in Murray's *Handbook for Egypt* (1888) as follows: "No Gothic architect in his wildest moments ever played so freely with his lines and dimensions, and none, it must be added, ever produced anything so picturesque as this. It contains all the play of light and shade, all the variety of Gothic art, with the massiveness and grandeur of the Egyptian style; and as it is still tolerably entire, and retains much of its color, there is no building out of Thebes that gives so favorable an impression of Egyptian art as this. It is true it is far less sublime than many, but hardly one can be quoted as more beautiful."

The Temple of Dendera takes its name from *Tentyris* or *Tentyra*, in *Coptic Tentore* or *Nikentore*. It has its origin in that of the goddess Hathor, the cow. *Tentyra* is probable taken from *Tei-n-Athor*, the abode of Athor or Hathor. It is in a superior state of preservation. The portico is considered a noble specimen of architecture. The temple, begun in the reign of the 11th Ptolemy, was completed in that of the Emperor Tiberius, though the sculptures and decoration were not finished till the time of Nero. In the Portico, the names of many Caesars are inscribed including those of Tiberius, Caligula, Claudius, and Nero. The oldest names here are of Ptolemy Caesarian, or Neo-Caesar, son of Cleopatra and Julius Caesar. The portrait of Cleopatra and her son are on the exterior back wall.

EGYPT ESSAYS ON ANCIENT KEMET

Egypt Essays Photo 34e. Karnak Temple of Amon. Beauty of Hieroglyphics, "Life, Health, Dominion, Stability."

Egypt Essays Photo 35. Karnak Temple of Amon. Entrance to the Temple of the Theban deity Amon, later Amon-Ra. Notice the Sphinxes of the Avenue leading to the entrance. These were placed here by Rameses II. Look carefully at the little figures between the sphinxes paws and beyond the entrance pylon, statues and the Second Pylon.

FREDERICK MONDERSON

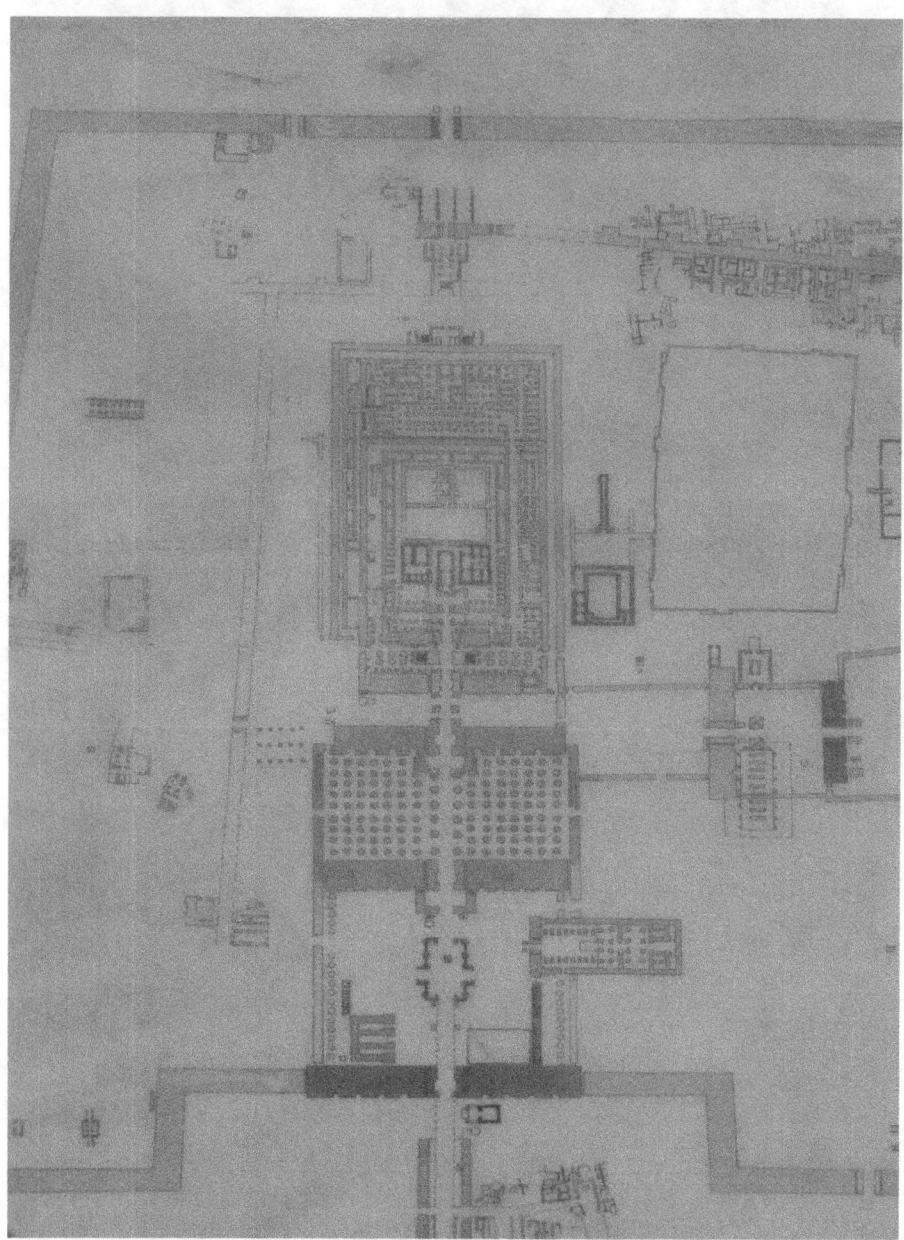

Egypt Essays Photo 35a. Karnak Temple of Amon. Plan of the temple with its principal features comprising the Central Group.

EGYPT ESSAYS ON ANCIENT KEMET

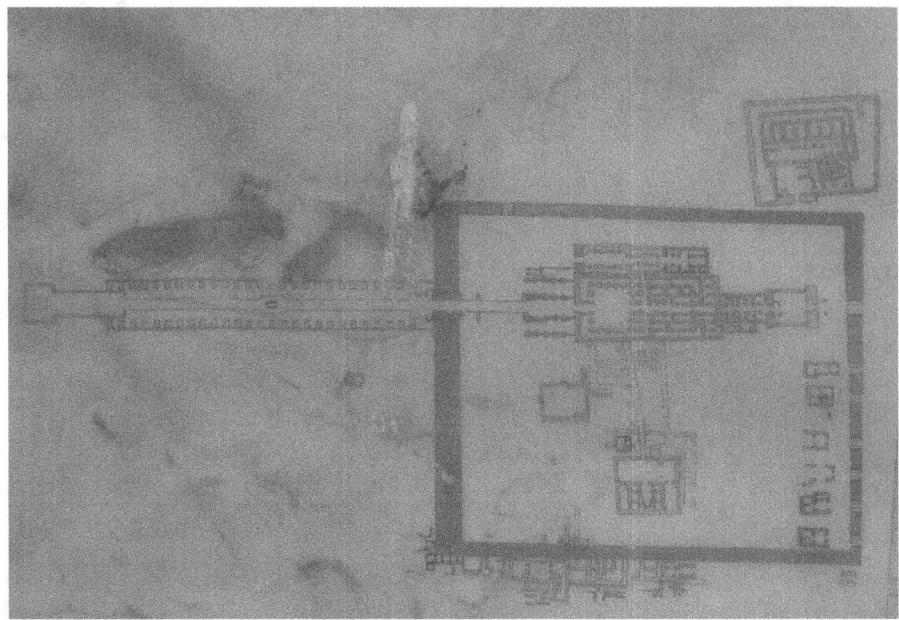

Egypt Essays Photo 35b. Karnak Temple of Amon. Plan of the Temple of Montu, and the principal features of the Northern Group of the Karnak Temples.

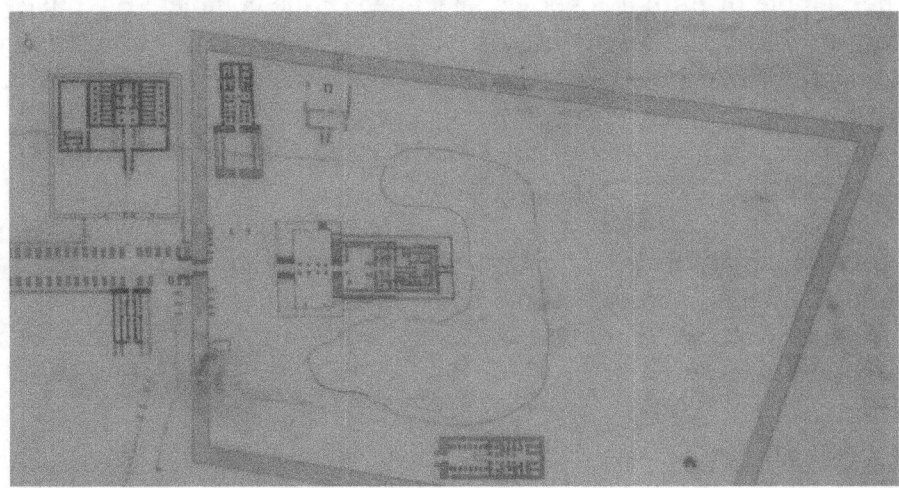

Egypt Essays Photo 35c. Karnak Temple of Amon. Plan of the Temple of Mut with its Sacred Lake, comprising the Southern group of the Karnak Temples.

FREDERICK MONDERSON

Egypt Essays Photo 35d. Karnak Temple of Amon. The "Gatekeepers." Mr. Showgi Abd el Rady (left), Chief of Security (right) and a friend (center).

The Temple of Edfu is a perfect specimen of the complete Egyptian temple. It is the best preserved of all temples in Egypt. It is similar in planning and in preservation compared to Dendera. However, Edfu also has uniquely preserved the propylon towers and the enclosure wall. Ptolemy Philopator, who built the sanctuary, founded Edfu and the chambers round it. He also built all the back part of the temple. The name of Ptolemy Philometer is found in the center halls, and their decoration is probably due to him. Ptolemy Philometer and Euergetes II; the latter of whom also built part of the enclosure wall, the other part being the work of Ptolemy Alexander I, constructed the portico. The pylon, or propylon, was either built or decorated by Ptolemy Dionysius.

The Temple of Kalabsha was dedicated to the Nubian God Mendulese, brother of Osiris. It was relocated on the present site by a German archaeological team who cut the temple into 16,000 pieces before reassembling it. It appears to have been built in the reign of

EGYPT ESSAYS ON ANCIENT KEMET

Augustus and though other Caesars, particularly Caligula, Trajan, and Severus made considerable additions to the sculptures, it was left unfinished. On the quay before the entrance, a granite statue bears the name of Thutmose III during whose time it was in existence. Rameses II's Temple of Beit Wali lies some ten minutes walk north of Kalabsha. It was relocated when the Nubian temples were threatened by the High Dam. This "damn" Dam created much dislocation for the local Nubian population which had to be relocated from their ancestral lands.

REFERENCES

ben-Jochannan, Yosef. *Abu Simbel to Ghizeh*: *A Guide Book and Manual.* Baltimore, MD: Black Classics Press, 1987.
Badawy, A. *A History of Egyptian Architecture* II. Berkeley, California: University of California Press, 1966.
Clarke, Sommers and R. Engelbach. *Ancient Egyptian Construction and Architecture.* Oxford University Press, London: Humphrey Milford, 1930.
Erman, Adolf. *Life in Ancient Egypt.* Trans H.M. Tirard. With a New Introduction by Jon Manchip White. New York: Dover Publications, (1894) 1971.
Haag, Michael. *Guide to Egypt.* London: Michael Haag, Limited, 1987.
Lundquist, John M. *The Temple.* New York: Thames and Hudson, 1993.
Maspero, Gaston. *Manual of Egyptian Archaeology.* New York: G. Putnam's Sons, 1926.
Murray's *Handbook for Egypt.* London: John Murray, 1888.
Wayne, Scott. *Egypt and the Sudan*: *A Travel Survival Kit.* Berkeley, California: Lonely Planet Publishers, 1987.

Abydos - A. Present entrance; B. First Hypostyle Hall; C. Second Hypostyle Hall; (1-7, R-L) Sanctuaries to Horus, Isis, Osiris, Amon, Ra-Horakhti, Ptah and Seti I. Inner Sanctuaries of Osiris; E. Sanctuary of Resurrection; F. Corridor of Kings; G. Passageway of

Throwing the Bull; H. Stairway to Temple of Osiris; K. Sanctuary of the Boats; L. Hall of Sacrifices.

Edfu - A. Pylon; B. Court; C. Pronaos; D. Hypostyle Hall; E. Antechamber and Upstairs to Roof; F. Antechamber; G. Sanctuary of Horus; H. Wall with decoration the "Corridor of Victory;" I. Nilometer.

Deir el Bahari - First Court with Lower Colonnade and First Ramp that splits this front into Northern and Southern Colonnade(nicknamed the "Fish" and "Obelisk Colonnades"); Second Court with Second Ramp that splits the Middle Colonnade having the Anubis Chapel and Birth Colonnade to the north or right and the Punt Colonnade and Hathor Chapel to the south or left. The Second Ramp leads to an Upper Terrace with recesses and entrance to the Upper Peristyle Court having the Holy of Holies (chapel to Amon) against the mountain. Off to the left there are chapels of Hatshepsut and Thutmose II and III. To the right is a chapel to Ra-Horakhty with an open air altar *in situ*.

Dendera - A. Court and Pronaos and Hypostyle Hall; B. Small Hypostyle Hall; C. Hall of Offerings; D. Hall of Ennead; E. Sanctuary; F-Z. Subsidiary Rooms.

Abu Simbel - A. Entrance; B. Great Pillared Hall; C. Small Pillared Hall; D. Vestibule; E. Sanctuary. Small subsidiary rooms left and right depict the king in different attitudes before the gods.

Philae - A. Chapel of Nectanebo; B. Stairway; C. The West Colonnade of 32 Columns; D. The (first) East Colonnade of 17 Columns; E. Chapels of Arsnuphis, Mendulese and Imhotep or Aesculapius; F. First or outer Pylon; G. Large Court with Mammisi or Birth House; H. Second East Colonnade of 12 Columns; I. Temple of Isis; J. Second Pylon; K. Double Portico; L. Sanctuary;

EGYPT ESSAYS ON ANCIENT KEMET

M. Gate of Hadrian; N. Kiosk of Trajan also called "Pharaoh's Bed;" O. Physcon's Temple; P. Gate of Diocletian.

Karnak - A newly Great or First Pylon; Open Great Court; Temple of Rameses III (right); Kiosk of Seti II (left); Taharka Column; East and West colonnades fronted by Sphinxes; all in First Court; Second Pylon; Hypostyle Hall with a. Sculptures of Seti I (left); b. Sculptures of Shishak (center); c. Sculptures of Rameses II (right); Hypostyle Hall; Third Pylon; Small Obelisk; Fourth Pylon; Large Obelisk; Fifth Pylon; Hall of Ancestors; Sixth Pylon; Sanctuary; Festival Temple of Thutmose III, Sacred Lake; "Cachette Court" on the North-South Axis; Seventh Pylon; Second Court; Eight Pylon; Third Court; Ninth Pylon, Fourth Court; Tenth Pylon.

Luxor - Entrance Pylon, Court of Rameses II with seated and standing statues, Site of Mosque of Abu 'el-Haggag (left); Hatshepsut's Obelisk (right); Colonnade of Amenhotep III ascribed to Horemheb; Court of Amenhotep III; Hypostyle Hall; the Sanctuary Shrine of Alexander; Birth House.

Ramesseum or Memnonium

Towers or Propylon, Modern Entrance, Area, Broken granite statue of Rameses II, Entrance between Pylon and Second Area with Osiride Columns, Traces of sculptures, Sculptures representing the wars of Rameses II, Sphinxes. The Grand Hall, Pedestals for statues, Sculptures of battle scenes, Chamber with Astronomical subject on ceiling, another Chamber with Sculptured scenes, Other Chambers.

FREDERICK MONDERSON

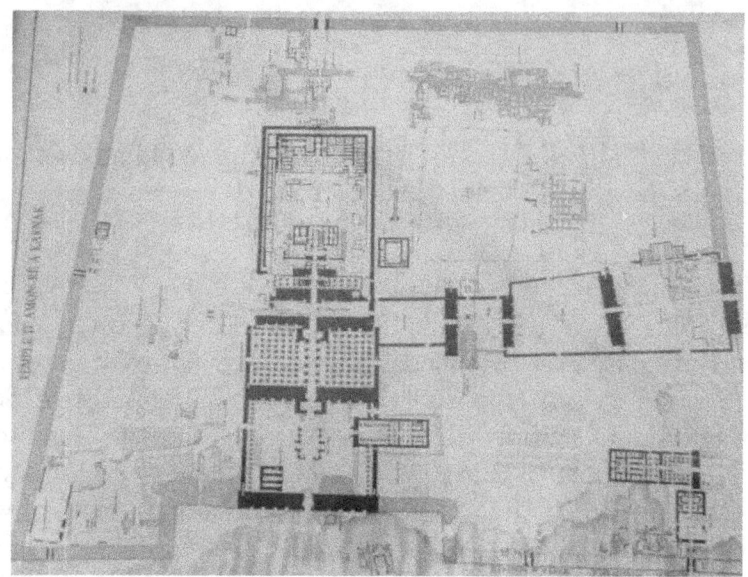

Egypt Essays Photo 36. Karnak Temple of Amon. Plan of the Temple of Amon-Ra at Karnak, with the ten Pylons (heavily indicated) and subsidiary structures within the Enclosure Wall.

Egypt Essays Photo 36a. Karnak Temple of Amon. The Kiosk of Seti II dedicated to the Theban Triad, Amon (center); Mut (left) and Khonsu (left).

EGYPT ESSAYS ON ANCIENT KEMET

Egypt Essays Photo 36b. Karnak Temple of Amon. Northern end of the Southern Colonnade in the "Great Court."

7.   THE PRIESTHOOD

In ancient Kemet, now Egypt, along the banks of the Nile River, one of the earliest professional organizations came into being, and from what we know, it is thus difficult to envision the society without such an essential institution as the Priesthood. This Priesthood, as a hierarchical bureaucracy, combined a number of functions - religious, political, scientific, educational, administrative, economic, and artistic - and came to exercise tremendous multi-dimensional power for the duration of dynastic rule. In this they proved a watchful, deferential, yet worthy opponent of the monarchy. Since their influence straddled this and the spiritual or other world. Such a state of affairs has led Rawlinson (1896: 288-89) to summarize: "The kings lived always in a considerable amount of awe of the priests. Though claiming a certain qualified divinity themselves, they yet could not but be aware that there were diverse flaws and imperfections in their own divinity – 'little rifts within the lute' - which made it not quite a safe support to trust to, or lean upon, entirely. There were greater gods than themselves - gods from whom their own divinity was derived; and they could not be certain what power or influence the priests might have with these superior beings, in whose existence and ability to benefit and injure men they had the fullest belief. Consequently, the kings are found to occupy a respectful attitude towards the priests throughout the whole course of Egyptian history, from first to last; and this respectful attitude is especially maintained towards the great personages in whom the hierarchy culminates, the head officials or chief priests, of the temples which are the principal centers of the national worship - the temple of Ra or Tum at Heliopolis, that of Ptah at Memphis, and that of Ammon at Thebes."

Egypt Essays Illustration 16a. Intricate details of engraved solid gold and precious stones of King Tut's third innermost coffin showing the mid-section of his arms grasping the symbols of power.

Significantly, in times of unity and division, peace and war, prosperity and stagnation, this body persisted. It expanded and transmitted the ancient Egyptian, African, Nile Valley culture - synthesizing, preserving and creating ideas and ethical, civil and

EGYPT ESSAYS ON ANCIENT KEMET

politico-religious structures for the propagation of the gods and kings thereby shaping the society's moral and ethical belief systems. In turn, pharaohs paid homage by building magnificent structures of worship endowed with prolific depictions of the kings in ritual attitudes towards the gods who had brought fame, fortune and festivals to their beloved land, and all associated largesse benefited the Priesthood handsomely.

Irwin (1946: 355) explained how the relationship between church and state evolved, and if we use ancient Kemet, Egypt, as part of that cultural mix of the old world and the ancient east, we get a better understanding of how the Priesthood brought itself into being. "An intimate relationship of church and state is traceable far back through human society. Early man's sense of dependence on the will of the gods and his belief in their immediate interference in human affairs gave him high place in community counsel and action to the spiritual adviser who, by theory, could tell just what the gods wished. The transfer of this special prestige into the politics of the ancient east is a familiar story. The monarchs in general either kept conveniently available a group of spiritual advisers or else paid such respect to the views of the hierarchy as to elevate the chief priest virtually into an important minister of the state."

Egypt Essays Photo 37. Karnak Temple of Amon. In the First or Great Court, sphinxes and the rear of the right half of the First Pylon. Notice the first or end column is incomplete, giving evidence of how these were first erected as squares then pounded into the finished and polished round columns.

FREDERICK MONDERSON

Egypt Essays Photo 37a. Karnak Temple of Amon. Eastern end of the Northern Colonnade in the Great Court, abutting the First Pylon.

Egypt Essays Photo 37b. Karnak Temple of Amon. Remains of an altar in situ in the Great Court with columns of the Norther Colonnade further on.

EGYPT ESSAYS ON ANCIENT KEMET

Egypt Essays Photo 37c. "The Gatekeepers." Chief of Temple Security (center) and two of his assistants.

We get an even better understanding of the situation that existed in the social order of ancient Kemet, Egypt, if we accept a theory of the tri-lateral relationship whereby, the Priesthood was endowed, and performed a service for the gods, the kings and the living and dead. In turn they came to exercise a whole lot of influence in every significant walk of Kemetic life. They ritualized the gods who bestowed their favors upon the pharaohs. These kings worshiped the deity, they were worshiped in turn as sons of God, and in this glorification they built magnificent temples to the deities and to themselves. These latter mortuary or funerary temples were intended that they might live for "millions of years." Within this dynamic, the Priesthood articulated its wealth of knowledge, resources and spirituality with continuing communion with deity from the earliest times.

FREDERICK MONDERSON

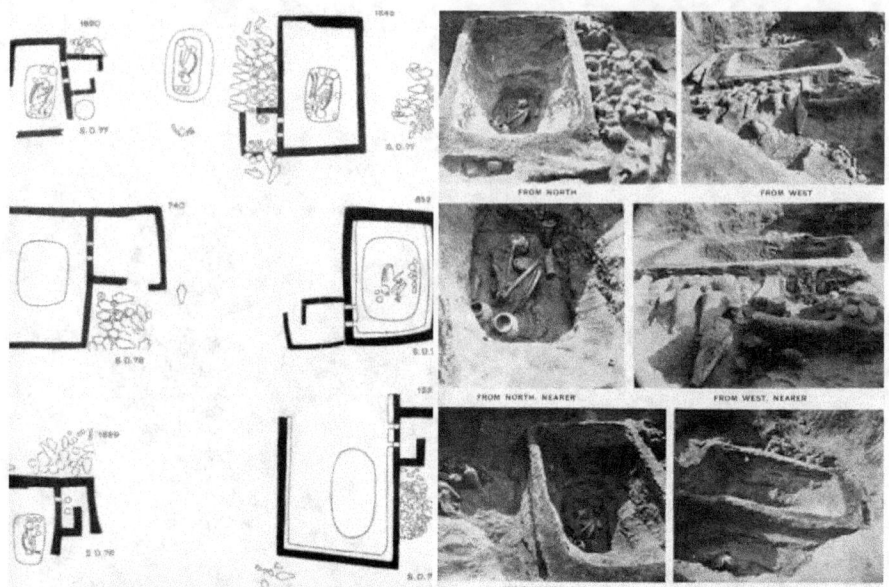

Egypt Essays Illustration 17. Tarkhan. Plan of small mastabas, with surface stacks of offerings (left); and tomb from different views with deceased in contracted position with goods of the grave nearby (right).

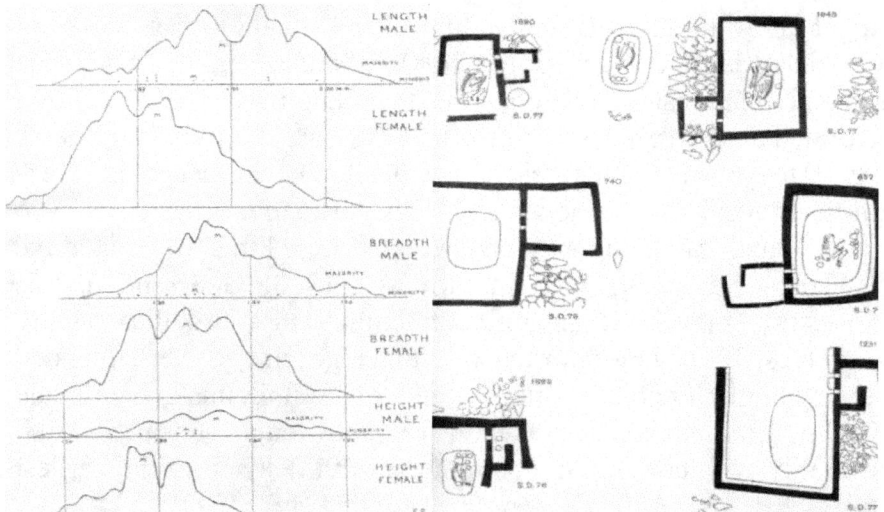

Egypt Essays Illustration 17a. Tarkhan Curves of Dimensions of Skulls (left); and Tarkhan Plans of Small Mastabas with Surface Stacks for Offerings (right).

EGYPT ESSAYS ON ANCIENT KEMET

Petrie supplies a perspective (1902: 11) that allows a closer look at the role of religion in the culture of ancient Kemet as the principal engagement of the Priesthood.

"The purpose of religion to the Egyptian was to secure the favor of the god. There is but little trace of negative prayer to avert evils or deprecate evil influences, but rather of positive prayer for concrete favors. On the part of the kings this is usually of the Jacob type, offering to provide temples and services to the god in return for material prosperity. The Egyptian was essentially self-satisfied, he had no confession to make of sin or wrong, and had no thought of pardon. In the judgment he boldly averred that he was free of the forty-two sins that might prevent his entry into the kingdom of Osiris. If he failed to establish his innocence in the weighing of his heart, there was no other plea, but he was consumed by fire and by a hippopotamus, and no hope remained for him."

Equally, Wilson (1946: 60), in attempting to explain the "principle of divine order" in the mind's eye of this ancient Egyptian, African, society explained it this way. "Because the Egyptians though of the world in physical, concrete terms and because the priesthood was the interpreter of what was divine, this 'word of god' came to be treated as a body of literature, the sacred writings, but it was still the directive speech given by the gods. A dead noble was promised every good and pure thing, in conformance to that writing of the word of god which (the god of wisdom) Thoth made."

Further elaboration by Wilson (1946: 60-61) is apt in the view the "... ancient Egyptian was self-conscious about himself and his universe; he produced a cosmos in terms of his own observation and his own experience. Like the Nile Valley, this cosmos had limited space but reassuring periodicity; its structural framework and mechanics permitted the reiteration of life through the rebirth of life-giving elements. The creation stores of the ancient Egyptian were also in terms of his own experience, although they bear loose general similarity to other creation stories. The most interesting advance lies in a very early attempt to relate creation to the processes of thought and speech rather than to mere physical activity. Even his 'higher' philosophy is given in pictorial terms arising out of Egyptian experience."

Egypt Essays Photo 38. Karnak Temple of Amon. In the First or Great Court, the eastern sphinxes fronting the east side columns of the Southern Colonnade. Notice the first or end column is incomplete, giving evidence of how these were first erected as squares then pounded into the finished round columns.

EGYPT ESSAYS ON ANCIENT KEMET

Egypt Essays Photo 38a. Karnak Temple of Amon. A surviving Sphinx of Tutankhamon in the Great Court.

Egypt Essays Photo 38b. Karnak Temple of Amon. Columns of the Southern Colonnade in the Great Court with the inner face of the First Pylon. Notice the last column, square blocks, that were pounded round in decoration.

Therefore, we see, as a body, the Priesthood assumed moral responsibility for creation of theological, ethical, and philosophical ideas that molded the culture from earliest times. Woldering (1965: 147) has shown how this body moved from and between the sacred to the profane world. All this was done in furtherance of political ambitions in the early evolving dynamics of the state. "As well as the monarchy, army and bureaucracy an important and dangerous part was played by the Temple of Amon at Karnak. The massive temple complex, which had been erected to the national god Amon, stood on the eastern embankment of the Nile at Thebes. Many bequests were made to it, and the priests who administered these riches were eventually able to acquire considerable power. They formed, so to speak, a state within the state, interfering in worldly matters and setting themselves up in opposition to the monarchy." Significantly, after a long and illustrious dynastic period where the priesthood exercised enormous influence, David could (1975: 33-34) still refer to this power as late as the time of the Greeks. "One section of the Egyptian community which the Ptolemies did attempt to placate was the Priesthood, perhaps because the priests wielded considerable power, and also because the ancient religion, based on the concept that pharaoh was the divine son who possessed Egypt, was an essential prop to the Ptolemies' economic and political rule."

Maspero XI (1904: 129-30), on the other hand, showed further how priestly practice and thought was expressed in the time of the Roman Period, at the very end of Kemetic civilization.

"The priests made a great boast of their learning and philosophy, and could each repeat by heart those books of Thoth which belonged to his own order. The singer, who walked first in the sacred processions, bearing the symbols of music, could repeat the books of hymns and the rules for the king's life. The soothsayer, who followed, carrying a clock and a palm-branch, the emblem of the year, could repeat the four astrological books; one on the moon's phases, one on the fixed stars, and two on their helical risings. The scribe, who walked next, carrying a book and the flat rule which held the ink and pen, was acquainted with the geography of the world and

EGYPT ESSAYS ON ANCIENT KEMET

of the Nile, and with those books which describe the motions of the sun, moon, and planets, and the furniture of the temple and consecrated places. The master of the robes understood the ten books relating to education, to the marks on the sacred heifers, and to the worship of the gods, embracing the sacrifices, the first-fruits, the hymns, the prayers, the processions, and festivals. The prophet or preacher, who walked last, carrying in his arms the great water-pot, was the president of the temple, and learned in the ten books, called hieratic, relating to the laws, the gods, the management of the temples, and the revenue. Thus, of the forty-two chief books of Thoth, thirty-six were learned by these priests, while the remaining six on the body, its diseases, and medicines, were learned by the Pastophori, priests who carried the image of the god in a small shrine. These books had been written at various times: some may have been very old, but some were undoubtedly new; they together formed the Egyptian bible. Apollonius, or Apollonides Horapis, an Egyptian priest, had lately published a work on these matters in his own language, named Shomenuithi, the book of the gods."

FREDERICK MONDERSON

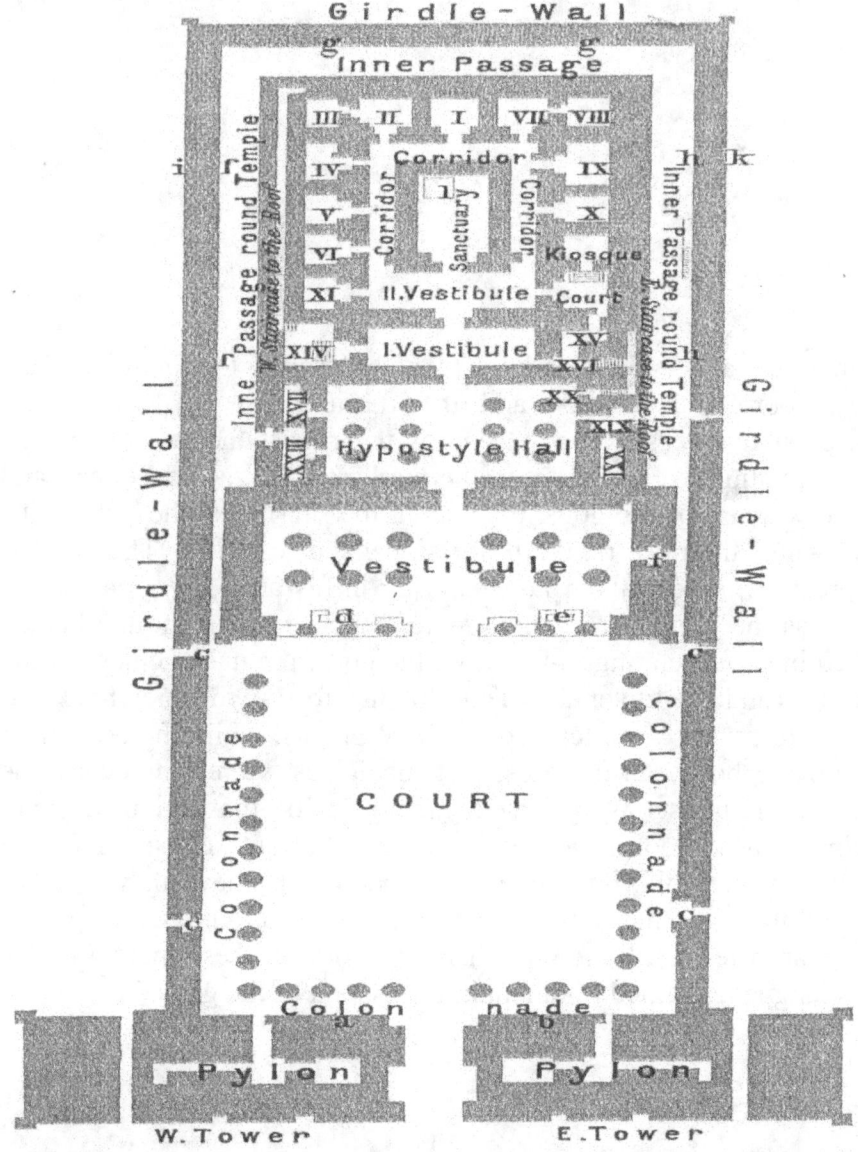

Egypt Essays Plan of the Temple of Horus at Edfu.

Carpiceci (1994: 141) also provided insights into how tradition was important as it helped to maintain stability in cultural practice of the society.

EGYPT ESSAYS ON ANCIENT KEMET

"From the third millennium on there were no basic changes in the rites performed in the temple except for a gradual increase in the participation, albeit still outside the temple, of the masses. Only initiates and priests together with the pharaoh were admitted within. Most of them awaited the 'rising of the god' in the large vestibule. And only 'those who were pure' could enter the 'hall of the rising,' in other words only the "Uab" priest who prepared the offerings and initiated the secret rites. At the back, in the heart of the sanctuary only the high priests and the pharaoh entered. Only they had access to the sacred bark, which 'bears the beauties of god,' and to the 'mysterious places' where the sacred objects were kept, and then they removed the seals and opened the doors of the tabernacle: god was finally 'visible.' New songs rose in the air: 'Oh wake great god, reawaken in peace. Full of serenity is thy reawakening.' The statue was washed, ornamented with linen wrappings, sprinkled with perfumed oils and the eyes and mouth were painted. Then came the offering of food perfumed with flowers. Every action was accompanied by a sacred dialogue addressed to the statue."

For a later age, and further, Maspero XI (1904: 130-31) introduced the comparison during the Graeco-Roman Period wherein circumstances of history had brought about changes in these same religious beliefs and practices of Millennia.

"But the priests were no longer the earnest, sincere teachers as of old; they had invented a system of secondary meanings, by which they explained away the coarse religion of their statues and sacred animals. They had two religions, one for the many and one for the few; one, material and visible, for the crowds in the outer courtyards, in which the hero was made a god and every attribute of deity was made a person; and another learned and intellectual, for the learned in the schools and sacred colleges. Even if we were not told, we could have no doubt but the main point of secret knowledge among the learned was a disbelief in those very doctrines which they were teaching to the vulgar, and which they now explained among themselves by saying that they had a second meaning. This, perhaps, was part of the great secret of the goddess Isis, the secret of Abydos, the betrayer of which was more guilty than he who should try to stop the baris or sacred barge in the procession on the Nile. The worship of gods, before whose statues the nation had bowed with unchanging devotion for at least two thousand years was now drawing to a close. Hitherto the priests had been able to resist all new opinions. The name of Amon-Ra had at one time been cut out from the Theban monuments to make way for a god from Lower Egypt; but it had been cut in again when the storm passed by."

Egypt Essays Photo 39. Karnak Temple of Amon. Obliquely opposite from the previous picture in the Great Court, another line of columns in a colonnade, the bases of columns of the Taharka Kiosk, a statue of Rameses II and the Second Pylon in the right rear.

EGYPT ESSAYS ON ANCIENT KEMET

Egypt Essays Photo 39a. Karnak Temple of Amon. A base and the one remaining complete Taharka Column in the Great Court.

FREDERICK MONDERSON

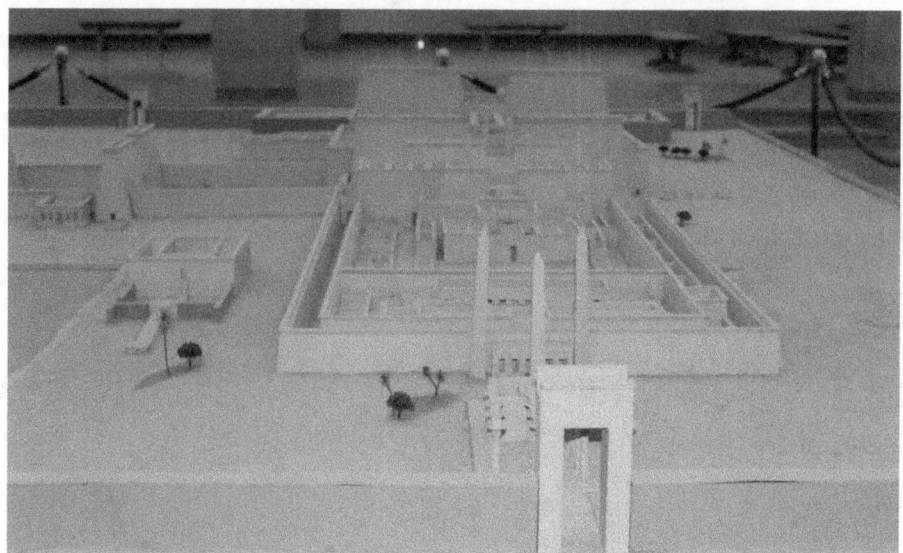

Egypt Essays Photo 39b. Karnak Temple of Amon. An artist rendition of the Temple of Karnak from the rear.

Leonard Cottrell's (1960: 24) book *The Anvil of Civilization* offers an interesting view of the Priesthood. From the earliest times, he wrote: "These men, bound together in 'secret societies,' sanctified and set apart by religious or pseudo-religious ritual, jealously guard the mysteries of their craft and transmit them only to their chosen successors. Some of these men, by reason of their higher intelligence, skill and knowledge, have become what we would call priests - intermediaries between common men and the uncontrollable forces to which they are subject. Rivaling them for power is another class of men, warrior-chiefs, on whom their peoples rely in times of danger. Sometimes, though not always, priest and chieftain are one."

Out of the religious syncretism of these ancient Nile Valley Africans, order in society emerged and helped to bequeath mankind a tremendous legacy of achievement in social civility, art, construction, government, medicine, and science. In this respect, the trailblazing Winwood Reade (1872: 8-9) provided a lively account of the people of ancient Kemet in his outstanding portrayal of *The Martyrdom of Man*.

"The Egyptians, as soon as they had won their harvests from the flood, were obliged to defend them against the robbers of the desert, and out of such wars arose a military caste. These allied themselves with the intellectual caste, who were also priests, for among the primitive nations religion and science were invariably combined. In this manner the bravest and wisest of the Egyptians rose above the vulgar crowd, and the nation was divided into two great classes, the rulers and the ruled. Then oppression continued the work which war and famine had begun. The priests announced, and the armies executed, the divine decrees. The people were reduced to servitude."

From a cosmological perspective this may be because Moscati (1962: 121) offers a glimpse of the issue of a role of the Priesthood. These individuals were active in the creation of Egyptian systems of theological and philosophical thoughts that so significantly influenced the development of man and civilization. Their role therefore was one of shaping behavior and practice and this lent a critical element of stability to the society. In a sense, they knew what the gods wanted and acted accordingly!

"Attempts to organize the pantheon were made by the educated elite, the priesthood, who apply themselves to the task of introducing order into the wide variety of existing beliefs. They also provide an organized account of the origins and laws of the universe. Thus the great theological systems come into being. At Heliopolis, the supreme gods are arranged in order of descent and relationship in an Ennead, which begins with the waters of the ocean, then set the sun and the other divinities in mated couples. At Hermopolis, on the other hand, the priesthood creates an Ogdoad, namely, a group of eight divinities from whom the sun emerges as the final result. Then at Memphis, it is the local god, Ptah, who creates the others, they being only parts of him: his tongue, his heart, his thought."

FREDERICK MONDERSON

The fourth center of worship, Abydos has a more illustrious history. For its divinity Osiris and his sister-wife, Isis worship persisted more fervently than the others lasting throughout the entire dynastic period. While all this manifested, the place where this divinity dwelt was also important. Accordingly, Erman (1907:39) wrote: "When the Egyptian named his temple the house of the god, the name was a literal expression of his belief: the deity dwelt in the temple as a man lives in his house, and the priests the servants of the god, who supplied him with food and attendance, were his household servants." The house of the deity, his temple, with its huge enclosure thus took on a rather meaningful role as think tank of dogged adherence to tradition and the ancestors in propagation of the culture, in the intellectual, spiritual, philosophical, and artistic veins of its creativity.

Maspero II (1904: 87) offered his commentary on the workings of the Priesthood, in the following statement: "Its administration was not vested in a single body of Priests, representing the whole of Egypt and recruited or ruled everywhere in the same fashion. There were as many bodies of priests as there were temples, and every temple preserved its independent constitution with which the clergy of the neighboring temples had nothing to do: the only master they acknowledged was the lord of the territory on which the temple was built, either Pharaoh or one of his nobles. The tradition which made Pharaoh the head of the different worships in Egypt prevailed everywhere, but Pharaoh soared too far above this world to continue himself to the functions of any one particular order of priests: he officiated before all the gods without being specially the minister of any, and only exerted his supremacy in order to make appointments to important sacerdotal posts in his domain."

EGYPT ESSAYS ON ANCIENT KEMET

Egypt Essays Photo 40a. Karnak Temple of Amon. Visitors mill about in the "Great Forecourt" as a guest snaps a photo of the Sphinx of Tutankhamon.

Egypt Essays Photo 40b. Karnak Temple of Amon. The Great Forecourt in modern image highlighting its important features.

FREDERICK MONDERSON

Egypt Essays Photo 40c. Karnak Temple of Amon. This individual is certainly in a hurry to deliver his birds and flowers. Notice his sandals and imagery on his apron.

Jacques Champollion's *The World of the Egyptians* (1971: 48) informs: "... in territorial possession, the entire priesthood was like a family with a vast inheritance, transmissible, according to known conditions, to its various members from generation to generation. These hereditary rights to land bore with them the hereditary obligation of priestly duties, because the nature of these duties determined the co-hereditary share reverting to each member of the family: it is on this basic principle that the entire Egyptian priesthood was founded.... Thus, the priests were married and their sons were priests. The great number of places of devotion, their rich endowments and the fertility of Egypt, these all easily explained how

EGYPT ESSAYS ON ANCIENT KEMET

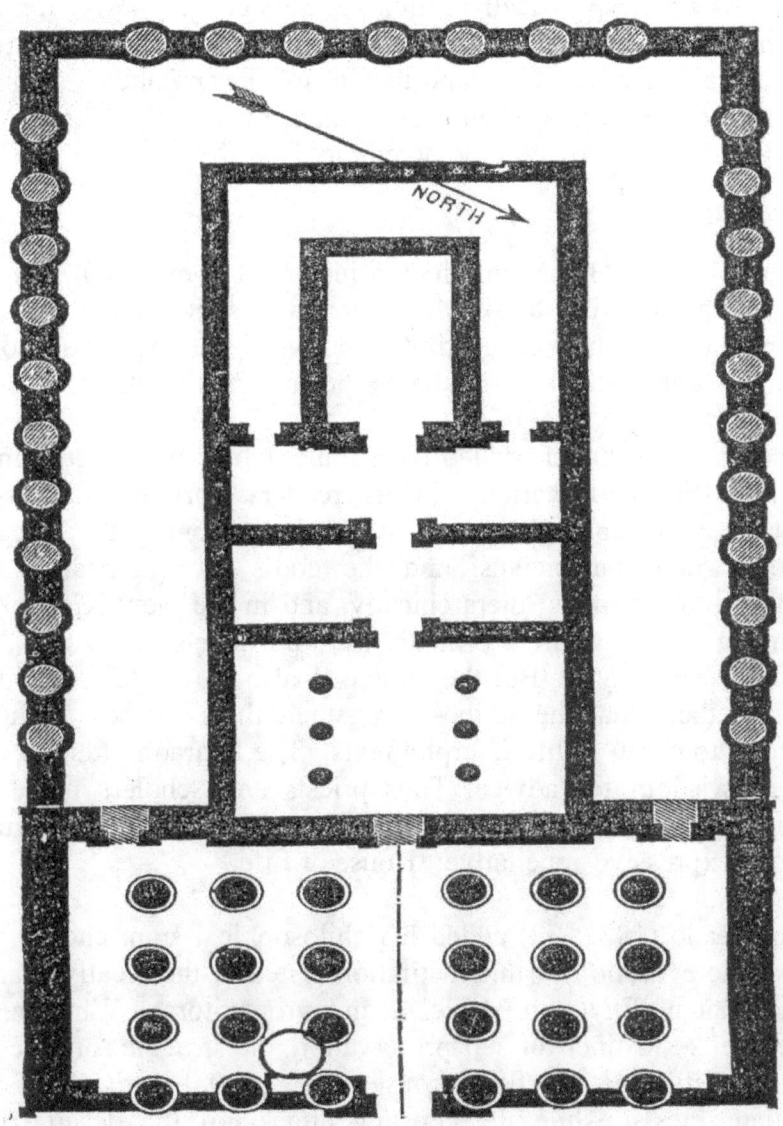

Egypt Essays Plan of the Temple of Esneh.

such a great number of priests could live in such affluence; and to these endowments and callings one must add the grants from the royal treasury for the numerous salaried duties which were reserved for their cast, including all the branches of public administration which were not specifically military. Therefore priests' families were made secure for life by the possible transmission of a share of the general inheritance, proportioned to the number of family members; there were also guaranteed their rank in the hierarchy of the priesthood, as this was also hereditary."

Moscati (1962: 123) has provided a historical comparison with the contemporary civilization of Mesopotamia in southwestern Asia, as to commenting on how the institution derives its strengths as a social system, in worshiping and ritualizing the ancient divinities.

"These practices center around the temple, where an inner chamber contains a list of its various classes: readers, purifiers, sacrificers, prophets, musicians. There is a female personnel too: singing women, women musicians, and the god's 'concubines.' This priesthood is organized hierarchically, and in the New Kingdom it acquires a clearly defined primate, the First Prophet of Amon, the High Priest of Egypt. But the temple is also the center of cultural life: it is there that the scribes foregather, their business being to compose, to copy, and to interpret texts. The Pharaoh often appeals to their wisdom for advice. Thus priests and scholars make the temple the center of religious and intellectual activity alike, earning for it the expressive appellative: 'House of Life.'"

Again, Reade (1872: 32) added his philosophical spin, choosing to believe the evolution of this institution rested in the creative daring of the ancient Egyptian, African, and progenitors. Wherein, he wrote, the "... instinct for self-preservation, the struggle for bare life against hostile nature first aroused the mental activity of the Egyptian priests, while the constant attacks of the desert tribes developed the martial energies of the military men. Next, the ambition of power produced an equally good effect. The priests invented, the warriors campaigned; mines were opened, manufactories were founded; a system of foreign commerce established; sloth was abolished by whip and chain; the lower classes were saddled, the upper class were spurred, the nation careered gallantly along. Finally, chivalrous ardor, intellectual passion, inspired heart and brain; war was loved for glory's sake; the philosopher sought only to discover, the artist to perfect."

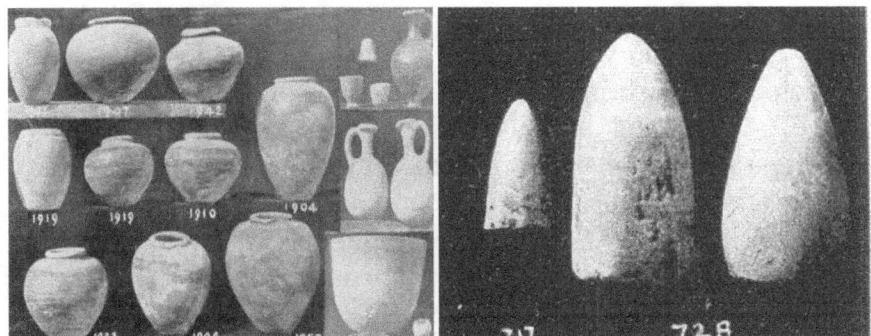

Egypt Essays Illustration 18. Foreign pottery of the First Dynasty and Fifteenth Dynasty pottery (left); as well as cones from the early period (right).

Egypt Essays Illustration 18a. Abydos Bracelets from the Tomb of King Zer (left); and Inscriptions of Kings Ka, Narmer and Sam (right).

FREDERICK MONDERSON

The land of Kemet is very dry, mysterious, cultural, full of history. It is artistic, philosophical, spiritual and religious. Boasting the earliest sense of theological consciousness these ancient Black Africans created religious systems and attendant intellectual, religious and mortuary and festive occasion with their dynamics. These helped to enshrine practices that came to enlighten and to influence later peoples and cultures, far and wide, then and now. Thus, religion played a significant role in the theocratic state. Very early, a bureaucracy was created around kingly and divine worship at their principal centers of theology Memphis, Heliopolis, Thebes, Abydos, and in the Mortuary cults at Giza, Sakkara, Abu Sir, etc, that had access to the inner workings of the practice. In fact, Ruffle (1977: 181) has pointed out: "The only persons to penetrate into the temple were the servants and priests of the god. Theoretically the king was the officiating priest at all times, but in practice his duties were delegated to local nobles and officials. These formed a non-professional priesthood, which served according to a fixed rota, living an ordinary secular life in the intervals. In the New Kingdom the priesthood changed and became largely professional, but many priests still wielded great political power." Nevertheless, from within the confines of their enclosures, accordingly Kamil (1984: 36) explained, "… the fabric of ancient Egyptian mythological tradition, which survived in embellished or mutilated form for thousands of years, was woven and re-woven, time and again, to justify new conditions to explain political trends; it was sometimes even entangled to promote a cause."

The Priesthood was thus, an established institution from the earliest times. During the archaic first and second dynasties, institutions of religion were established and essentially the major precepts of justice, honor, work and art were enshrined in practice. They thrived in the Middle and New Kingdoms, and prevailed until very late in Kemetic history, up and down the Nile River.

EGYPT ESSAYS ON ANCIENT KEMET

Egypt Essays Photo 41. Karnak Temple of Amon. On a broken stone, two images, one of an enthroned King holding an ankh and the other of a standing figure wearing an illustrated apron.

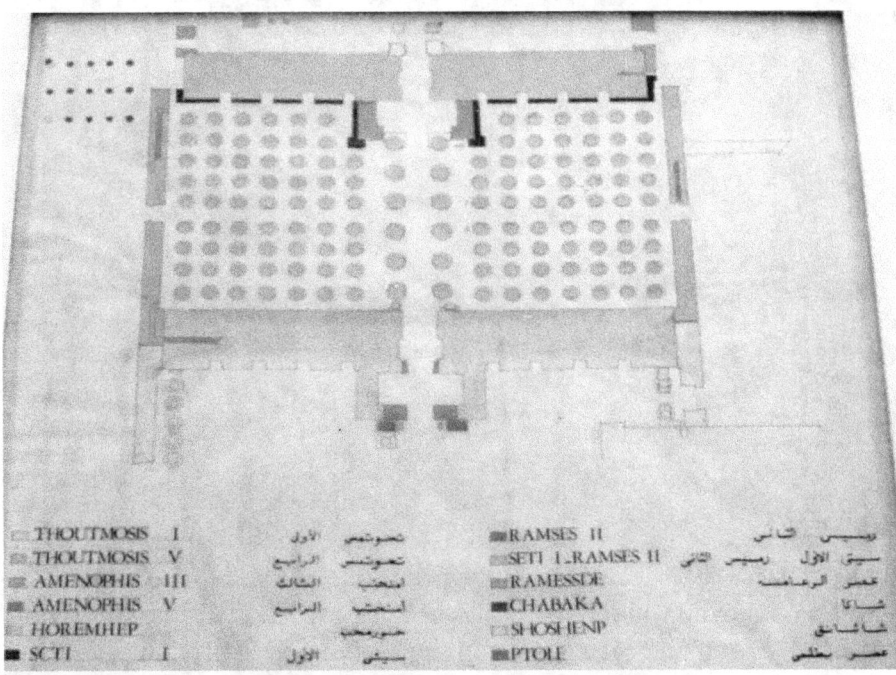

Egypt Essays Photo 41a. Karnak Temple of Amon. Plan of the Hypostyle Hall with the names of kings who did work there.

FREDERICK MONDERSON

Egypt Essays Photo 41b. Karnak Temple of Amon. Mr. Showgi (right) and his assistant Mr. Sayeed (left) stand before twin-statues of Amon and Rameses II in the Hypostyle Hall.

As early as the beginning of the Old Kingdom, with the king considered a god and theocracy the form of government, an "elaborate officialdom bureaucracy" helped fuse civil and ecclesiastical offices in the Pharaoh and his high officials. Throughout this period of great intellectual growth, artistic innovation, and devout religious beliefs and practices, remarkable accomplishments were achieved in education, architecture, astronomy, engineering, and medicine by the brotherhood.

Because of ever expanding administrative responsibilities, Petrie (1923 A: 123-24) explained how there were: "schools attached to the various offices, to prepare for the official work. The Priests were mainly the teachers for higher subjects of hieroglyphic writing, geometry, arithmetic and ethics. The oldest text book that we have is the repudiation of sins in the *Book of the Dead* that is in seven categories each of five statements a system adapted for finger counting."

The Victorian writer Reade's work, *Martyrdom of Man*, is classic for it was written in an age of revolutionary change in European society, in labor and in the literary press and expression. What is important is that it was written fifty years after Champollion deciphered the ancient Hieroglyphic script. Victorian England was in a heightened sense of adventure, go out and conquer the world. Write about it!

Reade (1872: 15-16) has supplied a picturesque glimpse of some aspects of the Priesthood as an institution, in the following statement.

"In the priesthood were included not only the ministers of religion. Priests were the royal chroniclers and keepers of the records, the engravers of inscriptions, physicians of the sick and embalmers of the dead, lawyers and lawgivers, sculptors and musicians. Most of the skilled labor of the country was under their control. In their hands were the linen manufactories and the quarries between the Cataracts. Even those posts in the Army which required a knowledge of arithmetic and penmanship were supplied by them: every general was attended by young priest scribes, with papyrus rolls in their hands and reed pencils behind their ears. The clergy preserved the monopoly of the arts, which they had invented; the whole intellectual life of Egypt was in them. It was they who, with their Nilometers, took the measure of the waters, and proclaimed good harvests to the people or bade them prepare for hungry days. It was they who studied the diseases of the country, compiled a pharmacopoeia, and invented the signs, which are used in our prescription at the present day. It was they who judged the living and the dead, who enacted laws which extended beyond the grave, who issued passports to paradise, or condemned to eternal infamy the memories of men that were no more."

The Priesthood possessed so much power, and to run a city like Thebes, the capital of Kemet, during the Middle and New Kingdoms, when that nation ruled the world, was indeed a tremendously fascinating experience. All this was thought-out in moral, spiritual and ethical development of the African personality as relished in glorification of their religious consciousness while building and exploring the arts, thereby molding human behavior near and far.

Again, in another aspect of development, comparison with the contemporary Assyrian civilization, Reade (1872: 16) points out equality frees the mind from the shackles of ignorance.

"Under the tutelage of these pious and enlightened men, the Egyptians became a prosperous and also a highly moral people. The monumental paintings reveal their whole life, but we read in them no brutal or licentious scenes. Their great rivals, the Assyrians, even at a later period, were accustomed to impale and flay alive their prisoners of war. The Egyptians granted honors to those who fought gallantly against them. The penalty for the murder of a slave was death; this law exists without parallel in the dark slavery annals both of ancient and modern times. The pardoning power in cases of capital offense was a cherished prerogative of royalty with them as with us; and with them also as with us, when a pregnant woman was condemned to death the execution was postponed until after the birth of the guiltless child. It is a sure criterion of the civilization of ancient Egypt that the soldiers did not carry arms except on duty, and that the private citizens did not carry them at all. Women were

EGYPT ESSAYS ON ANCIENT KEMET

treated with much regard. They were allowed to join their husbands in the sacrifices to the gods; the bodies of man and wife were united in the tomb."

Egypt Essays Photo 42. Karnak Temple of Amon. The Author, Dr. Fred Monderson stands between "The pillars of truth!"

FREDERICK MONDERSON

Even as all this occurred, "Growth in the wealth and political power of the nobles led them to rival the monarch in elaborate funerary preparations to reflect their newly acquired social status."

Funerary endowments made the Priesthood, or as Murray (1957: 17) explained it: "...a great rise of priestly power, for endowment of tombs meant the endowment of mortuary priests. So great was the importance of maintaining the offerings in perpetuity that warnings against the infringement of the endowment were sometimes inscribed on the wall of a tomb-chapel: 'As for any people who shall enter this tomb as their mortuary property, or shall do any evil thing to it, judgment shall be had with them before the great God.'"

Erman (1907: 123-24) offers an understanding regarding the expanding role of the mortuary priests in creating their own cottage industries, that also provided employment for their members.

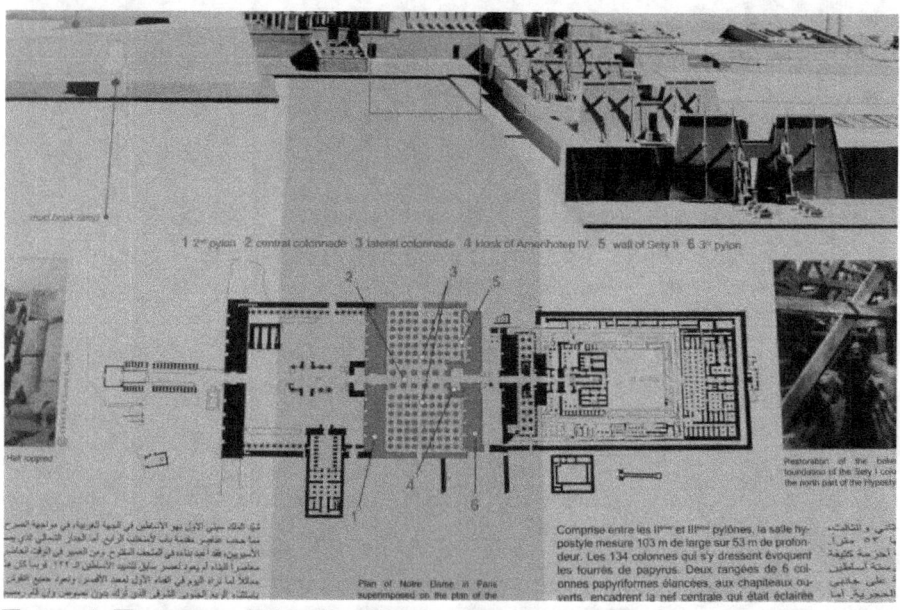

Egypt Essays Photo 42a. Karnak Temple of Amon. Plan of the temple showing the Hypostyle Hall accentuated with its many features, Processional Colonnade, Wall of Seti I, etc.

EGYPT ESSAYS ON ANCIENT KEMET

"When so large a staff (in the tomb of Mereruka there were forty-seven mortuary priests), was employed to take charge of the food brought for offerings, the amount of offerings must have been proportionately large. Here also apparently it was the example of the kings, who employed a large number of important people at their pyramids that was imitated. The old wholesome idea that sons and grandsons should tend the grave was no longer held; these important personages had too many other duties to allow them to undertake the regular charge of a tomb. So there remained no other alternative but to set filial piety on one side, and to provide for the deceased by a business arrangement.... These mortuary priests thus formed a colony at the great tombs, with settled orders, of varying ranks, and with regulations of their own."

Egypt Essays Photo 42b. Karnak Temple of Amon. Seti presents a "Table of Offerings" to Amon-Ra with Mut at his rear wearing the Red Crown. Both the king and gods are on the same plane.

FREDERICK MONDERSON

Herein lay the principles behind the enormous power of the Priesthood. For, later, during the New Kingdom, Wilson (1963: 171) supplies a connection between political and religious or priestly power, and what the ramifications were, these individuals being the principal administrators of the state: "The highest officials of the land under the Pharaoh were the High Priest of Amon at Karnak, the Vizier for Upper Egypt, the Vizier for Lower Egypt, and the 'King's Son of Kush' or Viceroy of Ethiopia. The last named position included three responsibilities; the delegated rule of the African Empire; the responsibility for gold mines of Nubia; and the command of the army in Africa, pharaoh having the responsible leadership for pushing the Empire in Asia. This viceroyship was often a training ground for the Crown Prince."

Within the dynamics of this imperial age of growth under strong leadership, the state went to great lengths to propagate the gods, through cultural, architectural and artistic innovations and the Priesthood was generally avant-garde in these efforts. Still, while their earliest beginnings may be shrouded in the mysteries of time, it is safe to argue the accepted date of the invention of the calendar at 4240 B.C., Nile Year 1, places the Priesthood there, and speculation as to how many thousands of years earlier, may still be valid.

In addition, reflecting on the growing power of the Priesthood, the Pharaoh as the principal religious figure in the land assigned the religious organization responsibility for worshiping and ritualizing the gods, and at times himself, as a son of god on earth. In this role, the Priesthood became a powerful body and the king endowed them with lands, and tax-free status. Breasted (1923: 574) notes that, "Priests and soldiers were exempt from taxation." As a result, this institution became self reliant and in symbiotic harmony as a community were able to perpetuate the religious, spiritual and political symbolism the king represented, which is to bring order, justice and harmony to the state.

Two of the earliest centers of religious and cultural rivalry were Memphis and Heliopolis. The former was situated on the eastern

EGYPT ESSAYS ON ANCIENT KEMET

bank of the Nile about 9 miles west of Cairo and the latter on the western bank some 16 miles further south. Such proximity enabled two theologies, the Heliopolitan Ennead and the Memphite Doctrine to share many similarities. In addition, with other centers at Abydos from the earliest times, and Karnak from the Middle Kingdom onwards, the Priesthood were hard at work molding the beliefs and practices of dynastic Kemet. Temples were built throughout the land as a hub of their activities.

Egypt Essays Photo 43. Karnak Temple of Amon. View of columns of the Processional Colonnade with remains of opening for the Clerestory which let light into the Hypostyle Hall.

Education was another serious concern of the Priesthood, and they became a sort of teachers college in that they became "teachers and exponents of religious and moral duty." Significantly, as a powerfully organized body, they practiced hereditary succession creating their own systems of loyalty and methods. In this, the eldest son succeeded his father. So much so, Wilson (1959: 171) writes: "The retention of position within a few trusted families and the interlocking of the highest offices may be illustrated with two or three examples. Hat-shepsut's Vizier for Upper Egypt, Hapu-Seneb, had been preceded in that office by his grandfather; but Hapu-Seneb was also High Priest of Amon, as his great-grandfather in that office. A certain Thutmose held the Vizierate for Lower Egypt, and his son Ptah-mose became High Priest of Ptah at Memphis."

Egypt Essays Photo 43a. Karnak Temple of Amon. With the Bull running alongside him and the protective vulture flying overhead, Seti dances before Amon as Min.

EGYPT ESSAYS ON ANCIENT KEMET

Egypt Essays Photo 43b. Karnak Temple of Amon. Barque of the God at rest in the Shrine, evidence some forty-odd uraei overhead.

Egypt Essays Photo 43c. Karnak Temple of Amon. From the feet displacement, the king seems in close embrace between gods such as Amon and Khonsu.

FREDERICK MONDERSON

Egypt Essays Photo 43d. Karnak Temple of Amon. Seti kneels to present two vessels to "Traveling Amon."

Petrie (1923 A: 120) elaborates even more commenting on a statement by a high priest whose worlds highlight the significance of titulary and position and how often persons get their start. The official boasted: "'The king has granted that my children being assembled in a tribe of my blood, he would establish them among the prophets of Amen, and my son is established by my side as second prophet, and sub-director of the royal palace on the west of Thebes; the son of my son will receive the titles of fourth prophet of Amen, divine father, officiant and priest.'"

The Ramesside Period of the XIXth Dynasty saw significant growth of the esoteric, philosophical, religious and theological roles and responsibilities of the Priesthood, particularly since Rameses II, the Grand Master, was a prolific builder and patron of the arts. This monarch added the "Ramessean Front" to the "Grand Lodge" at

EGYPT ESSAYS ON ANCIENT KEMET

Luxor Temple, and extended this home of Freemasonry even more. Even more, the Office of High Priest became hereditary in the reign of Rameses III.

Maspero, (1926: 186-87) a prolific writer in his own right commented on Old and New Kingdom tomb decoration. He provides glimpses of Rameses III in the fields of Aalu or heaven and the significance of regaining speech in the next life.

"Where the texts of Unas recount how Unas, now identified with the sun, sails on the celestial waters or enters the Elysian Fields, the scenes in the tomb of Seti I show Seti in the solar bark, and the scenes in the tomb of Rameses III show Rameses in the Elysian Fields. Where the walls of the pyramid of Unas have only the text of prayers recited over the mummy to open his mouth to give him the use of his limbs, to supply him with clothing, perfumes, and food, the tomb of Seti shows the mummy itself, and the ka statues that form the support of the double, the priests who are performing for them the opening of the mouth, who are clothing them, anointing them, and serving them with various dishes from the funeral banquet."

Elsewhere, and earlier, Maspero I (1904: 173-74) explained how the pharaoh also kept contact with the priestly body through the employment of civic titulary.

In explaining this Maspero wrote: "The Prince was the high priest. The whole religion of the nome rested upon him, and originally he himself performed its ceremonies. Of these, the chief was sacrifice, - that is to say, a banquet which it was his duty to prepare and lay before the god with his own hands. He went out into the fields to lasso the half-wild bull; bound it, cut its throat, skinned it, burnt part of the carcass in front of his idol and distributed the rest among his assistants, together with plenty of cakes, fruits, vegetables, and wine. On the occasion, the god was present both in body and double, suffering himself to be clothed and perfumed, eating and drinking of the best that was set on the table before him, and putting aside some of the provisions for future use. This was the time to prefer requests to him, while he was gladdened and disposed to benevolence by good cheer. He was not without suspicion as to the reason why he was so feasted, but he had laid down his conditions beforehand, and if they were faithfully observed he willingly yielded to the means of seduction brought to bear upon him. Moreover, he himself had arranged the ceremonial in a kind of contract formerly made with his worshipers and gradually perfected from age to age by the piety of new generations."

Ritualizing religiosity lets us therefore see a tradition of the high priest as head of an Egyptian, African, institution that is very old. Domiciled at Memphis at first, this premiere position in the Priesthood remained vibrant throughout dynastic rule gaining greater prestige in the New Kingdom. Nevertheless, Kees (1977: 162) has supplied an explanation in the following statement: "The earliest known High Priest of Ptah was called Ptah-shepses; he was the son-in-law of King Shepsekaf, was reared in the royal harem and apparently became high priest in the reign of Userkaf. The high priest bore the title 'Chief of the Craftsmen' and the Greeks identified Ptah with Hephaestus; but crafts belonged to him only inasmuch as he was Lord of the Earth." Wilkinson (1975: 46) in *Ancient Egyptian Jewelry* describes a "gold buckle and belt" belonging to Prince Ptah-Shepses who lived during the sixth dynasty. The author discusses this important artifact belonging to the noble, which he described as "... a gold buckle inlaid with carnelian, obsidian and turquoise hieroglyphs giving his name and titles. The belt itself is made of a thin band of gold with the threaded bead ornament fixed over it by means of a series of small golden tubes attached lengthwise on each end of the band. This band is 90.0 cm long and .5 cm wide. The ornament is composed of carnelian and gold beads threaded on gold wires in a geometrical pattern.... At each end of the belt a semicircular piece of solid gold covers the ends of the ornamental net." Naturally, the principal religious centers of worship each had their own center of worship but the High Priest of the national god enjoyed more prestige than the others.

EGYPT ESSAYS ON ANCIENT KEMET

Egypt Essays Photo 44. Karnak Temple of Amon. Another view of the columns with their open umbel columns comprising the Processional Colonnade in the Hypostyle Hall.

FREDERICK MONDERSON

Egypt Essays Photo 44a. Karnak Temple of Amon. Seti kneels to present two ointment jars to Amon as Min, balancing, not holding the flagellum. Notice the god's food, lettuce in rear.

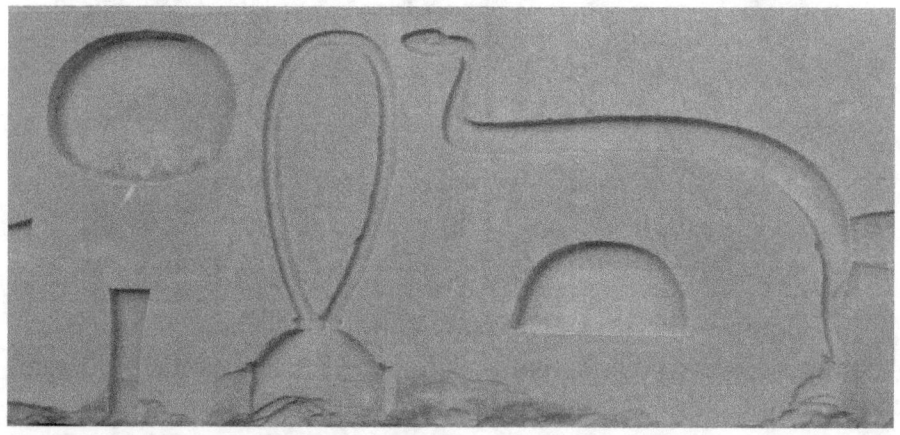

Egypt Essays Photo 44a. Karnak Temple of Amon. The beauty of "Sunk Relief."

EGYPT ESSAYS ON ANCIENT KEMET

Egypt Essays Photo 44b. Karnak Temple of Amon. While Seti kneels to have his name written in the "Tree of Life" (left); Sekhmet introduces him kneeling to Ra Horakhty in his shrine.

In further glimpses into the priesthood, Kees (1977: 163) adds: "It is scarcely fortuitous that we also find that the oldest-known high priests of Heliopolis - the Greatest of the Seers - combined in themselves the offices of Masters of Works and Leaders of the Expeditions to obtain raw materials along with that of directing the temple. We have seen this arrangement in practice in the case of Imhotep, the architect and master sculptor in the reign of Zoser. We find it again in the reign of Snofru: Kanufer, his eldest son, who later became vizier, Captain of the Royal Ships and Treasurer of the God. Similarly Meryib, the natural son of Chephren, who is buried in the cemetery surrounding the Pyramid of Chephren, styled himself Chief Architect and General (leader of the gangs of workmen) at the time when Dynasty IV was coming to an end. Rahotep, another general whose tomb is at Meydum and who was also certainly a son of Snofru belonged to this tradition as a leader of shipping and of youth organizations. It may be supposed that like Kanufer, he was one of those men of action who established Egypt's rule over Sinai. Kanufer, Meryib and Rahotep all bore the title 'Greatest of Seers,' like Imhotep. The explanation of this fact is not that these men were given the office of high priest as a reward for service abroad, but that they were appointed to an office centered in a place that was crucial for foreign commerce that is Heliopolis, the starting place for traffic to Sinai and Asia."

Later, at the end of the New Kingdom, Steindorff and Seele (1971: 254) wrote: "The Second half of the thirty-year reign of Rameses III was less prosperous than the first. Repeated wars, extensive and constant temple-building projects and the enormous gifts showered by the king upon the various temples of the land all combined to drain the treasury of the state. While the priesthood continued to enrich them-selves more and more, while the stables, granaries, and gold hoards of the temples increased to the bursting-point, the royal magazines and treasure-houses grew ever more nearly depleted. Means were actually lacking at the capital to deliver to the hungry workers their earnings of grain, revolts broke out in consequence, and strikes were resorted to in an effort to force on the government the payments of hard-earned dues."

Nevertheless, or, on the more positive side, Kees (1977: 279) reminds us during this age: "The high priest of Amun stood out as the only firm figure in a time of disintegration .... When Rameses had first attended the Festival of Opet at Karnak he had appointed Nebunenef, a former high priest at Dendera, to the vacant office of high priest of Amun, as the direct choice of the god himself. Since that time there had evolved in respect of the persons of the highest-ranking ecclesiastical official in Egypt a certain continuity which favored the preservation of the office within the same circle and even in the same family. This tendency can be clearly observed in the reigns of Rameses II and his successors in the persons of the high priests of Bekenkhons and Rone."

In this issue of succession, Kees (1977: 279-80) added further: "The high priest's successor was always one who had risen gradually to the highest office from the lower priestly ranks in the same temple. This tradition was probably lost in the anarchy that prevailed at the close of Dynasty XIX; but only about forty or fifty years later. After the death of Rameses III and his successors had followed in swift

EGYPT ESSAYS ON ANCIENT KEMET

succession, there arose in Karnak a new office, the subordinate offices of the prophets and of the chief steward of Amun; it thus secured firmly within its grasp the administration of the temple property."

Nonetheless, upward mobility was highly valued. Petrie (1923 A: 120) mentioned: "at Memphis Herodotus was shown a series of wooden statues, 345 in all, which were asserted to be those of the high priests in continuous order from father and son." Equally too, Francis Hawks' *Egypt and its Monuments* (1849: 178-79) tell the reader: "A passage in Lucian furnishes a peculiarly interesting parallel to the accounts of the Pentateuch concerning the practice of magic arts: - 'There was with us in the vessel, a man of Memphis, one of the holy scribes, wonderful in wisdom, and skilled in all sorts of Egyptian knowledge. It was said of him, that he had lived twenty-three years in subterranean sanctuaries, and that he had there been instructed in magic by Isis.'"

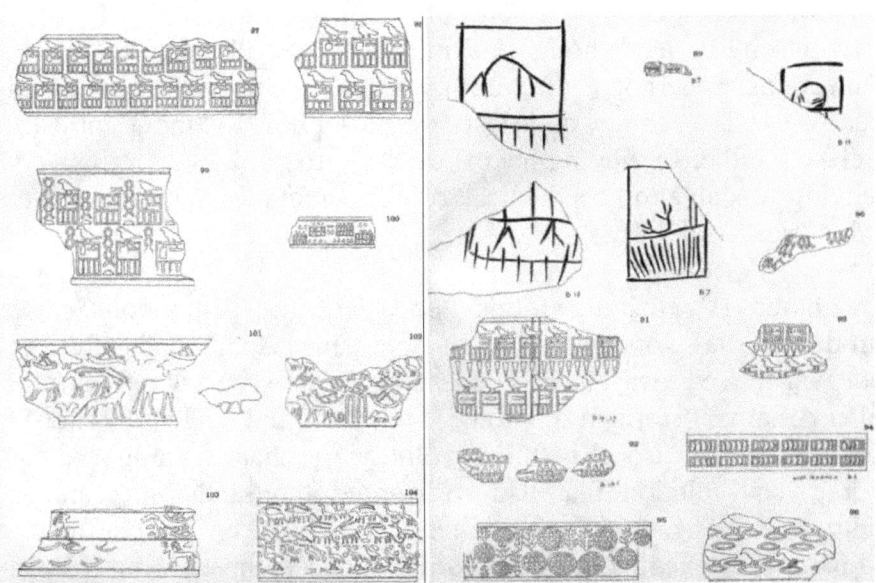

Egypt Essays Illustration 19. Abydos. Sealings of King Aha-Men (left); and of Kings Ka and Narmer (right).

FREDERICK MONDERSON

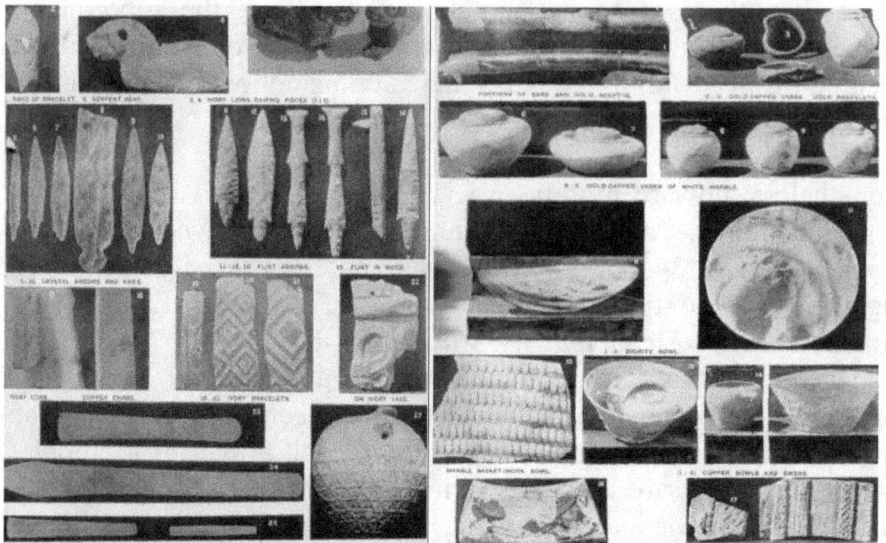

Egypt Essays Illustration 19a. Ivories from the Tomb of King Zer-Ta (left); and Tomb of King Khasekhemui (right).

Notwithstanding, and though lacking the powerful social or family connections, Sauernon (1962: 224) wrote accordingly, "a man could equally well become a priest by co-option, without priestly forebears, either by buying his office or by royal favor. In this way the King was able to keep a check on the sometimes alarming power of the Priesthood."

Amenhotep IV challenged this "power of the priesthood." He introduced the worship of Aton, the "one God," and after an upheaval moved away from Thebes and established his new city at Tel el Amarna, "Horizon of Aton." Steindorff and Seele (1971: 205-06) discussed an aspect of this revolutionary change brought about by the new religion that had overturned thousands of years of tradition. "The King's satellites, his courtiers and officials, following the example of their lord, espoused the new faith even though their hearts may not always have been in it. Notwithstanding the fervor which he devoted to his god, Amenhotep did not at first assail the cults of Amun and the other gods, nor did he hesitate to

EGYPT ESSAYS ON ANCIENT KEMET

appear in inscriptions and temple reliefs as a worshiper of Amun, Thoth, Seth, and other divinities."

Nevertheless, in the Amun reaction at the ascension of Tut-ankh-Amon and the restoration of Amun as Lord of the "throne of Thunder," first Jackson (1970: 110-111) tells us: "The career of King Tut was cut short by his untimely death at the age of seventeen years. The throne was taken over by a priest named Eye [Aye, Ai], whose reign was a disaster to the country; for during his brief rule all the foreign territories annexed by the great kings of Dynasty XVIII were lost. Then a general from the north, Horemhab, seized the throne from the Usurper, Eye, and brought the period of political decline to an end." Next, Steindorff and Seele (1971: 226) adds in spite of all that was going on: "The Priesthood were supplied with rich incomes, costly new barks for the Nile Procession and religious festivals were conducted and male and female slaves were presented to the temples." Even further, Johnson (1978: 81) shows how Amun, as represented by his priesthood aided Thutmose III's imperialism. He quotes Breasted who argued: "In the ancient East, monotheism was but imperialism in religion. The methods of Tuthmose were directly related to his Amunite theology. Hatshepsut appears to have tried to conciliate the priests of Amun at Karnak, but unsuccessfully; perhaps she was too deeply imbued with traditional Egyptian pantheism. Tuthmose was said to have been picked by the Amun priesthood, a tradition which probably enshrines the fact that he had their active support in claiming his royal rights. Certainly they became enthusiastic imperialists. Amun, as an unseen and mobile deity - we hear of 'Traveling Amun' - was well-adapted to imperialist purposes; made for export, as it were ...."

Egypt Essays Photo 45. Karnak Temple of Amon. Son of Ra cartouche of Rameses II on the underside of an architrave in the Hypostyle Hall.

Egypt Essays Photo 45a. Karnak Temple of Amon. More "Sunk Relief" indicating the feathers of Amon and "Health" and "Life."

EGYPT ESSAYS ON ANCIENT KEMET

Egypt Essays Photo 45b. Karnak Temple of Amon. Seti kneels to present a plant to "Traveling" Amon-Ra.

Even further, Johnson (1978) continued: "The idea of a theological contract was rooted deep in Egyptian conception of religion and justice: you cultivated the gods, and they in turn rewarded you. Thutmose conceived such a contract on a much larger scale: Amun promoted his imperialist schemes, and (being a traveling god) lent his authority and presence to centers of Egyptian power in Asia and Nubia. In return he received a lavish share of the commercial profits of conquest. These returns took the form of mining concessions, lands, immunities, monopolies, trading rights, slaves, as well as the sheer booty of ransacked cities, all of which were lavished on

Amun's temples and on the swarming and increasingly powerful priesthood which served them."

Again, this "power of the priesthood" is recognized when Wilson (1959: 272) reasons how the: "... effective grip of the High Priest of Amon upon the civil affairs and finances of the state may be shown by the distribution of offices within one family. Rameses-Nakht was the High Priest of Amon under Rameses IV. His father Meri-Barset had been Chief Tax-master and Rameses-Nakht's sons were to hold two of the most potent offices in the land: Nes-Amon and Amen-hotep successively as High Priest of Amon, and User-maat-Re-Nakht as Chief Tax-master and Manager of Pharaoh's Lands. Thus the priesthood of Amon could manage the finances of the state for its own benefit and withhold resources from the pharaoh as it desired."

Priestly power is demonstrated in the example of Rameses-Nakht who, while not commander of the army had acquired tremendous authority, resources and power concentrated in Upper Egypt, making him someone to reckon with. Rameses-Nakht's strength is explained by Wilson (1959) who wrote: "His son Amen-hotep, who held the High Priesthood of Amon from Rameses IV to Rameses XI, dared to sweep aside part of the pretense and violate one of the oldest canons of Egyptian art. The pharaoh had always been depicted in colossal size in proportion to all other Egyptians, who were only humans and not divine as he was. In a scene in the Temple of Amon at Karnak, we see Rameses IX recognizing the services of the High Priest Amen-hotep with decorations. Pharaoh is shown in his customary heroic size in proportion to the two bustling little officials who carry out his instructions, but Amen-hotep had the arrogance to have his figure carved in the same scale as the king. Furthermore, the composition makes him the focus of attention instead of pharaoh. Nothing could illustrate more clearly that reality which the texts piously ignored: that the king was only an instrument of a ruling oligarchy."

Thus we see, the Priesthood dramatically involved in the crucial arteries of the society, politics, economics, art, transmitting from generation to generation the skills and ideas necessary to serve the

EGYPT ESSAYS ON ANCIENT KEMET

society, do justice, do Ma'at, and learn and teach in the process, educate, while ensuring its own continuity and affluence. During the late period of decline, Budge (1972: 170) adds: "The influence of Amen and his priests at Thebes was felt in every grade of society, and it culminated when Heri-Her, the high priest of Amen, usurped the throne and founded the short-lived line of Priest- Kings at Thebes, about 1190-950 B.C. The same thing had happened about two thousand years earlier, when the priesthood of Ra at Heliopolis succeeded in making three of their high priests the first three kings of the Vth Dynasty."

Nothing more needs be said! Importantly, however, in addition to the sacerdotal priests, the bureaucracy comprised a class of Lay Priests who were assistants to the Pharaoh. "The chief of the lay priests was the deputy of god, and his assistant formed both his court and his council." Budge (1972: 171) explained even further: "The body of lay priests consisted of soldiers, sailors, handicraftsmen of all kinds, agriculturists, cattle-breeders, merchants, etc., all of whom made offerings to the common fund; but those who received wages from this fund were not called upon to make offerings. Most of the manual labor required by the lay priests was provided by their slaves, who were very numerous, some temples possessing as many as 682. Rameses III states, in the Harris papyrus No. 1, that in the course of 31 years of his reign he gave to the temples of Egypt 113,433 slaves."

FREDERICK MONDERSON

Egypt Essays Photo 46. Karnak Temple of Amon. Another cartouche on the underside of an architrave in the Hypostyle Hall.

EGYPT ESSAYS ON ANCIENT KEMET

Egypt Essays Photo 46a. Karnak Temple of Amon. Seti gestures toward Amon-Ra with Mut at his rear.

FREDERICK MONDERSON

Egypt Essays Photo 46b. Karnak Temple of Amon. While Thoth writes his name in the "Tree of Life," Rameses II kneels before the Theban Triad of Amon-Ra (enthroned), with Mut and Khonsu at her rear.

The climate has not changed significantly since ancient times. Dryness, humidity, and ennui from the heat of the sun caused great concern about purification of the body, echoing an old admonition "cleanliness is next to godliness." The priests shaved their heads every day. They also shaved the entire body every third day. Strict rules of purity also dictated that priests be circumcised and abstain from sexual contact during time of service in the temples. Erman (1907: 72) discussed this societal norm that: "Purity before all things was demanded of the Priests; it is no empty phrase that we find at the inner courts of the temples: Let everyone who enters here be pure! At the ceremony of the initiation of the Priests to the temple they actually bathed in the lake that was situated near the temple." They were reminded to also observe taboos of the local god, wherever the precinct was located. Sauernon (1962: 224) says the priests may "dress only in fine linen, wearing no wool nor leather which had been taken from a living animal." Erman (1907: 72) again admitting the dress was different from the ordinary folks of their culture, noted: "While the laity at this time clothed the upper part of the body, the priests merely wore the short skirt of the old kingdom, or the longer one of the middle kingdom, as though in this way they wished to show their connection with the past ages."

From the earliest times the priests wore linen clothing and papyrus shoes. Gold and silver shoes were used in religious ceremonies. Each priest had at least six pairs of papyrus and one pair of leather shoes. They bathe in cold water twice per day and twice per night. From their farms and industry the priests received daily a generous supply of bread, beef, geese and wine. However, some did not drink wine while the onion and pig were prohibited in their diets.

In the prehistoric period origins are difficult to trace. Still, in *Egyptian Religion*, (1923) Flinders Petrie has argued: "the office of the priest was more often developed from civil than from religious functions." As such, the emergence and function of the priestly bureaucracy, representing millennia of cultural continuity, is reflected in the names or titles they bore. In prehistoric times they were the "Servant of the Crown." Later, they became professionals and blended priestly and civil functions as "Great One of Medicine," "Chief, Commander of Workmen," and "Inundation Man." In Defense, they were "Splendid," "General," "Warrior," "Guardian who leads the Mesniu Troops of Horus." In religion, they were "Tongue of the God," "Lord of True Speech," "Opener of the Gates of Management," "Hider of Sins," "Servant of the Cow" (The Lady Isis), and "Guardian of the Guardian of the Pig." Many of these titles and even more honorific ones persisted throughout dynastic history. Erman (1907: 53) also pointed to the moral, dual roles of high officials for, "... the high judicial functionaries of the old kingdom are at the same time priests of the goddess of truth, physicians are priests of Sekhmat, the great artists are priests of Ptah."

The permanent staff in most temples was small, however, but the rotational priesthood was always very large. Duration of service was therefore a matter worked out for the priestly institution. In this respect, Sauernon (1962: 225) explained how service in the temples varied. "Each priesthood was divided into four classes of identical composition (the four phyles) which took turns to be in charge of the temple, its possessions and its ritual for a month. The same group would not be on duty again for another three months. During this time the priests returned to their villages to continue their lives as ordinary citizens."

Egypt Essays Photo 47. Karnak Temple of Amon. From the east of the Third Pylon, view of the Processional Colonnade with widows of the Clerestory to the right and on to the First Pylon in the rear, as visitors walk through.

EGYPT ESSAYS ON ANCIENT KEMET

Egypt Essays Photo 47a. Karnak Temple of Amon. Brother Nasser, son of Brother Abdul "Master of Karnak."

FREDERICK MONDERSON

Egypt Essays Photo 47b. Karnak Temple of Amon. Chief of Temple Security (right) and an assistant.

EGYPT ESSAYS ON ANCIENT KEMET

Egypt Essays Photo 47c. Karnak Temple of Amon. View of the Hypostyle Hall from the northern half, beyond the wall depicting the "Wars of Seti I."

Clearly, the civil experience of priests enabled them to become enmeshed in the social, economic, religious, political, cultural and intellectual lifeblood of the state. The governing principles being essential prerequisites for the civilization growth Africans descendants can boast of today. Also, the Priesthood as an institution itself made contributions as seminal think tanks, and therefore as colleges possessed extensive libraries. Petrie (1923) gives names of offices such as "Chief of the Palace," "Secretary," "Chief of the Architect," "Keeper of Granaries," "Keeper of Treasury," "Chief Justice" and "Keeper of the Armory," that are additional examples of their civic power.

From the time of the Old Kingdom onwards, in the Lower Kingdom, first Memphis then Heliopolis competed for primacy in politics and religion and in this rivalry, the intellectual wheels of this African civilization unfolded and progressed. At Memphis, Kamil (1984:

FREDERICK MONDERSON

37) writes the individual "High Priest, who was also the Chief artist, promoted his deity as the inspiration behind the metal-worker, carpenter and sculptor. However, in the areas surrounding Memphis, two other deities were revered: Sekhmet the lion-goddess and Nefertum a lotus-god. As Memphis expanded it drew those into its orbit. The problem of having three deities in a single area was early resolved by explaining Ptah as chief deity, Sekhmet as his consort and Nefertum as his son. United they formed the 'Memphite Triad.'"

Similarly, at Abydos Osiris, Isis and their son Horus comprised the Triad, whereas at Karnak it was Amon, Mut and their son Khonsu.

Thus, we see the Priesthood as theorists while they were also patron of the arts. The end result was the enormous rise in the wealth and power of this thrifty and creative ecclesiastic body.

Accordingly Petrie (ND: 74) notes: "Much light on the sources of the rise of the priesthood is given by the titles borne by the priests of the various capitals of the provinces or Nomes. Many of these refer to what were purely secular occupations in later times, and we thus learn that the priestly character was attached to the principal person, be he king, or leader in other ways. In one city it was the "King and His Loved Son" who were the priests, in another it was the "General," in another the "Warrior" who became the priest; elsewhere it was the "Great Constructor," in another city the "Great Commander of Workmen;" one city raised the "Manager of the Inundation" to the priesthood, and very naturally the "Great Physician" or medicine man became priest in another place. The "Eldest Son" was the tile of priesthood, much as the later kings made their eldest son high priest. A very curious view of the priestess proceeding the establishment of a priest is given by some cities; one where she was called the "Nurse," and the priest was the "Youth," and another city names the priestess the "Appeaser of the Spirit" and the priest the 'Favorite Child.'"

EGYPT ESSAYS ON ANCIENT KEMET

The wealth of the Priesthood increased from tribute and plunder of surrounding lands such as Nubia, Syria and Palestine. Often towns and cities were given as endowments to the priesthood. Pharaohs made generous contributions and endowments in their worship and mortuary temples. In addition, tributes from foreign conquests that funded extensive architectural construction were all part of the glorification of their father Amon. This largesse was the driving force behind the subsequent revolutions in the history of architecture. In this they also supported and sponsored art and music.

Endowments, tribute, and produce from priestly lands increased the wealth of the priestly body. In the endowment of the mortuary cults the priests gained their most significant influence, yet they were subordinate to the divine pharaoh. Wiedemann (1902: 48) noted: "The dedication is in the royal name, for in the Nile Valley Pharaoh was regarded as the appointed intercessor between his people and the god. He was himself of divine origin and sprang from the union of a god, usually the Sun-god Ra, with a mortal woman, generally the wife of his predecessor on the throne. As such he was certain to gain a ready hearing among the higher powers, whose circle he had left only for a short time and to which he hoped to return after death as a comrade and equal. In more primitive times the ruler himself had celebrated all acts of worship, among which making offerings for the dead was one of the most important. As the state developed and practical considerations prevented this many-sided activity, the prayers and offerings were still made in his name, in order to preserve and emphasize in any inter-course with the gods this ancient custom and duty."

FREDERICK MONDERSON

Egypt Essays Photo 48. Karnak Temple of Amon. Seti I in his chariot trampling some of his enemies as indicated on a wall north of the Hypostyle Hall.

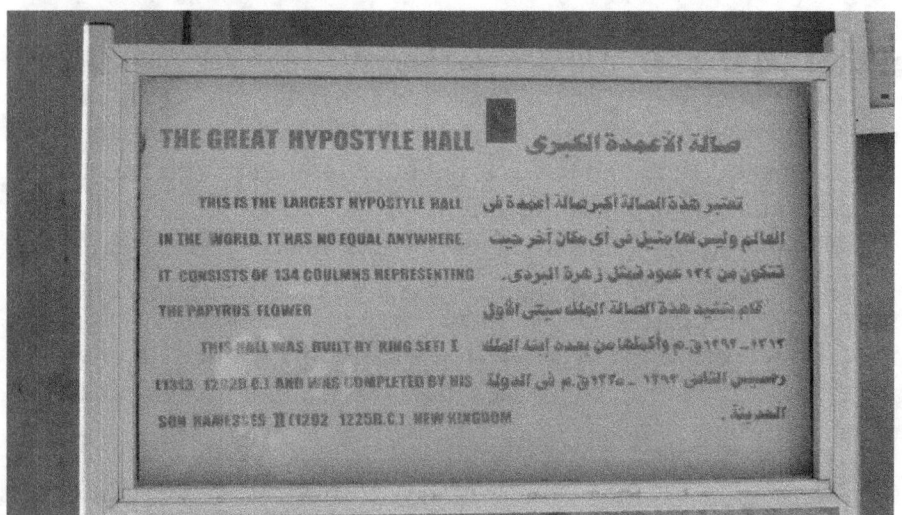

Egypt Essays Photo 48a. Karnak Temple of Amon. Description of the Hypostyle Hall.

EGYPT ESSAYS ON ANCIENT KEMET

Egypt Essays Photo 48b. Karnak Temple of Amon. The gods lay hands on Rameses II in the Hypostyle Hall.

Nevertheless, the importance of the Priesthood was further emphasized in their active role in non-religious matters, providing teachers and technicians as in the military and in practice of astronomy and learning, building, mummification and preparation of funeral ceremonies, farming, exploiting the Nile for irrigation, mathematics for surveying, and transport of quarried stone for greater building of secular and religious structures. Their role was paramount in the fine arts of statuary, painting and craftsmanships.

Sauernon (1962: 224) explained in addition to the priests, who were administrators of economic organization of the sanctuaries; there were doctors and other intellectual specialists who lived in the "Houses of Life." Each specialized in one area of expertise whether in medicine where ailments may relate to different organs and conditions of the body, arts, crafts, theology, hieroglyphs/Medu Netcher, building, etc., also. White explained further (1980: 51) the "main temples acted not only as the distributors of their own bounty, but of the royal bounty too. An entire population of civil servants, scribes, policemen, craftsmen, artisans and artists was fed and clothed from the priestly granaries and storerooms. The chief priests collected taxes on behalf of the king and doled out rewards and necessities as they saw fit. They were thus the instruments and regulators of the state economy and wielded enormous power." Sauernon (1962: 224) adds even more, in regards lay priests, inasmuch as these knowledgeable individuals. "...could, at the king's summons, represent the priests in a given temple. Among these specialists mention must be made of the 'Scribes of the House of Life,' the 'Sages,' the "Lector-priests," the 'Hour-watchers' (astronomer-priests, who decided when ceremonies should be performed) and astrologer-priests, learned in hemerology, who knew how to determine the lucky or unlucky character of the days of the year."

Having this skilled auxiliary at their disposal further increased priesthood power since their people were involved in: "management of the lands of the god, control over the collection of revenues, provisions for the altars and for the priests (who lived on the offerings placed on the altars) and negotiations with associated temples and/with the royal administration."

The titles of these religious officiants, lowest of the priests, was Uab, 'the washed' or purified man. He had to examine the animals for sacrifice and perform the routine of the temple. Maspero I (1904: 174-75) commented on physical cleanliness, as practiced among the priestly class.

He stated: "The officiating priest must carefully wash his face, mouth, hands, and body; and so necessary was this preliminary purification considered, that from it the professional priest derived his name of *uibu*, the washed, the clean. His costume was the archaic dress, modified according to circumstances. During certain services, or at certain points in the sacrifices, it was incumbent upon him to wear sandals, the panther-skin over his shoulder, and the thick lock of hair falling over his right ear; at other times he must gird himself with the loin-cloth having a jackal's tail, and take the shoes from off his feet before proceeding with his office, or attach a

EGYPT ESSAYS ON ANCIENT KEMET

false beard to his chin. The species, hair, and age of the victim, the way in which it was to be brought and bound, the manner and details of its slaughter, the order to be followed in opening its body and cutting it up, were all minutely and unchangeably decreed."

Next in the priestly hierarchy was the *Kher Heb* or reciter of liturgy and spells. Erman (1907: 54) says of the Ker Heb priest: "whose duty appears to have been to read the ancient rituals at the ceremonies, and whose second title scribe of the divine books, designates them as learned students of the sacred literature." Then came the *Her*, who was over the temple. Above him was the *Kherp* or director of the temples. There was also the *Sem* priest who conducted the feasts and worship of the king. Above these was the High Priest or Chief Divine Servant or *Neter Hemtep*. This individual was actually the pharaoh.

Egypt Essays Photo 49. Karnak Temple of Amon. King Amenhotep offers a vessel in this broken stone image.

FREDERICK MONDERSON

Egypt Essays Photo 49a. Karnak Temple of Amon. Broken stone with hieroglyphic inscription.

There were also priestesses, women, in the temples. First was the *Neter Hemt*, or Divine Wife of Amen and High Priestess of Thebes. Next was *Urt Kheneru Ne Amen*, Great One of the Harem of Amen. Then come the *Abyt* priestess, of various gods or goddesses. The *Sesheshet*, sistrum player and lastly, *Shemoyt*, the musician of various gods who rounds out this lot. Music and musical instruments were wonderful means of extending the meaning of the ritual. In this regard, Erman (1907: 48-49) has explained: "Music played no great part in the ceremonies, although later a glorious harp was a necessary part of the temple property in order to praise the beauty of the god in all his names in his processions. In general the musical performances were left to the priestesses, who clattered and rattled with their sistra and castanets before Hathor or some other deity, just as the ladies of the harem were accustomed to do, when dancing before their lord. It was the same with dancing, when occasionally at special religious festivals, the people expressed their joy at hearing and jumping."

EGYPT ESSAYS ON ANCIENT KEMET

The role of the women, however, was limited even though they outnumbered the male priests in the temples. Still, on the level of the gods, females perennially accompany the divinities in triads as Isis and Nephthys accompanied Osiris.

Herodotus is considered the "father of history," who visited Egypt/Kemet around 450 B.C. and wrote *The Histories*. Book II, *Euterpe* is devoted to Egypt. In this important historical and anthropological study, Herodotus recorded the thoughts of an Egyptian priest who had remained studying for many years underground in a temple. Such devotion shows the great respect the people of ancient Kemet, Egypt, had for learning "for its own sake and the respect it gave." The society crafted a practical and philosophical view of life that insisted students love learning like a mother. "Learn to write," admonished a wise sage, "there is no profession that is not governed. It is only the learned man who rules his-self." This seems an earlier version of an idea Aristotle; the Greek philosopher (384-322 B.C.), called *entelechy*, wherein, he believed that knowledge should be pursued for its own sake and not for some practical purpose. *Entelechy* thus becomes the reasoned mechanism, which transformed the individual into a knowledgeable and cerebrally useful member of society.

Education was thus high priority among the Priesthood. The priests of ancient Kemet taught justice and morals. They believed that justice should be the same for all. They also taught self-righteousness for the individual, self-restraint in one's doings, and love and respect for the family. As a barometer, the pharaoh, as the supreme father and judge, acted according to the philosophical beliefs of Ma'at, the goddess of equality, balance, order, goodness, whose emblem was a feather that was oftentimes shown above the goddess' head. The monarch feared judgment in the afterlife if he did not adhere to fairness. So as an example, in legal matters he often admonished judges to be severe in their actions and not show any partiality to the rich. Treat them as you would treat the poor, he said. Thus, "leaning to one side in a cause is abomination to the gods," became a philosophic pharaonic admonition, and the temples were foremost in teaching this belief.

FREDERICK MONDERSON

Karnak was indeed an academic institution of learning in addition to its many functions, viz., political, religious, spiritual, art, craft, etc., while Kemet ruled the world and Thebes its capital. Browder (1995: 124) cites Dr. Asa Hilliard in a paper presented at the 1984 Nile Valley Conference, regarding Karnak as a center of learning during the early New Kingdom. It was both a center of religion and education, since the two could not be separated in the minds of the Kamites. It housed an elite faculty of priest-professors. It has been estimated that at one time there were more than 80,000 students at all grade levels studying at *Ipet Isut* University (Abdullah, 1984). Both Luxor and Ramesseum enjoyed this luxury as centers of intellectual activities. In as much as Medinet Habu was a "carbon copy" of the Ramesseum, it stands to reason it also promoted intellectual activities. Thus, in their expanding roles, temples were at the center of religion, politics and education.

The faculty were called *Hersetha* or "teachers of mysteries," and were divided into departments (Meyer, 1900), as follows: (1) Mystery Teachers of Heaven (astronomy and astrology); (2) Mystery Teachers of All Lands (geography); (3) Mystery Teachers of the Depths (geology); (4) Mystery Teachers of the Secret Word (philosophy and theology); and (5) Mystery of Pharaoh and Mystery Teachers who examined words (law and communication)."

The priests taught self-righteousness is sinful, according to Petrie, and mankind should seek to avoid it. Further, they believed persons should have honorable dealings with god and men. As a way of life, violence should be avoided and one should remember one's religious obligations. The strong should show respect for the rights of the weak. Merchants should practice commercial honesty and try not to hinder the affairs of others. They also taught that the ancient Kemetic ideal was a man who should be strong, steadfast, and self-respecting. He should be active and straightforward, and quiet and discreet. He should also avoid covetousness and presumption.

Then, in a number of ways, Senmut can be considered an "Ideal man." According to Wilson (1959: 172), rising from humble

EGYPT ESSAYS ON ANCIENT KEMET

beginnings, this nobleman achieved social status and titles as "Hereditary Prince and Count, Seal-bearer of the King of Lower Egypt, Sole Companion, Steward of Amon; Overseer of the Fields, the Garden, the Cows, the Serfs, the Peasant-Farmers, and the Granaries of Amon; Prophet of Amon; Prophet of Amon's Sacred Barque; Chief Prophet of Montu in Hermonthis; Spokesman of the Shrine of Geb; Headman in the House of the White Crown; Controller of the Board Hall in the House of the Official; Steward of the King; Overseer of the Royal Residence; Controller of Every Divine Craft; Steward of the Princess Nefru-Re; Great Father-Tutor of the Princess Nefru-Re; Controller of All Construction Work of the King in Karnak, Hermonthis, Deir el-Bahari, the Temple of Mut at Karnak, and Luxor; and a 'superior of superiors, an overseer of overseers of construction works.'"

Egypt Essays Illustration 20. Tombs of Qa-Sen and Sekhemab-Perabsen (left); and Seth-Ath and of Den-Setui (right).

FREDERICK MONDERSON

Egypt Essays Illustration 20a. Steles around the Tomb of Zer-Ta (left); and Steles around the Tomb of Sen-Setui (left).

Significantly, then Senmut could not have achieved such social prominence had he not been a member of several priesthoods! In family relations, priests taught that a man should not be rude to a woman in her house. In this ancient African Nile Valley culture of Northeast Africa, the house belonged to the woman. That's even if the husband built or purchased it. She was the "Lady of the House," or "Mistress of the House." There was no "Master" of the house.

Though there was an occasional divorce, "marriage" or "unions" seems to always have been for life. "Children are sweet," is what they believed and taught. As such, the father did what he could for a dutiful son, who "should be regarded a true incarnation of the family spirit or Ka and treated with sympathy." The son, therefore, was taught "not to forget his mother and to remember all she had done for him." The daughter, however, was considered the heiress with property and lineage being passed down in the female line.

EGYPT ESSAYS ON ANCIENT KEMET

Egypt Essays Photo 49b. Luxor temple of Amenhotep III. Native Egyptian Guide in the "Ramessean Front beside an image of Nefertari enthroned.

FREDERICK MONDERSON

General associations with ancient Kemetic (Egyptian) culture emphasize pyramids, temples, tombs, art and mummification as part of the effort to explain trans-human metaphysical existence. Mummification and the climate had an important role in this process and it not only helped to preserve the remains of the wealthy and famous, but became the catalyst for experimentation in science, anatomy, medicine and surgery. With overseas expansion and migration, preservation of the body spread far and wide as Kemetic culture diffused so that many of their secrets are being used today in morticians' never ending work. Towards the end of dynastic rule, however, as Greeks, Copts and Christians mingled at this crossroads of the ancient world. Steindorff and Seele (1971: 131) reminded: "In fact, as the old religion gave way to the new, the knowledge of the hieroglyph writing, which during the Greco-Roman period had been largely confined to the native priesthood, was gradually forgotten."

Egypt Essays Photo 50. Karnak Temple of Amon. View of the Heraldic symbol of Egyptian unification, the lotus and papyrus, placed here by Thutmose III of the 18th Dynasty.

EGYPT ESSAYS ON ANCIENT KEMET

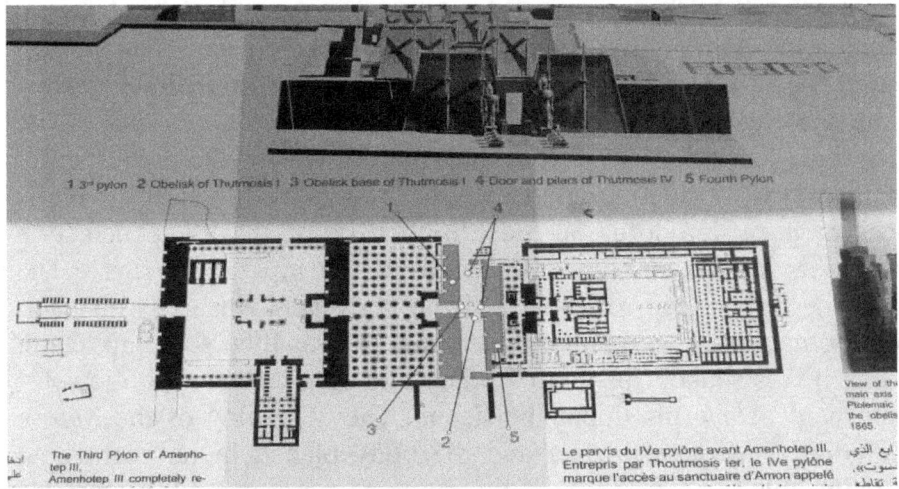

Egypt Essays Photo 50a. Karnak Temple of Amon. Plan of the Temple showing the Third Pylon and work of Thutmose I and Thutmose IV.

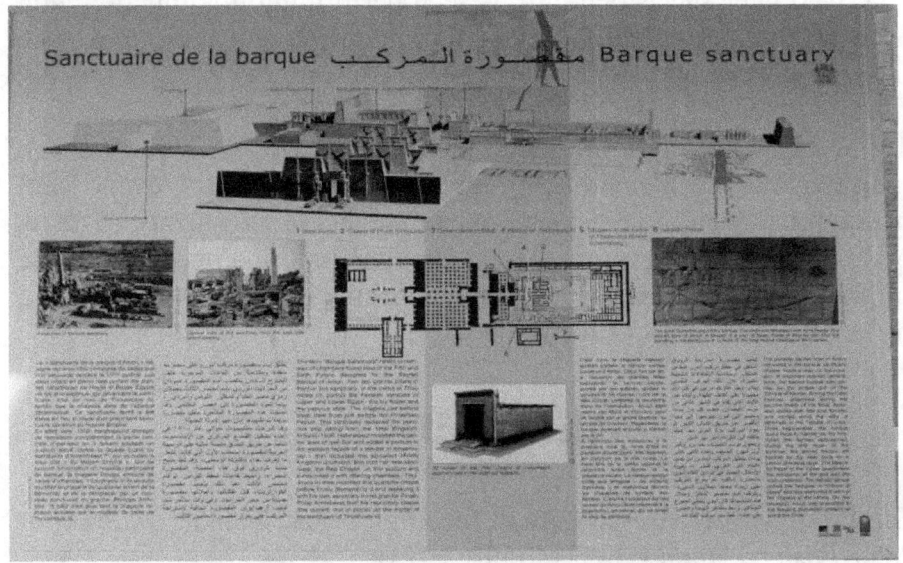

Egypt Essays Photo 50b. Karnak Temple of Amon. Plan of the Temple showing the "Barque Sanctuary" area.

The priests were responsible for the mummification of the dead before burial for which a fee was paid. Herodotus mentions three types of mummification for the Pharaohs and nobles, middle class and the poor. While the wealthy was often entombed in elaborate preparation, fanfare and sepulchral structures, the dryness of the soil has helped to preserve some bodies of the poor in shallow graves. Still, the earliest mummified body using this process is that of the Queen of King Zer of the first dynasty. However, the earliest fully resined body comes from Meydum in the third dynasty. Now, according to Herodotus, in preparing the body, it was opened by a long slit, usually on the left side from the hip to the ribs. The intestines were then removed and the body was washed with palm oil, aromatic spices, resin and perfume. It was then sewn up again. Next, it was soaked for up to 70 days and then studded with jewelry and magical charms under the linen. The "Opening of the Mouth Ceremony" was performed and the body placed in its coffin and sarcophagus for burial. As if linking dynastic craft with prehistoric beliefs, the gods in the afterlife, used an adze to perform the opening of the mouth ceremony. In Tutankhamon's tomb, the High Priest Ayi, who later succeeded him, is seen performing this function with adze and all. Generally made of iron, this tool's early existence poses important questions for the origins of iron.

These brief descriptions detail the role of the Priesthood as an indispensible mechanism being involved in and shaping every facet of Egyptian society. Whether science, medicine, art, taxation, trade, building or spirituality, they were involved and exerted a profound influence in shaping the moral, social, ethical, spiritual and metaphysical axioms of the society.

REFERENCES

Bierbrier, M. L. "Hrere, Wife of the High Priest Piankh." *Journal of Near Eastern Studies* 32: 311 (July 1973).
Breasted, J. H. *A History of Egypt*. New York: Charles Scribner's Sons, (1905) 1923.
_____. *Development of Religion and Thought in Ancient Egypt*. Philadelphia: University of Pennsylvania Press, (1912) 1972.
Browder, Anthony T. *Nile Valley Contributions to Civilization*. Washington, D.C.: The Institute of Karmic Guidance, (1992) 1995.

EGYPT ESSAYS ON ANCIENT KEMET

Budge, E. A. W. *The Dwellers on the Nile*. New York: Benjamin Bloom, (1885) 1972).
Carpiceci, Alberto Carlo. *Art and History of Egypt*. Florence, Italy: Bonechi, 1994.
Champollion, Jacques. *The World of the Egyptians*. Translated by Joel Rosenthal. Geneva: Minerva, 1971.
David, A. Rosalie. *The Egyptian Kingdoms*. New York: Elsevier-Phaidon, (1975).
"Egyptian Tomb Endowments." *American Journal of Archaeology* Vol. 44: (1942: 364).
Erman, Adolf. *Life in Ancient Egypt*. Translated by H. M. Tirard. London and New York: Macmillan and Co., 1894.
_____. *A Handbook of Egyptian Religion*. London: Archibald Constable and Co., Ltd., 1907.
Hawks, Francis. *Egypt and Its Monuments*. New York: George P. Putnam, 1849.
Herodotus. *The Histories*. Baltimore, MD: Penguin Books, (1954) 1973.
Jackson, John G. *Introduction to African Civilizations*. Secaucus, New Jersey, 1970.
Kamil, J. *The Ancient Egyptians*. Cairo: The American University in Cairo Press, (1976) 1984.
Kees, Herman. *Ancient Egypt: A Cultural Topography*. Chicago: The University of Chicago Press, (1961) 1977.
Maspero, Gaston. *History of Egypt and Chaldea*. Vols. I, II, and XI. London: The Grollier Society, 1904.
_____. *Manual of Egyptian Archaeology*. New York: G. P. Putnam's Sons, 1926.
Mertz, B. *Black Land, Red Land*. New York: Dodd, Mead and Co., (1966) 1978.
Murray, Margaret. *The Splendor that was Egypt*. New York: Philosophical Library, (1949) 1957.
"Occult Sciences in the Temples of Ancient Egypt." *American Journal of Archaeology* I: 470, 496.
Oswald, M. "Egyptian Tomb Endowments." *American Journal of Archaeology* 44: (July 1940: 364).
Petrie, W. M. F. *Egyptian Religion*. London: Constable, 1923.

FREDERICK MONDERSON

_____. *Social Life in Ancient Egypt*. New York: Houghton Mifflin Company, 1923.

_____. *The Religion of Ancient Egypt*. Chicago: The Open Court Press (ND).

Piccine, P. A. "In Search of the Meaning of Senet." *Archaeology* 33 (July-August 1980: 55-58).

Posner, Georges with Serge Sauneron and Jean Yoyotte. *A Dictionary of Egyptian Civilization*. London: Methuen and Co., Ltd., (1959) 1962.

"Priest Amidst Birds found in City of Dead." *Science News Letter* 36, (October 7, 1939: 231).

Rawlinson, George. *The Story of Ancient Egypt*. New York: G. P. Putnam's Sons; London: T. Fisher Unwin, 1896.

Ruffle, John. *The Egyptians*. Ithaca, New York: Cornell University Press, 1977.

Steindorff, George and Keith C. Seele. *When Egypt Ruled the East*. Chicago: University of Chicago Press, (1942) 1971.

White, J. E. Manchip. *Ancient Egypt: Its Culture and History*. New York: Dover Publications, Inc., (1952) 1970.

_____. *Everyday Life in Ancient Egypt*. New York: A Perigee Book, (1963) 1980.

Wiedemann, A. *The Realms of the Egyptian Dead*. London: David Nutt, 1902.

Wilkinson, Alix. *Ancient Egyptian Jewelry*. London: Methuen and Co., (1971) 1975.

Wilson, J. A. "Egypt" in *The Intellectual Adventure of Ancient Man*. Chicago: The University of Chicago Press, 1946.

_____. *The Culture of Ancient Egypt*. Chicago: The University of Chicago Press, (1951) 1963.

Woldering, Irmgard. *The Art of Egypt: In the Time of the Pharaohs*. New York: Greystone Press, (1962) 1965.

EGYPT ESSAYS ON ANCIENT KEMET

Egypt Essays Photo 50c. Temple of Mut. Under the shelter, colossal face of Goddess Mut.

Egypt Essays Photo 50d. Temple of Mut. Within the temple gate, ruins of the entranceway.

FREDERICK MONDERSON

Egypt Essays Photo 50e. Temple of Mut. Looking back through the broken Sphinxes of the Avenue towards Karnak with the Tenth Pylon in foreground and further on a crane at the Ninth Pylon.

Egypt Essays Photo 50f. Temple of Mut. Some of the broken statues of Goddess Sekhmet placed here by Amenhotep III.

EGYPT ESSAYS ON ANCIENT KEMET

Egypt Essays Photo 50g. Temple of Mut. Panoramic view of part of the temple with some columns still visible.

Egypt Essays Photo 50h. Temple of Mut. Another view of the grounds with the worker shed in rear.

FREDERICK MONDERSON

Egypt Essays Photo 50i. Temple of Mut. The Sacred Lake, after much labor was expended in repairing it, but unlike Karnak's it is not square but horse-shoe like.

Egypt Essays Photo 50j. Temple of Mut. Another view of the landscape with sphinxes and statues of Goddess Sekhment lie scattered.

EGYPT ESSAYS ON ANCIENT KEMET

Egypt Essays Photo 50k. Temple of Mut. More statues of Goddess Sekhmet before the Sacred Lake.

Egypt Essays Photo 50l. Temple of Mut. Some statues of Goddess Sekhmet still lie in the sand to be excavated.

FREDERICK MONDERSON

Egypt Essays Photo 50m. "The most beautiful tableau ever found in Egypt;" the back panel of Tutankhamon's throne, covered with sheet gold and richly inlaid, representing the king and his queen.

EGYPT ESSAYS ON ANCIENT KEMET

8. Sakkara

Some years ago, on an educational trip to the land of ancient Kemet, now Egypt, while at Sakkara, I scaled the barriers and approached the Step-Pyramid of King Zoser, built by his architect, physician and Vizier Imhotep, during the Third Dynasty. I touched this inspiring construction and said a prayer, thankful and awed to be in its reverenced and majestic presence. By the standards of eternity, this magnificent ancient Egyptian, African, architectural structure attests to the durability, creativity and accomplishments of the mind of ancient man of Africa. As a man-made creation, it has also defied time. Equally too, and often times we are told, time is afraid of the Pyramids, but the pyramids themselves must genuflect in the presence of their older relative, the Step-Pyramid of Sakkara, prototype of their own everlastingness. Clearly, these pathways of alpha and omega of African architectural consciousness stand as living testimony to the unconquerable force and creativity of the ancient African mind. In their technological genius, the ancient architects created these timeless wonders along the majestic Nile in adoration of Africa's Gods, Kings, women, people and culture. Importantly, subsequent achievements of world civilization were nurtured from these creative beginnings. Therefore, this glorious architectural legacy is extremely important in buoying the social process and educational efforts of African people worldwide. This makes efforts in search of ancient Kemet/Egypt culture an intellectual elixir that powers the search for knowledge and truth.

Egypt Essays Illustration 21. Prostration in presence of the deified King.

FREDERICK MONDERSON

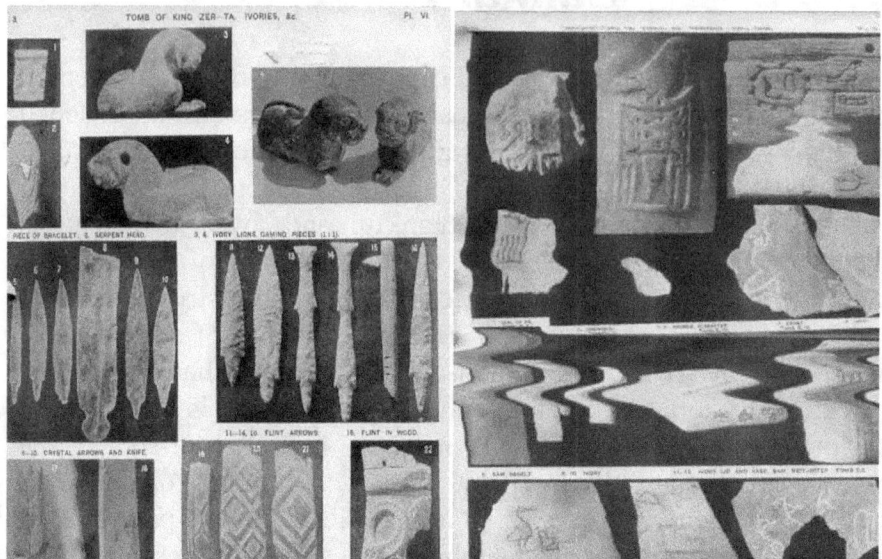

Egypt Essays Illustration 21a. Tomb of King Zer-Ta, Ivories; Seal of Ka, Narmer alabaster, ebony and ivory, etc.

Egypt Essays Illustration 21b. Ebony Tablet of King Mena of the Ist Dynasty (left); and Ist Dynasty Tomb of King Zer showing brick partitions to contain offerings.

In the rural and urban centers of this nation, African people need the strength and reassurance of such knowledge in their march of socialization, educational advancement, political and economic empowerment, and religious, spiritual and theosophical

EGYPT ESSAYS ON ANCIENT KEMET

rejuvenation, all necessary for the long haul. We recognize that as each generation is called upon to discover its purpose, and undergird its efforts to enhance its community, only knowledge of self, and a history of one's ancestral and cultural heritage, will enable them to read, research and conduct scientific inquiry to enlighten and educate the next link in the chain of Africa's progeny. With this knowledge base truthfully represented we can then stand mightily on the threshold of the future challenges and accomplishments, knowing that our part can assure our present and future. Then perhaps we can truly live Dr. King's dream.

Egypt Essays Photo 50n. Temple of Amon-Ra at Karnak. Wonderful view of Hatshepsut's obelisk against a blue sky.

FREDERICK MONDERSON

It's an accepted fact, in the architectural history of the world, the land and people of ancient Kemet stand supreme. Their innovative prototypes, genesis of architectural conventions and building practices have therefore influenced people, nations, religions, and the pageantry of history.

Egypt Essays Photo 51. Karnak Temple of Amon. Frontal view of the *Akh Menu*, "Festival Temple" of Thutmose III, beyond the "Sanctuary" and "Middle Kingdom Court." This is the last major structure on the East-West Axis.

Architecture is considered the greatest achievement of the human mind. In its evolution from the humblest beginnings, man has sought to praise, worship and ritualize divine beings in furtherance of his cultural development. Temples as places of worship and festivities, palaces as residences and centers of joviality and administrative functions, as well as civil structures to serve the ends of humanity, tombs as final resting places, and equally fortresses as barracks of military enterprise, all are examples of experimental architecture that produced the lasting masterpieces we find today at such places as Ghizeh, Karnak, Ramesseum, Luxor, Deir El Bahari, etc., being the crystallized building practices of ancient people's

EGYPT ESSAYS ON ANCIENT KEMET

genius. In these and collateral industries, ancient Africans excelled while the world was waking up to recognize the dawn of human consciousness and creativity. One such experiment took place at Sakkara.

The fame of Sakkara rests in its choice for tombs, constructing everlasting as burial site of the newly established city of Memphis. Not simply the Step Pyramid but massive mastabas equally tell of those significant building effort requiring even great administrative skill to coordinate the laying out of the ground, quarrying and transportation of the massive stone, art and architectural genius of the constructions and the organization of the necessary manpower that expertly erected these buildings.

Egypt Essays Photo 51a. Karnak Temple of Amon. View from the Great Court through the Taharka Column, Second Pylon, Processional Colonnade, and towards the Sanctuary at evening time as the sunlight casts its ebbing shadow back towards the Sanctuary.

This latter includes the support system of food, shelter and medical treatment. Sakkara served as the necropolis or cemetery of Memphis during its tenure as capital following Narmer's unification of the two kingdoms, and erection of the "White Wall," at c. 3200 B.C. or *Nile Year* 1040. This choice and the attendant reverence given the place allowed Sakkara to host the remains of pharaohs and nobles dating from the First Dynasty to the late period of Saite and even Persian and Ptolemaic rule. Significantly, the ideological nucleus of this sacred cemetery was the timeless funerary complex of King Zoser, a sprawling necropolis stretching for 8 kilometers long and one kilometer wide.

North of Zoser's structure is the North Necropolis containing the Serapeum, a number of tombs and the Pyramid of Teti to the north-northeast. In this northern half, the massive Serapeum was the burial place of the Apis bulls, sacred to the God Ptah, deity of Memphis, whose worship was inaugurated immediately after unification and start of the First Dynasty. Regarding this structure, Strelocke's (1965: 32) description tells, it "consists of a series of vaults in the form of underground corridors, nearly 10 ft. wide and 18 ft. high, passing under the desert sands for 1,148 ft. Left and right in chambers dug out of the solid walls, especially in the large vault are the granite sarcophagi of the sacred Apis-bulls. The 24 monolithic sarcophagi each weigh from sixty to seventy tons. The first, 328-ft. long corridor was cut out in the time of Rameses II. Psammetichus I (26th Dynasty) extended the vaults and the Ptolemies finished the complex."

To the east of this building lay a semicircle of statues of poets and philosophers including Plato, Heraclitus, Protagoras, Homer and Pindarus. Ptolemy I built all of these. Further north, in a semicircle reaching towards Teti's pyramid were the Mastabas of Ptah-hotep and Akhet-hotep, and Ti. Next are located Baboon and Ibis galleries, and the tomb of Hesi Re, whose gracefully wooden panel is now in the Cairo Museum. In addition, First Dynasty tombs of Kings Udimu, Ada, Zed, and Queen Merneith are there. Then come the Mastabas of Ankh-ma-hor, Kagemni, Mereruka and Ka-em-heset.

EGYPT ESSAYS ON ANCIENT KEMET

Egypt Essays Photo 52. Karnak Temple of Amon-Ra. Column (left) and pillar (right) in the *Akh Menu*, "Festival Temple" of Thutmose III.

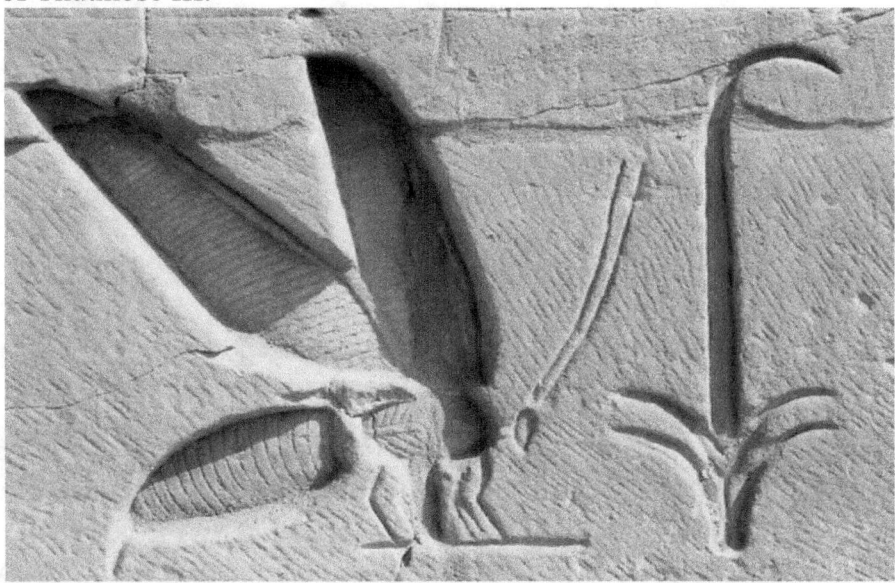

Egypt Essays Photo 52a. Karnak Temple of Amon-Ra. "Suten Bat" title of Pharaoh as "King of Upper and Lower Egypt/Kemet."

To the south lies the Southern Necropolis, in front of which is the Pyramid of Unas, with its mortuary temple, monumental gallery,

FREDERICK MONDERSON

causeway, sacred barks buried in large stone basins, a valley temple and its landing stage. Between the Causeway and Zoser's southern wall lie two rows of mastabas. In the first are Ha, Ishu Ef, Vizier Unefert, Unal Ankh, Princess Idut and Vizier Mehu. In the second row, the tombs of Queen Khenut and Bebet are found. Further southwest lies the Funerary Complex of Sekhemket. He was successor to Zoser and also built a Step-Pyramid. His funerary complex seems as if it was finished. Within its enclosure wall is the Mastaba of Mehu-ka-irer, Mastaba of Nefer-her-ptah and tomb of Ptah-iru-ke. It's believed there were at least two other Step-Pyramids built in addition to the great one. Watson (1987: 23-24) mentions a Step-Pyramid at Zawiyet el-Aryan, between Giza and Sakkara. Then he mentions: "A fourth Step-Pyramid complex might be concealed within the so-called Great Enclosure at Saqqara, the rectangular outline of which has been revealed west of Sekhemkhet's complex by Arial photographs. This, however, awaits excavation."

The more significant structure, however, is the mortuary complex of Zoser containing the Great Step-Pyramid, which is surrounded by an enclosure wall. This pyramid, in six steps, is about 193 feet high. Carpiceci (1994: 74) mentions a court with altar, storehouses, and dwellings for priests; mortuary temple with the pharaoh's sirdab; "House of the North;" "House of the South;" Heb-Sed Court with buildings and altar; small temple and temple with fluted columns; entrance of the Sanctuary and entrance "colonnade;" facade of the "Cobra Palace;" storerooms and portico; and the Court in front of the Great Step-Pyramid, with the three main altars. In the northeast corner of the complex, Zoser's statue was found in a walled-in stone area with two peepholes for him to look out. Because of its rarity, it is now in the Cairo Museum and a replica sits there.

EGYPT ESSAYS ON ANCIENT KEMET

Egypt Essays Photo 53. Karnak Temple of Amon-Ra. On his "Girdle Wall," Rameses offers two sistra (sistrum) to Mut as Hathor.

Egypt Essays Photo 53a. Karnak Temple of Amon-Ra. The majestic ibis is a manifestation among the many attributes of God Thoth, but the grace of the bird is in itself a major asset.

FREDERICK MONDERSON

While this complex boasts an architectural magnificence, its artistic beauty is itself breathtaking. Beneath Zoser's structure are beautiful blue faience tiles and decorated panels that show the Pharaoh celebrating the Heb Sed festival. On the other hand, the nobleman Mereruka was a 6th Dynasty Master of Ceremonies who built a large Mastaba with some 30 rooms. He has enormous space and there are six rooms for his wife Sesheshit and five for his son Meri-tety. This Mastaba of Mereruka depicts artistic renderings that show the slaughtering of cattle and processions of offering bearers and hunting and fishing scenes depicting people in boats along with birds, fishes, plants and animals.

Mariette discovered the *Mastaba of Ti* in 1865. It shows the sketched nobleman, a royal hairdresser of the 5th Dynasty, and his family sailing through the marshes and inspecting their workers. A hippopotamus hunt is sketched; fishes in the marshes as well as papyrus plants; birds being attacked by other animals and processions of men and women bearing offerings and importantly; the first evidence of people in motion. Haag (1987: 165) mentions the dual nature of many of Ti's representations: "Literally it is a hunt in the marshes; but symbolically it is Ti against the forces of evil and chaos. The hippopotamus was particularly feared and hated in ancient Egypt, but Ti together with a helpful crocodile is killing it. Fish and birds represented chaos, but here again man and animal are subduing them."

The Mastaba of Ptah-hotep represents this High Priest in offering scenes. There are water sports with rowers dancing in their boats. Fishes abound in the water below and individuals hold birds and animals as part of an enormous offering table before the Nobleman. The Mastaba of Kagemni has decorations showing a servant supplying seeds for birds in an aviary. Men are shown with the papyrus plant, along with birds and gazelles being led on cord as well as dancing girls. The Mastaba of Princess Idut has scenes of everyday life, administrators taking inventory, and seated scribes with their palettes and brushes making recordings. Also shown are servants butchering a bull and a water scene with men in boats

EGYPT ESSAYS ON ANCIENT KEMET

holding birds, animals and fishes, while crocodiles are shown in the water. However, while the art is a wonder to behold, the monumental architecture is timeless and awe-inspiring, and this revolutionary approach set the tone for millennia to come.

In an assessment of art and the architectural material nicety of these buildings, Firth (1928: 463) has written: "The perfection of the masonry makes it difficult to believe that these stone buildings are the oldest surviving in Egypt, but the imitation of brickwork and reed construction follows the law which makes every fresh change in material imitate the forms associated with the material previously in use, a stage which precedes the generalization of the constructional properties natural to the new material. This archaic limitation was in two generations left behind by the builders of the great Pyramids of the fourth dynasty, although the Egyptians retained the end columns in imitation of the lotus and the papyrus derived from the primitive constructions of their remote ancestors."

Egypt Essays Photo 53b. Temple of Mut. Another view of some of the buried seated statues of Goddess Sekhmet, showing more work to be done at the temple.

FREDERICK MONDERSON

Egypt Essays Illustration 22. Amenhotep III of the 18th Dynasty gives audience to one of his ministers.

Therefore, in looking back through time, history has recognized the genius of Imhotep in pioneering multi-tiered structures. These experimentations of the Third Dynasty set the stage for the "True Pyramids" of Giza in the Fourth Dynasty. Pyramids were built during the Fifth and Sixth Dynasties and as late as the Middle Kingdom. While these Old Kingdom structures contained both

EGYPT ESSAYS ON ANCIENT KEMET

"Mortuary" and later "Sun" or "Worship Temples," the transitional Middle Kingdom bequeathed to the New Kingdom a separation that encouraged Mortuary Temples erected on the west bank and Worship Temples on the east Bank of the Nile.

Sakkara, therefore, etched its name in the annals of art, architecture, and mortuary, religious, administrative, building and philosophic and scientific history. The originality and durability of its constructions was not simply a watershed of innovations, but provided the inspiration that influenced emerging developments in a number of fields of human endeavors that challenged and showcased the human spirit, its personality and inventive genius.

Through it all, African creativity and its technological innovations proved everlasting.

REFERENCES

Carpiececi, Alberto Carlo. *Art and History of Egypt: 5000 years of Civilization*. Florence, Italy: Bonechi, (1994).
"The Pyramids and Tombs." *American Journal of Archaeology* Vol. IV, 1900, p. 480.
"The Chapel of Unas." *American Journal of Archaeology* Vol. V. 1901, p. 332; SS *Times* July 15, 1901, Hilprecht.
"The Pyramid of Unas." *American Journal of Archaeology* Vol. VI. 1902, p. 6.; Maspero, *C.R. Acad. Insc.* 1901, pp. 614f.
"A Representation of the Manufacture of Seals." *American Journal of Archaeology* Vol. X. 1906, p. 334; Society *of Biblical Archaeology* Vol. XXVII. 1905, p. 286 (pl.) P.E. Newberry.
"Sakkara." *American Journal of Archaeology* Vol. XXXII. 1928, p. 71; *Ill. Lond. News* November 12, 1927, p. 861, (4 figs.).
"Sakkara." *American Journal of Archaeology*, Vol. XXXII. 1928 p. 354; *Ill. Lond. News* Jan 7, 1928, pp. 8-9 (6 figs. one in color.) Cecil M. Firth.
"Sakkara." *Ill Lond News* Feb 27, 1937, pp. 348-49. Walter D. Emery.

FREDERICK MONDERSON

"Sakkara." *American Journal of Archaeology* Vol. XL. 1938, p. 292; *Ill. Lond. News* June 4, 1938, pp. 1000-1001.

"Sakkara." *American Journal of Archaeology* Vol. XL. 1938 *Ill. Lond. News* Jan 4, 1939, p. 51.

"The Season of 1938 to 1939." *American Journal of Archaeology* Vol. VIIIL 1940, pp. 145-49, William Stevenson Smith.

"Sakkara." *American Journal of Archaeology* Vol. IIIL. 1943 *The New Pallas* Vol. VI, 1942, p. 26.

"New Finds at Sakkarah." Jasper Y. Brinton. *Art and Archaeology* Autumn 1949, pp. 141-144.

"The Step Pyramid at Sakkara." C. M. Firth. *Antiquity* Vol. 2, 1928, pp. 461-463.

"Sakkara." *American Journal of Archaeology* Vol. XL. 1936, p. 120. *Ill. Lond. News* January 2, 1937, p. 3.

"Sakkara." *American Journal of Archaeology* Vol. XL. 1936, p. 317. *Ill. Lond. News* February 27, 1939, pp. 348-49. Walter B. Emery.

"Royal Tomb at Sakkara." *American Journal of Archaeology* Vol. XL. 1936, p. 292. *Ill. Lond. News* February 12, 1938, pp. 247-49. Walter B. Emery, Director of Excavations Conducted for the Egyptian Government Service of Antiquities at North Sakkara.

"Sakkara." *American Journal of Archaeology* Vol. XLII 1938, p. 314. *Ill. Lond. News* January 14, 1939, p. 51. Zaki Effendi Y. Saad.

"Saqqara." *American Journal of Archaeology* Vol. XLVIII, 1944, p. 278; *Ill. Lond. News* February 26, 1944, pp. 247-49 (9 figs.) Guy Brunton.

"Egypt." *American Journal of Archaeology* Vol. L, 1946, p. 192.

"Egypt." *American Journal of Archaeology* Vol. XLVII, 1951, pp. 419-24 passim.

"Egypt." *American Journal of Archaeology* Vol. LIII, 1949, pp. 40-41.

EGYPT ESSAYS ON ANCIENT KEMET

Egypt Essays Photo 54. Karnak Temple of Amon-Ra. View of Thutmose I (left) and Hatshepsut's (right) obelisks among the ruins from southeast of the "Sanctuary."

Egypt Essays Photo 54a. Karnak Temple of Amon-Ra. From east of the "Sacred Lake," the "Seventh" and "Eighth Pylons" along the East/West Axis.

9.   UPPER EGYPT/KEMET

The flow of the Nile from south to north is the way ancient Egypt/Kemet and Nubia were oriented geographically, politically, economically, religiously and socially. However, most Western, European and American historiographic representations and teaching techniques orient the river and its culture from north to south. Exploring this contradiction, Upper Egypt/Kemet, the south, from Elephantine Island and the Temple of Isis on Philae Island (now Agilka), represented one of the two large divisions of the country during pharaonic rule. This region extended as far north to the apex of the Delta to include Memphis, the Giza Plateau and Sakkara. In the Middle and New Kingdoms, the southern border stretched deep into Nubian territory. The other large division of the United Upper and Lower Kingdoms, the North, comprised essentially the Delta region.

Egypt Essays Photo 54b. Karnak Temple of Amon-Ra. A vulture with outstretched wings, hold a Shen ring above Horus image wearing the Double Crown with uraei sporting other rings.

Throughout dynastic times the land was further subdivided into districts. The Greeks called these districts nomes. From the first dynasty, a noble family ruled each nome, and each of these was an aspirant to pharaonic rule. The number of these nomes seems to have varied. Old Kemetic records generally gave 44. Pliny gave the same number; Strabo and Diodorus listed 36. The usually accepted number is 42. Of these 22 were in the South or Upper Egypt/Kemet and 20 were in the North or Lower Egypt/Kemet. Each nome had its own capital and in the earliest times its local god. The seat of the hereditary governor was located in the Nome's capital. He was called a Nomarch. In the configuration of regional power, from the Middle Kingdom onwards, the south emerged supreme owing to the primacy of Amun in religious, economic, political, architectural and artistic efforts and the daring, dreams and dramatics of men and women of great and noble aspirations.

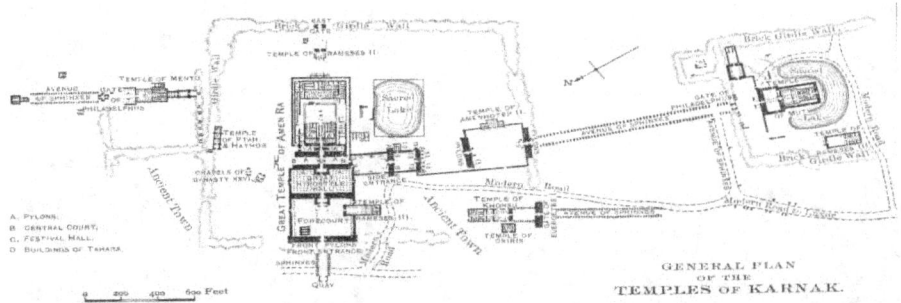

Egypt Essays General Plan of the Temples of Karnak.

H. Brugsch, in *Egypt under the Pharaohs* explained, the "capital" of "these nomes formed the central point of the particular divine worship of the district which belonged to it." He pointed out, the "sacred name of the Nomes have handed down to us the names of the temple, of the chief deity, of the priests and priestesses, of the holy trees, and also the names of the town-harbor of the holy canal." Even further Brugsch indicated, ancient records provide evidence regarding, "cultivated land, and the land which was only fruitful during the inundation, and much more information, in such completeness, that we are in a position, from the indications contained in these lists, to form the most exact picture of each Egyptian nome in all its details, almost without any gaps."

In the prehistoric period, nomes existed with their own peculiarities, viz., economic activities, industry, nome standards, deities, sacred animals, fortifications for defense, etc. They were parts of the north/south regional division of the country. The Narmer Palette depicts the conquest of the southern over the northern region by the earliest chieftain and warlord. The feat of Narmer's mobilization of a significant southern military force, sailing downstream, conquering and collecting his enumerated booty, attests to the size of his own forces. It may be also that he had inner Africa as his backyard and this provided the wherewithal for the great warrior tradition and the syncretized cultural creativity he unleashed lasting for the duration of dynastic rule.

Egypt Essays Photo 54c. Karnak Temple of Amon-Ra. From south-east of the Sacred Lake the two obelisks and ruins of the Hypostyle Hall.

A significant symbol of the unification was the White Crown to represent *The Upper Kingdom*; Red Crown to represent *The Lower Kingdom*; and a united Red and White Double-Crown to represent the *United Kingdoms of the North and South*; in this "Holy Land" of ancient Kemet. The Lotus represented the symbolic plant of the Upper Kingdom and the Papyrus of the Lower Kingdom, as other pharaonic symbols. The *Suten Bat* titulary designation King of the Upper and Lower Kingdoms remained one of the first of five kingly names for much of dynastic rule. The other names were his *Golden Horus, Horus, Two Ladies*, and *Son of Ra titles*. Ever since,

EGYPT ESSAYS ON ANCIENT KEMET

throughout its 3000 year history, the north and south vied for supremacy in art, politics, agriculture, religion, and economic relations from its nascent Archaic or Thinite Period, through the Middle Kingdom and especially New Kingdom, Late Period and the Ethiopian Ascendancy in the XXVth Dynasty. These areas of societal dynamics grew exponentially and added luster and resurgence to a nation that had begun to fail in some respects. This was continued in the Saite, Persian, Assyrian and Greek and Roman Periods though to a lesser extent. Much of this is considered the age of the warrior tradition.

The ruler of each nome performed a feudal obligation to the pharaoh. This relationship required the Nomarchs to pay taxes to the national treasury. In their nomes they had to supply "corvee labor" for national projects such as canal and road building and their repairs and upkeep. They also had to supply recruits for the national army, particularly in times of war. When the Pharaoh visited a nome, its Nomarch was responsible for the hospitality of the king. They were also responsible for maintaining local police, and a Judiciary whose function was to administer justice impartially.

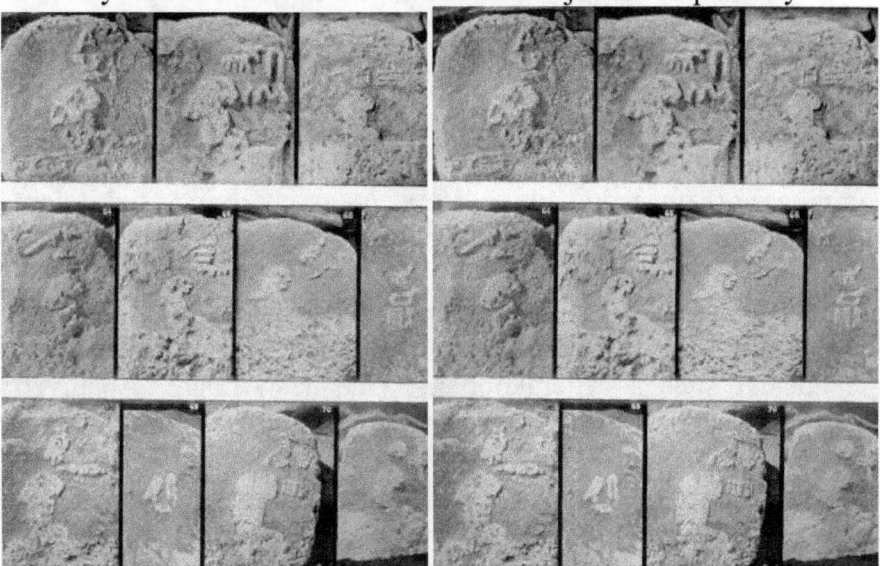

Egypt Essays Illustration 23. Steles around Tomb of Zer-Ta and Steles around Tomb of Den-Setui.

FREDERICK MONDERSON

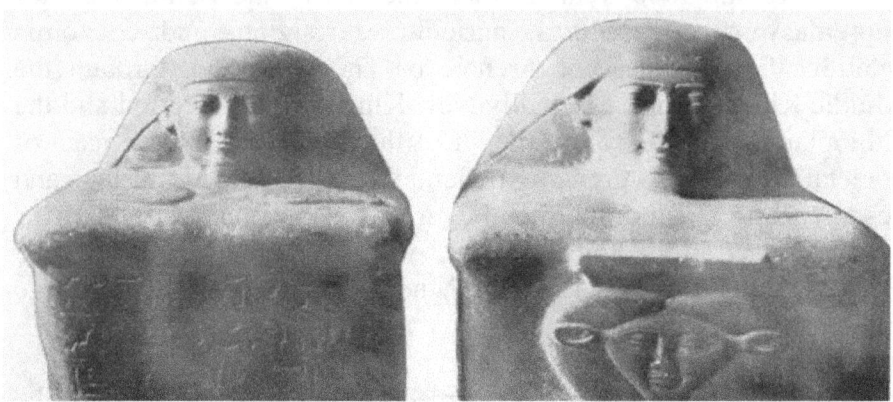

Egypt Essays Illustration 23a. Statues of Hor (left); and Pakhouroi (right). One with Inscription (left) the other with Hathor head (right).

In *Atlas of Ancient Egypt*, John Baines and Jaromir Malek point out, the Nomes of Upper Egypt had their numbers fixed by the fifth dynasty. They cite as reference the Kiosk of Senwosret I, the "White Chapel," (Twelfth Dynasty 1970-1936 B.C.) at Karnak, that gives recorded lengths of each nome along the river. For Lower Egypt, the definitive number of 20 nomes was not set until the Graeco-Roman Period, which is after the Late Period and Persian and Assyrian conquests. However, notwithstanding, the 22 Nomes of Upper Egypt/Kemet, were properly defined and established by the beginnings of dynastic rule. Here is another and significant evidence of Southern Supremacy.

Many pre-dynastic and early Dynastic cultures were located in the southern land, home of the first three Nomes. This area includes such ancient sites as Hierakonpolis, Naqada, Armant, Abadiyeh (Hu), Naga Ed-Der, El Kubaniya, El-Kab, Edfu, Badari, Mostagedda, Matmar, Ballas, Naqada, and Kharga and Dakhleh Oases and Gebelain. Thebes boasted twin cities of Luxor and Karnak as well. The sepulchral Valley of the Kings, Queens, Nobles and Artisans are important repositories of funerary, artistic and architectural remains in Upper Egypt/Kemet. This prominence, the God Amon, and its antiquity gave the south its powerful role in the affairs of the state. In addition, the Islands of Philae and Elephantine, and towns such as Aswan, Edfu, and El Kab provide valuable links to the origins of cosmological, theological, philosophic, scientific and mathematical beginnings along the Nile, in Northeast Africa. Together with Kom el-Ahmar, and Abydos with its pre-dynastic forts, temples and cemeteries, these sites hold keys to earliest origins man's intellectual quest and this was an African experience. Egypt is African! It has been and it is now!

New evidence indicated the pre-Pharaonic beginnings at Nabta Playa in the Western Desert millennia in the making before 3500 B.C; and in the Eastern Desert at least 1000-years before "Winkler's Mesopotamians" wrongfully credited with making polygraphs on the ridges and caves situated on the highlands.

Egypt Essays Photo 55. Karnak Temple of Amon-Ra. Looking past Thutmose I's obelisk, through the "Processional Colonnade" and on to some of the throngs of people who visit daily.

FREDERICK MONDERSON

Egypt Essays Illustration 24. "Stele of Choi" (left); and "Stele of the Mireacle of Aahmes I" at Abydos (right).

For archaeologists, cemeteries proved virtual reservoirs of information, supplying enormous evidence of historical and cultural significance. Certainly the Eastern Desert highlands has been explored for early engravings but not for graves that require separate effort. Importantly, Barbara Adams (1987) mentioned the preservative nature of the hot climate and dry sands in *Predynastic Egypt*, when she enumerated parts of the wealth found in graves of the pre-dynastic period. The category of pottery was decorated with "nature objects and geometric patterns." These simple patterns would later evolve into more complex representations. Coloring of pottery was by natural fire or hand painting. From the work of archaeological excavation, it was discovered, the "predynastic tombs revealed stone mace-heads; metal tools such as needles, chisels and adzes." Goldsmiths worked jewelry such as "bracelets and rings; flint tools and weapons, both exotic and utilitarian ivory, pottery and

EGYPT ESSAYS ON ANCIENT KEMET

stone human and animal figurines, ivory, stone shells and glazed composition (faience) beads and amulets; slate cosmetic palettes; ivory, bone and shell spoons, dishes, combs, bracelets and hairpins; leather and textile clothes and containers; and baskets, resins and plant food forms."

While most of these artifacts were recovered from graves, in settlements, on the other hand, "pottery sherds and stone implements are usually the most abundant finds, although some organic remains, particularly wooden posts and animal bones, can be salvaged by careful excavation."

Waset, of the indigenes became *Thebes* of the Greeks and *Luxor* of the Arabs. It was the religious capital for the significant middle years in the nation's development. As the center of an enormous empire, Upper Kemet/Egypt orchestrated the affairs of state for the two lands during the Middle and New Kingdoms. This region also boasted the largest, most important, and surviving temples in all of the land. The kings of the Middle and New Kingdom worshiped the great god Amon-ra who resided at Thebes and favored their daring and generosity.

Luxor is situated on the east bank, and has temples of Amon, Mut, Khonsu, Montu and Ptah, the major Theban deities. Though Ptah's principal temple was located at Memphis, he was one of those "National" gods of Egypt. There are other temples built at Luxor chiefly by Thutmose III, Amenhotep III and Rameses II and III. Amenhotep or Amenhotep III, the 18th Dynasty Pharaoh, was the great-grandson of the military genius Thutmose III, the "Napoleon of far antiquity." Kemet reached the pinnacle of its cultural expansion during Amenhotep's reign. He built the Temple of Luxor close to the banks of the Nile, just south of the city. An Avenue of Sphinxes by way of the Temple of Mut connected it to the enclosure wall of the temple of Karnak.

Even when Egyptian military strength was past its peak, economic conditions within the capital were sound. Jill Kamil in *Luxor: A Guide to Ancient Thebes* says of the New Kingdom: "Trade was connected with wealth pouring in from the distant provinces of the empire." The empire then had come to encompass almost all Western Asia including Palestine, Syria, Phoenicia and the northern parts of the Euphrates, Nubia and Libya. They contributed "great wealth brought by loaded caravans." Among the merchandise of exchange were "gold, silver, metal-ware, ivory and timber, spices for the deity's taste and strange and exotic plants to roam in private gardens." Great wealth was lavished on the god Amun whose priesthood, in praising, worshiping and ritualizing the gods of ancient Kemet, helped bring great success to the warrior pharaohs and bounty to the state. Much of this was endowed to Amon and his priests which aided temple construction. Temple's walls, ceilings and columns were encrested with religious, historical, cosmological and artistic inscriptional masterpieces that when applied to priestly creativity advanced science, astronomy, mathematics, and medical practice, thrust humanity along the panoramic road of civilization development.

Egypt Essays Photo 56. Karnak Temple of Amon-Ra. Ruins of the "Ninth Pylon" and a crane for heavy lifting. The "Tenth Pylon" (right) is further on.

EGYPT ESSAYS ON ANCIENT KEMET

Karnak is also located on the east bank of the Nile at Thebes. It comprises the Great Temple of Amon, with precincts to the deities Mut, the mother goddess, and Khons, the moon god, their son, of the Theban Triad. A temple of the war god, Montu, and numerous smaller temples and chapels round out the wide array of architectural works dating this temple complex to over two thousand years in expanding construction. That is from the time of the 12th Dynasty to after the Roman invasion in 30 B.C., *Nile Year* 4210. Some scholars have argued for a greater dating of Karnak, placing a significant temple there at 4000 B.C., *Nile Year* 240.

Western Thebes, across the river, contained numerous mortuary temples built by some of the most outstanding Pharaoh. Mentuhotep I, Mentuhotep II, Hatshepsut, Amenhotep I, Amenhotep II, Amenhotep III, Thutmose I, Thutmose II, Thutmose III, Thutmose IV, Seti I, Rameses II, Rameses III, Rameses VI, Merneptah, all built temples on the west bank of the Nile. These were considered these King's "Mansions of Millions of Years." Some kings as Amenhotep III built palaces, as he did for his wife Queen Tiy that she may reside on the West Bank at a place called Malcata. Rameses III of the Twentieth Dynasty erected Medinet Habu temple and with a palace, the last major New Kingdom construction. Perhaps with the exception of Mentuhotep (Middle Kingdom) and Hatshepsut (New Kingdom), all these temples had a palace for the king to reside in when he visited the temple.

There are other temples and sites of significance to the visitor. In ancient times there was much activity during pharaonic and noble burials and during the "Opet Festival," "Feast of the Valley," and other festivals. Among others, the Temples of Medinet Habu and the Temple of Hathor at Deir el-Medina and others, when lit on those festive and holy days, convey an aura that added to the majesty to make this region culturally, the most fertile artistic and architecturally as well as archaeologically in all of Egypt, ancient Kemet; fact is in all the world. This is why young African-Americans and all people in search of scientific truths need immerse in study to gain familiarity and knowledge of the ancient cultural

FREDERICK MONDERSON

heritage that lit up human history. In this, they must defend Egypt as African.

In the Western Necropolis, or burial places, are located the Valley of the Kings ("Biban el-Moluk") in Arabic, the Valley of the Queens ("Biban el-Harim") and Valley of the Nobles. The Valley of the Kings today contains some 70 royal tombs. Recently, a major tomb was found containing the resting-places of 36 sons of Rameses II was discovered. After that a new valley has yielded the tombs of Aiy and Amenhotep III now open to tourists. Nevertheless, regarding the celebrated boy king, Tutankhamon whose tomb was discovered by Howard Carter in 1922, Professor John H. Clarke liked to say he: "was a minor king who got a major funeral." These remarks relate to circumstances surrounding religious conflict between Amun and the Aten worship of Amenhotep IV, Akhenaten, during the Amarna Age.

Queens were interred in the Valley of the Queens (*Biban el-Harim*). However, while Queen Hatshepsut had a tomb there, and having also built the Deir el-Bahari temple, she constructed a tomb in the Valley of the Kings. After she usurped the throne to rule as King of Egypt. Most importantly, this queen intended to build a tunnel from the mortuary temple to her tomb in the Valley of the Kings. She intended to be taken directly from the funerary temple's ceremony to the tomb internment site. Despite her builders' failure to accomplish this feat due to the softness of the soil, the architectural and engineering feat of such a venture was well within the capability of Kemetic technology, as the earliest tunnels date to the Pyramid Age of the Old Kingdom. However, and more important, this and other darings caused the Ramessides to look dis-favorably on her.

EGYPT ESSAYS ON ANCIENT KEMET

Egypt Essays Photo 57. Karnak Temple of Amon-Ra. Statues along the North/South Axis in the "Cachette Court" and before the "Seventh Pylon." These statues do not face the Axis but face parallel to it. Conversely, on the main East/West Axis, the statues face the Axis which is the path of the Sun God!

This animosity was generated primarily because she reigned as king from the time of her ascendancy to the pharaonic throne until Thutmose III ended her rule. In addition, Hatshepsut dressed as a man and wore a customary false beard. The nobleman, Senmut, her architect, built extensively for his mistress and shared great power and influence. Thutmose III was her younger brother whose throne she usurped. She reigned until his party of followers was strong enough to challenge Senmut's party dominance in support of the Queen and finally unseat her. In vengeance, Thutmose's adherents removed all inscriptions with her name. They also destroyed many of her statues and works, though Deir el Bahari and the obelisk at Karnak that was dedicated to her father Thutmose I and Amon were spared utter destruction though they did get some share of his vengeance. Deir el-Bahari was also dedicated to the Goddess Hathor, and there was equally a shrine for Anubis. Thutmose III also built a ten-foot wall surrounding both of her obelisks at Karnak. While the wall and one obelisk have fallen, the other obelisk still stands to this day. The fallen one lies near the "Coca Cola Temple" beside the Sacred Lake. This lake was fed by underground springs linking the sacred Nile to this solemn place within the temple of Karnak, *Iput Isut*.

Egypt Essays Photo 57a. Karnak Temple of Amon-Ra. The Temple of Amenhotep II placed perpendicular to the north/south axis.

EGYPT ESSAYS ON ANCIENT KEMET

Rameses III also constructed a temple at Karnak. Thus, Karnak, the "most select of places," boasted temples, altars, courts, a sacred lake, vestibules, enclosure walls and decorated and ruined walls, obelisks, kiosks, chapels, columns, statues, stelae, and reused blocks. There were gardens, vineyards, crafts and schools where astronomy was studied and taught; a school where art was encouraged and theology and religiosity were taught and practiced.

There are Royal Tombs at el-Kurna dating back to the XIth Dynasty, Dra Abu el-Naga to the XVIIth Dynasty, and XVIII-XXth Dynasty Kings in the Valley, including the spectacular tomb of Tutankhamon. The village that housed workmen of the period is called Deir el-Medina. There are also rock-cut tombs dating from the sixth Dynasty down to the Greco-Roman period that are located at Beni Hasan in Middle Egypt/Kemet.

At Nagada and Tukh, are predynastic and early dynastic cemeteries. They contain mastaba tombs of the reign of Aha, of the First Dynasty. Coupled with Abydos, which had cemeteries of most of the nobility, including early Dynastic Royal Tombs, they can represent important sources for history and early development of Upper Nile Valley culture. The prominence of Abydos, site of the head of Osiris, and where Seti I and Rameses II built temples not discounting Petrie's "Ten temples at Abydos" allowed it to boast wondrous inscriptions and some of the most beautiful and surviving artwork in all the land. It is also the only place to see the setting up of the Tet of Osiris, his backbone. Also important, it is the only surviving temple dedicated to seven deities.

Egypt Essays Illustration 25. Stele of Tehuti, a royal kinsman of the King's throne and Ka-priest of the King. XIIth Dynasty (left); and Limestone sepulchral stele of Nbekht-Anher dated in the 7th year of the reign of Khakauri Usertesen (Senusert III) III. XIIth Dynasty (right).

EGYPT ESSAYS ON ANCIENT KEMET

Egypt Essays Photo 57b. A native Egyptian Guide stands before the south side of the Eighth Pylon with its statues placed here by Thutmose III.

Dendera or the sixth Nome is part of an area that includes the fourth, fifth, seventh, and eighth and ninth Nomes. In this area are located Thebes, Koptos, Dendera, Diospolis Parva, Abydos and Thinis. In-as-much as a great deal has been recovered these ancient sites still contain many remains, yet to be excavated. The evidence therefore holds, Africa and Ethiopia spoke through Upper Egypt/ancient Kemet, and can be considered the anvil upon which Kemetic/Egyptian culture impacted so significantly upon the ancient world, allowing that legacy to be foundation in western fields of thought and artistic practice. Here is overwhelming evidence as to why, in most cases, the influence of the south always seemed to rule supreme over the north. While the south, however, held religious and economic relevance, the lower land had political, economic and administrative significance. This northern region was the gateway to Asia as well as the entranceway into Africa. Yet still, when the nation was divided or invaded, help came in great abundance from the south as in the case of the great military generals Narmer, Mentuhotep, Ahmose, and Piankhy, Shabaka, and Taharka who

FREDERICK MONDERSON

unified the country. These uniters of the two lands were great Egyptians, Africans, whose ethics, mentality, courage and creativity, are worth emulating by today's young Black scholars and citizens.

REFERENCES

Adams, Barbara. *Predynastic Egypt*. Bucks: Shire Publications, (1988).

Baines, John and Jaromir Malek. *Atlas of Ancient Egypt*. New York: Facts on File, (1980).

Brugsch, H. *Egypt Under the Pharaohs*. Vol. I. London: John Murray, Albemarle Street, 1881.

Budge, E. A. Wallis. *Dwellers on the Nile*. New York: Robert Blum, Publishers, Inc., (1972).

Carpiceci, Alberto Carlo. *Art and History of Egypt*. Florence, Italy: Bonechi, 1994.

Egypt Essays Photo 58. Karnak Temple of Amen-Ra. From the south along the North/South axis, view of the southern face of the "Ninth Pylon" constructed by Horemhab.

EGYPT ESSAYS ON ANCIENT KEMET

10. TEMPLE OF ISIS AT PHILAE

The Temple of Isis of Philae offers one of the most amazing sites in today's Egypt reflective of the ancient culture establishing links with the earliest architectural and artistic construction method and religious thinking and practice. The temple is a sight to behold as one approaches from the river for it seems to rise out of the water, a short distance from the High Dam at Aswan. Up close and as one penetrates its interior structure, the temple reveals its magnificence that sets it apart from most others of this age. Even as one leaves after an exhilarating visit, its beauty seems to beckon as if saying: "Come back soon!" Maspero says of the Temple of Isis at Philae, now relocated to Agilka Island, that retains much of its color, but "there is no building out of Thebes that gives so favorable an impression of Egyptian art as this. It is true it's far less sublime than many, but hardly one can be quoted as more beautiful."

From the earliest times, it was believed the source of the Nile was connected with the Island of Philae, making it a very special place in Egyptian cosmogony and religious practice. This may be because, as Strelocke (1965: 52) wrote: "Just before the northern tip of the island are a number of rocks with inscriptions-boundary stones marking the southernmost limits of the Pharaonic Kingdom." Of course, at different times the border extended way beyond this Aswan region. Nevertheless, this meant the Temple of Isis was built in Nubia, Land of the Ethiopians. However, and significantly, while the Head of Osiris was buried at Abydos, his heart was thought to be buried at Philae, making the Goddess's temple even more special. Morally, in the worship of Isis, such principles as Ma'at-balance, beauty, order, truth, etc., were foremost and rightfully embodied African womanhood. Here we see the essential roots of the complimentarity of African male-female principles of cooperation, respect, love and faithfulness in full operation.

FREDERICK MONDERSON

Egypt Essays Photo 59. Luxor Temple of Amenhotep III. Sphinxes line the Dromos or "Avenue of Sphinxes" give access to two seated statues, one of two remaining obelisks, and one of four remaining standing statues entrancing the temple. Look closely, beyond the entrance opening another seated statue and beginning of the columns of the "Processional Colonnade."

Egypt Essays Photo 59a. Luxor Temple of Amenhotep III. A broken head from a seated statue of Rameses II.

EGYPT ESSAYS ON ANCIENT KEMET

Egypt Essays Photo 60. Luxor Temple of Amenhotep III. This gentleman claims to be the "Keeper of the Temple."

Blending the principles of nature with architecture and art, the Kemetic/Egyptian artist achieved quintessential mastery of the materials and complexity of his art form, viz., wood, stone, metal, painting, sculpture, architecture, etc. However, with Greek inventiveness came changes in size, structure, art motifs and inscriptions whether in temples, or on civic projects, stelae, correspondence, etc. Nevertheless, and yet, underscoring this view, Smith (1981: 422) could argue: "Alexandrian artists, in general, made little more than a playful use of misunderstood Egyptian motifs, much as such Egyptian elements entered into the fashionable decorative scheme of Imperial Rome or as they were revived in Napoleonic France."

Yet still, Bratton (1987: 22) boasts proudly: "No Sumerian, Babylonian or Persian sculpture can compare with the Egyptian in draftsmanship, mastery of form or sense of proportion. No ancient sculpture except possibly the Greek has such a universal appeal. Goethe recognized the classical nature of the Egyptian sculpture in his comparison of the 'black basalt' figures with the Greek 'white marble.'"

For a better understanding of the period, we need to take notice of the benefits of cultural syncretism generated in the interaction, during Graeco-Roman rule in Egypt, 332 B.C. to 395 A.D. (*Nile Year* 3908-4635). The dynamics of the rich heritage of the Nile helped in cultivating many positive and constructive contributions for the period, particularly in the proliferation of literature. So much of Graeco-Roman classical literature in papyrus was recovered in Egypt, and now housed by the hundreds of thousands, in European institutions, there is hardly a doubt Egyptian culture influenced the creation or evolution of Greek genius!

Egypt Essays Illustration 26. Herdsmen giving accounts of cattle.

EGYPT ESSAYS ON ANCIENT KEMET

An Obelisk found at Philae and now at Kingston Hall in Dorsetshire, England, played a significant part in the decipherment of Hieroglyphics/*Medu Netcher*, to which Champollion is rightly credited with so much.

However, we need to remember, an equal number of negative and destructive acts were also associated with foreign rule in Egypt. Modern "rescue" of antiquities, particularly papyrus were often clothed in skullduggery, thievery, and usurpation. Enumerating these negatives allows mention of the conquest and incorporation of Egypt/Kemet into the Graeco-Roman military and culture complex. With this came the arrogance and the audacity of some rulers who assumed god-like stature under playful guises of worshiping and glorifying the native deities. This notwithstanding, the Temple of Isis on Philae, so close to the earliest views of the origin of the source of the Nile, that King Zoser of the Third Dynasty, who built his Step-Pyramid at Sakkara, once enquired of the priests of the Temple of Isis, whether this was indeed the source of the Nile. So the temple must be envisioned as very early manifesting cosmic, etiological, esthetical and ethical relevance in the evolution of Egyptian culture. Therefore, clearly and significantly, evidence of African theosophy, theology, spirituality, metaphysics, linked to the Nile River in its flow from interior Africa, can be searched for and seen in this mound of genesis.

In as much as Toby Wilkinson's discoveries in the Eastern Desert and Bauval and Brophy in the Western Desert at Nabta Playa provide evidence for reconsideration of pharaonic beginnings and that these inhabitants influenced the culture complex around Philae, Aswan, Abu Simbel and Upper Egypt, more than "1000 years before Winkler's Mesopotamians," more credence needs be accorded these Africans in not simply laying the foundations but propelling the culture to its great achievements.

FREDERICK MONDERSON

Egypt Essays Photo 60a. Luxor Temple of Amenhotep III. A close-up of one of the surviving sphinxes of the Dromos.

Egypt Essays Photo 60b. Luxor Temple of Amenhotep III. Seated statues wearing the "White Crown" of Rameses II outside and a seated statue beyond the "Pylon" beside the "Processional Colonnade."

EGYPT ESSAYS ON ANCIENT KEMET

Among the negatives may be mentioned one Ptolemaic pharaoh of Egypt, who replaced the head of the crocodile god Sobek. In its stead he placed his head or features on the body of this ancient and important deity. Such a caricature is shown at Sobek's temple at Kom Ombo where pronounced differences in representational art are seen. Also, during the Ptolemaic and Roman period of rule, Egypt came under more active and thorough foreign administration. In this regard, heavy taxes were levied against the people. In another, the nation's agricultural bounty was used to feed peoples of the eastern and northern Mediterranean. This land, in Northeast Africa, first fed the Hellenistic world and later as a Province became the breadbasket of Rome. It also served to advance European states' mercantile and political interests in the region.

In addition, because the Greeks had been such harsh rulers during the Ptolemaic dynasty, the Roman invasion of 30 B.C., *Nile Year* 4210, led by Julius Caesar, was "welcomed" by the people to end Ptolemaic rule over Egypt. Yet still, the resulting fiasco between Cleopatra, Ptolemy, Julius Caesar, Mark Anthony, Caesarian and Octavian, represented a shameful and infamous culmination of the history and culture of a proud people. Then again, some scholars would say, Cleopatra, an "African Queen," played all the cards she was dealt in the ancient world's changing geo-political dynamics of empire during the waning twilight of the history of her people who were pioneers in inventions, art, craft, religion and science.

Even more, as developments unfolded, the Romans occupied the city of Alexandria, named after the son of Philip of Macedon. This port, however, had existed from the earliest times. Though the famous Alexandrian lighthouse was located here, very few other contributions to the city have survived to this day. However, the more famous Alexandrian School of philosophers and later Christian thinkers did flourish here and their impact on that region and later Western civilization was constructively enormous. In this profound literary and philosophic expression, Thebans were significantly represented in the *intellectual body politic* of this age. The shaping of western theology, epistemology, aesthetics and ethics synthesized well at the end of the majestic Nile, from whence Central Africa's cultural effluence flowed and Africans were in the forefront making lasting contributions in this growth of the human mind.

Lastly, and most important, Alexandria housed a famous library of great significance to ancient Kemet. Here was accumulated one of the ancient world's great repository of esoteric, philosophic, religious and scientific knowledge. This "light of the ancient world" was accumulated over thousands of years. In 30 B.C., while engaging Kemetic/Egyptian forces, the Romans burnt the sacred collection. The loss of this library sounded the death-knell for ancient Kemet, as its traditions were recorded, preserved, and practiced. Some scholars further believe the last priests who possessed the secret knowledge of the culture and keys to understanding the ancient hieroglyphic writings were all put to death. If so, this must have had a significant impact and so contributed to the culture's demise.

Egypt Essays Photo 61. Luxor Temple. Cartouche of Rameses II *Usr-Ma'at-Ra* beside his seated statue before the "Pylon."

EGYPT ESSAYS ON ANCIENT KEMET

Egypt Essays Photo 61a. Luxor Temple of Amenhotep III. The last of four standing statues of Rameses II outside the "Pylon."

Equally too, without question there were some positive contributions made during this last breath of ancient Kemet. These were

FREDERICK MONDERSON

highlighted beyond the architectural wonders of Philae, Kalabsha, Kom Ombo Edfu and Esna. The Greek writer, Herodotus of Helicarnus visited Kemet/Egypt in c 450 B.C. He is considered the "father of history." Yet, the *Annals* of Tuthmose III's wars in Asia are recounted on the walls of the great temple at Karnak more than a millennium earlier. In addition, the wars of Rameses II against the Hittites are recounted on the walls of the entrance to Luxor Temple, Abu Simbel and the Ramesseum, all built by that pharaoh. The question is then: "Were these works by 'native Egyptian/Kemetic historians?'" The significance is that Greeks and later Europeans and their American descendants "name" people and events from their Eurocentric perspective, for purposes of control and dominance.

This notwithstanding; Herodotus made several important contributions to understanding Egyptian/Kemetic history and culture. He is credited with the statement "Egypt is the gift of the Nile" though it has been argued Hecataeus of Miletus, who visited before him, may have made the same statement or observation. Nonetheless, an early traveler, Herodotus, wrote his *Histories* in nine books. Book II, *Euterpe*, was devoted entirely to Egypt. Ethnologically and historically, this book helped preserve many vestiges of the culture based on Herodotus' observations and talks with priests, the intellectuals of their day. Thanks to him, we know much regarding the flora, fauna, fishes, festivals and frolics of the Nile Valley culture; though he dismissed the idea of melting snow atop mountain peaks in Central Africa, source of the rich effervescence of the Nile.

EGYPT ESSAYS ON ANCIENT KEMET

Egypt Essays Photo 61b. Luxor Temple of Amenhotep III. Beyond the First Pylon, an ancient survival refurbished with mud-bricks in structure and columns.

Important, both anthropologically and ethnologically, Herodotus' statement that: "Egyptians, Colchians and Ethiopians" have "broad noses, thick lips, and were burnt of skin" has elicited extensive commentaries, both positively and negatively. However, while Herodotus depicted these people of Africa, he did not say with whom he compared their features. Today more than ever, this ethnological description is important in the reclaiming of Egypt as African.

Egypt Essays Illustration 27. The weighing of the Heart of Ani, the scribe, in the Great scales in the Judgment Hall of Osiris (From the Papyrus of Ani (left); and Horus, the son of Isis, introducing the Scribe Ani, who has been declared to be a "Speaker of Truth" by Thoth, into the presence of Osiris; the Scribe Ani kneeling before Osiris, from the Papyrus of Ani (left).

FREDERICK MONDERSON

One of Herodotus' lasting contributions, moreover, was his attempts to understand funerary practices along the Nile, which he wrote on extensively. From his *Histories* and the *Lives of Plutarch*, a later Greek writer, we have an accurate description of funerary behavior and the process of mummification. Plutarch wrote on the "Myth of Osiris and Isis," for which the Temple of Isis on Philae had been the nucleus of this cult. Here Osiris' heart was buried, after the Goddess had located it in her faithful and relentless search and lamentations following her husband's murder at the hands of his evil brother Seth and aided by accomplices.

Following Herodotus, Manetho of Sebennytus is the next important writer on ancient Kemet. Manetho was a Kemetic/Egyptian Priest of the second century B.C. He lived during the reign of Ptolemy II (285-247 B.C.). This knowledgeable writer with access to the most ancient sacred and esoteric knowledge is responsible for dividing Kemetic/Egyptian history into 30 dynasties from Menes to Alexander 3200-332 B.C. His book *Aegyptopica* has not survived except in fragments and commentaries by ancient writers such as Josephus and Eusebius.

Egypt Essays Photo 61c. Luxor Temple of Amenhotep III. View of the area east of the Great Pylon.

EGYPT ESSAYS ON ANCIENT KEMET

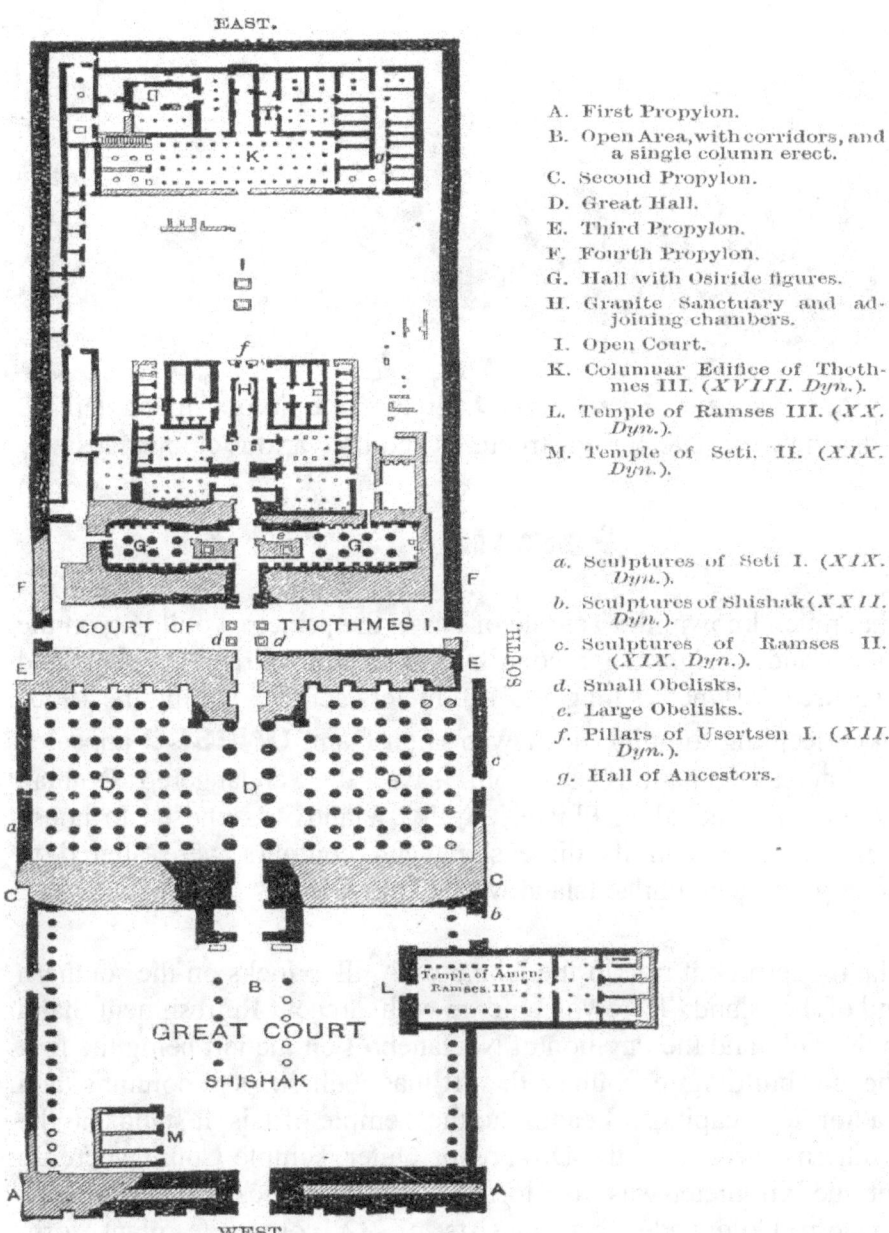

Egypt Essays Plan of Karnak Temple.

FREDERICK MONDERSON

Egypt Essays Photo 61d. Luxor Temple of Amenhotep III. From the west, late period structures and the various colonnades.

Part II.

That much known, the Temple of Isis is the principal building on the island and a significant contribution of the period. The island measured 450 meters long and 150 meters across. During the 1960s upon deciding to build the Aswan High Dam, **UNESCO** appealed to interested nations to help save the endangered Nubian monuments, including Philae. Agilka Island was chosen to house Philae temple, and its dimensions and contours were altered to exactly replicate Philae Island with its monuments.

The modern boat ride to the Island of Agilka docks on the southern end of the island. Here you emerge with a recent Refreshment Stand to the right and the Pavilion of Nectanebo I on the left being the first ancient building encountered. It has bell-shaped columns and Hathor head capitals. Leading to the Temple of Isis, it stands on the southern entrance of the Dromos or Outer Temple Court where an antique Nilometer was also located. In this majestic court with its Western Colonnade that consists of 32 composite plant form columns with reliefs, according to Wayne (1987: 276) the Roman Emperor Tiberius is shown "offering gifts to the gods, the capitals of

EGYPT ESSAYS ON ANCIENT KEMET

varying plant motifs, no two alike." The East Colonnade consists of 17 columns in an unfinished state. To the right of the court and at the southern end of the east colonnade is the *Temple of Aresnufi*, near midway is the *Temple of Mandulis* and at the northern end is the *Temple of Imhotep*. Deified as the Greek *Aesculapius*, Imhotep became the Kemetic/Egyptian God of Medicine, having practiced as a physician two thousand years before Hippocrates, the western "father of medicine."

Budge I (1969: 523) states that an inscription on a door of Imhotep's Temple read: "Great one, son of Ptah, the creative god, made by Thenen, begotten by him and beloved by him, the god of divine forms in the temples, who giveth life to all men, the mighty one of wonders, the maker of times, who cometh unto him that calleth upon him wheresoever he may be, who giveth sons to the childless, the chief Kher-heb (the wisest and most learned one), the image and likeness of Thoth the wise."

Egypt Essays Photo 62. Luxor Temple of Amenhotep III. "Ramessean Front." On the southeast wall of the "Great Court," sons of Rameses II in Procession to the Temple of Luxor illustrated to the far left.

FREDERICK MONDERSON

Egypt Essays Photo 62a. Luxor Temple of Amenhotep III. "Ramessean Front." One of the fat cows led by priests in the procession of the sons of Rameses II.

Egypt Essays Photo 62b. Luxor Temple of Amenhotep III. "Ramessean Front." Rameses II sits enthroned within a shrine with flags being flown above him.

EGYPT ESSAYS ON ANCIENT KEMET

At the end of the Dromos is the First Pylon of the temple with its two massive towers that are 120 feet wide and 60 feet high. On the exterior face are colossal sculptures of divinities and Ptolemy Philometer swinging his battle-axe over a batch of bound prisoners. The name of Nectanebo is found on this pylon, to the left.

The Temple of Isis was begun by Ptolemy Philadelphus and Arsinoe, and completed by succeeding monarchs; among whom are Euergetes I, Philometer, his brother Euergetes II, with two Cleopatras, and Ptolemy the elder son of Auletes, whose name is found in the area and on the pylon. Many of the sculptures of the exterior are of the later epoch of the Roman emperors, Augustus, Tiberius, Claudius, Domitian, Nerva and Trajan.

The principal entrance through the First Pylon is that of Philadelphus. The second entrance is that of Nectanebo. These portals lead into the Central Court of the Temple of Isis. To the east is a colonnade, called the second Eastern Colonnade boasting 7 columns. To the west is the *Mammisi* or Birth House aligned with the entrance of Nectanebo. The Birth House has columns in front and at its rear. Further east of the *Mammisi* is the new Nilometer, which leads down to the river. The average length of the cubit on the Nilometer is 1 ft. 8.9 in., being almost the same as that of the average cubit on the Nilometer of Elephantine Island.

At the northern end of the court on a different axis is the Second Pylon of the temple proper, of a much smaller size than the First Pylon. This second pylon is actually the First Pylon of the Temple of Isis. The eastern tower of the Second or rather First Pylon bears an inscription, which mentions grants of land made to the temple by Ptolemy Philometer and Ptolemy Euergetes II. This Gate of Ptolemy at the Second Pylon or "First Pylon" leads to a Pronaos or Hypostyle Hall with 10 gigantic columns, all remarkable for the brilliancy of the colors still remaining on their capitals. The walls and ceiling are covered with astronomical and other subjects, and figures of divinities. In this hall, and in other parts of the temple, the presence of the cross may be taken as evidence of the existence of the church of St. Stephen, into which this temple is said to have been turned at the end of the sixth century.

This Hypostyle Hall entrances into three chambers in succession, of which the last was the Sanctuary, a monolithic granite shrine. On the wall is a representation of Ptolemy Philadelphus, suckled by Isis. On either side of these chambers are other rooms, in the first of which on the right will be found the latitude and longitude of the island, as taken by the scientific members of the French expedition. Near this room is the entrance to crypts and hidden passages, similar to those at Denderah. From the corresponding lateral chamber on the opposite side a staircase leads to the terrace. During the Graeco-Roman Period, the divinity's corporeal form was taken to the roof to be bathed in the rays of the Sun God Re.

On the left, at the top of the staircase, is a small room covered with interesting sculptures relating to the death and resurrection of Osiris. Flaubert's commentary, according to Wayne (1987: 278) states: "In one of the upper rooms, scenes of embalming: in the corner to the right a woman on her knees lamenting, her arms raised in despair; here the artist's observation cuts through the ritual of the conventional form." From Greek ex-votos in this chamber, we learn the interesting fact that the worship of Isis and Osiris was still carried on at Philae in A.D. 453, more than 70 years after the *Edict of Theodosius* abolishing the religion of ancient Kemet.

On the east side of the Temple of Isis, is a small Temple of Hathor, built by Ptolemy VI Philometer and Euergetes II. Wayne's (1987: 179) description states, the "colonnade was decorated during the reign of Augustus with amusing carvings of music and drinking-apes dancing and one playing a lute, dwarfish Bes beating a tambourine, while Augustus offers a festal crown to Isis." To the north of this are remains of what appears to have been an arched gate with steps down to the river. To the south of this is Trajan's Pavilion, called "Pharaoh's Bed." It is an oblong rectangular building of the late date surrounded by an inter-columnar screen with 14 columns adorned with beautifully carved floral capitals. The temple was roofed with stone slabs, supported on wooden beams,

EGYPT ESSAYS ON ANCIENT KEMET

the sockets of which still exist. Trajan is shown offering incense and wine to Isis, Osiris and Horus.

Egypt Essays Illustration 28. Cast in bronze of the head of a portrait-statue of Tutankhamon in the Egyptian Museum in Berlin (left); and seated figures of khamuast and his wife, XVIIIth Dynasty (right).

In conclusion, the Temple of Isis at Philae, called "Pearl of the Nile" by Herodotus, has also been called "vision of Paradise" as it seems to rise out of the sacred waters of the Nile. Procopius c. 540 A.D. (*Nile Year* 4780) states, according to Keating (1975: 185), at Philae; "the last stronghold of the ancient gods was reduced and their worship passed into memory. But the temples remained in romantic view for posterity to wonder at." Somewhat similar to the modern approach, Amelia Edwards wrote of the inundation at the turn of this century as Keating (1975: 185) reported: "The approach by water is quite the most beautiful. Seen from the level of a small island, with its palms, its colonnades, its pylons, seem to rise out of the river like a mirage. Piled rocks frame it in on either side, or purple mountains close-up the distance. As the boat glides nearer between glistening boulders, those sculptured towers rise higher and even higher against the sky. They show no sign of ruin or of age. All looks solid, stately, perfect. One forgets for the moment that anything is changed. If a sound of antique chanting were to be borne along the quiet air - if a procession of white-robed priests aloft the veiled ark of the God, were to come sweeping round between the palms and the pylons - we should not think it strange."

Egypt Essays Photo 63. Luxor Temple of Amenhotep III. The "Kiosk of Hatshepsut" dedicated to the Theban Triad and usurped by Thutmose and later Rameses II stands in the "Ramessean Front."

Egypt Essays Photo 63a. Luxor Temple of Amenhotep III. "Ramessean Front." Alignment of column bases.

EGYPT ESSAYS ON ANCIENT KEMET

Egypt Essays Photo 63b. Luxor Temple of Amenhotep III. "Ramessean Front." Statues seemingly coming out from between the columns. White Crown heads lie on the ground.

This observation was made following the temple's submersion due to the first or "Low Dam" at Aswan during the Inundation. Even more importantly, however, Bratton (1968: 264) has quoted the words found on one of the portals of the temple.

"The Holy Mound is the sacred golden domain of Osiris and his sister Isis. It was predestined therefore from the beginning (of the world) ... Let there every day be divine service by the appointed high priest; let there be a libation to Isis, Lady of Philae, when the libation of each day is poured. Let there be no beating of drums or playing of harps or flutes. No man shall ever enter here; no one, great or small, shall tread upon this spot. None here shall raise his voice during the sacred time of the days when Isis, Lady of Philae, who is enthroned, shall be here to pour the libation each tenth day. Isis, Lady of Philae, will embark for the Sacred Mound on the holy days, in the sacred bark of which the name is ... (effaced)."

One is therefore constantly reminded of Dr. ben-Jochannan's admonition that a particular decorum must be paramount for all visitors and that certain parts of the temple in reverence, must not be entered by African-American visitors. Still, some misguided brothers and sisters insist they enter those sacred and prohibited domains and bathe in the power of its aura. We must insist they not do so, for too often Europeans and Arabs disrespect the temple by doing just that. Nevertheless, the Temple of Isis is one of the great repositories of African spirituality, cosmic force, religiosity, artistic and architectural accomplishments as well as philosophical, epistemological and scientific knowledge that African-Americans can take great pride in. As a result, we must teach the children to honor, worship and respect the notion of African womanhood in all its godliness and pristine beauty that the Temple of Isis came to represent for this makes us all proud and strong.

REFERENCES

Baines, John and Jaromir Malek. *The Atlas of Ancient Egypt*. New York: Facts on File, 1980.

ben-Jochannan, Yosef A. A. *From Abu Simbel to Ghizeh*. Baltimore, MD.: Black Classics Press, 1989.

Bratton, Fred Gladstone. *A History of Egyptian Archaeology*. New York: Thomas Y. Crowell, 1968.

Budge, E. A. Wallis. *Dwellers on the Nile*. New York: Benjamin Bloom, Inc., 1972.

_____. *Gods of the Egyptians*. 2 Vols. New York: Dover Publishers, Inc., (1904) 1969.

Carpiececi, Alberto Carlo. *Art and History of Egypt*. Florence, Italy: Bonechi, 1994.

Chalaby, Abbas. *All of Egypt*. Italy: Bonechi, 1995.

Haag, Michael. *Guide to Egypt*. London: Michael Haag, 1987.

Herodotus. *The Histories*. Translated by Aubrey de Selincourt. Revised, with an Introduction and Notes by A. R. Burn. Baltimore, MD.: Penguin Books, (1954) 1976.

Hobson, Christine. *The World of the Pharaohs*. London: Thames and Hudson, 1987.

Kamil, Jill. *Upper Egypt: Historical Outline and Descriptive Guide to the Ancient Sites*. New York: Longman Inc., 1983.

Keating, Rex. *Nubian Rescue*. New York: Hawthorn Books, Inc., 1975.

EGYPT ESSAYS ON ANCIENT KEMET

Magi, Giovanna. *Aswan*: *Philae*, *Abu Simbel*. Italy: Bonechi, 1989.
Obenga, Theophile. *Ancient Egypt and Black Africa*. Chicago: Karnak House, 1992.
Smith, W. Stephenson. *The Art and Architecture of Ancient Egypt*. New York: Penguin Books, (1958) 1991.
Strelocke, Hans. *Egypt*: Polyglot Travel Guide. Cairo: Lehnert and Landrock, 1965.
Thomas, Angela P. *Egyptian Gods and Myths*. Bucks: Shire Publications, 1986.
Wayne, Scott. *Egypt and the Sudan*: *A Travel Survival Kit*. Berkeley, Calif.: Lonely Planet Publications, 1987.

Egypt Essays Photo 64. Luxor Temple of Amenhotep III. More bases of the columns of the Peristyle Colonnade in the "Ramessean Front."

FREDERICK MONDERSON

Egypt Essays Photo 64a. Luxor Temple of Amenhotep III. Another view of the columns featured in the previous image, in the northwest corner of the "Ramessean Front" "Peristyle Court."

Egypt Essays Photo 64b. Luxor Temple. From the southwest, view of the magnificent "Processional Colonnade" with its 14-open calyx columns enclosed by two short walls whose inner face depict the journey to and from Luxor to celebrate the "Opet Festival," the purpose for the Temple of Luxor.

EGYPT ESSAYS ON ANCIENT KEMET

11. THEBES

Thebes of the Greeks and Romans, *Luxor* of the Arabs and *Waset* or *Tape* of the people of ancient Kemet/Egypt, equally *Thaba* of the Memphitic dialect of Coptic, is home to the most splendid ruins of ancient civilization. So much so that, nine out of ten visitors to the Nile Valley, travel and come to this important nucleus of the Upper Kingdom and capital of the Empire during the Middle and New Kingdom, to see its temples, courts, statues, tombs, art, etc. In the perennial north/south competitive balance so important to its history and the stability and vibrancy of the state, Erman (1894: 16) has written, "... in the time of the Old Empire the Delta was far behind the southern part of the country in civilization. The civilization of Lower Egypt progressed slowly. We find traces of this process in the names of places in Upper Egypt, e.g., Thebes and Edfu. The colonists from the south carried the names of their old homes to their new settlements, in the same way as our colonists have done in America."

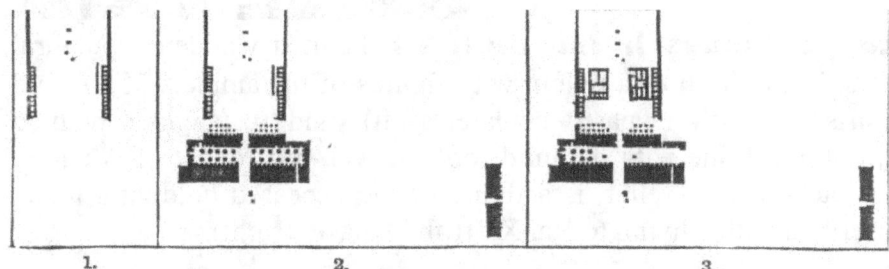

1. Karnak before the time of Thothmes I., B.C. 1633.
2. Karnak during the reign of Thothmes I.
3. Karnak during the reign of Queen Hatshepsut, B.C. 1600.

Egypt Essays Plan of the Temple of Karnak during the reigns of Thutmose I and Hatshepsut.

Sauernon (1962: 282) believed, Thebes "is still the place where Egyptian architectural genius demonstrates its most enduring and successful results." It is also the place where patronage of the arts has helped depict the wonderful heritage of this great ancient

FREDERICK MONDERSON

African City. Breasted's (1923: 149) geographic description locates Thebes, "the Heliopolis of the south," along the mighty waterway.

Egypt Essays Illustration 29. Painted wooden sepulchral chest in the form of a pylon, with figures of the amulets of Isis and Osiris, XXVIth Dynasty or later (left); and rectangular painted limestone shrine with pyramid roof, of Ani, a gardener of Amarna. On each side, in relief, is a figure of the deceased holding a tablet inscribed with a hymn to Ra, XVIIIth Dynasty (right).

"Some four hundred and forty miles above Memphis, and less than one hundred and forty miles below the first cataract, along the stretch of Nile about forty miles above the great bend, where the river approaches most closely to the Red Sea before turning abruptly away from it, the scanty margin between river and cliffs expands into a broad and fruitful plain in the midst of which now lie the mightiest ruins of ancient civilization to be found anywhere in the world. These are the wrecks of Thebes, the world's first great monumental city."

EGYPT ESSAYS ON ANCIENT KEMET

In hieroglyphic it is written AP or APE, with the feminine article T-APE, the meaning of which is said to be "head," Thebes being the "head" or capital of the Upper Kingdom. Homer, in the *Odyssey*, 477; XIV, 257; visits Egypt and Erman (1894: 21) recounts: "Royal Thebes, Egyptian treasure-house of countless wealth who boasts her hundred gates, through each of which with horse and cart two hundred warriors march."

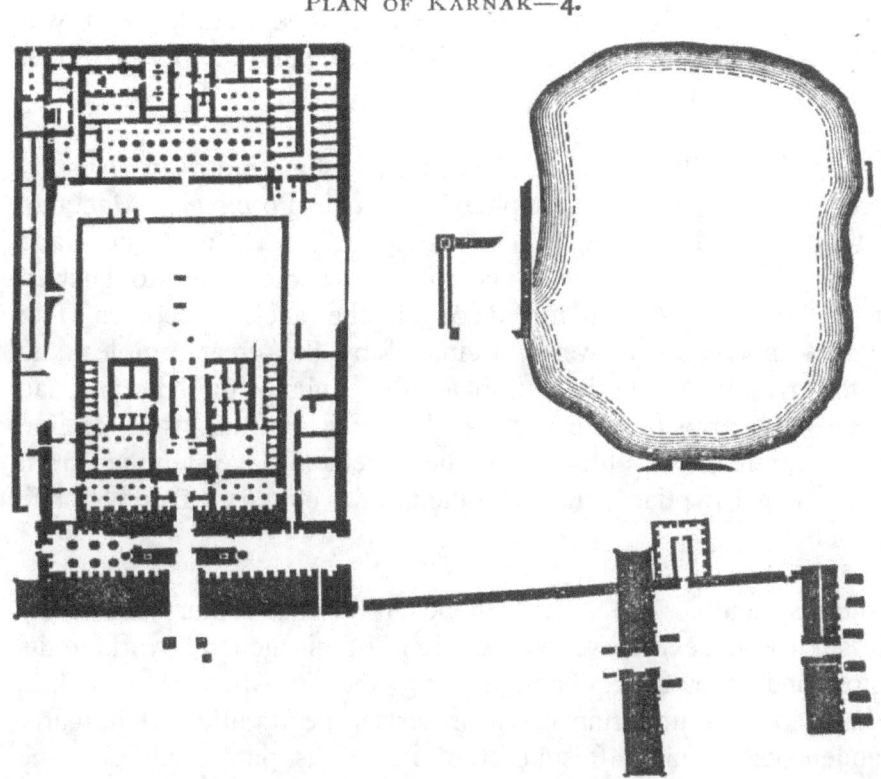

Karnak during the reign of Thothmes III., B.C. 1600.
From Mariette, *Karnak*, Pl. VI.

Egypt Essays Plan of Karnak Temple during the reign of Thutmose III.

Homer is an interesting character, for Diop (1991: 153) accordingly states: "All the anachronisms of the Homeric poems, pointed out by

FREDERICK MONDERSON

M. I. Fineleu, might be explained by using Egypt as a reference: the sumptuous 'palaces,' bearing no relationship to the Mycenaean 'palaces,' rather remind one of those of the city of 'Thebes of the hundred gates,' and it is now known that this verse of Homer refers to the city of Thebes at the time of Ramses III. If Homer visited Egypt - and this fact is attested to by Greek tradition - it was probably during the time of the XXVth Sudanese Dynasty, under Piankhi or Shabaka, around 750 B.C."

Nahum III. 8-9; some say Hecataeus, but more importantly Herodotus, "Greek Philosophers" Solon, Porphyry, Manetho, Strabo; all had commentaries on Egypt/Kemet, or Amon and Thebes. Many other Greeks visited Egypt and traveled to Thebes. Fagan (1975: 14-15) believed of all the ancient peoples, the: "Greeks and Romans were fascinated by the great temples and mighty pyramids that still dominated the banks of the Nile and had obviously been there for centuries. The basic institutions of religion and government were thought by the Greeks to have stemmed from the Ancient Egyptians, the inhabitants of a country full of strange wonders."

Diodorus Siculus, who visited Thebes in the first century before the Christian era, devotes several sections of his general work to its history and appearance. Though he saw the city when it had sunk to quite secondary importance, he preserves the tradition of its early grandeur-its circuit 140 staid, the size of its public edifices, the magnificence of its temples, the number of its monuments, the dimensions of its private houses, some of them four or five stories high - all giving it an air of grandeur and beauty surpassing not only all other cities of Egypt, but of the world.

EGYPT ESSAYS ON ANCIENT KEMET

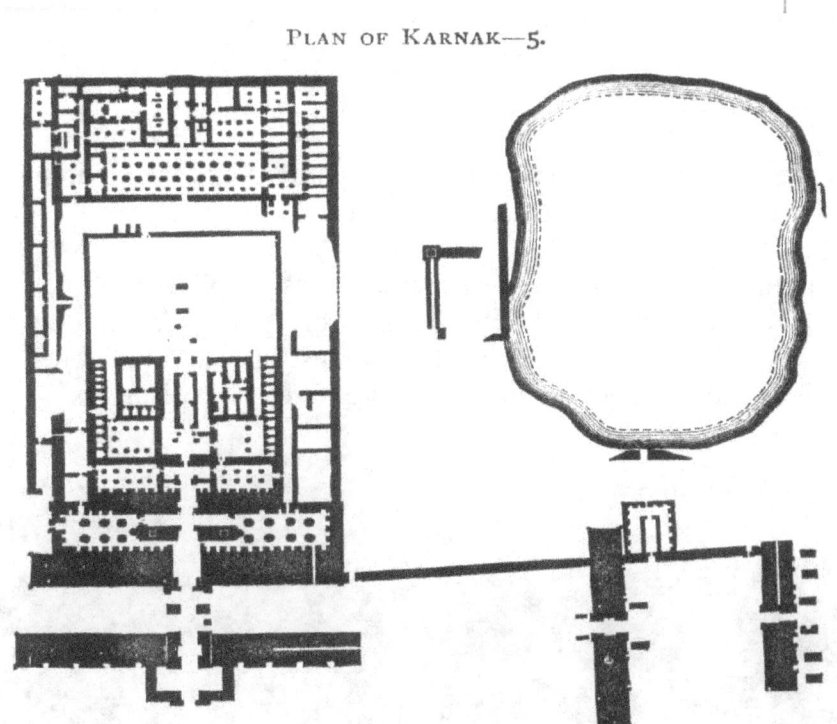

Karnak during the reign of Amenophis III., B.C. 1500.
From Mariette, *Karnak*, Pl. VI.

Egypt Essays Plan of Karnak Temple during the reign of Amenhotep III.

John Jackson, in *Introduction to African Civilizations* (1970: 109-110), supplies a more modern view of this endearing city. "Thebes itself expanded into a great metropolis with walls nine miles in circumference. On the outskirts of the city were the elegant mansions of the nobility, some containing fifty or sixty rooms, and halls with the walls covered with colorful paintings, and embellished with costly inlaid furniture, beautiful vases, and attractively carved ornaments and utensils of ebony, bronze, and ivory. Along the great river, temples were built by the order of the king, and were linked together by avenues of sphinxes. Around the mansions and temples were tree-shaded boulevards and flower gardens and the environing landscape was enhanced by a series of lakes."

Explaining the emergence of early cities, Uphill (1988: 54) introduces an interesting observation of town planning with cosmological and theological implications that allowed Theban engineers and architects to align structures over great distances.

Egypt Essays Photo 65. Luxor Temple of Amenhotep III. Ascent into the "Peristyle Court of Amenhotep III" with its closed bud calyx capitals, an attractive magnet for photographers captivated by the "play of sun and light" reflected in the waning evening sun.

EGYPT ESSAYS ON ANCIENT KEMET

Egypt Essays Photo 65a. Luxor Temple of Amenhotep III. Columns of the Hypostyle Hall beyond the "Court of Amenhotep III."

"Looking from the first pylon at Karnak a line-up with the temple of Hatshepsut at Deir el-Bahari appears immediately significant, because it is next to the Eleventh Dynasty temple of King Mentuhotep (2060-2010 B.C.). This pharaoh reunited Egypt after a long period of division and used his new great resources to create a splendid new capital, the first known major city to be laid out on axial lines in ancient times. Previously kings had done this for pyramid complexes with a causeway connecting the valley temple to the upper part of the complex, but here is a scheme stretching for 3 miles (5km) across the valley of the Nile itself."

Referring further to the strategic planning involved in the Mentuhotep mortuary structure, Uphill (1988: 54) continued: "Starting from the king's tomb in the western mountain, it aligns with central Karnak, where remains of the period have been found. A causeway 3/4 mile (1.2 km) long descended from the court of the temple to reach a valley entrance building, where there may have been a priests' town and canal to the river. On the plan of Thebes a line drawn continuing the causeway ends up in the Karnak area, where the royal residence must surely have been. The Twelfth Dynasty kings, although ruling from the north, maintained a major administrative center here and huge halls and other buildings have been found at the rear of the sacred lake at Karnak."

Strabo, also visiting Thebes much later, at the beginning of the Christian era described the city, shrunk in size. "'Vestiges of its magnitude still exist which extend 80 stadia in length. There are a number of temples, many of which Cambyses mutilated. The spot is at present occupied by villages. One part of it, in which is the city, lies in Arabia; another is in the country on the other side of the river, where is the Memnonium.' Strabo makes the Nile the dividing line between Libya and Arabia."

In addition, Strabo supplied a splendid description of the seated Memnon. In fact, the colossal of Amenhotep III, called "Hama and Chama," by the natives. These stood at the entranceway of the king's temple, destroyed in 27 B.C.

EGYPT ESSAYS ON ANCIENT KEMET

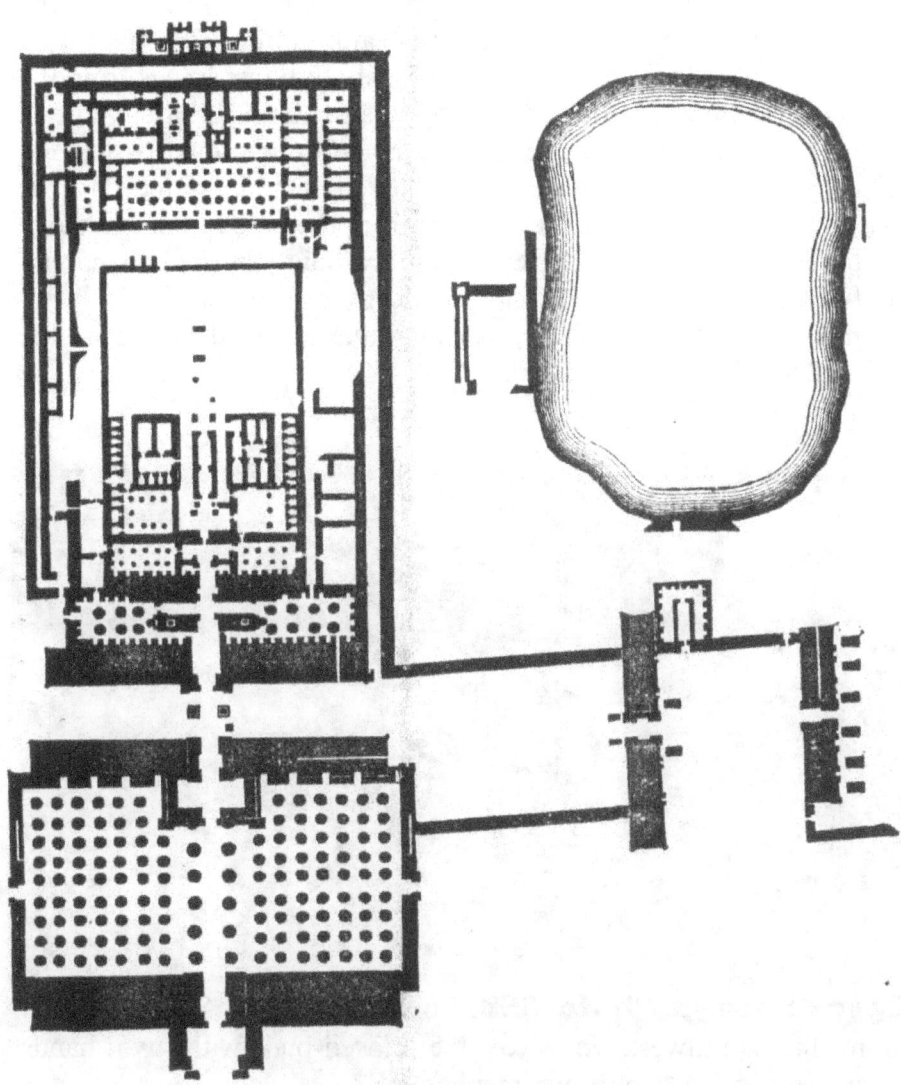

Plan of Karnak—6.

Karnak under Rameses II., B.C. 1333.
From Mariette, *Karnak*, Pl. VII.

Egypt Essays Plan of Karnak Temple under Rameses II.

FREDERICK MONDERSON

"Here are two colossal figures near one another, each consisting of a single stone. One is entire; the upper parts of the other, from the chair, are fallen down - the effect, it is said, of an earthquake. It is believed that once a day a noise, as of a slight blow, issues from the part of the statue which remains in the seat, and on its base. When I was at those places, with Aelius Gallus, and numerous friends and soldiers about him heard a noise at the first hour of the day but whether proceeding from the base, or from the colossal or produced on purpose by some of those standing around the base, I cannot confidently assert. For, from the uncertainty of the cause, I am inclined to believe anything rather than that stones disposed in that manner could send forth sound."

Egypt Essays Photo 65b. Luxor Temple of Amenhotep III. From the southwest, view of the closed-bud with two bands colonnades in the "Court of Amenhotep III."

This is clearly skepticism on the part of Diodorus! Next Lucian, another ancient commentator, described Egypt; then Pliny speaks of Thebes as "a hanging city," i.e. built upon arches, so that "an army could be led forth from beneath the city while the inhabitants above were wholly unconscious of it."

EGYPT ESSAYS ON ANCIENT KEMET

Philostratus' *Life of Apollonius*, Euphantus, Proclus, Aelian, Eudoxus, and down through the ages, Jesuit Father Claude Sicard, Thomas Shaw, Granger of Dijon, Pococke, Norden, Volney, Denon, Bruce, Higgins, etc., all these writers were fascinated with ancient Kemet/Egypt and the culture of the Thebaid and thus, they splendidly recounted some of its more enduring aspects. Equally, in modern times, a proliferation of visitors have written and expanded knowledge of these ancient Africans. Archaeological excavations have unearthed architectural creativity at Thebes, and ethnological and physiological data. Plus, on both banks of the river, there is evidenced an impressive array of worship and mortuary temples, tombs and other civil structures of this grandeur. Artists too have produced great replicas of the ancient cultural artifacts while publishers have had a bonanza printing and distributing the unearthed information that attests to trailblazing innovations in art and architecture. Kees (1977: 252) made the argument: "Thebes is a city of temples, the great temples of the gods on the eastern bank of the river at Karnak and Luxor and the royal mortuary temples on the west bank running from Qurneh in the north to Medinet Habu in the south where the land begins to rise in the direction of Armant (the ancient Hermonthis). Even in the outlying temples like that of Monthu at Medamud, far in the east across the fields, and that of el-Tod, south of Luxor, where the desert hills again come close to the river, there is more still standing than in the whole municipal areas of Memphis and Heliopolis.

Statuary, an important art and commercial industry, was even more an honor that a few distinguished individuals had bestowed upon them. Again Kees (1977: 264) provides a glimpse of this important feature and its role in the social hierarchy. "Such statues also represent those officials wearing the gold of honor or other special marks of distinction such as the double heart which Sennufer, the Mayor of Thebes under Amenhotep II, wears on his breast to signify that he was in possession of the king's heart. Statues of Amenhotep, son of Hapu, were also set up at Karnak, apparently near the pylon of Amenhotep III, at the colossal feet of his sovereign."

FREDERICK MONDERSON

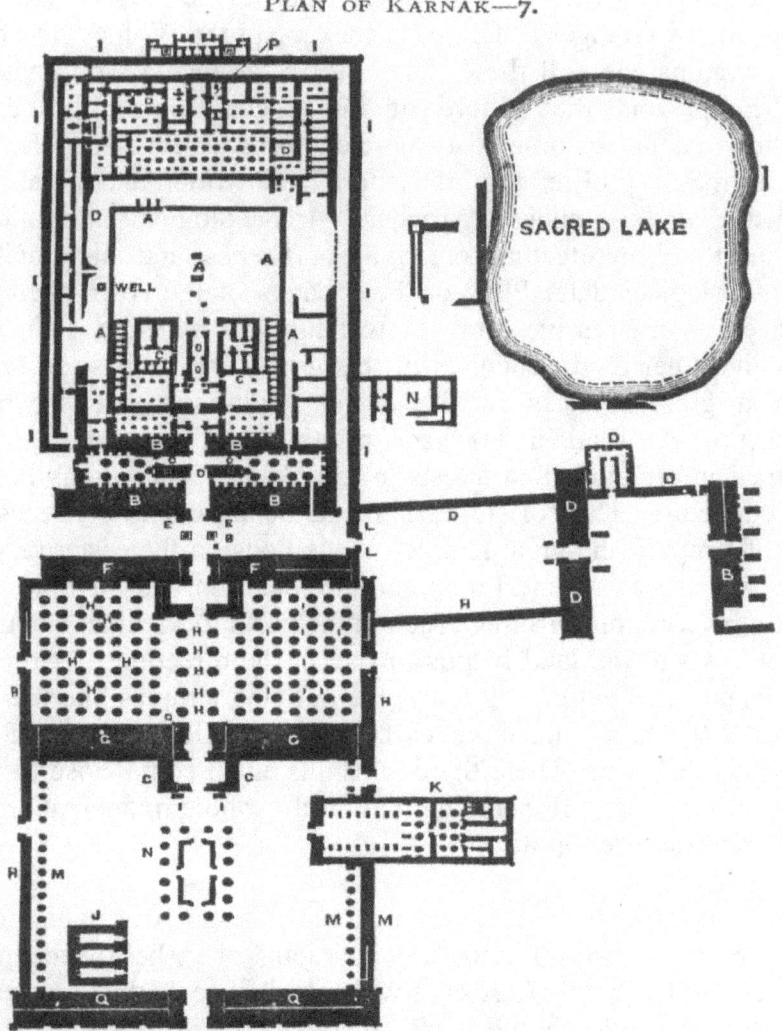

Karnak under the Ptolemies. From Mariette, *Karnak*, Pl. VII.

A. Walls standing before the time of Thothmes I.
B. Pylons built by Thothmes I.
C. Walls and obelisks of Hatshepset.
D. Walls, pylon, etc., of Thothmes III.
E. Gateway of Thothmes IV.
F. Pylon of Amenophis III.
G. Pylon of Rameses I.
H. Walls and columns of Seti I.
I. Columns, walls, and statues of Rameses II.
J. Temple of Seti II.
K. Temple of Rameses III.
L. Gateway of Rameses IX.
M. Pillars and walls of the XXIInd dynasty.
N. Pillars of Tirhakah.
O. Corridor of Philip III. of Macedon.
P. Chamber and shrine of Alexander II.
Q. Pylon built by the Ptolemies.

Karnak Under the Ptolemies from Mariette.

EGYPT ESSAYS ON ANCIENT KEMET

Egypt Essays Photo 66. Deir el Bahari Temple of Queen Hatshepsut. From the northeast, the "Birds' Eye View," of the Temple with its colonnades.

Egypt Essays Photo 66a. Deir el Bahari Temple of Queen Hatshepsut. Coming down the Mountain, view of the "First Ramp" and the "Fishes and Birds" and the "Obelisk" Colonnades.

FREDERICK MONDERSON

Egypt Essays Photo 66b. Deir el Bahari Temple of Queen Hatshepsut. A better view of the principal features of the temple. The opening below leads to the Tomb of Senmut, Queen's architect.

Even further, the mega-necropolis of the Theban massif, also called *Tanthryris*, as being under special protection of Hathor, who is sometimes called President of the West, contains the Valley of the Kings, Valley of the Queens, Valley of the Nobles and Valley of the Artisans. Combined, these areas reveal majestic architecture in temples and tombs with the most stupendous painted relief decorations and with frescoes that depict the fundamental concepts and elements of the ancient African cosmological, theological, religious and ethical belief systems. In addition, social themes of agricultural practice, technical skills, festivals and family life, all represented in picturesque art depicted in temples on the east bank and temple and tombs on the west bank of this Upper Egyptian/Kemetic capital, where indigenous creativity experimented with and gave birth to conventions of building in brick, then stone. Even more, architectural daring encouraged stone quarrying land and river transportation of massive pieces of such material, requiring mobilization of enormous manpower and innovations in boat-building and navigation, so necessary for the great distances these materials had to be transported. The resulting erection of magnificent pylons, courts, halls, obelisks, etc., and creation of Sacred Lakes as at Karnak and Luxor, Deir el Bahari, Ramesseum, Medinet Habu, Malcata, with juxtaposed gardens whose blooming and wonderful flowers were decorative and part of the daily ritual, etc., reveal construction techniques, as Browder has indicated, where "some elements are explainable, while others remain difficult to comprehend."

Looking to the causes of the power and prosperity of Thebes we see principally behind its geographical strategic significance, three sources - trade, manufacture, and religion. As such, its position as fourth Upper Kingdom Nome enabled *Waset*, the "scepter," to exploit its economic position and benefit politically by being distant from northern and foreign influences and threats. "The parallel ridges which skirt the narrow Nile Valley upon the east and west from the northern limit of Upper Egypt, here swept outward upon either side, forming a circular plain whose diameter is nearly ten miles. Through the center of the plain flows the river, usually at this point about half a mile in width, but at the inundation overflowing the plain, especially upon the western bank, for a breadth of two or more miles. Thus the two colossal statues, which are several hundred yards from the bed of the low Nile, have accumulated about their bases alluvial deposit to the depth of seven feet."

Even more important, trade during the Empire was extensive and Maspero V (1904: 32-33) describes this enterprise between Thebes, Memphis and the Asiatic cities, that came whether by vessel or caravan, and how these early nations had worked out mutual tax arrangements for merchandise coming from beyond their borders. This trade with the cities he write, "comprised slaves destined for the workshop or the harem, Hittite bulls and stallions, horses from Singar, oxen from Alasia, rare and curious animals as elephants from Nii, and bers from Lebanon, smoked and salted fish, live birds of many-colored plumage, goldsmiths' work and precious stones, of which lapis-lazuli was the chief, wood for building or for ornamental work - pine, cypress, yew, cedar, and oak, musical instruments, helmets, leathern jerkins covered with metal scales, weapons of bronze and iron, chariots, dyed and embroidered stuffs, perfumes, dried cakes, oil, wines of Kharu, liquors from Alasia, Khati, Singar, Naharaim, Amurru, and beer from Quodi."

Economic benefits also accrued to Thebes from its relations with adjacent lands to her west and south, crossroad of a great trade route. We see: "Its position on the Nile, near the great avenues through the Arabian hills to the Red Sea, and to the interior of Libya through the western desert, rendering it a common entrepot for the Indian trade on the one side, and the caravan trade with the gold, ivory and aromatic districts on the other and its comparative vicinity to the mines which intersect the limestone borders of the Red Sea, combined to make Thebes the greatest emporium in Eastern Africa, until Alexandria turned the stream of commerce into another channel."

The "Long Egyptian staples" of cotton proved superior from time immemorial and the Theban priesthood extensively produced the highest quality cotton clothing in the land. Indigenous craftsmanship was well refined and many imported raw materials, Maspero (190, V: 35) explained, were made "by means of native industry, worked up and exported as ornaments, vases, and highly decorated weapons, which in the course of international traffic, were dispersed to all four corners of the earth." In addition, the Amun priesthood's craftsmen worked glass, pottery and jewelry renowned as artistic and social possessions, as well as icons of divinity. Trade items as gold, ivory, gems, aromatics, incense, skins, etc., flowed to Thebes from Nubia. Altogether, the dynamics of this wealth was transformed into the architectural splendor of Egypt/Kemet in its magnificent temples, palaces and tombs, some of which still mystify today.

During the heyday of the imperial New Kingdom, Thebes' sacred sanctuary of Amon was considered the "throne of the two lands" signifying the enormous spiritual, philosophic, scientific and mechanical power and influence buttressed by the accompanying wealth of the Amun priesthood. The god's estates comprised

EGYPT ESSAYS ON ANCIENT KEMET

impressive and lucrative tracts of tax-exempt real property and the priesthood had care of extensive quantities of gold. The significance of Thebes can be further shown in a legal land precedent case, as a function set in the office of the Vizier, as explained by Breasted (1923: 240) who notes, "in cases concerning land in Thebes he was obliged by law to render a decision in three days, but if the land lay in the 'South or North' he required two months. This was while he was still the only vizier; when the North received its own vizier such cases there were referred to him at Heliopolis."

With devastating implications, Kamil (1986: 10) places the Theban priesthood at the head of subsequent events at the end of the New Empire. For, accordingly: "The monuments raised throughout the land during the New Kingdom, particularly those in Upper Egypt, reflect the wealth and prosperity of the nation. Unfortunately, the pharaohs fell under the domination of the high priest of Amon at Thebes, until eventually one of them seized the throne. In the 21st Dynasty, the country was once more divided: Upper Egypt was ruled by the high priests at Thebes, and Lower Egypt succumbed again to foreign invasion: Tribes of Libyan origin, Kushites from beyond Nubia, the Assyrian conquest and then, following a short lived revival known as the Saite Period, came the Persian invasions, and finally the Greek and Roman occupations."

More important, in all this, the "Opet Festival" was one of the most joyous occasions celebrated for the Theban deity, where processions of priests ventured beyond the enclosed walls of their temples. Murnane (1983: 64) offered an explanation regarding this drama involving divinity. "Amon journeyed from his temple at Karnak twice a year - once to visit the mortuary temple of the reigning king on the west bank of the Nile during the 'Feast of the Valley' and again to rest in the 'Inner Chambers [Opet] of the South' at Luxor, some two kilometers from Karnak. It was at this time that Amun, the state god visited his counterpart, the Amun who resided in Luxor Temple."

FREDERICK MONDERSON

Egypt Essays Photo 67. Deir el Bahari Temple of Queen Hatshepsut. The Tomb of Vizier Nespakashuty (664-610 B.C.) on the slope of the mountain.

Egypt Essays Photo 67a. Deir el Bahari Temple of Queen Hatshepsut. From the "Birds' Eye View, the "Second Court," "Second Ramp" and "Middle" and "Upper Colonnades."

EGYPT ESSAYS ON ANCIENT KEMET

This resulting fame and the dynamics of the imperial historical process later attracted foreign conquerors whose strategies insisted that Thebes be destroyed. Such therefore, was the attitude principally of the Assyrians under Cambyses, who did untold damage to the city and African culture. DuBois (1971: 138) tells how Ashurbanipal declared, "I captured Thebes like a flood."

Edfu and Dendera, "Graeco-Roman temples," rest on much older foundations of New Kingdom and earlier sacred places. Here, mirroring Amon's voyage from Karnak to Luxor, at the 'Feast of Beautiful Meeting' during the third month of summer, "Hathor arrived at Edfu on the afternoon of the New Moon." After elaborate welcoming ceremonies, the statues of the two gods (Horus of Edfu and Hathor of Dendera) were placed inside the Birth House, where they spent this and every succeeding night until the festival's conclusion at the Full Moon. Emphasizing the joviality in this festival Murnane (1983: 65) explained during the "New Kingdom at Thebes, there were about sixty yearly festivals, some of them lasting several weeks."

From the classical visitors, viz., Herodotus, Diodorus, Josephus, Africanus, Pliny, Strabo, etc., commentaries abound that attest to Thebes' religious and strategic significance, wealth, manufacturing potential, opulence and power. Further, because of its dynamism, art treasure troves and theological and philosophical creative spirit, Thebes enjoyed a mystique of multidimensional proportions that allows its easily qualifying as the most remarkable ancient city on the face of the earth. Its significance is even further projected in a consistent characterization of powerful Black African pharaonic personalities, manifesting along the banks of the sacred Nile, in the form of Mentuhotep, Senusert, Amenemhat, Aahmes-Nefertari, Thutmose I, Hatshepsut, Queen Tiy, Tutankhamon, Horemhab, the Ramessides, and a host of others, the greatest adherents of Amon, whose efforts and representation have been influential in the development of art, architecture and religious beliefs and practice. Today its eternal nature beckons and the modern visitor can be easily transported through time to experience, through the palm

FREDERICK MONDERSON

trees, horse cabs, nearby villages, "tricksters of Luxor," Thebes' power, vibrancy, vitality and mysticism. It's teaching of *Ma'at*, viz., balance, order, uprightness, justice, etc., was and is still invigorating in itself and this is experienced by most visitors.

Much of the ancient majesty began to be revealed to the modern world following Napoleon's expedition and discovery of the Rosetta Stone in 1799, the basis for Champollion's decipherment of Hieroglyphics in 1822. Fagan (1975: 257) says of this remarkable scholar: "Champollion was born on December 23, 1790, in Figeac, France, the son of an impoverished bookseller. At the age of five he was able to read. When eleven, he was taken to visit the mathematician Jean Baptiste Fourier, who had been a member of Napoleon's Commission. Fourier seems to have inspired the young Champollion with the desire to break the secrets of hieroglyphs. By the time he was seventeen, Champollion had learned Hebrew, Arabic, Sanskrit, Persian, and other eastern languages, as well as English, German, and Italian. Soon he was adding Coptic to his repertoire, in the belief that the language of Christian Egypt might have retained something of Ancient Egyptian speech."

Egypt Essays Illustration 30. Fishing for statues in Karnak Temple's "Cachette Court" under the direction of Legrain.

EGYPT ESSAYS ON ANCIENT KEMET

Egypt Essays Illustration 31. Further fishing for statues in the "Cachette Court" with the 7th Pylon in background to the rear (left); and finding a statue of Merenptah of the XIXth Dynasty (right). In this "Cachette Court, in foreground to the 7th Pylon, Legrain discovered some eight thousand statues in golden bronze, and more than five hundred in granite, basalt, beryl, limestone, petrified, and other materials. Almost all the discoveries bear historical inscriptions. This find is said to be the most important since Mariette's famous discovery of the Serapeum at Memphis. Important that these statues last handled by the ancient Egyptian and discovered under the cloud of fanfare do not have their noses broken!

Egypt Essays Photo 68. Deir el Bahari Temple of Queen Hatshepsut. A surviving Hathor Head column in the Hathor Shrine.

EGYPT ESSAYS ON ANCIENT KEMET

An antiquarian culture emerged in Europe following Napoleon's unearthing of the scientific, artistic, theological and philosophic knowledge of the ancient people of Kemet, the Egyptians. These antiquarians, their societies, institutions, emerging publishers and readership, not simply collected antiquities and wrote commentaries, but also began the gradual and later systematic archaeological excavation that peaked at the end of the 19th century. As a result of the emerging and scientifically systematic archaeological excavation of the Nile between 1870 and 1900, and conventions agreed to between 1900 and 1915, helped Europe to dominate much of the 20th century's historical interpretations of Nile Valley experience. As such, distortions abound in the historiographic record whether in museums, texts, video, lectures, discussions, and understandings. Therefore, in an age of being politically correct, when current intellectual interpretations undergird the historical record and support the primacy of European hegemonic dominance of world history, critical comparative analysis provides motivation and stimulus necessary for some meaningful reconstruction in African historiography.

Egypt Essays Photo 68a. Deir el Bahari Temple of Queen Hatshepsut. View of the Ramesseum from the mountain above Deir el Bahari.

FREDERICK MONDERSON

Egypt Essays Photo 68b. Deir el Bahari Temple of Queen Hatshepsut. Untold numbers of visitors come to Deir el Bahari to view and appreciate this wonderful architectural experiment of the Queen and her architect Senmut. The opening leads to the Tomb of Senmut.

IN HISTORY

Menes, when he moved his capital from *This* or *Thinis* to Memphis may have founded the City of Waset or Thebes. Diop does identify Narmer or Menes as Theban. He also identified Osiris as Theban. Nevertheless, who knows, however, when Thebes' habitation actually began. Spencer (1993: 18) exhibits: "Two fling hand-axes roughly chipped to shape from cores. Palaeolithic, before 100,000 B.C. From Thebes." Jackson (1972: 211-12) quotes Lady Lugard, who wrote, during the earlier period: "The people of Ethiopia colonized to the north and west. Amongst their colonies to the north, one of the most important was Thebes. Thebes and Meroe together founded the colony Ammonium in the western desert, and through Thebes the religion of Meroe was carried into Lower Egypt. It was at a much later period, about 1500 B.C. that Egypt returned upon Meroe and conquered it."

EGYPT ESSAYS ON ANCIENT KEMET

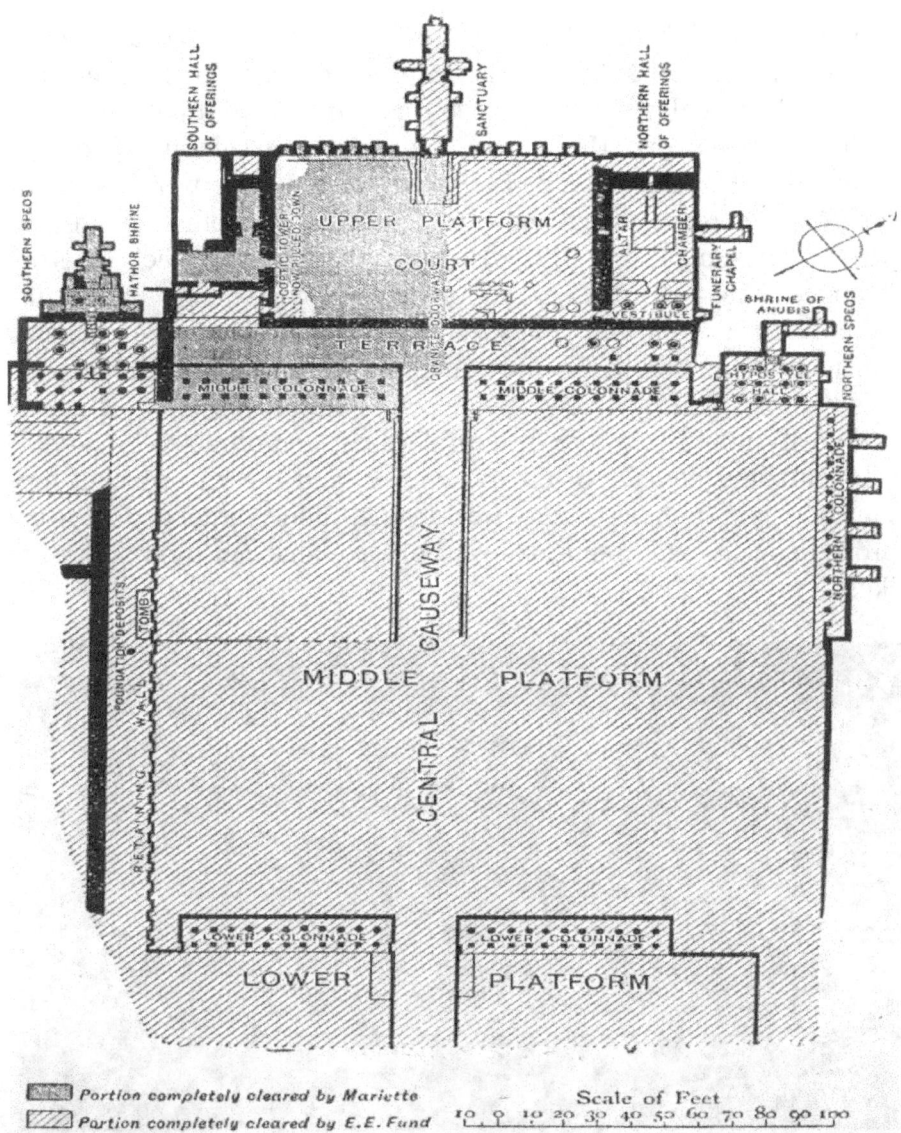

Egypt Essays Plan of Hatshepsut's Temple at Deir el Bahari.

Lurker (1991: 16) credits its illustrious history with the emergence and triumphs of Amun as state god in the Middle and New Kingdoms. During the XIIth Dynasty Amenemhat moved the capital from Thebes to a region in Middle Egypt, at Lisht. With the second rise of Thebes, Hatem (1982: 29) makes the argument: "Moving its capital south to Thebes, Egypt extended its influence northward to Palestine and Syria (as far as Mesopotamia and Media), westward to Barka and Tomedia, and southward to the borders of Ethiopia." Portman (1989: 8) added there were "houses, workshops, gardens, lakes and palaces spread on both sides of the Nile." Jackson (1970: 109-10) again commented, "Thebes itself expanded into a great metropolis with walls nine miles in circumference. On the outskirts of the city were the elegant mansions of the nobility, some containing fifty or sixty rooms, and halls with the walls covered with colorful paintings, and embellished with costly inlaid furniture, beautiful vases, and attractively carved ornaments and utensils of ebony, bronze, and ivory.... Around the mansions and temples were tree-shaded boulevards and flower gardens and the environing landscape was enhanced by a series of lakes."

Egypt Essays Photo 69. Deir el Bahari Temple of Queen Hatshepsut. A crowd has gathered to view events of the "Virgin Birth" at the "Birth Colonnade," to the left; while to the right, a visitor leaves the "Anubis Shrine."

EGYPT ESSAYS ON ANCIENT KEMET

Egypt Essays Photo 69b. Deir el Bahari Temple of Queen Hatshepsut. Shrine of Hathor. Image of the goddess with a female face, cows ears, big wig and surmounted by a capital with cows wearing horns at its front.

The city itself was indeed remarkable, wrote Portman, for during the period of its ascendance to its "zenith architecture, the arts, mathematics and medicine flourished in the greatest city the world had ever known." As to its nomenclature, the monuments seem to indicate three distinct names for Thebes, that of "Nome, a sacred name, and the name by which it is known in profane history."

The sacred name of Thebes was Amunei "abode of Amon" the ram-headed deity worshiped at Karnak and Luxor, and in the mortuary temples, at that city. This prominence remained during the Late and Graeco-Roman Periods. "No-Amon is the name of Thebes in the

FREDERICK MONDERSON

Hebrew Scriptures (*Jer.* XLVI. 25; *Nahum* III. 8). Ezikel uses *No* simply to designate the Egyptian seat of Ammon, which the *Septuagint* translates by Diospolis (*Ez.* XXX.14, 16). Gesenius defines this name by the phrase 'portion of Ammon,' i.e., the possession of the god Ammon, as the 'chief seat of his worship.'"

ARCHAEOLOGY

Because of its historical, religious and architectural ruins, Thebes has attracted a most impressive array of archaeologists and other scholars whose excavations in temples, tombs, cemeteries, cataloguing of antiquities and publication of their work have helped to supply data to make this aspect of ancient history as complete as possible. New Kingdom tombs supplied abundant cultural evidence of religious beliefs, social practice, agricultural exercises, technological enterprises, entertainment, war, civil administration, and titulary, as these interacted in the dynamics of this city of awe, beauty, spiritualism and mystique.

As an example of technological expertise and cultural opulence, Kamil (1984: 141-42) explained how the architects of Thebes' heyday decorated their mortuary structures in the Valley of the Kings. "Their tombs are hewn out of solid rock and inscribed with sacred texts from the Book of the Dead (developed from the Coffin Texts of the Middle Kingdom which were appropriated and revised selections of the Pyramid Texts of the Old Kingdoms). The smallest tomb is that of Tutankhamon which was found intact and contained the priceless treasures with which the world is now familiar. The largest belongs to Seti I. It is 100 yards in length and contains fine sculptured wall paintings in perfect preservation."

Interestingly, though the Ramesside kings would later move their capital to the Delta, they chose to be buried at Thebes and greatly beautified the city. In the process of exploration and excavation in the modern age of imperialism, what Brian Fagan called the "Rape of the Nile" ensued. The adventures of marauding collectors

EGYPT ESSAYS ON ANCIENT KEMET

enriched museums and private collections worldwide such that today cities as Boston, London, Manchester, Oxford, Brooklyn, New York, Chicago, Philadelphia, Detroit, Paris, Turin, etc., all possess significant reservoirs of the ancient African "culture in captivity." Importantly also, the work of credible scholars has helped reveal fundamental studies in mathematics, technology, medicine, astronomy, botany, zoology, navigation, architecture and geology, as practiced on the Nile, at a time when ancient Africans were originators of civilization and study of the fundamental sciences that govern the world.

Even further scholars working at Thebes helped create conventions for study and practice of archaeology and anthropology, as well as aiding new understandings in biology, pottery making, mummification and art. This is why the first "information age" with its archaeological and anthropological reports and resultant oral discussions with written commentary lasting from 1870-1930 is as important as foundation in contemporary understanding of the ancient culture along the Nile.

Who worked at Thebes?

Auguste Mariette was one of the earliest and most indefatigable of archaeologists who worked at Thebes. He "secured" the gold cache of Queen Aa-hotep for the Cairo Museum. Greener (1966: 190), quotes an earlier visitor Deveria and companion of Mariette, in 1859 who had written: "To our great surprise the jewels all bore the name of Aahmes, a king of the 18th dynasty, while that of Queen Aa-hotep was not once mentioned. The workmanship is finer than any of the same kind known, and there are about two kilograms of gold, marvelously worked, incrusted with stones and colored enamel." In an imperial age, the efforts of these excavators and scientists were driven by geo-political, economic, academic, cultural and scientific considerations. Gaston Maspero, the Frenchman became Curator of the Cairo Museum and did extensive excavations at Thebes during his tenure. He cleared Luxor Temple "below" the Abu el-Haggag mosque. In his time, many of the Cairo Museum's displays were created.

Critical scholars now see bias in his museum display representations. Diop, in *The African Origin of Civilization: Myth or Reality*, takes Maspero to task for misrepresentation of the historical record. This critique forces Maspero to be seen in a different light. Yet still, Maspero was a prolific writer, whose works became standard texts as archaeological sources with important historical and artistic data necessary for reinterpretations in the inductive methodological process of questioning theories, generating new hypotheses and creating new interpretations of history. Moorey (1988: 5) provides a summary of the significant developments in the archaeological study of the ancient past at the start of the Twentieth Century. "The Frenchman August Mariette (1921-1881) laid the foundations of the Egyptian Antiquities Service, created a National Museum of Antiquities and strove to control the wholesale expropriation of antiquities. The Germans Karl Brugsch (1927-94) and Adolf Erman (1854-1937) pioneered the systematic study of the Egyptian language and the Englishman W. M. F. Petrie (1953-1942) founded Egyptian archaeology on firm principles of accurate observation, precise recording and rapid publication."

EGYPT ESSAYS ON ANCIENT KEMET

Egypt Essays Photo 70. Deir el Bahari Temple of Queen Hatshepsut. On the north wall of the "Birth Colonnade," Thutmose III makes a presentation to "Sokar, Theban God of the Dead."

Egypt Essays Photo 70b. Deir el Bahari Temple of Queen Hatshepsut. The Queen's soldiers who came out to greet the two obelisks returning from Aswan to be erected at Karnak.

FREDERICK MONDERSON

On October 9, 1899, eleven columns of the Hypostyle Hall of the great temple at Karnak fell and the work of restoration fell to the Frenchman Legrain. He did extensive work of clearance and restoration at Karnak and made a fabulous discovery of several thousand statues in the famed Karnak "Cachette Court," north of the Seventh Pylon.

Lythgoe was part of the New York Metropolitan Museum of Art's expedition to Thebes. His efforts were recounted in that institution's Bulletin.

Egypt Essays Illustration 32. Craftsmanship ancient and modern: Ancient Greek and Egyptian Art discovered in Egypt: The Treasure of Touk-El-Garmous.

Howard Carter worked for two decades in the Theban area and the Valley of the Kings, hoping for a big discovery. The eighteen-nineties and first decade of the Twentieth Century was a time of intense rivalry between scholars, institutions and nations as concessions for digging became objects of high stakes. Bratton (1968: 139) offers light on efforts expended to secure artifacts and scientific data. "The most important modern expedition to the Valley was begun in 1902 by Howard Carter, Arthur Weigall, and

EGYPT ESSAYS ON ANCIENT KEMET

Egypt Essays Photo 71. Deir el Bahari Temple of Queen Hatshepsut. An attentive Guard on duty on the "Upper Terrace" before the Colonnade with a few surviving Osiride statues of the Queen.

FREDERICK MONDERSON

Edward Ayrton for the Service of Antiquities. Edward J. Quibell and Gaston Maspero also participated in this series of excavations financed by the American Theodore M. Davis. In 1903 Carter found the tomb of Thutmose IV, whose mummy was among those discovered in the burial chamber of his father, Amenhotep II. Between 1903 and 1912 the Davis expedition also discovered the tombs of Queen Hatshepsut, Horemheb, and Queen Tiy."

Carter was also employed by Lord Carnarvon, a very generous patron. Finally, in 1922, Carter discovered the Tomb of Tutankhamon, one hundred years after Champollion's decipherment of the ancient language. Lord Carnarvon, as Howard Carter's patron, had underwritten the cost of his digs. Carnarvon also, in the course of his interests had accumulated an extensive collection of artifacts on ancient Kemet, and "his share" of the spoils from King Tut's treasure enriched these. After the discovery of King Tut's tomb, Lord Carnarvon was at its opening and he died mysteriously, immediately after, from an insect bite. The press and others attributed this to a curse on the person who disturbed the king's remains.

Egypt Essays Photo 71a. Deir el Bahari Temple of Queen Hatshepsut. "Portico" entrance to the "Sanctuary" in the "Upper Court" with the mountain as a backdrop.

EGYPT ESSAYS ON ANCIENT KEMET

Egypt Essays Photo 71b. Deir el Bahari Temple of Queen Hatshepsut. While pillars and columns alternate in this temple's Colonnades, the "Middle Colonnade" boasts columns.

Egypt Essays Photo 71c. Deir el Bahari Temple of Queen. Previously people could climb the mountains to get a "Bird's Eye" view of the temple but now that is no longer allowed.

FREDERICK MONDERSON

Arthur Weigall was an archaeologist and journalist, who after King Tut's discovery, wrote extensively and colored the interpretation of the subject of ancient Egypt in the minds of millions of Europeans and Americans who now became avidly interested in the phenomenon of the Nile Valley cultural experience. Regarding Blacks in Kemet/Egypt, he seemed to write with a pejorative vindictiveness that by today's standards is unbelievable racist.

James H. Breasted was the first American Egyptologist whose work helped and became a mainstay of the University of Chicago Oriental Studies and "Chicago House" at Luxor. His *History of Egypt*, *Ancient Records of Egypt*, and *Development of Religion and Thought in Ancient Egypt* are milestones in study of the culture of ancient civilization along the banks of the river in North-East Africa.

Emery was instrumental in placing first and second dynasty royal tombs at Sakkara to complement those at Abydos, thereby signaling pharaoh's dual nature as King of Upper and Lower Egypt/Kemet. His discovery raised the question of whether the Abydos or Memphite tomb was the real one or a cenotaph or "dummy tomb."

Winlock and the Metropolitan Museum of Art Staff, including N. de Garis Davies, did extensive work at Thebes and allowed that institution to begin and expand its collection. The Museum's *Journal* was initiated and instrumental in publishing works of excavation while chronicling its own acquisition from bequests, excavations or purchase, etc.

H. R. Hall worked with Edouard Naville for a number of years at Deir el Bahari recounting the work of excavation done on Mentuhotep's XIth Dynasty temple, copied 500 years later by Hatshepsut's architect, Senmut. Edouard Naville, a Swiss Egyptologist, worked constantly at Deir el-Bahari for more than a decade and brought to light much information regarding Middle Kingdom and New Kingdom architectural and cultural history. First he cleared Hatshepsut's Temple at Deir el Bahari then he accidentally discovered and then cleared Mentuhotep's temple.

EGYPT ESSAYS ON ANCIENT KEMET

Alan Gardiner did extensive linguistic work in hieroglyphics, translations, commentaries and reviews. In the climax of a brilliant career he was knighted in England. Oxford University's Llewellyn Griffith also did linguistic interpretations at Thebes. Theodore Davis was a wealthy American archaeologist who extensively excavated at Thebes and made many important discoveries including that of the parents of Queen Tiy.

WARFARE

WARFARE at Thebes is represented in a number of places including temples, tombs and civic structures. The German scholar Von Bissing in the *American Journal of Archaeology* mentions one such recounting. He tells of a conflict between Intef and Mentuhotep, during the formative years of the Theban consolidation on eve of challenging the unstable rule of the IXth and Xth Dynasties to form the XIth Dynasty and Middle Kingdom in wake of the Old Kingdom collapse at the end of the VIth Dynasty. The war of liberation to oust the Hyksos by Sekenenra and his sons Kamose and Aahmose mobilized the Thebans as did Narmer's effort to conquer, unify the land and begin dynastic rule and resulting pacification.

After the wars of Seti I, the *Battle of Megiddo* is a famous conflict in which Thutmose III exemplified superior battlefield strategy in surprising and defeating a significant force in Southwest Asia, as part of his imperial expansion into that region. His incessant militarism nullified resistance of these princes for decades while untold wealth flowed to Thebes and into the coffers of the Amun priesthood.

The *Battle of Kadesh* involved Rameses II whose victory resulted in the world's first treaty that set the stage for regulated international relations. It was a most publicized event, being displayed on pylons of his most significant constructions at Abu Simbel, Karnak, Luxor, Ramesseum, Abydos, and even on papyrus. This King was indeed a prolific builder who equally expropriated the works of others.

Nevertheless, his own creations were prodigious that he left an indelible impression on the architectural history of his time.

Egypt Essays Photo 72. Ramesseum, Mortuary Temple of Rameses II. Remains of a seated statue, four Osiride statues of the King, a broken head on the ground and stairs to the vestibule before the "Hypostyle Hall."

The *Battle Against the Sea Peoples* occurred during the Twentieth Dynasty reign of Rameses III, where he fought to repel confederated enemies of his beloved land. His victory is commemorated at his mortuary temple at Medinet Habu and in the temple he built in the great court at Karnak. This temple, oriented south to north at Karnak, was perpendicular to the central east to west axis aligned with structures across the Nile.

EGYPT ESSAYS ON ANCIENT KEMET

Egypt Essays Photo 72a. Ramesseum, Mortuary Temple of Rameses II. Looking past the massive columns into the "Hypostyle Hall," centerpiece of this testament to a great pharaoh.

FREDERICK MONDERSON

Egypt Essays Photo 72b. Ramesseum, Mortuary Temple of Rameses II. Looking out from within the "Hypostyle Hall" at the columns that reflected the grandeur of its builder.

EGYPT ESSAYS ON ANCIENT KEMET

Warrior Pharaohs in an Age of Imperialism Expansion and accumulation of wealth

The chaos of the First Intermediate Period came to an end with the emergence of the Intefs and Mentuhoteps of the XIth Dynasty who seized power and proclaimed themselves Kings of the Upper and Lower Kingdoms. Wilson (1951: 106) explains how: "For nearly a century Thebes fought Herakleopolis and its ally, Assuit. Finally, about the middle of the twenty-first century, this Eleventh Dynasty at Thebes defeated the northern state and went on to extend her sway and to present to her successor, the Twelfth Dynasty, a relatively united land."

According to Wayne's (1987: 13) insightful observations, this second "golden age" of ancient Kemet was a period of prosperity. "With political order came economic stability [and] social and artistic development. Thebes prospered for about 250 years. Tombs and temples were built throughout Egypt - the remains of which can be seen today in almost every Egyptian town. The Pharaohs Mentuhotep, Amenemhet and Sesostris built monuments at Lisht, and Dashur, Hawara and Lahun - all of which are near the Faiyum and Saqqara."

These successes were due primarily, added Wilson (1951: 126) since the: "visible form of the Middle Kingdom rule was that the Theban dynasts were accepted as gods, sons of Re, and absolute rulers through the perpetuation of the traditional dogma." Equally, in summing up the politics, art and religious juxtapositioning that developed, Aldred (1985: 109) added, "The rulers of Heracleopolis fell heir to the Memphite workshops, while rival princes of Thinis, Dendera, Mo'alla, Asyut and Thebes developed their own versions of Sixth Dynasty traditions in splendid isolation."

FREDERICK MONDERSON

Significantly, a remarkable Heb Sed statue of Pharaoh Mentuhotep II one of several, was found at Deir el Bahari and now in the Cairo Museum. This rarity, which Smith describes as having "black flesh," was found in his mortuary temple at Thebes, the oldest temple at Thebes and the most complete of all the older temples that have survived. In addition to the extensive use of pillars, one court having a Peristyle with ten rows of eight, a number of statues depict the monarch in pharaonic regalia, as ruler of the Upper and Lower Kingdoms. Of these latter: "the most complete is the seated example found in a subterranean chamber of the temple, representing the king clad in a jubilee robe and wearing the Red Crown of Lower Egypt. Wide staring eyes with their long inner canthi and outer paint stripe, the eyebrows in relief, and the thick lips with edges defined by sharp ridges, the heavy chin and the muscles emphasized round the corners of the mouth and nose, are derived from the mannerisms of the late Sixth Dynasty ...."

A stele of Intef, son of Myt, now in the Brooklyn Museum, according to AJA XXI (1917: 208) tells, the "inscription dates from the time of Nebhepetra of the eleventh dynasty, and contains copies of the contracts for offerings to be made and ceremonies to be performed at his tomb."

Moorey (1993: 20) contends, the XIIth Dynasty was a: "Period of outstanding achievement, later regarded as an historic golden age. Important political changes and a series of forceful rulers, whose portrait statues are among the most remarkable surviving examples of Egyptian art, helped ensure the central government's authority. The capital was moved from Thebes to a site, south of Memphis, on the border of Upper and Lower Egypt and the rulers were buried in pyramids at Lisht, Lahun, Dashur and Hawara."

In the Twelfth Dynasty Mentuhotep was canonized and regarded as the Titulary deity of the Deir el Bahari precinct. Subsequently, and not in conflict, Lurker (1991: 20) shows how across the river: "Amenemhet I of the Twelfth Dynasty advanced the Theban god Amon to the position of new State god. He was also accessible to the simple classes of society in his animal manifestations, a ram and

EGYPT ESSAYS ON ANCIENT KEMET

a Nile goose. In the Theological system of his priesthood, however, he was the 'invisible one,' the soul (ba) of all things. The names of Egyptian gods could be described as words with symbolism."

Wilson adds even further (1963: 133), regarding this symbolism: "Running through the names of the Twelfth Dynasty there is frequent repetition of the term Ma'at, "truth" or "justice," or Ma'at, "true" or "just." Amen-em-het II took the names "He Who takes Pleasure in Justice" and "the Just of Voice." "Senusert II was "He Who Makes Justice Appear." Amen-em-het III was "Justice Belongs to Re," and Amen-em-het IV was "Just of Voice is Re."

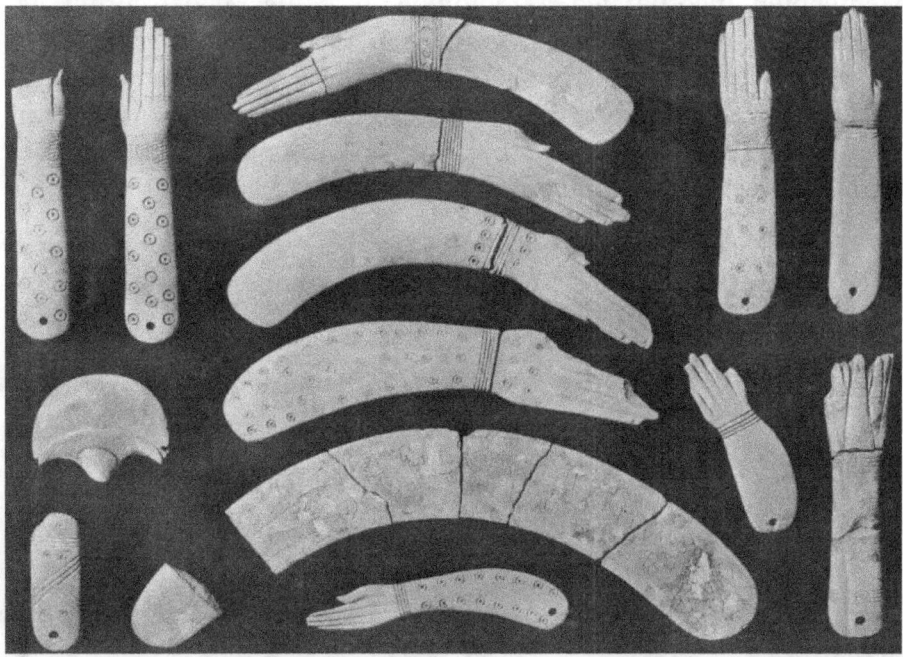

Egypt Essays Illustration 33a. A group of carved ivory wands, all found in one burial shaft, near the pyramid of Amenemhat I at Lisht, described as "Amuletic in character. Made to protect their owner from the fearsome creatures he expected to encounter in the Under-world."

FREDERICK MONDERSON

Even more, Hart (1990: 22) added seeming to characterize a deity who could possess men of such caliber: "There is a conflation of all notions created into the personality of Amun, a synthesis which emphasizes how Amun transcends all other deities in his being 'beyond the sky and deeper than the underworld.' Time and again the Egyptian poet-priests tried to interpret Amun's inexplicability. His mystery is contained in his name - since his essence is imperceptible, he cannot be called by any term that hints at his inner nature, and so the name of Amun has the underlying notion of 'hidden-ness' and probably best translates as 'the one who conceals himself.'"

Additionally, Aldred (1985: 115) recognized the temple of Mentuhotep incorporated a multitude of deities underscoring its multi-faceted theological expression. As such, it "served not only the cult of the dead king, but also those of Osiris, to whom the dead king assimilated, Hathor the goddess of this hilly area of western Thebes, Amun, the god of Karnak on the river opposite, and Mentu, the falcon-headed god of the entire Thebaid."

Egypt Essays Photo 73. Ramesseum, Mortuary Temple of Rameses II. The Colonnade is the majesty of this masterpiece of the Pharaoh.

EGYPT ESSAYS ON ANCIENT KEMET

Egypt Essays Photo 73a. Ramesseum, Mortuary Temple of Rameses II. The temple in its essentials with Osiride figure before the "Portico" and "Clerestory" above the "Hypostyle Hall."

Egypt Essays Photo 73b. Ramesseum, Mortuary Temple of Rameses II. Column bases in the "Hypostyle Hall."

In expressing their religiosity, the people of ancient Kemet created three types of temples during the Middle and New Kingdoms especially. These included the worship temple, the mortuary temple and the processional temple where the god rested when away from his sanctuary. In addition to the statues, stelae, frescoes, etc., these structures were decorated with sunk and raised relief. In the three types of temple, sunken relief, as a decorative motif, seems more frequently used to recognize art forms. Aldred (1985: 118) gives a noted example: "The little peripteral kiosk which was built at Karnak, in the precincts of the local god Amon, for the jubilee of Sesostris I, shows this style in a greatly developed form with rather those parts which receive the full glare of the daylight, and raised relief for architraves and pillars that are in partial shade. This kiosk, modest in its dimension, is of an austere perfection in its proportions and in the expert carving of its carefully arranged texts and scenes. It is one of the few non-funerary temples to have survived from the period." In this structure, the god is styled "Amun-Bull of his mother, the goddess Mut."

Lack of strong leadership at the end of the Middle Kingdom resulted in anarchy that was exploited by an invading horde of Asiatics. Sekenen-Ra II inherited the war of liberation to expel the Hyksos. These foreigners had invaded and ruled the "North Country" for almost a century, while Thebes retained more than a measure of autonomy. The Theban rulers had used "Medjay" solders, known as "Pan-grave People," who entered Kemet in great numbers from regions south of Aswan during this time. The Hyksos "tent-dwellers" came at the end of a great literary and intellectual tradition, and as the kids say, "Can't touch this," they contributed little to the culture they found, but easily generated the most intense nationalist resentment. Aldred (1985: 140) tells us: "It was a line of vassal princes in Thebes, forming Manetho's Seventeenth Dynasty, who in the sixteenth century B.C. felt themselves strong enough to challenge their Hyksos overlord, and eventually under the leadership of Amosis, to overthrow them and reunite Egypt and Nubia." The war of liberation, in fact, started over an insolent hippopotamus remark, survived an unsuccessful coup d'état at home while the army was in the field, thanks to Tetisheri (Ah-hotep), and ended in the expulsion of the foreigners, establishment of the Eighteenth Dynasty, and beginning of the New Kingdom.

EGYPT ESSAYS ON ANCIENT KEMET

Tetisheri was a remarkable African queen. Her beauty was etched in bravery, loyalty and courage. While her husband, Seqenenra II, was away fighting in the war of liberation, a palace coup broke out, instigated by "Tety the Handsome." Fearlessly, she rallied the faithful who had remained at Thebes, put down the uprising and secured the throne for her dynasty.

Kamose was the son of Seqenenra and Tetisheri. He continued the war after his father was felled on the battlefield with an axe blow to the head. He began expelling the Hyksos and militarization of the Kemetic forces. The *Carnarvon Tablet* No. 1, AJA XVI (1913: 525) speaks of this pharaoh and his Theban wars with the Hyksos. "The substance of the inscriptions is briefly this: In the seventh year of Kamose, the Hyksos, with Avaris as their capital, controlled the Delta and Middle Egypt as far as Cusae; Kamose, with headquarters at Thebes, governed Upper Egypt as far as Assuan; Ethiopia was in the hands of a third prince, whose name is not given. By command of the god Amon, the Theban king went north to drive back the 'Asiatics,' with an army composed of Nubian mercenaries and captured Teta, the son of Pepa, in the city of Nefrus."

Ahmose, his brother, completed the military build-up and imperial, expulsion, and expansion, while reorganizing the kingdom. He established the Eighteenth Dynasty, and began building for the emergence of "Amon as Lord of Thebes." Breasted (1959: 313) reasoned, "... with the expansion of the Egyptian kingdom into a world empire it was inevitable that the domain of the god should expand." He was so successful and well liked, throughout the land, Kees (1977: 244) supports the view, "clearly, therefore, Ahmose was regarded in Abydos as possessing peculiar sanctity just as his wife Aahmes-Nefertari and her son Amenhotep I were regarded at the same time in the West City at Thebes."

Throughout the period of the Old Kingdom, Bierbrier (1989: 13) noted, "the pyramid remained the ideal design for royal burials for over a thousand years, although rulers occasionally had to resort to modified forms in times of political uncertainty. The rulers of the Eleventh Dynasty at Thebes were buried in rock-cut cliff-tombs with adjoining temples and possibly also with pyramidal super-structures. The powerful kings of the Twelfth Dynasty reverted to the traditional design."

Adding further to this recognition, Breasted (1923: 252) informs, "We find Ahmose therefore in his twenty second year opening new workings in the famous quarries of Ayan or Troja, opposite Gizeh, from which the blocks for the Gizeh pyramids were taken, in order to secure stone for the temples in Memphis, Thebes (Luxor) and probably elsewhere. For these works he still employed the oxen which he had taken from the Syrians in his Asiatic wars. None of these buildings of his, however, has survived. For the ritual of the state temple at Karnak he furnished the sanctuary with a magnificent service of rich cultus utensils in precious metals, and he built a new temple-barge upon the river of cedar exacted from the Lebanese princes."

Egypt Essays Photo 74. The Tomb of Sen-nefer. Thoth and Ra-Horakhty sail in their boat, with others while to the left, Sen-Nefer stands in another frame.

EGYPT ESSAYS ON ANCIENT KEMET

Egypt Essays Photo 74a. The Tomb of Sen-Nefer. Sen-Nefer and his wife before the gods.

Egypt Essays Photo 74b. The Tomb of Sen-Nefer. Thoth introduces Sen-Nefer to enthroned Osiris colored green, which is actually a form of black.

FREDERICK MONDERSON

In the wake of the Hyksos expulsion, constant warfare changed the nature of the state and militarism became a noble profession. This is best explained by Breasted (1923: 254) who wrote: "The wealth, the rewards and the promotion open to the professional soldier were a constant incentive to a military career, and the middle classes, otherwise so unwarlike, now entered the ranks with ardor. Among the survivors of the noble class, chiefly those who had attached themselves to the Theban house, the profession of arms became the most attractive of all careers, and in the biographies which they have left in their tombs at Thebes they narrate with the greatest satisfaction the campaigns which they went through at the Pharaoh's side, and the honors which he bestowed upon them."

Complementing these biographies of the New Kingdom, art in tombs, on temple walls and in civic places, looked to traditional designs of earlier periods and maintaining the highest quality. Aldred (1985: 147) notes accordingly, the "reliefs of Amosis and Amenhotep I at Karnak show a departure from the style of their immediate predecessors, who were still working in the traditions of the late Thirteenth Dynasty, and a return to the inspiration of the early Middle Kingdom." In addition, Amenhotep I followed Ahmose, and Breasted (1923: 254) says of this Pharaoh who carried arms to the Asiatic princes, making them conquered vassals of ancient Kemet: "Whether from this war or some other source he gained wealth for richly wrought buildings at Thebes, including a chapel on the western plain for his tomb there, and a superb temple gate at Karnak, later demolished by Thutmose III. The architect who erected these buildings, all of which have perished, narrates the king's death at Thebes, after a reign of at least ten years."

Thutmose I succeeded Amenhotep I as King of Upper and Lower Kemet/Egypt, and, according to Breasted (1923: 264-65) this King "Thutmose I was able to begin the restoration of the temple so neglected since the time of the Hyksos. The modest old temple of the Middle Kingdom monarch was no longer in keeping with the Pharaoh's increasing wealth and pomp. His chief architect, Ineni, was therefore commissioned to erect two massive pylons, or towered gateways, in front of the old Amon-temple, and between these a

EGYPT ESSAYS ON ANCIENT KEMET

covered hall, with the roof supported upon large cedar columns, brought of course, like the splendid silver-gold-tipped flag staves of cedar at the temple front, from the new possessions in the Lebanon. The huge door was likewise of Asiatic bronze, with the image of the god upon it, inlaid with gold."

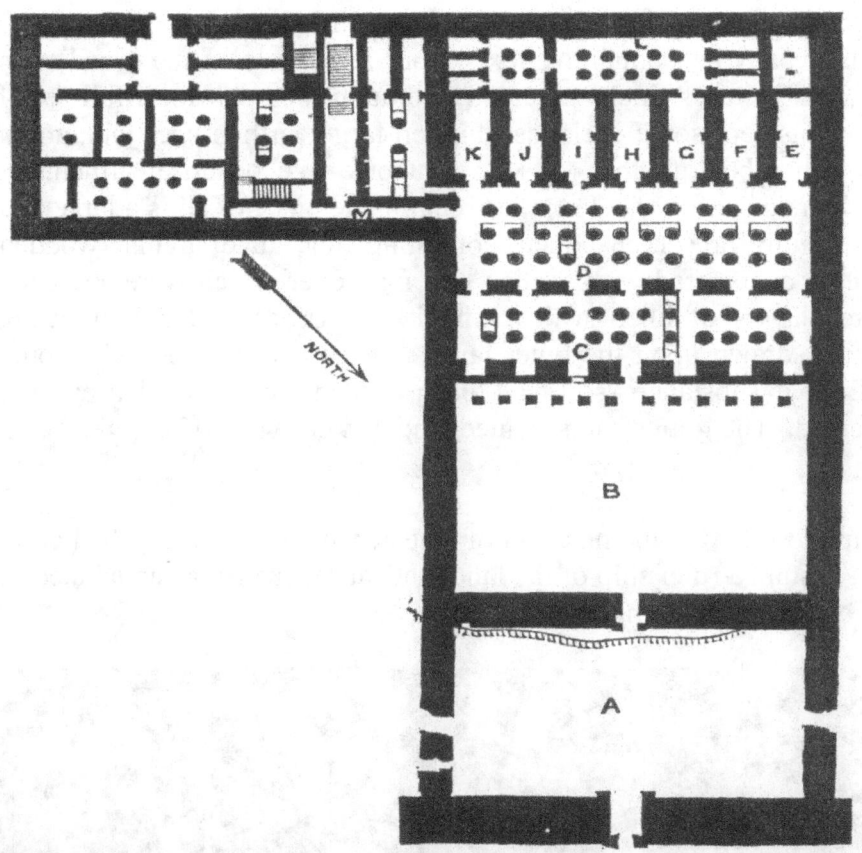

Egypt Essays Plan of Seti I's Temple to Osiris at Abydos.

American Journal of Archaeology IX (1905: 373) mentions the curator of the Egyptian Department of the Metropolitan Museum of Art mentioning the acquisition of "The Sarcophagus of Thutmose I, from the tomb of Queen Hatshepsut, in the Valley of the Tombs of the Kings, at Thebes."

FREDERICK MONDERSON

The tomb of Thutmose I was discovered in May 1899, by Loret. This king was the first monarch to be buried in the Valley of the Kings. *American Journal of Archaeology* IV (1900: 243-44) reported: "The tomb is a small one, of only two chambers. It has been rifled and the mummy unwrapped. But the robbers had wrapped it up again and restored it to its mummy case. In the tomb was a papyrus containing texts from the Book of the Dead with colored pictures finely executed; a draught-board, with a full set of draughtsmen; some garlands; thirteen large earthen beer jars, and a large number of other vessels; weapons, two beautiful armchairs; and remains of food. The most remarkable piece of all is a large and beautifully preserved couch, consisting of a quadrangular wooden frame, overspread with a thick rich mat, over which were stretched three layers of linen with a life-size figure of the god of death, Osiris, drawn upon the outer layer. Over this, mingled with some adhesive substance, soil had been spread, in which barley was planted. The grains had sprouted, and had grown to a height ...."

Thutmose II was the husband of Hatshepsut and when he died early she assumed ruler ship of the land that caused, as Breasted labeled it, "The Feud of the Thutmosids."

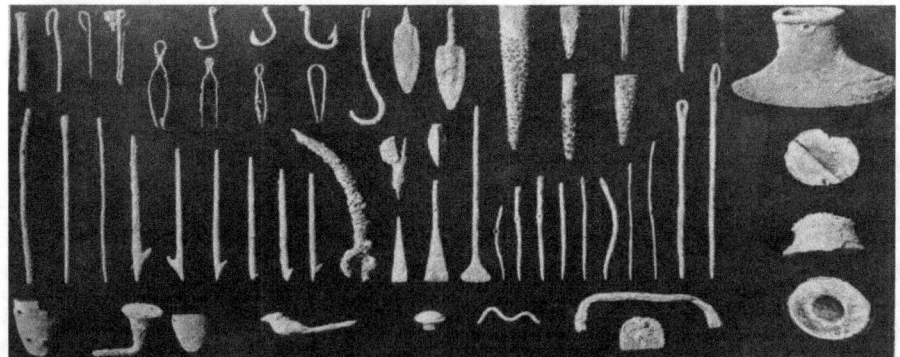

Egypt Essays Illustration 34. Copper implements found at Lisht during the time of the XIIth Dynasty, including "Nails, tweezers, fish-hooks, and harpoons, lance and arrow heads, rasps, needles, and Axe-Head."

EGYPT ESSAYS ON ANCIENT KEMET

Thutmose III was one of the greatest generals of history, a warrior pharaoh and a mighty builder who won great fame at Megiddo for outwitting and subduing his Asiatic rivals there and elsewhere. Breasted (1959: 314) thought, "Thutmose III was the first character of universal aspects, the first world-hero. As such he made a profound impression upon his age. The idea of universal power, of a world-empire, was visibly and tangibly bodied forth in his career." This pharaoh was successful in subjugating western Asia, Fairservis (1962: 134) through his daring an effective and efficient military machine. "In no less than seventeen campaigns into Asia, which even took him twice across the Euphrates, Thutmose III annihilated resistance. His army was organized into divisions complete with units of bowmen, axe-men, and spearmen, and of course the crushing power of clouds of chariots. Ships carried supplies to bases in Palestine and Phoenicia, while communication was sustained by a system of interlocking garrisons."

Waxing philosophic, Diop (1991: 92) notes, "Thutmose III, Son of God, meaning son of Amon-Ra, was guided by his father during all of his conquests: he held the sword of the faith and of divine truth." Breasted (1959: 313) explained Thutmose's actions in the following statement where the king remarked his god, Amon of Thebes was so mighty, "He seeth the whole earth hourly." As a result, endless wealth poured into Thebes during his reign. His successes were overwhelming and even further, Diop (1991: 93) wrote: "The chiefs of Syria rushed to pay tribute and to take the oath of loyalty .... Gold, silver, bronze, lapis lazuli, all that constituted the treasury of the Hittite princes passed into the coffers of God (Amon). The leaders had to give their sons as hostage.... Besides the annual tribute, the leaders of the Retennu agreed to contribute by supplying food to all stations where the Pharaoh and his army arrived." Records of his reign have shown contemporary art of a high quality.

FREDERICK MONDERSON

Egypt Essays Photo 75. The Tomb of Sen-Nefer. Sen-Nefer and his wife pay respects to the Gods.

Egypt Essays Photo 75a. The Tomb of Sen-Nefer. Sen Nefer sails the heavens with the principal gods led by Isis and Thoth.

EGYPT ESSAYS ON ANCIENT KEMET

After he had examined the mummy, Maspero V (1904: 41-42), provided an interesting contrast of how the artist has helped distort the personality of Thutmose III. "Its appearance does not answer to our ideal of the conqueror. His statues, though not representing him as a type of manly beauty, yet give him refined, intelligent features, but a comparison with the mummy shows that the artists have idealized their model. The forehead is abnormally low, the eyes deeply sunk, the jaw heavy, the lips thick, and the cheekbones extremely prominent; the whole recalling the physiognomy of Thutmosis II, though with a great show of energy. Thutmosis III is a fellah of the old stock, squat, thickset, vulgar in character and expression, but not lacking in firmness and vigor."

According to *American Journal of Archaeology* XXV (1921: 86), in 1906, E. Schiaparelli and the Italian Archaeological Mission excavated the Tomb of Kha situated in a "little valley of the Libyan chain near the plain of Thebes, Hatshepsut, who built at Karnak, Luxor and Deir el Bahari, challenged male supremacy to rule the "Golden Throne of Horus." She began repairing religious structures that had been in dis-repair while the Hyksos "ruled in ignorance of Ra." Her architect Senmut's tomb ceiling was decorated, according to Childe (1951: 173) with a style of early astronomy traceable to Middle Kingdom experiments, "with stellar clocks or calendars built on the diagonal principle." Gillings (1981: 87) mentions Senmut's tomb, "at Thebes, where the New York Metropolitan Museum of Art conducted an expedition, obtaining an arithmetic computation on an ostracon that was subsequently translated." In addition to his extensive building projects at Thebes, Senmut quarried and transported two red granite obelisks from Aswan, in a seven-month period, and erected them for his beloved queen at Karnak. Habachi (1987: 27) conjectures: "When the obelisks finally arrived at Thebes, they must have been greeted with much ceremony. From Deir-el-Bahari come scenes of soldiers running, holding aloft branches raised in greeting. Sacrifices were made and offerings presented to the gods. It was undoubtedly a great day for Hatshepsut and her courtiers and the citizens of Thebes. In an adjacent scene, the queen is shown presenting the obelisks to Amun-Re, king of the gods."

FREDERICK MONDERSON

Putting this queen in perspective, Aldred (1985: 151) has assessed: "The first great enterprise to stimulate new artistic activity at Thebes was the building of Hatshepsut's great mortuary temple at Deir el-Bahari, in which she associates herself with her 'father,' Amun of Thebes. The site was already dominated by the earlier monument of Mentuhotep II, which provided a challenge as well as an inspiration, to her architect in planning a colonnaded structure on three levels built with the white Theban limestone."

Another effort of equal importance is the work of the *Antiquities Service* in 1920-1921. The *American Journal of Archaeology* XXVI (1922: 342-43) reported: "At Thebes the sarcophagus of Queen Hatshepsut has been removed to the museum from its difficult position in an isolated valley to the south of the Valley of the Queens. She had prepared this place for herself when she was only a queen. After, when she had usurped the actual sovereignty, she had another sarcophagus made and placed in the Valley of the Kings."

The length of the reign of Amenhotep II has puzzled scholars for a number of years. Maspero thought it "lasting ten years at most." So too did Llewellyn Griffith. However, Hall (1912: 107) reflecting on the king's ascension, quoted General Amenemheb: "When the morning dawned, the Sun rose and the heavens lighted, King Aakheperura, son of the Sun, Amenhotep, to whom life is given, was established upon the throne of his father and assumed royal titulary." Hall (1912: 108) additionally offered his considered view in response to a theory of the length of the king's reign. "Dr. Tofteen thinks that Thutmose ruled Thebes and Amenhotep the North, as Thutmose always bears in his later years, the title 'ruler of Thebes,' while Amenhotep likewise and persistently called himself 'ruler of Heliopolis!' These are mere meaningless titles: Amenhotep was called 'divine prince of Heliopolis,' merely to distinguish him from his father, 'divine prince of Thebes.' Rameses III was also called 'prince of Heliopolis,' and Amenhotep III, 'prince of Thebes;' but we do not assume therefore that the one ruled in the North only, the

EGYPT ESSAYS ON ANCIENT KEMET

other in Thebes only: We know that they ruled over the whole country without a co-regent."

In a subsequent article, Hall (1912: 107) discussed Llewellyn Griffith's contention that: "Amenhotep's reign was a short one, rejecting the combined evidence of Manetho and the (perhaps doubtful) wine-jar inscription which gives 'year 26.'" *American Journal of Archaeology* XIII (1909: 479) holds to the view of Griffith that, "There is no clear evidence for believing that his reign continued longer than between three and seven complete years, and that it was probably but four to five years long." However, in response, wrote Hall, "But I do not see that the arguments he brings forward from the absence of documents later than the fifth year, are of any greater weight than those which he rejects. An argument from the silence of the monuments is a very risky one." Nonetheless, during his reign, Amenhotep II faced rebellion in Asia and Nubia after he followed his father Thutmose III, whom he closely resembled, to the throne. This grandson of Hatshepsut crossed the Orontes and quickly subdued the nations of Naharian, Nii, Akaiti, Alasia, Mittani and the Hittites, all within a blitzkrieg campaign that lasted three to four months. Then he turned his attention to the upper Nile and with great severity crushed the Nubians.

FREDERICK MONDERSON

Egypt Essays Photo 75b. The Tomb of Sen-Nefer. Ra-Horakhty in his boat with baboons at fore and aft.

Maspero V (1904: 46) explained Amenhotep II "had taken prisoner seven chiefs in the country of Tikhisa, and had brought them, chained, in triumph to Thebes, on the forecastle of his ship. He sacrificed six of them himself before Amon, and exposed their heads and hands on the facade of the temple of Karnak; the seventh was subjected to a similar fate at Napata at the beginning of his third year, and thenceforth the sheiks of Kush thought twice before defying the authority of Pharaoh."

In his groundbreaking History of Ancient Egypt, Breasted (1923: 326) tells of the magnificent architectural work Amenhotep did as part of the greater building efforts of the Eighteenth Dynasty. "In Thebes he built his now vanished mortuary temple on the west side of the river, by that of his father, while in the Karnak temple he restored the long dismantled hall of Hatshepsut's obelisks, setting again the columns which she had removed and richly adorning them with precious metal. He recorded the restoration on the wall which his father had built around the obelisks of Hatshepsut to hide their inscriptions forever from view. Besides a small colonnaded

EGYPT ESSAYS ON ANCIENT KEMET

structure at Karnak, he also built at Memphis and Heliopolis, restoring the neighboring quarries of Troja; but all his works there have perished."

Conspiracy and distrust marked the later years of his reign owing to his not having sons with powerful claims to the throne, in order to marry his heiresses, the princesses, Khuit and Mutemuau. Thutmosis IV, a young prince, of minor standing, who resided at Memphis, "the White Wall," was out riding, rested and fell asleep in the shadow of the Great Sphinx at Gizeh. The god Ra-Harmachis appeared to him in a dream and said: "'Behold me, gaze on me, O my son Thutmose, for I, thy father Harmarkhis-Khopri-Tumu, grant thee sovereignty over the two countries, in both the South and the North, and thou shall wear the white crown and the red crown on the throne of Sibu, the sovereign, possessing the earth in its length and breadth ....'"

Egypt Essays Illustration 35. An Egyptian village that existed from about 1700 B.C., showing a group of houses at Lisht built against the side of the Pyramid of Amenemhat I, after it had been plundered and reduced to ruin.

All this if he would clear away the sand that had engulfed it, he would become king. He did the clearance and was able to succeed his father. Having done so, he erected the "Dream Stele" that now resides between the paws of the Great Sphinx at Giza.

The Tomb of Amenhotep II was discovered by Loret in 1898, wherein Prof. Wiedemann gave an account of his work there. According to *American Journal of Archaeology* III (1899: 59), regarding the Tomb of Amenhotep II: "The tomb itself has the ordinary shape of the royal king-tombs of the eighteenth and nineteenth dynasties. A passage leads downwards into the mountain; then follows a staircase, and then some rooms. The principal of these has a roof supported by quadrangular pillars and painted blue with golden stars, in imitation of the night heaven into whose realm the king had now entered. The walls were covered with appropriate representations. The sarcophagus, made of sandstone, was standing in a niche on a block of alabaster. Besides that of Amenhotep II, nine other mummies were found in a small chamber to the right without names, but the others are proved by their inscriptions to be those of Thutmose IV, Amenhotep III, Seti II, Setnakht and Rameses IV, VI, and VIII. These mummies had evidently been removed from their original tombs in ancient times, probably to be deposited in a safer place. The floor of the newly found tomb was covered with gifts offered to the dead pharaoh. In the tomb were also found four human corpses not embalmed, but merely dried."

Analysis of the notion of "culture in captivity" can be applied to an artifact from the tomb of Tuthmose IV and how similar precious treasures are scattered in various collections. *American Journal of Archaeology* XVII (1913: 270) mentions T. D. Lee's detailed discussion of: "The Girdle of Rameses III" for many years preserved in the Liverpool Museum. "With the exception of some fragments of tapestry found in the tomb of Thutmose IV it is the oldest known example of a woven pattern. It is 17 feet long and tapers from 5 to 1 7/8 inches in width. The cartouche of the king is written in black ink about a foot from the wide end. It is of linen woven in five colors blue, red, yellow, green, and the natural color of the linen. It is remarkably well preserved."

EGYPT ESSAYS ON ANCIENT KEMET

Egypt Essays Photo 77. Medinet Habu, Mortuary Temple of Rameses III. Alignment into the Temple, while above the entrance, the King smites Egypt's enemies.

Egypt Essays Photo 77a. Medinet Habu, Mortuary Temple of Rameses III. The "First Pylon" to the Temple of Rameses III, 20th Dynasty.

FREDERICK MONDERSON

Egypt Essays Photo 77b. Medinet Habu, Mortuary Temple of Rameses III. Colored black, Amon-Ra sits enthroned with his consort "watching his back."

EGYPT ESSAYS ON ANCIENT KEMET

Egypt Essays Photo 77c. Medinet Habu, Mortuary Temple of Rameses III. Osiride statues decorated this "Second Court" of the temple.

Egypt Essays Photo 77d. Medinet Habu, Mortuary Temple of Rameses III. A small "Ramp" elevates to the next level, this time the "Hypostyle Hall" area of the temple.

FREDERICK MONDERSON

Following Thutmose IV, the reign of Amenhotep III is considered one of the most prosperous, a time of the "Golden Age." Still, Haag (1987: 210) held to the view: "In the century that passed between the Asian conquests of Thutmosis III and the reign of Amenhotep III, artistic and architectural restraint gave way to an overblown imperial style, expressed at Karnak by the Third Pylon built by Amenhotep and his start on the great Hypostyle Hall. Empire introduced foreign influences and new wealth to the country, required an enlarged bureaucracy, and upset the status quo. Amun, who had lent his sword to Pharaoh's victories, saw the coffers of his priesthood and of the old aristocracy from which it was drawn swell with tribute, and so their power grew."

The king married Tiy, a commoner, for whom he built a castle, called Malcata. Tiy must have been a remarkable woman, who though "thought to be Syrian" looks "more Nubian than the Nubians!" Even further, Haag (1987: 210) continued, this queen "was given unusual artistic prominence alongside her husband, and her parents, Yuyu and Tuyu, were buried in splendor in the Valley of the Kings. Pharaoh and temple no longer represented identical interests."

In regards pharaoh's architect who was also his namesake, "Amenhotep, Son of Hapu," a genius who achieved brilliance in his construction of line and mass as in the Central Court and Processional Way at Luxor, the Processional Way or Colonnade at Karnak, and his extensive works at the Temple of Soleb in Nubia, these monuments are considered the great nurseries of classical Kemetic architecture. Amenhotep was later deified and a Demotic Ostraka published in *American Journal of Archaeology* XVII (1913: 526-27) reported: "It is a fragment of the usual pale red-brown clay of Theban ostraka, of irregular form measuring roughly 10.5 cm along the right-hand end by 9 cm. at its greatest width. The text is written in a very neat hand resembling that of the Senta papyrus, and may date from about the middle Ptolemaic time. It states the result of a supplication made to the god Amenhotep on behalf of a sick man; and the ostracon is probably the original answer given by the priest on behalf of the god."

EGYPT ESSAYS ON ANCIENT KEMET

Though little known, the Temple of Soleb represented a classical piece of this craftsman's handiwork. Fairservis (1962: 138) describes the erection of the Temple of Soleb. "The scheme involved a columned entrance hall which led to a pylon gate through which one had access to a succession of magnificent colonnaded courts terminating in a now vanished 'holy of holies' complex of inner rooms. Part of the splendor of this building was the sculpture of lions and sphinxes which lined the way to the temple entrance."

Equally, Breasted (1923: 341) assesses the work of the Theban School who had accomplished so much in art and architecture. "Under the fingers of such men as these the old and traditional elements of Egyptian building were imbued with new life and combined into new forms in which they took on a wondrous beauty unknown before. Besides this, the unprecedented resources of wealth and labor at the command of such an architect enabled him to deal with such vast dimensions that the element of size alone must have rendered his building in the highest degree impressive."

Even further, Breasted (1923: 242) continued: "Of the two forms of temple which now developed, the smaller is not less effective than the larger. It was a simple rectangular cella or holy of holies, thirty or forty feet long and fourteen feet high, with a door at each end, surrounded by a portico, the whole being raised upon a base of about half the height of the temple walls. With the door looking out between the graceful columns, and the facade happily set in the retreating vistas of the side colonnades, the whole is so exquisitely proportioned that the trained eye immediately recognizes the hand of a master who appreciated the full value of simple fundamental lines."

FREDERICK MONDERSON

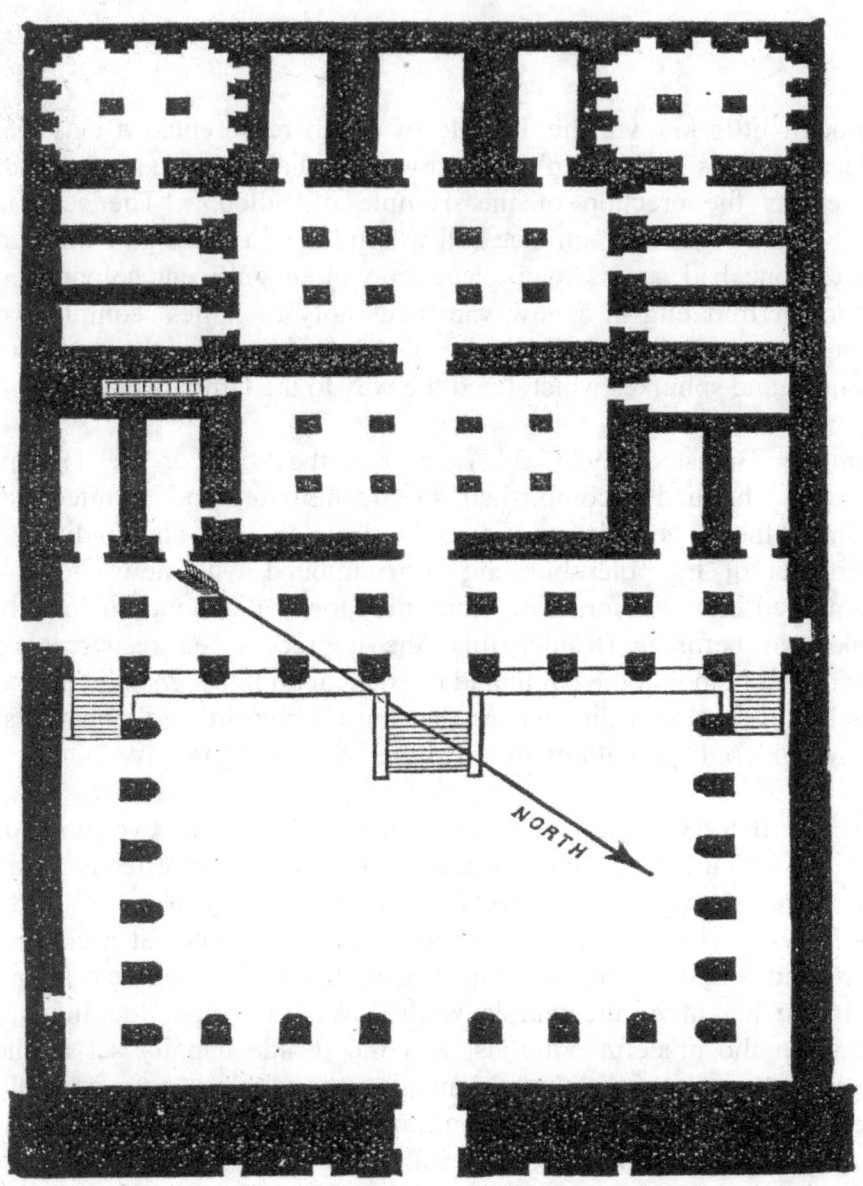

Egypt Essays Plan of the Temple of Rameses II at Abydos.

EGYPT ESSAYS ON ANCIENT KEMET

In the mind's eye of the ancient Africans along the majestic Nile River, Karnak and Luxor were quintessential primeval spots whose holiness, in radiating light and inspiration, brought immense fame, fortune, festivals, and fun to their lives. These early attempts to evolve ethical standards molded human behavior and interaction in a society that was blest through belief in the African divinities.

The stupendous beauty of the great Hypostyle Hall has elicited the most intense commentary for its massive exactness, and the numerous questions it instantly poses regarding construction, religion, theosophy, science, etc. Breasted (123: 343-44) has opined: "The great hall was laid out with a row of gigantic columns on either side of the central axis, quite surpassing in height .... Being in every respect masterpieces of exquisite proportion, with capitals of the graceful, spreading papyrus-flower type. These columns are higher than those ranged on both sides of the middle, thus producing a higher roof over the central aisle or nave and a lower roof over the side aisles, the difference in level being filled with grated stone windows in a clearstory. Thus were produced the fundamental elements in basilica and cathedral architecture, which we owe to the Theban architects of Amenhotep III."

In addition to the Karnak clearstory, Clarke and Engelbach (1990: 173) point to others. "They are also found in the temple of Seti I, in the Ramesseum at Thebes, and in the temple of Khonsu at Karnak. They seem to have given way in later times almost entirely to the practice of using screen walls between the pillars forming the first hypostyle hall of the temples. At any rate, in the Ptolemaic and Roman temples, such as Edfu and Dendera, no clerestories were used."

FREDERICK MONDERSON

Egypt Essays Photo 78. Medinet Habu, Mortuary Temple of Rameses III. Disfigured Osiride statues of the King in the "First Court." Notice the elevated steps to the "Second Court."

Egypt Essays Photo 78a. Medinet Habu, Mortuary Temple of Rameses III. One side of this "Court" with "Osiride Figures" and Columns.

EGYPT ESSAYS ON ANCIENT KEMET

Egypt Essays Photo 78b. Medinet Habu, Mortuary Temple of Rameses III. The other side of this "Court" with "Osiride Figures" and Columns.

Within a decade of his son Amenhotep IV's ascension, the empire was engulfed in a religious revolution, Amon against the Aten! The new religion, with roots to his father and mother, developed at Thebes. In *American Journal of Archaeology* XVIII (1914: 503). Wiedemann mentions, "Scarabs of Amenhotep III," which read: "The use of scarabs as a means of making known his religious feelings, his personal characteristics, and his famous deeds, to his subjects and to posterity, were quite in accordance with the usual practice of Amenhotep III. The most popular fact recorded on the king's scarabs was his marriage with Tii. Among the titles given to Amenhotep III the most interesting is that which connects him with the Aten; it is evidence that the Aten-cult did not arise after the accession of Amenhotep IV, but had already been planned in the time of Amenhotep III."

Nevertheless, Breasted (1923: 361) pointed out: "In the garden of Amon, which his father had laid out between the temple of Karnak and Luxor, Amenhotep located his new temple, which was a large and stately building, adorned with polychrome reliefs. Thebes was now called "City of the Brightness of Aton," and the temple-quarter 'Brightness of Aton the Great;' and the sanctuary itself bore the name 'Gem-Aton,' a term of uncertain meaning." We now know that 'Gem-Aton' was located in Nubia.

Soon, however, this "irrepressible conflict" exploded. While Erman (1894: 45) argued for gradualism, in this respect, he wrote: "Had he been content to establish this worship officially only, to introduce it gradually, and to let time do its work, his efforts might have been crowned with success; but he tried violence, and therefore, his innovation in spite of momentary results, had no duration."

Even further, Erman (1894: 45-46) continued: "He endeavored to exterminate all remembrance of the old gods, and especially he declared war against the great god of his ancestors, Amon, whose name he erased from all the monuments. He changed his old name containing the name of Amon to Chu-en-Aten, the 'splendor of the disk,' and as the capital, where his famous forefathers had lived, was filled with memorials in honor of Amon, the puritan king resolved to live no longer in such an idolatrous place. He therefore forsook Thebes, and built a new town, the 'Horizon of the Sun's Disk,' near the modern Tell el Amarna."

EGYPT ESSAYS ON ANCIENT KEMET

Egypt Essays Illustration 36. At Tell El-Amarna, a stone table for offerings sits in front of a doorway, made of stone and painted red (left); and a Besom and paint-brushes, wickerwork stand, and fiber-ring for balancing the tray on the head (right).

The significance of this revolution is its recognition of the role of the sun. Akhenaten first recognized the 'Aten,' as a primary aspect of science in human existence. This is underscored when Erman (1894: 262) refers to the Hymn to the Aten as: "the living-sun disk, besides whom there is no other." "He created all things, 'the far-off heavens, mankind, the animals, and the birds; all eyes are strengthened by his beams, and when he shows himself all flowers grow and live; at his rising the pastures bring forth, they are intoxicated before his face, all the cattle skip on their feet, and the birds in the marshes flutter with joy.' It is He 'Who brings in the years, creates the months, makes the days, reckons the hours, he is the lord of time, according to whom men reckon. These ideas and expressions are similar to those found in the hymns to the sun-god in the older religion; the innovation brought in by Chuen'aten therefore was essentially the idea that the one God, 'the God living in truth,' was to be an article of real faith, and no longer merely a phrase."

From his work of excavating in the tombs of Egypt, Von Bissing reproduced eight reliefs as stated in the *American Journal of Archaeology* XVIII (1914: 503) which sought to explain "the figures of Ramose and his wife, two wall paintings, and a sketch for a relief, all of which show the realistic style of Amenhotep IV or its effect upon the style of artists under his successors." Nevertheless, the overthrow of the Aten cult did not bring strong leadership until the Ramesside, XIXth Dynasty. Rameses I, then Seti I and finally Rameses II were not only adherents of the Amon cult but equally strong advocates of building mortuary and worship structures. Seti I left evidence of his good relations with the workers, and in that respect, Childe (1954: 123) enumerated, "he provided each of the thousand laborers employed on building his temple with '4 lb. bread, 2 bundles of vegetables and a roast of meat daily, and a clean linen garment twice a month'!" Equally, Blackman, in *American Journal of Archaeology* XXII (1918: 87) noted "a relief at Karnak depicts Horus and Seth purifying Sethos I before officiating in the temple of Amon." Even further, Blackman (1918: 91) discussing this Karnak relief, on the one hand recounted the admonition: "'I have purified thee with life and good fortune, so that thou art rejuvenated like thy father Amun' points to the pharaoh's rebirth in the capacity of Son of the Sun-god rather than in that of embodiment of the god.'"

Breasted (1923: 443) on the other hand, commenting on the stupendous architectural constructions of this "great" pharaoh has written, at "Thebes, Rameses II spent enormous treasure and vast resources of labor in the completion of his father's mortuary temple, another beautiful sanctuary for his own mortuary service, known to all visitors at Thebes as the Ramesseum; a large court and pylon in enlargement of the Luxor temple; while, surpassing in size all buildings of the ancient or modern world, his architects completed the colossal colonnaded hall of the Karnak temple, already begun under the first Ramses, the Pharaoh's grand-father."

EGYPT ESSAYS ON ANCIENT KEMET

Egypt Essays Photo 79. Medinet Habu, Mortuary Temple of Rameses III. Decorated columns behind pillars. Notice the base for each is different: column bases are round; pillar bases are square.

FREDERICK MONDERSON

Egypt Essays Photo 79a. Medinet Habu, Mortuary Temple of Rameses III. Amon-Ra, painted Black, sits among the gods and goddesses.

EGYPT ESSAYS ON ANCIENT KEMET

Egypt Essays Photo 79b. Medinet Habu, Mortuary Temple of Rameses III. Rameses makes a presentation to enthroned Osiris who sits alongside Isis and Hathor.

Among the distinctions credited to the Ramesseum, the Egyptian Mathematical Leather Roll (E.M.L.R.) and the Rhind Mathematical Papyrus (R. M. P.) we're told, were "discovered in some ruins of the Ramesseum at Thebes, and later acquired by Rhind. The papyri came to the British Museum in 1864, and have remained there ever since. The E. M. L. R. is roughly 10 inches by 17 inches; because of its very brittle condition, it remained unrolled for more than 60 years."

In the continuing revelations of the ancient culture, *American Journal of Archaeology* XIII (1918: 202) mentions the settlement of a lawsuit by a deified king, in the time of Rameses II from an inscription found at Abydos and now in the Cairo Museum. "At the top of the stele is shown the boat of Aahmes I carried on the shoulders of eight priests. In front of it the plaintiff, Pasar, priest of Osiris, stands with raised arms. Below are nine lines of hieroglyphs, and in the lower right hand corner the figure of Mesmen, father of Pasar. Another inscription found at Sakkara in 1898 seems to refer to the same case. It appears that in the reign of Aahmes I a certain Nesha received from the king an estate, which he bequeathed to his descendants stipulating that it should not be divided. In the year of Rameses II, two hundred years later, the courts permitted the division; but Pasar, son of Mesmen, appealed the case to the statue of the deified Aahmes as it was being carried in procession and the statue by nodding confirmed his claim to the estate."

Rameses III was the last great king of the New Kingdom whose mortuary temple at Medinet Habu, was equally the last major building project of the New Kingdom. Of this wonderful structure, Breasted (1923: 486) wrote: "On the western plain of Thebes, at the point now called Medinet Habu, he built a large and splendid temple to Amon, which he began early in his reign. As the temple was extended and enlarged from rear to front the annals of his campaigns found place on the walls through successive years following the growth of the building until the whole edifice became a vast record of the king's achievements in war which the modern visitor may read, tracing it from year to year as he passes from the earliest halls in the rear to the latest courts and pylons of the front."

Again Breasted (1923: 487) continued: "There was a sacred lake before the temple with an elaborate garden, extensive out - buildings and magazines, a palace of the king with massive stone towers in connection with the temple structure, and a wall around the whole forming a great complex which dominated the whole southern end of the western plain of Thebes, whence from the summits of its tall pylons one might look northward along the stately line of mortuary temples, built by the emperors."

Breasted (1923: 487) further added: "Other buildings of his have for the most part perished; a small temple of Amon at Karnak, which Ramses, quite sensible of the hopelessness of any attempt to rival the vast Karnak halls, placed across the axis of the main temple

EGYPT ESSAYS ON ANCIENT KEMET

there, still bears witness to his good sense in this respect. Some small additions to the Karnak temple, besides that of Mut on the south of the Karnak group, a small sanctuary for Khonsu only begun by Rameses III, sanctuaries of which little or no trace has been discovered at Memphis and Heliopolis, and many chapels to various gods throughout the land have for the most part perished entirely or left but slight traces."

From the XXIInd Dynasty came Sheshonk, of whom Breasted (1923: 529-30) informs, "... by his origin controlled Heracleopolis, and he and his family after him maintained close relations with the High Priest of Ptah at Memphis. Not later than his fifth year, he had also acquired Thebes. He attempted to hold its support to his house by appointing his own son as High Priest of Amon there; but it still remained a distinct principality, capable of offering serious opposition to the ruling family in the Delta."

It's interesting that White (1970: 5) points out, "whereas the Theban Pharaohs remained at Thebes for religious and sentimental reasons, the kings who ruled from Tanis, Sais and Bubastis were compelled to do so for motives of political strategy."

FREDERICK MONDERSON

Egypt Essays Photo 80. Medinet Habu, Mortuary Temple of Rameses III. Amon-Ra enthroned smells his flowers in his Shrine, while a defaced Mut stands to his rear.

EGYPT ESSAYS ON ANCIENT KEMET

Egypt Essays Photo 80a. Medinet Habu, Mortuary Temple of Rameses III. Fat cows in procession and above cows being slaughtered.

Breasted (1923: 530) says further: "Sheshonk was able to return with great plunder with which to replenish the long depleted Pharaonic coffers. He placed a record of the tribute of Palestine and of Nubia, of which he had now gained control, beside those of the great conquerors of the Empire on the walls of the Karnak temple at Thebes .... With his treasury thus replenished Sheshonk was able to revive the customary building enterprises of the Pharaohs which had been discontinued for over two hundred years. He beautified Bubastis, his Delta residence, and at Thebes undertook a vast enlargement of the Karnak temple. His son Yewepet, who was High Priest of Amon there, dispatched an expedition to Silsileh to secure the stone for an enormous court and pylon which were to complete the Karnak temple on the west and give it a magnificent front toward the river."

First Khasta, then Piankhy subdued Thebes during the XXIV Dynasty, then the XXVth Dynasty finally conquered and held the entire country. In this regard, Breasted (1923: 553) wrote, Shabaka, a significant ruler of the XXVth Dynasty: "... showed great partiality to the priesthood and favored the temples. His restoration of an ancient religious text of great importance in the temple of Ptah rescued and enabled us to employ in this work one of the most remarkable documents surviving from ancient Egypt. At Thebes he reinstated Amenardis, his sister, who must have been temporarily expelled by Osorkon III. Together with her, he built a chapel at Karnak, and his building operations necessitated an expedition to the distant quarries of Hammamat. We also find records of his temple restorations at Thebes, and it is evident that he governed Egypt at least in his relations with the temples, precisely as a native Pharaoh would have done."

The next significant ruler of the XXVth Dynasty was Taharka, styled "Emperor of the World." Accordingly, Breasted (1923: 554-55) summed up Taharka's building efforts. He stated: "For some thirteen years Taharka ruled his kingdom without interference from Asiatic princes, and he was able to execute buildings of minor importance in Tanis and Memphis, and more considerable monuments in Thebes."

DuBois (1971: 137) provides an important commentary on the Kiosk of Taharka in the Great Court at Karnak. He states: "Taharka's building at Karnak was planned as one of the most striking in the ancient world. The temple built at Thebes had a relief representing the four courts of the four quarters of the Nilotic world: Dedans, the great God of Ethiopia, represents the south; Sop, the eastern desert; Seek, the western desert; and Horus, the north. According to Petrie: 'this shows how southern was the center of thought when the whole of Egypt is reckoned as the north. Some writers say that Taharka led expeditions as far as the Strait of Gibraltar."

EGYPT ESSAYS ON ANCIENT KEMET

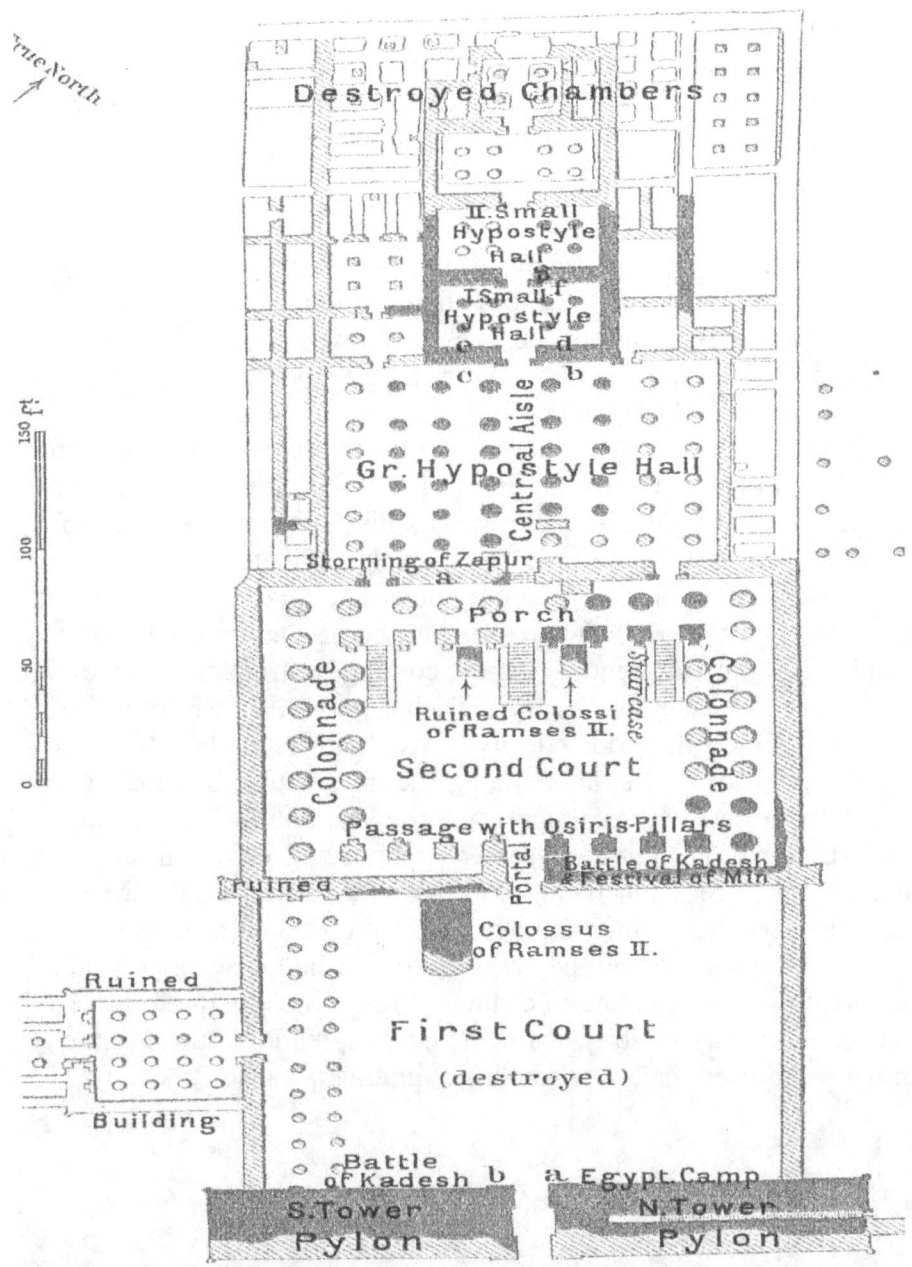

Egypt Essays Plan of the Ramesseum, Mortuary Temple Rameses II.

FREDERICK MONDERSON

The destruction of Thebes resulted after Kemet could not field vigorous leadership and its forces could no longer contain the rising tide of Asiatic expectations. This as much we are told in Breasted's (1923: 559-60) commentary: "The rich cultus images, the gorgeous ritual furniture and implements, with which the pious Theban prince, Mentemhet, had equipped the temples, fell a prey to the fierce Assyrian soldiery, while 'two enormous obelisks, wrought of bright silver, whose weight was 2,500 talents, the adornment of a temple-door,' which they carried off to Nineveh, indicate the wealth still remaining in the temple of the long devastated nation. The story of the ruin of Thebes spread to all the peoples around. When the prophet Nahum was denouncing the coming destruction of Nineveh, fifty years later, the desolation of Thebes was still fresh in his mind as he addressed the doomed city: 'Art thou better than No-Amon [Thebes]. That was situate among the rivers, that had the waters round about her; whose rampart was the sea, and her all was of the sea? Ethiopia and Egypt were her strength and it was infinite; Put and Lubim were thy helpers. Yet was she carried away, she went into captivity: her young children also were dashed to pieces at the top of all the streets: and they cast lot for her honorable men, and all her great men were bound in chains.' From this time the fortunes of the venerable city steadily declined and its splendors, such as no city of the early orient had ever displayed, gradually faded."

EGYPT ESSAYS ON ANCIENT KEMET

Egypt Essays Illustration 37. A Baboon-God Shrine revealed, showing a recessed image of Thoth as a Baboon-Headed God (Cynocephalus) with a light-shaft (left) to illumine it. An underground chapel at Hermopolis whose walls contained a mummy.

FREDERICK MONDERSON

RELIGION: THRONE OF THUNDER

The state god of Thebes, Amon, emerged into prominence in the Middle Kingdom and in the New Kingdom had become even more powerful. Fused into Amon-Ra, "King of the Gods" whose precinct was the "Throne of Thunder" his influence spread far and wide. Budge (1969, II: 22) explained how worship of Amun-Ra expanded beyond the country but most particularly in Upper Egypt, where its centers were: "Thebes, Hermonthis, Coptos, Panopolis, Cusae, Hermopolis Magna, and Herakleopolis Magna; in Lower Egypt they were Memphis, Sais, Xois, Metelis, Heliopolis, Babylon, Mendes, Thmuis, Diospolis, Butus, and the Island of Khemmis ...." The forms of Amon were many. Budge II (1969: 17) further indicates: "In many scenes we find Amen-Ra with the head of a ram, when he usually wears the disk and uraeus, or the disk only. In this form he is called 'Amen-Ra, lord of the thrones of the two lands, the dweller in Thebes, the great god who appeareth in the horizon, or Amen-Ra, lord of the thrones of the two lands, governor of Ta-Kenset (Nubia).'"

Mokhtar (Second Edition: 4) gives the size of Karnak as "an area of 1,210,380 sq. Mt. There was a magnificent wall encompassing the temple, other temples and the sacred lake. There was also the wall surrounding 61 feddans capable of containing ten middle-sized European churches. This proves the extent of venerating the God Amon-Ra." The Theban deity, Amon, his wife Mut and son Khonsu, notwithstanding, the fame of Thebes rests not only in its architecture but in its arts. As an example, Seti II built a Kiosk to the three gods in the Great Court at Karnak and Hatshepsut also did at Luxor temple in the "Ramessean Front." Regarding the art, Murnane (1983: 117) mentions the "black granite bust of the Fourth Prophet of Amun and Mayor of Thebes, Montuemhat [No. 935 in Room 24 in the Cairo Museum] east of Center is one of the triumphs of ancient portraiture: the man's advanced age and his intelligence are delineated with a subtlety that makes all but superfluous the receding hairline shown as well."

EGYPT ESSAYS ON ANCIENT KEMET

Egypt Essays Photo 81. Medinet Habu, Mortuary Temple of Rameses III. Rameses offers a platter to an enthroned Black Amon-Ra.

FREDERICK MONDERSON

Egypt Essays Photo 81a. Medinet Habu, Mortuary Temple of Rameses III. Rameses prepares to pour a libation and incense enthroned Amon-Ra with Mut at the god's back.

Nevertheless, it was the religion and spirituality of Thebes that motivated the great adherents of the worship of Amon. In this regard, Diop (1991: 320) sums up this great Theban belief system: "In the cosmogony of Thebes, the god Amon will say: 'I am the God who came by himself, and who was not created.'" Frankfort (1963: 31) shows also that the god's house of worship has similar means of coming into existence. As regards the Temple of Isis on Philae, a sacred place of great antiquity, Frankfort (1963: 31) has written: "The names of the great shrines at Memphis, Thebes, and Hermonthis explicitly stated that they were the 'divine emerging primeval island' or used similar expressions. Each sanctuary possessed the essential quality of original holiness; for, when a new temple was founded, it was assumed that the potential sacredness of the site became manifest. The equation with the primeval hill received architectural expression also. One mounted a few steps or

EGYPT ESSAYS ON ANCIENT KEMET

followed a ramp at every entrance from court or hall to the Holy of Holies, which was thus situated at a level noticeably higher than the entrance." That is, as one penetrated into the temple, the floor rose and the ceiling got lower, placing the sanctuary of the god on the highest location in the temple.

Naturally, there were symbolisms and manifestations that characterized Amon. His alter ego was the God Min. Amon was also seen as a goose and a ram. He had some 75 names but most important his crown was distinctive. The head-wear of Amon, according to Andrews (1993: 16) was: "a low round crown surmounted by the sun-disk of Re and two tall feathers, perhaps a pictorial reference to his name Imn means 'hidden' and hence 'the wind,' and only ruffled feathers could indicate his unseen presence."

THRONE OF POWER

The name Legrain has etched a place in the annals of Karnak, for in addition to his archaeological excavations and repairs to the temples; he discovered thousands of statues in the famed "Cachette Court."

Thebes was indeed a special place for in addition to their contributions to worship temples; pharaohs built mortuary temples or Temples of a Million years, in the Theban necropolis. Within a stretch of a few miles on the West Bank of the Nile, at Thebes a number of temples were located. This is enumerated, according to Sauernon (1962: 282) showing: "Medinet Habu to the south, the Ramesseum in the center and Deir el-Bahari and el-Qurna further north; on the edge of the desert, the colossi of Memnon are the only remains of the temple of Amenhotep III." Carpiceci (1994: 88) adds Seti I, Mentuhotep I, Thutmose III, Hatshepsut, Rameses VI, Mentuhotep II, Amenhotep II, Thutmose IV, Merneptah, a Ptolemaic temple, Thutmose I, Amenhotep and Thutmose II, all the greatest kings, littered the Theban landscape with mortuary temples to celebrate their death.

Cosmologically, the entrance to the underworld lay at Thebes, above Hatshepsut's splendid mortuary temple, the Christian "Convent of the North," Deir el-Bahari. When the deceased was about to enter the world of the next life, he entered through this sacred "gate." The vicinity abuts the Valley of the Kings where today 70 royal burials have been identified and excavated. Some were entered from ancient times, some only in the modern era. Choice of this site for burial dates to Thutmose I. He resolved to move from burial on the plains to the more secret valley. Thutmose III's tomb lies at the very end of the valley in an elevated spot.

J. Baillet describes graffiti he found, according to *American Journal of Archaeology* XXXV (1921: 292-93), in the tombs of the Valley of the Kings near Thebes. "He has collected more than 200 of these. The greater number is inscribed on empty spaces of the walls, or in corners of the pictures; some actually deface the decorations of the tombs. Graffiti have been found in ten of the forty-five known tombs, probably those, which were most accessible, and oftenest shown to travelers. The positions of some of these signatures have shown that the talus of debris which half closed the tombs is not of modern or medieval origin, but existed before the Ptolemaic period. The names represent a great variety of nationalities-Egyptian, Carthaginian, Greek, Roman, Tracian, etc., and show that visitors to the tombs came from all parts of the Mediterranean world, even from Massilia and Spain. Many professions and occupations are mentioned." Aldred (1985: 158) mentions the "full repertoire of statuary in the middle of the eighteenth dynasty tombs at Thebes, notably those of Rekhmire and Kenamon."

VALLEY OF THE QUEENS

Valley of the Queens, *Biban el-Harim* in Arabic, and *Set Neferu* "seat of beauty" was excavated by the Italian Ernesto Schiaparelli from 1903-1906, when according to "The Valley of the Kings and The Queens," English Edition (1995: 19), he discovered "about eighty tombs, many of which were seriously damaged; some of them featured traces of fire whereas others were reduced to stables. They contain the mortal remains of queens and princes from the XIX to

EGYPT ESSAYS ON ANCIENT KEMET

the XX Dynasty; therefore, they can be dated from 1300 B.C. to 1100 B.C."

Valley of the Nobles held the remains of those who served the pharaohs and built structures that depicted their social and civic standing in the society. Poplar tombs there are those of Kiki, Nakht and Sennufer in the Valley of the Artisans at Deir el Medina where they were interred: "As workmen on the royal tombs, these craftsmen were considered the 'holders of secrets' and therefore made to dwell in a village surrounded by walls. Workmen's houses were small and simple; built alongside each other in dried brick; their interiors were whitewashed. Generally speaking, they consisted of a tiny entrance, a reception hall, a second room and a kitchen. Sometimes, but not often, they had a canteen and terrace. Nothing has remained of a probable decoration."

The more famous tombs include that of Sennedjen. According to "The Valley of The Kings and The Queens," he was a "Servant in Truth Square and official of the necropolis at the time of the XIX Dynasty; perhaps, on account of the liveliness and freshness of its decoration, it is the most beautiful tomb of the necropolis. The main room of the tomb is more or less intact and is all that remains of the sepulcher; all the furniture contained therein is now on display at the Cairo Museum."

Egypt Essays Illustration 38. An Open-Air chapel at one of the entrances to the subterranean galleries at Hermopolis. A view showing the desolate site of the City where baboons and ibis were held sacred, and part of the excavations (left); mud-brick building beyond the balustrade of sandstone pillars containing an embalmer's workshop and a chamber where pilgrims paid fees for the mummification of baboons and ibis brought as offering.

FREDERICK MONDERSON

CONCLUSIONS

The meaning of these ruins is indeed significant for they portray a people whose efforts seem as if to withstand time. In their beliefs and practices, in education, technology, religion, art, agriculture and intellectual and creative daring, these Africans influenced the course of history. This legacy of the children of Africa and its people, have indeed been engines of human progress. For today's young, these accomplishments can provide tremendous motivation for them to be meaningful participants in universal human drama, for two of the most significant things, man and civilization began in Africa, and Thebes ruled the world as its capital city more years than any other civilization.

Egypt Essays Photo 82. Hathor's Temple at Dendera. The classic columned hall entrance to the Temple. Each column sports a different capital, with the outer ones sporting Hathor Heads.

EGYPT ESSAYS ON ANCIENT KEMET

Egypt Essays Photo 82a. Hathor's Temple at Dendera. An image from the "Crypt," showing some secrets of the temple.

FREDERICK MONDERSON

Egypt Essays Photo 82b. Hathor's Temple at Dendera. Horus, in size and beauty, evident a major player in this temple.

EGYPT ESSAYS ON ANCIENT KEMET

REFERENCES

Aldred, Cyril. *Egyptian Art*. London: Thames and Hudson, 1980.

Andrews, Carol. *Amulets of Ancient Egypt*. London: Thames and Hudson, 1994.

Bierbrier, Morris. *The Tomb-Builders of the Pharaohs*. Cairo: American University Press, (1982) 1989.

Bratton, Fred Gladstone. *A History of Egyptian Archaeology*. New York: Thomas Y. Crowell, 1968.

Childe, V. Gordon. *What Happened in History?* Baltimore, MD: Penguin Books, (1942) 1954.

Clarke, Sommers and R., Engelbach. *Ancient Egyptian Construction and Architecture*. New York: Dover Publications, (1930) 1990.

Erman, Adolf. *Life in Ancient Egypt*. New York: Macmillan and Co., 1894.

Fagan, Brian. *The Rape of the Nile: Tomb Robbers, Tourists and Archaeology in Egypt*. New York: Charles Scribner's Sons, 1975.

Fairservis, Walter A. *The Ancient Kingdoms of the Nile*. New York: New American Library, 1962.

Frankfort, Henri, Mrs. H.A. Frankfort, John A. Wilson, and Thorkild Jacobson. *Before Philosophy*. Baltimore, MD: Penguin Books, (1946) 1963.

Greener, Leslie. *The Discovery of Egypt*. New York: Dorset Press, 1966.

Haag, Michael. *Guide to Egypt*. London: Michael Haag, 1987.

Habachi, Labib. *The Obelisks of Egypt: Skyscrapers of the Past*. Cairo: American University in Cairo Press, (1984) 1987.

Hart. George. *Egyptian Myths*. London: British Museum Publications, 1990.

Hatem, M. Abdel-Kader. *Life in Ancient Egypt*. Cairo: Al Ahram Commercial Press, 1982.

Jackson, John G. *Introduction to African Civilizations*. Secaucus, New Jersey: The Citadel Press, (1970).

_____. *Man, God and Civilization*. New Hyde Park, New York: University Books, Inc., 1972.

Lurker, Manfred. *The Gods and Symbols of Ancient Egypt*. London: Thames and Hudson, (1974) 1980.

FREDERICK MONDERSON

Kamil, Jill. *The Ancient Egyptians*. Cairo: The American University Press, (1976) 1988.

Kees, Herman. *Ancient Egypt*: *A Cultural Topography*. Chicago: University of Chicago Press, 1977.

Mokhtar, Wafaa Moh. *Karnak*. Second Edition: Cairo: Al Helal Trading and Press, No Date.

Moorey, P. R. S. *Ancient Egypt*. Oxford: Ashmolean Museum, 1988.

Murnane, William J. *Ancient Egypt*. New York: Penguin Books, 1983.

Portman, Ian. *Luxor*: *A Guide to the Temples and Tombs of Ancient Thebes*. Cairo: American University Press, 1989.

Sauernon, Serge in George Posener's *Dictionary of Egyptian Civilization*. London: Methuen and Co., Ltd., 1962.

Spencer, A. J. *Early Egypt*: *The Rise of Civilization in the Nile Valley*. London: British Museum, 1993.

Uphill, Eric P. *Egyptian Towns and Cities*. Bucks: Shire Publications, 1988.

The Valley of the Kings and the Queens. English Edition. Italy: Centro Stampa Editoriale, 1985.

White, J. E. Manchip. *Ancient Egypt*: *Its Culture and History*. New York: Dover Publications, 1970.

Wilson, J. A. *The Culture of Ancient Egypt*. Chicago: University of Chicago Press, (1951) 1963.

Egypt Essays Illustration 39. Egyptian ships in full decorated sail.

EGYPT ESSAYS ON ANCIENT KEMET

Egypt Essays Illustration 39a. A beautiful Ptolemaic chalice in light-blue faience: One of several vessels of fine workmanship found in the subterranean tombs at Hermopolis (left); and a faience bowl in deep rich blue from the sacred city of Hermopolis: An under-side view showing the curious pattern of the decoration.

12. TEMPLE OF KARNAK: THE MAJESTIC ARCHITECTURE OF ANCIENT KEMET

The Temple of Karnak, "Throne of Power," is a profound and majestic architectural construction, the grandest in all the land of ancient Kemet, today's Egypt, in Northeast Africa. In fact, when we think of significant milestones in the history of architecture, and particularly in the Nile Valley, Karnak stands supreme for its creativity, beauty, majesty, grandeur, massive exactness, and double-axis, east and west, and north and south. Today's remains, in superb defiance of the ravages of time, still evoke great reverence, awe and inspiration. Comprising such great beauty, the Temple of Karnak, in the Precinct of Amun, principal deity of the Theban Triad, is an aggregate of worship temples whose buildings extended over a period of two thousand years. Here pharaohs vied with each other to erect structures in honor of the mighty deity Amon-Ra,

FREDERICK MONDERSON

"Lord of the thrones of Two Lands," the sun god; his wife, Mut, the earth goddess; and their son, Khonsu, the moon god comprising the Theban Triad. In Lurker (1991: 123) a photograph depicts how "Rames-Nakht, High Priest of Amun, kneels to present a small shrine upon which are represented the Theban Triad of Amun, Mut and their son, Khons. From Karnak. XX Dynasty, c. 1120 B.C. Egyptian Museum, Cairo." The war-god Montu also had a temple to the north of Amon's at Karnak. Today the temples of Mut, Khonsu and Montu are closed to visitors.

Circumstances of the last few years has caused security apparatus to be installed that screens all visitors who come in multitudes to enjoy the wonderful spectacle known as the Temple of Karnak.

Baines and Malek (1980: 92) rather succinctly explained how Karnak Temple was arranged. "The layout of the great temple can be described as a series of pylons of various dates, with courts and halls between them, leading to the main sanctuary. The earliest are Pylons IV and V built by Tuthmose I; from then on the temple was enlarged in a westerly and a southerly direction."

Even further, Baines and Malek (1980: 92) added: "Nearly 20 other small chapels and temples are within the precinct of Amun, including a temple of Ptah built by Tuthmosis III, Shabaka, the Ptolemies and Tiberius (north of the Great Temple, close to the enclosure wall), and a chapel of Osiris Heqadjet "Ruler of Time, of Osorkon IV and Shebitku (northeast of the Great Temple, close to the enclosure wall)."

Such grandeur in architectural construction, utilizing exact mathematical and scientific principles so amazed young Champollion, Sauernon (1962: 42) quotes his statement: "No ancient or modern people have thought of art or architecture on such a sublime scale so vast and so grandiose as that of the ancient Egyptians. They thought in terms of men 100 feet tall." Elsewhere, Aldred (1987: 33) mentions Belzoni, agent of Henry Salt, the British Consul. Then, Belzoni, the "strongman Egyptologist" wrote, "In the 19th Century the remains of Karnak and Luxor were like those of a

EGYPT ESSAYS ON ANCIENT KEMET

city of giants, who after long conflict were all destroyed, leaving the ruins of their temples as the only proof of their former existence."

Throwing more light on these discussions, Habachi (1987: 52) has pointed to two recurring themes throughout the temples comprising the Precinct of Amun. "One showing the god Amon or Amon-Re - Presenting the king with a sword with which he might smite his enemies and the other portraying the king offering the gods rich tribute and prisoners captured during his visits."

Standing remains support the view that the earliest temple began in the Middle Kingdom. However, use of this site, in the 4th Upper Kingdom Nome, may extend to the beginnings of Pharaonic rule and into the prehistoric period. This area was contemporary with other centers and deities that held prominence in the early age of dynastic rule. The first twenty-two nomes stretched from Biga above Aswan and Elephantine to Memphis in the north. Baines and Malek (1980: 15) explain these political divisions with their statement. "The 22 nomes of Upper Egypt were fixed by the 5th Dynasty, and their lengths along the river are recorded in the Kiosk of Senwosret I at Karnak. For Lower Egypt the definitive number of 20 nomes was not established until the Greco-/Roman Period. The total number of 42 had a symbolic value: there were 42 judges of the dead, and the early Christian writer, Clement of Alexandria (2nd century A.D.), states that the Egyptians had 42 sacred books."

FREDERICK MONDERSON

Egypt Essays Photo 83. Hathor's Temple at Dendera. Ceiling of a chapel to Goddess Nuit, depicting the divinity giving birth to the sun in the morning and swallowing it in the evening.

EGYPT ESSAYS ON ANCIENT KEMET

Egypt Essays Photo 83a. Hathor's Temple at Dendera. A Thoth ape with knives in the "Setting up the Tet" Osiris ritual.

Additionally, in the position as seat of great learning and wisdom, during the Middle and New Kingdom, Karnak and Thebes sparkled. As such, Baines and Malek (1980: 90) believed, the "temple of Amun was ideologically and economically the most important temple establishment in the whole of Egypt." In theological, cosmological and political dynamics, it was considered "the location of the emergence of the primeval mound at the beginning of time. It was the supreme 'city' and all other towns in Egypt could only try to imitate it and would only achieve pale reflections."

FREDERICK MONDERSON

Egypt Essays Illustration 39b. Portrait of Queen Aahmes-Nefertari, wife of Aahmes, founder of the New Kingdom and Mother of Amenhotep I shown wearing the Queen-Mother Crown represented by a vulture headdress surmounted by a vulture atop a mortar.

Significantly, if it could be imagined what the pathway to heaven would be like, the walk through Karnak Temple seems just as exhilarating an inspiration, in this "the most Select of Places." The aura, majesty and symbolism surrounding the home of the great Theban Triad, where "Amun Lord of Karnak" resided, particularly

EGYPT ESSAYS ON ANCIENT KEMET

intoxicates those privileged to behold this site as they are invigorated and rejuvenated by its sacred and profound vitality. This, as the visitor beholds the wondrous testaments of artistic and pictographic panorama that undergirded the epistemological, philosophic, religious and festive efforts of praise and ritualizing of the Egyptian, African god, Amon.

Egypt Essays Illustration 40. Vulture in flight with outspread wings and clutching an ankh in its talons as shown in the restored "White Chapel" of Senusert I at Karnak (left); and the reconstructed "White Chapel" of Senusert I of the XIIth Dynasty and now in Karnak Temple's Open Air Museum.

Now, to understand the nature of the temple, one has to familiarize oneself with the historical circumstances surrounding the emergence of the Amun priesthood, and how this body influenced successive pharaohs to glorify the deity through their works of architectural splendor. Monarchs lavished enormous endowments of wealth in gold, cattle, spices, slaves, etc., on Amun who brought success, fame and fortune to his most ardent supporters. Equally, we can also trace the evolution of the worship of Amun. In this regard, Steindorff and Seele (1971: 134) have offered their view. Accordingly, the "cosmic god Amun was transferred from Hermopolis to Karnak in the Eleventh Dynasty so that he eventually became the local god of Thebes and later through identification with Re, as 'King of the gods,' the national god of the New Kingdom."

Syncretism, or combining of gods, enabled "Hathor and Isis," wrote Steindorff and Seele (1972: 143), to be "considered the same person, while Amon of Karnak, Min of Coptos, and later even Khnum of

FREDERICK MONDERSON

Elephantine were combined into a single divinity." This is one reason why the mighty Amun, his precinct, city, region and state, enjoyed the power it did in the ancient world.

That is, until challenged by the Amarna Heresy. In building his temple beyond the eastern gate at Karnak the new king had to confront the grandeur of Amon. Amenhotep IV, 'Amon is Satisfied' changed his name to Akhenaton, 'He who is Beneficial to Aton,' and became increasingly concerned with his new disk worship. In this, he began to feel uncomfortable within the Precinct of Amon.

Maspero (1904, V, 82) has expressed the view rightly that: "Thebes had belonged to Amen so long that the king could never hope to bring it to regard Atenu as anything but of inferior rank. Each city belonged to some god, to whom was attributed its origin, its development and its prosperity, and whom it could not forsake without renouncing its very existence."

This inherent denial caused Akhenaton to choose Amarna to build his new city Akhenaton 'City of the Horizon' and temple 'Mansion of the Obelisk,' 'Shadow of Ra.' He drew up the plans himself. Ikhnaton also taught his artists new techniques of representing nature and the human form that contradicted the traditional mode of representing these subjects, particularly the Pharaoh. His mother Queen Tiy, and advisers Ay and Commander of the Egyptian Forces, General Horemhab, moved to strategic Amarna, along with a retinue of supporters, their families and property. There he began to write and praise the Aton, solar disk.

In Akhenaten's *Great Hymn to Aton*, Obenga (1992: 19) wrote, "One sees more than a text of monotheism and expressions of faith. It reveals an exact knowledge of nature which is surprisingly scientifically precise when compared to modern scientific knowledge."

After this Aton turned with a vengeance on Amon. Akhnaton decreed, according to Payne (1964: 128-29) that: "the name of the district where the Amon Temple was located was to be changed to 'The Brightness of Aton, the Great' and Thebes itself, the City of Amon, was to be renamed, 'The City of the Brightness of Aton.' His animosity was directed purely against Amon, for Prisse D'Avennes 'found at Karnak on fragments of the temple, the names of other divinities than Atonu worshiped by Khuniatonu." Maspero (V, 1904: 89) pretty well explained how the king felt. "The other gods, except Amon, were sharers with humanity in his benefits. Atonu prescribed him, and tolerated him only at Thebes; he required that the name of Amon should be effaced wherever it occurred, but he respected Ra, and Horus and Harmakhis - all, in fact but Amon: he was content with being regarded as their king, and he strove rather to become their chief than their destroyer."

Anger at the principal deity of the triad did not extend to the consort. For as Maspero (V, 1904: 82) again informed: "The proscription of Amon extended to inscriptions, so that while his name or figure, whatever could be got at, was chiseled out, the vulture, the emblem of Mut, which expresses the idea of mother, was avoided." Despite this destruction, in King Tutankhamon's return to Thebes, Amon reemerged as principal deity particularly under the succeeding dynasties of Ramesside kings, great adherents of Amon.

It seems rather natural that Amon's adherents would return vengeance for the proscription they suffered. Erman (1907: 69-70) explained an attitude of Amon's priests in the following statement in exhortation of their deity.

They cried: "Woe to him who injures thee! Thy city endures, but the city of him who injures thee has perished. Shame upon him who commits sacrilege against thee in any land.... The sun of him who knew thee not has set; but he who knows thee, he shines; the sanctuary of him who injured thee lies in darkness, and the whole earth is in light."

Powerful! Amon as Great God in universal beneficence!

FREDERICK MONDERSON

Interestingly, that power, in its spiritual, intellectual, revitalizing and awe-inspiring significance, is ever present today. The visitor is impressed by the stupendous remains with their timeless, esoteric mystique and artistic wonderment that reflect the deep sense of commitment of early Africans of ancient Kemet in their sweet communion with deity.

Secular and religious festivals as the Heb-Sed, Opet, and agricultural festivals were celebrated with great reverence and joviality. In one particular festival, the "Feast of the Valley," Bierbrier (1989: 97) explained, the "sacred image of the god Amon was brought across the river to visit the mortuary temples of the deceased ruler." The "Opet Festival" represented Amun's journey to Luxor, the *Southern Isut*, to engage in worshiping and enjoying Hathor/Mut, his wife.

Egypt Essays Illustration 41. The earliest stone building ever found: Two third dynasty chapels excavated from the Step Pyramid at Sakkara, with fluted columns 2500 years older than the earliest one known of Greek construction (left); A bowman-charioteer illustrated showing the king, Rameses II, in blue crown with reins attached to his waist as he fires his arrow (right).

Mention can be made of Percy E. Newberry's "An Egyptian Gardener: The Tomb of Nakht" that shows the nobleman, who under Thotmose III, 'held the office of head gardener of the gardens attached to the Temple of Karnak.' One of his duties was to supply flowers daily to the main and subsidiary temples for their services and ceremonies. Nakht is depicted in his tomb: "presenting Thutmose III with a huge bouquet, five feet high, and composed of

EGYPT ESSAYS ON ANCIENT KEMET

papyrus, lotus flowers, cornflowers, and poppies, interspersed here and there with fragrant fruits of the mimusopsi, a tree not now found in the gardens of Egypt, but well known at the present day in India. Some of these garlands have been found in the ancient cemeteries of Egypt, buried with the dead."

For the civil garden, a tomb of the nobleman Amten, who owned several estates, could be used as comparative reference. In another article "Ancient Egyptian Gardening," Newberry mentions this, the oldest garden yet discovered, as explained by Amten. "'The boundary wall,' he writes, 'was 200 cubits (i.e. 350 feet) in breadth, and the same in width; the garden inside it was planted with beautiful trees, and a very great pond was excavated in its center, the surrounding garden being planted with fig-trees and vines. When the 'writing for the royal prescript had been made, a very great vineyard was planted, which yielded me wine in great quantity. I trained two acres of vine hidden in the interior of the wall, and I planted trees around it.'"

Egypt Essays Photo 84. Osiris Temple at Abydos. The view from a distance shows six openings between the columns on each side of the middle or principal entrance. There were altogether seven entrances before Rameses closed all but the center one.

Egypt Essays Photo 84a. Osiris Temple at Abydos. Columns of the "Second Hypostyle Hall" showing the rise to the platform housing the shrines of the seven deities.

Egypt Essays Photo 84b. Osiris Temple at Abydos. Isis and Seti I set up the Tet or backbone of Osiris. Notice the kneeling figure. Four versions of the "Pillar" are indicated.

EGYPT ESSAYS ON ANCIENT KEMET

Egypt Essays Photo 84c. Osiris Temple at Abydos. An enthroned goddess from the nearby temple of Rameses II at Abydos.

FREDERICK MONDERSON

In examining this ancient culture, it ought not be forgotten, racist scholarship, here as in other places in Africa, have tried to falsely claim European authorship of many significant achievements made on the African continent, under the banner of the "Hamitic Hypothesis." This pseudo-scientific theory, now refuted, held "all evidence of civilization or high culture found in Africa was brought there by people of a white morphology." In this vein, such pseudo-scientists have sought to claim as foreign, great Egyptians, Africans, whose influence on the world stage has been memorable. I say this to create an example of the enormous power of ancient African persona, spirituality, tenaciousness and creativity to draw attention to attendant problems of ascribing their accomplishments to foreigners.

Dr. ben-Jochannan (1990: 40-41) strongly favored the Egyptian, African, Rameses II; a great warrior pharaoh, high priest, military strategist, imperial colonizer, conqueror, engineer, builder, and father and husband. However, yet another authority claimed Rameses to be of Syrian origin! For, in addition to his stupendous building projects, this monarch was involved in *The Battle of Kadesh*, one of the most memorable military engagements of the ancient world. On an imperial expedition to Asia, he set out with four regiments, Amun, Ra, Ptah, Sutekh, with the king in the vanguard force. He pushed with great fervor and ran ahead of his troops. Other Corps accompanying his effort were named the "Tribes of the Pharaoh," the "Tribes of the Beauty of the Solar Disk," etc. As night fell, the princes of the Kadesh Confederacy who had set an ambush sprung their trap on the unsuspecting Egyptian/Kemetic monarch and descended upon his encampment. He thereupon called upon Amon-Re, his father, beseeching the great Theban deity, reminding that he and his ancestors had praised and glorified him in the most stupendous manner and that Amon should never allow the likes of these foreigners to be the better of him. With that the king sprang into action, seized his equipment, grabbed his chariot, charged the enemy then rallied his forces and rode out of the orchestrated trap, linking up with his main force. Winning the

EGYPT ESSAYS ON ANCIENT KEMET

day or night as it was, he was able to broker a peace treaty in good terms with the confederacy.

This wonderful account was enshrined on the walls of his temples at Abu Simbel, the Ramesseum, Abydos, Luxor, and Beit Wali and at Karnak. They're also papyrus versions of the treaty with the Hittites. Importantly, this pharaoh, purportedly a Syrian, calling upon an Egyptian, African, god in Asia, is one aspect of the awe and might of Amon and the Theban social and religious system represented in his name. Is this a profound example of trilateralism? Of course, Rameses II, the great African, was not Syrian. However, he did call upon his father, the ancestral god Amon, "Lord of Karnak," an African God, to give strength, courage and fortitude, while he battled foreigners and continued to propel the nation of Kemet, Egypt, and Africa, to the prominence it enjoyed. Maspero (1904) tells us the king enjoyed great luxury even on military expeditions. He carried a portable shrine where he could make morning presentations to the deity. How religious and how profound for a pharaoh, as was so customary for these ancient Africans?

In order to more properly experience the Temple of Karnak, one needs to understand the archaeological history surrounding the site. The fate of Karnak got special attention with the fall of columns in the Hypostyle Hall on October 3, 1899, due to a mild earthquake. At Karnak, archaeologists had unveiled a mass array of ancient art in statues, stelae, obelisks, decorated blocks, columns, pylons, and walls. These were natural canvases of divinely inspired creative expressions of literature and art in praise of Amon buttressing spirituality but creating vistas in science, medicine and other social conventions.

Woldering (1963: 148) has pointed out, "The Egyptian word for Karnak is *Ipit Isut* or 'counter of the palaces' i.e., the assembly place of all the Egyptian deities, whose visiting gods had their chapels in the national temple, where they were worshiped." Many archaeologists did extensive work to repair and clear this temple.

FREDERICK MONDERSON

The Frenchman, Legrain was lucky to unearth several thousand statues in "their attitudes of the rank, in limestone, in black or pink granite, in yellow or red sandstone, in schist, in alabaster ...." in the "Cachette Court." Portman (1989: 39) reminded, the "Cachette Court" was "erected by Tuthmose III, the walls were decorated by Rameses II and bare the text of the latter's treaty with the Hittite King Metwallis. There is also a long list of the victories of Merenptah (1221-1214 B.C.)."

Bratton (1968: 178) discussed Le Grain's work at Karnak where: "From December 1903 to July 1904 he found 456 stone statues, seven sphinxes, and 8,000 bronzes. In the 1904-05 Season he recovered 200 stone statues and additional bronzes. All of these were drawn out of the water of the Cachette."

Granted, modern archaeology did much for the recovery and systematization of the historical record of the Nile Valley. It exposed profound social, spiritual and scientific axioms that in their dynamism as engines of civilization development have guided the human experience along the pageantry of history. However, we must, in an effort at African historiographic reconstruction, recognize the hunger and limitations of many of the "plunderers" seeking ancient knowledge in the tombs of the sacred ancestors along the Nile. Modern analysis of the archaeological and anthropological record have also helped color the history of interpretation of this data, and thus project a distorted view of the ancient African culture of Kemet. To this end, Afrocentric historiographic reconstruction needs only attempt a correction of the record through re-examination, particularly records of a century ago. Then the "records of the ancient records" were unearthed, analyzed, catalogued, distributed and disbursed to private collections, museums, and governments, where these now adorn their exhibits.

EGYPT ESSAYS ON ANCIENT KEMET

Egypt Essays Photo 85. Osiris Temple at Abydos. Another view before shrines provides a look at an interior of great mystery and symbolism.

Archaeology has helped realize, the religious significance of Amun can be seen in his pantheon, whose composition included, Budge (1934: 162) enumerated: "1. Amen-Ra at the head of the Southern Apt (Luxor), the Lord of Heaven, and his gods; 2. Mut, Lady of Heaven, Mistress of the World. 3. Khonsu, Nefer-hetep. 4. Min with symbol and temple. 5. Isis. 6. Neb Khnemu (Thoth). 7. *Ma'at*. 8. The Lady of Amenti (Hathor). 9. Osiris. 10. Un-Nefer-Khenti-Amenti. 11. Horus of the Two Horizons. 12. He of the Embalment Chamber. 13. Het-Her (Hathor). 14. Governor of the House of the Physician. 15. Nephthys."

FREDERICK MONDERSON

Egypt Essays Photo 85a. Osiris Temple at Abydos. An enthroned goddess from the nearby temple of Rameses II at Abydos.

Archaeology has helped realize, the religious significance of Amun can be seen in his pantheon, whose composition included, Budge (1934: 162) enumerated: "1. Amen-Ra at the head of the Southern Apt (Luxor), the Lord of Heaven, and his gods; 2. Mut, Lady of

EGYPT ESSAYS ON ANCIENT KEMET

Heaven, Mistress of the World. 3. Khonsu, Nefer-hetep. 4. Min with symbol and temple. 5. Isis. 6. Neb Khnemu (Thoth). 7. *Ma'at*. 8. The Lady of Amenti (Hathor). 9. Osiris. 10. Un-Nefer-Khenti-Amenti. 11. Horus of the Two Horizons. 12. He of the Embalment Chamber. 13. Het-Her (Hathor). 14. Governor of the House of the Physician. 15. Nephthys."

Egypt Essays Photo 86. Osiris Temple at Abydos. Inner chambers depict more formalism and mystery.

FREDERICK MONDERSON

Egypt Essays Photo 86a. Osiris Temple at Abydos. Part of the "Osireion" in the temple's rear. This mysterious region was always surrounded by water fed by underground springs connected to the Nile.

Concomitantly, in this respect, Hart helped supply an important view of numbers in Kemetic pantheism when he explained (1990: 13) the composition and number significance. "The nine deities can be restricted to the genealogy devised at Heliopolis, but the notion of a coterie of gods and goddesses was transferable; the temple of Abydos had an Ennead of seven deities, while there were fifteen members of the Ennead in the Karnak temple. Probably, because signs grouped in threes in Egyptian hieroglyphs conveyed the idea of an intermittent plural, the concept of nine gods and goddesses indicates a plural of plurals, sufficient to cover a pantheon of any number of deities in any temple."

EGYPT ESSAYS ON ANCIENT KEMET

Egypt Essays Photo 86b. Osiris Temple at Abydos. Another enthroned goddess from the nearby temple of Rameses II at Abydos.

FREDERICK MONDERSON

The Theban Priesthood became a powerhouse, even though they were four principal religious sites where various deities were worshiped, as at Memphis, Ptah; Heliopolis, Ra; Osiris at Abydos; and Amen at Thebes, manifesting at Karnak and Luxor, and in the valley across the river. Their wealth entrenched particularly in the New Kingdom, included tens of thousands of individuals, specialists, accumulated knowledge, scientists, artisans, astronomers, mathematicians, engineers, medical men, embalmers, and also acres of land, buildings, ships, agricultural groves, and flower gardens. Great learning flourished here and this made Karnak the intellectual, religious and spiritual capital of ancient Kemet, and as such, "light of the ancient world." Thus, even from great distances, men looked with confidence to the promise and symbolism of this great and holy mound of creation, Karnak. One could well imagine Thutmose I, Thutmose III, Amenhotep II, Amenhotep III, Seti I, Rameses II, Rameses III, on any one of their many military expeditions, praising Amen in morning devotion, at their portable shrines, before the day's battle. The same can be said for the Middle Kingdom monarchs Mentuhotep, Amenemhat, and Usertesen and everyone in their sequence. All this occurred while the wheels of ethics and science at Karnak guided education, architecture, astronomy, art, music, science, gaiety, spirituality and reverence.

KARNAK: THE POWER

Though the history of Thebes dates to the earliest formation of the nomes, the buildings still standing at Karnak and those that have provided inscriptions of a historical significance tell the temple was begun by the Middle Kingdom pharaohs. This may be because, we see signs of the primacy of Amen during the XIIth Dynasty when kings took his name as Amenemenes, and became his staunchest adherents. However, there is reason to believe the site of Karnak is built on even earlier foundations that were made of more perishable materials, possibly extending the sacredness of the site to the emergence of time measurement, the very beginning of the Calendar, at *Nile Year* 1, at 4240 B.C. Pier (1916: 91) is less ancient

EGYPT ESSAYS ON ANCIENT KEMET

saying: "The prehistoric implements which have been found within site of the great Karnak pylons [and] .... Karnak itself provides relics which take us back to the period of the Second Dynasty or about 3000 B.C."

In-as-much as the Middle Kingdom was a period of consolidation, reorganization, expansion and artistic, linguistic and cultural growth; the glory days of the New Kingdom surpassed this in splendor and represented the third "golden age" of pharaonic rule. Its rise stemmed from the nucleus of pharaonic rule, Thebes and the strength and wealth of inner Africa. While Tetisheri and Sekenen-Ra began the war of liberation against the Hyksos in the XVIIth Dynasty, it was their son Kamose, and his brother Aahmose (Aahmes) who expelled the "Shepherd Kings." Aahmes married (Aahmes)-Nefertari, his sister and ancestress of the XVIIIth Dynasty. Her portrait in the British Museum depicts a "coal-black Ethiopian" Queen bejeweled in long-flowing fashionable attire, wearing the Red, White and Blue Tricolor, 1500 years Before Christ, and, thousands before the 20 or so modern nations whose flags are so designed.

FREDERICK MONDERSON

Egypt Essays Photo 87. Osiris Temple at Abydos. Wearing the leopard skin, the King, assisted by Hathor as Isis, presents a plant to Osiris, in full "Traveling Regalia."

EGYPT ESSAYS ON ANCIENT KEMET

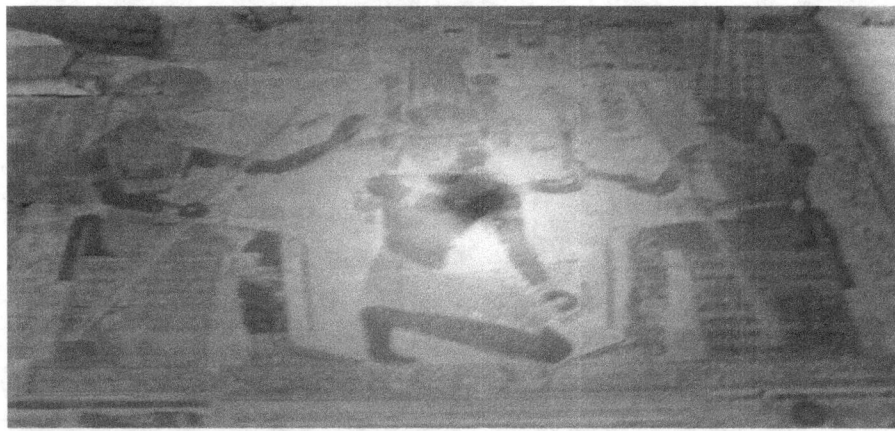

Egypt Essays Photo 87a. Osiris Temple at Abydos. Seti kneels between enthroned gods as Amon-Ra gives him an instrument of power and Ra-Horakhty pats him on the back.

Establishing the capital at Thebes, Aahmose reaffirmed the primacy of the south, for as Payne (1964: 76-77) would write: "Ahmose announced that Amon, the Theban city-god, was henceforth to be worshipped as 'King of the Gods.' For it was Amon, Ahmose believed who had led him to victory against the 'vile' Hyksos." After this, warrior pharaohs, Amenhotep I, his son Thutmose I, the latter's daughter Hatshepsut, and sons, Thutmose II and Thutmose III; the last king's son Amenhotep II, Thutmose IV, Amenhotep III, and Horemheb, Rameses I, Seti I, his son Rameses II, Seti II and Rameses III, Bubastites, as well as Taharka, and Greek and Roman rulers, all built at Karnak. These kings, whose efforts sought to enhance and placate the various shrines of the deities, contributed their unique part to the whole structure.

FREDERICK MONDERSON

Egypt Essays Photo 87b. Osiris Temple at Abydos. Seti offers an instrument to enthroned Amon-Ra, painted Black!

EGYPT ESSAYS ON ANCIENT KEMET

Particularly, the Late Period was one of continued expansion of the temple and a continuation of the artistic representation of the earliest periods. Greek pharaohs encouraged the religious and political significance of this site through their repairs and erection of small structures as porticos and porches at Karnak. These latter pharaohs built principally at Philae, Kom Ombo, Edfu, Esna, Dendera, Elephantine, and Kalabsha.

In ancient times, a quay at the riverside allowed pharaoh to visit the temple Precinct of Amun for presentations at festivals, holy days, and important constructions. The same way that a canal connected the Temple of Karnak with the Nile River, a canal also connected Karnak with Luxor Temple, the "Southern Isut."

At the Quay the pharaoh entered a canal that brought him to today's built-up plaza before the Avenue of Sphinxes that entranced the First Pylon of the Temple of Karnak where two now broken and buried statues stood. In modern times, two small obelisks of Seti II remain, before the entrance is approached from a raised platform. Here, double rows of 200 feet long Avenue of Criosphinxes with head of rams and the small statue and name of Rameses II leads to the temple. Since the Sanctuary of the original temple dates to the Middle Kingdom, therefore there's a reverse order in the history of the buildings one encounters in a visit to Karnak Temple. As a result, and because of its vastness, Sauernon (1962: 142) comments, "Karnak is a world in which one could be completely lost." So it's best to stay with the guide or valuable monuments in the site could be overlooked.

The **First Pylon** was built by the Ethiopians to wall the **Great Court**, and stands 370 feet wide, with the standing tower 140 feet high, and the structure 50 feet thick. We can quote Simpkins (1989) for "comparison, the west front of St Paul's Cathedral in London is 170 feet wide and 137 feet high." One of the two-propylon towers retains a great part of its original height, but has lost its summit and cornice. The tower on the north (left) could have been climbed for a spectacular view of the temple and the surrounding area. However, this was discontinued because of an accident to a visitor. The full breadth of the wall was perforated with holes for fastening timbers that secured flagstaffs of the various representative gods, usually placed in front of these propylaea. No sculptures have ever been added to either face nor was the surface leveled to receive such decorations. Therefore, the structure can be considered unfinished. At the doorway, Kamil (1976: 39) mentions an inscription, "recording the latitude and longitude of the chief temples of the Pharaohs as calculated by the group of scholars accompanying the army of Napoleon to Egypt." There is an aerial photograph of the greater enclosure wall and a plan of the entire area at this entrance. On the inner-face of the southern propylon an embankment remains and provides clues as to how these higher structures were erected.

The **Great Forecourt**, called the "Court of the Bubastites" is 376 feet long and 338 feet wide, for an area of 93,000 square feet. Shishak of the XXIInd Dynasty built this Court and Maspero considers that he intended to roof over the columns but never completed the work. In the southeast angle of the court, there is a set of sculptures containing the names of the XXIInd Dynasty kings. Here Kamil (1980: 42) tells us: "this scene commemorates the victory of Shishak of the Bible over Rehoboan, son of Solomon, the King of Judah, when Solomon's temple was robbed of its riches. Beneath Amon is the goddess Mut holding a club, bow and quiver, leading five rows of captives carved in perfect symmetry. To the right Sheshonk is grasping a group of captives by the hair and striking them with his raised club."

There are covered corridors on either side of the Court, two colonnades to the north and south. Taharka contributed a Kiosk of a double line of five columns down the center, of which only one remains. However, while the standard number of columns in this kiosk is given as 10, Sir Bannister Fletcher's diagram provides a number of 12, whereas Mariette provides his diagram with 16 columns. The surviving Taharka column stands 69 feet tall with open papyrus capitals. It took two years to dismantle and to re-erect

EGYPT ESSAYS ON ANCIENT KEMET

the Taharka column by modern restoration efforts, for fear it would collapse at the turn of the Twentieth Century. Ruffle (1977: 93) informs, Taharka also built "two smaller colonnades at the Temple of Khonsu and Montu." There was much prosperity during the reign of Taharka and this success enabled the pharaoh to build extensively as he did at Thebes and elsewhere. Taharka built a colonnade at Medinet Habu, mortuary temple of Rameses III.

Egypt Essays Illustration 42. A kneeling statue of Hatshepsut with its face damaged and missing parts of both arms, while another kneeling statues stands nearby.

FREDERICK MONDERSON

The corridors of the Court at Karnak are 50 feet high. The temple of Rameses III interrupted the colonnade of the south. At the western end of this southern colonnade there's evidence of how the columns were erected. The colonnade on the north presents an even front of 18 columns. A chapel for the barque of the Theban Triad was dedicated by Seti II and located in the northwest corner of the court. In this Kiosk, the barque of Mut is on the left and Amun in the center, with Khons to the right. Beside it a flight of seven steps, on either side of which were granite statues of Rameses II, only one of which now remains, much mutilated.

Rows of Sphinxes lie in front of the northern and southern colonnades. These belonged to the Avenue of Criosphinxes before the **Second Pylon** was erected by Rameses I. Towards the **Second Pylon**, stands the monumental statue of Rameses II and the Lady Binta Anta. His name was usurped and so some tourist guides attribute it to Rameses III. Later High Priest and king Pinudjen of the Twenty-First Dynasty again usurped it.

In the southeast corner, intersecting the southern colonnade is the 170 foot long Temple of Rameses III of the XXth Dynasty, resting on a perpendicular axis to the main temple. It was built as a single unit without any additions, therefore different from the larger Karnak structure. At this point, Maspero (1926: 107) has indicated, "The temple was built as an image of the world, as the Egyptians imagined it to be."

EGYPT ESSAYS ON ANCIENT KEMET

Egypt Essays Photo 88. Osiris Temple at Abydos. Seti presents a platter to enthroned Isis.

FREDERICK MONDERSON

Egypt Essays Photo 88a. Osiris Temple at Abydos. Seti makes a presentation of Ma'at to enthroned Ra-Horakhty.

EGYPT ESSAYS ON ANCIENT KEMET

Egypt Essays Photo 88b. Osiris Temple at Abydos. Ra-Horakhty gives life to the nostrils of Rameses II, from his nearby temple at Abydos.

Two sandstone statues of King Rameses III stand in front of the pylon, wearing the Double Crown above the Nemes Headdress. In this temple, stands a Peristyle Court with two rows, left and right, of

Osiride Figures and a Hypostyle Hall, of which Simpkins (1987: 6) has written, "eight bud-capital-decorated columns with reliefs showing the monarch, making offerings before various gods." On the west wall, Murnane (1983: 238) points to scenes, "illustrating the yearly progress of the ithyphallic form of Amun, who was related to the god Min of Coptos and represented the principle of exuberant fertility in nature." All stand before the Sanctuary.

The wealth of Amun during the later New Kingdom was immense. Pier (1916: 100) mentions an inscription of Rameses III regarding Karnak: "'Its beauty is unto the dome of heaven, its august pillars are of electrum,' and Amenhotep II says: 'I made for Amon a hall in Karnak, a thing of wonder unnumbered in decorations of gold, unnumbered in decorations of malachite and lapis lazuli, bright with flowers and filled with slaves.'"

Erman (1907: 71) further informs regarding the size of land holding and other forms of wealth as represented by three of the principal centers of worship. During the later New Kingdom, under Rameses III, he noted, the: "temple of Amon at Thebes possessed 926 square miles of land and 81,322 serfs, as well as 421,362 head of cattle. Heliopolis had 166 square miles of land, 12,963 serfs, and 45,544 head of cattle; while the respective numbers for Memphis, which was far behind, were nearly 11 square miles, 3,079 serfs, and 10,047 cattle."

Management of such wealth, Erman (1907: 71) believed needed a "complete administrative organization, where distinguished persons served as superintendents of the treasury, of the land, granaries, cattle, or peasantry, with scribes and soldiers, architects, sculptors, painters, and all classes of minor officials." Of course, the "Garden of Amon" is included for it bloomed with beautiful and varied flowers.

At the end of the Eighteenth Dynasty, Horemheb built the Second Pylon, after the Amarna Heresy. He used blocks from Akhenaton's dismantled sun temple in its construction. His actions are rationalized in the statement of Portman (1989: 30) whose wise assessment states: "The re-use of blocks served a triple function: first, they make convenient filling for the pylon; second, the outrageous stones had to be hidden somewhere; and third, the inscriptions, being so recently dedicated to a solar deity, could not be sullied with a burial beyond the gates. All in all, a neat solution to an awkward heresy, and eminently Egyptian." Rameses I also gets credit for the Second Pylon for his name is engraved there.

The Pylon had four groves for flagstaffs. Ptolemy VI Philometer and Ptolemy IX Euergetes II of the Greek Period erected an intervening door. The lintel of this doorway is missing, but the jambs are well preserved. Simpkins also mentions sculptures showing Horemheb, the "king sacrificing to the gods of the temple and the sacred barque of Amun going to the temple."

Beyond this entranceway lies the Hypostyle masterpiece, a stupendous work of artistry and science that required quarrying, transportation, coordination and erection of untold tonnage of stone. The great hall was cleared and its columns strengthened in the winter of 1885.

However, eleven columns in the Hypostyle Hall fell in October of 1899. As a result, efforts to re-erect them and preserve this wonderful structure have enabled moderns to obtain a better perspective of the significance of this 54,000 square feet of architectural magnificence. This Hypostyle Hall, Maspero V (1904: 172-173) explained: "... measures one hundred and sixty-two feet in length, by three hundred and twenty-five in breadth. A row of twelve columns, the largest ever placed inside a building runs up the center having capitals in the form of inverted bells. One hundred and twenty-two columns with lotiform capitals fill the aisles in rows of nine each. The role of the central bay is seventy-four feet above the ground, and the cornice of the two towers rises sixty-three feet higher."

FREDERICK MONDERSON

Light penetrated into this hall through a sort of clerestory, remains of which may still be seen on the south side. Simpkins compares the columns "with Trajan's Column in Rome. Each of the open flower capitals has room for about 100 persons to stand."

Egypt Essays Photo 88b. Osiris Temple at Abydos. Ra-Horakhty gives life to the nostrils of Rameses II, from his nearby temple at Abydos.

Importantly, Dr. ben-Jochannan (1989: 175) has written of this holy place: "The Great Northern Temple of Warit (Karnak) Upper Egypt, North East Africa is too much for anyone to try and complete in ten [10] years, and much less in a cordial single day by any group .... This can only be considered the 'appetizer' for the 'main-course' - your fifth [5th] or sixth [6th] return visit to this colossal wonder of the

EGYPT ESSAYS ON ANCIENT KEMET

world by Africa's sons and daughters from the Americas or so-called Diaspora."

Egypt Essays Photo 89. Osiris Temple at Abydos. Enthroned Isis offers ankh or life to Seti's nostrils.

FREDERICK MONDERSON

Egypt Essays Photo 89a. Osiris Temple at Abydos. Carrying three vessels in each hand, Rameses II dances in an image from his nearby temple at Abydos.

Moreover, Gaston Maspero V (1904: 172) also expressed the provocative view: "We long to know who was the architect possessed of such confidence in his powers that he ventured to design and was able to carry out this almost superhuman undertaking. His name would be held up to almost universal admiration besides those of the great masters that we are familiar with, for no one in Greece or Italy has left us any work which such simple means could produce a similar impression of boldness and immensity."

In regards the age of this hall, the 12 massive columns of the Processional Way were built by Amenhotep III, "The Magnificent," who also built the "Temple of Luxor" as well as the "Temple of Mut" and the "Temple of Khonsu." Here and elsewhere he ushered in new forms of architecture, particularly at the "Temple of Soleb" in Nubia. Evidently, Sekhmet, the lion goddess was a favorite of his, for as Armour (1989: 130) says, he "placed several hundred statues of her in his temple dedicated to Mut." The king also created extensive tracts of land nearby to serve as gardens supplying flowers to the temple daily, all this after he had ascended the "Golden Horus Throne of his Ancestors" to rule for thirty-six years.

However, assigning ownership to the Hypostyle Hall, Maspero (1926: 93) explained, "Rameses I conceived the plan, Seti I finished the building, Rameses II almost completed the decoration." Pier (1916: 97) added, "Rameses I inscribed his name upon one column, Seti's name appears upon seventy-nine and the remaining fifty-four bear the names of a number of later kings." The image of the god Min appears 16 times in this Hall. Ruffle (1977: 173) also added, "Merenptah recorded his victory in a relief at Karnak in the foundation of the Hypostyle Hall." Others such as Payne believed Horemheb, Rameses I's predecessor conceived of the idea first.

This notwithstanding, Portman described the Hypostyle Hall as a "mysterious mixture of the delicate and the massive, the exuberant and the overwhelming; the light of faith wrapped in the gloom of formalism." Cosmologically, he believed: "the petrified forest has its roots in the idea of the temple as a microcosm of the world. Out of the primeval waters Nun emerged the first island; on this island creation took place. The sky, the air, the dew, the plants and animals, all in their turn, took form at the beginning of time. This ideal world is shown in the typical decorations of a temple hall - a midnight sky with stars and astral beings on the ceiling, a riot of vegetation and animal life (quick or dead) on the walls and their growth of columns topped with papyrus or lotus buds."

FREDERICK MONDERSON

Even further, Maspero V (1904: 172) added in summation, "It is impossible to convey by words to those who have not seen it, the impression which it makes on the spectator."

Egypt Essays Photo 90. Osiris Temple at Abydos. Thoth restores life to Osiris.

At the east-end of the Great Hall, the Third Pylon built by Amenhotep III, had been the entrance to the temple and remained so up to the reign of Rameses I. Baines and Malek (1980) mention numerous blocks from earlier buildings reused in this pylon: "A sed-festival shrine of Senwosret I (the "White Chapel") now re-erected to the north of the hypostyle hall, shrines of Amenhotep I and Amenhotep II, as well as Hatshepsut's Red Chapel, so-called for its material (red quartzite) and Thutmose IV, and a pillared portico of the same king."

EGYPT ESSAYS ON ANCIENT KEMET

Egypt Essays Photo 90a. Osiris Temple at Abydos. Isis gets intimate with Seti who smells her garment.

FREDERICK MONDERSON

Egypt Essays Photo 90b. Osiris Temple at Abydos. Three Horus images carry vessels, from the nearby Rameses II temple at Abydos.

Muller (1963: 670) explained how, "Thutmosis I expanded the plan of the Middle Kingdom sanctuary towards the West in order to gain space for a new shrine and subsidiary rooms. He enclosed the expanded sanctuary on three sides with a wall, and the fourth became the pylon." Thutmose I's architect Ineni, who had served Amenhotep I, also helped Thutmose III to erect some of his structures. Ineni erected four obelisks in the Central Court between the Fourth and Fifth Pylon. Today only one obelisk stands here. We are told by Simpkins, the "shaft is of red Aswan granite, 71 feet high, weighs 143 tons. It is the second highest of the greater extant obelisks - the Marius (Heliopolis) obelisk of Senusert I weighs 22 less."

KARNAK: THE GLORY!

The Fourth Pylon built by Thutmose I, is of smaller size and passes 14 truncated columns built by the king. Here a 40-foot vestibule leads to the Hall of Osiride Figures where Thutmose III placed 26

EGYPT ESSAYS ON ANCIENT KEMET

engaged-Osiride statues against the Western Wall. Hatshepsut placed two obelisks there. We are told: "In it are Two Obelisks of red granite like the others, but of large dimensions, the one now standing being 97 feet 6 inches high. This is the second tallest obelisk in the world, being surpassed in height by that of St. John Lateran at Rome. The latter obelisk was erected by Thutmose III at Heliopolis. It is 105 feet 7 inches high." On the north side of the base of one of her still standing obelisks, Hatshepsut, who thought Karnak, 'a holy place from immemorial time,' wrote an inscription. Accordingly, Pier (1916: 99) says of the Queen, she stated: "Having smelted electrum, I placed one half upon their shafts unheeding the mutterings of men for since the utterance of my mouth is law in all that cometh out of it, I cannot retract that which I have already uttered. So hear me then! I placed on them the finest electrum, and I weighed it by the bushel even as if it was corn. My majesty myself did cry the number of the weight."

While this part of the building bears the name of Thotmose I and has his standing obelisk, the other standing obelisk bears the name of his daughter Hatshepsut, while another of hers lies fallen beside the Sacred Lake, near the "Coca Cola Temple." Thutmose III encased the Queen's standing obelisk and this preserved it, particularly during the Amarna Period. Altogether Hatshepsut erected two pairs of obelisks at Karnak. Evidence of four obelisks is depicted on the Middle Colonnade at Deir el Bahari temple. The first pair of her obelisks was cut at Aswan, shipped, transported and erected by Senmut her architect and this was accomplished in seven months. Such an accomplishment is considered a monumental effort. Senmut built extensively to win favor for her rule where at Karnak she worshiped her father and Amun. To win public support for her rule, Hatshepsut proclaimed herself a child of immaculate birth and this event was recorded at her Mortuary Temple at Deir el Bahari, across the river on the West Bank. Khnum, who made man on his potter's wheel, according to Amour (1989: 142), is made to say to Hatshepsut: "I am forming you of substance of Amun, god of Karnak. I give you the land of Egypt and her people, and I will have you appear in glory as king in the name of Horus. You will be supreme among men, as has been commanded by your father Amen-Ra."

As indicative of her commitment to Karnak and the state, many concepts initiated by Hatshepsut became standard cultural and festive practice down through dynastic rule.

Additionally, Habachi (1987: 66) mentions a statement by Queen Hatshepsut, who, when criticized as being neglectful of the great god Amon, affirmed: "I have not been neglected of the city of the Lord of the Universe, rather I have paid attention to it. I know that Karnak is the Horizon [of heaven] Upon Earth, the august ascent of the First Occasion, the Sacred Eye of the Lord of the Universe."

Amenhotep replaced Senmut as architect and erected the second pair of obelisks between the fifth and sixth pylons on occasion of the queen celebrating her jubilee. Senmut had erected the first two obelisks between Pylons Four and Five where Thutmose I had placed his four.

Next is the ruined Fifth Pylon of Thutmose I. The Hall of Records was built by Thutmose III and here priests recorded tribute to the temple. The hall originally had 16 columns and Osiris statues. Thutmose I's architect Ineni left an inscription in which he wrote, as Habachi (1987: 57) tells, "I saw to the erection of two [great] obelisks, having built an august boat 120 cubits in length and 40 cubits in width in order to transport these obelisks. They arrived safe and sound, and landed at Karnak." One still stands between the Fourth and Fifth Pylons.

Thutmose III built the Sixth Pylon. On the west face are some of the celebrated Geographical Lists, containing the names of 1200 towns, the king conquered, of which 628 remain. Not to be outdone by Hatshepsut or their father, Habachi (1991: 72) continued: "Thutmosis III set up at least seven obelisks in Karnak and two more in Heliopolis, but none of these still stands in its original place. They seem to have been erected for his first five Jubilees, celebrated

EGYPT ESSAYS ON ANCIENT KEMET

successively in the thirtieth, thirty-fourth, thirty-seventh, fortieth, and forty-third years of his reign; although two of the obelisks (apparently, from the numbers written below, meant to represent two pairs of his obelisks at Karnak) are depicted in a scene showing the treasure which he offered to Amun-Re in celebration of the military campaigns in which the god had given him success."

Egypt Essays Illustration 43. A splendid alabaster offering plate found near the grave of Ti-Mery, "Chief of the king's linen chamber" at Sakkara (described as one of the best single finds) (left); and fragments of broken statues of Queen Hatshepsut, buried at her death (right).

For further clarification, Habachi (1991: 73-76) informs of Thutmose III's work. He states: "Of the three pairs of obelisks erected at Karnak, one stood to the south of the Seventh Pylon; the upper part of one of these is now in Istanbul, while fragments of its mate remain at Karnak. A second pair stood to the west of the obelisks raised by Thutmosis III's grandfather Tuthmosis I. The pedestals of these were recently unearthed from beneath the foundations of the Third Pylon …. The seventh and last of the Karnak obelisks of Tuthmosis III, a single one, is the largest surviving obelisk, with a height of 36 meters. Only its foundation remains in the eastern part of the Great Temple at Karnak."

FREDERICK MONDERSON

Egypt Essays Photo 91. Osiris Temple at Abydos. Anubis greets Seti I.

EGYPT ESSAYS ON ANCIENT KEMET

Egypt Essays Photo 91a. Osiris Temple at Abydos. Another part of the "Osireion" set-up some believe since the time of the Old Kingdom.

FREDERICK MONDERSON

A small vestibule in front of the granite gateway of the towers forms the facade of the court before the Sanctuary. In a hall before the Sanctuary stood two heraldic granite columns that were, Murnane (1983) wrote, "carved with the Egyptian Lotus (north) and the Papyrus of Upper Egypt (South) - thus expressing the union of the two lands before Amun ...." Here are also statuettes of Amon and Amunet, erected by Tutankhamon and later usurped by Horemheb. After the Amarna Heresy, Steindorff and Seele (1971: 224) quoted Tutankhamon as declaring, he was "beloved of Amen-Re, Lord of the Thrones of the Two Lands, the foremost of Karnak."

The actual Sanctuary or "Holy of Holies," is a mass of ruin, considering the number of assaults it suffered at the hands of invading forces. Yet still, some of the chambers are still standing, and are covered with sculptures of the XVIIIth Dynasty.

In the large Open Court immediately past the sanctuary are some polygonal columns with the cartouches of Usertesen I, of the XIIth Dynasty, in the midst of fallen architraves of the same era; showing that the original construction of the sanctuary dated from that era.

Egypt Essays Photo 91b. Osiris Temple at Abydos.   The immediate entrance to the temple's central opening.

EGYPT ESSAYS ON ANCIENT KEMET

Muller (1963: 670) argued: "The nature of this god and his cult and the ceremonial procession in his honor determined the initial form and subsequent development of the sanctuaries. Sanctuaries were constructed at Karnak and in the Theban area, at Tod and Medamud, as early as the Middle Kingdom. The structures of the New Kingdom could therefore fall back on local tradition."

So, while the construction of the Sanctuary dates to Senusert I, Thutmose III, who tore down Hatshepsut's Red Chapel in place, rebuilt it. The Sanctuary in situ bears the name of Philip Arrhidaeus, half-brother of Alexander the Great, who restored it.

Muller explained the inner shrine at Karnak consisted of an elongated granite-walled room that is accessible from the west through a portal and has a window opening to toward the east. The barge of the god rested on a support in this chamber. Murnane (1983: 231) pointed out, "The walls are covered with scenes illustrating the episodes of the offering rite with Amun appearing in his usual anthropomorphic guise and also in the ithyphallic form he shares with Min, the god of fertility."

Regarding the god's "movement" by procession, Pier (1916: 100) explained, "... the gold figure of the Sun-god Amon" was "taken from this building on some such grand occasion as the accession of a Pharaoh, the New Year's Feast or a Feast of Victory." Murnane describes the sanctuary's nearby illustrations, in the statement: "from the suite of rooms just south of the Sanctuary it is possible to see the full sequences of scenes showing the progress of the rituals during the annual feast."

From remains of architraves it shows Senusret I's temple was decorated. Manfred Lurker's illustration (1991: 32) depicts the "Sedge and bee, symbols of Upper and Lower Egypt, aspects of the titles of Senusret I (1971-1928) carved on the processional Kiosk he built in the temple of Amun at Karnak, Middle Kingdom, XIIth Dynasty." In another illustration Lurker (1991: 86) informs "The vulture goddess Nekhbet, together with her companion, the snake goddess Wadjet, symbolized the two ladies' protectors of the two lands. They are shown resting on two baskets. XII Dynasty. Detail from a Processional Shrine of Senusert I."

To the East of the Central Court is Thutmose III's columnar edifice, the *Akh Menu*, the last major building along the central axis. Of course, there is a temple of Rameses II further east, not of the same size or shape or as spectacular. Nevertheless, this "Festival Hall" of Thutmose III measures 144 feet wide and 52 feet deep and stands at a right angle or perpendicular to the Sanctuary. The exterior wall is entirely destroyed except on the North side.

Murray's *Handbook for Egypt* (1888) explained: "Parallel to the four outer walls is a row of square pillars, going all round, within the edifice, 32 in number; and in the center are 20 columns, disposed in two lines, parallel to the back and front row of pillars. But the position of the latter does not accord with the columns of the center. An unusual caprice has changed the established order of the architectural details, the capitals and cornices being reversed, without adding to the beauty or increasing the strength of the building. The latter, however, had the effect of admitting more light to the interior." Regardless of argument, this is the earliest form of the "clerestory."

EGYPT ESSAYS ON ANCIENT KEMET

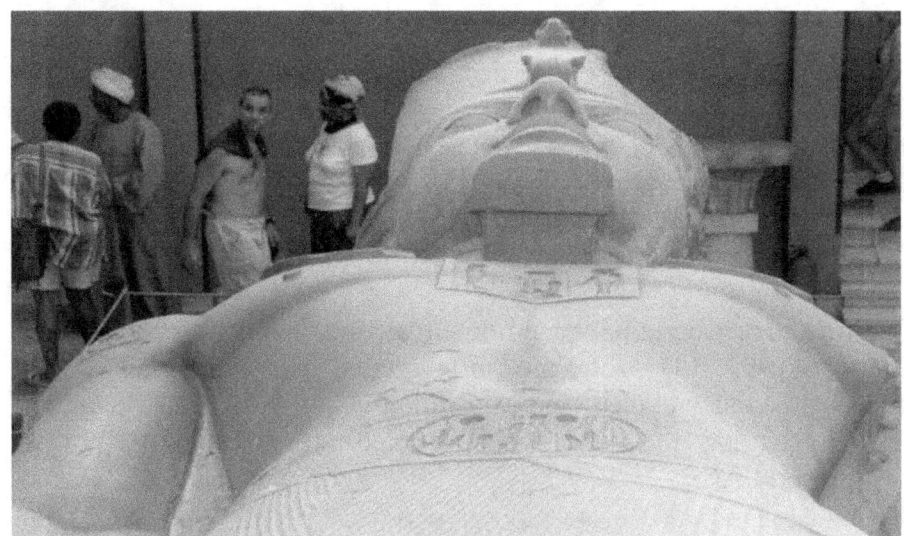

Egypt Essays Photo 92. Memphis Museum. The fallen colossus of Rameses II lies majestically as visitors mill around regularly at the Museum built around this statue.

Regarding its architectural details, Muller (1963: 670) explained, "It is the earliest basilica with the nave elevated above the side aisles, and its ceiling was supported by 'tent pole' columns. The fenestrated exterior walls rest on square pillars that also supported the stone ceiling beams covering the two aisles." Murnane (1983: 233) has argued that the *Akh Menu*, as a memorial temple, "encompasses a number of features - jubilees, reliefs, suites dedicated to chthonic and solar deities, chapels for ancestor worship - that are normally found in shrines dedicated to the cult of the ruler, particularly the king's mortuary temples." Diop, (1991: 87) on the other hand, believed the world-view of Thutmose III was essentially stated as, "The king in the righteousness of his heart, reigns, accomplishing the divine will."

On some of the columns of Thutmose III's "Festival Hall" are traces of walls of a Christian church, and pictures of saints, among whom is a conventional representation of St. Peter.

FREDERICK MONDERSON

In the southwest corner of the Festival Hall was located the famous *Karnak Tablet of Kings*, or "Hall of Ancestors," listing 62 of Thutmose III's predecessors. When it was discovered in 1825, only 48 of these names were legible. In 1843 this prized artifact was stolen and shipped to *Bibliotheque Nationale de Paris*, by Prisse D'Avennes, and now rests in the Louvre Museum.

Creating a broader understanding of ancient Kemetic chronology, Spencer (1993: 14) wrote, the "monumental lists which include the kings of the early dynastic period are known as the Karnak, Saqqara and Abydos lists, the last of which, located in the temple of Seti I, is best preserved."

To the east of the "Hall of the Ancestors" lies the "Zoological Garden" of Karnak, showing birds, flowers, fruit, cattle and other animals seized by Thutmose III in a South-West Asia campaign during his 25th year. Thaneni, Thutmose III's military historian or chief scribe, wrote the *Annals* of Thutmose III primarily about the "Battle of Megiddo." Steindorff and Seele (1971: 60) give three different lists of the conquered cities. On the north/south Axis, a list on the Seventh Pylon is a "catalogue of the Southern lands and Nubian peoples which his majesty subjugated."

Meanwhile, at the "Festival Hall," Clarke and Engelbach (1990: 158-59) points out there is no drainage system for the roof. "The blocks have no joint-troughs between them, and are not cut to facilitate the flow of water over them. Possibly there was a thick layer of mortar or plaster over the whole roof."

On the southern side adytum are the vestiges of a colossal hawk, seated on a raised pedestal, and within sculptures containing the name of Alexander, who did restoration work to it. To the rear of this building was a small chapel with a sanctuary where Thutmose III was worshipped, just before Rameses II's smaller structure.

EGYPT ESSAYS ON ANCIENT KEMET

Egypt Essays Illustration 44. Early indication of wrestling as part of military training.

The Sacred Lake is located south of Rameses II's "Girdle Wall" and to the east of Pylons Seven and Eight. It is 600 feet long and 360 feet wide and 12 feet deep. It was "connected by underground channels to the Nile." Here priests of Amon cleansed themselves for the temple ritual. Simpkins (1987: 20) mentions, the "sacred barques of the Theban Triad floated in the Festival of Opet at flood time. The sacred boats were decorated, and statues of the gods were placed upon their canopies." Additionally, Maspero V (1904: 70), in enumerating works under Thutmose III, points to the "outline of the sacred lake, on which the mystic boats were launched on the nights of festivals, was also more symmetrical and its margin edged with masonry." Sauernon places a tomb of Osiris to the south of the Sacred Lake. Flower gardens also stood in this area while rooms for Osiris were placed to the north of the *Akh-Menu*.

A statue in the Munich Museum found at Karnak contains an inscription of Bekenkhonsu, of the XIXth Dynasty, where he was described as "skilled in art, and the first prophet of Amen." Accordingly, however, not at Karnak but Luxor Temple, the inscription refers to: "I performed the best I could for the people of Amen, as architect of my lord. I executed the pylon of Rameses II, the friend of Amen, who listens to those who pray to him (thus he is named), at the first gate of the Temple of Amen. I placed obelisks at the same made of granite. Their height reached the vault of heaven; propylon is before the same in sight of the city of Thebes, and ponds and gardens, with flourishing trees. I made two great double doors of gold. Their height reached to heaven, I caused to be made a double pair of great masts. I set them up in the splendid court in sight of his temple.'"

The earliest name found on any of the buildings of the Great Temple of Amon at Karnak, is that of Usertesen I. By his other name Amenemenes I, Grimal (1992: 160) indicated: "He undertook important building works at Karnak, from which a few statues and a granite naos (which must have contained a cult statue) have survived. It is even possible that it was Amenemes I who established the original temple of Mut to the south of the precinct of Amon-Re. Traces of his building works have also survived at Koptos, where he partly decorated the temple of Min; at Abydos, where he dedicated a granite altar to Osiris; at Dendera, where he consecrated a gateway, also in granite, to Hathor; and at Memphis, where he built the temple of Ptah. He also had a pyramid built for himself at el-Lisht, about fifty kilometers south of Memphis."

EGYPT ESSAYS ON ANCIENT KEMET

Egypt Essays Photo 92a. Memphis Museum. Side view of the "Sphinx at Memphis."

Egypt Essays Photo 92b. Memphis Museum. *Suten Bat* title with Ma'at, more than likely Rameses II's cartouche.

FREDERICK MONDERSON

Egypt Essays Photo 92c. Memphis Museum. In the "Memphis Garden," a visitor pauses to take a photo of a colossal statue of Rameses II.

We know that Senmut started the Temple of Mut in Asher during Hatshepsut's reign. This is consistent with Breasted's view (1923: 344) that credits Amenhotep III with building: "a temple to Mut, the goddess of Thebes, where his ancestors had begun it, on the south of Karnak, and excavated a lake beside it. He then laid out a beautiful garden in the interval of over a mile and a half, which separates the Karnak from the Luxor temple and connected the great temples by avenues of rams carved in stone, each bearing a statue of the Pharaoh between the fore-paws." Let us not forget, in explanation, pharaohs have always torn down structures and rebuilt on the same site. Such a scenario can account for the names of Usertesen, Senmut and Amenhotep being linked to the Temple of Mut.

Royal palaces and villas lined the Avenue of Sphinxes connecting Karnak with Luxor. Illustrations by Tutankhamon in the Temple of Amenhotep III's Processional Colonnade, show the water procession to Luxor, when Amon would visit during the "Opet Festival." On the return trip priests in white robes shouldered the god's bark along the Avenue of Sphinxes.

EGYPT ESSAYS ON ANCIENT KEMET

Sesostris I erected a Kiosk in an unknown spot at Karnak that can now be seen with special permission in the "Open Air Museum," north of the Great Court, and through the opening in its Northern Colonnade. This kiosk is called the "White Chapel." Trigger, et al (1989: 189) mention a "Thirteenth Dynasty stele from Karnak records the flooding of the temple of Amen." Even further, Trigger et al (1989: 173) have deduced, the "main source for the Theban revolt is a pair of stelae (and a scribal copy of one of them) erected in Karnak temple by Kamose and dated to his year 3" after which his brother Ahmose completed the expulsion of the Hyksos and established the New Kingdom with Amun triumphant. The latest name appearing at the Temple of Amon "Lord of Karnak, Master of Heaven," is that of Alexander II, in a small chamber in the *Akh Menu* of Thutmose III. Hurry (1987: 104) tells of a mural image, where: "In the temple of Ptah and Hathor at Karnak, Imhotep with Ptah and his consort Hathor are seen sculptured on the walls and worshiped by King Thutmosis III."

Herein is recounted a wonderful artistic, architectural, as well as theological, epistemological, and metaphysic and spiritual heritage, that African people can connect with. Knowledge of this cultural history that gave birth to science, mathematics, medicine, engineering, construction, riverain transportation, and agriculture, can provide significant inspiration for children of the ancestors residing in urban and rural settings across America who do not know their true history and heritage. Karnak lasted as long as it did and was influential because beneath its religious base, Ma'atian ethics and morality were prime factors in Amon's efforts to uplift humanity.

REFERENCE

Armour, Robert A. *Gods and Myths of Ancient Egypt*. Cairo: American University in Cairo Press, (1986) 1989.
Baines, John and Jaromir Malek. *Atlas of Ancient Egypt*. New York: Facts on File, 1980.

ben-Jochannan, Yosef. *Abu Simbel to Ghizeh*: *A Guide Book and Manual*. Baltimore, MD. : Black Classics Press, (1987) 1989.

_____. *The African Called Rameses* ("*The Great*") II *and the African Origin of "Western Civilization."* New York: Alkebu-Lan Book Associates, 1990.

Bierbrier, Morris. *The Tomb Builders of the Pharaohs*. Cairo: American University in Cairo Press, (1982) 1989.

Bratton, Fred Gladstone. *A History of Egyptian Archaeology*. New York: Thomas Y. Crowell Co., 1968.

Breasted, John H. *A History of Egypt*. New York: Charles Scribner's Sons, (1905) 1923.

Budge, E. A. Wallis. *From Fetish to God in Ancient Egypt*. Oxford University Press and London: Humphrey Milford, 1934.

Carprieci, Alberto Carlo. *Art and History of Egypt*. Florence, Italy: Case Editrice Bonechi, 1994.

Clarke, Sommers and R. Engelbach. *Ancient Egyptian Construction and Architecture*. New York: Dover Publications, Inc., (1930) 1990.

Diop, Cheikh Anta. *Civilization or Barbarism*: *An Authentic Anthropology*. Brooklyn, New York: Lawrence Hill, 1991.

Du Bois, W. E. B. *The World and Africa*. New York: International Publishers, (1946) 1971.

Erman, Adolf. *A Handbook of Egyptian Religion*. London: Archibald Constable and Co., Ltd., 1907.

Grimal, Nicolas. *A History of Ancient Egypt*. Oxford/Cambridge, USA: Blackwell, (1988) 1993.

Haag, Michael. *Guide to Egypt*. London: Michael Haag, 1987.

Habachi, Labib. *The Obelisks of Egypt*: *Skyscrapers of the Past*. Cairo: The American University in Cairo Press, (1984) 1987.

Hart, George. *Egyptian Myths*. London: British Museum Publications, 1990.

Hobson, Christine Hobson. *The World of the Pharaohs*. London: Thames and Hudson, 1987.

Hurry, Jamieson B. *Imhotep*: *The Egyptian God of Medicine*. Chicago: Ares Publishers, Inc., (1926) 1987.

Kamil, Jill. Luxor: *A Guide to Ancient Thebes*. 2nd Edition. London: Longman, (1973) 1980.

Lurker, Manfred. *The Gods and Symbols of Ancient Egypt*. London: Thames and Hudson, 1991.

EGYPT ESSAYS ON ANCIENT KEMET

Maspero, Gaston. *History of Egypt, Chaldea, Syria, Babylonia, and Assyria*. XII Volumes. London: The Grolier Society, 1904.

_____. *Manual of Egyptian Archaeology*. New York: G. P. Putnam's Sons, 1926.

Mertz, Barbara. *Temples, Tombs, and Hieroglyphs*. New York: Dodd and Mead, (1964) 1978.

Muller, Wolfgang. "Egyptian Art." *Encyclopedia of Art* (1963: 618-710).

Murnane, William C. *The Penguin Guide to Ancient Egypt*. New York: Penguin Books, 1983.

Newberry, Percy E. "An Egyptian Gardener: The Tomb of Nakht." *Scientific American Supplement* No. 1231 (August 5, 1899).

"Ancient Egyptian Gardening." *Scientific American Supplement* No 1256 (January 27, 1900: 20138-39).

Obenga, Theophile. *Ancient Egypt and Black Africa*. London: Karnak House, 1992.

Payne, Elizabeth. *The Pharaohs of Ancient Egypt*. New York: Random House, 1964.

Petrie, W. M. F. *Religious Life in Ancient Egypt*. London: Constable and Co., (1924) 1932.

FREDERICK MONDERSON

Egypt Essays Photo 93. Memphis Museum. Colossal standing statue wearing the White Crown.

Pier, Garrett Chatfield. "The Great Temple of Amon Ra at Karnak." *Art and Archaeology* Vol. IV No 2 (August, 1916: 91-100).
Polyglot. *Travel Guide Egypt*. Cairo: Lehnert and Landrock, (1965).
Ruffle, John. *The Egyptians*. Ithaca, New York: Cornell University Press, 1977.
Sauernon, Serge. "Karnak" in George Posener's *A Dictionary of Egyptian Civilization*. London: Methuen and Co., Ltd., (1962).
Simpkins. *The Temple of Karnak*. Salt Lake City, Utah: Simpkins, 1982.
Smith, W. Stevenson. *The Art and Architecture of Ancient Egypt*. New York: Penguin Books, (1958) 1981.
Spencer, A. J. Early Egypt: *The Rise of Civilization in the Nile Valley*. London: The British Museum, 1993.

EGYPT ESSAYS ON ANCIENT KEMET

Trigger, B. G., B. J. Kemp, D. O'Connor, and A. B. Lloyd. *Ancient Egypt*: *A Social History*. Cambridge at the University Press, 1989.

Wayne, Scott. *Egypt and the Sudan*: *A Travel Survival Kit*. Australia: Lonely Planet, 1987.

Woldering, Irmgard. *The Art of Egypt*: *The Time of the Pharaohs*. New York: Greystone Press, 1963.

Egypt Essays Photo 93a. Memphis Museum. Sign indicating a Sarcophagus of Amenhotep of the 19th Dynasty.

Egypt Essays Photo 93b. Memphis Museum. One of the souvenir vending stalls on the Museum grounds.

FREDERICK MONDERSON

13. THE TEMPLE OF LUXOR

The Temple of Luxor is a magnificent piece of classical Kemetic architecture that is near 1300 feet long and some 181 feet wide. Its orientation towards Karnak temple helped it to become a twin force in worship of the great god Amon at Thebes. In this, its purpose for being built is one for festival of the God Amon. That is, the purpose of the temple of Luxor is the celebration of the "Opet Festival." It is one of the best preserved of the ancient temples surviving from the time when indigenous pharaohs ruled ancient Kemet. As the Temple of Rameses III, in the Great Court at Karnak is a single structure and different from the larger temple, so too the Temple of Luxor, as built by Amenhotep III during the XVIIIth Dynasty, was conceived as a single structure. More significantly, this temple's conception enjoyed compounded knowledge of Old Kingdom, Middle Kingdom and early New Kingdom temple building practice.

By the river's side, crafts of quarrying, shipbuilding and water transportation of great sized stone from distant regions, aided the construction of this quintessential structure of ancient Kemetic religious worship and esoteric knowledge. It became the "grand lodge" of spiritual, theosophical and epistemological teaching, practices and experiences of ancient Egypt, in northeast Africa. The lights of tradition shined brightly here! Under Amenhotep III, "the Magnificent," great-grandson of the mighty warrior pharaoh Thutmose III, the empire was intact, vibrant, at the pinnacle of its "Golden Age." Yet, within a decade of his rule, his son Amenhotep IV, Akhenaten, had ushered in a mighty religious, cultural and artistic revolution that brought great turmoil to the land. This aside, many great achievements in temple construction underscore Amenhotep III's many virtues.

A great builder, Amenhotep III erected the Third Pylon at Karnak and the massive Processional Way Colonnade, central to the Hypostyle Hall, was his brainchild. This pharaoh constructed the Temple of Mut in Asher, begun by Senmut, Hatshepsut's architect.

EGYPT ESSAYS ON ANCIENT KEMET

He placed hundreds of statues of the lion-goddess Sekhmet in the Temple of Mut. He also built a sacred lake for its vulture goddess. As the second deity of the Theban Triad, recognition and worship of Mut dates to the beginnings of worship of Amun, "Lord of Karnak" and "Master of the World." Similarly, as much as the temples of Amon and Mut were linked to earlier structures, the Temple of Luxor was erected on an earlier Twelfth Dynasty shrine from where the name of Pharaoh Sobek-hotep of the XIIIth Dynasty, has been recovered. This Middle Kingdom structure may have been built on even earlier sacred foundations, perhaps dating to the start of dynastic rule.

Egypt Essays Illustration 45. Tutankhamon's canopic chest, a gem of Egyptian sculpture showing the gold dada and guardian goddesses.

Nonetheless, existing evidence indicates, after the war of independence, and founding of the Eighteenth Dynasty and beginning of the New Kingdom, Ahmose built a temple at Luxor. The Kiosk to the Theban triad built by Hatshepsut and usurped by Thutmose Iii now residing in the "Ramessean Front," was probably connected to this temple. Amenhotep tore this smaller temple down and erected a monumental masterpiece in Kemetic architecture. Here, and elsewhere, particularly at the Temple of Soleb in Nubia, Amenhotep III experimented with new forms of architecture. This original Temple of Luxor was conceived as a single construction, while Rameses II of the XIXth Dynasty added a court and pylon showing an axis that more properly oriented this temple with the Precinct of Amon at Karnak and so avoiding the river. Beyond this second axis, West (1987: 168) in quoting Schwaller de Lubicz wrote this "curiously skewed complex is strictly aligned upon three separate axes. Without exception, every wall, colonnade, hall and sanctuary is rigorously aligned upon one or the other of these axes." West (1987: 168) wrote even further: "The axes are chiseled into the sandstone floor of the Temple and obviously served as a guide for the earliest stage of construction. Thereafter, this floor was covered over in white limestone, but the subsequent construction continued to be rigorously aligned to the invisible axis!" Additionally, Schwaller de Lubicz subscribes to the view, according to West (1987: 197) that "man is not a 'product' of the universe, nor a 'scaled model' of it; he is to be regarded as an embodiment, its 'essence' incorporated in physical form."

EGYPT ESSAYS ON ANCIENT KEMET

Egypt Essays Photo 94. Memphis Museum. Anubis atop the sarcophagus with that "thousand yard stare."

Nevertheless, however we view the juxtaposition of Rameses' addition, on a distinct axis, knowledgeable critics as Maspero V (1904: 126) could still write: "The whole structure lacks unity, and there is nothing corresponding to it in this respect anywhere else in Egypt. The northern half does not join on to the southern, or the two parts might be regarded as having once formed a single edifice which had become divided by an accident, which the architect had endeavored to unite together again by a line of columns running between two walls.

However, an interesting comment is made regarding irregularities in Kemetic architecture, particularly at some temples such as here at

FREDERICK MONDERSON

Luxor and Philae. In this regard Maspero (1926: 94-95) later wrote: "At Luxor the building progressed methodically under Amenhotep III and Seti I, but when Rameses II wished to add to what had been done by his predecessors, an easterly bend of the river obliged him to deviate in the same direction. His pylon is not parallel with the boundary wall of the last court of Amenhotep III, and his colonnade forms a distinct angle with the general axis of the previous work. At Philae the deviation is even greater. Not only is the larger pylon out of line with the smaller one, but the two southern colonnades diverge considerably and naturally do not accord with the plan."

In orientation with the greater Amun temple at Thebes, a Dromos or Processional Way of Sphinxes as well as a canal linked Luxor with Karnak. Bratton (1968: 183) mentions "1400 sphinxes" along the two mile path that were "10 feet long, 4 feet high and mounted on 5 feet tall pedestals." Amenhotep III also constructed the palace of Malcata across the river for his Queen Tiy. It had a lake for her to sail on. Here they retired while the Aten controversy developed during his son Amenhotep IV's reign. According to Ruffle (1977: 70-71) Malcata was a "huge estate incorporating parade grounds and small chapels, large audience halls, decorated with painted walls, ceilings, and floors, villas for government officials, offices, kitchens, workshops, and huts for the servants."

Then again, the origin of this Luxor Temple may be linked to the fact of Karnak being crowded and the pharaoh who had married the beloved Queen Tiy chose this site to represent another light in the constellation of sites of worship to Amun. He had a great repository of knowledge, observations, scientific data and expertise that surrounded the worship at Karnak. After all, this deity had brought great fame and fortune requiring festivals to the nation and the Theban capital. All this, while the south reigned supreme following the expulsion of the Hyksos and great cultural growth during the glorious XVIIIth Dynasty when ancient Kemet became the "light of the ancient world." On the other hand, regarding origins, Hobson (1987: 139) mentions, "a lightly carved relief shows the celebration of the Opet festival, the reason for the existence of the Temple of Luxor." Even further, Hart (1990: 10-11) points to a unique aspect

EGYPT ESSAYS ON ANCIENT KEMET

of the Luxor Temple, for like Hatshepsut's Temple at Deir el-Bahari, they "reveal Amon deserting his mysterious confines in the sky for union with the reigning Queen of Egypt, thereby fathering the future monarch." This "divine birth" helped to strengthen the king's claim to the throne of the Sun god. During Amenhotep's reign art, architecture, science, medicine, literature, mathematics, mummification, astronomy, and engineering achieved a high level, and the period was rightly called "the Golden Age."

The people of ancient Kemet called the site of Luxor *Waset*. The Greeks considered it a part of *Diospolis Parva* and in Arabic it is called *El Uksor* or *Abou el Haggag*. The name, Luxor, or *El Kosoor* signifies "the palaces," from the temple there erected by Amenhotep III and Rameses II. In time the name became *Luxor*, and on a regional basis, it represented both sides of the river. Dr. ben-Jochannan likes to say to visitors, regarding this city, "You buy cotton at Aswan, leather at Luxor and gold in Cairo." Of course, you buy books where you get them!

Next, we can turn to David (1993: 83) who enumerated the names of early travelers and scholars to visit Luxor including: "Norden, Denon, Wilkinson, Burton, Lhote, Champollion, Minutoli and Lepsius." The Scottish artist David Roberts visited the site in 1838. However, even more interesting is the tale told by Fagan (1975: 74) that when Napoleon's troops turned the bend at Thebes on January 17, 1799, and they beheld the two temples of Karnak and Luxor: "The division came to a spontaneous halt and burst into applause. 'Without an order being given, the men formed their ranks and presented arms, to the accompaniment of the drums and the band.'"

The modern public approach to the Temple of Luxor is from the east beside the Abu Haggag Mosque Plaza. Previously the entrance had been from the west where the monuments of Rameses II dominate the entranceway view. In ancient times, Maspero V (1904: 68) who cleared this temple in the 1880s, wrote "the naos rose sheer above the waters of the Nile, indeed its cornices projected over the river, and a staircase at the south side allowed the priests and devotees to embark directly from the rear of the building."

FREDERICK MONDERSON

Egypt Essays Photo 95. Memphis Museum. Horus on the Sarcophagus.

EGYPT ESSAYS ON ANCIENT KEMET

In front of two stone towers, now remain one of two standing obelisks and two seated statues and one of four standing statues of the king, split by the entrance pylon or gateway. At the bases of these seated statues the Nile gods unite the land, and conquered enemies of Kemet from north and south, are displayed. Lurker (1991: 97) recognized these and adds, "Originally there were six statues of Rameses II (1304-1237 B.C.), before the pylons, one seated and two standing at either side." The red granite obelisk is covered on four sides with hieroglyphic or *Medu Netcher* inscriptions whose beauty rests in the admirable style of their execution and depth that in many instances exceed two inches. This obelisk measures 84 feet in height. At its base baboons greet the sun god. The other obelisk was given to the French king Louis Philippe in 1831, shipped to Paris and erected in the Place de La Concorde in 1836. This obelisk, also of red granite, is 77 feet tall and rests on a pedestal. Ben-Jochannan (1989: 179) gives a "weight of two hundred and twenty-six [226] tons, approximately." Haag (1987: 200) informs of the French desire for an obelisk after Josephine's brazen request of Napoleon. "Goodbye!" she said. "If you go to Thebes, do send me a little obelisk!"

Sadly, Flaubert while standing in front of the Temple of Luxor in 1850 had written: "'The obelisk that is now in Paris was against the right-hand pylon. Perched on its pedestal, how bored it must be in the Place de la Concorde! How it must miss its Nile! What does it think as it watches all the cabs drive by, instead of the chariots it saw at its feet in the old days?"

A century later, according to Haag (1987: 200-01) Cocteau wrote: "the plinth of the obelisk removed to Paris 'was surrounded by the low reliefs of dog-faced baboons in erection.' This was not thought to be proper and so the monkey's organs have been cut off." Habachi (1987: 11) has also written: "On the pedestal of the eastern obelisk, which is still in situ, the king boasted that 'he made a large obelisk [called] Rameses-Beloved-of-Amon [the rising sun].' The western obelisk which is now in Paris was named 'Rameses-Beloved-of-Atum [the setting sun].' On the eastern obelisk the king is called 'Beloved of Harakhti [the rising sun].' While on the western one he is styled 'Beloved of Atum.' The names of each obelisk and the epithets on them correspond to the rising of the sun in the east and its setting in the west."

Today, this decoration of the front elevation to the temple faces the Dromos or partially restored Avenue of Sphinxes of Nectanebo that leads towards Karnak, three miles away. A Chapel of Serapis and Chapel of Hathor of the Roman period were within a great enclosure wall encapsulating a great court or open area before the pylon and fronting the Avenue of Sphinxes.

Egypt Essays Illustration 46. Released from its Sarcophagus, the coffin containing Tutankhamon's mummy rests in quiet solitude.

When we think of the significance of a Temple as at Luxor, we need examine the cosmological, theological and ethical thought and practice of adherents of the cult of such a structure. In this regard, Portman (1989: 15) has described the temple in ancient Kemet as being the "mansion of a living god."

EGYPT ESSAYS ON ANCIENT KEMET

The incomprehensible and mysterious power of creation, embodied in the god, was worshiped with elaborate ritual behind massive stone walls. At the same time the temple was the seat of spiritual authority! The god's wishes were communicated to the world by a priesthood whose position naturally gave them great influence in affairs of state.

The priesthood also had a significant hand in training architectural, logistics, labor and administrative hierarchical officials of the state. Most importantly, they erected temples wherein their god resided and these structures reflected the socio-economic and political standing of this deity in the wider landscape of dynastic times. Further, Maspero (1926: 54-55) mentions customary practice at the "... building or rebuilding of a temple to place deposits under the foundation consisting of small squares of the building materials and models of the tools employed. Also a number of amulets, which were probably intended to secure by magic the safety of the temple. The foundation deposits are generally found in a layer of clean sand marvelously fresh and uninjured."

Egypt Essays Photo 96. Sakkara. Home of the Step-Pyramid. Classic picture of the Step-Pyramid at Sakkara, built by Imhotep for Pharaoh Zoser of the Third Dynasty.

FREDERICK MONDERSON

Even more, as the French archaeologist and Curator of the Museum of Antiquities in Cairo, Maspero (1926: 55) wrote: "Many of the objects are inscribed with the name of the founder of the temple, and it was by means of its intact foundation deposits that one of the ruined temples to the south of the Ramesseum was identified as that of Queen Tausert of the end of the Nineteenth Dynasty, although all its walls were razed to the ground .... Among the glazed objects found in this deposit were scarabs, plaques, and models of offerings, besides many beads. The metal objects include adze, knife, axe-head, hoes, and chisels, made in thin sheet copper. There were also jars and cups, an ebony cramp, and a model corn-grinder."

In this way, the Temple of Hatshepsut can throw light on the question of ceremony at consecration of that structure. It can serve as parallel light to understand such at the construction of Luxor Temple. Deir el Bahari foundation deposits furnished "numerous models of workmen's tools, including the wooden centerings used in constructing brick vaulting. These were neatly inscribed in blue ink with the cartouche of the foundress Hatshepsut." Therefore, it's believed, the same practice applied at Luxor as at Deir el Bahari. Here Maspero V (1904: 55-56) wrote, "Two deposits at the western entrance of this temple afford evidence of a ceremony customary at the foundation of a temple. An animal was slain and the flesh laid on a floor of clean sand over which the blood was allowed to drip; vessels containing unguents and wine were smashed and their contents together with grains of corn were poured into the cache in addition to the offering of flesh and blood."

Finally, four colossi of Rameses II stood against the base of the pylon whose walls are decorated with reliefs that depict Rameses' campaigns against the Hittites, at the Battle of Kadesh. The court scribe Pentaurt, in 1285 B.C. wrote this account; right after the young king ascended the throne. The pylon itself is 79 feet high and 213 feet wide. The scenes on the pylon: "were studied," David (1993: 84) wrote, "by Rosellini and Champollion, Erentz and Breasted. A general account of the temple was published by Gayet in 1894." Polyglot (1965: 40) explains the illustrated depiction on the pylon regarding disposition of the campaign, wherein we see,

EGYPT ESSAYS ON ANCIENT KEMET

"(left: council of war, the camp, the King battling from his war chariot; right: the King as archer, the flight of the Hittites, the enemy fortress)." The chariots, horses, shields taken from the enemy as well as the holy place that held the ark of the nation in a tent, are also represented. This event was retold on major works of Rameses II as at Abu Simbel, Ramesseum and Karnak, among others. A parasol shades the king's chariot. There is also a papyrus version of the tale.

In interpreting this scene, West (1987: 173-74) argued that the representation of this pylon and circumstances surrounding the Battle of Kadesh itself is even more significant in the esoteric message it imparts. "The purpose of this complex relief is the depiction of the battle between the forces of light and darkness. Having vanquished the enemy, the king can enter the temple; to enter the temple, all obstacles in the external world must be overcome. This is why the battle scenes are all on the exterior of the Temple walls."

At the doorway of the Pylon itself is the name of Shabaka, and on the abacus of the columns beyond, that of Ptolemy Philopator, both added at a later epoch. Beyond the Pylon is the forecourt of Rameses II consisting essentially of the "Ramessean Front," a Peristyle columnar masterpiece.

The Great Court of Rameses III, measures 190 feet by 170 feet and is surrounded by a Peristyle, according to Jill Kamil (1976: 27) of: "smooth-shafted papyrus columns with lotus-bud capitals." Bratton (1968: 183) added that the columns of the Court are as such, but "show the decadence of the Ramesside period." On the other hand, Baines and Malek (1980: 87) describe the columns of this colonnade as: "... arranged in a double row around its sides, and are interrupted by a shrine consisting of three chapels (bark stations) of Amun (center), Mut (left) and Khonsu (right), built by Hatshepsut and Thutmose III and redecorated by Rameses II. It was the existence of this shrine which caused the considerable deviation of the axis of the buildings of Rameses II from that of the earlier temple of

Amenhotep III." Originally, this temple had some 230 columns throughout.

Egypt Essays Photo 96a. King Tutankhamon and his wife in an intimate mood.

In the northeastern corner rests the Mosque of Abu Haggag, the patron saint of Luxor, who came from Syria in the 13th Century A.D., to preach Islam. The line of direction no longer continues the same behind this court, the "Ramessean front having been turned eastward; which was done in order to facilitate its connection with the great temple of Karnak, as well as to avoid the vicinity of the river."

This meant that the Pillared Portico or Massive Processional Way Colonnade has a length of about 170 feet and is part of the temple on its original axis. Names on these massive columns show

EGYPT ESSAYS ON ANCIENT KEMET

Amenhotep III, the original builder and Tutankhamon, Seti I, Rameses II, Seti II, and Horemheb, monarchs who did repairs to the structure. The 14 papyrus columns with open capitals stand 52 1/2 feet tall and conceal abaci with the name of Tutankhamon. Regarding the natural beauty of this colonnade, Kamil (1980: 28) has written: "In the early morning and towards the sunset heavy shadows are cast between the seven pairs of columns and the interplay of light has long been exploited by photographers as it slants from heavy architrave to calyx capitals down the slender shaft of this colonnade." Even further, adding to this beauty, Polyglot (1965: 40) explained the reliefs on both side of the wall, in which the "New Year's Festive procession of the Sacred Barques from Karnak to Luxor and back can be seen were executed by the order of Tutankhamon." The west wall shows the procession from Karnak while the east wall shows the return journey. Wayne (1987: 188) adds: "The Opet Festival is depicted in great detail with the king, the nobility and the common people joining the triumphal procession of Amon, Mut and Khons from Karnak." This festival that occurred during the Nile flood lasted for "twenty-four days of merry-making." Armour (1989: 146) has provided even more when he explained: "The festival opened with dancing girls who accompanied the priests of Amun as they carried the barge holding the statue of the god to the water's edge. Then men towed the barge up river to the other temple while the audience clapped, animals were sacrificed, and acrobats tumbled joyously. Finally at the second temple offerings were made to the holy triad of Thebes."

We now arrive at the Colonnaded Court of Amenhotep III that is 167 feet long and 147 feet wide. Pemberton (1992: 94-95) identified this splendid work in the following description. "The court of Amenhotep III, whose elegant double colonnade of papyrus-bundle columns, testifies to the skill of the royal architect, Amenhotep, son of Hapu." The structure is surrounded by a Peristyle of 12 columns in length and 10 in breadth, for a total of 32. Woldering (1963: 155) believed, "the closely-packed papyri-form columns and subdued light served to remind participants in the procession of the mysterious and solemn purpose of their festivities, and to put them into a proper state of awesome respect for the statues of the gods in the adjoining chapels." Even further, Woldering (1963: 155) added: "The style of the flowering period of the New Kingdom is characterized by soft and graceful lines and curves and a harmonious symmetry between the various elements." Art as characterized in the temple influenced other building efforts and art in general, especially statuary.

Behind this Court is a space occupying the whole breadth of the building, the hypostyle hall, divided into chambers of different dimensions, the center one leading to a hall of four rows of six each column. Beyond this is another hall with four columns with three at the side, immediately before the entrance to the isolated sanctuary, with one row of three columns on both sides. On the East of the hall is a chamber containing some curious sculpture, representing the accouchement of Queen Maut-m-Shoi, the mother of Amenhotep. This is an interesting phenomenon in the history of ancient Kemet. Budge (1972: 86) mentions four such experiences, in tracing it back to the fifth dynasty to a woman named Ruttet, wife of a priest of Ra of Sakhaby.

"These children were declared to be the sons of Ra who in human form, had companied with her. The same story is told about Queen Hatshepsut and Amenhotep III, who were held to be begotten by Amen-Ra, and according to the narrative of the *Pseudo-Callisthenes* (Book 1. Chap. 8), Alexander the Great was the son of Amen (Ammon), who took the form of Nectanebo, the last king of Egypt, and begot him by Queen Olympias.

EGYPT ESSAYS ON ANCIENT KEMET

Egypt Essays Photo 97. Sakkara. Home of the Step-Pyramid. Classis view of the world's first colonnade, enduring for 3000 years.

In the temple, the original Sanctuary was perhaps destroyed by the Persians; but the present one was rebuilt by Alexander (the son of Alexander, Ptolemy being the Governor of Egypt), and bears his name in the following dedicatory formula: "This work (?) made he, the king of men, lord of the regions, Alexander, for his father Amen-Ra, president of Tape (Thebes); he erected to him the sanctuary, a grand mansion, with repairs of sandstone, hewn, good, and hard stone, in lieu of? (that made by?) His majesty, the king of men, Amenhotep." Maspero V (1904: 68) added even further: "The sanctuary was a single chamber with an opening to its side, but so completely shut out from the daylight by the long dark hall at whose extremity it was placed to be in perpetual obscurity."

Behind the sanctuary is a large room with two rows of six columns and further in another room with four columns. The larger room of columns is ornamented with rich sculpture, much of which appears to have been gilded.

A second Hypostyle or Great Columnar Hall preceded the Sanctuary. This was rearranged by a Roman Legion who chose to make their chapel here. Near the great columnar hall is one of the old chambers, measuring 34 feet 6 inches by 57 feet 1 inch, with a semicircular niche. The walls are covered with Frescoes of late Roman time; and it was evidently a court of law with the usual tribunal, in which are painted three figures larger than life wearing the toga and sandals. The center one holds a staff or scepter (Scipio) in the right hand and a globe in the left; and near him was some object now defaced.

The two other figures have each a scroll in one hand. On the walls to the right and left are the traces of figures, which are interesting from their costume; and on the sidewall to the East are several soldiers with their horses, drawn with Great Spirit. The colors are much damaged by exposure, but have been lately cleaned and the frescoes can now be distinguished. They probably date after the age of Constantine. The costumes are remarkable; and some of the men wear embroidered upper garments, tight hose, and laced boots, or shoes tied over the instep.

The false wainscot, dado, below is richly colored in imitation porphyry and other stones incrusted in patterns, and is better preserved than the frescoes of the upper part, where the old gods of Kemet/Egypt in bas-relief have outlived the paintings that once concealed them. There appears to be traces of a small cross, painted at one side of the tribune, and the figures have a nimbus round their heads, but without any of the character of Christian saints. Nor did the early Christians confine the nimbus to saints.

Behind the temple is a stone Quay, apparently of the late era of the Ptolemies or Caesars, since blocks bearing the sculpture of the former have been used in its construction. Opposite the corner of the temple, the river takes a more easterly direction, and points out the original course of the river, which continued across the plain now lying between it and the ruins of Karnak, and which may be traced by the descent of the surface of that ground it gradually deserted. The southern extremity of the quay is of brick (probably a Roman addition), and indicates in like manner the former direction of the stream. When the temple was first built, the river seems to have flowed close under its walls.

EGYPT ESSAYS ON ANCIENT KEMET

To the east of the temple, an Open Air Museum houses broken stone recovered in the temple's excavation and work continues in restoration of the Processional Colonnade.

Egypt Essays Photo 98. Karnak Temple of Amen-Ra. Figure with a head of two birds holds a knife.

REFERENCE

Armour, Robert A. *Gods and Myths of Ancient Egypt*. Cairo: American University in Cairo Press, (1986) 1989.
ben-Jochannan, Yosef. *From Abu Simbel to Ghizeh*. Baltimore, MD: Black Classics Press, 1989.
Bratton, Fred Gladstone. *A History of Egyptian Archaeology*. New York: Thomas Y. Crowell Company, 1968.

FREDERICK MONDERSON

Breasted, James H. *A History of Egypt*. New York: Charles Scribner's Sons, (1905) 1923.

Budge, E. A. W. *Dwellers on the Nile*. New York: Benjamin Bloom, Inc., Publishers, 1972.

David, Rosalie. *Discovering Ancient Egypt*. New York: Facts on File, 1993.

Egypt Essays Photo 98a. His wife presents King Tut with a bouquet of flowers.

EGYPT ESSAYS ON ANCIENT KEMET

Fagan, Brian. *The Rape of the Nile*. New York: Charles Scribner's Sons, 1975.
Haag, Michael. *Guide to Egypt*. London: Michael Haag, 1987.
Hobson, Christine. *The World of the Pharaohs*. London: Thames and Hudson, 1987.

Egypt Essays Photo 98b. Hathor and Mut on Papyrus.

FREDERICK MONDERSON

Egypt Essays Photo 98c. Memphis Museum. Sign indicating more of the glory of the ancients.

Lurker, Manfred. *The Gods and Symbols of Ancient Egypt*. London: Thames and Hudson, (1987).
Pemberton, Delia. *Ancient Egypt: Architectural Guide for Travelers*. San Francisco: Chronicle Books, (1992).
Portman, Ian. *Luxor: A Guide to the Temples and Tombs of Ancient Egypt*. Cairo: The American University in Cairo Press, (1989).
Ruffle, John. *The Egyptians*. Ithaca, New York: Cornell University Press, 1977.
West, John Anthony. *Serpent in the Sky*. New York: The Julian Press, (1979) 1987.

EGYPT ESSAYS ON ANCIENT KEMET

14. ABYDOS

The city of Abydos has held fame from the beginnings of Egyptian civilization for here is where tombs of the first and second dynasties have been found. Military fortifications exist from this earliest period. Equally too, temples have been discovered from that time, designed for active participation in the Osirian Drama. In this, connection and having subscribed to and participated ethics and ritual, the dead had hopes of being resurrected same as the great god, Osiris. Much of this pageantry characterized the site's use during the Old Kingdom.

The kings buried at Abydos of the first and second dynasties also built tombs at Sakkara that is with the exception of Narmer, who only had one tomb. Scholars, however, have debated which of the two sets of tombs is the real one and which a "cenotaph" or dummy tomb. In all likelihood, the Abydos tomb is the real one and the Memphis tomb the cenotaph. Some of the archaic tombs were attacked by fire indicating internecine struggles between the kings and dynasties, perhaps due to religious reasons.

With time, Abydos grew in importance and pharaoh after pharaoh through the Old Kingdom built temples here indicating its significance. By the end of the Old Kingdom Osiris seems to have replaced the jackal god Khenti-Amenti as the principal divinity at Abydos and this is perhaps due to early recognition of the universality of the Osirian promise.

During the First Intermediate Period, Breasted (1923: 150-51) thought Abydos, "the fortress of the Port of the South." Even more, by the emergence of Theban supremacy in the Middle Kingdom, Abydos became the "Door of the North." In the Imperial Age, Hagg (1987: 187) informs further: "Frequently on the tomb walls at the Theban necropolis you see the mummy of some notable making the voyage by river to Abydos." The burial voyage along the Nile with weeping relatives became a favorite art theme after the "democratization of the afterlife" that so characterized the New

Kingdom. Now, unlike during the Old Kingdom when only the Pharaoh and a few notables could get to heaven, now all deserving persons who lived a good life could so aspire. To live by the precepts of Ma'at was a sure way to stand truthfully in the Hall of the Double Maati.

Egypt Essays Photo 98d. A stone boat at rest on the grounds of the Cairo Museum of Egyptian Antiquities.

Even more important, while the fortunes of the various deities and centers of worship and learning, viz., Re at Heliopolis, Ptah at Memphis, and Amun at Thebes, were dependent upon the monarch, dynasty or religious preference of the time. Abydos remained popular throughout dynastic rule. This may very well be, because, of all the Nile Valley cosmologies, the "Myth of Osiris" is the only one in which the deity, according to *American Journal of Archaeology* XVI (1912: 256) had "a complete legend, which set forth all his history, his parentage, birth, marriage, death and resurrection." More particularly, F. Legge in *Society of Biblical Archaeology* XXIII (1911: 135) further explained, how Osiris' "cult extended over the whole country and never seems to have depended upon any priestly corporation or college."

EGYPT ESSAYS ON ANCIENT KEMET

Egypt Essays Photo 99. Sakkara. Home of the Step-Pyramid. Another view of the wall enclosing the "Great Court" with uraei on the cornice.

Egypt Essays Photo 99a. Sakkara. Home of the Step-Pyramid. Image of the Step-Pyramid under construction.

FREDERICK MONDERSON

Egypt Essays Photo 99b. Sakkara. Home of the Step-Pyramid. Ptah (center) flanked by two other divinities. The one on the right may be an image of Ptah for he seems to hold the emblems.

So clearly, the antiquity of Abydos is affirmed from before the pyramids down to the Ptolemies and Caesars. At this site, Petrie also found evidence of kings before Menes, such as Ka, Zeser, Narmer and Sam. Narmer may very well be Menes. At an even earlier date, *American Journal of Archaeology* mentioned: "square oval pits, pre-dynastic tombs with their contracted burials - the bodies not mummified but protected by a layer of matting. 'These tombs belonged to a people who had attained to the Neolithic state of culture.'" Of the earlier Palaeolithic inhabitants of Abydos, crude flint implements lay scattered on the surface of the desert.

Votive offerings from Narmer, uniter of the two lands and founder of the First Dynasty, have survived from this site. Smith (1981: 30) also added, "We know that ivory and stone figures of men and women were placed on votive offerings in the archaic temples at Hierakonpolis and Abydos." Therefore, from the rich and mighty to the poor and lowly, all dreamt of a pilgrimage and the chance to be

EGYPT ESSAYS ON ANCIENT KEMET

part of the Osirian Drama as a reward for a considered life, directed and dictated by Ma'atian principles and behavior. *Ma'at*, who was a Theban deity, is represented by a feather. Importantly, the significance of ethical practice was here underscored.

Abydos is also the site where Petrie discovered ten successive layers of temples reaching back to the beginning of dynastic rule. So, from pots to painting, Abydos has thus etched its name in the annals of immortal places of eternity where theological, spiritual and social ideas syncretized to influence the pageantry of religious and historical experience. In this process, early Africans on the Nile created a legacy for posterity that is particularly enlightening and instructive in religious beliefs and practice as well as in all forms of knowledge, from building, law, medicine and art to mathematics, theology, astronomy and science.

A whole cadre of scholars including Belzoni, Mariette, Amelineau, Petrie, Caulfeild, Quibell, Mace, Garstang, MacIver, Peet, Naville and Margaret Murray, as well as the Egyptian Exploration Fund and the Egyptian Research Account, has worked the site of Abydos. Belzoni, the "strongman Egyptologist," was one of the first Nineteenth Century "raiders of the Egyptian ark," who looted the land while contributing little to develop the emerging science of Egyptology or could be beneficial to today's study of classical African civilization along the Nile River. Some Afrocentric scholars argue the discipline of Egyptology is simply Europe's way of explaining this African phenomenon, yet is not scientifically accurate in its portrayal of ancient Africa in the Nile Valley.

Mariette, the indefatigable scholar, worked the site of Abydos but Petrie seems to have spent more time at Abydos than all other archaeologists. Petrie first discovered ivories and other objects that enabled him to identify kings mentioned by Manetho and the *Abydos Tablet*, as belonging to the First dynasty. These names corresponded with hawk or banner names discovered earlier by the Frenchman Amelineau at Abydos, between 1895 and 1899. So much so, by February 1901, Petrie had found "thirty inscriptions of Menes and his predecessors, some fine jewelry of the queen of Zer,

FREDERICK MONDERSON

the successor of Menes, some forty inscriptions on stone and ivory of Zer, about sixty tombstones with names of royal household, ivories, tombstones, and other objects of King Den (fifth Dynasty), besides numerous other objects of interest."

Egypt Essays Photo 100. Sakkara. Home of the Step-Pyramid. Colossal painting of Ptah-Hotep as he does his rounds.

EGYPT ESSAYS ON ANCIENT KEMET

Egypt Essays Photo 100a. Sakkara. Home of the Step-Pyramid. In the religious belief system, the deceased needed a statue for the spirit to return to. Several statues made this more likely.

FREDERICK MONDERSON

Egypt Essays Photo 100b. Sakkara. Home of the Step-Pyramid. Laborers at work doing their many chores.

Egypt Essays Photo 100c. Sakkara. Home of the Step-Pyramid. Another view of the entranceway, providing shelter for workmen.

EGYPT ESSAYS ON ANCIENT KEMET

On June 29, 1903, Petrie penned a letter to the *London Times* giving an account of his work at Abydos where he had discovered ten successive temples. Here he informed: "The main result was proof that Osiris was not the original god of Abydos. The jackal-god, Wepwauwit, and the god of the west, Khentiamenti, were honored here till the twelfth dynasty. About the time of the fourth dynasty the temple building seems to have been replaced by a great hearth for burnt offerings, which was full of votive clay substitutes for sacrifices. An ivory statuette of Cheops [Khufu] of the finest workmanship shows for the first time the features of this king."

Petrie further explained how artistic achievements of this early age show "many of the ivory carvings of the first dynasty show great delicacy and refinement, and a figure of the aged king for subtlety and character ranks with the best work of Greece and Italy." Maspero (1926: 309) also added, "The seated figure of Khufu found at Abydos is only 5 inches high, but it is of perfect and most delicate workmanship."

The Egypt Exploration Fund excavated Abydos in 1912-13 and discovered beneath the wind-swept sand, "burnt wood, pot-shreds, animal bones, and decaying vegetable matter." Beneath this: "Two hearths, each about 20 feet in diameter, were buried in ashes, from which came arrow-heads, borers, scrapers, knives, and saws. A cylindrical seal shows four animal forms, one of them possibly an elephant. A small copper chisel was found. Grain was ground on flat slabs of stone. The abundance of bone attest a meat diet, the bones cracked to extract the marrow.... In one corner was a primitive furnace, 23 jars, arranged 12 and 11, packed close together and bolstered by vertical firebricks. Masses of charred logs suggest a slow-heat furnace for keeping things warm for a long time."

The next year eight additional prehistoric furnaces were unearthed. "The largest consisted of thirty-seven jars. In every case the jars were placed side by side in two rows supported by fire-bars of clay, and the whole was surrounded by other fire-bars. There had been a roof, and there were stoke holes in the walls. The fire made of twigs was between the jars. In addition, remains of wheat proved these grains were parched." In a twelfth dynasty tomb, was found, "an amethyst necklace four feet long, and in another the figure of a dancing girl bending backwards until her hands touch the ground." However, Petrie discovered the most significant find of jewelry found at Abydos in the tomb of Den.

Proximity of Abydos to *This* encouraged the first and second dynasty kings to build their tombs near the early capital of the Old Thinite Nome. In the area, tombs of the first and second dynasties, or Thinite kings, were discovered and excavated at the end of the last century. From these finds the names of the earliest kings of Egypt were supplied. This site therefore helped Petrie to reconstruct the early succession of the dynastic kings.

Egypt Essays Illustration 49. A sculpture never meant to be seen; part of the roof of the Sarcophagus room, showing the Goddess Nuit swallowing the sun at evening time.

EGYPT ESSAYS ON ANCIENT KEMET

Such kings as Narmer (Mena), his wife Neithhotep, and son and successor Hor-Aha were buried at Abydos. In their tombs, looted very early after internment, names were recovered from jar sealings and other artefactual remains. Uadji, Udimu, Enezib, Semerkhet, Ka and Queen Meryet-Nit were also buried at Abydos. These were First Dynasty kings and a queen. The Second Dynasty kings Hotepsekhemui, Ra-neb, Neteren, Sekhemib-Perabsen, Sendji, Neterka, Neferkara, Kha-sekhem and Kha-sekhemui were also buried here. Aldred (1980: 45) points to architectural departures using stone, the more durable material, for these final resting places, when he states: "The Cenotaph of King Den at Abydos has been floored with granite brought from Aswan on the far southern frontier. The burial chamber of King Khasekhemwy was built of limestone blocks rather than mud brick."

The other Thinite kings, excepting Narmer, built a second tomb at Sakkara. The construction of this second tomb, whether for cosmological, theological or political reasons, has led scholars to debate whether the Memphis or Abydos tomb could be considered the real one and which a cenotaph or "dummy tomb." However, Abydos is the most likely seat of the body, for in the myth of Isis and Osiris, the head of the dead god is buried here.

Throwing some light on the discussion regarding antiquity of the site, Pemberton (1992: 67) wrote: "Even after the transfer of authority to Memphis during the second dynasty, the great antiquity of Abydos, the Thinite necropolis, assured its continued religious significance; its status reinforced by the identification, of the tomb of Djer, a First Dynasty king, as that of Osiris, Lord of the Underworld." Subsequent to Petrie's work, researches have shown continued prominence of this area throughout dynastic times. So, for much of this time, the area remained a cemetery for royalty and animals held sacred by the ancient Egyptians. Wayne (1987: 178) pointed out: "The cemetery between Kom es Sultan and Seti's temple includes burials of dogs, falcons and ibises as well as cenotaphs or actual graves of those ancient Egyptians who wanted to be forever in the company of Osiris."

FREDERICK MONDERSON

Egypt Essays Photo 101. Ghizeh. View of the Sphinx, the Great Pyramid of Khufu, and some of the throngs of people who visit this site on a daily basis.

Egypt Essays Photo 101a. Ghizeh. Not only camels but horses are another way to get around.

EGYPT ESSAYS ON ANCIENT KEMET

Egypt Essays Photo 101b. Ghizeh. Naturally, motor vehicles are essential. The guys in white are Tourist Police who make an extraordinary effort to provide security for tourists.

In the later New Kingdom, during the Ramesside XIX-XX dynasties, this site was again accorded special status. Rameses I, Seti I, and Rameses II did lasting architectural work here. Seti I began his mortuary structure, the Temple of the Kings at Abydos that was finished by his son and successor, Rameses II, who built his own temple here. Jill Kamil's *Upper Egypt: Historical Outline and Descriptive Guide to the Sites* believed Seti's Temple possessed, the "finest relief sculpture of the age found in the Nile Valley."

Nineteenth century travelers and scholars revealed much about the culture and history of ancient Kemet and Abydos. In fact, in 1864, Dumichen discovered and excavated the temple and disclosed a remarkable document, significant in efforts to reconstruct ancient Kemetic chronology. In the southern wing of the Temple of Seti I was located the famous "Corridor of Kings." Here the "list of kings" or *Tablet of Abydos* "on the right wall, upper two registers" contained the names of seventy-six kings enclosed in cartouches in this gallery. The names of the kings from Narmer to Seti I are listed in chronological order. This find significantly aided efforts to determine the order of kings from the Ist to the XIXth Dynasty. There is a second *Tablet of Abydos*, from the Temple of Rameses II, that's now in the British Museum. So much so, Mariette Pasha supposed "the kings whose names are given on these two tablets, are those who had more particularly been connected with Abydos, either through having been born there, or having added to and embellished the city; just as the list of kings engraved by Thutmose III, in what is called the 'Hall of Ancestors,' taken from Karnak, and now at Paris, contains the names of those who more particularly benefited Thebes."

At Abydos, in a chamber to the west of the passage containing the King List, Seti I is shown assisting his son Rameses II, represented as a boy, to catch a wild bull. Some guides insist its Rameses instructing his son Merenptah. Other pictures show young king in a sacrifice, and also fowling, assisted by a number of divinities.

Five cartouches in the king list contain no names. These blanks represent the "Kings" Hatshepsut, Akhenaton, Tutankhamon, Smenkhare, and Aye. Hatshepsut's name is excluded because she ruled as "king," wore male clothes and a "beard." She built a temple larger than her ancestor Mentuhotep II, of the XIth Dynasty did. She also built a tomb in the Valley of the Kings (*Biban el Moluk*) rather than retain her first tomb in the Valley of the Queens (*Biban el Harim*). This daring female ruler planned and began to construct a tunnel from her mortuary temple at Deir el Bahari to her tomb in the Valley of the Kings. In the mortuary ceremony, she intended to be taken directly from the temple to her internment. Unthinkable, for a woman, in such an age! The other missing cartouches contain individuals associated with the religious revolution or Amarna heresy. These were Amenhotep IV, Tutankhamon, Smenkhare, and Aye.

EGYPT ESSAYS ON ANCIENT KEMET

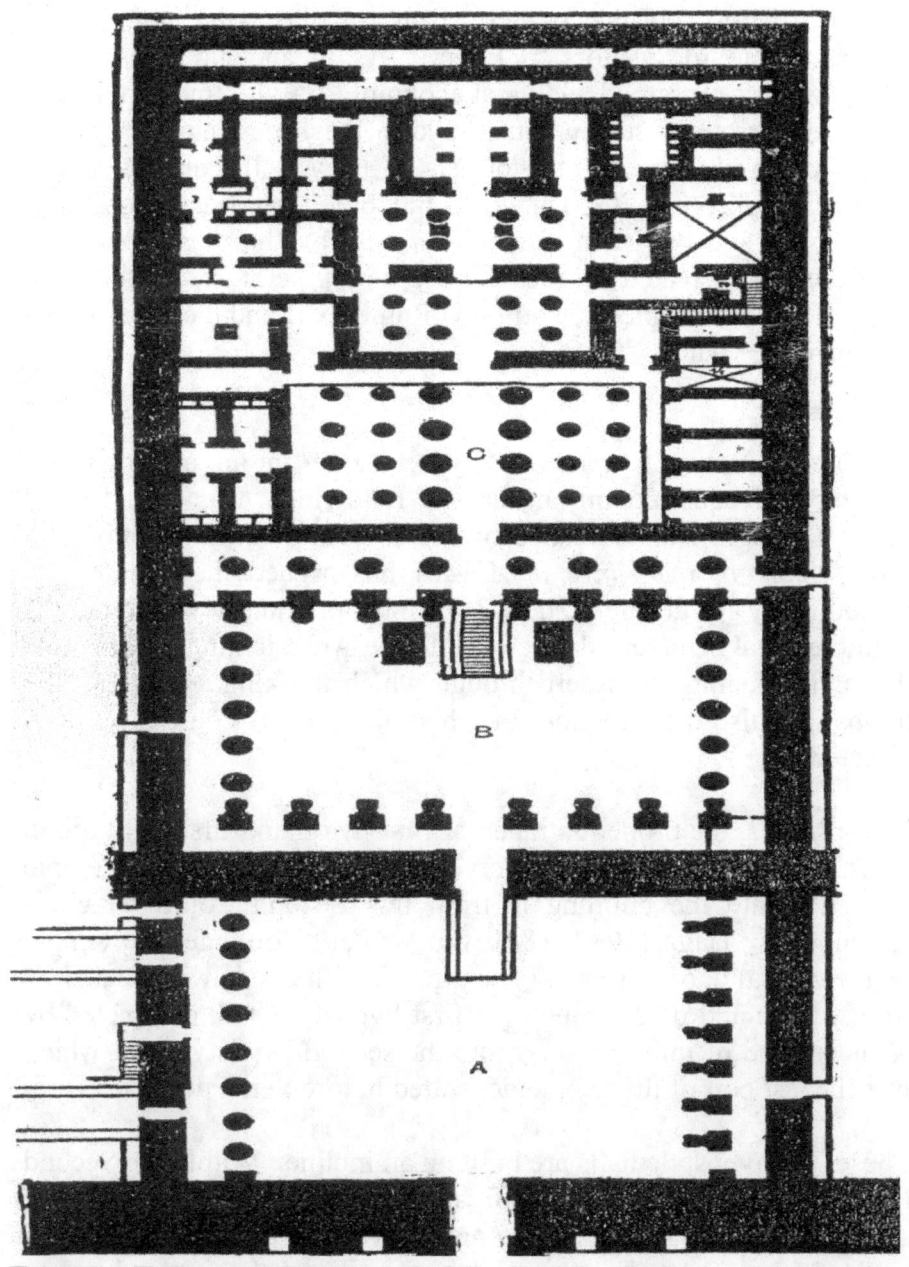

Egypt Essays Plan of Medinet Habu, Mortuary Temple Rameses III.

FREDERICK MONDERSON

Today Abydos, on the western bank of the Nile, remains an important site for visitors to Egypt. As in ancient times, when Abydos was a crossroad and great economic activity transpired here, in the modern town surrounding Abydos, local merchants conduct a lively business catering to tourists. They sell galiebas, bags, jewelry, books, film for cameras, and other hand-made artifacts. Cold sodas and bottled mineral water sold by the merchants, help ease the thirst created by the 120-degree temperatures of the area. Even more, the temples of Seti I and Rameses II and the Osireion all fascinate the visitor.

Seti I's mortuary temple at Abydos, done in an age of great architectural construction and artistic renderings, was built for his father Rameses I and finished by his son Rameses II. Caulfield's *The Temple of the Kings at Abydos* has argued the temple was symbolically for all the predecessor kings and that its orientation is with the royal cemetery dating back to the Archaic kings. He points to a pylon facing the desert through which the king could visit the tombs, but also the direction for which the prayers could have been directed.

Nevertheless, the proper entrance or first pylon and first court are in ruins. The second court is preserved. Thus, entrance to the Temple of Seti I into the building is from this Second Court, which is explained by Hagg (1987: 188) who wrote: "You enter the temple by the central door of seven. (The three on either side were sealed by Rameses II) and pass through the first hypostyle hall, completed by Rameses and of inferior work, into the second hypostyle hall which was the last part of the temple decorated before Seti's death."

These two hypostyle halls are built on an incline. Within the Second Hypostyle Hall, from right to left, are Seven Shrines dedicated to the divinities Horus, Isis, Osiris, Amon-Ra, Ra- Horakhte, Ptah, and Seti I, the deified king. The seven deities required the seven doors to properly enter their respective sanctuaries. Mentioning the architectural layout of the colonnades of the first and second hypostyle halls, Woldering (1963: 187) explained: "The papyrus-

EGYPT ESSAYS ON ANCIENT KEMET

bundle columns in the two halls have cushioned-like bases and smooth bulging shafts; they resemble the natural proto-type only in their calyx-leaves, suggested by low relief. The shafts of the columns themselves are covered with figures and inscriptions, so that the plant motif is completely lost from view. The columns themselves are massive and clumsy."

Egypt Essays Photo 102. Ghizeh. The "Great Pyramid of Khafra" viewed from the desert.

Egypt Essays Photo 102a. Ghizeh. Two of the Great Pyramids, Khufu (left) and Khafra (right) viewed from a local street near the Mena House Garden Hotel.

FREDERICK MONDERSON

Egypt Essays Photo 102b. Ghizeh. Still another look at the "Great Pyramid of Khafra" from a local street and near the hotel.

In the south wing of the temple are found the Hall of the God Sokar and famous corridor of kings, containing the list of kings or *Tablet of Abydos*, with a nearby stairway leading outside.

Behind the temple stands the Osireion, thought to be the burial place of Osiris. Discovered by Margaret Murray, this "Cenotaph of Seti I" was also worked by Naville. The structure is remarkable for a number of reasons. First, thought to be a cenotaph or mortuary temple, it is the only Nile Valley structure surrounded by water. It is sunk into the earth at a level reached by water. There is a central hall surrounded by ditches and seventeen rock-hewn niches. Each has a ledge in front of it. There is also an antechamber, a transverse chamber and an arched ceiling. These are decorated with scenes of the underworld and Egyptian cosmogony. Featured here are "Sky Goddess Nut and the Earth Goddess Geb, and Shu the god of the atmosphere."

The nearby Temple of Rameses II was built, of "fine grained limestone, black granite, rose granite, red and brown sandstone, and flawless alabaster." It was dedicated to Osiris and the deified

EGYPT ESSAYS ON ANCIENT KEMET

Rameses II. From its walls was taken the mutilated *Second Tablet of Abydos* now in the British Museum. In 1818, this document with its cartouches or oval rings was discovered by Mr. Banks, having been carried away by M. Mimaut, the French Consul-General, and sold in Paris, finally making its way into the British Museum.

Both the Entrance Pylon and First Court are now destroyed. The Second Court has a colonnade supported by rectangular pillars and contains Osiride statues of Rameses II. The First and Second Hypostyle Halls, each containing eight rectangular pillars, supported the roof. This roof has now collapsed. The Sanctuary is preserved. Throughout this temple interesting hieroglyphic scenes with fresh paint survive from the XIXth Dynasty, over 3,000 years ago. The religious depictions include priests bearing flowers and sacrificial animals towards the temple and processions of people singing, clapping hands, blowing trumpets and carrying banners. On the outside of the temple are battle scenes of Rameses' wars with the Hittites. These show scenes of hand-to-hand combat.

Egypt Essays Illustration 50. View of the Central hall of the "Osireion," recognized as the Cenotaph of Seti I (left); and in the foreground two steps leading down to the "Primeval Waters" and behind them two holes to take the shrines into where the tomb of Osiris was found (right).

At Abydos, two forts remain; one reaching back to the Archaic Period. The fort North of K'om es Sulta'n is enormous, and surrounded by double walls, that stand 12 ft. apart. The structure was whitewashed. Clarke and Engelbach (1990: 210) dated "the brick wall bounding the area at Abydos known as 'Kom el-Sultan' to the Middle Kingdom. The outer face of the inner wall is furnished with massive square buttresses. The height of each wall averages 40 ft., but must originally have been greater. The length of the whole building is 410 ft. and the breadth is about 220. Under the flooring of this building an enormous number of Ibis mummies have been found, each interred in an earthen jar. The God of Writing, Thoth was also worshiped here and the ibises were the animals sacred to him."

Finally, when we consider the great holy places of this world, we need to remember; the idea of holiness, judgment, resurrection, eternal life, and eternity grew out of the first appearance of religious consciousness and god's communion with man at Abydos, the land of ancient Kemet, in North-East Africa. As Africa's children have accepted and today worship God in the many forms and manifestations of their experiences, we need to remember also, God first appeared in Africa, his converts were African, and his first children were African. So as the first has become last, we need remember, the last shall be first one day!

Now Africa's children need to be taught that not simply religious belief, but also scientific thought, social relations, cultural practice, the development of knowledge, engineering, astronomy, government, the arts and concepts and principles associated with life and death, were also African inventions and experiences. Moral teachings and ethical practices were Africa's gifts to human progress. Thus, the genius of Africa's people and environment was quintessential to the genesis of human life and culture on earth. What a legacy for those in need of moral, ethical, spiritual and practical examples on which to base and enrich their lives. As the ancient Africans of Kemet/Egypt ordered or regulated their lives on the fundamental principles of Ma'atian thought of balance, order, justice, equality, and fairness, so too we can teach our young, that in quest of these godly qualities can prepare us to overcome any obstacles and even reach into the heavens. If we work diligently and

EGYPT ESSAYS ON ANCIENT KEMET

sincerely for self, family, community and nation, we are certain to be rewarded with everlasting life and pleasant remembrance. Then we need not fear the second judgment or the second death. We live in the thought of the significance of a wonderfully rich heritage that can provide lasting foundations upon which to create perspective, vision, analysis, strategy and hope, as we face a new century and millennium.

Egypt Essays Photo 103. Ghizeh. View of the Mena House Garden Hotel as seen from the street.

REFERENCE

Aldred, Cyril. *Egyptian Art*: *In the Days of the Pharaohs*. London: Thames and Hudson, (1980) 1985.
Armour, Robert A. *Gods and Myths of the Ancient Egyptians*. Cairo: American University in Cairo Press, (1986) 1989.
ben-Jochannan, Yosef. *From Abu Simbel to Ghizeh*. Baltimore, MD: Black Classics Press, (1987) 1989.
Breasted, John H. *A History of Egypt*. New York: Charles Scribner's Sons, (1905) 1923
Clarke, Sommers and R. Engelbach. *Ancient Egyptian Construction and Architecture*. New York: Dover Publishers, Inc., (1930) 1990.
Haag, Michael. *Guide to Egypt*. London: Michael Hagg, 1987.
Kamil, Jill. *Upper Egypt*: *Historical Outline and Descriptive Guide to the Sites*. London: Longman, (1983) 1986.

FREDERICK MONDERSON

Maspero, Gaston. *A Manual of Egyptian Archaeology.* New York: G. Putnam's Sons, 1926.

Smith, W. Stevenson. *Art and Architecture of Ancient Egypt.* New York: Penguin Books, (1959) 1981.

Wayne, Scott. *Egypt and the Sudan: A Travel Survival Kit.* Berkeley, California: Lonely Planet Publications, 1987.

Wilkinson, Alix. *Ancient Egyptian Jewelry.* London: Methuen and Co., 1971.

Woldering, Irmgard. *The Art of Egypt in the Time of the Pharaohs.* New York: Greystone Press, 1963.

Yoyotte, Jean in Georges Posener's *A Dictionary of Egyptian Civilization.* London: Methuen and Co., Ltd., (1959) 1962.

Egypt Essays Illustration 50b. "An exquisitely worked vulture" shown in flight with outspread wings, and clutching in its talons an ankh (the sign of life) Part of a mural relief in the restored temple of Senusert I at Karnak in the "Open Air Museum."

15. THE DANCE, MUSIC, MUSICAL INSTRUMENTS

The dance, accompanied by some form of music is one of the oldest, aesthetic expressions in Africa. Gods, kings, nobles, and just plain folks participated in and enjoyed the dance. Whether for social relaxation, banquet festivities, in religious function, on military expeditions, an accompaniment to working, or simply when boating

EGYPT ESSAYS ON ANCIENT KEMET

down the Nile River, music was always pleasing to the soul, and a wonderful form of enjoyment. When we consider the enormous strides humanity has made in musical expression and its assistance in developing language and other social conventions, the significance of music becomes even more apparent. Budge I (Osiris: 243) quoting Sir H. H. Johnston in *The Uganda Protectorate II*, mentions five dances performed in "Black Africa." These were: "(1) The dance to celebrate the birth of twins; it is danced by men and women, and the gestures are obscene; (2) the death dance, which is danced by both sexes; (3) the dance of the sexual initiation ceremony, which is danced by both men and women; (4) the wedding dance in which only women join; (5) the dance which takes place in seasons of drought to propitiate the good spirit and bring down rain."

It is not certain if these specific dances were done in Kemet/Egypt. However, Budge II (Osiris: 253) further commented, "the chief African peoples regard ceremonial dancing before a god as an act of worship .... 'the dance of the god,' the 'god' being presumably, Osiris, and we are justified in assuming that this 'god' had his special dance, which was not generally known in Egypt." This suggests an "other" African source both for Osiris and the dance. In Kemet, the "Black land," it appears that the king danced on religious and ceremonial occasions and probably did at any number of palace banquets to celebrate marriage, accessions, victories in war or at any of the numerous festivals including the "Heb-Sed," and "Opet," "Feast of the Valley," etc., celebrated throughout the united lands. More-so, it is again shown by Budge I (Osiris: 233) that, "Egyptian bas-reliefs of all periods contain many illustrations of kings dancing before Osiris and other gods."

FREDERICK MONDERSON

Egypt Essays Photo 104. Cairo Museum of Egyptian Antiquities. Kashida Maloney of Brooklyn, beside a "Hathor Head" figure.

Egypt Essays Illustration 50c. A gold pectoral depicting the Ba-bird that was the king's spirit with a diadem similar to that actually found on King Tut's head.

EGYPT ESSAYS ON ANCIENT KEMET

Egypt Essays Photo 104a. Cairo Museum of Egyptian Antiquities. Broken stone showing the king in adoration and offering Ma'at.

The earliest representation of such a ritual as the king dancing before a god involved Semti (Hesepti) of the First Dynasty so depicted on an ebony tablet in the British Museum. Displayed in the

FREDERICK MONDERSON

Third Egyptian Room in table case L, No. 123, this plaque also records several events in the reign of this king. Here Budge (1885/1972) recounts that minimally clothed: "The king is seen wearing the crowns of the north and south and in his right hand he holds his whip and in his left a paddle." Elsewhere, Budge I (Osiris: 33) describes other features of the illustration of Semti. There he notes, "... on each side of him are three signs, which represent objects that were associated with dancing. The king, I believe, is dancing, though his back is turned to the god, and this representation appears to be the prototype of all the scenes, down to the Ptolemaic Period, in which the king dances before his god."

Indeed this notion of dancing was a ritual enjoyed throughout dynastic rule. On the great Mace-head of King Narmer, uniter of Upper and Lower Kemet/Egypt, three men are seen dancing. Elsewhere, on a limestone relief from the Zoser temple complex at Sakkara, the king, according to Woldering (1963: 78) is "shown performing a ritual dance. Wearing the crown of Upper Egypt/Kemet and carrying a ceremonial whisk, he is shown in the ritual dance, as part of the festivities connected with the jubilee of his accession to the throne. In another representation from this early period the king is shown involved in an agricultural pursuit, where the dance is ritually performed to ensure prosperity in the endeavor."

The next depiction of royal involvement with the dance occurs in the Fourth Dynasty, dating to the reign of King Assa. Budge I (Osiris: 232-233) mentions a high official called Ba-ur-tet who "brought from Punt a tenk (Twa/Pygmy), who knew how to dance 'the dance of the god'... and was said to come from the land of the spirits."

Pepi I ruled as king in the VIth Dynasty. In a text of his pyramid, Budge I (Osiris: 232-233) distinctly mentions the "Pygmy dancers of the ...." It read: "Come northward to the court immediately; thou shalt bring this dwarf with thee, which thou bringest living, prosperous and healthy from the land of the spirits, for the dances of the god, to rejoice and (gladden) the heart of the king of Upper and Lower Egypt, Neferkere, who lives forever. When he goes down

EGYPT ESSAYS ON ANCIENT KEMET

with thee into the vessel, appoint excellent people, who shall be beside him on each side of the vessel; take care lest he fall into the water. When (he) sleeps at night appoint excellent people, who shall sleep beside him in his tent; inspect ten times a night. My majesty desires to see this dwarf more than the gifts of Sinai and of Punt ...."

Breasted (1923: 140) says the boy king promised "Harkhuf a greater reward than king Isesi had given to his 'treasurer of the God,' Burded, when he brought home a dwarf from Punt."

Egypt Essays Illustration 51. In the foreground, steps leading down to the "Primeval Waters" and behind them, the place for a shrine of Seti as Osiris, ruler of the other-world; a corner of the Island representing the "Primeval Hill" (left); and in the background, one of the cells for the "Guardian Spirits;" on the right, the ledge of the Island, the "Primeval Hill," the "Primeval Waters" of the Cenotaph (right).

FREDERICK MONDERSON

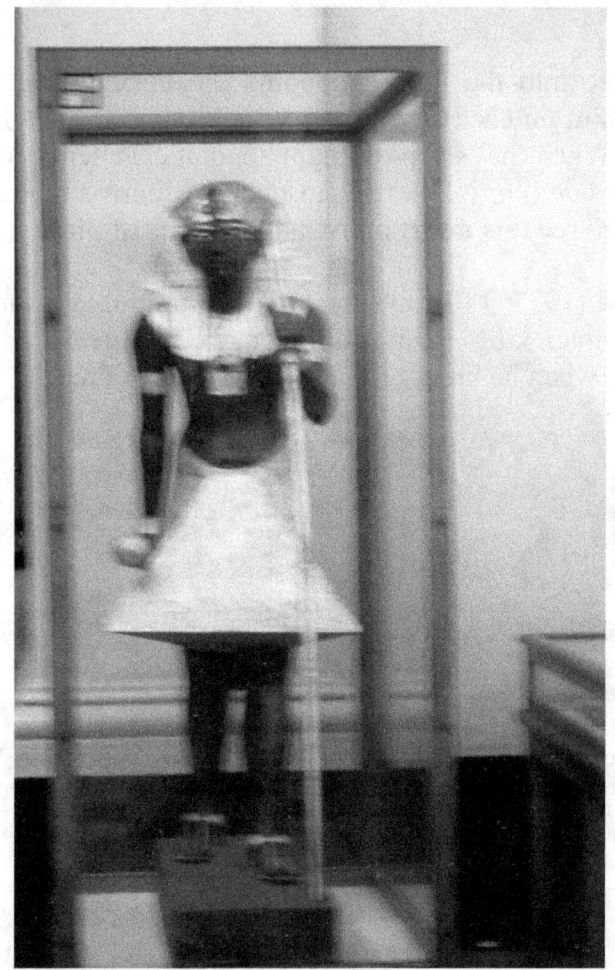

Egypt Essays Photo 105. Cairo Museum of Egyptian Antiquities. The first of two statues of King Tutankhamon, painted black, to reflect his color.

On another abstract, Budge I (1904: 233) provides a clear indication of the sacredness and high regard for these dancers of the Twa people that a king of Kemet "considered it an honor to him in the other world, if he could dance like a pygmy before Osiris, and proves clearly that the object of the dance was to comfort, cheer and strengthen the deity whose special dance he danced."

EGYPT ESSAYS ON ANCIENT KEMET

Egypt Essays Photo 105a. Cairo Museum of Egyptian Antiquities. Tutankhamon as a bronze sphinx attacking Nubians painted black!

FREDERICK MONDERSON

Egypt Essays Photo 105b. Cairo Museum of Egyptian Antiquities. Bronze plaque of the boy king attacking a lion.

In *Osiris and the Egyptian Resurrection*, Budge I (234-235) provides an enlightening description recorded in *Albert Nyanza* by

EGYPT ESSAYS ON ANCIENT KEMET

Sir Samuel Baker, who made a visit to Katchiba, King of Obbo. The quotation is a bit lengthy, but it characterizes the intensity, drama and significance of the dance.

"The king determined upon a grand dance, and soon the nogras (drums) were beaten, pipes and flutes were soon heard gathering from all quarters, horns brayed, and men and women formed a circle. Each man held in his left hand a small cup-shaped drum, formed of hollowed wood, one end only being perforated, and this was covered with the skin of the elephant's ear. The dance commenced by all singing remarkably well a wild but agreeable tune in chorus, the big drum directing the time, and all the little drums striking at certain periods, with such admirable precision, that the effect was that of a single instrument. The dancing was most vigorous ... the figures varying continuously, and ending with a 'grand gallop' in double circles at a tremendous pace, the inner ring revolving in a contrary direction to the outer; the effect of this was excellent. Although the men wear a skin slung across their shoulders and loins, the women are almost naked, and instead of wearing the leather apron and tail of the Latukas, they are contented with a slight fringe of leather shreds, about four inches long by two broad, suspended from a belt. The unmarried girls are entirely naked, or wear three or four strings of small white beads, about three inches in length, as a covering. The old ladies wear a string round the waist, in which is struck a bunch of green leaves, the stalk uppermost. Here we have a complete parallel with King Pepi, whose earnest desire was to dance before the god."

Religion was central to life in ancient Kemet/Egypt as well as other African peoples. This important parallel with the peoples south of Egypt finds support in the *Papyrus of Hunefer*, a nobleman of the XIXth Dynasty, which states inter alia, "we came from the foothills of the Mountains of the Moon where the God Hapi dwells." The Mountains of the Moon are thought to be Mounts Kenya and Ruwenzori on the plains of East Africa. Hapi is another name for Osiris who is also a god of the Nile.

FREDERICK MONDERSON

King Sesostris I reigned in the XIIth Dynasty. On the detail of a limestone pillar, the king is shown; Woldering (1963: 120) wrote accordingly, "performing a ritual dance before the god Min at Coptos, and also a relief on a pillar depicting the god Ptah embracing the king."

Another example of the king dancing before a divinity comes from the New Kingdom. Here Thutmose III of the XVIIIth Dynasty is shown, according to Budge in *Dwellers on the Nile* (1972: 132) where he is "wearing the Khnum headdress, with ankh and *waz* scepter in right hand and offers a bird while dancing before the goddess Hathor."

At a much later time, the god Bes is shown dancing on a column in the small chapel at the Temple of Isis. Throughout, these examples show the significance of the dance to the king and the gods. That meant, Budge (1972: 31) states, "... the person who knew how to dance the dance of the gods was an honored and respected person."

Art in the form of sculpture, architecture and pictorial decoration, particularly in tombs, depict musicians, singers and dancers that paint a lively picture of daily life in ancient Kemet/Egypt with bustling preparations for the afterlife.

In the Mastaba of Ptahhotep, who was a high official of a king of the Fifth Dynasty, is an excellent collection of wall decorations. This form of sepulcher and later tombs became a prototypal place where scenes of dancing, musical scenes, particularly at banquets, with musicians and their instruments, were represented and have come down to us.

EGYPT ESSAYS ON ANCIENT KEMET

Egypt Essays Photo 106. Cairo Museum of Egyptian Antiquities. The second statue of the King painted Black!

FREDERICK MONDERSON

Egypt Essays Photo 106a. Cairo Museum of Egyptian Antiquities. Statues of the young king painted gold.

Egypt Essays Photo 106b. Cairo Museum of Egyptian Antiquities. Hathor as a calf, among King Tut's possessions.

EGYPT ESSAYS ON ANCIENT KEMET

Polyglot's *Egypt Travel Guide* (1965: 32) describes the Mastaba of Ptahhotep, where: "Nearly all the walls, corridors, chambers, and rooms are decorated with reliefs, which illustrate Ptahhotep life - with his servants, dogs and monkeys, with singers, harpists and dwarfs; Ptahhotep sacrificing or taking a meal, on a tour of inspection of the provinces, busy with state affairs."

The creation and enjoyment of music as an aesthetic, was an early part of the consciousness of Nile Valley man who ushered in civilization. Music as a cultural mode of expression is traceable from the mythical traditions; and, the people of ancient Kemet believed their God Asar/Osiris was a patron of music. Further, they believed, this deity had his scribe the God Tehuti (Thoth) invent music, and as well, some other instruments. Thoth is also credited with inventing writing, arithmetic, sculpture and a system of astronomy. Among the 42 "priestly books" attributed to Thoth, there were two books of the singer. Anthropologically speaking, the God Bes represented music, dancing and food. Among his other attributes during Roman times was as god of wine (Bacchus, thus "bacchanal") and protector of women at childbirth. Though dating to remote antiquity among the gods, Bes is preserved playing a tambourine in a decoration of the small temple of Hathor at the Temple of Isis. Today at Aswan, in southern Kemet/Egypt traditional Nubians dance, sing and play instruments similar to those of antiquity. Some aspects of ancient Kemet dance forms are thus preserved and can be observed in any properly orchestrated trip to Egypt.

During pharaonic times music was played at annual festivals and parties or banquets. There were titles such as 'the Superintendent of the singing,' 'superintendents of the royal singing,' and 'superintendent of the singers of Pharaoh,' and again 'superintendent of the singers of all the gods.' Temples and palaces had orchestras that played vocal and instrumental music. Instrumental music was played at funerals and this soothed the saddened condition of the mourners. Soldiers used drums along with flag signals in wars. Boatmen sang and played varied instruments in their sometimes serene and sometimes exhilarating

FREDERICK MONDERSON

voyages up and down the Nile. Baikie IX (1917: 34) believed: "The singers seem at all periods to have marked the rhythm by clapping the hands - in fact, this simple method of marking time is so inseparable in the Egyptian mind from the idea of music that the word 'to song' is written in all periods by the hieroglyph of a hand. Blind performers were not unknown - a representation from tell el-Amarna shows a blind harpist accompanying several blind choristers who mark the rhythm with the clapping of hands."

Dance, instruments and musical praxis in a dynamic and enduring civilization as Kemet, raised the fine art of manufacturing the delicate and balanced musical instruments, to the level of an "industry." Therefore, it can be argued that dance, music and instruments were among early Nile Valley cultural gifts as part of universal aesthetics.
This essay examines a variety of themes and artifactual survival in dance, music and musical instruments from ancient Kemet.

Beethoven, the musical genius, it was argued, had "Moorish" blood implying he was Negro, African or had what we would call African American features. Authorities differ on the "racial Origin" of this musical great. Writing in *Sex and Race* vol. III, J. A. Rogers (1944: 306) supplies "Notes on Beethoven" showing that: "Beethoven was German and because his portraits are usually shown with a white tone and abundant hair nearly every one thinks of him as white." Rogers' beliefs on Beethoven's color is based on commentary supplied by the musical genius' biographers, that are included here as follows: Fanny Giannatasio del Rio "mulatto;" May Byron "swarthy;" Alexander Wheelock Thayer "negroid;" Frederick Hertz "negroid;" Brunold Springer "negroid;" Brunold Springer "negro;" Emil Ludwig "dark."

EGYPT ESSAYS ON ANCIENT KEMET

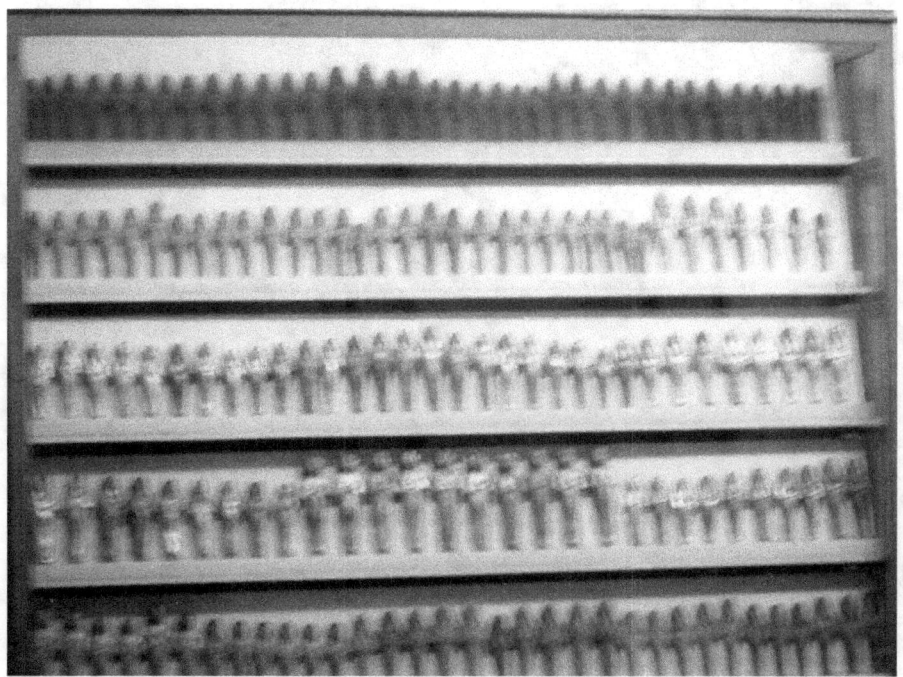

Egypt Essays Photo 107. Cairo Museum of Egyptian Antiquities. Part of the ushabti collection that accompanied Tutankhamon into the afterlife.

FREDERICK MONDERSON

Egypt Essays Photo 107a. Cairo Museum of Egyptian Antiquities. A beautiful piece of furniture for the king's personal effects.

EGYPT ESSAYS ON ANCIENT KEMET

On Beethoven's writing-table Naumann (1882: 36) mentions a framed copy of an inscription from the Temple of Sais, which ran thus: "I am all that is, that was and that will be; no mortal has lifted my veil." It's believed that the veil belonged to Auset/ Isis, the goddess to whom Kemet man and woman also attributed the origin of music.

Naumann (1882: 34) further tells us that on an island of the Upper Nile, the German Egyptologist Brugsch found the following inscription supposed to date from the time of the fifteenth dynasty: "Epra-He, the great, Prince of Kusch, and singer to his Lord Amon." These examples are only added to support the indication of the proximity of Egyptian/Kemet deities to music in early Northeast Africa.

The philosopher Plato is quoted as saying (Gnomon, 1882: 37) of the Egyptians/people of ancient Kemet that "in their possession are songs having the power to exalt and enable mankind, and these could only emanate from gods or god-like men." This early accolade of early African cultural and aesthetic creativity is indeed noble.

A number of classical authors have commented on Kemet/Egyptian dance, music and musical instruments. The first such commentator was Herodotus of Halicarnassus who traveled the Nile around 450 B.C. and wrote *Euterpe*, Book II of his *Histories*. This History of Egypt provides some interesting eyewitness accounts of Nile Valley culture that is a constant source of debate among scholars of early civilization. Baikie (1917: 33) says: "Herodotus (ii. 79) speaks of his surprise at finding that the song called Maneros by the Egyptians, a dirge said to have been named after the son of the first king of Egypt, was similar to the Cyprian dirge Linor or Alinios."

FREDERICK MONDERSON

Egypt Essays Illustration 52a. Causeway of Khafra, from the Mortuary Shrine at the Pyramid to the Valley Temple (the so-called Temple of the sphinx) – A threefold way, finely paved with limestone.

Egypt Essays Illustration 52b. Aerial photographs of the Subterranean Cenotaph of Seti I in the foreground, with its pillared hall representing the "Primeval Hill" rising out of the "Primeval

Waters;" and, one of the earliest arches in architecture: The five course arch of bricks, which was closed after the ritual of the burial of the dead, had been performed.

In *The History of Music*, Chappell (1874: 50-51) makes an interesting observation regarding early Egyptian/African origin of the musical scale and how it had close proximity to the Greek "origin" of musical systems. The author's statement is quoted in its entirety below: "Nichomachus, quoting Pythagoras and Plato, tell us that the Egyptians ascribed twenty-eight sounds to the universe, calling it "twenty-eight soundings." So the Egyptians must have had twenty-eight sounds, i.e., twenty-eight notes in their scale. That is the precise total number of Greek notes, in their greater and lesser perfect systems combined, and including all their scales - Diatonic, Chromatic, and Enharmonic, neither in Egypt or in Greece was there an actual limit to twenty-eight sounds, because all scales were transposable, but only twenty-eight notes could be defined starting from any given pitch. Euclid, Nicomachus, Aristides, Quintilianus, and others enumerate the Greek scales and their notes, and all authors are agreed as to the number being precisely twenty-eight. This most remarkable coincidence between Egypt and Greece seems nevertheless to have escaped the observation of historians of music. If it stood alone it would almost suffice to prove the origin of Greek music. The number is too peculiar to have arrived at by accident, within a compass of only two octaves."

Diodorus Siculus flourished around 60 B.C. and wrote on Egyptian/Kemet music. Baikie (1917: 33) made the following commentary regarding ancient Egyptian music based on writings of the classical authors. "They confine themselves to general observations, none of which carry us very far, and some of which are demonstrably inaccurate." Diodorus (I. 80), indeed, is responsible for an observation on the subject, which led, for a time: "It is unfortunately impossible to derive much information with regard to the mistaken idea that the Egyptians were an unmusical race. 'It was not customary,' he says, 'for the Egyptians to practice music, because they considered it effeminate and undesirable.' On what grounds his statement is based it would be difficult to say, and he himself admits that the Greek poets and musicians visited Egypt in order to improve their art."

Egypt Essays Photo 108. Cairo Museum of Egyptian Antiquities. Seated figure of the Goddess Sekhmet.

Another avid commentator on Kemet/Egypt, Strabo is credited with preserving the view that the Ethiopians founded Egypt as a colony. Strabo, who lived during the time of Christ also, commented on Egyptian music. Baikie IX (1917:33) says: "Plato ascribes a very high antiquity and a very noble character to the sacred music of the

EGYPT ESSAYS ON ANCIENT KEMET

Egyptians, whose rules concerning it were, according to him, most rigid, only certain things being allowed by Government. This is confirmed by Strabo (XVII, 1), who says, 'the children of the Egyptians were taught letters, the songs appointed by law, and a certain kind of music, established by government, to the exclusion of every other;' and, further, that vocal and instrumental music was usually admitted in the worship of the gods, especially at the commencement of the services, except in the temple of Osiris, where neither singers nor players on the flute or the lyre were allowed to perform."

Egypt Essays Photo 108a. Cairo Museum of Egyptian Antiquities. More jewel and other personal boxes of the king.

FREDERICK MONDERSON

Egypt Essays Photo 108b. Cairo Museum of Egyptian Antiquities. A duck or goose painted black to represent its color.

Two classical writers who commented on Egyptian music were Dion Cassius and Clemens Alexandrinus, both living around 200 A.D.

While clapping of the hands may have been the first employment of musical instruments, the Tambourine is probably the first instrument and the earliest form of the drum. There were two types of tambourines, a square or sometimes oblong and a round one. Women most usually played this instrument, found in temples and used at funerals and other ceremonies. A round tambourine is shown being played by the god Bes at the Temple of Isis/Auset, formerly on Philae but now on Agilka Island.

The Drum proper was both long and short types. There were three kinds of drums. The first was a small hand-drum, two or three feet long, covered with parchment at both ends, and braced by cords.

EGYPT ESSAYS ON ANCIENT KEMET

The second type of drum was 1 1/2 ft. high and 2 ft. broad. There was a double drum variation of this one that's found as part of a decoration of Horemheb, XIXth Dynasty. The large drums were beaten with sticks. Some sticks were padded. A third type of drum is identical to the Darabukker, a closed vessel with parchment over the mouth that the modern Egyptian plays.

The Sistrum was a form of rattle. Its *Medu Netcher*/hieroglyphic name is *seshesh*. Mainly employed at religious ceremonies, it was principally used by females to drive away evil spirits. Naumann (1882: 52) held that the people of Kemet/Egypt "attributed to the sistrum the power over evil spirits and believed at its sound the evil Typhon fled."

In *Wisdom of the Egyptians* Petrie (1940: 57) mentions two types of sistrums. "There is the emblem of Hat-hor, with a face bearing horns, and a building placed over it, thus reading Hat-Her; and there is also a rattle placed over a head of Hathor and lotus flower. The first is seen carried by Hathor, the queen as priestess of Amenhotep III at Thebes and in the Amarna period. Rameses II is shown carrying a sistrum while adoring Hathor. These are not instruments of sound but purely emblematic and appear in religious scenes."

Petrie (1940: 57) also notes the sounding Sistrum first appears at Beni Hasan, XIIth Dynasty, where it is borne by a servant and in this instance has no religious significance. Still, by the time of the XVIIIth to XXth Dynasties there were five variations of this musical instrument. Petrie further shows (1940: 57) that these were carried by a servant to the Vizier Rekh-ma-ra; held by Amarna princesses; by all daughters of Rameses II at Sabua, Derr, and Abu Simbel; and Queen Nefertari at Medinet Habu. Significant to the expropriation and export of African art and cultural motifs, Petrie (1940: 58) further adds: "Actual sistra of bronze are in the British Museum, Berlin, and at University College, with bust of Horus on the top, of Roman age. Also at U.C. is the blue glazed head of a sistrum of Amenhotep II and late fragments of Apries, Aahmes, and Nekhtnebef."

FREDERICK MONDERSON

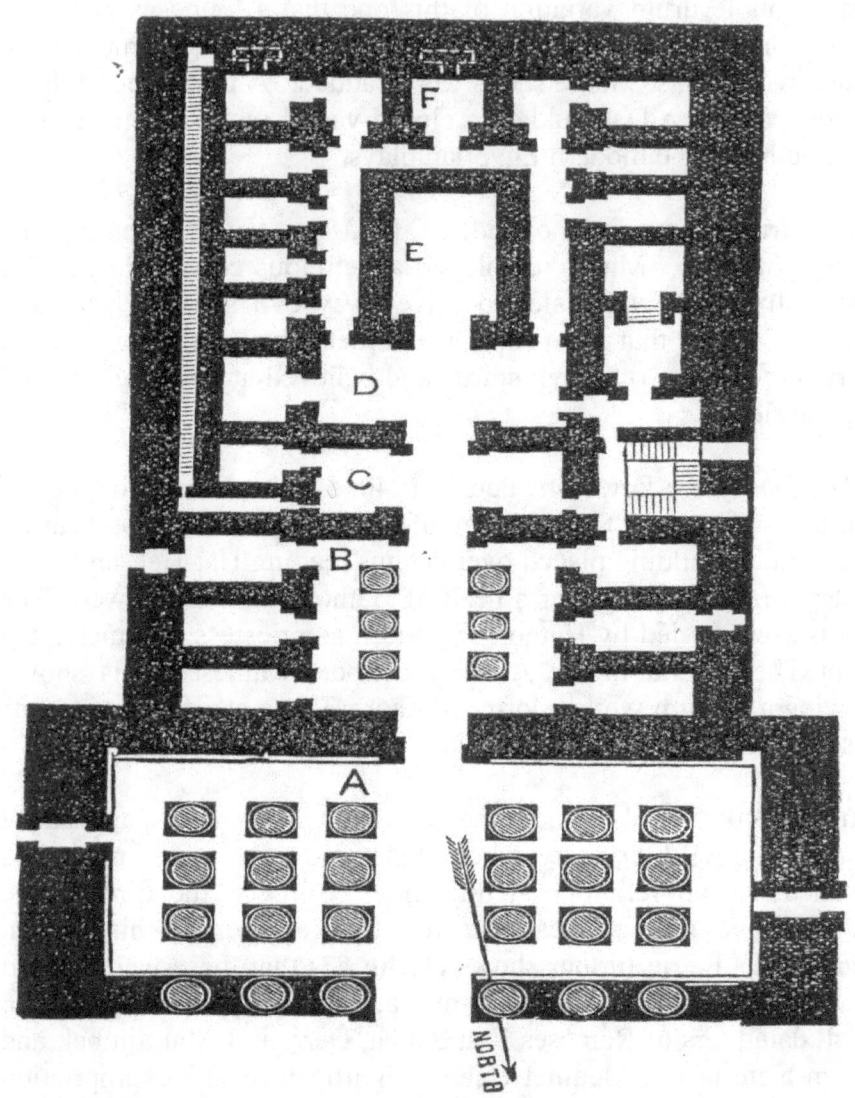

Egypt Essays Plan of Hathor's Temple at Dendera.

Naumann (1882) describes the sistrum as consisting "of a frame of bronze or brass, crossed with three or four metal bars and was furnished with an ornamented handle; at the end of these bars were

EGYPT ESSAYS ON ANCIENT KEMET

moveable pieces of metal for the purpose of producing a jingling noise when the instrument was struck with a metal clapper."

Trumpets, generally made of wood, were used for civil and military purposes. There were two types. There was a long conical type with an open end. Then there was a shorter form.

The Flute is one of the few instruments that have survived from the Old Kingdom. In the earliest times they were originally made of bone and rested on the ground. The number of finger holes numbered six or seven.

Egypt Essays Photo 109. Cairo Museum of Egyptian Antiquities. Kings and gods of early Egypt.

FREDERICK MONDERSON

Egypt Essays Photo 109a. Cairo Museum of Egyptian Antiquities. Old and Middle Kingdom Kings of Egypt.

Pipes were of two varieties, the single and double type. The single pipe was generally made of reed with four finger holes. Sometimes they had three, five or more holes. Both single and double pipes were played with a vibrating reed held within the mouth. The mouthpiece was made of ivory. The Lute had a long straight stem. This instrument varied in shape and the number of strings. Petrie (1940: 59) remarked that the lute looked similar to the Nefer sign and has supplied three facts to prove the separate nature of the figures.

(1) The marks on the body of the Nefer are never found on a lute, and the stem of the lute crossing the body is never seen on a Nefer.

(2) The lute has pegs only on one side; the Nefer has projections on both sides.

(3) The Nefer was figured as early as the first dynasty, on the black cylinders; the lute does not appear till the XVIIIth dynasty. The real source of the Nefer sign, meaning "good," is echoed in the tradition in Horapollo, "a man's heart hung from the windpipe means the mouth of good man."

Dancers also played the Lute. Engel (1864) noticed one in the Berlin Museum that appears to have 13 strings instead of 10. He added; a similar but smaller one was in the Leiden Museum.

EGYPT ESSAYS ON ANCIENT KEMET

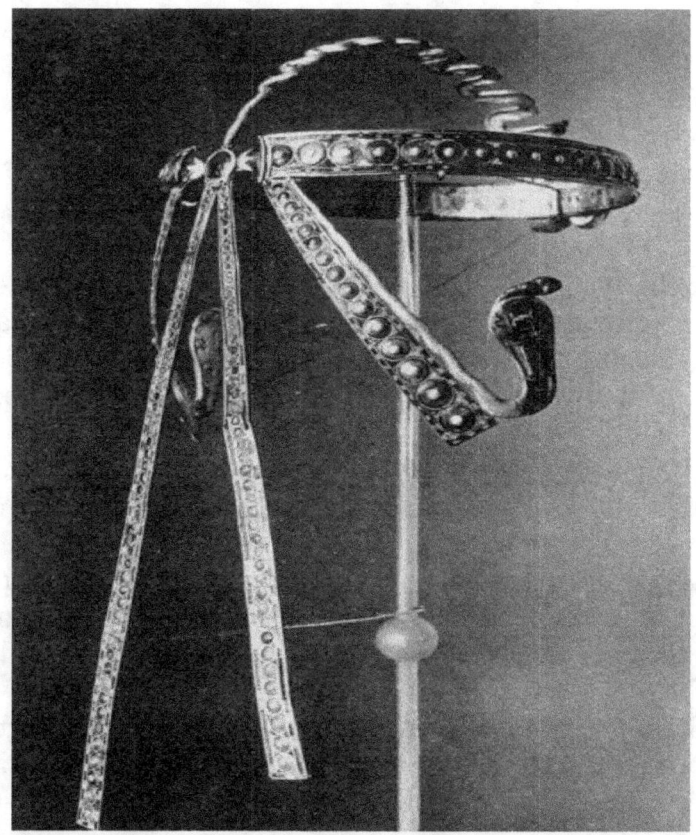

Egypt Essays Illustration 53a. Tutankhamon's gold diadem showing gold uraei on the side appendages and from behind, the symbolic bow at the back, the ribbons and side appendages.

The Sancho had a bowl body and curved neck. It's somewhere between the lute and harp. Naumann (1882) wrote the Temple of Dakkeh contains an image showing "fire-god Ptah playing a harp."

The Harp is a musical instrument indigenous to the Nile Valley. Representations show different sizes, shapes with varied number of strings. While all had strings, only some had tuning pegs. Some harps had stands and could be played standing, sitting or kneeling. The harp had a long snout, and slightly curved beam with various strings. It sometimes expanded at the waist. Some harps had double strings. Interestingly, Petrie (1940: 61) adds: "The representations often show only half of the strings, which were in double row; and of 63 harps there are 8 in which there are many more sets than strings, often double the number, and there are two instances of the two sets of strings crossing each other, proving the double set. Thus about one in six was double-strung. There is no evidence of three rows of strings, as in some Welsh harps."

In the twelfth dynasty, Naumann (1882: 50) writes, the base of the harp increased in size and it served as a large resonance body; and in the New Empire the bow form and bent outline of the harp disappeared entirely and was succeeded by the triangular shape.

The harp became a favored royal instrument during the Ramesside years. Baikie IX (1917: 34) wrote, "... the greatest elaboration of the harp is reached in the time of dynasties XIX and XX. The representations of priests playing the harp in the tomb of Ramessu III show instruments which are not only distinguished by the number of their strings, but are also very elaborately decorated, the framework being carved and inlaid with gold, ivory, tortoise-shell, and mother-of-pearl, and ornamented with various figures." Wherein, Gnomon (1882: 50-51) could add regarding expansion of its strings employing more elaborate decoration.

Egypt Essays Photo 110. Cairo Museum of Egyptian Antiquities. Mainly New Kingdom Pharaohs.

EGYPT ESSAYS ON ANCIENT KEMET

Egypt Essays Photo 110a. Cairo Museum of Egyptian Antiquities. Late Period Pharaohs.

"During the period of its greatest perfection it had thirteen, eighteen, twenty-one, and even twenty-six strings, and was most probably played only by priests and kings, which may in some degree account for its elaborate ornamentation. The framework was carved in the richest and most elegant manner; inlaid with gold ivory, tortoise-shell, and mother of pearl; and is further ornamented with mythical figurines, or with the heads of gods, goddesses, sphinxes, and animals. It was sometimes decorated with colors, the edges covered with Morocco velvet, imparting to it a bright and cheerful appearance."

The Medu Netcher/hieroglyphs name of this instrument was *bunion beni*. The harpist was described as "*Seb an ben*" meaning "scraper of the horn."

The Trigonon is a triangular form of the harp that looks more like a lyre. It had a wooden frame that was sometimes covered with leather. As many as 20 strings could be mounted on this instrument. "It had no tuning pegs," Engel (1864) wrote, "but the strings were affixed to the upper part of the frame and were tuned by being wound round a rod which was inserted into the lower part of the frame."

FREDERICK MONDERSON

The Lyre first appears in the XIIth Dynasty and had sometimes six, seven or eight strings. The Tamboura is a lute like a modern guitar. The Gong was made of metal and designed to give a gong sound to exit.

Crotola are Clappers or Castanets and mentioned by Naumann (1882: 38) who describes a scene on the walls of a catacomb dating from the time of the seventeenth dynasty. Here, "the departed master and his consort are represented as listening to the performance of female singers accompanied by two harps and one flute, while a little girl is beating time with the well-known Egyptian wooden clappers." Two pairs of Egyptian Cymbals are on display in the British Museum.

Bells have for long been a part of religious and civil ceremonies. Bells are on display in the British Museum. It can be conjectured that bells played a musical part in Egyptian/Kemet architecture. When pharaonic builders employed the bell motif capitals instead of papyrus, lily or lotus, and even Hathor Head types, they probably intended this instrument to resonate its sacred vibes on sacred and civil occasions.

REFERENCES

Baikie, James. "Egyptian Music." *Hastings Encyclopedia of Religion and Ethics* Vol. IX (1917: 33-36).
Breasted, James H. *A History of Egypt*. New York: Charles Scribner's Sons, (1905) 1923.
Budge, E. A. Wallis. *Dwellers on the Nile*. New York: Benjamin Bloom, Inc., Publishers (1885) 1972.
_____. *Osiris and the Egyptian Resurrection*. 2 Vol. New York: (1911) 1973.
Chappell. *The History of Music*. 1874.
Davidson, Basil. *African Civilization Revisited*. Trenton, New Jersey: Africa World Press, 1991.
Engel. *History of Music* 1864.
Naumann. *History of Music* 2 vol. 1882-1882.

EGYPT ESSAYS ON ANCIENT KEMET

Petrie, W. M. Flinders. *The Wisdom of the Egyptians*. London: Bernard Quaritch, 1940.
Rogers, J. A. *Sex and Race*. 3 Vols. New York: Helga Rogers, 1944.
Woldering, Irmgard. *The Art of Egypt: The Time of the Pharaohs*. New York: Greystone Press, (1962) 1963.

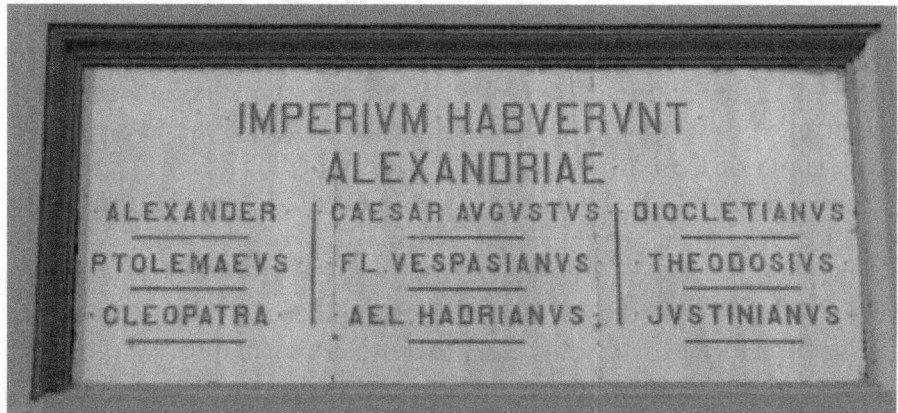

Egypt Essays Photo 111. Cairo Museum of Egyptian Antiquities. Graeco-Roman Pharaohs.

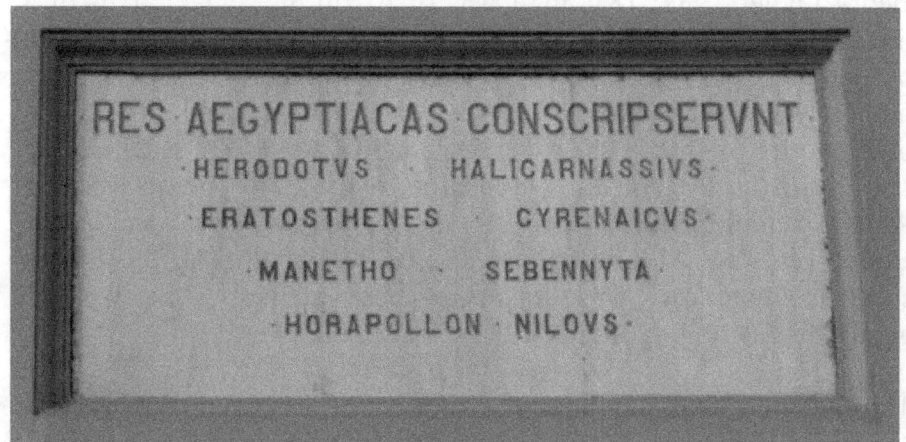

Egypt Essays Photo 111a. Cairo Museum of Egyptian Antiquities. Commentators on Egypt.

FREDERICK MONDERSON

16. AFRICAN ART

African Art is older than man, for man himself is art from Africa! Importantly, however, African man, in conscious domestication of himself after long thought and experimentation with early tools, envisioned the forest, savannah, hillsides, mountains, valleys, rivers and animal and vegetative forms of life, along with man, displayed on the African landscape as potential artistic subjects and canvass for his art. From such juxtapositioning with nature, man was able to create some of the earliest art themes and motifs. From the Sahara "Tassili Frescoes" in the north; stone age art of Tanzania; and the so-called Bushman art of South Africa; art of the Nile Valley; together with Nok art; and later art throughout the Western Sudan; Africa today boasts the earliest historical landscape on the face of the earth. Here artists, canvases, materials and nature, as models, came to reflect and represent the great mysteries and conceptions, art depicts as it expresses a number of esoteric and cosmological representations based on practical applications of life's many experiences.

Henry Lhote (1987: 181) in "Oasis of Art in the Sahara" tells of a time when the: "Sahara was green, millennia ago, man hunted buffalo and drove cattle over grasslands where giraffes browsed and hippos wallowed in Lakes." Here he mentions, among a multitude of artworks of that era, an "archer stands poised in sandstone at Tassili-n-Ajjer." From this collection, over 4,000 paintings in the Algeria remote massif, "plateau of the rivers," were dated near 12,000 years ago. Lhote, collected some 8,000 colored prints of this spectacular gallery, and considers these artifacts "the world's greatest collection of prehistoric art."

The author's Tassili time-line suggests four major styles that "dominate the numerous artistic traditions of successive cultures." The *Round Head* style began before 6,000 B.C. or 1760 *Before Nile Year* 1 beginning at 4240 B.C. The Round Heads depict, "Featureless faces and rounded heads" that characterize a period of

EGYPT ESSAYS ON ANCIENT KEMET

stylized painting and may have lasted some 2,000 years. Figures vary in size, some reaching more than 15 feet in height.

The *Pastoral* frescoes appear ca. 5000 B.C. (760 *Before Nile Year* 1). Here, Lhote's (1987: 183) reproductions introduce "Herders of unknown origin" who developed a "naturalistic style depicting scenes from everyday life. Compared with the Round Head, these works show greater concern for detail and composition."

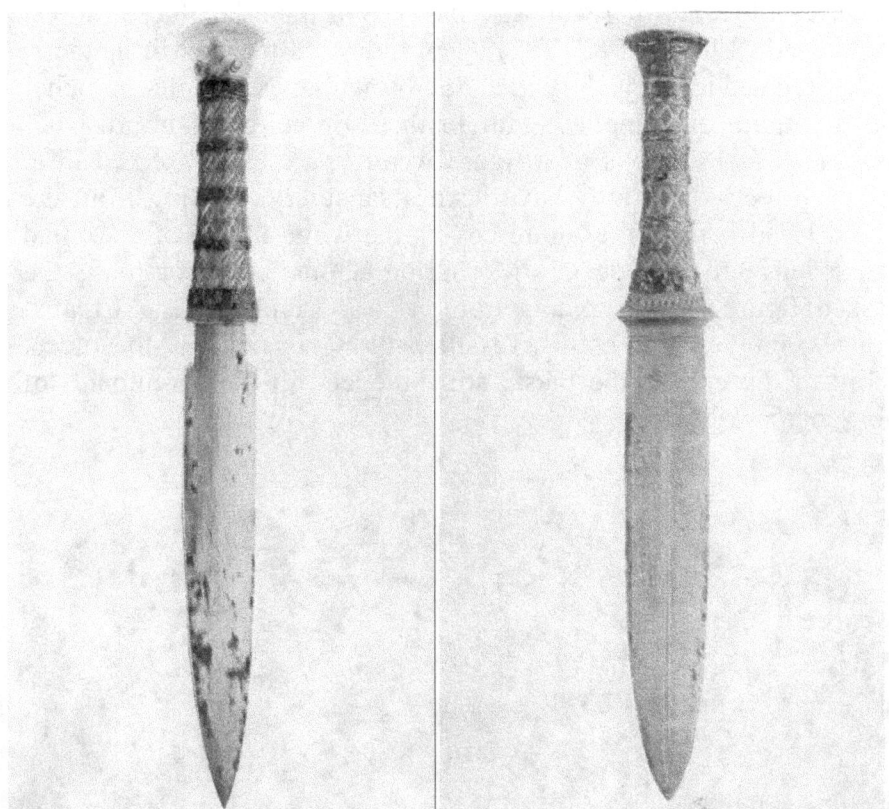

Egypt Essays Illustration 54. An important milestone in the development of civilization: one of the two Tutankhamon daggers, with an iron blade resembling steel and in perfect condition (left); and, with a blade of gold and richly ornamented haft, one of two magnificent daggers found on Tutankhamon's mummy (right).

FREDERICK MONDERSON

The *Horse* period began about 1200 B.C. (*Nile Year* 3040) and, according to Lhote, "Horse-drawn chariots reflect contact with cultures from the eastern Mediterranean." *Camel* period begins around 100 B.C. (*Nile Year* 4140) for, "As the Sahara became more arid, the camel - more suited to the climate - replaced the horse." As to the Pastoral period, Lhote (1987: 182) continued, the "features of the archer painted during the Pastoral period, suggest to me the presence of black peoples."

Modern art lovers often wonder what type of materials these earliest artists used. Lhote (1987: 182) again indicated the Tassili painters, x "favored shades of yellow, red, and brown, made by mixing ocher with a liquid, and applied with feathers or animal-hair brushes." Lhote (1987: 187) tells of a figure wearing a mask observed in a: "… deep recess that may have been a sanctuary. Dating from the Round Head period, the figure covers the white image of a woman whose legs are still seen. Measuring about five feet high, the masked figure sprouts plants from its arms and thighs. Created about 7,000 years ago, this Tassili painting is perhaps the oldest record of the cult of the mask, still practiced in the ceremonies of sub-Saharan tribes."

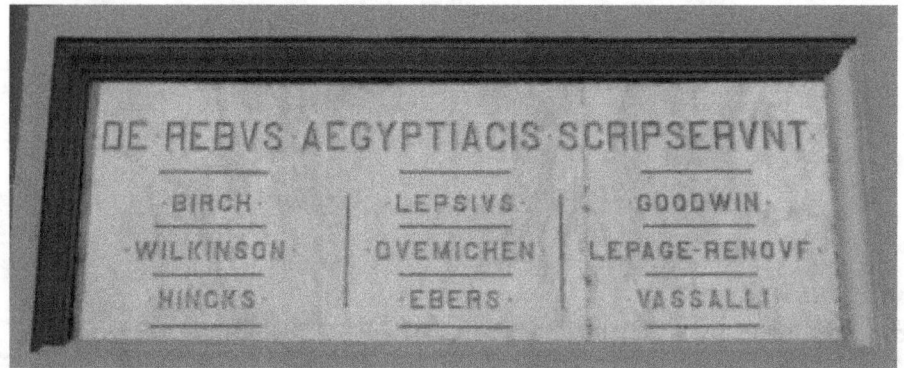

Egypt Essays Photo 112. Cairo Museum of Egyptian Antiquities. 19th Century scholars who worked to make Hieroglyphics a sound language and advance the discipline of Egyptology.

EGYPT ESSAYS ON ANCIENT KEMET

Egypt Essays Photo 112a. Cairo Museum of Egyptian Antiquities. The lintel above the doorway entrance to the Museum.

On one particular canvas with giraffe head and horns of wild sheep and other figures, the "expedition discovered 12 superimposed layers painted during a period of perhaps 2,000 years." To this revelation, Lhote (1987: 191) reasoned: "It is not known why different artists used the same locations. Some sites may have offered a better painting surface than others or held special religious importance. Perhaps the act of painting filled a ceremonial function more important than the artwork itself."

Elsewhere in East Africa, the anthropologist Mary Leakey and her husband Louis, from 1935 through 1951 (*Nile Year* 6175-6191) discovered and catalogued 186 rock-painting sites. This extensive gallery supplied 1,600 individual scenes, over a 500 square mile area in Tanzania. Through Mary Leakey's (1983: 86) article in *National Geographic Magazine* entitled "Tanzania's Stone Age Art," we are helped in understanding an archaeological study of man's distant past that brings to us the startling conclusion: "Those long-ago works of art tell us, for example, that Stone Age man in Africa wore

FREDERICK MONDERSON

clothing, had a variety of hairstyles, hunted, danced, sang, played musical instruments, and may even have known the secret of fermenting spirits."

For these early East African painters, in many respects similar to those of the Tassili artists, painting materials were of principal concern. Their choice of colors is interesting for "the predominant red was made from ocher, which is derived from iron ore. Black probably came from manganese, and bird droppings may have provided the basis for the white."

From these early and humble beginnings, Leakey (1983: 92) tells us: "The beauty and delicacy of some of the paintings are extraordinary, particularly when one considers that those ancient artists did not erase or correct their work as modern painters do. There is no blurring strokes or abrasion of rock surfaces that would have resulted from rubbing or scraping out of lines. Perhaps the artists sketched in rough shapes first with charcoal or some other medium that has not survived."

These prehistoric artists were obviously hunter-gatherers rather than a pastoral people. Leakey (1983: 92) continued: "Stone age painters took certain artistic license. They often exaggerated the salient features of various animals. For example, snakes are shown with more loops than they normally have. The kudu, an antelope with horns that always have fewer than three complete spirals, is sometimes depicted with as many as eleven spirals. Roan antelopes with their characteristically large ears are drawn with that feature greatly exaggerated."

Stone Age artists tended to be selective of subjects on the basis of size. Small creatures as hydraxes, hares, and little antelope are rarely depicted. Though, they are known from heaps of bones left after the hunter's meals. In contrast, Leakey (1983: 99) commented on choice of larger themes and remarked, "... the artists concentrated instead on large animals such as elephants, giraffes, rhinos, and the carnivores. Plainly, the killing of a large animal, which would provide food for many people, was considered of greater

EGYPT ESSAYS ON ANCIENT KEMET

significance than an average small kill. Thus the number of elephants painted probably does not reflect the number killed, but rather importance of such events."

Alfred Friendly has spent a great deal of time chronicling "Africa's Bushman Art Treasures." From Cape Town in South Africa to just below Lake Victoria in Central East Africa, the author discovered more than 2,000 sites where these more recent Stone Age artists left depictions of the African fauna known to them, including "elephants, giraffes, felines, serpents, birds, fish, and the Bushman's principal diet - rebook, eland, springbok, hartebeest." This background and models, Friendly (1963: 849) wrote, created a "gallery filled with thousands upon thousands of exhibits, each one a gem or a collection of gems, displayed against a natural backdrop of mountain, valley, or broad savannah." He further remarked: "Such is the gallery of Bushman paintings in Africa, fabulous and infinitely rewarding to the observer, whether art lover, naturalist, archaeologist, or mere sightseer."

Egypt Essays Photo 113. Cairo Museum of Egyptian Antiquities. The Goddess Hathor personified atop the entrance to the Museum.

FREDERICK MONDERSON

Egypt Essays Photo 113a. Cairo Museum of Egyptian Antiquities. An Egyptian manifestation of the beautiful decorating the entrance.

EGYPT ESSAYS ON ANCIENT KEMET

Egypt Essays Photo 113b. Cairo Museum of Egyptian Antiquities. M. Dourgnon, architect, who had the vision to build such a structure.

Combining these surviving ancient art expressions we can help construct a more complete view of African man creating art in his many habitations and circumstances, as he pictured and represented nature throughout the continent.

Interestingly enough, Friendly's (1963: 854) interpretation regarding the representations left by these early artists, allows a glimpse back into times when scant records exist for much of this.

"In all respects, the early Bushman was the classic Old Stone Age man. He was a hunter and food gatherer; he had no agriculture whatsoever. As a hunter, he had no fixed abode, being obliged to follow the game on its migrations. Accordingly, he had only the fewest and lightest possessions: stone, bone, and wooden weapons and tools; a weighted stick to dig edible roots and tubers; a few skins for clothing or for the rigging of a windscreen when he was encamped away from his beloved rocks. He spun no cotton, made almost no pottery, and domesticated no animals. His vessels were gourds and shells of ostrich eggs, the source of his jewelry as well." Friendly (1963: 854) further instructed, the "essence of the Bushman's world," was represented in his art work, where he left, "illustrations of the most central aspects of his life, his times and his temperament, examples of the basic techniques of his artistry; revelations of his arsenal, his religion, his economics - even of his disposition."

Finally, Friendly (1963: 857) wrote, quoting Malan who recalled what Dr. W. H. Bleek, the classic authority on "San" or "Bushman Lore" had written, "... these animal headed Bushmen represented sorcerers; he found them somewhat reminiscent of the Egyptian mythological representations in which animal heads were placed on human bodies. Bleek added: This fact of Bushman paintings illustrating Bushman mythology gives at once to Bushman art a higher character and teaches us to look upon its products not as the mere daubings of figures for idle pastime, but as a truly artistic conception of the ideas which most deeply moved the Bushman mind and filled it with religious feelings."

These graphic examples can serve as vivid reminders of the nature and purpose of African art and sculpture, being careful observations of nature as the mind evolved through the countless centuries upon centuries of inquiries and experimentation. Therefore, early man's pristine and subsequent creations of art to express his religious concerns, questions about nature, philosophic speculations, conceptions of beauty, etc., became important aesthetic mediums employed in Africa to portray art-science fusion with their metaphysical implications and dynamics. So, with the aid of scientific consciousness, art and sculpture came to be viewed as beautiful and timeless works of artistry that have expressed cosmological and social themes in the life history of various African peoples.

EGYPT ESSAYS ON ANCIENT KEMET

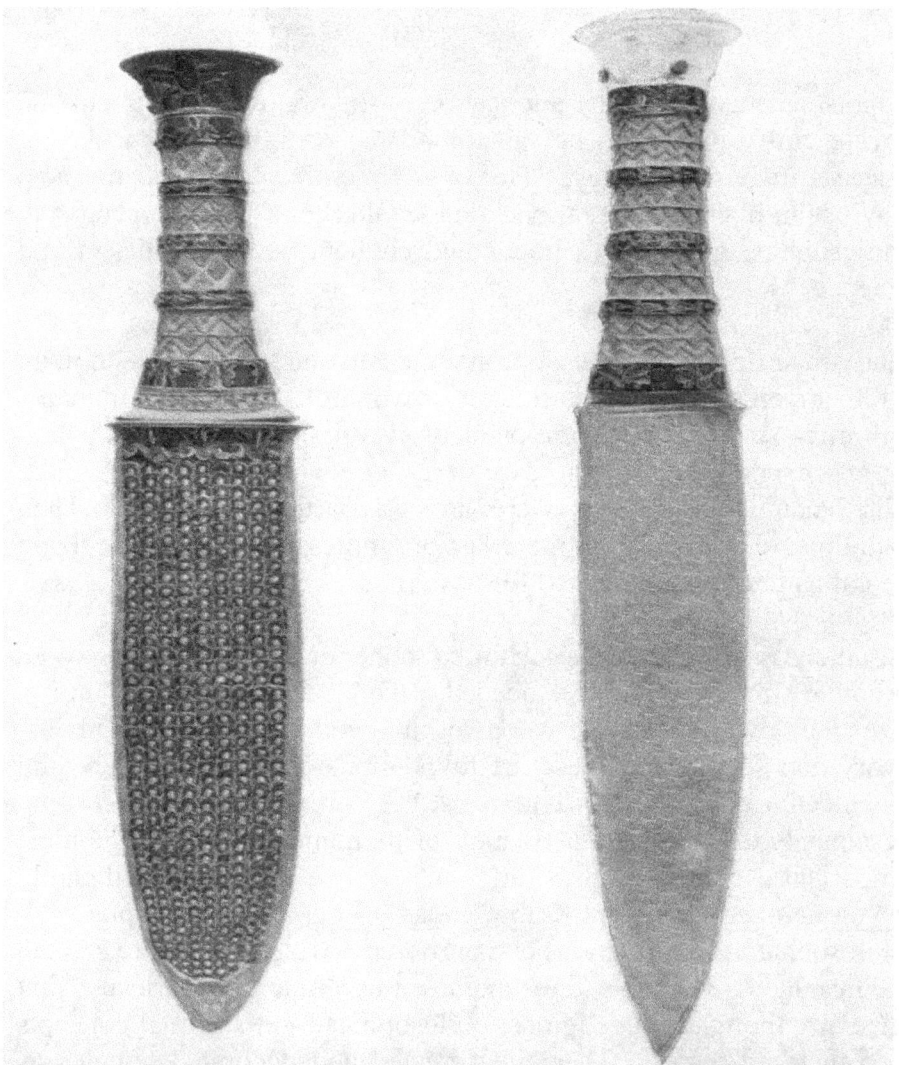

Egypt Essays Illustration 55. In their sheaths: The same two daggers shown above unsheathed, that on the right having a rock-crystal knob on the shaft (left); and the other side of the left hand sheath beautifully embossed with wild animals (right).

These rhythmic vibrations in the undulative evolutionary history of Africa, teaches us all, thousands of years ago man first domesticated himself. Later, art and philosophy were his next additions. His first technology, the hand-axe, was a work of art that became more

FREDERICK MONDERSON

sophisticated with further application of the brain to experiment and create craft. At night, he sat around the campfire after a day of success in hunt and feast. Here tools were repaired and the next day's hunt planned. As far back in the Old Stone Age, man began to philosophize about life's hopes and challenges, its mysticism and science.

Early man first asked questions about death and the sky. He thought of the moon and planets as sources of wondrous creativity. In man's primitive state animals were painted on walls of caves. This belief, in his superstitions, sought favor and success in the next day's hunt. His technology or tools were an early artistic creation. Then painting aided in creating more lasting impressions of an ethical and moral nature to be preserved for posterity.

In idleness he may have whittled bone or stone against wood. Another time he may have needed a wooden tool for some utility. This led down the road to woodworking, and later industry in bone, ivory and stone. On these art foundations science, sculpture and architecture were blended to construct some of the most lasting testaments to early man's creation of monumental art. Of its most important contributions, art in Africa was significantly revolutionized in ancient Kemet, today's Egypt. It served practical, philosophic, religious and social purposes. Art and sculpture created a message. Using nature themes these ancient Africans first mentally thought out religious, philosophical and spiritual concepts and their processes. Then they erected and decorated temples as places of worship and adoration of their gods, in veneration for favorable gifts in return. Such emblems as hawk, lion, scorpion, jackal, or pelican were the earliest forms of the anthropomorphic quintessence of theosophical creation which was splendidly thought-out by the earliest African theologians along the banks of the Nile River in North-East, Africa.

EGYPT ESSAYS ON ANCIENT KEMET

Egypt Essays Photo 114. Cairo Museum of Egyptian Antiquities. Rosellini, the Italian linguist and archaeologist who worked alongside Champollion to lay the foundation for the discipline.

Egypt Essays Photo 114a. Cairo Museum of Egyptian Antiquities. Champollion, the master who cracked the Hieroglyphic Code in 1822, but died in 1832.

Petrie's "Egyptian Art" in Volume I of Hastings *Encyclopedia of Religion and Ethics* (1909: 862) explains how the Divine Forms were represented: "The compound theology of sacred animals and deities resulted in a variety of strange combinations. The animal element is always the head, placed upon a human body for a deity; a human head upon an animal body is used only for a sphinx, emblem of a king, and for the ba-bird, emblem of a soul. The combination of animal heads on human bodies is found in the second dynasty (Set, on seals of Perabsen) and the fourth dynasty (Thoth, on scene of Khufu); and it became very unusual in later times."

Dress was an important aspect of the deity, for as Petrie mentions, "The gods are usually clad in the oldest form of close-fitting waist-cloth; it is always older forms of dress that are thought appropriate for religious or artistic purposes, and in Babylonia the oldest figures of worshipers are entirely nude. The gods never wear the projecting peaked waistcloth common in the Old and Middle Kingdoms."

Petrie indicated further, "Another primitive piece of costume was the animal's tail, hung at the back from the belt. This is shown as a bushy tail, like a fox's, on the archaic hunters, carved on a slate palette. It appears on all kings from the first dynasty onward (... figure of Rameses IV.... the kneeling Hatshepsut, where it is brought forward). And it gradually becomes almost universal for gods after the early ages.... It can be seen on the figures of Horus and Thoth, in the long form, and thinner than usual. Four principal ceremonies depicted in illustrations are Sacrifice, Offering, Laying on of Hands, and Purification. Again, as depicted in some of the first forms of art, we see that illustration in "early sculptured tombs the sons of the deceased are shown as trapping birds, and sacrificing the ox, for the festival in their father's honor. It is rare to find representations of sacrifice later, such as this example of the nineteenth dynasty. Burnt-sacrifice was a foreign importation, and is only known in pictures at Tell el-Amarna (eighteenth dynasty), and in a description at the Ramesseum (twentieth dynasty)."

This idea of the offering is very significant for we see the pharaoh in many attitudes of communing with deity. Whether making an incense, liquid, or food offering, the king represents the people in expressing their religiosity. This form of private and royal art came to portray the profound philosophic tenets early Africans were

EGYPT ESSAYS ON ANCIENT KEMET

privileged to create as they established the axioms of human progress measured by the arts, sciences, technology and religion, all guided by ethical behavior.

An interesting commentary can be interjected here, for as Petrie in "Egyptian Art" Volume I, Hastings *Encyclopedia of Religion and Ethics* (1909: 863) has indicated: "The Egyptian never burnt incense on an altar, but always in a metal censer held in the hand. It was a long metal rod, with hand holding a cup for the burning incense at one end, and a hawk's head at the other end; in the middle of the length was a pan or box in which the pellets of incense were kept ready for burning. The heat requisite to light it was obtained by using a hot saucer of pottery placed in a cup, on which the resin fused. When the incense was burnt, the saucer was removed and thrown away, and thus no cleaning was required for the metal cup."

The art of the incense holder is interesting and significant. To recall, Bruce Williams discovered at Qustol in Nubia, evidence of the "World's Earliest form of Monarchy," published in *The New York Times*. He commented on displayed illustrations depicting the enthroned monarch wearing a white crown and showing a palace facade, royal barge, incense burner, etc. This form of religious expression is therefore directly linked to Africa before ancient Kemet/Egypt certainly came into being. It indicated a creative African man, whose art has left representation of his expression, depicting connections with a higher form of metaphysical, spiritual, theological and theosophical consciousness.

"Laying on of the hands," wrote Petrie in *Religion and Ethics* "was represented as being done by the gods, in order to impart the Sa. This was a divine essence which the gods drank from the heavenly 'lake of the Sa,' and which the earthly images of the gods could impart to beings and to priests who knelt before them. The benefit was not ceaseless, but required renewal from time to time. The same form of laying on of hands was used, as in our illustration, for conferring the kingship; the inscription reads, 'giving of the kingship of both banks of the river, the complete office, to his daughter, *Maat-ka-ra*' (Hatshepsut)."

FREDERICK MONDERSON

Egypt Essays Photo 115. Cairo Museum of Egyptian Antiquities. Samuel Birch, master Egyptologist whose efforts were instrumental in guiding the young science.

Egypt Essays Photo 115a. Cairo Museum of Egyptian Antiquities. Case "Stand by Your Man" in the Museum Gardens.

Purification was the last and most significant ceremony performed by the priests or pharaoh. Petrie repeats the old adage: "Personal cleanliness was strictly observed by the priests; and the purifying of

EGYPT ESSAYS ON ANCIENT KEMET

the king was performed symbolically by the gods.... Each god holds a vase from which he pours out a stream over the king. It is stated that Ramessu 'is purified with life and power.'"

Egypt Essays Photo 115b. Cairo Museum of Egyptian Antiquities. A facade view of this magnificent structure, repository to a glorious past.

Egypt Essays Photo 116. Cairo Museum of Egyptian Antiquities. The Mariette Memorial that pays tribute to the greatest Egyptological minds.

Gold was an essential metal to represent things religious, spiritual; and working such the early craftsmen of the Old Kingdom were able to create some of the highest standards for ancient Egyptian/African art. Petrie notes further: "the Egyptian often describes large objects as covered with gold, which was usually of considerable thickness. The reliefs were usually worked in hard stucco and then thickly gilded and burnished. The art of high burnishing upon a stucco base was kept up till Roman times. The sets of vases for the purification ceremonies and further libations of wine were kept on wooden stands.... A stand with water jars, covered with lotus flowers, and with bunches of grapes placed below it. On another stand at the extreme left is a figure of the king kneeling, offering a large ankh, or sign of life; this is crowned with flowers, and has convolvulus and vine growing up beneath it. Another stand at the extreme right has a figure of the king offering a large bouquet of flowers. A main part of the religious art was spent on these statuettes of the king making a great variety of offerings. Unhappily all this wealth of figures has perished, and only a few fragments remain to give reality to the innumerable pictures of the temple riches shown upon the walls."

In addition, the ancient Africans craftsmen further expanded their technological or artistic repertoire by building tombs, temples, pyramids, and palaces. Housing, villages or settlements, towns and even fortresses reflected their art, some of a permanent nature, some as fleeting structures. Therefore, architecture and monumental portrait sculpture are best examples of Egyptian art. Ceramics is also a significant art medium that exhibits much artistry and contains purposeful historical evidence.

In regards to painting and sculpture, the first artists were not tied to an arbitrary canon of proportions, but were desirous of representing what they saw as exactly possible. The oldest painting yet found is now in the Cairo Museum depicting a flock of geese pasturing. It comes from a tomb at Meydum. Also discovered from this earliest time were two statues from another tomb also at Meydum, and dated to the reign of Snefru.

Murray (1888) has indicated: "In the goldsmith's art the excellence of every work is remarkable, though the mechanical finish is

EGYPT ESSAYS ON ANCIENT KEMET

sometimes inferior to the design and execution of the more ornamental portions. The jewelry of Queen Aahotep, in the Boulak Museum, shows more taste in color and design than actual skill in workmanship. Metal work was much developed under the pharaohs of the Middle Empire and retained its vitality to a late period. Bronze statuettes of great beauty were made even down to the Roman times. Pottery was another manufacture in which the ancient Egyptians excelled at all periods; the finest examples occurring under the XIXth Dynasty. They were also acquainted with glass from an early time."

The crafts, that created these majestic works of art then, were parents of art. Their masterpieces were created in workshops. Precious and semi-precious metals were worked. They yielded much beautiful jewelry and wooden works. Stone was used in architecture. Together, these accomplishments can tell much about the art and aesthetics of the people. Hence, works of quality are associated as timeless art produced by ancient African artistry, in Nile Valley cultural flowering, that came to impress and fascinate people of both the ancient and modern worlds. Therefore, through the art medium, Africa could be considered the Mother of Invention. An interesting interjection made here can underscore this view of Mother Africa.

The *American Journal of Archaeology* published "Tools and Weapons" about Professor Flinders Petrie's book of the same name. Here Petrie undergirds the view of Egypt and Africa's predominant role in technological developments that came to have such an impact on later civilizations. Imagine what influence the following information throws upon the social, cultural, architectural, and military development upon subsequent cultures, particularly in those areas of the world as America and Europe where much of Africa's artifacts are held in captivity.

FREDERICK MONDERSON

Egypt Essays Illustration 56. A fine Egyptian Balsamary inscribed Green Duck-Egg (left); and Black Balsalt head of King Amasis II (right).

The *American Journal of Archaeology* XXII (1918: 441-42) indicated: "Professor Flinders Petrie has published under the auspices of the British School of Archaeology in Egypt and Egyptian Research Account a work entitled Tools and Weapons. It is concerned particularly with implements from Egypt although many illustrations are drawn from other parts of the world. He discusses in turn the plain blade axe, the socketed axe, the double axe, adzes and picks, the adze and hoe, the lug adze, the hoe, the chisel, the knife, the symmetric knife, the sword, the dagger, the spear-head, the arrow, the throwing-stick, slings and bullets, harpoons, fish-hooks, scale armor, rasps and scrapers, artisans' tools. Builders' tools, the saw, the sickle, the pruning-hook, shears, razors, leather cutters, tweezers, borers, pins and needles, implements for spinning and weaving, agricultural tools, the horse-bit, the spur, stamps for branding, fire-hooks, manacles, fish-spears, flesh-hooks, shovels, ladles, spoons, mortars and pestles, fire-drills, stirgils, the bolt, lock and key, pulleys, compasses, chains, and tools used in casting."

EGYPT ESSAYS ON ANCIENT KEMET

In this ancient African society craftsmen, therefore, worked in a variety of mediums of metal and stone including limestone, grey granite, basalt, alabaster, and syenite. They also worked bronze, copper, lead, bronze and lead-electrum, slate, serpentine, steatite, quartz crystal, and hematite. Such materials as black quartz, sandstone, malachite, blue glass, white glass, burnt syenite helped expand the repertoire of African art. Not mentioned here is cobalt, which was early used by the people of ancient Kemet.

A. Wiedemann (Jan 10, 1893: 113) informs about a small quadrangular Egyptian amulet, which from the "description of Lepsius appears to date from the later time of the New Empire, turned out to be a dark blue opaque glassy flux, painted with cobalt. An oblong dark blue glass-bead was painted likewise with cobalt; the quantitative analysis gave 2.86 per cent oxide of cobalt; and another glass bead contained 0.95 per cent oxide of cobalt."

Even further Wiedemann (1893: 114) tells, the "blue frits of the time of Rameses III, at Tell el Iehudije were painted often with cobalt. The mineral was therefore used by the Egyptians though the blue color was usually obtained from copper."

Beautiful rock-cut Tombs of the Nobles line the hills of Elephantine Island at Aswan. These wondrous works of mortuary art retain early links with interior Africa. Since background is important in creating and viewing works of art, the high view with Aswan below is nature's art. The magnificent panoramic view from these hills is art in choice to build here.

FREDERICK MONDERSON

Egypt Essays Photo 116a. Cairo Museum of Egyptian Antiquities.

Egypt Essays Photo 116b. Cairo Museum of Egyptian Antiquities.

EGYPT ESSAYS ON ANCIENT KEMET

Egypt Essays Photo 116c. Cairo Museum of Egyptian Antiquities.

Art in many of the tombs, on the high cliffs, portray African beliefs in the afterlife. They adorn the tradition of Egypt as African and retain visible links to Kemet's early past. It is also a challenge to the modern visitor, brave enough to scale the 135-odd steps to the summit. Here the intense heat of the desert has preserved beautiful and realistic African art. Recent studies show the Egyptians got many materials and ideas from their southern neighbors. In reality we must look to Central Africa for Egyptian origins. These early cultural dynamics call attention to art as reflective of science and religious beliefs.

African art and science, we now know pioneered metallurgy, mining, and smelting processes. The chemistry of working in gold, copper, electrum, silver, iron, tin and lead is a wonderful experience. However, the drawbacks are intense heat, callused hands and an offensive smell. Yet, these minor impediments are a small price to create such beautiful art.

FREDERICK MONDERSON

With their primitive smelting technology African craftsmen built bowl furnaces. Then they improved the bowl furnace and created a sophisticated shaft furnace. This was far more effective in providing heat. Such a technological improvement was art and it created art.

In innovation, today respected for their work of timelessness and ingenuity, these ancient African metallurgists, in experimentation, decreased the top of the bowl. According to Bernd Scheel in *Egyptian Metalworking and Tools* (1989: 11-34), they then shaped the inside. This change developed more lome in the structure. The bellows passed through the mud bricks. Then it stroked the charge through the Lome to smelt the metal. The hot liquid would then exit through the tap hole and into the slag pit.

The early metallurgists worked gold into sheets. This was also the way they prepared copper. They made sandals and other jewelry that now adorn fine museums in Brooklyn, New York, London, Paris, Berlin, etc.

Early art in ancient Kemet retained its propaganda nature. The earliest forms of such representations are on slate palettes. The most famous of these is the *Narmer Palette*; where the king is shown wearing the White Crown of Upper Kemet/Egypt and the Red Crown of Lower Kemet/Egypt. Scholars reason that this pharaoh is responsible for uniting the two lands and choosing the united red and white Double Crown as a symbol of unification. The significance of this artifact is the propaganda role it played in establishing conventions in art and social customs that were key elements of unification.

However, the most important art innovation introduced during this time was the register. It became the dividing line between pre-dynastic disorder and dynastic order, in art and society. The *Narmer Palette*, in raised relief, shows the king as monumental in scale to his subjects. This depiction of the king in a convention of social classes remained in much of pre-dynastic and dynastic art. Other early artistic portrayals of the pharaoh show him engaged in agricultural ceremonials, ritual worship, smiting Egypt's/Kemet's

EGYPT ESSAYS ON ANCIENT KEMET

enemies and dancing before the Gods. These attitudes were symbolic and also helped to serve propaganda purposes. Nevertheless, it was the artist who rendered the images for us. Public art, on the facades of enclosure walls and other public places were introduced for the common use. But, other art, in tombs, particularly, were never meant to be seen by anyone after the internment. That is why the irreverence of some modern visitors seems to desecrate these holy places and the philosophic and religious intent of their creators.

Egypt Essays Photo 116d. Cairo Museum of Egyptian Antiquities.

FREDERICK MONDERSON

Egypt Essays Photo 116e. Cairo Museum of Egyptian Antiquities.

Conventions of such beginnings set the stage, order, stability and unchanging reality of Kemetic and African art. Together with the canon, or set of rules, for representing the human figure, art changed yet remained traditional and timeless. Classical art, certainly dating to the Old Kingdom, remained the ideal well past the New Kingdom and into the Late Period. It was the quintessential imitative style that represented the permanence of the society bequeathed by the gods. The influence of the Greeks after Alexander's conquest in 332 B.C. brought new innovation that still looked to the African past for inspiration. Nevertheless, an interesting observation can be made at the Graeco-Roman double Temple of Kom Ombo, dedicated to the gods Sobek and Haroeis, the Older Horus. Here in many friezes, Queen Cleopatra can be seen with one of her upper female anatomical parts exposed.

Still, from the earliest times, the human body was represented in a particular manner based on order. The people of ancient Kemet used a Canon of Proportion to represent the human body. This changed slightly from period to period. In the Old Kingdom or Pyramid Age, 2680-2240 B.C. (*Nile Year* 1560-2000), they used 13

EGYPT ESSAYS ON ANCIENT KEMET

divisions for the height of a man. Petrie (1940: 54-55) notes, these included, "2 for the head, 1 to the armpit, 4 to the fork, 2 to the knee, 4 to the ground." For the position of the figure during the Dynastic Period, 3000-30 B.C. (*Nile Year* 1240- 4210), they used a rule that "a vertical line must pass the edge of the wig, or center of the head, the middle of the waist, equidistant between the knees and between the heels."

The New Kingdom began at the expulsion of the Hyksos, Asiatic nomads, who essentially overran Kemet and ruled for a century, from their stronghold in the north. With today's hindsight, an interesting aside can be interjected here. We know very much about Upper and Lower Egypt, Northern and Southern Egypt. So, from this time, can we also begin to speak of native and foreign Egypt? In the wake of the resulting Kemetic imperialism, the wealth, glamour and opulence of the New Empire, built its art upon those earlier developments of the Old and Middle Kingdoms.

The "Canon of Proportion" emerged as a rigid yet accurate mechanism that further highlights the artistic contributions of these ancient Africans along the Nile. During the New Kingdom, the Canon of Proportion for the human body changed. Now, the height of a standing figure was divided into 19 units. Petrie (1940: 54) further explained, the "head down to the top of the shoulders is 3 units, divided at the top of the forehead and base of the nose. From the shoulders, 4 units to the waist, then 6 to the knees, and thence 6 to the ground."

There was some difference for seated figures. These seated figures were, Petrie (1940) continued, "15 squares high. Thus assigning 19-15 = 4 units to the thigh bone. The seat is 5 units over the ground."

As the civilization entered its decline by the XXVIth Dynasty, the artists adopted a third canon. Here again, Petrie (1940) has informed us, the "figure became 22 1/2 or 22 1/3 units high; of this increase 1/3 unit is in the head, 2 units in trunk and 1 unit in the lower leg."

FREDERICK MONDERSON

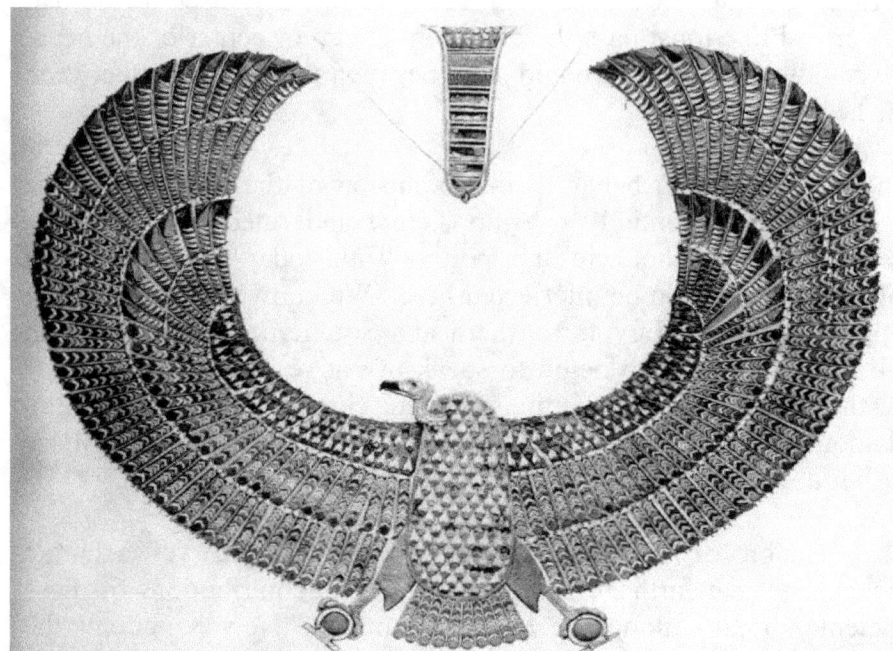

Egypt Essays Illustration 57. Composed of 255 separate gold plaques, finely inlaid, and threaded together by means of tiny eyelets: "The Collar" is a wonderfully flexible pectoral-showing (top center) the Gold wire by which it hung from the king.

While the Kemetic artists had Canons of Proportions for the human figure, these were mainly for standing or seated models. In addition, however, there were many examples of figures in motion. Petrie (1940: 55) further explained how the "long rows of wrestlers at Beni Hasan in the XII Dynasty," dancers, acrobats, and "field workers in action in the XVIII Dynasty" show movement. These representations depict how readily the "instantaneous positions were grouped and reproduced." Significantly, however, as early as the XIth Dynasty, in the mortuary temple of Mentuhotep at Deir el Bahari, the artist Mertisen was first to boast of "being able to depict people in motion." With this innovation the artist blended color in

EGYPT ESSAYS ON ANCIENT KEMET

further experimentation and thus enhanced the quality and texture of painting.

The life of the artist was pleasing yet austere. They made funerary art that was timeless yet designed to never be seen by the human eye. They specialized in various crafts, but generally speaking they were exposed to intense heat, developed callused hands, and often exuded an offensive smell. This aside, the strict division of labor aided the creation of beautiful works of art that defied time, while exhibiting the greatest of finished artifacts, so adored by modern art lovers.

These foundations of art developed in guilds controlled by the palace or wealthy nobles as well as the priesthood. In these highly organized arrangements Michalowski (No Date) has indicated, "... one specialist made the designs, another worked in plaster, and other specialized in stone cutting in relief sculpture, in carving statues, in finishing and polishing them, in decorating temple walls, and so on. The jeweler's art also had specialist categories; workers, who washed the gold, did enamel work, and there was even a category of beard stringer."

He argued, in theory, no single workman did an entire piece. Those individuals equated with our "foreman" or "overseer" inspected the work of the artist and used coloring marks as a corrective. "Black was used for outline, while alongside, red was used to indicate corrections."

The ruling class comprising the Gods, Pharaoh, and high dignitaries represented the official portrait. Their formal poses were shown in painting, sunk, raised and painted relief and statuary, as shown in temples, palaces, on public monuments, in quarries and in tombs. They were shown striding or seated. To represent these, the artist was bound to observe the rules of canon when portraying this "upper crust" of society. Nevertheless, ostraka, sometimes pottery bits or chips of stone were used as "sketch pads." Here, sometimes, the artist deviated from the established norm and created caricatures that would not be associated with the "official standards" for art.

FREDERICK MONDERSON

The pharaoh especially was shown in an official portrait. Generally depicted with all kingly panoply, any defects or shortcomings he had were concealed by an elaborate costume. Michalowski (ND) again tells, the king "... was a god, a living Horus, and as a divinity his body had always to be represented as timelessly youthful."

The administrative bureaucracy was the second class of artistic models. Because of their closeness with the local people the artist did not strictly adhere to the convention that bound the first more formal portraits. These latter were presented showing "only the most obvious facial characteristics." Whereas, we see, governors or mayors were shown with "sagging flesh, prominent bellies, and thick legs, but in a dignified posture carrying a staff."

Egypt Essays Photo 116f. Cairo Museum of Egyptian Antiquities.

EGYPT ESSAYS ON ANCIENT KEMET

Egypt Essays Photo 116g. Cairo Museum of Egyptian Antiquities.

Artistically, the main difference between the way the top two classes, the nobility and the administrative bureaucracy, were represented was in the modeling of the body. Michalowski (No Date: 188) believed, the "conventions of timeless youth was obligatory for the first group, whereas dignitaries were shown more realistically."

The third group of the society comprised a vast array of workers. In the mastaba tombs of the Vth and VIth Dynasties as represented, Michalowski (No Date: 188) mentions, "reliefs of laborers, harvesters, herdsmen, and artisans at work in warehouses, fields, pastures, and workshops. There are also fishermen and boat builders, musicians and dancers." In representing this group, the artist was free to deviate from the canon and represented this group more as they were. This may be because, for Michalowski (No Date: 189) they show "realistic scenes of common people possess great expressive power."

Scribes were generally shown either in the standing or seated position. The wooden relief figures of the famous third dynasty scribe Hesire, found at Sakkara, is now at the Cairo Museum. It stands 44 7/8 inches. He is shown holding his working tools and the SEKHEM rod, emblem of executive officials. In this as in so many examples, the diagram of canon for this Old Kingdom masterpiece of realistic art required, notes Michalowski (No Date: 174), a different canon. He shows this to be "18 rows of squares, as follows: 'From the top of forehead to base of neck, 2 rows; from neck to knees, 10 rows; from knees to soles of feet, 6 rows. An additional row for the hair above the forehead was not included in the total of 18 rows.'" The other posture of the scribe was the seated position. The finest known statue of a scribe comes from the Vth Dynasty and is housed in the Louvre, Paris. Here the subject, according to Michalowski (ND) is shown: "Wearing a loin cloth, he is seated with legs crossed, an open roll of papyrus on his knees, and a reed pen in his right hand. It is made of painted limestone and stands 20 7/8 inches. At a much later time the scribe was represented in a more obscure way simply as a block statue, with face and writings on the block."

The question is always asked whether there was realism in ancient Kemetic/Egyptian Art. If the term realism is defined in broad concepts as denoting, "the effort to represent a given phenomenon in its most typical form, and the fact recorded by the artist has thus a general significance that every viewer can grasp. In this sense, Egyptian art was certainly realistic." How else would the artisans record such profound religious and social testimony to their life and culture? This is particularly evident, when these early artists, as civilization trailblazers were engraving the *Tabula Rasa* of human progress in so many fields of artistic and science fusion.

Nevertheless, Kemetic/Egyptian painting and sculpture of the Old Kingdom can be summed up as follows, as Michalowski (ND: 190-91) explained:

"1. The canon was a unique historical phenomenon and has a peculiar indigenous character.

EGYPT ESSAYS ON ANCIENT KEMET

2. It was the result of a lengthy process of observation and experimentation, which culminated in an art, based on the most typical forms of nature; as such, the canon was formulated in terms of certain constant proportions.

3. The aim of the canon was to record phenomenon in the most legible and understandable manner, to reflect reality in both its visual and its social aspects.

4. The canon performed an important function in the ideological superstructure, serving the ruling class by perpetuating the conviction that the existing social function was by glorifying the gods and the Pharaohs.

5. The canon was essential to the maintenance of artistic quality and standards of workmanship."

The resulting quality of Kemetic art can be found in Cairo, Luxor, Aswan, and other museums worldwide. Here the art-science fused notion fueled by religious conviction is seen in artifacts of wood, papyrus, metal and stone. Much of these glorified the culture, or adorned temples and noble people. Today many of these are far from home, a "culture in captivity," highlighting foreign institutions. Nevertheless, such pieces provide important evidence of daily life and sacred festivals celebrated by Africans along the Nile, Northeast Africa. Now, if we include Charles Finch's revelations regarding archaeological work at Katanda and the Ishango bone with "mathematical markings;" African Art extends for many millennia.

FREDERICK MONDERSON

Egypt Essays Photo 116h. Cairo Museum of Egyptian Antiquities.

Egypt Essays Photo 116i. Cairo Museum of Egyptian Antiquities.

EGYPT ESSAYS ON ANCIENT KEMET

Much cultural evidence of early Africa is contained in the tombs of pharaohs and nobles. These survivals are found mainly in the Valley of the Kings, at Thebes. Many other sites in Egypt have yielded their beautiful trove of wealth. Thebes, however, has given and preserves much cultural wealth and history, more than anywhere else on earth. The majesty of Kemetic/Egyptian, African Art, in painting, sculpture and architecture is here represented in its greatest glory.

The site of Thebes in Southern Egypt attracts thousands of visitors each year. They all remain in awe at the artistic and cultural accomplishments of the ancient Africans. Elsewhere in Africa, the same art quality can be imagined. However, throughout the continent, much art has not survived because of environmental factors. Moreover, throughout the artistic landscape, from Egypt to South Africa art served a particular purpose whether religious, military, economic, social or agricultural. Art's purpose in Africa is not like art appreciation in Europe, where art is made to hang on walls, to be viewed by art lovers and the curious.

Moving to other areas, the art of the Western Sudan is traceable to the Nok discoveries at Jos, Nigeria. To complement this, numerous other sites in the Sahara hold evidence of early African art in the form of paintings depicting plant, animal and human life experiences.

Egypt Essays Illustration 58. A side view of the right profile of the sphinx undergoing repairs after the paws were uncovered in excavation (left) and a back view of the famous monument under scaffolding (right).

FREDERICK MONDERSON

Bernard Fage's *History of West Africa* included interesting insights into the early history of this region. He explained fragments of coal were found at Nok sites that dated "greater than 39,000 years." Whether such sites were continuously occupied is uncertain. What is certain, by inference, many thousands of years ago, great regions of the continent seemed inhabited and producing art, though much of it has not survived. To underscore, this belief Freeman-Granville (1976: 6) gives the following dates for other occupational sites in North Africa, such as: Hawa Fata c. 38,750 to 2,910 B.C.; Malewa Gorge 31,000 B.C.; Matjes in Southern Africa gives dates at Pomongwe 33,570-19,700 B.C.; Florisbad c. 39,000 to 17,000 B.C.; and Mufo in the Congo at c. 12,500 B.C. Conjecture would let us believe these early Africans had thought out the fundamental human questions regarding nature and science. If they did, then their art may have shown it. However, not much has survived. Again, Freeman-Grenville (1976: 4) calls attention to sites at Kanyatsi along the Upper Nile, having relationship to Olduvai, and Yayo in Chad. At Ain Hamech, Algeria; at the Atlas Mountains near Casablanca and at Makapan, Sterkfontein and Taung in South Africa, all dated approximately c. 1,800,000 B.C. After 500,000 B.C. many sites were in early occupation. Lochad in Zimbabwe, Broken Hill and Victoria Falls in Zambia, Ismalia and Kalambo Falls, Kharga Oasis in Kemet, Khodaine, Tachengitin, Algeria and Sidi Zin in Tunisia round out Early Stone Age culture in Africa.

The Later Stone Age boasted sites of occupation as follows: Freeman-Grenville (1976: 6) gives: "Kalambo Falls, 41,000-7,500 B.C.; Pomongwe, North of the Limpopo 33,570-19,700 B.C.; Florisbad, 39,000-17,000 B.C.; Matteo River 10,800+-6,500 B.C.; Malewa Gorge near Lake Victoria, 31,000 B.C.; Mufo in the Congo at 12,500 B.C.; Fashi, near Chad, at 19,350-19,750 B.C.; El Daba at the Libyan Mediterranean coast at 38,750-2910 B.C." For sure, as indicated, the illustrious African historical and cultural heritage has had ample time to experiment and create foundations for art.

EGYPT ESSAYS ON ANCIENT KEMET

Egypt Essays Photo 116j. Cairo Museum of Egyptian Antiquities.

Egypt Essays Photo 116k. Cairo Museum of Egyptian Antiquities.

FREDERICK MONDERSON

Nevertheless, following the 6,000 B.C. Round Head style of the Tassili painters, Nok revealed stratification showing occupations at 3500 B.C. (*Nile Year* 740), 2000 B.C. (*Nile Year* 2240), 900 B.C. (*Nile Year* 3340), and 200 A.D. (*Nile Year* 4440). Therefore, tools from this society let scholars consider Nok a "transitional" culture, from stone to metal workings. These early "African" artists at Nok also worked tin and iron.

In their excavations of these sites, archaeologists at Nok discovered, wrote Bernard Fage, a "couple of human heads" in pottery. They also found parts of a human head and foot. Reinforcing these revelations, Fage explained, Nok produced "well fashioned pottery." Clearly, it can be argued that Africans in this area must have developed other crafts. Then their craftsmen can be considered pioneers in working the various mediums. Therefore, from North Africa through the Saharan and Nok sites, the East and South Africa regions show evidence of sensitive and fresh African art. The analogy of "Bushman art" in the essence of his world as depicted, can be applied to all those ancient areas of habitations where no art has remained to portray their early lifestyles and beliefs.

Such descriptions can only help strengthen the view of an early African culture with great antiquity. More importantly, this early cultural ethos laid the foundations for other areas such as the Western Sudan where art came to play an important role.

Islamic scholars recount the history of the Western Sudan. They provide primary sources for this period. Here is recounted the growth and expansion of Medieval African states. Successes of these empires were attributed to trade, good government and strong armies. Islam also played a pivotal role. The new religion helped, yet destroyed Ghana, aided Mali and was also a factor in Songhai's growth and destruction.

In higher education we see literacy flourish and produce works of intellectual art represented in academic manuscripts. Philosophy, law, astronomy, mathematics and medicine were taught at the Universities of Sankore, Djenne and Timbuktu, in West Africa. The

EGYPT ESSAYS ON ANCIENT KEMET

Tarikh es-Sudan and *Tarikh al-Fattah* are sources of Western Sudan literary art. These chronicles recount the history of *Bilal es-Sudan*, "land of the Blacks." They speak of the art of the period that was primarily supported by the state. Thus, royalty was a supporter of art that blended African conventions and social needs with Islamic beliefs and building practices. Here also a cultural infusion created new innovations in African architecture.

Nevertheless, despite the importance of the large states, the Western Sudan still had no uniform art style. Still, in this dichotomy, economic factors influenced art from this region. Agricultural practices supported sedentary hoe farming, with millet, maize and rice as staples of their society. To support farming activity craftsmen demonstrated technological creativity in the tools they produced. In this, their crafts were grouped into two classes, blacksmiths and professionals.

Blacksmiths made metal tools for farming, domestic purposes and military uses. They also did some gold work. These blacksmiths, possessing tremendous metaphysical insights, also served as a theosophical-religious medium between this and the African spirit world. Professionals on the other hand utilized gold in various forms of jewelry. In a land where gold was found in great abundance, goldsmiths flourished. The gold of the Western Sudan became legendary. E. W. Bovill's *The Golden Trade of the Moors* (1970) mentions gold production was large as late as the start of the sixteenth century. Much of the gold-trade by that time had been diverted to the Atlantic coast. This rerouting of trade came after the destruction of Songhay by the forces of the Islamic Moroccan al-Mansur, and his mercenaries who introduced into the Western Sudan.

Bovill (1970) has pointed out, "gold from the Gold Coast was accounting for an amount that has been estimated at about one-tenth of the total world supply at that time." This was an immense total from one small region. Mining gold and supporting industries helped the development of other crafts in wood and metals, creating a wide array of implements to foster commercial exchange and to

FREDERICK MONDERSON

undergird cultural, social and religious practice. International, regional and local markets developed as a result, from the Trans-Saharan trade. Here could be found a wonderful array of crafts that expressed African art designed for the commercial markets. In these markets one could find cloths, thread, straw hats, mats and calabash bowls. Much of these had geometric and other forms of decorative patterns. Craftsmen worked in glass beads, did leather work and made iron hoes. Gold, nevertheless, characterized the "Golden Age of West Africa."

Egypt Essays Photo 116I. Cairo Museum of Egyptian Antiquities.

From the time of ancient Ghana, the Trans-Saharan trade exported some nine tons of gold annually. Much of this was in the form of well-worked jewelry. The state utilized coins of gold. Goldsmiths worked with twisted thread and ingots, using a variety of art mediums. Craftsmen produced weapons of iron and copper. Those who worked for the king made royal weapons of gold. Goldsmiths made bracelets, rings and necklaces. For bravery, the state awarded "toe rings" of gold. These are reminiscent of Kemetic pharaohs awarding the "Gold of Valor" for similar activity.

EGYPT ESSAYS ON ANCIENT KEMET

Egypt Essays Photo 116m. Cairo Museum of Egyptian Antiquities.

The sword scabbard worn by the royal interpreter and instruments played by musicians of the king, were made of gold, attesting to a craftsmanship unsurpassed. Ceremonial sabers, lances and arrow quivers were made of gold. Also, the trappings of horses as well as such utensils as royal dinner plates were made of gold. Royal dogs were leashed in gold. Therefore, African artists can be credited with working in fertile fields to produce some of the most profound forms of social and religious ceremonial expressions in praise of deity, and the growth, development and advancement of society.

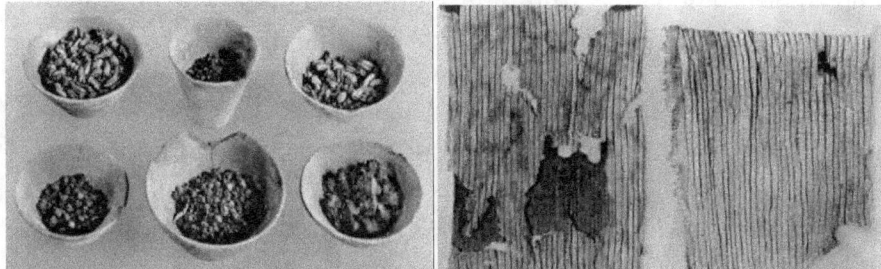

Egypt Essays Illustration 59. A parallel to "The contents of a modern corner-stone," saucers of fruit for her "Eternal provision" showing part of a foundation deposit from Hatshepsut's temple (left); and scraps of pleated linen from the tomb of the eleventh-dynasty Queen Neferu, showing "Still retaining the folds ironed into them from four thousand years ago" (right).

FREDERICK MONDERSON

17. NORTH AFRICA: EGYPT, KUSH

Today, the history of North Africa - mainly Egypt, Kush and Ethiopia, is constantly being re-examined owing to the deluge of new information providing new analyses questioning earlier assumptions, often hurriedly arrived at. In this, we must pay some attention to familiarizing our youth with the significance of their continued interest in ancient Kemetic studies because of its relevance for the future. So that by 2027, as the Afrocentrists would say; we'll be ready to understand the issues of historical distortion; include omission; and readily defend Egypt as African.

In the last half of the 19th and first half of the 20th Centuries, scholars did extensive work of excavation in Egypt and elsewhere in the Nile Valley. Power players effectively created an area called the "Middle East" and made Egypt a part of it. They used the great desert, Sahara, as a dividing line in Africa. This division was presented as existing for all time. The creation effectively blocked out any role for Ethiopia, Kush and Africans, in development of the Egyptian/Kemetic high culture. Here we see a skillful conspiracy between developments in the field, ambassadors as political operatives, the people who sponsored their expeditions, and those who published their reports and books. The general public came to accept their view as the truth and so manufactured misinformation molded the presentation of historical perception and distortion became the order of the day. The logical question then posed is, "On how many other historical events have people been misinformed?" This situation brings to mind one of the more interesting works in the Afrocentric literature corpus entitled *What They Never Taught You in History Class* (1983), Indus Kati Kush, published by Luxxor Publications.

Herodotus, the "father of history" visited Egypt in 450 B.C. He wrote the *Histories* and devoted Book II, called *Euterpe*, to Egypt, ancient Kemet. This early traveler observed and commented that the "Egyptians, Ethiopians and Colchians" were similar. They had "thick lips, broad noses, woolly hair" and were "burnt of skin," or

EGYPT ESSAYS ON ANCIENT KEMET

otherwise Black. The Greek philosopher Aristotle in his book *Physiognomonica* is quoted as saying, "Egyptians and Ethiopians are cowards for they are black." He also argued that some northern whites were equally cowards, because they were white! He tried to find the middle ground in the debate on color like so many areas of critical inquiry and so found the Greeks as being the ideal. This may have had to do with their Mediterranean origin. Of course, we know his science of bravery was wrong! However, and fundamentally, he did label these Africans "black," and this too was based on his observations, as did Herodotus.

Egypt Essays Photo 116n. Cairo Museum of Egyptian Antiquities. Hippolito Rosellini.

FREDERICK MONDERSON

Egypt Essays Photo 116n. Cairo Museum of Egyptian Antiquities.

Diodorus Siculus, another ancient writer, claims the Ethiopians told him they founded Egypt as a colony. In addition, many other writers of antiquity regarded the peoples of Africa, namely Egypt, Ethiopia, Kush, etc., as mainly one people. In this regard, critical contemporary scholarship on Egypt and the Nile Valley has shown that during the periods of the Old Kingdom, Middle Kingdom and New Kingdom, there were extensive contacts with the lands to the south of Egypt/Kemet. Much data supports the view this area produced the predecessors of the pharaohs and the fundamental units of
These were, for the most part, peaceful economic and trade contacts with the land of Yam, Punt, Warit, Kush, etc., to the south of Egypt. However, there were also during these periods, numerous military campaigns conducted to the south of Egypt/Kemet to secure trade privileges and preempt military threats from that region. This was

EGYPT ESSAYS ON ANCIENT KEMET

indeed a period of intensive interaction between all the peoples of the Nile River region.

An article published in *The New York Times* on March 1, 1979 showed evidence of the world's earliest monarchy found in Nubia, at Qustul to the south of Egypt. Dr. Bruce Williams, of the University of Chicago, has detailed how the symbols we associate with pharaonic power in Egypt/Kemet were found in Nubia in 3400 B.C. At the start of the Egyptian dynasties 3200 B.C., viz., these were very much in use as enthroned pharaoh, white crown, disk of the sun, whip, flail, royal barge, incense burner, flora and fauna evidence, etc. This interesting insight is partly explained and reinforced by Aldred (1980: 96) who held, the "dignity of the king demanded that he should be seated upon a throne or standing upright, wearing his crowns and carrying his scepters." Particularly important, moreover, this evidence of monarchy is 200 years before such symbolism appeared in Egypt/Kemet. Such a discovery lent strong support to Diodorus' statement that Ethiopia founded Egypt as a colony.

Cheikh Anta Diop in *The African Origins of Civilization: Myth or Reality* has documented the cultural continuity and interaction between Egypt and Ethiopia. He has also shown that Egypt was a Black civilization; the Egyptians were Black, and whatever Whites in this early culture were few and latecomers. Importantly, such a demographic mix had enabled early Nile Valley Blacks to found the Old Kingdom with its magnificence that has been so instrumental in later Egyptian and global cultural growth. Importantly, much of this was accomplished even as the ancient world, for the most part, was just awakening from it long slumber in the mist of history.

In the history of African-American experience with Egypt/Kemet and the Nile Valley as a whole, the twentieth century has offered tremendous opportunities. This has resulted from an evolved and unconquering intent to identify with Black "ancestors" and the ancient African cultural legacy that has advanced civilization. Significantly, the Nineteenth Century, despite contemporary ignorance, has provided extensive evidence of early Black

FREDERICK MONDERSON

Nationalist identification with Egypt. In 1990, Dr. John Henrik Clarke of Hunter College of the City University of New York, presented a wonderful lecture given at Aswan, Egypt, where he sketched a poignant picture of Caribbean and African-Americans' quest for Egypt. This provided a significant point of departure for today's nationalists, particularly the Afrocentrists. So, the work of these scholars set the stage for arming our young people, in learning, teaching, writing, in the twenty-first century, with a sound understanding of their cultural history. So, by 2027 they will certainly be ready, armed with credible and irrefutable knowledge.

More importantly still, the African-American youth, particularly those of the inner city, have either not been educated or mis-educated about their connection with the Nile Valley and Egypt, the land of ancient Kemet. The urban schools, especially in the large industrial and economic centers as New York, Chicago, Cleveland, and Detroit, have not addressed the issue either. They have failed to integrate an understanding of the connection between the African-American youth particularly, and so many others in general.

Egypt Essays Photo 116o. Cairo Museum of Egyptian Antiquities.

EGYPT ESSAYS ON ANCIENT KEMET

Egypt Essays Photo 116p. Cairo Museum of Egyptian Antiquities.

Fortunately, however, there have been a number of credible African and African-American scholars who have labored unendingly to educate all about the African ancestors in Egypt. From the beginning of the 20th Century, W.E.B. Du Bois began articulating the intellectual nationalist movement of African-Americans in the country. Quite frankly, we could go back to the earlier stalwarts, David Walker, Martin Delaney, Frederick Douglass, etc. W.E.B. Du Bois wrote *The Negro* in 1915. In spite of the paucity of source material available to him in the United States and despite the preponderance of archaeological and anthropological data, forming emerging histories, particularly those vitriolically distorted, Du Bois demonstrated the blackness, certainly the mulatto nature of Egypt or Kemet. Even more, he had followed in the footsteps of European writers whose iconoclastic attitudes pointed out and attacked the incubated process of systematic distortion of the relevant African historical record, wherein the fundamental blackness of Kemet was underscored. In *The World and Africa*, Du Bois synthesized his earlier positions and much of his ideas have withstood the test of time. Marcus Garvey, Duse Mohammed, and Carter G. Woodson also educated us about the blackness of Egypt, at a time when Blacks could hardly afford to study this ancient African culture.

The early scholars, in spite of their troubles with the times, had understood the significance of King Tut-ankh-Amon, when Howard Carter discovered his tomb in 1922. These critical scholars also worked so the ancestors of their day could read, research, study, and understand the fight to reclaim Egypt/ancient Kemet, as African. Their work was undertaken and handed down as legacy to the next generation.

Then along came another generation of critical African historians in the persons of J. A. Rogers, Dr. John H. Clarke, John Jackson, John Huggins, Dr. Y. ben-Jochannan, and Dr. Ivan Van Sertima. Cheikh Anta Diop came from Senegal in West African, Leonard Jeffries, and Leonard James from the New York area and Walter Rodney and G. M. James from the Caribbean. Dr. Carruthers, Wade Nobles, Na'im Akbar, and a host of others, particularly from the *Association for the Study of Classical African Civilizations*, were equally focused on the issue. They all preached, taught and wrote books in an attempt to educate the young and old of the African and African-American community. Their message was clear, Egypt is African! Egypt is Kemet and Kemet is African!

Egypt Essays Illustration 60. The entrance to Neferu's tomb showing "The ancient tourists' entrance" dated to 3500 B.C. when the tomb was blocked up (left); and scraps of sculpture and a wall torn down by ancient robbers that bears "The names of Tourists who had scribbled on the walls 35 centuries ago."

EGYPT ESSAYS ON ANCIENT KEMET

African-American young people of today must come to a sense of understanding about the forces arrayed against them. They must develop critical operational skills that are essential for their survival. They must visit and utilize the great libraries and institutions of cultural and historical importance, that African ancestral artifactual evidence help maintain. They must learn the difference between primary and secondary sources. They must understand the significance of critical comparative historical analysis. They must master the criteria for critical reading and reasoning as important tools in their intellectual growth. They must understand and operationalize the eight major social sciences in life situations that are critical to their development. This application of historical analysis will enable them to give purpose to the work that must be undertaken.

The African-American inner city youth must study, understand and claim the glories of Egypt/Kemet as their legacy. They must study art, architecture, anthropology, and archaeology. French, German, Greek, Coptic and Hieroglyphics are all fundamental disciplines in study of this glorious ancient African past, and these must be attempted at an early age. Only then will they be able to take their places as teachers, writers and defenders of their heritage in the face of rampant racism and cultural genocide, spawned by global white supremacy.

The African-American youth must therefore study Egypt/Kemet. They must research and teach in the twenty-first century just as their elders and ancestors have done in this and past centuries. Only then will they reclaim their cultural heritage and history, to be strong in a fast-paced and changing world.

FREDERICK MONDERSON

Egypt Essays Photo 116q. Cairo Museum of Egyptian Antiquities.

Egypt Essays Photo 116q. Cairo Museum of Egyptian Antiquities.

18.   TIME MEASUREMENT

Can you imagine what would happen if all the world's clocks went on strike or stopped working? The world would be in chaos. Modern man in the post-technological age would be lost. However, those who know the story of the birth and development of time

EGYPT ESSAYS ON ANCIENT KEMET

measurement would not really be affected to a great extent. Time is measured, according to Breasted (1915) in "discontinuous fragments and continuous flow." An example of discontinuous fragments is the way Native Americans measure time. For instance, when asked one's age, the reply would generally be "fifty winters" or "twenty snows." Each represented a season and that person could be 50 or 20 years old respectively. Another example is the way the British use the term "fortnight" to mean 14 days, or "sen-night," to mean seven nights.

The ancient Egyptians and the Nile Valley measured time in continuous flow. These early Africans used five types of yearly measurements. Therefore, it can be reasoned, the ancient Greeks never invented or added anything to the calendar created by the people of ancient Kemet/Egypt Nile Valley Africans.

The first of these recorded periods was the "Luni-Solar Year." Ancient man in Egypt/Africa saw that the seasons come at an interval of about 12 moons. His understanding of this happening became the science of astronomy from which mathematics flowed, and ultimately geometry was used to create large scale building projects. The second of these yearly measurements was the "Stellar-Solar Year." It was due to nature's cycle or seasons. Also, ancient man's observance of the reappearance of a prominent star or group of stars was important. This happened after an elapse of time. Thus, the inundation or overflowing of the Nile River and the coming of the seasons provided the basis of the "Stellar Calendar," in use by modern man. There is no such thing as a lunar year or lunar calendar, based on the moons. The Prophet Mohammed used the moon to regulate the Muslim year. Their religious calendar has only 354 days. The Islamic festival *Ramadan*, for example, if celebrated one year in April, six years later, would be celebrated in June.

Next is the *"360-Day Year."* In the tomb of an Egyptian nobleman named Senmut of the New Kingdom, a star map depicted on the ceiling records the 360-Day Year. Apparently, this knowledge was known long before him, possibly a reproduction of a still older version, perhaps 3000 B.C., or over five thousand years ago.

FREDERICK MONDERSON

Ancient Egyptian/Kemetic scholarly priests observed a group of stars on the horizon every 10 days. The group of stars was called constellations. Their ten-day appearances were called decans. In the course of 1 year, there were 36 constellations of these decans, which amounted to 360 days. While the figure 360 was not the exact length of the year, it was important in many ways. It had figured in the division of the circle of 360 degrees, important in geometry, arithmetic, astronomy, astrology, and time measurement. This helps us understand that ancient Africa was the birthplace of these sciences that rule the world today.

The priests were learned men in African civilizations along the Nile River. It was their job to record and keep all knowledge. By studying the flow and rise of the Nile River they learned that the *360-Day Year* was too short! They set-up Nile gauges or Nilometers at Abu Simbel in Nubia and Elephantine or Aswan at the First Cataract. One was also at Memphis. There were others at Kom Ombo and Edfu, and perhaps at all the major temples. One was at Memphis. Such instruments were cut into the rocks to measure the volume of the river. These Nilometers helped the priests see that the Nile did not reach its height at the end of the 360-day period. It needed another five-plus days to reach its peak. This they added or intercalated and called them the days of the birth of the gods Osiris, Isis, Seth, Nephthys and Horus.

The early morning risings of the Dog-Star Sirius helped to measure the length of the year. Though this only appeared after 1460 years, their records show risings dating before 4,000 B.C. when the calendar was begun. The ancient Kemetic priests then introduced the *365-Day Year* by adding or intercalating five days. Conversely, the prophet Mohammed prevented his followers from adding to their calendar. That is why it is not fixed today.

The five days that were added by the priestly scholars of ancient Kemet became feast days. They were called days of the birth of the Gods Osiris, Isis, Seth, Nephthys, and Horus. This event is significant as an aspect of ancient Kemetic Mythology. There were four principal religious centers with their attendant schools of

EGYPT ESSAYS ON ANCIENT KEMET

thought or "College of Cardinals." Each created its own cosmogony. Osiris worship was based at Abydos, Ptah at Memphis, Ra at Heliopolis and Amun, later Amun-Ra, at Thebes, with the latter gaining great prominence during the golden imperial ages of first, the Middle Kingdom, then, later, the New Kingdom.

Egypt is a dry country that gets an average of 3 inches of rain per year. Much of it falls between Cairo and the Mediterranean coast. Sometimes, for several years, it never rains at Abydos, Thebes, Aswan, etc. This is unlike the United States that gets an average of 76 inches of rain per year. So, the Myth of Osiris and Isis finds parallel with the land being dry or like-death in the summer. Its rebirth or resuscitation came with the life giving waters of the Nile. This became a natural and yearly event that flooded and fertilized the land. After the flood, Kemetic farmers planted their seeds and waited for a rich harvest. The natural process seemed linked to the Osirian Drama. Then again, some scholars have argued that the mythology of ancient Kemet was purely solar in origin.

Egypt Essays Photo 116r. Cairo Museum of Egyptian Antiquities.

FREDERICK MONDERSON

Egypt Essays Photo 116s. Cairo Museum of Egyptian Antiquities. Jean Francois Champollion.

Cheikh Anta Diop has argued the people of ancient Kemet knew their 365-Day Year was a bit off. They knew it lost one-half day every two years and one full day every four years. They knew this when the calendar was introduced in 4241 B.C. or 4240 B.C., the beginning of what is called the Nile Year calendar. They knew the Civil Year slipped back into the Solar Year. Thus, they had known the Leap Year! However, instead of adding one day every four years, they added one year every 1460 years when the Dog Star Sothis or Sirius reappeared.

In 46 B.C., Julius Caesar introduced the Egyptian/Kemetic Calendar in Europe. He added one-quarter day to make the 365-1/4 Day Year. The Julian calendar was named after him. In 1582 A.D. Pope Gregory XIII changed the western Julian calendar and replaced it

EGYPT ESSAYS ON ANCIENT KEMET

with the Gregorian calendar, in use in the West. Today we still add one extra day in February every four years and call it a Leap Year.

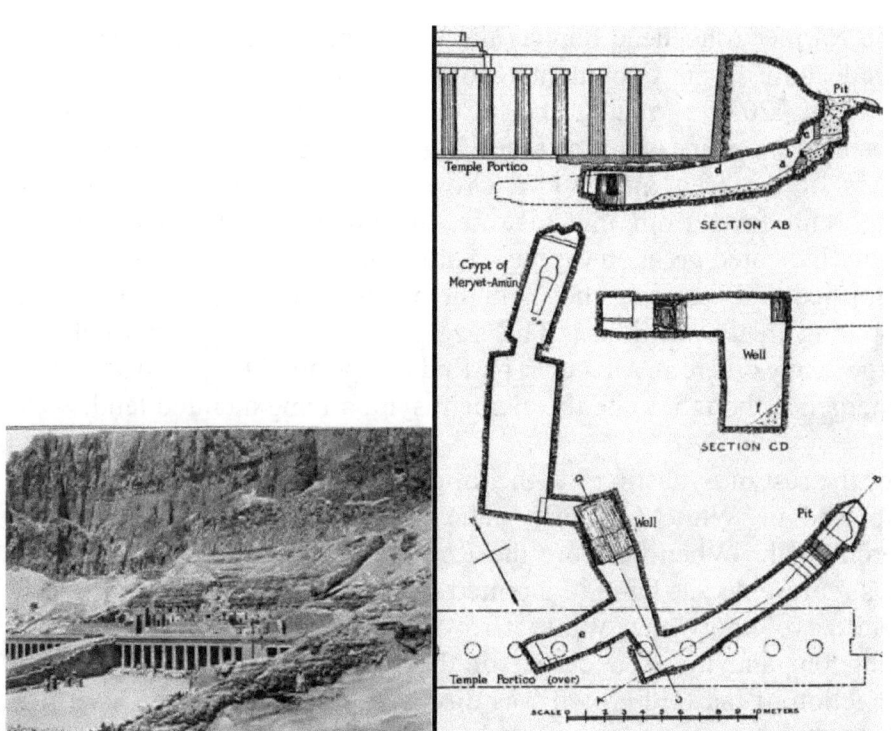

Egypt Essays Illustration 61. The first step in the discovery of the tomb of Meryet Amun beside the temple of Hatshepsut (left) and Plan of the tomb of Meryet-Amun (below) the ground plan and (above) the sectional plan.

19. PHARAONIC CROWNS, NAMES AND REGALIA

The White Crown, the Red Crown and the Double Crown remained symbolic of Pharaonic rule in Kemet for three thousand years. These three crowns came into prominence at the start of the first dynasty about 3200 B.C. On the Narmer Palette we see the King wearing the White or *Uatchetu* Crown of Upper Kemet. On the obverse, we also see him wearing the Red *Tesherth* Crown of Lower Kemet.

The Narmer Macehead depicts the king seated with Queen Aahotep beside him. This document records Narmer's capture of 400,000 cows, 1,420,000 goats, and 120,000 captives. Scholars who reasoned his wars were to unite Upper and Lower Kemet/Egypt, or lands of the Red and White Crowns realizes also a number of important facts from this historic "document." The size of the booty indicated great emerging wealth was at stake. The numeration informed the reader their mathematics was highly advanced, counting in the millions. The size of his captives lets us believe large armies were involved. The Red and White Double Crown that emerged is thought to be the element symbolizing a united land.

For the rest of dynastic rule, the king was sometimes shown wearing the Red or White Crowns. These seemed to be more or less ceremonial. When he wore the Red and White Double Crown, he was represented as King of a united Upper and Lower Kemet/Egypt. While we know the White Crown was symbolic of the Upper Kingdom and the Red crown of the Lower kingdom; the earliest depiction of the Red crown was discovered in the Eastern Desert of Upper Egypt.

At the end of the VI Dynasty or Old Kingdom, the centralized system of government that united ancient Kemet broke down. The First Intermediate Period was ushered in. It lasted for the VII, VIII, IX, and X Dynasties. There was non-stop warfare and disruption in the land during this period. The culture was set back. No one was able to unify the land. No king wore the Double Crown to signify the united country at this time.

A Theban Prince named Intef united Upper Kemet/Egypt as far north as Abydos. He wore the White Crown. Next he set in motion the conquest of Lower Kemet/Egypt which resulted in the founding of the XI Dynasty to begin the Middle Kingdom. Mentuhotep I was his successor and was probably the first Middle Kingdom pharaoh to

EGYPT ESSAYS ON ANCIENT KEMET

claim the Double Crown. Some scholars feel there was a connection between the names of Intef and later Mentuhotep II. Instead, however, Mentuhotep I, II, III may very well be the same person who changed his name over time as his fortunes improved.

Egypt Essays Photo 116t. Cairo Museum of Egyptian Antiquities.

In the classic work on *The Art and Architecture of Ancient Egypt*, W. Stephenson Smith has described Mentuhotep's statue found in his temple at Deir el-Bahari. This structure was the inspiration for Queen Hatshepsut's temple right next to it built some 500 years later by the Queen's architect Senmut. Smith wrote, "This King is certainly the outstanding personality of the early Middle Kingdom." In his tomb in a room under his temple was found a statue, wearing ceremonial *Heb Sed* attire and now in the Cairo Museum. Smith (1957: 160) reports: "In the chamber was found a seated sandstone figure six feet high. It was painted, and represented the king in Heb-Sed dress wearing the red crown of the north and with black flesh."

FREDERICK MONDERSON

We could infer from this there was another statue of the king similarly seated, painted and wearing the white crown.

Egypt Essays Photo 116u. Cairo Museum of Egyptian Antiquities. Pleyte

From the earliest times the King of Egypt had five names. These are given in J. A. Wilson's *The Culture of Ancient Egypt* (1975). They are again given in Baines and Male's *Atlas of Ancient Egypt* (1980). The first of these was the *Horus* name, written on a rectangular object. The King was considered the Son and descendant of the God-King, Horus. The second or *Nebty* name represented his relationship with the two ladies, the Vulture Goddess Nekhbet of Upper Kemet and the Cobra Goddess Uadjit, of Lower Kemet. The third or *Insibya* name was his Horus of Gold name, which had some mystical significance.

The King's prenomen or Throne name most often came before his cartouche or oval. This *Nesubat* name symbolized a reed for the south and a bee for the north. Thus, he was King of Upper and Lower Kemet/Egypt. The name in the cartouche was his nomen or personal name. This was his *Son of Ra* name linking him to the

EGYPT ESSAYS ON ANCIENT KEMET

divine Sun God. However, both his *Nesu Bit* and *Son of Ra* titles are often in cartouche.

On the other hand, Dr. ben-Jochannan has pointed out the king of Egypt/Kemet actually had nine names, but scholars seldom discuss more than the regular five. The King was considered a "Perfect God" which carried a name. He had a name when he led the army in battle. He had a name when he presided over any festival at the temple, and so on.

In the Middle and New Kingdom, Kemet conducted a very aggressive and imperial foreign policy. There were many wars and the king wore a *Kepresh* Blue War Crown, from the New Kingdom onwards. Aldred (1980: 159) has given an illustration of the pharaoh wearing the "blue crown on a Red granite relief from a fallen obelisk of King Tuthmose III kneeling to be crowned by the god Amun, in the great temple of Amun at Karnak." Actually, this is Hatshepsut whose obelisk lies beside the Sacred Lake. Aldred (1980: 186) again had cause to comment on changes in art and costume of the time of the Ikhnaton revolution during the later 18th Dynasty, during which "innovations of the Amarna sculptors persisted for the next three reigns. The lappets of the Nemes head cloth revived the Thirteenth Dynasty fashion of an inner border. The Blue Crown became taller and more upright, and acquired streamers that hang down the nape of the neck, eventually assuming a broader shape and a ribbed appearance. Contemporary changes in dress are also reflected both in statuary and relief."

In addition to depicting a basalt head of a statue of King Amenhotep III wearing the Blue Crown, Aldred further tells of the Saite Period of the XXVIth Dynasty. Here a black basalt head of King Apries "reveals the peculiar details of the late version of the Blue Crown, with its flat tabs, curved parietal seams and a rolled border to the lower edge."

The God Amon wore a crown with tall plumes and a Solar Disk. Also, the God Osiris wore the Atef Crown, which was the White Crown with plumes, horns and Uraeus. He is generally shown in the mummified form with scepter and flagella. Another crown of significance was the "Queen Mother Crown." Queen Aahmes-Nefertari, foundress of the XVIIIth Dynasty, wears one of the earliest surviving examples of this headgear. This "coal black" Ethiopian beauty is shown bejeweled, wearing the Queen mother crown and wearing the fashionable red, white and blue, "tricolor" dress. Lastly, the most informal crown was the Nemes Headdress. It was worn from the Middle Kingdom onwards. This crown was made of cloth and surmounted by a Uraeus or cobra symbol. On the outer east and west walls of the temple of Dendera are friezes depicting the 23 crowns associated with the culture of ancient Kemet/Egypt.

Egypt Essays Photo 116v. Cairo Museum of Egyptian Antiquities. Dr. Gaston Maspero

EGYPT ESSAYS ON ANCIENT KEMET

Egypt Essays Photo 116w. Cairo Museum of Egyptian Antiquities.

Jewelry seemed to accentuate the use of crowns particularly those worn by princesses. Murray (1949: 115) reminds of the lotus flower and indicates, "... it is possible that a crown of this flower was part of the royal insignia." Again, according to Murray (1949: 115) the: "Forget-me-not crown of a princess of the XIIth dynasty shows beauty of color and delicacy of design; so also does the buttercup crown of Queen Ta-usert of the XIXth dynasty."

Murray (1949: 277) further discusses the Middle Kingdom jewelry found at Dashur, where she notes: "The Dashur jewelry consisted of three pectorals, two crowns, bracelets with inlaid clasps, belts of gold cowries and lion-heads, bead necklaces and a great number of small objects. The pectorals show the most consummate craftsmanship; each one is different in design as they belong to different periods, and are only alike in the fact that each has as the central motif the name of the Pharaoh in whose reign it was made. The pectoral, which is second in date, is of the time of Senusert III and has a peculiarly interesting design. It is made, like the two others, of a thick plate of gold on which the design has been cut out; the design has been so arranged that though at first sight it appears to have greatly weakened the ornament, the points of contact of the various parts make it thoroughly strong, the bending lotus, for example, is attached to the wing of the vulture and the tail of the lion."

Egypt Essays Illustration 62. Top of the brickwork blocking the entrance of the tomb, and the rubbish filling the pit: straw basket-lids and bits of a coffin (left); and corridor of the tomb from the entrance: *Shawabti Boxes* and (beyond) Baskets of the 18th Dynasty (right).

Murray (1949: 277), again in comparison, states: "The Lahun jewelry is of the same type, with the exception of the crown. This is a circular band of gold to fit around the head, ornamented at intervals with rosettes inlaid with colored stones like the Dashur pectorals. At the back is a lotus in gold, from which spring two gold feathers, the emblem of Amon; three long streamers hang down, one on each side of the face and one at the back. The interesting part of the workmanship, apart from the beauty of the object itself, is that the crown takes to pieces and could be packed into a small compass for traveling. The streamers are merely hooked on, the feathers and the lotus fit into sockets and can be slipped out; the rosettes also can be slipped out, and the band round the head can be unhooked and laid out flat. The rest of the jewelry was in beauty and workmanship equal to the royal find at Dashur."

EGYPT ESSAYS ON ANCIENT KEMET

Other symbols of Pharaonic power included a Nekheb whip or flail. The king also had a crook and *Aba*, *Hedj* and *Waz* scepters. The king celebrated the Heb-Sed festival or jubilee, after 30 years of rule. The duration of time for this festival is not absolute since some Pharaohs celebrated several Sed-Festivals. Here the King wore a royal lion's tail to symbolize him being a mighty hunter. There was also a *Wadjet Eye*, and the *Ankh*, symbol of life. There was also a *Djed Pillar*, symbolizing Osiris' backbone or strength.

The monarch of ancient Kemet wore many hats throughout his lifetime. He was Prince, Pharaoh, and "God" or "Son of God." Interestingly enough, the first record of the Pharaoh we have comes from the Narmer Palette, though there is some evidence of earlier kings, such as Scorpion, from the pre-dynastic period. Nevertheless, Narmer, on the Palette is depicted as a conqueror from Upper Egypt/Kemet, the South, who subdued the North, Lower Egypt/Kemet, and united the two lands under one kingdom. On the Narmer Macehead we see the king seated with his wife Queen Aahotep nearby. They had a son Aha, who succeeded his father to the throne as Pharaoh.

Narmer set up a monarchy as the form of government. Next, the administrative system that governed was set up. As conqueror who led the army from the South, he defined the nature and role of the army in internal and external relations. It is believed he further determined the type of weaponry the army came to use. He seems to have chosen the weapons we came to associate with the king, such as dagger, Macehead, bow and arrow, etc.

Then, the Pharaoh's regalia, viz., crowns, the sacred symbol of the Uraeus upon his brows, whip, flail, crook, tunic, girdle, beard, even royal slipper of gold, as well as symbols of stability, health, long life, etc., were established. On the Narmer Palette he is shown with his sandal bearer. The king is also shown smiting the enemy with his mace and as a true conqueror with his captives. The raised relief sculpture of the palette shows him as a colossal figure in relationship to his subjects.

FREDERICK MONDERSON

Egypt Essays Photo 117. Imhotep Museum at Sakkara. This building houses artifacts relative to the world's first multi-genius.

Narmer established a shrine for the God Ptah at Memphis and began the deity's religious worship and ritualizing there. His role as builder was begun with construction of the major "white wall" he built at Memphis, the nation's new administrative capital. The Pharaoh was responsible for the inspection of public works such as irrigation projects of canals, basins, embankments, wells and lakes to conserve water in a desert country. The records show the king, after the first dynasty inspecting the frontier and establishing his authority by "going round the wall" and "uniting the lands of Upper and Lower" Kemet/Egypt. The head of the Kemetic State assumed the function of head of the army, chief administrator and high priest who performed religious functions. These rituals were especially important according to J. Manchip White's *Ancient Egypt*.

"The enemy whose onslaughts Pharaoh resisted was not only the host of Libyans, Nubians, Bedouins and Asiatics who lured on Egypt's physical boundaries, but also the spiritual enemy in the shapes of Seth and Apophis. The powers of darkness, though constantly vanquished, attempted ceaselessly to overthrow Egypt by blighting the crops, obstructing the flow of the Nile, causing floods or preventing the sun from rising."

EGYPT ESSAYS ON ANCIENT KEMET

As such, the pharaoh unceasingly worshipped and ritualized the Gods or was in turn ritualized as their earthly representative. This way he hoped to insure divinely sanctioned good fortune for his state. This communion with deity began the higher sciences of religion, theology, theosophy, cosmology, spirituality, etc. Further, the "spiritual potency of the king, on which the well-being of his subjects depended, was enhanced by the purity of his breeding. Theoretically the actual blood of the sun god had been transmitted by Horus into the royal veins." This caused the priesthood to take great pains in ensuring prolific procreation for the Pharaoh, and as far as possible, very limited marriages outside the royal family.

The Pharaoh ruled by *Ma'at*, a philosophy of justice, which meant "that which is straight, balanced, ordered." Budge (1969: 416-17) pointed out the symbol of the Goddess Ma'at was a feather oftentimes seen on her head but sometimes in her hand. He wrote, the people of ancient Egypt/Kemet "used the word in a physical and a moral sense, and thus it came to mean 'right, true, real, genuine, upright, righteous, just, steadfast, unalterable, etc.; The goddess Ma'at was, then, the personification of physical and moral law, and order and truth."

We read further in Budge (1969: 417-18) of a hymn to Ra. It read as follows: "The land of Manu (i.e., the West) receiveth thee with satisfaction, and the goddess Ma'at embraceth thee both at morn and at eve; the god Thoth and the goddess Ma'at have written down thy daily course for thee every day: may I see Horus acting as steersman [in the boat of Ra] with Thoth and Ma'at, one on each side of him." In a further hymn Qenna says: "I have come to thee, O Lord of the gods, Temu-Heru-khuti, whom Ma'at directeth;' Amen-Ra is said to 'rest upon Ma'at,' i.e., to subsist by Ma'at; Ra is declared to 'live by Ma'at;' Osiris 'carries along the earth in his train by Ma'at in his name of Seker.' In her capacity as regulator of the path of the Sun-god Ma'at is said to be the 'daughter of Ra,' and the 'eye of Ra,' and 'lady of heaven, queen of the earth, and mistress of the Underworld,' and she was, of course, 'the lady of the gods and goddesses.'

FREDERICK MONDERSON

Therefore, these facts considered, the king's actions were closely scrutinized. In the afterlife he was judged based on his actions while on earth. So he structured his rule with the view 'Justice was defined as what Pharaoh loves,' wrongdoing as 'what Pharaoh hates.' He was the rule of law in the state and the final refuge of appeal. However, there were few cases that reached this high level of litigation.

Pharaoh Amenemhat III ruled in the Twelfth Dynasty, during the Middle Kingdom. He had in his employ a high official who spoke to his children and summed up what was the universal belief throughout Kemet regarding his master, as well as the symbol of Pharaonic rule.

'He is the God Ra whose beams enable us to see. He gives more light to the Two Lands than the sun's disc. He makes the earth more green than the Nile in flood. He is the Ka (i.e., the guardian spirit). He is the god Khnum who fashions all flesh. He is the goddess Bast who defends Egypt. Whoever worships him is under his protection. But he is Sekhmet, the terrible lion goddess, to those who disobey him. Take care not to defy him. A friend of Pharaoh attains the rank of Honored One, but there is no tomb for the rebel. His body is thrown into the river. Therefore listen to what I tell you and you will enjoy health and prosperity.'

In the religious realm the King exercised the most profound influence on Kemetic culture. Kings continued a tradition of prehistoric times when, based on the Osiris legend, the Gods were regarded as Kings of Upper and Lower Kemet/Egypt. Each ruled a number of centuries and some only years.

According to Erman's *Handbook of Egyptian Religion* (1907) and reliance on the *Turin Papyrus*, the order of reigns were: "Keb, Osiris, Seth and Horus succeeding in order, then Thoth and Ma'at; then all manner of lesser Gods, and finally, the human kings, the Servants of Horus, end the prehistoric period."

EGYPT ESSAYS ON ANCIENT KEMET

20. THE NILE RIVER

The Nile River, flowing through Northeast Africa, enabled early man to people a d domesticate a valley and to raise a civilization. In a desert culture, this life giving source became an important part of the religious beliefs, festivals and ceremonies that sprang up along its banks. It is the longest river in the world and the only major river that runs south to north. All other major rivers, whether the Mississippi, Ganges, Tigris-Euphrates, and Amazon, the Rhine, Volga, etc., run north to south. Measuring 4,132 miles (6,648 kilometers) it drains an area estimated at 1,293,000 square miles (3,349,000 Square Kilometers). Its basin includes parts of the modern African states including Tanzania, Burundi, Rwanda, Zaire, Kenya, and Uganda, most of the Sudan, Ethiopia and the cultivated part of Kemet. It supports a present day population of nearly 100,000,000 people. This is indeed amazing.

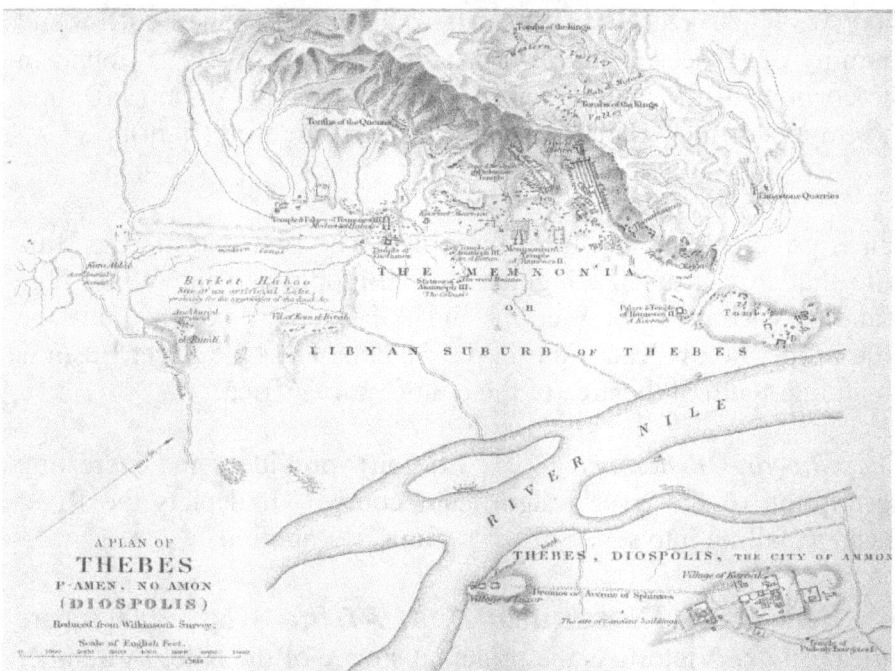

Egypt Essays Illustrations 63. Plan of Thebes showing both sides of the river with principal monuments.

FREDERICK MONDERSON

Egypt Essays Illustration 63a. The inner coffin and mummy of Princess Entiu-Ny, a later burial (1000 B.C.), found in the corridor of the above tomb of Queen Meryet-Amun (left); and the empty coffin of Entiu-Ny on the brink of the well (right).

Three principal streams form the Nile. The first two are the Blue Nile that flow from the highlands of Ethiopia and the White Nile that flows from Lakes Victoria and Albert. The Atbara joins the Nile proper below Khartoum in the Sudan. The Nile River Basin is about one-tenth of the area of the continent of Africa.

Encyclopedia Britannica (10th Edition) provides an interesting description of the river's significant course. It depicts the River Basin as falling into seven major regions, we are told.

1. ***The Lake Plateau of East Africa***. The 26,000 square miles of Lake Victoria is the principal source of the Nile. A number of other lakes and head-streams feed into this basin.

EGYPT ESSAYS ON ANCIENT KEMET

2. *The Bahr el-Jebel at Nimule.* The Nile enters the Sudan rapidly over the steep slopes and gorges and is called the Bahr el-Jebel, the "River of Mountain."

3. *The White Nile.* The White Nile is about 500 miles in length, and is the main branch of the Nile that supplements two-sevenths of its volume.

4. *The Blue Nile.* The Blue Nile drains from the lofty Ethiopian highlands north by northwestward, where it descends from a height of 6,000 feet above sea level. Its reputed source is a small spring considered holy by the Orthodox Church of Ethiopia. From here a small stream, the Abbai, flows down to Lake Tana, a fairly shallow lake (with an area of about 1,400 square miles) that lies 6,000 feet above sea level. While the White Nile at Khartoum is a source of almost constant volume, it is the Blue Nile that contributes most to the Nile floods. The flood occurs in Egypt beginning in September as a result of the seasonal rains, the river receives from its torrential tributary streams.

5. *The Atbara.* The Atbara is the last tributary of the Nile. It merges into the mainstream nearly 200 miles north of Khartoum. It rises in Ethiopia at heights of 6,000 to 10,000 feet above sea level, not far from Gondar, to the north of Lake Tana.

6. *The North of Khartoum* stretches into what is called the United Nile, where two parts can be distinguished. The first part, which runs from Khartoum to Wadi Halfa, is just about 930 miles in length. The river is never far from the desert, and the desert often forms the riverbank. The second part consists of the stretch from Wadi Halfa where the river enters Egypt to Cairo. Here the Nile Delta opens a stretch along which cultivation is feasible.

7. *The Nile Delta.* North of Cairo, the head of the alluvial plain of Lower Egypt, the walls of the plateau that form the Nile

FREDERICK MONDERSON

Valley becomes ill defined. They diverge from each other, leaving between them the triangular lowland that forms the Nile Delta. In the first century A.D., the Greek geographer Strabo described the Nile as having seven tributaries. The flow has since been controlled so that the river now flows across the Delta to the sea through two main tributaries, the Rosetta and the Damietta branches.

Herodotus, who visited Egypt in 450 B.C. is credited with the saying "Egypt is the gift of the Nile." In fact, however, that saying may really be attributable to Hecataeus of Miletus who lived about one hundred years before Herodotus visited Kemet. He was a reputed traveler and historian who wrote *Travels Around the Earth*, only fragments of which are extant.

Nevertheless, the river permeated every aspect of the life of the ancient Egyptian/Kemetic people. It impacted in every way, whether administration, agriculture, art, astronomy, leisure, festival celebration, cosmology, death, religion, taxes, transportation and warfare.

W. M. F. Petrie, in *Social Life in Ancient Egypt* writes, the Vizier or Prime Minister, was able to keep abreast of taxes and receipts of all local officials. His job was helped by reports of the state of the Nile and this became a guide to future taxation. Taxation was based on the height of the inundation and the estimated amount of crops which could be raised. Taxes were also raised on some types of river traffic that fell within the purview of the Vizier. "The regulation of Nile Traffic was also his duty, directing the cargo boats, pilots and steersmen." Such sources of revenue enriched the treasury.

From time immemorial the Nile has been the benefactor of agriculture along its banks. It has aided farming, the mainstay of the Kemetic economy. Pharaoh's role in the construction of dams and dykes enabled extensive tracts of land to come into cultivation. These artificial measures of irrigation deterred the encroaching desert. Today, two main canals run parallel to, one on each bank, of the river. From here, the notion of "checker-board pattern" of irrigation enabled further protection and distribution of the water, bringing even greater areas under cultivation.

The predictable behavior of the Nile allowed the pharaohs to harness unemployed farmers during the inundation. Many were employed for construction of their pyramids, tombs, and other forms of social, civil and religious architectural structures. The Pyramid group at Giza, especially, was built during this period. So too were those at Sakkara and the more southerly pyramids at Abusir, Meydum, etc., all juxtaposed to massive mastabas. Such use of the unemployed for national architecture construction is mentioned in Herodotus' *Histories* Book II, *Euterpe*. Many other architectural projects, particularly those at Luxor and Karnak, as well as other religious sites such as Abydos and Abu Simbel, Edfu, Esneh, Dendera, Kom Ombo, Kalabsha, Deir El Bahari, the Ramesseum, Medinet Habu, etc were probably built during this time.

The stones for many of the large projects were quarried far to the south and floated down river on barges. The industry of such river transportation became a science. These tasks were easily accomplished when the river was in flood. In addition, they were more easily moved to their final destinations while the river was still high. Obelisks in particular were quarried at Aswan, where the best stones were located. They were then transported down-river to their sites of erection. Two of Queen Hatshepsut's obelisks were dug at Aswan by Senmut and transported and erected at Karnak, within a period of seven months.

Astronomy and astrology were conjoined with certain seasonal behaviors of the river. However, though much is known about astronomy and the early development of Kemetic consciousness, not much is really known about their astrology. They did have lucky and unlucky days throughout the year.

Too often the Greeks are credited with the discovery of the zodiac. When reference is made about the Kemetic zodiac, the chart at

FREDERICK MONDERSON

Dendera is most often referred to. It is emphasized that this temple was built during the Ptolemaic or Greek period. Yet, Petrie (1923) informs: "Priesthood had also the care of the calendar, like the Pontifex in Rome. Astronomy was therefore a study with them, and they have left us one part of their work in the horoscopes on the temples of the XIX dynasty and Ptolemaic times."

What's interesting is the Dendera and other Ptolemaic zodiacs are thought to be copies or reproductions of the XIX Dynasty, at least. Additionally, the XIX Dynasty zodiac, in all probability is a copy of a much earlier one. In wake of missing information, especially on Kemet, rational deduction must be used in archaeological sleuthing. Keep in mind, as much as we know about ancient Nile Valley civilizations, we probably base it all on no more than 15% - 20% of all there is to know!

So, the Nile River featured prominently in Kemetic Cosmogony. These ancient Africans believed that once a person attained heaven, which was a replica of their beloved Kemet, he or she could roam about. However, such freedom required the person to know the districts of Kemet, which were replicated in heaven. Equally, they had to know the names of the gods of the various districts or gates in heaven.

E. A. W. Budge in *The Gods of the Egyptians*, Vol. I, expresses the view, the people of ancient Kemet/Egyptians had to recite prayers of various kinds to gain the goodwill of the gods of the Four Corners of the sky. They did this to "be able to pass at pleasure along the eastern Delta of heaven and without opposition presupposed the favor of Sept and Temu." Further, they wanted to have the power to drink the waters of the celestial Nile. This meant they needed the favor of the god Khnemu, the Lord of the Island of Elephantine. This island, the Kemetic people believed, was located near the source of the Nile. Thus, its acceptance reinforced in their cosmological beliefs, that there was a heavenly Nile.

EGYPT ESSAYS ON ANCIENT KEMET

When the Pharaoh and other wealthy persons died their bodies were prepared for burial. After the mummification process, a most elaborate Nile voyage carried the deceased to a ceremony at the Holy City of Abydos, in Upper Kemet/Egypt. At this site, the world's first holy city of pilgrimage, the priests recited prayers. They also performed ceremonies to unite the deceased with the God Osiris. This ritual was necessary since the deceased was en-route to meet the god Osiris in the afterlife. After the ceremony at Abydos, the deceased traveled along the Nile to the place of final internment. This last Nile journey became symbolic and important for a number of reasons.

First, many people could not be buried at Abydos, the burial place and site of the temple of Osiris and site of the worship of the god. The real estate was very costly. To make the voyage to this pilgrimage site was a first introduction to the judge of the dead. Second, the symbolic journey on the Nile mirrored the journey on the celestial Nile on the way to the Hall of Judgment in heaven. Third, the Nile water was considered sacred and to be associated with it in any way was a powerful plus for the deceased. Finally, the priests poured libations on the deceased in the mortuary ceremonies, and this water came from the Nile.

Significantly, the worship of this important river by the people of ancient Kemet/Egypt is similar to other worship of the forces of nature found elsewhere in Africa. Such an important practice ties Kemet to its antecedents and cultural manifestations in Africa.

Budge in *Osiris and the Egyptian Resurrection* Vol. II supports such beliefs. In this regard, he wrote: "If we compare the worship or reverence paid by the Egyptians to the spirits of certain trees or to the spirits of the Nile, or to the spirits of the gods, with the worship of spirits of like character by modern Africans we find its theory and practice to be identical."

FREDERICK MONDERSON

Egypt Essays Illustration 64. A shattered head of Hatshepsut belonging to a headless statue now in Berlin showing the Queen without the conventional Royal Beard.

Many African peoples and especially those of ancient Kemet/Egypt worshiped their ancestors. They believed the spirits of their ancestors were located in statues and figures. There were nature-spirits of all kinds. So too were the spirits of gods. When it pleased these entities, they took up their abode in symbolic figures, in living animals, and in totems, living and dead. However, from first to last there is no evidence whatsoever that the Africans worshiped a figure or symbol, "whether made of metal, wood, stone, porcelain, or any other substance, unless they believed it to be the abode of a spirit of some kind." Budge continued, "… far from fetishism being

EGYPT ESSAYS ON ANCIENT KEMET

peculiarly characteristic to the Egyptian religion, it seems to me that this religion, at all events in its oldest forms, was remarkably free from it."

So, from the earliest times of the pre-dynastic period the Nile was used as a waterway for transportation, trade, warfare, and leisure sailing. It was the life-blood of agricultural pursuit. It had religious significance, was associated with astronomy, helped in development of mathematics, building, festivity, etc. Thus, in every aspect the great river was a part of the life and existence of the Kemetic/Egyptian person and civilization, along the Nile River, in Northeast Africa.

Egypt Essays Illustration 64a. Close-up of Tutankhamon's death mask showing the king with his scepter and flagella or whip.

FREDERICK MONDERSON

21. KEMETIC TECHNOLOGY/SCIENCE

Throughout history Kemetic technology has withstood time, and showcased the genius and indomitable spirit of ancient African architectural and industrial creativity. Technology's proliferation was demonstrated in building construction, boat building, and a vast number of industries that fed the various trades. Craftsmanship was renowned, and the Kemetic culture excelled in quarrying, transportation, mining, the development of irrigation facilities, civic projects, and a number of metal, papyrus, wood, stone, bone and ivory workings. These ancient Africans of Egypt have produced the type of architecture, art, and jewelry of lasting durability and beauty modern man has come to associate with timeless ancient Kemetic/Egyptian craftsmanship and technical expertise. As the world becomes more sophisticated technologically, young students of African ancestry need know, not only the intellectual and esoteric bases of most knowledge were created by the African ancestors, but the most fundamental and technical contributions to human progress were also Africa's gifts.

The application of Egyptian/Kemetic technology dates to the pre-dynastic period when housing structures evolved from the simplest types. In *Egyptian Towns and Cities*, Eric P. Uphill (1988: 6) mentions "the earliest Egyptian dwellings appear to have been simple reed huts or even wind-breaks rather than caves as in Paleolithic Europe." These Nile Valley Africans were fortunate to have at hand desirable materials for building. As their technical skills advanced they moved to work with more complex materials creating architectural wonders still fascinating visitors to their modern sites.

Essentially, there were three principal types of materials available for building in ancient Kemet. The first of these consisted of various kinds of leaves as well as reeds, rushes, papyrus, and palm ribs. When wood was used significantly, in dwelling structures, builders knew, "two kinds of planks could be made from two species

EGYPT ESSAYS ON ANCIENT KEMET

of palm trees, the date and the dom." In addition, Uphill (1988: 6) points out: "Acacia (*nilotica*) and tamarisk were other local woods useful for house buildings. Only later, when very large beams were needed for roofing palaces or making columns and temple flagstaffs, were cedar and other imported woods, used extensively."

As a decorative motif, palm fronds, with open and closed buds, and papyrus, influenced the design of column and capital. For much of dynastic rule, papyrus, lotus and palm were the principal forms of the capital that decorated forests of columns adorning mortuary and worship temples, along the Nile. The Hathor Column, the Osiride Pillar or column, and even the "Tent Pole Column," once used in Thutmose III's Festival Hall, the *Akh Menu*, in Karnak Temple at Thebes, were unique, not being used often.

The second type of material to evolve in their technological repertoire included mud, wattle and daub, and the basis of modest domestic buildings. This gave way to mud-brick. Bricks were made from Nile mud. Uphill (1988: 7) has again demonstrated that brick making was a "highly involved art which had to be learnt over a long period and used wooden molds of various sizes. Much of the old materials and practices are still being used today." Uphill (1988: 7) even further points out: "The best bricks were built with chopped straw, but quite a useful brick could be made by using sand instead. Normally they were simply dried in the sun; although baked clay tiles were used for special functions. Mortar was merely mud of similar consistency to the brick." Clay tiles were used in the Step-Pyramid at Sakkara, built by Imhotep for Pharaoh Zoser, 3rd Dynasty, 2600 B.C.

The third type of building material utilized was stone. As the art of construction became more sophisticated, Uphill (1988: 7) explained, "houses and domestic buildings and later temples and tombs were built entirely of stone." In palaces and houses of the wealthy, stone was mainly reserved for, "column bases and sometimes door-cases and window grilles. Wooden column shaft bases could suffer damage from wet rot or insects, and stone bases acted as a protection and were much wider than the wooden shafts."

FREDERICK MONDERSON

Kemetic technology was also applied to the construction of irrigation projects as lakes, dams, dykes, canals, and embankments. Militarism and imperialism dictated fortresses be constructed in occupied areas as in Nubia and elsewhere in Asia, where the state's interests were centered.

Fortifications were also built to protect towns and other settlements from hostile neighbors, in the period before unification. Early settlements were laid out in a determined pattern. Much later, towns and cities with more complex structures of housing patterns with street and social infrastructure were developed. The layout and development of the plan of Ikhnaton's new city at Amarna is a classical example of "ready construction." Here they experimented with new motifs and designs that were erected on virgin soil.

Angela P. Thomas (1988: 53) has explained: "The surveying, measuring and planning of the major roads and buildings presented few problems for there were no earlier structures on the site to take into account. Construction started with the heart of the city, the central official quarter, with its temples, palaces and administrative buildings. The Great Temple to Aten and a smaller Aten temple were constructed of stone and as sun temples they contained unroofed courts and processional ways leading to the altars, which were also open to the sky. The walls were decorated with relief scenes and the temples provided with statues."

EGYPT ESSAYS ON ANCIENT KEMET

Egypt Essays Photo 118. Sakkara, Home of the Step-Pyramid. From between the Colonnade looking out into the Great Court.

Egypt Essays Photo 118a. Sakkara, Home of the Step-Pyramid. From the Great Court looking toward the Colonnade.

Further, Thomas (1988: 530 notes: "Most of the secular buildings, as was normal, were built mainly of mud-brick with elements like column bases, lintels and door frames of stone, and columns, doors and roofing timbers of wood. By the side of the temples were their storehouses and stretching behind were the various government offices. Between the two temples was a house of the king, his state office, which was eventually connected by a bridge across the road

FREDERICK MONDERSON

to the vast official palace complex with its halls, courts, colonnades and gardens."

Egypt Essays Photo 119. Since the deceased needed an extra head or body as an insurance in the afterlife, several increased the chances of survival.

Egypt Essays Photo 119a. Sakkara, Home of the Step-Pyramid. Reserve statues, to ensure survival of the deceased in a private tomb. Again, several statues gave the deceased several chances of survival.

EGYPT ESSAYS ON ANCIENT KEMET

The pyramids are the most famous showcases of ancient Kemetic technology. The timeless group at Giza has defied the imagination and been commented on by travelers for thousands of years. These mathematically precise funerary structures have amazed indigenous Africans and foreigners from far and wide. The pyramid idea evolved in order to create a more lasting resting-place for the pharaoh or God-king after death. Such was the system of belief in the Old Kingdom which had a solar connection and orientation. The ideas developed during this period, permeated the duration of pharaonic rule and later influenced the world. Here is presented a shining example, young people, in search of roots, can be proud of.

Herodotus, who visited Egypt/Kemet in 450 B.C., was one of the first Europeans to comment on the purpose of the pyramids. However some credit Hecataeus with this distinction. Nevertheless, in Aubrey De Selincourt's (1972) translation of the *Histories*, the "father of history" reported, it took 100,000 men working twenty years to build the Great Pyramid. Traditional belief holds that pharaohs used the unemployed indigenous population to build pyramids during the inundation, when the river was flooded, the farmers were idle and stone could be quarried and flooded on flat-bottomed boats over long distances. The grandiose magnificence of these projects awed a pharaoh's contemporaries by demonstrating his wealth and power. In addition, the organizational skill involved in the giant project attests a high level of administrative and technological expertise, accomplished by early builders, when much of the world still remained in architectural ignorance.

These monoliths grew out of a pattern of trial and error; with each attempt the threshold of architectural sciences was advanced. The first of these structures are rooted in the mastaba concept, wherein the Step-Pyramid emerged out of the first and second dynasty sepulcher tombs of the kings and their nobles. Mastaba means bench in Arabic. The tombs resembled benches built by Arabs outside their houses. The later true-pyramid grew out of the attempt to make taller mastabas that were more pointed to the sun or the heavens, in early identification with a solar religious concept of deity.

FREDERICK MONDERSON

Most persons are aware of the Step-Pyramid at Sakkara. This monumental religious structure historically highlights the beginning of Kemetic architectural innovation. In his construction techniques, Imhotep innovated many architectural features that became standard in subsequent building practice. Nevertheless, according to Philip Watson in *Egyptian Pyramids and Mastaba Tombs*, there are three others.

Egypt Essays Illustration 65a. A bowman-charioteer firing his arrow in stride in an Abu Simbel illustration.

In 1950, Z. Goneim, an archaeologist, discovered a second Step-Pyramid at Sakkara. This structure was erected for Pharaoh Sekhemkhet who reigned for only six years. Watson further indicated, excavations have revealed the "essential elements of a seven-stepped pyramid, a paneled enclosure wall and a south tomb comprising a rectangular mastaba built over a deep burial shaft." Even further, he suggests, "similarities in the substructure of this pyramid and that of Zoser." The burial chamber was approached down a sloping ramp from the north side. Its descent gave access to one-hundred and thirty-two underground magazines and to four galleries that were associated with the funerary chamber.

EGYPT ESSAYS ON ANCIENT KEMET

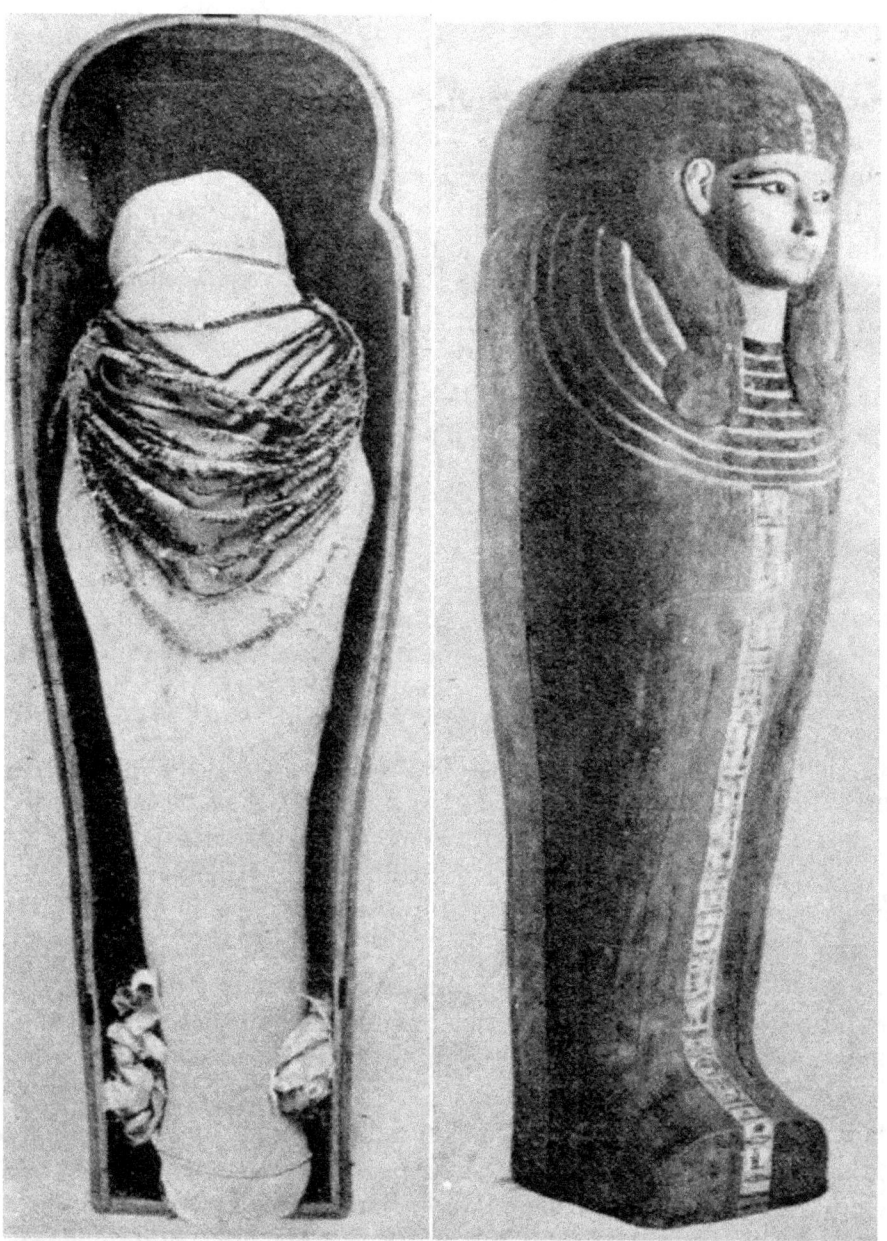

Egypt Essays Illustration 65b. The mummy of Queen Meryet-Amun in its place inside the coffin, in her newly found tomb (left); and stripped of its gold casing by ancient tomb-robbers: The lid of Meryet-Smun's inner coffin (right).

FREDERICK MONDERSON

Another Step-Pyramid was identified at *Zawiyet el-Aryan*, between Giza and Sakkara. This building was called the Layer Pyramid and probably belonged to King Khaba. It was never finished! Still, another Step-Pyramid complex might be concealed within the so-called "Great Enclosure at Sakkara." Aerial photographs have revealed its rectangular outlines to the west of Sekhemkhet's tomb, also of the Third Dynasty.

The Fourth Dynasty experienced the move to create a true pyramid. The origin of these monoliths may be found in similar shaped structures that can be found, littering the southern Kemetic landscape, creating "natural pyramids." Here the winds have shaped these forms that attest to the conflict between the elements and the elevated lands, naturally creating that visible permanence and durability. The pyramid may also be explained as sitting on the top of an obelisk with a sacred symbol dedicated to the Sun God Re. An obelisk is simply a pyramid upon a long high base.

The Bent-Pyramid at Dashur was constructed after the Step-Pyramid but before the True-Pyramid. Snefru, the first king of the Fourth Dynasty, or the last king of the Third Dynasty built the original True-Pyramid. His successor Khufu, the Greek Cheops, built the Great Pyramid at Giza. Khufu's son and grandson, Khafre and Menkaure, whom the Greeks called Chephren and Mycerinus, built two others. The Giza-Pyramid group is some of the best-preserved in all of that ancient land. Tourists, owing to their proximity to the Cairo environs, most often visit them.

Many smaller pyramids were built in the Fifth and Sixth Dynasties. Still, others were raised in the Middle Kingdom. Nevertheless, all pyramids, regardless of size, were housed in a mega-complex comprising a large expanse of land and numerous other buildings. A priestly bureaucracy, whose work of perpetuating the memory of the deceased, was encouraged through kingly and noble endowments, to serve the god and the emergent cult of the dead.

EGYPT ESSAYS ON ANCIENT KEMET

Egypt Essays Photo 120. Sakkara, Home of the Step-Pyramid. A great man sits before a "Table of Offerings" still showing good color.

Egypt Essays Photo 120a. Sakkara, Home of the Step-Pyramid. Part of the entourage bringing goods to the same great man.

FREDERICK MONDERSON

In this regard, the "Components of a Pyramid-Complex" of the Old Kingdom included: A very tall Enclosure Wall to conceal whatever happened within; a Valley Temple received the deceased on arrival; Causeway; and Sun or Funerary Temple provided for the Ritual of the Dead. In the enclosure was a Sacrificial Altar; Heb-Sed Festival Pavilion to celebrate the pharaoh's rejuvenation; the Main Pyramid for the Pharaoh; and smaller Subsidiary Pyramids for the Pharaoh's wives and sisters. Also included were a Sphinx; Obelisk; Magazines for Storage; "Dummy Buildings" symbolizing the union of the Upper and Lower Kingdoms' Nomes, of which there may have been 42; and Mastaba tombs for nobles who served the Pharaoh. There was also a place where the Pharaoh could do a run to symbolize him traversing the entire land. Finally, solar barks or boats for the Pharaoh to sail across the sky, like the sun god, were enclosed. Khufu had five such "solar vehicles."

The symbols of these mountains of stone were not the sum total of ancient Kemetic technology. Mohammed Saber in *Pyramids and Mastaba Tombs* points out the discovery of the world's earliest tunnel at Giza. The Pyramid of Khafre had two temples. They were the Valley Temple and the Sun or Mortuary Temple. A Causeway that was covered with fine limestone connected these two temples. "It seems that this causeway was used only by the Pharaoh and the chief-priest during the procession from the Valley Temple to the Mortuary one."

As such, those persons who wished to move from one side to the other had to make a lengthy detour. This involved a distance of three kilometers. Therefore, their planners, as Mohammed Saber (ND: 112) demonstrates, "solved this difficulty by hewing a tunnel under the causeway; it facilitated the connection between the two sides of the causeway .... Needless to say that the discovery of this tunnel caused the astonishment of all people, for it revealed the inventive genius of their ancient architects."

EGYPT ESSAYS ON ANCIENT KEMET

In ancient Kemet, the Craft of Metallurgy began far back in the pre-historic Badarian culture, between 4500-3600 B.C. (260 *Before Nile Year* 1 and *Nile Year* 640). In *Egyptian Metalworking and Tools*, Bernd Scheel (1989: 7) argued that the development of trades and crafts were closely connected with social evolution in society. These specializations developed "with the process of settlement, the transition from food-collecting to food-producing economies and the domestication of animals and plants."

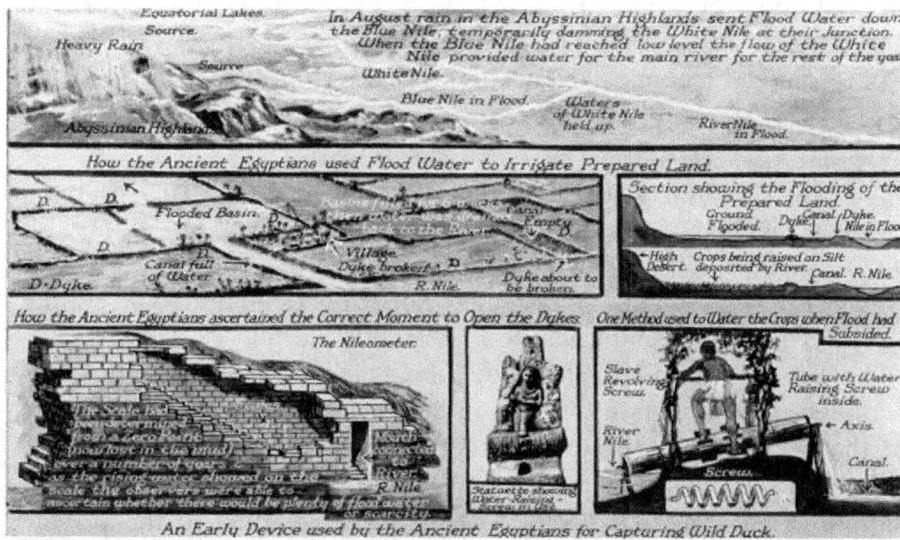

Egypt Essays Illustration 66. Examples of how the Ancient Egyptians applied principles to irrigation, fowling, agriculture and harvest.

Nevertheless, copper was the first metal worked by craftsmen in the Badarian Period. As such, it marked the start of the Metal Age in Kemet/Egypt, Northeast Africa. Copper tools and weapons were manufactured simply by open-mold casting. According to Scheel (1989: 9), such gains meant "melting, casting and smelting metals from ores required a sophisticated pottery industry, which would then have served as a basis for acquiring the technique of producing high temperatures using charcoal and developing smelting furnaces and melting crucibles."

FREDERICK MONDERSON

Division of labor and specialization of crafts are early additions in cultural development. In Kemet, industry became so sophisticated a proliferation of crafts developed including joiners, carpenters, wood sculptors or carvers and leather workers. There were also stonemasons, quarry workers, stone sculptors and textile workers. Other professions included barber, manicurists, doctors, agricultural workers and butchers. They all needed skills and tools for their professions.

What we call trades or Guilds of Medieval Europe, for example, produced leather workers, wood workers, stone workers, potters or metal workers, who were all strictly organized. There were artists who scaled heights to paint those majestic depictions on ceiling architraves, walls, columns, courts, Hypostyle and Peristyle Halls, and even tombs. Management, technical teaching and administrative dynamics were handled by inspectors or "Overseers of the Workshop" who supervised standards and quality of work. Scheel (1989) has indicated, a "workshop could be attached to a temple or to a royal palace. Others were attached to the private household of a king's son or to the household of a high official or monarch."

Some workers did not belong to a state owned palace workshop. They could be part of a private household of the king. At times and as a special honor, the king would have the palace craftsmen do work for private individuals.

EGYPT ESSAYS ON ANCIENT KEMET

Egypt Essays Photo 121. Sakkara, Home of the Step-Pyramid. From beyond some ruins looking at the roof of the Colonnade and towards the Step Pyramid in the rear.

Egypt Essays Photo 121a. Sakkara, Home of the Step-Pyramid. Part of the sand-covered ruins of the surrounding area.

FREDERICK MONDERSON

The people of this marvelous human experiment made great preparations for the afterlife by building and decorating their tombs. Many such tombs showed various scenes and themes with the owners and their families. They included rural life, fishing, fowling and the desert hunt. Funerary rites and dynamics of the afterlife were also depicted. The wealthy or noble dead are shown in sport and recreation. Animals such as dogs, donkeys, sheep, goats, gazelles and pigs were shown. In addition, a wide variety of ducks, geese and even cranes were all part of the funerary offering scene. They also show such domesticated wild animals as gazelles, oryx, and hyenas.

Most important, these tombs have depictions of the professions and various industries. Here we get evidence of many early crafts, pottery making, wine pressing and even circumcision. Wrestling, music and dance, playing board games and even war scenes also decorate the walls of some tombs.

Extremely colorful representations begin with early dynastic tombs such as those of *Ti* and *Ptahhotep* at Sakkara of the Vth Dynasty. Then there is *Periankh* at Meir and *Mereruka* at Sakkara; both of the VIth Dynasty. *Kheti* at Beni Hasan, *Thehutihotep* at el-Bersha and *Sarenput* at Aswan, all belong to the Middle Kingdom.

By the time of the great pharaohs of the New Kingdom, tombs became more elaborate. They provide much more information on mining, smelting, melting, casting and plate production. There are depictions of bowl and shaft furnaces, crucibles, dish bellows, reed blow pipes and molds. Wooden and stone anvils, various types of hammers and smoothing and chasing stones are also represented.

The *Tomb of Rekh-Mi-re* at Thebes and the *Tomb of Puy-em-re*, also at Thebes, are New Kingdom sources of metalworking and tools. The *Tomb of Two Sculptors* and the *Rock Tombs of Deir el-Gebraw*i also provide valuable information of the arts and professions.

A wide variety of tools are represented in these tombs and elsewhere. Specializations became so profound that every

EGYPT ESSAYS ON ANCIENT KEMET

profession had a different set of tools. There were those who worked in rock such as quarrymen, stone cutters, stone masons, and stone sculptors. They used stone, copper and later bronze chisels. Metal picks, wooden mallets and stone hammers as well as metal wedges were used in their many projects.

In bead-working, drills were used. There were hollow rotating drills and chert drills used in a variety of fields. Bow drills were used in woodworking. Carpentry tools also included axes, adzes, chisels, saws, shavers and hammers. All mallets and hammers had wooden handles. Wood was also used in everyday and funerary objects. Carpenters made beautiful chairs, stools, chests, draughtboards, scribal palettes, tables, beds, canopies, headrests, scales and sticks or staffs. They also made combs, hairpins, boxes and spoons. Agricultural tools such as wooden hoes, plows, and sickles were produced. Tools were made for individual professions such as barbers and tanners.

Working with metals and other forms of manual labor was difficult and messy work. Most sons followed their fathers in whatever craft they practiced. There was, however, the occasional son who had intellect. His father would not want him to follow in the same line of work. The best example of this is told in the "Satire of the Trades." The model here is the youth being encouraged to become a scribe or intellectual.

FREDERICK MONDERSON

Egypt Essays Photo 122. Sakkara, Home of the Step-Pyramid. An area filled with debris (left); and a cleared area descending to a tomb (right).

A father named Khety from the XIIth Dynasty had the perennial task of speaking to his son Pepi about working hard in school in order that he could become an official. Either the boy cultivates the intellect his father reasoned; otherwise he would become a craftsman and work hard all his life. Khety told his son, he never saw a goldsmith on important business. Interestingly, metal workers faced hot furnaces. Their hands were wrinkled and they smelled worse than scraps of fish. Many other trades were just as difficult and unpleasant. Therefore, study hard in school, the lad was told, and he would become a scribe.

The crafts were generally divided into skilled and unskilled workers. "The skilled workers were blacksmiths, coppersmiths, engravers and gilders. The skilled workers knew about metallurgy, chasing, annealing or casting metals. The unskilled workers started fires,

EGYPT ESSAYS ON ANCIENT KEMET

fanned fires by means of blowpipes or bellows, and cleaned and polished metal artifacts." During the Ramesside Period, of the late New Kingdom, shaft furnaces achieved 1200 degrees Centigrade (2200 degrees Fahrenheit) temperatures to work various metals. The intense heat helped to expand tool making for the various trades.

Metal tools for working leather included hide scrapers, leather-cutting knives, awls and needles. The craftsmen produced leather ropes, writing materials, arrow quivers, kilts and tents. They covered wooden stools, and tied tools like axes, hammers, adzes, and plows to their handles. Chariot equipment included harness, saddles and whips. Workers also made sandals.

Dressmaking tools included needles, pins, cutting-out knives, and scissors worked by separate fingers. Agricultural tools such as bronze hoes, plows and metal-edged sickles were made. According to A. Lucas in *Ancient Egyptian Materials and Industries* Egyptian medical instruments included, "shears, surgical knives, and saws in their creations." There were also different kinds of probes, small hooks and spatulas. All were used in surgery, dentistry, gynecology, and general medicine. Other metal implements included various knives used as weapons and tools; especially those used by butchers. Plates were made of copper and bronze.

The crafts were also useful to these ancient Africans along the Nile who attached an importance to personal hygiene. These early Black Africans disliked shaggy beards and overall hairiness. So razors and special toilet implements were made. Their repertoire included tweezers, razors, and knives. They shaved their faces, necks, armpits, limbs, chests, and pubic regions frequently.

From the metals gold, copper, lead, silver, and tin, four principal alloys were made. These were copper and tin for bronze and a lead and copper alloy. Gold and silver made electrum, while copper and zinc made brass.

In addition, the dictionary defines minerals as a substance obtained by mining. In that case, a number of minerals were also mined in

FREDERICK MONDERSON

ancient Kemet/Egypt. These included, according to Lucas, alum, used in tanning leather, in dyeing and for medical purposes. Cobalt was used as an abrasive with drills and saws for working hard stones. Graphite was sometimes used in beads. Manganese Compounds were used to implant purple color to glaze and glass. It was also used as eye paint.

Mica was used for mirrors, decorating caps and pendant necklaces. Natron consists of sodium carbonate and sodium bicarbonate. This was used in purification ceremonies, especially in the mouth. Further, it was also used for the manufacture of glass, glaze, and in blue and green frits used as pigments. Again, natron was used for cooking, in medicine, for bleaching and in mummification. Salt was used for seasoning food, preserving fish and also in mummification. Sulfur was used in mummification.

Egypt Essays Photo 123. Sakkara, Home of the Step-Pyramid. Entrance to the Akhnaton Carpet School where wonderful rugs are made.

The beauty of the Kemetic state was the lasting political stability it provided. With the exception of the few Intermediate Periods, the government was enduring. Political stability is always important for economic growth, to encourage division of labor, development and

EGYPT ESSAYS ON ANCIENT KEMET

specialization of crafts, and expansion of trade aided by improvements in transportation where ideas and crafts were spread.

The rich resources of the land were well exploited by the craftsmen. These early Africans were the genesis of their own genius. They had no one to imitate. Therefore, in applying African wisdom and ingenuity in the ancient world, Nile Valley Kemet harnessed its resources and spoke for emerging Africa. That voice is being heard thousands of years later. And, Africa's sons and daughters who have such a proud and wonderful cultural heritage are responding vigorously to that voice.

TAXATION

All governments depend on taxation to carry out their functions. In ancient Kemet/Egypt this was no different. A number of laws and officials were charged with regulating and collecting taxes demanded by the state. The basic forms of taxes were those levied on products and on labor. The state imposed heavy burdens and land-food rents on the wealthy. There were taxes on rights of passage over certain lands. Taxes also took the form of tribute exacted from conquered peoples and states. It is believed that the Kemetic/Egyptian craftsmen and traders also had to pay some form of taxes, especially in times of war. However, the main sources of taxes were of three types. The taxes on officials, taxes on agricultural produce and taxes as tribute from foreign vassal states. All in all, taxes played an important role in the culture.

FREDERICK MONDERSON

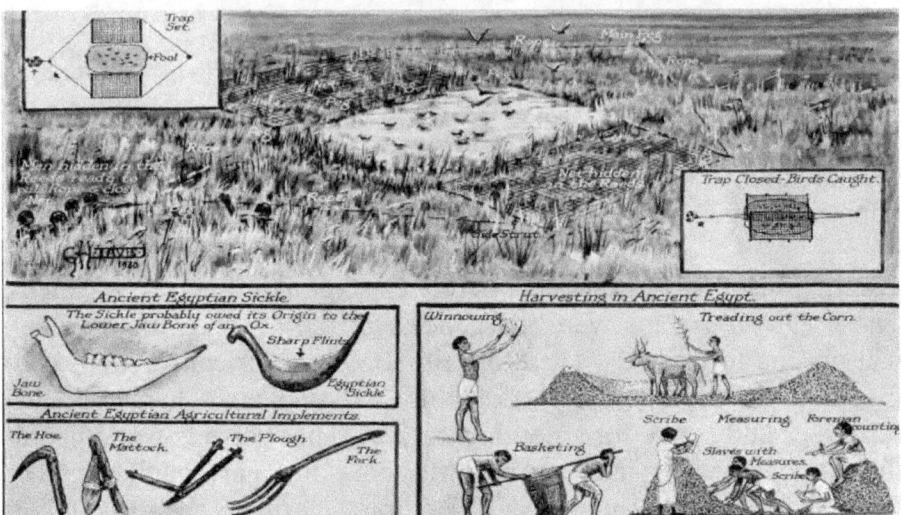

Egypt Essays Illustration 67. Illustrations depicting the Ancient Egyptians method of agricultural tools and effort.

From the earliest times, Kemet/Egypt has been an agricultural society dependent on the Nile River. The Inundation season lasted for four months. The height or size of the flood determined the expected yield of the harvest. This meant the Kemetic/Egyptian surveyors and administrators who were concerned with surveying and numbers came to rely on their Nile gauge or Nilometers.

The Nilometers were placed strategically at Semneh in Nubia. One is still visible from the high ground at Abu Simbel. There is another at Elephantine, ancient Kemet's southern border, one at Philae, and one at Memphis in Middle Egypt. There is another in the well at Kom Ombo and an old one at Edfu in addition to the one beside the outer corridor. Why the old one at Edfu? It is difficult to tell, since the temple is well removed from the river, as we know it.

In *Dwellers on the Nile*, E. A. Wallis Budge (1972: 109) explains what the Nilometers were. According to him, the Nilometer is a "pillar or slab, standing in a sort of well. It is cut into a scale divided into cubits (the cubit is 21 1/3 inches), and kirats (the kirat is 1/24th part of a cubit)." A flood too high could mean destruction of boundary markers, property, animals, and so on. One too low could

EGYPT ESSAYS ON ANCIENT KEMET

mean famine. The ideal has been twenty-five and twenty-six and a half inches.

Since the "Inundation of the Nile" removed all land boundary marks, this meant that surveyors had to re-survey the land on an annual basis. This required the use of good record keeping, architects and geometry. As a result, knowing or predicting the extent of the river's rise enabled the inspectors to determine what the size of taxes should be. This in turn was based on the projected yield in crops produced by farmers.

The regulation of taxation based on the river's bounty is very old. It dates back to the earliest organized society of the first dynasty or before. All lands were registered and taxed except those owned by the priests. This group, because of their special functions of service to the state, for the most part, was declared tax-free. Nobles' estates were registered and the size of their households counted. The taxes they paid were "in kind" and amounted to one-fifth of produce.

The general public was taxed on products. There were food dues of baskets of vegetables, eatables, and bread and fodder supplies made to the registry office. So too were dues in linen, yarn and cordage as well as common and precious metals. There was a poll tax and levy of labor for cultivation and harvesting of royal lands. Digging and maintenance of irrigation canals and embankments were a part of the corvee' system required by the state.

FREDERICK MONDERSON

Egypt Essays Photo 124. Cairo Museum of Egyptian Antiquities. A defaced Sphinx stands before the entrance as throngs of people prepare to enter (left); and an enclosed pair of statues in the garden area where photography is permitted though "banned" inside (right).

From the earliest times the king was associated with the inauguration of some public works. These ranged from digging or opening the irrigation canals, to building dykes, basins and, even an artificial lake. These water-troughs ran parallel to the Nile and would trap the inundated water when the river retreated. The trapped water was used in time of need to decrease the long wait until the next inundation. Therefore, the pharaoh's role in the ceremonial opening or construction of these facilities became important. The *Scorpion Macehead*, from the pre-dynastic period, portrays the king holding what seems an agricultural tool as if to open the season for planting. The priests then ritualized the ceremony in a way of blessing the enterprise and to ensure its success.

EGYPT ESSAYS ON ANCIENT KEMET

The importance of maintaining the canals, dykes, and embankments in a workable state should be mentioned. This irrigation helped to create a checkerboard pattern of stored water running in canals vertical and horizontal to the Nile. These measures extended the existing space under cultivation. They also served as a waterway for light sailing craft that could move people and supplies inland. These canals provided useful water when the Nile's volume was low. There was also a tax for passage across such lands owned by the king.

By the time of the XVIIIth Dynasty, taxes for the general masses were more widespread and extensive. The power and size of the temple holdings, however, had expanded and their tax-exempt status remained essentially in effect. The period of imperial expansion intensified into Nubia, Palestine and Syria. The end result was a massive inflow of wealth to the state, which gave ever-increasing amounts to the temples and priesthood.

The Treasury Department, under the Vizier and an extensive host of officials, was busy. These administrators managed the numerous storehouses, granaries and stables of the state. The taxes they collected were in turn redistributed. This satisfied the state's obligations of wages, etc., due "in kind" produce.

The Pharaohs of the New Kingdom occupied lands in Nubia as far as the third through sixth cataracts. Here the Nubian goldfields were located. A Viceroy or "Prince of Kush and Overseer of the Southern Lands" was appointed to administer this region. J. A. Wilson's (1975) *The Culture of Ancient Egypt* explained that the Prince of Kush's domain extended from "El Kab in Upper Egypt to the Southern frontier of the Empire which, from the time of Thutmose III was located in the District of Karoy, in the region of Napata."

The Viceroy's functions were extensive. They included the exploitation of the mines, the encouragement of free flow of commerce and stamping out any forms of rebellion. From this area would be sent to the Treasury Department at Thebes, Wilson (1975) specifies, "gold, either in the form of dust packed in sacks or in the rings which were the nearest approach to coin known to the ancient Egyptians; various kinds of cattle; male and female slaves; and the ships laden with ivory, ebony, and every other beautiful product of the land in addition to the yield of the harvest."

A similar kind of duty was exacted of the lands to the north, Palestine and Syria. From Palestine came useful wood, the conifers, which were highly valued in an almost treeless Kemet/Egypt. Here they were used for "building and manufacture of large and small articles of furniture, chests, small dishes and the like." It was an impressive sight, Wilson (1975) discloses, when the "Chief of Retenu, and all the northern lands came from the ends of the earth, bowing in humility, bearing their tribute on their backs." Wilson continued that pictures of tribute bearing foreigners became a "favorite subject chosen for the wall paintings used in the decoration of their tombs by the dignitaries in charge of the reception of the tribute."

More importantly, however, was the tribute from Syria. From this region the payment included, Wilson (1975) denotes, "male and female slaves who were assigned to work in the construction of temples and public buildings or to labor in mines and quarries; horses and chariots; great herds of all kinds of cattle, sheep and goats." In addition, the tribute from the "north-land" of Syria included, "rarer animals such as elephants and bears; incense, oil, wine and honey; ivory and desirable metals, including gold, copper and lead; semi-precious stones, especially lapis lazuli and rock crystal."

The taxes also numbered "countless manufactured products of Syrian craftsmanship, including gold and silver and pitchers, some of which were remarkably executed in the form of animal heads."

Therefore, taxation was a tremendous source of revenue in ancient Kemet/Egypt. As such, a huge bureaucracy grew up around it. They were paid in kind. What is more important, however, is the effective administration of the system. Therefore, this began a

EGYPT ESSAYS ON ANCIENT KEMET

whole history of African administrative functions in major social systems and organizations of this and other societies. It is thus clear when given the opportunity Africans can administer large bureaucratic structures.

Egypt Essays Photo 125. Two bird images from the Sakkara area.

ROSETTA STONE

The "Rosetta Stone" was discovered by a French Officer of Engineers on the Rosetta Branch of the Nile River in July of 1799 (*Nile Year* 6039). During this time, the French Emperor Napoleon was at war in Europe with Britain and her allies. Napoleon lost a major battle at Waterloo. He then retreated to Egypt in Northeast Africa.

For many years prior, travelers spoke of the wonderful sites of ancient Kemetic/Egyptian culture in that timeless land, along the Nile. So, when Napoleon moved his army to "winter" in Egypt, he took a large contingent of savants or scholars to study the ancient culture. His scholars did numerous artistic, graphics and linguistic studies of the emerging ancient Kemetic culture. In addition,

FREDERICK MONDERSON

finding the Rosetta Stone was one of the biggest discoveries of the Eighteenth Century. This stone held the key to ancient Kemetic writing called *Medu Netcher* by the indigenes and hieroglyphics to the Greeks. After the treaty ending the Napoleonic Wars, the Rosetta Stone was given to the British and taken to London. It is now in the British Museum. There is a second such stone in the lobby of the Cairo Museum, Egypt; this, however, is a replica of the original!

In 1971 (*Nile Year* 6211), the Trustees of the British Museum published a book called the Rosetta Stone. In this work the Rosetta Stone is described as a "black basalt, 3 feet 9 inches in length, 2 feet 4 1/2 inches width, and 11 inches in thickness." It contained three languages with the same message. First, the *Medu Netcher*, from the earliest times was used for state and ceremonial documents. Jar sealing and inscriptions are other uses of this form. Hieratic, a cursive form of Hieroglyphics was used during the time of the Greeks. Then, there is Greek.

The third or Greek inscriptions were copied and sent to all universities in Europe after Napoleon's discoveries. Rev. Stephen Weston, who knew how to read ancient Greek, deciphered the text of the Greek part. Scholars who worked to decipher the ancient language of Kemet included Mr. Sylvester De Sacy and Mr. Akerblad, a Swedish diplomat. Other scholars in the giant effort included Mr. Thomas Young, Mr. W. J. Bankes and Jean Francois Champollion (1790-1832) or (*Nile Year* 6030-6072).

Mr. Champollion was a linguist who could read many languages including Coptic. The Copts of Egypt were some of the descendants of the people of ancient Kemet. Champollion used the structure of their language to crack the Code of Hieroglyphics.

EGYPT ESSAYS ON ANCIENT KEMET

Egypt Essays Illustration 68. Amenhotep IV, Khu-en-Aten, worshipping the solar disk along with his wife and kids.

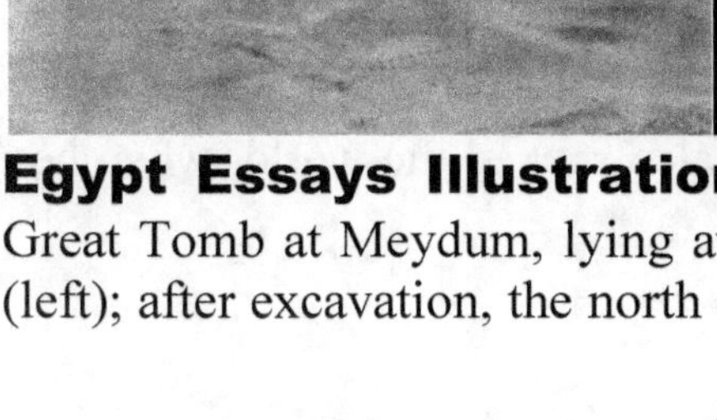

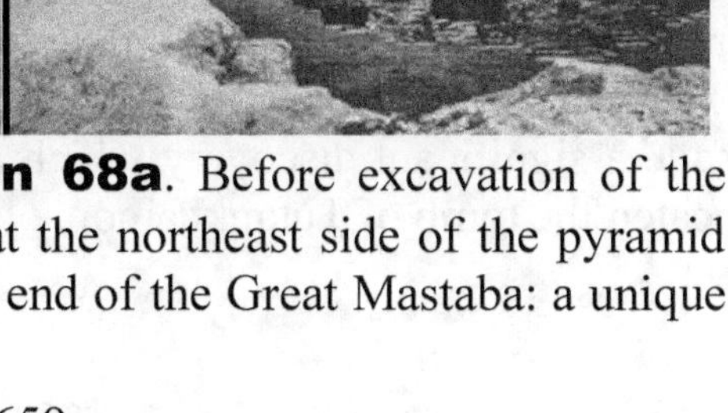

Egypt Essays Illustration 68a. Before excavation of the Great Tomb at Meydum, lying at the northeast side of the pyramid (left); after excavation, the north end of the Great Mastaba: a unique stepped type, showing the high brick retaining wall foreground, and rubble core beyond built in three stages (right).

First he realized there was an oval which the French called the "Cartouche." These Cartouche ovals were tied by sacred rope and contained royal names. Scholars observed in the Greek text, certain royal names were repeated many times. One Cartouche in the *Medu Netcher* repeated itself six times. In the Greek Text, the name Ptolemy repeated itself six times also. So, each *Medu Netcher* symbol was identified and compared with the symbol in Greek. Soon this worked. The same thing was done for Cleopatra. Through this method of comparative analysis and reconstruction the Code of the ancient language was finally deciphered by Champollion in 1822 (*Nile Year* 6062).

Accordingly, Kemetic priests in the inscription of the Rosetta Stone praised the Greek Pharaoh Ptolemy V, Epiphanes, King of all Kemet/Egypt. He was crowned in the eighth year of his reign. The event occurred on the fourth day of April in the ninth year of his reign. It mentions the king's titles, his love for the Gods, the People and Kemet. Next, it lists donations of money and corn he gave to the temples. He reduced some taxes and debts. He also released prisoners, and reduced fees and dues. Lastly, he repaired and rebuilt temples, ruined shrines, and sacred buildings.

Champollion died in 1832 (*Nile Year* 6072), ten years after he had broken the Code of *Medu Netcher* or Hieroglyphics. He had barely attained the age of forty-two years old. After his great discovery in 1822 (*Nile Year* 6062), he set about working a great deal. He wanted to read as many hieroglyphic tests as fast as he could, as fast as possible. This was designed to help later scholars. From the great labors of such scholars, the science of Egyptology was begun. Exactly 100 years later in 1922 (*Nile Year* 6162), Howard Carter made a significant discovery which also rocked the world, when he located the tomb of Tutankhamon.

EGYPT ESSAYS ON ANCIENT KEMET

For years, Carter worked for Lord Carnarvon, an English patron, exploring Egypt, the land of ancient Kemet, in Northeast Africa. Very early he realized that there was a young king named Tutankhamon who had reigned for some six years. When he was about to finally give up in his searches he made the most famous discovery. Tutankhamon was a "minor king of the XVIII Dynasty who got a major funeral," as Prof. John H. Clarke often said. The wealth of this burial highlighted the glory of ancient Kemet. Today, King Tut's tomb in the Valley of the Kings still contains his mummy. This royal cemetery is located at Thebes in Upper Egypt. So, the key to a glorious past was an inscribed rock called the Rosetta Stone, now captive in the British Museum.

The interesting thing about Tutankhamon is the distorted way he was and is presented to the general public. In the famous "Tut Mania" tour of the United States, during the 1970s, the classic representation of the boy king turned out to be an alabaster bust. This material is clear or white reinforcing the false view the king was white. From the earliest times, it seems, two such statues were placed before the burial chamber to accompany the dead into the afterlife. However, because tombs were not found intact, this is the only time such statues were found in situ, though from records about the Valley of the Kings, bits of broken wooden statues were found lying about but their significance was often overlooked. Talk about distortion of history!

Imagine the consternation in America, when young Black boys and girls - in churches, cornfields, on the streets and on farms across this nation - are confronted with this reality. Some with bootstraps and others without boots, and many who never got the opportunity to observe a young Black boy like themselves, who ruled that great African nation thousands of years ago. This was too much! Thus, the organizers of King Tut's tour of America choose the "white" alabaster model, as smoke and mirrors, as symbol of the monarch. All things done in secret come to light one day!

Now, his Black color is evident in the two statues placed to guard the burial chamber that are now in the Cairo Museum. This is

FREDERICK MONDERSON

important to know in order to counter the conspiracy. Second, this evidence is significant in establishing the dynastic link with Aahmes-Nefertari and her family. If we add the accepted Black statue of Mentuhotep of the eleventh dynasty, clearly the Black presence seems to run rather deep in this ancient African society. Third, manner and form of color representation seems also to play a significant role. When we juxtapose a case in Cairo Museum with this idea we see the need for further inquiry.

Egypt Essays Photo 126. Karnak Temple of Amon-Ra. From the north, view of a crane atop the Ninth Pylon on the North/South Axis; Hatshepsut (left) and her father Thutmose I's Obelisk (right); and ruins of the Hypostyle Hall further right.

For instance, a case in the Cairo Museum, Second Floor, portrays a panther with black skin akin to statues of powerful Eighteenth Dynasty monarchs as Amenhotep II and III. Wooden statues seem to be the only ones that properly portray the racial color of the ancient peoples of Kemet. Stone statues were most never painted. Invariably, when we see wooden statues, if they are painted it is generally black or a very dark brown. Rameses I and Rameses II in the British Museum, the already mentioned Tutankhamon statues,

EGYPT ESSAYS ON ANCIENT KEMET

Hesy Re, and those of Amenhotep II and III, among others, that we know about, have resisted wood decay. These artifacts are indeed important in the struggles for Egypt, the land of ancient Kemet.

NARMER

Some 5,000 years ago before our age, there was a great Pharaoh named Narmer, who was also known as Menes. In the *Medu Netcher* language Narmer's name is written as a fish and chisel. He was the first historical king who united the kingdoms of Upper Kemet and Lower Kemet. Before his unification Kemet/Egypt had cultural and economic growth and unending warfare. As monarch of the Upper Kingdom in the south, Narmer conquered the Lower Kingdom in the north, and established the United Kingdom of ancient Kemet/Egypt.

Narmer, a warrior king whose home was Thebes, situated his capital in the Nome of *Thinis* or *This*. *Thinis* is near Abydos in the south of Kemet. Abydos contains some of the oldest forts and also some of the most important early Pharaonic internments. It was the world's first Holy City of Pilgrimage, where the God Osiris was buried. As King of Upper Kemet/Egypt, Narmer chose a White Crown called the *Hed jet*. He recognized the lower Kemetic kingdom, whose symbol was the Red Crown, called the *Deshret*. To show that the two kingdoms were united he chose a Double Crown, called the *Sekhemti*, a combination of both the Red and White Crowns. When the two crowns were united into one Double Crown, it was known as the "Lady of Power" or the "Lady of Flame." For the next 3,000 years the Double Crown became the symbol of a unified Kemet.

We know of Narmer from the Narmer Palette, a commemorative ceremonial palette made of slate. It was found at the great temple of Hierakonpolis, in the Upper Kingdom. On one side he is shown wearing the White Crown. On the other side he is shown wearing the Red Crown. There is another document called the ceremonial "Narmer Macehead." This is an extremely important document on which the king depicted his capture of 120,000 men, 400,000 oxen and 1,420,000 goats.

The use of symbols in the first document helps us understand the conquest and unification of ancient Kemet/Egypt. The figures of the second document show signs, Petrie (1940: 24) wrote, denoting each decimal place, "completely fixed exactly as they were used during thousands of years afterwards." The figure of goats meant these Africans of Kemet had account keeping up to millions already developed by Narmer's time. Further, in mythology, the gods gave "millions and millions of years" of life which recognized the conception of these big numbers. This reinforced the view that their system of numeration was highly developed.

Since *Thinis*, near Abydos in the south, was far from the center of Kemet, problems of political control developed. So, Narmer changed the direction of the Nile River and built a "white wall." At this location he built the City of Memphis which was more centrally located for national administrative reasons. This city then became Narmer's administrative capital, at the start of dynastic rule. The move had political, economic, military, social and religious ramifications for the newly emerging united state on the Nile River.

Some scholars say Narmer chose the new center of power to check the autonomy of the Northern Kingdom. Others think it was an economic move aimed at Levantine trade. Even more, Narmer controlled the copper mines of Sinai. From there, he could encourage and safeguard trade with the Mediterranean area. He also sent expeditions to the eastern desert. At Memphis the king built a temple to the God Ptah. From here, he also introduced temple worship and the cult of the Apis Bull. Thus, Narmer is credited with introducing central government, kingship and secular and religious practices in ancient Kemet/Egypt. His conquest of the Lower Kingdom represented the first major descent of the Nile with a purposefully mobilized military force.

EGYPT ESSAYS ON ANCIENT KEMET

Egypt Essays Photo 126a. Karnak Temple of Amon-Ra. From the north, view of a crane atop the Ninth Pylon on the North/South Axis; Hatshepsut (left) and her father Thutmose I's Obelisk (right); and ruins of the Hypostyle Hall further right.

Egypt Essays Photo 127. Karnak Temple of Amon-Ra. The "Red Chapel" of Hatshepsut. A kneeling Hatshepsut offers a vessel to enthroned Amon-Ra (top left); and (top right) her image is defaced doing the same; while below she offers two plants to members of the enthroned Theban Ennead.

FREDERICK MONDERSON

Egypt Essays Photo 128. Karnak Temple of Amon-Ra. The "Red Chapel" of Hatshepsut. Whether kneeling or standing before the enthroned Ennead, Hatshepsut's image is erased.

Narmer was married to Queen Aahotep. They had a son named Hor-Aha who succeeded his father as King or Pharaoh of ancient Kemet. Narmer was buried at Abydos in tomb B-10; a small brick lined pit approximately 11 by 9.4 meters. On the other hand, his Queen Aahotep was interred at Neggadeh, also in the south of Kemet. Her son, Hor-Aha built the Queen's tomb, a remarkable structure measuring 53.4 by 26.7 meters. Clearly Narmer represents the link between prehistoric and dynastic Kemet. His choice of Abydos as a burial site set a precedent for the kings of the first and second dynasties. These early kings also built second tombs or cenotaphs at Memphis, as if to recognize and celebrate the dual nature of their power embodied in kingship of the state. In addition, the system of government, religious practices and religious beliefs introduced by him remained, essentially, in effect for much of dynastic rule.

It is generally believed that the Priesthood in ancient Kemet first introduced mathematics or counting. In the very remotest times there was a need to count wealth. Administrators surveyed the land

EGYPT ESSAYS ON ANCIENT KEMET

and collected taxes based on expected agricultural yield. This aspect of the society's economy made mathematics a necessity.

According to Petrie (1940: 24) in *Wisdom of the Egyptians*, this culture had "started in historic times with an excellent notation, purely decimal, for each place of unit up to millions." The *Book of the Dead* gives even higher figures. For the first set of the system, representation was not that difficult. Each sign is repeated as often as required up to nine. The unit was commonly made by a stroke, but in later times it was represented by a short piece of rope. The ten was a piece of rope, bent. A hundred was a circle of rope. For a thousand, the sign is the initial of khaa, a measuring cord. Thus, Petrie (1940: 24) makes clear, the "initial symbol of numbering was the length of rope. The finger used for 10,000 seems to be a phonetic rebus. The tadpole for 100,000 is the sign of multitudes. The man with hands raised for 1,000,000 is the sign of everlastingness or eternity."

Scholars came to an understanding of numbers from a discovery of a "row of totals" that were "found inscribed on a flake of flint of the Ist dynasty, in a tomb, along with stone palette for ink, with numbers 40, 320, 88, 60, 44, and three. Another existing set of numbers is on a flake of ostraka from Meydum, of the IIIrd dynasty." The only missing numbers in this set are one, five and however, the method of writing these existing numbers allow for representing the missing ones.

Fractions were used for food, especially those given to workmen. The following is a typical fraction problem. If half a dozen men have ten loaves to divide for the day's work, each receives a loaf, and then the remaining 4 loaves are halved, and each takes a half, and the remaining halves must be cut into six pieces, so each has 1 plus, 1/2, plus 1/6. This gives each worker 1 and 3/4 loaf.

The storage of grain from the Nile harvest was an issue from the very earliest times. Also, gauging as a form of building was used to make circular granaries. They used a disc of 9 diameters representing the area of a square of 8. This was based on 3.184 as

FREDERICK MONDERSON

approximating to Ti, or Pi. Another example was 22/7 or 3.1428 instead of 3.1416.

Measurement standards became regularized by the time of the pyramid builders of the Old Kingdom. The skill of leveling had progressed remarkably. Coordinates were used in the building of structures on slopes. The early pyramid builders visualized planes, and would put the sloping plane upon a wall, and also on an inclined wall. Then they would construct a sloping face anywhere in the same area between the two. Thus a building plan could be laid out truly over ground however uneven.

Egypt Essays Illustration 69. The Great North Wall of the Mastaba (here 56 ft. high): A view showing the depth of the foundations (left); and ancient leveling marks on the Mastaba: "6 cubits" – The level shown by a horizontal line.

EGYPT ESSAYS ON ANCIENT KEMET

22. Warfare

It was the army from the south that helped Narmer subdue the north to unify Kemet. That army helped to maintain the political structure begun in the Archaic Period. They helped support the evolved theocratic state throughout the Old Kingdom. At the end of this period, the wars of the First Intermediate Period, helped create the state of anarchy in the country. This lasted throughout the VII-X Dynasties.

The southern war machine under Intef and Mentuhotep reunited the country and formed the Middle Kingdom. It was their army that subdued, expanded and reinforced the reorganization and expansion of the Middle Kingdom. Amenemhat and Usertesen were other names of Middle Kingdom pharaohs who attacked Libya, held Sinai and extended Kemetic control beyond the First Cataract. J. A. Wilson's *The Culture of Ancient Egypt* supplies a description of this latter area where the dynastic rulers were constantly engaged militarily.

"The policed frontier of the Middle Kingdom lay at the Second Cataract, but Egyptian interests extended further to the south. The arable and hospitable territory between the Second and Third Cataracts is both narrow and inhospitable. South of the Third Cataract the Nile Valley widens out and affords greater possibility for cultivated fields and particularly for pasturelands. The Third Cataract itself is hazardous for navigation because of hidden rocks in the rapids."

Even further, Wilson (1975) discloses: "Nevertheless, that area is worth commercial cultivation. Just south of the Third Cataract and its dangerous rapids lies the modern town of Kerma, possessing a modest agricultural and trading importance and serving as the northern limit of the good land to the south. Under the Middle Kingdom Kerma was an outlying trading post and trans-shipment point for vessels and land caravans; Egypt maintained a resident colony there for commercial and political adventure, with a fortified trading post known as 'The Walls of Amen-em-het, the Justified.'"

These Middle Kingdom Pharaohs left a number of inscriptions at Aswan and regions to the south. James Henry Breasted's *Ancient Records of Egypt*, Vol I describes what was undoubtedly a military expedition against the Nubians of Wawat in lands to the south. He wrote: "The most important of Mentuhotep's monuments is the relief on the rocks at Shatt el-Regal, near Aswan, where, accompanied by his mother, a lady not of royal lineage, he receives the homage of his vassal, King Intef, who is ushered into the royal presence by Mentuhotep II's chief treasurer, Kheti, with the following inscription: 'year 41, under (the majesty of) Nibkhrure (Nb-hrw-r) came the wearer of the royal seal, sole companion, chief treasurer, Kheti, born of Sitre, triumphant; and sent to Wawat ....'"

Egypt Essays Photo 129. Karnak Temple of Amon-Ra. The "Red Chapel" of Hatshepsut. In this instance, while the Ennead's image has been destroyed, Hatshepsut's has escaped the destructor's hands and she presents two vessels and a "Table of Offerings."

EGYPT ESSAYS ON ANCIENT KEMET

Egypt Essays Photo 129a. Karnak Temple of Amon-Ra. The "Red Chapel" of Hatshepsut. With nutrients placed before the Gods of the Theban Ennead, Hatshepsut's image stands erased.

Again, according to Breasted, the Twelfth Dynasty King Amenemhet I, left the following inscription nearly half-way up to the second cataract "'Year 29, of the King of Upper and Lower Egypt, Sehetepibre (Ship-yb-r, Amenemhet I), living forever. We came to overthrow Wawat ....'"

This then, shows clearly that warfare seemed a principal preoccupation of the kings up to this time. Addressing this enterprise, in *Ancient Egypt*, Jon M. White believes that warfare had become a lucrative economic enterprise during the Middle and New Kingdoms. For, according to him, "... not only were successful officers rewarded with bounties, splendid ceremonial weapons and gold necklaces known as the 'Gold of Valor,' but they also received grants of land from the royal estates. When not on active service with their regiments they were given token posts in the service of the Pharaoh or the Nomarchs"

Further, White makes known, "during the Middle and New Kingdoms, the army was recruited at need from the Nomes, each of which raised a levy of between five hundred and a thousand militiamen for specific campaigns."

However, as the Middle Kingdom waned, it was anarchic warfare that resulted in the Second Intermediate Period. At this time, a more

FREDERICK MONDERSON

united force of Asiatics called Hyksos invaded Lower Kemet and established the XV and XVI Dynasties. This happening was concurrent with the XIII and XIV Dynasties that ruled Upper Kemet/Egypt. The XVII Dynasty began a protracted war of liberation that lasted for 50 years in the effort to expel the Hyksos. It has been argued, the only significant contribution that the Hyksos made to ancient Kemet was the introduction of a four-sided type of military fortification. They were also credited with introducing the horse into ancient Kemet and perhaps some musical instruments.

In the war of liberation to end the Second Intermediate Period, one of the principal combatants who fell was Sekenenra, whose mummy, in the Cairo Museum, shows he died from an axe wound to the head. His son Kamose whose brother Ahmose, expelled the Hyksos and founded the XVIII Dynasty and New Kingdom, carried on the war. It should be emphasized, the XVIIIth is actually a continuation of the XVIIth Dynasty, but because it represented an important period, a new dynasty is commenced, for convenience, really! Thutmose I continued the fight and overran Palestine.

Egypt Essays Illustration 70. Made to mislead tomb-robbers: A stairway in the west side of the Mastaba, leading down to a "blind" tunnel beneath it (left); and a Diagram of the Construction of the mastaba with the position of the "6 Cubits" level mark (in No. 5) indicated just above the words "stage" (right).

EGYPT ESSAYS ON ANCIENT KEMET

The significance of the Hyksos sojourn and their expulsion from Kemet was the transformation of the nation's military into an effective fighting machine. Here we see the forerunners of the modern great African and African-American strategists who have fought those terrific battles of military and civil engagement.

From Narmer, Zoser, Khufu, Khafra and the Middle Kingdom kings Menkaure and Intef and Mentuhotep, and Amenemhats and Usertesens, then the New Kingdom warrior Pharaohs, Sekenenra, Kamose, Ahmose, Tuthmose I, II, III, Amenhotep I, II, III, Rameses I, Seti I, Rameses II, and Rameses IV then Piankhy, Shabaka Shabataka and Taharka, we can chronicle a litany of great Africans, whose warlike prowess remained unmatched.

Interestingly, throughout history, these great African warriors are matched by others who have taken the field as formidable military and civilian commanders in defense of Africa and its progeny. Hamilcar, Hasdrubal and Hannibal Barca of Carthage in North Africa, and the Kings of Ghana, Mali and Songhay, Mansa Musa, Sundiata Keita, Sunni Ali and Askia Mohammed achieved remarkable historical stature. During the European Slave Trade in Africans, Equiano and Amistad, and the African statesmen and generals of the Nineteenth Century, Shaka, Samori, Ceteyayo, Behanzin, Yohannes IV and Menelik II, Fredrick Douglas and Edward Wilmot Blyden, Sojourner Truth and Harriet Tubman are notable. In the Twentieth Century, Booker T. Washington, W. E. B. Du Bois, Marcus Moziah Garvey, Kwame Nkrumah, Sekou Toure, Patrice Lumumba, Julius Nyerere, Haile Selaisse, George Padmore, C.L.R. James, Caseley Hayford, Albert Luthuli, Roy Wilkins, A. Philip Randolph, Mary McCloud Bethune, Lorraine Hansberry, Sonny Carson, Conrad Worrill and Jitu Weusi, have all been tested in the many great civil engagements to defend the people and the land. They were all warrior kings and statesmen and states-women who left indelible impressions on the historic Kemetic and world landscape. Many were born into warfare, while others had warfare civil and military, thrust upon them as the unfolding reality and glory of Kemet's place and the role of Africa and its sons, and daughters actively engaged in ancient and modern history dynamics.

Egypt Essays Photo 130. Karnak Temple of Amon-Ra. The "Red Chapel" of Hatshepsut. To the left, Hatshepsut (Cartouche *Ma'at-Ka-Ra* above) offers two plants to Amon-Ra, while to the right; the now defaced Queen offers flowers to Min version of Amon.

Egypt Essays Photo 130a. Karnak Temple of Amon-Ra. The "Red Chapel" of Hatshepsut. While the Queen offers food with both hands to Min as Amon-Ra (left); she offers flowers with one hand (right) to Min balancing, not holding, the flagellum.

EGYPT ESSAYS ON ANCIENT KEMET

In the New Kingdom, following the war of liberation to expel the Hyksos, the chariot as a war machine came into being. It gave the Egyptian/Kemetic military personnel great mobility and striking speed. This terrorized their adversaries, especially the Syrians who fought two major conflicts with Tuthmose III at Megiddo and later against Rameses II at Kadesh.

Throughout ancient Kemetic architectural landscape, a number of battle scenes are represented on the monuments to attest to Pharaoh's exploits. Such places as the Ramesseum, Medinet Habu, Luxor, Karnak, Beit el Wali, Derr and Abu Simbel, are replete with descriptions of the various wars of the kings.

The Ramesseum or Mortuary Temple of Rameses II was erroneously called the Memnonium and the tomb of Osymandyas, of Greek Fame. Nevertheless, for architectural symmetry and sculptural elegance, the Ramesseum matches any other Kemetic monument. The sculptures are much more interesting than the architectural details but they have suffered over time.

On the north face of the eastern pyramidal tower or propylon is represented the capture of several towns from an Asiatic enemy, called in the hieroglyphic the Khetas, now known as the Hittites, whose chiefs are led away by the victorious people of Kemet/Egypt towards their camp. Several of their towns are introduced into the picture, each bearing its name in hieroglyphic or *Medu Netcher* characters, which state them to have been taken in the fourth year of King Rameses II.

Diodorus Siculus mentioned the ruins of Medinet Habu along with three others at Karnak, Luxor and Ramesseum. Strabo also mentions Thebes' "many temples, the greater part of which Cambyses defaced." The early Christians also did much to deface the monuments of ancient Kemet/Egypt and some of this is evident today.

FREDERICK MONDERSON

On the walls of the Great Temple and Palace of Rameses III at Medinet Habu, many scenes depict that monarch's battles with the Mediterranean enemy. On the front walls the king smites his suppliant captives in the presence of Amen-Ra, who, on the N. E. side appears under the form of Ra, the Physical Sun, with the head of a hawk. An ornamental border, representing "the chiefs" of the vanquished nations, Europeans, Asiatic and African, extends along the base of the whole front; and on either side of the oblong court or passage of the center Rameses offers similar prisoners to the deity of the temple who says: "Go, my cherished and chosen, make war on foreign nations, besiege their forts, and carry off their people to live as captives."

Egypt Essays Illustration 71. Another part of the structure designed to mislead tomb-robbers: The mouth of the "Blind" tunnel (left); and originally walled and roofed: A chapel or offering niche, on the east side of the Mastaba (right).

EGYPT ESSAYS ON ANCIENT KEMET

23. EGYPTIAN MEDICINE AND THE SCIENCES

The people and culture of ancient Kemet reached a high level of medical know-how. They were well ahead of their time in examination, treatment, and prescription of remedies for many illnesses. To treat the sick they used magic and made medicine from plants and minerals. These advances required knowledge of the science of physiology, botany, zoology and mineralogy.

Manetho was an Egyptian priest of the third century Before Christ. During this time the Greek or Ptolemaic Dynasty ruled the land. He wrote a *History of Egypt* from the earliest times, when Gods ruled that ancient African country. Manetho grouped the kings into dynasties and began the chronology we use today. Though he made some mistakes in his method, he classed the dynasties into periods. These were I-X, XI-XX, and XXI-XXX Dynasties. Modern scholars created the terms Archaic, Old Kingdom, First Intermediate Period, Middle Kingdom, Second Intermediate Period, New Kingdom, Third Intermediate and Late Period. These scholars, however, finding Manetho's divisions and groupings of the dynasties convenient and he "trustworthy," have retained them.

Egypt Essays Photo 131. Karnak Temple of Amon-Ra. The "Red Chapel" of Hatshepsut. The ark at rest with victuals and unguents nearby.

FREDERICK MONDERSON

Egypt Essays Photo 131a. Karnak Temple of Amon-Ra. The "Red Chapel" of Hatshepsut. Symbols - "Life, Stability, Dominion."

Importantly, according to that author, Athothis, who was the son of Narmer of the First Dynasty, practiced medicine. However, no known records have survived to support this claim. The implications stemming from such a belief are that the art of medicine had become highly developed in the millennium of the pre-dynastic Badarian, Amratian and Gerzean or Naqada cultural developments. This meant there was an accumulation of medical lore and practice going back possibly thousands of years. One modern writer believes the practice of medical cure may go back beyond ten thousand years, making us believe that herbal remedies were probably very old.

A little later after Athotis, the first physician whose name is recorded in history appeared. This meant the first medical person to stand out from the past with any form of distinction was Imhotep who lived about 2800 B.C. He knew the sciences of astronomy and mathematics. He was the world's first multi-genius and Chief Physician of King Zoser. This great Egyptian African intellectual lived during the Third Dynasty, at the start of the Old Kingdom. His greatest deeds were in the fields of architecture, government and medicine. Imhotep built the Step-Pyramid at Sakkara for King Zoser. Such an architectural accomplishment attests to the level of technology reached at this early age. His most lasting works,

EGYPT ESSAYS ON ANCIENT KEMET

however, were in the fields of medicine, magic and as a sage or wise man.

As a wise man, his ideas were taught from generation to generation. He was described as a "master of poetry" and "patron of the scribes." Imhotep is credited with the philosophy of the ages, which is, "Eat, drink and be merry, for tomorrow we die." The *Westcar Papyrus* provides some of his magical feats. However, the *Ebers*, *Oxyrchynchus* and *Edwin Smith Surgical Papyri* mention his advances in medicine and cures for many illnesses. Temples were built to worship him and one survives in the Dromos before the Great Pylon to the Temple of Isis of Philae, now Agilka Island.

Books were written about him and this helped his profession by generating systematic study of medicine. A cult grew up around his name and work as a doctor and this encouraged the study, teaching and practice of medicine. Steindorff and Seele's *When Egypt Ruled the East*, mentions eight more or less medical works.

Imhotep made great contributions to the gentle art of healing. The people of ancient Kemet/Egypt regarded him as a demi-god and the Greeks identified him their God of Medicine, Aesculapius, mentioned in the Hippocratic Oath.

This elevation to divinity to reserved only for special persons. In fact, Petrie (1932: 104-05) has shown that this deification of humans was indeed a rare occurrence. For that matter, he wrote: "The Egyptians denied the deification of other than kings, as Herodotus reports 'that in 11,340 years no god had on the form of a man.' This number is connected with 341 generations, at three in a century, from the first king to Sety priest of Ptah in the time of Sennacherib, 701 B.C."

There were, however, sages like the Greek heroes, who almost reached deification. Imhotep, the wise physician of Memphis, seems by the veneration paid to him, to have been canonized, and statuettes of him are often found.

FREDERICK MONDERSON

Egypt Essays Illustration 72. Beautiful Queen Hatshepsut dressed as a man in head-dress and kilt, but with a distinctly female face (left); as it appeared before restoration, the beautiful marble statue of Hatshepsut, with the head and other fragments found and rejoined to the seated body from Berlin (right). Notice the statue on the left has both hands while the right one has the hands missing.

Another individual who had achieved this high distinction, according to Petrie (1932: 105) was Amenhotep, Son of Hapu, who "was a great architect and administrator under Amenhotep III; he had two seated figures placed in the temple of Karnak. In inscriptions on these, people were told to come to him as an intercessor before Amen. There was a shrine to him and Imhotep, where he is said to be a deity, and the son of the Apis bull and Hathor. Manetho states that 'Amenhotep, son of Paapis, was one

EGYPT ESSAYS ON ANCIENT KEMET

that seemed to partake of divine nature, both as to wisdom and the knowledge of future things.'"

From the earliest times, temples were built to him at such places as Thebes, Philae, Edfu, and in Nubia. The people of ancient Kemet/Egypt deified Imhotep for his medical skills, and also because he was one of them who became a god. Since the gods were so remote, the locals were glad to identify with someone they had experienced. They had seen the mighty stone structure at Sakkara he constructed for King Zoser. This step-pyramid laid the foundation for building the pyramids and other forms of construction in the Old, Middle, and New Kingdoms that stood as legacy to the Greco-Roman Periods. Standing majestically and permanently at the beginning of Egyptian architecture, his work initiated many decorative features that became standard in later building practice.

Egypt Essays Photo 132. Karnak Temple of Amon-Ra. The "Red Chapel" of Hatshepsut. While Mut in Red Crown embraces Hatshepsut, image of Hatshepsut, having escaped the destroyer, presents two plants to enthroned Amon-Ra.

FREDERICK MONDERSON

Egypt Essays Photo 132a. Karnak Temple of Amon-Ra. The "Red Chapel" of Hatshepsut. Saluting and looking back at Amon, Min, and Amon again.

Technologically speaking, Imhotep is at the foundation of what A. Rupert Hall and Marie Boas Hall treats in the work *A Brief History of Science.* They wrote that: "a surplus of labor, combined with an exceptionally complex cult of the dead, created the elaborate tombs and monuments familiar to us as pyramids and obelisks. The colossal size and careful workmanship of these great structures suggest to the modern eye a complex technology."

Even further, Hall and Hall point out, these ancients, built "with wedges and stone hammers to split the rock, sledges and ropes to drag the stones to the building sites, ramps from one level to another up which successive courses were hauled, levers to propel the stone into place, and water used to check when all was level. The Egyptians had no wheels or pulleys in the Pyramid Age (from 2700 to 200 B.C.), and the secret of their success was unlimited manpower, patience and a strong artistic sense."

"One of these old treatises deals not with human diseases but with veterinary medicine. Of the remaining seven, four are of diverse nature, containing a mixture of purely medical material and a number of prescriptions or recipes for home uses, that is, cosmetic suggestions such as methods for dying grey hair, and formulas of a magical character."

EGYPT ESSAYS ON ANCIENT KEMET

Likewise, Steindorff and Seele (1957) confirm, "three of the papyri, however are thoroughly homogeneous. One is a treatise on gynecological disorders; another, of which fragments only are preserved, deals with conception, sterility, and the sex of the unborn child; the third is concerned with surgery."

The level of medical practice reached by the Egyptians was higher than that of their neighbors in their time and place. Since the Kemetic doctors were so skilled and specialized; to be treated by one, psychologically and physically, helped the patient to recover even quicker. These doctors also treated kings and queens of other lands. Kemetic medical men were exceptional and such famous rulers as Cyrus and Darius of Persia sought these excellent physicians and their services. Petros de Baz (1975: 21) reveals, "Egypt was regarded as the medical center of the ancient world." Newsome (1983: 128) has written of these ancient medical specialists of Kemet: "(1) They produced the world's first physicians who for millennia enjoyed the reputation of being the most skilled in the world. (2) They produced the world's first medical knowledge and literature. (3) They influenced and contributed to Hippocrates, the Hippocratic tradition and the development of medicine in ancient Greece."

As early as the Old Kingdom, these African priests controlled the practice of medicine. They were general doctors but many specialized on different parts of the body. Herodotus tells us of their specialization. "One ministered to the eye, another to the chest, another to the limbs. None trespassed on the anatomy of the other." Overtime, they treated more than 250 diseases. Rogers' *World's Great Men of Color* Vol. I. (1972: 39) mentions diseases treated by these physicians including 15 of the "abdomen, 11 of the bladder, 10 of the rectum, 29 of the eyes, and 18 of the skin." Their early medical men knew how to tell a disease by the "shape, color or condition of the visible parts of the body." Looking at the skin, hair, nails, and tongue, showed how well a person was. They also treated illnesses, Rogers (1972: 39) points to such as "spinal tuberculosis, gall-stones, appendicitis, gout, arthritis, and dental caries." They

FREDERICK MONDERSON

treated body aches, various fevers, coughing, broken bones, cuts and other types of ailments.

Kemetic/Egyptian doctors performed surgery, listened to the heart, and thought it the seat of all things. Imhotep it is said knew of the circulation of the blood 4,000 years before it was known in Europe. Further, these medical men were familiar with the positions and functions of the stomach, lungs, and other vital organs. They knew the significance of hygiene in the recovery of illnesses. The brain's usefulness, however, was not fully understood. It was easily set aside during the mummification process. Some arguments are made about prehistoric mummification of the brain. Since these Nile Valley Africans believed in an afterlife, preserving the body became a highly developed art. In this practice, their skilled practitioners came to know much about anatomy and physiology when preparing a corpse for the burial and afterlife.

Frederick Newsome's (1983: 127) essay: "Contributions to the Early History of Western Medicine" in *Blacks in Science: Ancient and Modern*, edited by Ivan Van Sertima, begins with the statement: "During several millennia, blacks in ancient Egypt made numerous contributions to medicine and were acknowledged as the inventors of the art of medicine .... They contributed to the development of medicine in ancient Greece. Ancient writers, including Herodotus, Isocrates, and Diodorus, affirm this. Modern presentations of ancient medicine, however, deprive blacks of the knowledge of their early contributions to medicine by ignoring or subtly misrepresenting the black identity of the ancient Egyptians."

The language, *Medu Netcher* or hieroglyphics contain ample evidence of the use of anatomical parts to represent signs and symbols. In this regard, Newsome (1983: 128) makes known: "Many of the signs which represent consonants, vowels, things, and concepts are well-reproduced animals and parts of anatomy. Graphical reproduction of anatomical parts requires knowledge of anatomy. This is also true of sculpture and embalming which, as is well known, they also practiced. Anatomical parts for which there were signs include: the pupil of the eye, the cornea, the heart, the

EGYPT ESSAYS ON ANCIENT KEMET

trachea, the lungs, the vertebral column, the long bones, the brain, the meminges, the spinal cord, the ribs, the intestines, the spleen, the male and female genitals, the uterus, and, possibly, the kidney."

To treat a wide variety of ailments, these medical experts used herbal remedies and made medicine from plants and minerals. Some hold the view ancient African medicine was tied to holistic practices. This became the basis of their long-standing intelligent application of inquiry and practice that produced such success. While it is believed this build-up of medical know-how may be more than 10,000 years in the making, who knows when early man first began tending to wounds and remembered cures that worked and had willing students to pass along such knowledge.

An extensive list of herbal or vegetable medicine is often listed in Kemetic pharmacopoeia. Dr. Finch's (1983: 146) essay, "The African Background of Medical Science" in *Blacks in Science* contained the view: "Like all African peoples, the Egyptians had a large *Matura medica*, using as many as 1000 animal, plant, and mineral products in the treatment of illness. Night blindness, caused by vitamin A deficiency, was treated with ox livers, known to be rich in vitamin A. Poppy extract - the source of opium-was used to treat colicky babies. Modern physicians use paregoric - whose active ingredient is opium - for exactly the same purpose. Patients with scurvy - caused by vitamin C deficiency - were fed onions, a known source of vitamin C. Castor seeds, the source of castor oil, were used to make cathartic preparations. Mandrake and herbane, sources of belladonna alkaloids, were also known and used. The belladonnas possess properties that stimulate the heart, decrease the stomach motility, dilate the pupils and cause sedation. The Egyptians dispensed their prescriptions as pills, enemas, suppositories, infusion, and elixirs in accurate, standardized doses, causing some to wonder if they had separate pharmacies and pharmacists."

FREDERICK MONDERSON

Egypt Essays Photo 133a. Memphis Museum. The Memphis colossal lying in the prone position.

J. B. Hurry's (1987: 80) *Imhotep: The Egyptian God of Medicine* also mentions "castor oil, aloes, coriander, caraway, gentian, and turpentine ...." Petros de Baz (1975: 21) believes, it "appears that as early as 6,000 B.C. meadow Saffron was given internally. (This was rediscovered by an Austrian physician, Von Stork, in the 18th century under the name of Colchie.)" The record also mentions myrrh, juniper, fennel, herbane, linseed, and peppermint. Hurry (1987: 80) further includes such minerals as "lime, soda, salts of lead, iron, sulphate of copper, and magnesia" as some of the ingredients of their medicine. Other cures they used came from certain animal bodies including fats and blood from the ox, lion and hippopotamus."

The *Ebers Papyrus* mentions remedies, Hurry (1987: 81) discloses including, "sedatives, hypnotic, expectorants, tonics, astringents, purgatives, diuretics, disinfectants and antibodies." Lucas (1989: 271-326) has supplied an extensive chapter on "Mummification" in which a number of mineralogical, botanical and zoological materials were used medicinally and their inclusion here is appropriate. The author speaks of lime, salt, natron and the manner, in which it is used, as well as alum, beeswax, bitumen, cassia, cinnamon, cedar oil, cedri succus, cedrium, henna, honey, juniper berries, and various ointments. Onions, palm wine, resins - glue, gum, and miscellaneous, sawdust, spices, wood pitch and wood tar, are some of their liquids.

In the next chapter entitled "Oils, Fats and Waxes" Lucas (1989: 330) further mentions almond oil and various animal fats. These are contained in the statement. "Since the ancient Egyptians kept cows, sheep and goats, it is only natural that they should have been acquainted with the fats of these animals, including milk fat, and many different fats are mentioned in the texts, notably ox fat, goose fat, and white fat, and also, according to Breasted, 'butter.'" Lucas (1989: 330-31) further reveals: "An ointment for making the hair grow mentioned in the *Hearst papyrus* was made of gazelle fat, serpent fat, crocodile fat and hippopotamus fat, and in the *Ebers papyrus*, a remedy for the same purpose consisted of the mixed fats of the lion, hippopotamus, crocodile, cat, serpent and antelope. Goose fat was an ingredient in many remedies, and the fat or oil of a variety of other animals is also prescribed."

Belanos oil, ben oil, castor oil, colocynth oil, lettuce oil, linseed oil and malabathrum oil were imported from India. They were made from the leaves of cinnamon, as well as olive oil, radish oil, safflower oil, and sesame oil representing a wide repertoire of healing agents that could be called to provide soothing treatment. The uses, for which these oils were put, coupled with the herbal and mineralogical elements of the pharmacopoeia of the ancient Kemetic people, attest to their high attainments in care and preservation of the body. Lucas (1989: 336) provides some uses for these substances in his statement. "Oils and fats were employed in ancient Egypt for eating, cooking and illumination; for anointing both the living and the dead; for libations; as a base for perfumes; as medicines and vehicles for medicines and doubtless for many other purposes."

In summary, the ancient Africans of the Nile Valley, those of Kemet particularly, made great gains in medicine and treatment of their

FREDERICK MONDERSON

patients. Whether in the "houses of life" for royal and civil/public healing, and for treatment of armies on the move, the art of medicine was well done thousands of years ago. Many of these ideas never reached Europe until much later. Imhotep was therefore the first physician to stand out from the mist of history with more than a measure of success. Robert A. Armour's *Gods and Myths of Ancient Egypt* (1987: 135) described him as, the "god who sent sleep to those in great pain and suffering. He was believed to treat men's illnesses while they were alive, and help prepare their bodies for eternal life after their death."

Later the Greeks deification of this African personality seemed a very good idea. He was a part of the Triad of Memphis that included Ptah, Sekhmet and Imhotep. Armour (1987: 135) again tells of the small inscription over the door at Philae from the reign of Ptolemy V. In this, Imhotep is called the "great one, son of Ptah, the creative god, made by Thenen, begotten by him and beloved by him, the god of divine forms in the temples, who gives life to all men, the mighty one of wonders, and maker of times, who comes unto him that calls upon him wheresoever he may be, who gives sons to the childless, the wisest and most learned one, the image and likeness of Thoth the wise."

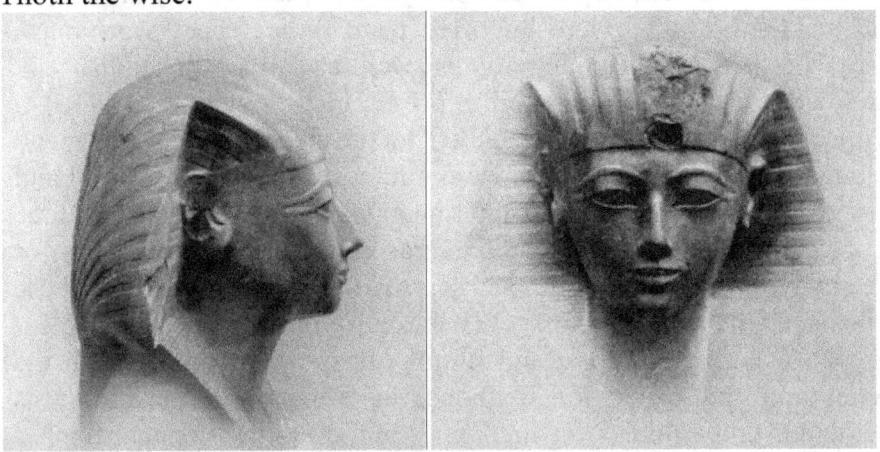

Egypt Essays Illustration 73. Profile of Queen Hatshepsut without her beard (left); and full face view of the Queen. Notice her nose is not broken. As in other frames where the body is broken.

EGYPT ESSAYS ON ANCIENT KEMET

In addition, Newsome (1983: 134) adds: "Many of the well-known Greek philosophers and scientists went to Egypt to be educated and transported their acquired knowledge upon returning to Greece. These include Thales (600 B.C.), Solon (575 B.C.), Pythagoras (550 B.C.), (Plato 375 B.C.), Eudoxus of Cnidus (360 B.C.) and others. This we are told by Isocrates (400 B.C.), Diodorus Siculus (50 B.C.), Strabo (20 A.D), Josephus (75 A.D.), Plutarch (100 A.D.), Diogenes (200 A.D.), and Iamblichus (300 A.D.)."

Newsome (1983: 134) has added further, indicating: "James, ben-Jochannan, and Christian give complete, modern treatments of the Egyptian influence on Greek philosophers. With the exception of Eudoxus, who was a physician, as well as a mathematician and astronomer, these sources are more informative about the travels and education of Greek philosophers than physicians. One of these philosophers, Pythagoras, played a major role in early Greek medicine.... It is reasonable to assume that many Greek physicians as well as philosophers studied in Egypt. Galleon, who himself studied in Egypt, supports this assumption."

Today, young African-American students especially should try to become doctors. When they are certified they will take the "Hippocratic Oath." It is named after the "Father of Medicine" Hippocrates, who practiced medicine 2300 years after Imhotep. They should know, however, that the God *Aesculapius*, praised in the oath is really Imhotep, an ancestor, from the land of ancient Kemet, today's Egypt, in Northeast Africa. They should know also Imhotep's wisdom was indeed a renowned part of his gifts to his African race. Rogers (1972: 39) gives his title from the inscription at Philae, "Chancellor of the King of Lower Egypt; Chief under the King of Upper Egypt; Administrator of the Great Mansion; Hereditary Noble, Heliopolitan High Priest, Imhotep."

While he is credited with the best-known saying "Eat, drink and be merry for tomorrow we shall die," the literature also contained surviving fragments of his wisdom. Morris Bierbrier's (1989: 81) *The Tomb Builders of the Pharaohs* mention texts at Deir el Medina

FREDERICK MONDERSON

in which Imhotep's wisdom is coupled with other great ones from ancient Kemet, whose "wisdom texts were admired and remembered through the ages." Accordingly, the inscription read: "Is there one here like Hordjedef? Is there another like Imhotep? There have been none among our kindred like Neferti and Khety, that chief among them. I recall to you the names of Ptahemdjedhuty and Khakheperreseneb. Is there another like Ptahhotep or like Kaires?"

Frederick Newsome (1983: 129) mentions another inscription to the deified Imhotep, which read, "Turn thy face toward me, my lord Imhotep, son of Ptah. It is thou who dost work miracles and who are beneficent in all thy deeds."

In addition, I agree, the African American youth should be taught about all the great philosophers of ancient times, including Socrates, Plato, Aristotle, Pythagoras, etc., but they must also be taught about these mentioned African great men.

Egypt Essays Illustration 74. A clothes-basket belonging to Queen Meryet-Amun, sister and wife of Amenhotep II and daughter of Thutmose III (left); and a little basket of Queen Meryet-Amun decorated with ostriches, some 3500 years old (right).

EGYPT ESSAYS ON ANCIENT KEMET

Navigation is another science these people of the Nile mastered very early. Because of the role of the Nile River in their lives, boat building developed as an industry, early in the pre-dynastic, for we see them on pottery even before Amratian or Naqada I Period.

The simplest boats were made of papyrus stalks lashed together and used by the poorest native. In *Atlas of Ancient Egypt* Baines and Malek (1980) provide some interesting insights regarding methods of dating the earliest boats. Here they disclose evidence of dating provided by: "(1) appearance of the hull, (2) the method of steering, (3) the type of the mast and sail, (4) the vessel's paddles and oars, (5) the disposition of the deckhouses, and (6) unusual features."

In the pre-dynastic period boats were features on early pottery from such sources as the painted tomb at Hierakonpolis. It is interesting that in the earliest theological and theosophical conceptions of such centers as Heliopolis where Ra and Atum were worshiped, the sun god had the most primitive of boats to ride the skies. Later, as the culture matured, the sun bark became more sophisticated, bespeaking the religious and artistic evolution. In modern parlance, the Sun god Ra first rode the skies in a "Model T Ford" and later in a "Cadillac with the Norstar System!"

Other methods of identifying boats from the pre-dynastic period supplied by Baines and Malek (1980) included: "(1) sometimes, though not always, sharply upturned prow and stern (even large Nile craft were made mostly of papyrus or similar material); (2) one or more large steering oars; (3) rectangular sail; (4) and (5) paddles in two groups (uninterrupted by central deckhouse); (6) prow decoration of tree branches (?); standard close to deckhouse."

During the Old Kingdom there were some improvements in ship design. Baines and Malek (1980) again state, such vessels could be identified through the following: "(1) 'classical' Egyptian hull shape (wood now the main building material), often with animal-head

FREDERICK MONDERSON

prow; (2) several large steering gear; (3) usually bi-pod mast, probably trapezoidal sail, usually more tall than wide; (4) from 5th Dynasty oars."

In the Middle Kingdom, there were further improvements of ship building where we see, Baines and Malek (1980) state briefly: "(1) higher stern; (2) steering gear operated by a helmsman standing between the massive rudder post and the usually single large rudder oar; (3) single mast, lowered and supported on a formed stanchion when sailing downstream; (5) deckhouse forward of the rudder post."

Egypt Essays Photo 134. Memphis Museum. The statue of Rameses II, again in the prone position, from the left side.

EGYPT ESSAYS ON ANCIENT KEMET

Egypt Essays Photo 135 Memphis Museum. An offering table with the depression for blood to run out.

By the time of the extensive river traffic of the Imperial New Kingdom, we see additional innovations in ship construction. Here Baines and Malek (1980) confirms in the New Kingdom there were: "(1) large range of specialized types; (2) steering gear with usually two rudder oars, operated by a helmsman standing in front of the rudder post; (3) sail more wide than tall; (5) castles forward and aft, with centrally placed deckhouse."

By the end of the New Kingdom and into the Late Period, there was a tendency towards a higher stern. Nevertheless, while the Nile River and surrounding Mediterranean and Red Seas were plied for everything from trade, war, funerals, fishing, transportation, festivals, etc., there was also some evidence of Atlantic Ocean voyages.

In the *Histories*, Herodotus mentions the Pharaoh Necho, around 600 B.C., sent Phoenician sailors, on a three-year voyage to circumnavigate Africa. Much more important, some years ago, in a letter

FREDERICK MONDERSON

written to the *Journal of African Civilizations* by the late Dr. Cheikh Anta Diop. He was one of few and the only Black African scholar, permitted to be in the room in Paris where specialists examined and repaired the mummy of Pharaoh Rameses II to stem its deteriorating state. Dr. Diop mentions residues of "New World" tobacco found in the intestines of the mummy. Based on this he posited the view that the Pharaoh Rameses II may have sent expeditions by ship, to the "New World" and they brought back smoking tobacco. This revelation is significant for the science of navigation in the fourteenth century Before the Christian era.

SCIENCE

Science developed in ancient Kemet without the regular designation of this discipline being fully applied. John Pappademos' (1983: 177-78) work "An Outline of Africa's Role in the History of Physics" depicts how textbooks distort this aspect of science. He tells, "We have made a survey of 17 textbooks of physics and physical science issued since 1970 by leading U.S. publishing houses. The texts were distributed among both calculus and non-calculus types as well as some introductory physical science and or astronomy texts (since, courses in physical science and astronomy are frequently taught in physics departments). Both college-level and high school-level books were examined. The texts were selected at random for the requirement that they be published since 1970 (in order that they would be likely to be in current use)."

He comes to the conclusion based on his survey, "currently used U.S. physics and physical science texts do indeed tend to reinforce racial stereotypes." Pappademos (1983: 178) has argued: "No black scientist is pictured in any of the books, nor is a single black scientist credited with any contribution. The picture of science in general and physics in particular that emerges from these books without exception is that the cradle of physics was in Europe and that it owes its present development entirely to the scientists of the U.S. and Europe (rarely other than white males)."

EGYPT ESSAYS ON ANCIENT KEMET

This led that author (1983: 179) to conclude, "... from the above results of the survey that by neglecting the contribution of non-whites (particularly blacks) the 17 texts belittle their contributions and effectively promote the view that the progress of physics owes little or nothing to the intellectual ability and labor of other than whites."

John Henrik Clarke (1979: 82) in his "African-Americans in Science and Invention: A Bibliographic Guide" mentions the important contributions of African people to science and invention by quoting John M. Weatherwax in *The African Contribution.* The latter author held that: "Early Africans made hooks to catch fish, spears to hunt with, stone knives to cut with, the bolo with which to catch birds and animals, the blowgun, the hammer, the stone axe, canoes and paddles, bags and buckets, poles for carrying things, bows and arrows. This was a period in the early history of mankind called the Old Stone Age. African inventions were already the start of man's use of power. Africans gave mankind the first machine. It was the fire stick. Knives and hammers and axes were the first tools. It is the making of tools that sets man apart from and in a sense above all living creatures. Africans started mankind along the tool-making path. From the blowgun of ancient Africa, there followed, in later ages, many devices based on the same principle. Some of those are: the bellows, bamboo air pumps, the rifle, the pistol, the revolver, the automatic, the machine gun - and even those industrial guns that puff grains. African hunters many times cut up game. There still exist, from the Old Stone Age, drawings of animal bones, hearts and other organs. These early drawings are a part of man's early beginnings in the field of anatomy."

FREDERICK MONDERSON

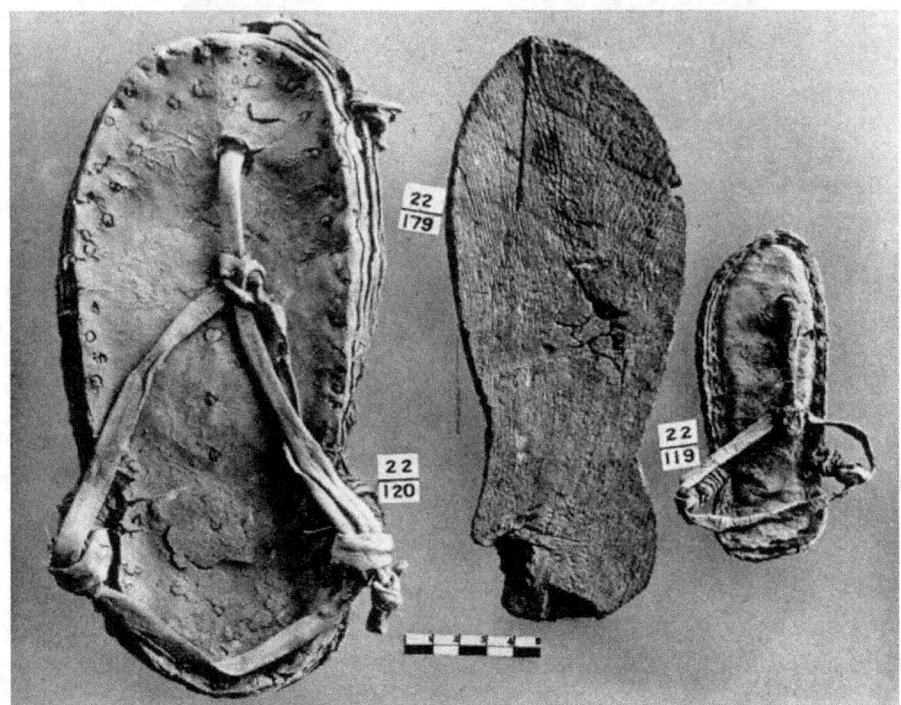

Egypt Essays Illustration 75. Sandal footwear, 3000 years old, a man, child's and wooden pattern used for cutting out soles in the center.

In *Wisdom of the Egyptians*, Flinders Petrie (1940: 8-22) mentions 10 elements of observational astronomy in the development of this Nile Valley culture, of ancient Kemet. These advances in science were the *Observed Year, 360-day Year, 365-Day Year, 365 1/4 Day Year, Lunar Year, Four Kalendars, Precession, Hieroglyphs of Seasons, Cycle Periods*, and *Early Festivals*.

The *Observed Year* marks man's earliest attempts to view time in a circular manner with a set number of days forming the cycle. It is aided by establishing a definite position of the sun at rising and setting, then using some annual phenomenon as a gauge to test it. In this case, it was the annual behavior of the Nile River.

The *360-Day Year* started from the convenience of twelve months of 3 times 10 days each. Elsewhere we are told, in the night sky of

EGYPT ESSAYS ON ANCIENT KEMET

ancient Kemet/Egypt, a group or constellation of stars appeared every 10 days. These were called decans. In the course of one year, 36 decans appeared. Since 10 times 36 equals 360, here is associated the fundamental notion of 360 degrees of a circle that so helped to revolutionize mathematics.

The *365-Day Year* is a result of intercalating five days, which were named the days of the birth of the gods Osiris, Isis, Seth, Nephthys, and Horus.

How and Wells (1912: Vol. I, 159) have supplied some insights. Their statement is as follows: "The Egyptians were the first people who definitely adopted a solar year of twelve months with thirty days in each; this began July 19 (according to the Julian calendar), i.e., 1st of Thoth according to the Egyptian, which was about a month in advance of the real solar year. On this day Sirius (Sothis) is first visible in the morning, in the latitude of Memphis. This coincides with the beginning of the rise of the Nile. Five days were added at the end of the year."

How and Wells, Vol I (1912: 159) further commented on the contributions to science by the people of ancient Kemet: "Brugsch says they had anticipated the Julian calendar, and to every fourth year added an extra day, i.e., making it a leap year. Certainly J. Caesar was said to have derived his calendar from Egypt. (*Dio. Cass.* XLIII, 26). This view seems to be a mistake. Ptolemy Euergetes (238 B.C.) by the *Decree of Canopus*, tried to introduce this (i.e., the Julian) system, but in vain. The Egyptians, however, recognized that their common year and the real year (the 'Sothic Year') did not agree. They knew that the 'common year' grew later and later; hence the calculation of the 'Sothic period' of 1460 years (= 1461 'common years'), at the expiration of which the mistake had rectified itself (1/4 day per year for 1,460 years = a year of 365 days). The first 'Sothic period' is said to begin 4241 B.C.... Hence the date of the appearance of the calendar is fixed for this year, 'the first certain date in the world's history.'"

FREDERICK MONDERSON

The *people of Ancient Kemet before 4000 B.C. knew the 365 1/4-Day Year*. According to Cheikh Anta Diop (1986: 78) in "African Contribution to World Civilization: The Exact Sciences" published in *Nile Valley Civilizations*, Edited by Ivan Van Sertima. Here he expresses, "... the Egyptians knew that the civil year of 365 days was ¼ of a day shorter than the solar year. This meant that their civil year slipped steadily backward through the solar year, 1/2 a day every two years and one day every four years."

Further Dr. Diop (1986: 78) believed: "... as early as the fourth millennium B.C., the Egyptians had already created the leap year. However, it is remarkable that they preferred to choose a time-lag of 1,460 years in order to add a whole year instead of adding one day every four years. Indeed, this time period of 1,460 years is the period which separated the two helical risings of Sothis."

The *Lunar Year* was fixed by the months of the moon. Petrie has shown that twelve months of 29.530 days each amounted to 354.36 or 10.88 days short in the year. This is the calendar used by the Muslims. The Prophet Mohammed prohibited his followers from intercalating or adding to their calendar. The ramifications of this is shown by Breasted (1915) in "The First Fixed date in History" regarding the Celebration of the Festival of Ramadan. For example, if the Festival of Ramadan is celebrated in April this year, it will be celebrated in June six years from now to symbolize the short duration of the "Muslim Year.' Still, modern Egypt is the only country that has used Four Kalendars. These were (1) a lunar (Muslim) Kalendar in official use, (2) a fixed seasonal Kalendar in agricultural use, (3) a true Kalendar in European use, and (4) a Greek Kalendar in religious use.

Precession or "precession of the equinoxes," according to Pappademos as quoted by Petrie, refers to the "very slow, cyclic changes in the coordinates of the fixed stars that takes place with a period of some 26,000 years." Petrie (1940) points out: "The date of the Equinox preceded the star date, and this precession of the equinoxes was due to the change of direction of the earth's pole wobbling round the pole of the orbit. Hence the star date of the

EGYPT ESSAYS ON ANCIENT KEMET

heliacal rising of Sirius, which was determined on the 1st of Thoth in A.D. 139, had been on 18 Mesore in B.C. 1317, on 6 Mesore in B.C. 2775, on 1 Mesore in 3385, on 24 Epiphi in 4235, on 14 Epiphi in 5705 and on 1 Epiphi in 7471 B.C."

It is interesting, some scholars believe in order to measure one Precession implies another, possibly two others. On the other hand, Dr. Charles Finch III began with two Precessions and posited there and four for 78,000 and 104,000 years. From the one of 26,000, this may mean 52,000, or even 78,000 years of stargazing. Mind-boggling! Being argumentative, or should I say speculative, in view of modern research giving greater attention to Central African beginnings, an interesting proposition presents itself. After much debate as to the tenacity of the Dogon of West Africa, to know of the star Sirius, scholars very reluctantly have conceded, 'Okay,' but they must have gotten this knowledge from the Egyptians, or people of ancient Kemet. It's plausible to ask, did the Egyptians get this knowledge from the Dogon or some other African people from Central Africa?

The *Hieroglyphic of Seasons* was based on the three seasons of four months each. Petrie (1940) makes known: "These were the season of *aakhet* written as a growing plant, *pert* as a house sign, and *shemu* with a water sign. These signs obviously refer to the period of growth, November to February, and the living in a house after that from March to June, and the inundation from July to October."

The Temple of Kom Ombo boasts one such calendar of seasons that also depicts a method of counting the various days of the month.

The *Cycle Periods* range from the 25-year period of the Apis Bull, to the 520-year period of the Phoenix. The Early Festivals are first shown being celebrated in the IV Dynasty and where we find identified the fixed year, the vague year, the great year and small years. In seeking to clarify this, we look to Petrie (1940) who has responded: "The fixed year cannot be anything but that of 365 1/4 days; the vague year must be that of 365 days. Then the other two, of 360 and 354 days, are called the great and small year, and as they only occur in one list they were certainly the least important."

Richard J. Gillings' (1981: 236) *Mathematics in the Time of the Pharaohs* has shown how the measuring of the day came into being from observation of the rising of Sirius and the emergence of the decans. "The measuring of the days by the helical risings gave rise to the system of decans, in which each chosen star would serve its duty of noting the last hour of night for 10 days (or nights), so that there would be 36 decans distributed through the mornings of the year. Of course, not all decans would be visible through any given night. At the time of the inundation, when Sirius rose helically, 12 decans rise during the night, and thus the "hours" of the summer night were determined. In winter there would be more decans visible; thus the length of hours varied slightly, both for the seasons and for the nighttime and daytime. We see here the origin of the division of the day into 24 hours that is now universally adopted."

To complement ancient Kemetic advances in science, Petrie (1940) also mentions some 28-firsts in instrumental astronomy attributed to these of ancient Africans. These included the *Sun's Altitude*, *Sun's azimuth*, *Clepsydra*, *Plumb-line Pendulum*, *Star Observation*, *Parts of the Body*, *and the Inundation*, among others.

The *Sun's Altitude* was determined in a method of dividing and measuring the sun during the day. The instrument used in achieving this end "had a raised end to cast a shadow, and divisions for the hours along a horizontal bar. This was represented as a hieroglyph, with a plumb-line hanging to fix the level of the base on which the hours were read." The *Sun's Azimuth* can be observed in the "direction of the sun casting the shadow of an upright stick; or else by a projection from a wall casting a shadow on the wall."

The *Clepsydra* was a method of deciding the time by water dropping in and out of a graduated vessel. The *Plumb line Pendulum* was probably in use from the very earliest times in ancient Kemet. The fact is that, as Petrie (1940) specifies, "29.157 ins. (the diagonal of the 20.62 ins, cubit), which was the basis of all land measure, is the

EGYPT ESSAYS ON ANCIENT KEMET

length which the pendulum would swing 100,000 times in 24 hours, exactly true at Memphis altitude." While Petrie supplied such scientific insights, it's interesting to know, whether Narmer's scientists knew of this when he chose Memphis to be his capital at the founding of dynastic rule? Fascinating!

Star Observation is recorded in the tombs of Rameses IV and Rameses X in the Valley of the Kings. The outlines of the constellations, according to Petrie, were: "The first step is to lay out, for the first time, a star map of the XVIII dynasty, by finding the hour meridians, and the pole, of that age on a globe, and transferring them to this map. As the proper motions of the stars amount to a degree or two in the interval, it is of no consequence to lay out nearer than that, especially as we only have whole hours defined, of 15 degrees each."

Lastly, *Parts of the Body* present a puzzling feature in the star list because each star is assigned both by words and by diagram - to one of seven positions of the body, (1) right arm, (2) right ear, (3) right eye, (4) middle of breast, (5) left eye, (6) left ear, (7) left arm.

The *Inundation* or over-flooding of the Nile River played a very important and crucial role in the development of Kemetic/Egyptian civilization. Moreover, because the river could have various types of impact on the inhabitants of Kemet it came to dominate the lives of all. W. E. Knowles Middleton in *The Scientific Revolution* believed: "The Nile was also partly responsible for the interest of the Egyptians in astronomy, since they came to associate its flooding with the apparent position of the sun among the stars. But astronomy also had religious uses, for the sun was an object of worship, and the moon and the planets were believed to affect the affairs of men."

MATHEMATICS

Mathematics is another field the ancient people of Kemet excelled in the ancient world. The Narmer Macehead is the earliest representation of numbers where the king is shown indicating he had captured, as Budge (1972: 5-6) confirms, "... cows, 400,000, goats, one million, four hundred and twenty-two thousand, and captives, one hundred and twenty thousand." With the consolidation and expansion of the society of the earliest period, Zaslavsky (1983: 113) writes in regards to mathematics among these early Africans: "In ancient Egypt the flooding of the Nile River necessitated annual re-division of the land. Private ownership of land and the ability to produce a surplus of commodities enabled the owners to exchange their products for their private gain or to store them for further use. Thus arose the need for a system of weights and measures."

Mathematical operations of addition, subtraction, multiplication, division, and the use of fractions are recorded in Egyptian papyri in connection with the practical problems of the society.

Zaslavsky (1983: 115) adds further comments on mathematical and other forms of knowledge developed by this African culture. We are told: "But many centuries before their time the Egyptian priests had developed a complete curriculum for the training of their members. This included philosophy, writing, astronomy, geometry, engineering, and architecture. Indeed, the upper-class Greeks completed their education by studying with Mesopotamian or Egyptian teachers."

Budge (1972: 190) denotes further, "The Egyptians were not naturally great mathematicians, and they owed their knowledge of the higher branches of the subject to the Greeks. They used the decimal system, but traces of a duodecimal system are found in the 12 hours, the 12 months and in the 36 (12 X 3) decans.... Addition and subtraction were often used; multiplication and division were difficult, for the multiplication table was unknown."

The *Rhind Papyrus* in the British Museum, No. 10057, provides arithmetic and geometry problems of ancient Kemet/Egyptian teachings. Barbara Mertz (1978: 206-07) has indicated: "The Egyptians used a decimal system in which a single stroke

EGYPT ESSAYS ON ANCIENT KEMET

represented one. Two strokes stood for two, and so on, up through nine. Ten rated a separate sign, like a croquet hoop. From eleven to nineteen the figures were formed by adding the requisite number of strokes to the ten symbols. Twenty was two croquet hoops, twenty-one was two hoops and a stroke. Besides ten and one, the only other numerals that had separate signs were one hundred, one thousand, ten thousand, one hundred thousand, and one million. There was no zero."

In this mathematical development is contained the "Egyptian forerunner of the Mother Goose rhyme." In this, Lumpkin (1986: 105) discloses: "As I was going to St. Ives, I met a man with seven wives ...," had no narrow, practical purpose. It is problem 79 of the Ahmose Papyrus, which lists: 7 houses, 49 cats, 343 mice, 2,401 spelt, 16,807 hekat, and the sum of 19,607." Even further, "problem 33 of the Ahmose papyrus requires" accordingly as Lumpkin (1986: 105) suggests "the addition of $16 + 1/56 + 1/679 + 1/776 + 10 + 2/3 + 1/84 + 1/1358 + 1/4074 + 1/1164 + 8 + 1/112 + 1/1358 + 1/1552 + 2 + 1/4 + 1/28 + 1/392 + 1/4753 + 1/5432$. The sum is 37! The Egyptians used their equivalent of the least common denominator and red helping numbers (new numerators) to find the answer."

To meet the demands of the Inundation, surveyors used geometry to re-survey the land after the water had retreated and boundary marks were removed. Efficiency in this correlation was directly tied to taxation and other forms of record keeping. Mertz's (1978: 209) description of their geometry held that: "they could calculate areas of triangles, trapezoids, rectangles, and circles, and there were problems for similar elementary volumes, including a correct computation of the volume of a truncated pyramid. This was the last impressive achievement of Egyptian mathematics; equally admirable, perhaps, was their value 3.16 for pi, which is reasonably accurate. It has been claimed that the Moscow mathematical papyrus gives a solution for calculating the area of a hemisphere, but Professor Neugebauer thought a simpler interpretation of the problem is more likely."

FREDERICK MONDERSON

Lumpkin (1983: 102) has also indicated: "Geometry, literally the measurement of the land, required a high technology in addition to theoretical mathematics. The famous 'rope stretchers' to whom Democritus compared himself, used special ropes, twisted of many fine strands to assure high stability and constant length." Lumpkin (1983: 102) demonstrates further in relation to the practice of agriculture as a mainstay of the society: "An efficient irrigation technology, efficient central administration and the skill of the farmers of ancient Egypt made possible a large food surplus, enough to support the mathematicians, teachers and other intellectuals."

In addition, while Lumpkin (1983: 101) discusses the subordinate role Kemetic/Egyptian mathematics has come to play in the History of Mathematics quotes George Sarton, the Encyclopedist of science, that: "It is childish to assume that science began in Greece. The 'Greek miracle' was prepared by millennia of work in Egypt, Mesopotamia and possibly other regions. Greek science was less an invention than a revival."

Further, Lumpkin (1986: 102), in outline, expresses the view that, "Important stages that preceded the modern age in mathematics included the prehistoric, ancient, classical, Middle Ages, and the Renaissance. In each of these periods the mathematics of the Nile Valley played a leading role." In fact, "the first task of the European Renaissance concerned the need to bring Europe up to the higher level of African and Asian knowledge, then expressed in the Muslim civilization."

QUARRYING

Quarrying is an industry long practiced by the ancient dwellers on the Nile. Its origins may be shrouded in the past but certainly became known after the double burials of the Thinite Kings, with their tombs at Abydos and Memphis and some domestic construction using stone. However, quarrying had been fully developed in the Old Kingdom in order to construct the Step-Pyramid and later different types of pyramids.

EGYPT ESSAYS ON ANCIENT KEMET

Egypt Essays Illustration 76. A painted clay pot found in a 14th Century B.C. workmen's village at Tell El-Amarna (left); and another painted clay pot also found at Amarna.

In *Dwellers on the Nile* E. A. W. Budge (1972: 124-25) explained: "… tombs and funerary monuments and statues, and the Pyramids of Giza, Sakkara, and Meydum prove that the quarrymen and stonemasons were great masters of their crafts, and suggest that they formed a very numerous and important section of the artisan classes. These stone workers formed an important class among the artisans since they were able to supply materials for building throughout the dynastic period. The insatiable demands for stone during the New Kingdom, is a measure of the importance of these men working in stone. Stone is found throughout the ancient land."

"The principal quarries were those," Budge (1972: 125) discloses, "of Tura, opposite Memphis, Kes in Middle Egypt, Wadi Hammamat, those near Abydos and at Jabal Silsilah, Syene, and there were quarries in many parts of Nubia." There were also quarries located at Aswan where some of the finest stone was located. The stones mostly quarried were fine white limestone, alabaster, and sandstone. They used both yellowish limestone and crystalline limestone, as well as red, grey and black granite, basalt, diorite, and porphyry. For inlaid work on statue, jewelry and other objects, craftsmen used lapis-lazuli, malachite, carnelian, sard, and red, yellow and black jasper.

The modern town of Tehneh or Wadi Tehneh lies about 30 miles south of the Middle Kingdom cemetery of Beni Hasan. In ancient times it was worked as a quarry. Its significance today is that the trenches at the top of the hill show a peculiar mode of choosing a quarry, and of hewing square blocks of stone. Another instance is met with near the North West angle of the second pyramid of Giza.

"In ground breaking they began leveling the surface of the rock to the extent admitted by the nature of the ground, or the intended area of the quarry. A deep trench, forming a parallelogram surrounded this space. With one of its sides open, this facilitated the removal of stones. Then they cut other parallel trenches along its entire length, about 7 or 8 ft. apart. Still others were cut right angles to the parallel trenches until the whole was divided into squares. The blocks were then cut off according to their required thickness."

"One of the quarries of Tehneh had been divided in this manner. The outer trenches of two others have been traced, to a depth of 21 ft. In some parts their direction is less regular. The former parallel lines reveal some trenches were about 1 1/2 and 2 ft. broad, and the squares measure from 6 1/2 to 7 ft. 1 in. each way. The estimated length of the trench quarry being 126 ft. by 32 ft. in breadth. This location has enabled quarrymen to separate stone from the rock and roll it to the halls below without the trouble of carriage."

By dividing the blocks into squares enabled them to remove a succession of blocks of the same dimensions. Several layers of rock were cleared. They continued to work downwards as long as the rock remained good. Such things as circular blocks used for drums, bases, or capitals of columns were rounded off the corners. This finish, in many instances, was done right there at the Tehneh quarry.

EGYPT ESSAYS ON ANCIENT KEMET

In the *Manual of Egyptian Archaeology*, G. Maspero (1926) describes the method some ancient workmen used to obtain the blocks of stone. "They quarried such places as Turah and Massarah. These quarries lie opposite Memphis and Silsileh, 145-km. south from Luxor. The walls are grooved with parallel lines, some horizontal; some sloping from left to right. This method revealed fashioned blunted chevrons enclosed in a rectangular frame of grooves an inch, or an inch and a half wide, and nine or ten feet in length. Methods of quarrying left scars scratched to the tools of the ancient workmen. This shows the method quarrymen used to obtain their blocks. They made sketches on the rock in red ink. The members of the *Commission L'Egypte* published diagrams and squared designs of several capitals found in the quarries of Gebel Abu Fedah. These outlines were drawn, and the vertical incisions were made by means of a long metal chisel. This latter was driven in perpendicularly or obliquely by powerful blows from a mallet. Horizontal detachments were made as bronze and wooden wedges were inserted in the direction of the rock strata. Many blocks were worked several times before final detachment from the rock. Often after the first working, blocks were abandoned if they had any flaws. The unfinished obelisk of Queen Hatshepsut at Aswan was one such project the quarrymen abandoned. Equally too, due to geological faults at Tehneh there are drums of columns only half disengaged."

Some of the best stone was located at Aswan. Here many notables quarried projects to be transported and erected for their monarchs elsewhere. Queen Hatshepsut's obelisks were quarried here and erected at Karnak by Senmut and his successor in that function, Amenhotep. Both these architects left inscriptions at Aswan. Nevertheless, the three main building stones used by the people of ancient Kemet were limestone, sandstone and granite. Red and black granite was located only in the Aswan area. Labib Habachi in *The Obelisks of Egypt* expresses this view. "While stones were quarried at Aswan and transported elsewhere, the most important quarries were those of the islands of Elephantine and Seheil. Here we have those near the Unfinished Obelisk south of Aswan and those in Shellal opposite the Island of Philae." There were vast quantities of quartzite on the West Bank of the Nile opposite Aswan, between the Monastery of St. Simeon and the tombs at Qubbet el-Hawa. These spots round out the location for good stone.

Singer (1956: 858) in his **Index of Subjects** provides a wide selection of artifacts and industries associated with the idea of technology among these ancient Africans. Subject matter covered includes art, painting grounds, painting media, varnishes, and ink, and pigments. Boats and ships, boring and drilling, building construction, calendar system, copper reproduction, cosmetic arts, domestication of animals, dyes and dyeing, fire making, lighting, food: culinary arts, cultivation of food plants, preservation of food, and gold mining are mentioned. Iron production, irrigation, cisterns and wells, dams, Nile flood and water lifting devices are covered.

In conclusion, ivory work, and the language, *Medu Netcher* or Hieroglyphics written in alphabetic and syllabic signs, as well as mathematics, together with measurements and standards of capacity are some forms of technology. Weights, metallurgy, fine metal work, and tools and weapons are also gifts of these ancient Africans. The art of mummification, pleasure-gardens, pottery, kilns, religion, rope making, and salt production provide ample latitude for arts and craftsmanship. Looms and textiles, transport, draught-animals and chariots treated with alum, silver and lead production are mentioned. Viticulture, wheeled vehicles, the potter's wheel, and woodwork were all associated with the arts and crafts of industry and technology, credited to the people of ancient Kemet. This is the legacy of Africans and African-Americans. This is the prize we must insist the young focus on for the next century. How did these ancient African ideas influence the development of civilization is the question we must continue to seek answers to.

EGYPT ESSAYS ON ANCIENT KEMET

24. THE CONSPIRACY AGAINST ANCIENT EGYPT

Introduction

In order to investigate this issue, the interrogative hypothesis "Is there substantive evidence that omissions and distortions, misstatements and outright fabrication in ancient Egyptian studies has occurred?" is very much appropriate. Such a position, from a detached stance, allows a fair inquiry into the intent and purpose for which this falsity is perpetuated and objective scholarship has not effectively dealt with the problem. Perhaps the purpose of overlooking such distorted and unscholarly writing with their untenable propositions "under the glaring light of the living room" is more sinister and pernicious than generally thought. A principal prognostication regarding the events surrounding this issue is the intent of denying a meaningful role of Africans in ancient Egyptian civilization, to wit, as Afrocentrists have argued the German scholar Hegel took "Africans out of Egypt and Egypt out of Africa."

In ancient times, the term "Mysteries of Egypt" had to do with the esoteric and philosophic drama of temple ritual and all forms of knowledge developed particularly as they were controlled by the Priesthood. It's understandable that as man's consciousness developed in the emergence from the mist of antiquity, great bodies of knowledge were accumulated in the fields of science, art and technology. Access to this life changing process and experience was restricted to organizational initiates or handed down practically from father to son.

This practice continued for more than two thousand years and as word leaked out about the "Wisdom of the Egyptians," destructive invading hordes vented their wrath on Egypt when the state had ceased to provide the leadership and tenacity as expected of an imperial power. On the other hand, ancient visitors with an

FREDERICK MONDERSON

inquisitive bent came to Egypt in search of knowledge, wisdom, enlightenment, and adventure, anything that would lift their consciousness above the ignorance of their countrymen at home. In the latter case, one of the earliest Greek visitors was Hecataeus of Abdera, who rightly called Egypt "The gift of the Nile. Then Herodotus came and got credit for the same statement. We know Socrates, Plato and Aristotle visited Egypt as Ivan Van Sertima tells.

Egypt Essays Photo 136. Luxor Temple of Amenhotep III. Baboons in erection at base of remaining Luxor Obelisk. On the other in Paris, the French severed the penis.

EGYPT ESSAYS ON ANCIENT KEMET

Egypt Essays Photo 137. Native Guide "Showgi" Abd el-Rady (center) and friends outside the Tomb of Inherkha.

All visited Egypt, learned new ideas and even got credit for formulating new theories that took the Egyptian millennia to develop through trial and error testing. Thus, the tradition of the esoteric nature of Egyptian knowledge helped color the concept of the "Mysteries of Egypt." That is to say, those to whom bits of knowledge were given were to not only claim original authorship, but unintentionally spread the word about the "Mysteries of Egypt" that would resonate down through the ages.

FREDERICK MONDERSON

Egypt Essays Photo 138. Native Guide "Showgi" and friends in a startled mood.

For nearly two thousand years tales of the "Mysteries of Egypt" and the exploits of Africans as benefactors of goodness, moral quality, viz., Homer's "long lived Ethiopians," praises of other Greeks, all propelled the Africans to almost god-like stature, simply because Egypt could only be admired not possessed by the evolving modern man. The key to Egyptian *Mdw Ntr* writing called hieroglyphics lay in the egg awaiting the great minds that would later decipher its secrets and unleash an avalanche of interest in ancient Egyptian, Nile Valley, antiquities and history. Naturally, much of this came about because of an accident of history. The war in Europe, following the French Revolution, forced Napoleon to retreat to Egypt to "winter" and "lick his wounds."

The British followed him and there was fought the "Battle of the Nile" which was actually fought in the Mediterranean. From these encounters a number of subsequent developments took place that forever changed the face and landscape of ancient and Egyptian history, perception, presentation, propagation and interpretation. The first of these developments was the French fascination with the art and architectural accomplishments of these early Africans whose influences had far-reaching implications for medieval and early Modern European cultural and artistic development. The

EGYPT ESSAYS ON ANCIENT KEMET

Description of Egypt Napoleon's savants or scholars (wise men) produced remains a classic of Egyptian studies two centuries later. No other work has done as extensive and comprehensive an assessment as this classic. Concomitant with this publication, Count Volney wrote his *Ruins of Empire*.

Equally Count Denon was the first modern artist to paint a picture of the Sphinx of Ghizeh in its intact form. He would later write that elements from Napoleon's artillery regiment shot off the nose and disfigured the face of the Sphinx because of its Black African or Negro god-like facial features that had remained to awe throughout the glorious achievements of the Old, Middle and New Kingdoms, the Late Period and beyond the Assyrians, Persians, Greeks, Romans, Arabs, Turks, etc., who came, wreaked havoc, showed some appreciation, conquered and stayed. Perhaps they asked the sphinx and he told them, all that he had seen as he looked out into eternity.

Egypt Essays Photo 139. "Showgi" Abd el Rady with more friends.

FREDERICK MONDERSON

Everyone knows to change custom and tradition is a difficult aspect of human experience. Many scholars ascribe the Sphinx to Khafre, builder of the Second Great Pyramid at Ghizeh, during the Fourth Dynasty. Any cursory glance at the Sphinx will reveal its African facial features. Therefore, if we accept it's the likeness of Khafre, then it's easy to assign this king, his father Khufu and his son Menkaure to the African race. In as much, the Senegalese scholar Cheikh Anta Diop has argued, the formative years and foundations of Egyptian Civilization, the Predynastic and Archaic periods and the Old Kingdom were created by a people of African physiognomy, claims to the contrary notwithstanding. As such, this eruditely research and articulated view debunks the Caucasoid origins of Egyptian civilization for Diop has shown the first significant influx of foreigners came with the Hyksos invaders, after the fall of the Middle Kingdom. That is, sometime proximate to 1900-1800 B.C.

Nevertheless, other scholars have attributed an age of almost 10,000 years to the Sphinx, arguing that while evidence links the Sphinx of Khafra, it's simply because he did repairs to the monument and so inscribed his name to it.

Egypt Essay Photo 140. While conducting his tour, Native Guide Hasan Elian signals to his friend, the author and photographer.

EGYPT ESSAYS ON ANCIENT KEMET

If we fast-forward to the New Kingdom, Hatshepsut built the Kiosk of Amon, Mut and Khonsu, the Theban Triad, at Luxor Temple in the "Ramessean Front." This was certainly before Amenhotep III built his temple there. This meant, there must certainly been a Middle Kingdom temple standing at Luxor when Senmut, the Queen's architect, erected the Kiosk. The temple standing there, Amenhotep III tore down to erect his classical masterpiece with its inspiring Processional Colonnade. As the colonnade was unfinished, Tutankhamon completed it and inscribed his name. Later Ay, Horemhab, Rameses I, Seti I and Rameses II did repairs and inscribed their names. Rameses II, in constructing the "Ramessean Front" addition to the Temple of Luxor, repaired Hatshepsut's Kiosk, which Thutmose III had appropriated, and inscribed his name as a backlash against the queen. For anyone now knowing this, history would ascribe the Kiosk to Rameses II because his name is there.

Elsewhere, at Karnak, the Eighth Pylon has a unique history. Hatshepsut built this Pylon. Thutmose III appropriated it, erased her name and inscribed his. Later in the dynasty, during the Amarna Revolution, Akhnaton, also known as Amenhotep IV, Amenhotep III and Queen Tiye's son, erased the name and image of Amon and inserted that of the Aton and his name. In the "Ramesside Restoration," Seti I erased the Aton's name and reinserted the name of Amon alongside his name. Therefore, the name being there on a particular monument is simply not sufficient to ascribe ownership to that particular individual.

Fate is sometime rather strange and perhaps it was the same artillery officers who shot at the Sphinx, and who probably made the discovery of the Rosetta Stone. This single piece of rock has had the most far-reaching influence and implications in the history of human progress than any other inanimate object known to man. The Guides at the Cairo Museum boast the institution has 120,000 authentic pieces and one imitation, the Rosetta Stone. The original is in the British Museum whose agents wrested it from the French after their defeat at the "Battle of the Nile." Fortunately the French had made a "frieze" that was shopped across Europe challenging scholars to decipher it.

The Rosetta Stone is a tri-lingual inscription of Greek, Demotic and Hieroglyphic, inscribed on black basalt in which pharaoh Ptolemy Epiphanes V, is praised by priests for his tax concessions and assistance to the temples during the Second Century B.C. The third or ancient Green part was translated first and those with knowledge of Coptic, a derivative of ancient Egypt, began to do comparisons with the Greek.

Egypt Essays Photo 141. Sakkara, Home of the Step-Pyramid. An area filled with debris (left); and a cleared area descending to a tomb (right).

EGYPT ESSAYS ON ANCIENT KEMET

Egypt Essay Illustration 77. Colonnade at Sakkara perpendicular to the passage that entrances the Great Court (top right) during early excavation and without the shelter later added.

Akerblad, Young and Champollion made the most progress and by 1822 the latter announced to the world his success in deciphering Hieroglyphics. Recent revelations have indicated contrary to ancient beliefs the Romans killed the last priest who understood the language; there were Egyptian priests as late as 1850 who lived underground and had kept alive the knowledge of how to read and write hieroglyphics. No one knows what pressures were brought to bear on these priests to divulge their knowledge to aid decipherment.

Nevertheless, because Champollion was a brilliant linguist, proficient in English, French, Ancient Greek, and Coptic, his efforts were the most successful and he got full credit for cracking the "Code of Hieroglyphics." It's often commented on how proud and excited he was with his successes that he endeavored to decipher every inscription he could get his hand on. He worked so feverishly that within 10 years, from 1822 to 1832, he dropped dead from exhaustion, after having bequeathed the world his priceless accomplishment. All this notwithstanding, and whereas, the world lauded Champollion for his cracking the Code of Hieroglyphic, not much attention has been paid to his writings on initial observations of the nature of the people of ancient Egypt and their neighbors. He certainly recognized the Black African nature of the ancient Egyptians and other Africans and the then inferior position of their Caucasian counterparts.

Cheikh Anta Diop in *The African Origin of Civilization*: *Myth or Reality* has a chapter entitled "Recent Falsifications of History" in which he exclaims: "The birth of Egyptology was thus marked by the need to destroy the memory of a Negro Egypt at any cost and in all minds." Then he examines and analyses the original letters of Champollion to his younger brother. Equally, he has shown how the brother distorted Champollion's message as if he was a part of the cartel, a la Hegel, who had begun and were forcefully propagating the false foundations of a Caucasoid Egypt.

According to Diop (1974: 46-47), Champollion wrote regarding the races of man known to the Egyptians of their day.

"Right in the valley of Biban-el-Moluk, we admired, like all previous visitors, the astonishing freshness of the paintings and the fine sculptures on several tombs. I had a copy made of the *peoples* represented to the bas-reliefs. At first I had thought, from the copies of these bas-reliefs published in England, that these peoples of different races led by the god Horus holding his shepherd's staff, were indeed nations subjects to the rule of the Pharaohs. A study of the legends informed me that this tableau has a more general meaning. It portrays the third hour of the day, when the sun is beginning to turn on its burning rays, warming all the inhabited countries of our hemisphere. According to the legend itself, they wished to represent the inhabitants of Egypt and those of foreign lands. Thus we have before our eyes the image of the various races of man known to the Egyptians and we learn at the same time the great geographical or ethnographical divisions established during that early epoch. Men led by Horus, the shepherd of the peoples,

EGYPT ESSAYS ON ANCIENT KEMET

belonging to four distinct families. *The first, the one closest to the god, has a dark red color,* a well-proportioned body, kind face, nose slightly aquiline, long braided hair, and is dressed in white. The legends designate this species as *Rot-en-ne-Rome*, the race of men par excellence, i.e., the Egyptians.

There can be no uncertainty about the racial identity of the man who comes next: he belongs to the Black race, designated under the general term *Nahasi*. The third represents a very different aspect; his skin color borders on yellow or tan; he has a strong aquiline nose, thick, black pointed beard, and wears a short garment of varied colors; these are called *Namou*.

Egypt Essays Photo 142. Sakkara, Home of the Step-Pyramid. Entrance to the Akhnaton Carpet School where wonderful rugs are made.

Finally, the last one is what we call flesh-colored, a white skin of the most delicate shade, a nose straight or slightly arched, blue eyes, blond or reddish beard, tall stature and very slender, clad in a hairy ox-skin, a veritable savage tattooed on various parts of his body; he is called *Tamhou*."

Diop continued Champollion's letter to his brother. "I hastened to seek the tableau corresponding to this one in the other royal tombs and, as a matter of fact, I found it in several. The variations I observed fully convinced me that they had tried to represent here the inhabitants of the four corners of the earth, according to the Egyptian system, namely: 1. The inhabitants of Egypt which, by itself, formed one part of the world...; 2. The inhabitants fo Africa proper: Blacks; 3. Asians; 4. Finally (and I am ashamed to say so, since our race is the last and the most savage in the series), Europeans who, in those remote epochs, frankly did not cut too fine a figure in the world. In this category we must include all blond and white-skinned people living not only in Europe, but Asia as well, their starting point. This manner of viewing the tableau is all the more accurate because, on the other tombs, the same generic names reappear, always in the same order. *We find there Egyptians and Africans represented in the same way* [Diop's Italics.] which could not be otherwise; but the Namou (the Asians) and the Tamhou (Europeans) present significant and curious variants. Instead of the Arab or the Jew, dressed simply and represented on one tomb, Asia's representatives on the other tombs (those of Ramses II, etc.) are three individuals, tanned complexion, aquiline nose, black eyes, and thick beard, but clad in rare splendor. In one, they are evidently Assyrians; their costume, down to the smallest detail, is identical with that of personages engraved on Assyrian cylinders. In the other, are Medes or early inhabitants of some part of Persia. Their physiognomy and dress resemble, feature for feature, those found on monuments called Persepolitan. Thus, Asia represented indiscriminately by any one of the peoples who inhabited it. The same is true of our good old ancestors, the Tamhou. Their attire is sometimes different; their heads are more or less hairy and adorned with various ornaments; their savage dress varies somewhat in form, but their white complexion, their eyes and beard all preserve the character of a race apart. I had this strange ethnographical series copied and colored. I certainly did not expect, on arriving at Biban-el-Moluk, to find sculptures that could serve as vignettes for the history of the primitive Europeans, if ever one has the courage to attempt it. Nevertheless, there is something flattering and consoling in seeing them, since they make us appreciate the progress we have subsequently achieved."

EGYPT ESSAYS ON ANCIENT KEMET

It is interesting that Diop produces this letter because not only did Champollion's brother twist his ideas, but seldom do we have any writers who mention the implications of this revelation.

First the American, then the French Revolution produced an age of intellectual boldness that within a few decades, man's powers of reason expanded immensely. The idea of the *Encyclopedia* came into being and the French Philosophes and the British and German counterparts created all manner of philosophical paradigms based on the teaching of the Greeks, Romans, Medieval and even early Modern philosophers whose intellectual foundations we now know were traceable to ancient Egypt and Africa.

However, by 1800 AD, because the European trade in African bondsmen was at its height a new movement, grounded in prejudice, racism, and white supremacy ideology emerged to deny the role of Africans in Egypt.

The German philosopher Wilhelm Hegel was a standard bearer of this movement that so stained the intellectual consciousness of European and even some Africans that the idea of a Caucasoid Egypt began to take hold. So powerful has this line of thought been espoused, even the masses of non-intellectual Europeans embolden and made proud by a white over Black mentality to this day trumpet this false notion. This falsity existed, nevertheless, side by side with the works and revelations of scholars such as Volney, Denon, Godfrey Higgins and much later, Gerald Massey, Kersey Graves, Raymond Dart, Albert Churchward and even Patti and Greaves whose scholarship revealed the greatness and intellectual contributions of Africans in Egypt, and who this fact became distorted along the way.

FREDERICK MONDERSON

Egypt Essays Illustration 78. A statue of King Amenhotep IV, Akhenaten, found at Karnak Temple.

The decipherment of Egyptian hieroglyphics set in motion a number of things that developed and created significant spin-off throughout the Nineteenth Century. The first of these was an enormous interest in the study of the ancient monuments. This in turn had an equally enormous impact on later archaeological excavations and rapid print of reports that fed the emerging readership of the "Penny Press" in such places as England and elsewhere on the continent of Europe. By the end of the 19th Century, a whole slew of organizations especially from England, including The Egypt Exploration Fund, founded by Amelia Edwards and Stanley Lane-Poole; and the Egypt

EGYPT ESSAYS ON ANCIENT KEMET

Research Account to spearhead Nile Valley excavations with the intent of rapid publications of reports on every conceivable site in Egypt. Much of this activity was matched by German, French, Swedish interests. Turkish, Polish and other nationals interests came later but equally held their own.

American institutions as the Metropolitan Museum of Art, Brooklyn Museum, Boston Museum of Fine Arts, Philadelphia Museum, and schools as the University of Chicago, Harvard, California, etc., began sponsoring excavations to Egypt and secured the beginnings of their collections. These institutions of higher learning and exhibit each published a Journal extolling the rapid revealing ancient knowledge and the progress of their acquisition process as well as reports on their field work and any other interesting developments taking place at the time. Universities that did not sponsor excavation expeditions subscribed to books published on the subject so that old universities such as Columbia, Harvard, Yale, etc., subscribed to all the books as they came out year after year.

The phenomenon as Brian Fagan entitled "The Rape of the Nile" began to unfold following discovery of the Rosetta Stone and Champollion's decipherment. There were no rules governing antiquities in Egypt at its early time in the 19th Century so the country lay prostrate and inviting to adventurers and antique treasure seekers.

This reminds me and is a sort of parallel. I was being chauffeured in Cairo on way to Sakkara. My driver's name was Gala. El Sawy. Trust me, there are a great many cars in Cairo! We came close to a collision and as a driver in the passenger seat; I instinctively moved my foot to mash the brakes. He noticed! I said: "I'm a driver too." He replied: "Ah! You drive with the rules. There are no rules for driving in Cairo." Now to return to my topic!

FREDERICK MONDERSON

Egypt Essays Photo 143. Cairo Museum of Egyptian Antiquities. A defaced Sphinx stands before the entrance as throngs of people prepare to enter at rear.

Ring leaders in the "Rape of the Nile" included the British Consul Salt and Belzoni, the "strongman Egyptologist;" As one Sgt. Major once said: "If it's not tied down, I'll move it." These antiquities

EGYPT ESSAYS ON ANCIENT KEMET

hunters stole everything they could get their hands on, large or small as they began to reveal the gifts of the ancients. Some things were purchased from native Egyptian dealers who were beginning to realize there's money to be made in Egyptian antiquities. Everyone got into the act to secure antiquities and to sell to institutions, governments, and private collectors. And so it continued for more than a century as the "Rape of the Nile" laid the foundation for the grand museum collections that would later stun and entertain visitors. All this occurred before the Egyptian authorities decided to impose some rules for antiquities excavation and collection for export.

It's interesting how in 1881 with the discovery of the "Deir el Bahari cache of Royal Mummies" one report boasted how this find would now put the Boulak, today's Cairo Museum of Egyptian Antiquities, on par with such European Museums as Turin and later the Louvre.

As all this madness unfolded, a few voices could be heard "crying in the wilderness" about the *Destruction of Ancient Monuments in Asia and Africa*, specifically Egypt. Those antiquities removed from Egypt were never "gift wrapped" by some clerk in a Bazaar. The rascals, thieves and plunderers, who stole those objects, viz., statues, columns, stela, paintings, sarcophagi and their lids, obelisks, jewelry, mummies, coffins, etc., used all manner of tools and strategies to uproot and remove those objects from their positions *in situ*. In the process much damage was done to the monuments.

In my researches, I discovered in ancient times temples were destroyed in two different ways, other than by some natural disaster as an earthquake. In the first instance, whether internecine struggles between the adherents of rival deities and theologies, who attacked the other's temple out of spite; or, invading forces whose initial intent and target was the state's principal god's temple that they wrecked before retreating. A good example of the first is the conflict unleashed in the Amarna Revolution when Amenhotep IV, Akhnaton's god Aton decreed the name of his rival Amon should be erased and his temple attacked. When the Aton was overthrown by

FREDERICK MONDERSON

Amon's people, they in turn attacked and destroyed the Aten's temple, his city Amarna and his name where it could be found.

On the other hand, invading forces, at first the Hyksos, who came after the Middle Kingdom, wrecked much destruction of temples and other infrastructure before they settled down to live in Egypt amidst the destruction they had unleashed. It's no wonder these invaders were expelled by the 17th and 18th Dynasty kings who later founded the New Kingdom glory days or "Golden Age" of Egypt. Concommmitantly, with the efforts at expulsion, Egypt became a military and imperial power. In the second same instance of destruction of temples, the Assyrians and Persians destroyed much, hauled away a great deal and left a bad taste in Egypt. Many temples were destroyed by them, principally Karnak and Luxor, home of the Theban and Empire god Amon-Ra. One could well imagine "Their March through Egypt" or "spreading of locust" mentality as they scorched the earth from Delta to Luxor. If their actions at Karnak and Luxor were such one could well imagine the wake of destruction they left in their path up and down the Nile in their invasion and retreat.

Conversely, when the Ethiopians invaded Egypt and founded the 25th Dynasty, they respected the culture, according to Piankhi, "of the ancestors." The Ethiopians built and repaired structured, brought stability and prosperity to Egypt and defended her against foreign hordes. Alas, they were pushed back into Nubia or Ethiopia when the hordes returned with their evil intent to wreak further destruction. In their retreat, the Ethiopians did not destroy! However, as modern scholars "fine tune" the history of this period, the time of Ethiopian rule in Egypt gradually diminishes.

To the Greeks and Romans, equally, can be attached the label or term "appreciative conquerors." First, the Greeks were amazed at the color of the Egyptians, as well as the high level of intellectual, religious, scientific, art and architectural and medical knowledge and social, philosophic and ethical standards the Egyptians had attained. The Greeks employed a two pronged strategy of oppressing the people yet paying "lip service" to the religious establishment, the

EGYPT ESSAYS ON ANCIENT KEMET

Priesthood, which played a significant role in the culture. Greek rulers who became Pharaohs of Egypt started and completed temples and also repaired structures throughout the land. Surviving temples are at Edfu, Kom Ombo, Esneh and Philae, among others.

Equally too, Greek travelers and scholars visited Egypt in search of adventure and knowledge and would write volumes later. Many gave credit for the sources of their knowledge. Nearing the end of the 20th Century, as critical Afrocentric scholarship developed and the truth about ancient Greece and Africa unfolded, the many names of Greek visitors and philosophers who studied in Egypt became known. Yet, the anti-Afrocentrists have sought to down-play these ancients' observations and commentaries of the Nile Valley peoples among whom they visited and lived.

The second type of temple destruction occurred in a more orderly manner. When a pharaoh wanted to build a great temple he generally chose a site already sacralized by an existing older temple so he systematically and orderly dismantled the older structure to make way for the new one. Oftentimes bricks or stone from the older temple would be reused as foundation fill for walls, beds of colonnades or as fill for pylons. Nevertheless, it was the Egyptians who willingly and in an orderly manner dismantled or destroyed t their temples.

FREDERICK MONDERSON

Egypt Essays Photo 144. Karnak Temple of Amon-Ra. From the north, view of a crane atop the Ninth Pylon on the North/South Axis; Hatshepsut (left) and her father Thutmose I's Obelisk (right) and ruins of the Hypostyle Hall further right.

By mid-19th Century the European intellectual assault on Egypt had begun to pick-up steam. As the museums of Europe and other academic institutions could now boast of having extensive collections, a sort of "possession is nine-tenths of the law" mentality emerged. This sort "cart before the horse" syndrome in essence argued "Since we Europeans have all these antiquities, then naturally the ancient Egyptians were Caucasians." Naturally, this did not go well with the visual images of the monuments so the linguistic argument was put forward. A whole slew of arguments were proposed for the origins of the Egyptians and as a result, distortion and omission became the order of the day. The claim that Ancient Egyptian was a Semitic-Indo-European language was reinforced with a number of arguments laying out routes in which the Caucasoid Indo-European peoples was thought to enter Egypt.

EGYPT ESSAYS ON ANCIENT KEMET

Egypt Essays Photo 145. An Egyptian Guide to the Tomb of Userhat in the South Assasif.

Pardon my digression, but let me make this point. Today the racists mount a "bald-face" false claim that the ancient Egyptians were Caucasians. The argument shifted from being Indo-European to Caucasoid to Caucasian. Comparatively, the Cairo Museum contains the Mahepra Papyrus, Number 142, which shows a very dark individual who stands before Osiris. In many instances Osiris is shown on papyrus as being black or even green as a symbol of fertility. Would you believe, green and blue were the "ancient black!" Nevertheless, in this case, while Mahepra's face is clearly evident, the Osiris before whom he stand has his face and arms erased or disfigured. This may appear purposeful, simply because if Mahepra's ethnicity is questioned, he stands before a Black image of Osiris, it does not take much to connect the dots. Are you following this line of argument? Nonetheless, the note-card attached to the display, done by Gaston Maspero, indicated that the tomb of Mahepra was discovered by Loret in 1899 at Thebes. He was described as the "Fan-bearer and child of the Nursery, Mahepra", of the 18th Dynasty, during the reign of Amenhotep II, son of Thutmose III. The card reads: Mahepra "may have been the son of Thutmose III and a Negress." Even further, it continued: "A detailed examination of his mummy which showed that he died at about 20 years of age also showed that he was Negroid, but not actually a Negro."

How interesting, Caucasoid to Caucasian but Negroid not Negro. It can here be pointed out that the word Negro was a 16th Century A.D. invention by the Spanish and therefore any translation of ancient texts that inserts the name Negro is suspect. Let's face it, the name Negro, according to the book: *The Word Negro: Its Even Intent and Use* is a racist term. In some translations, the Egyptian kings are made to say vile things about Negroes of Nubia. Dr. Ben Carruthers has argued these modern translators have put racist rhetoric in the minds and mouths of the ancient kings who never knew such things!

Another example can be made as part of the distortion and omission argument in the repertoire of the falsification of ancient Egyptian history. The famous American Egyptologist James Henry Breasted produced the classic *Records of Ancient Egypt* in 5 Volumes (1905-1907) by the University of Chicago.

Everyone knows the notion of "pick of the crop" means you choose the best in any lot, particularly if you intend to display it to the public with the intent of conveying a message. Practically everyone is familiar with the idea of "The White Man's Burden."

During the Slave Trade perpetrated by Europeans on Africans from 1441 to the 1880s, European behavior has been described as "Naked Imperialism." With the abolition of the slave Trade and the "Second coming of Europe to Africa" the tactic changed to "Enlightened Imperialism." This meant the Africans shall pay the Europeans in land, raw materials and mineral resources for rescuing them and "bringing the light of Christianity and civilization to Africa."

First and foremost, Christianity was not brought to Africa, as the *African Origin of Christianity* has been demonstrated by Gerald Massey, ben-Jochannan and John Jackson.

The "Immaculate Conception" has its origins at Abydos where this is clearly evident in Seti I's Mortuary Temple to God Osiris, the

EGYPT ESSAYS ON ANCIENT KEMET

world's earliest site of pilgrimage. The death and resurrection of the savior is as old as the time when the gods ruled Egypt. Osiris was a good king, of divine origin, who taught his people love, compassion and industry. Out of jealousy, his evil brother Seth and his cohorts beguiled, entrapped, killed and mutilated Osiris. His faithful wife Isis and sister Nephthys (the two Marys?) with the help of divine messengers Thoth and Anubis reconstituted and resurrected the god who became the judge of the dead and ruler of the underworld. The belief in the salvation, promised for the faithful permeated Egyptian civilization for the millennia of its existence. Because of the potency of the Osiris belief system, while the Egyptians, the first people to emerge from the mist of antiquity with a true sense of religious and spiritual consciousness, had many gods whose fortunes rose and fell, Nevertheless, the Osiris cult remained consistent throughout.

Second, the first Christian Nation to exist was the African nation of Ethiopia, who has held steadfastly to Christianity despite the many challenges it faced from neighboring peoples who practiced other faiths.

Egypt Essays Photo 146. Karnak Temple of Amon-Ra. The "Red Chapel" of Hatshepsut. A kneeling Hatshepsut offers a vessel to enthroned Amon-Ra (top left); and (top right) her image is defaced doing the same; while below she offers two plants to the enthroned Ennead.

FREDERICK MONDERSON

Third, as Jesus the Christ anguished on that perilous march to be crucified at Calvary, it was an African Simon of Cyrene who came to his assistance and helped bear the cross. That humanistic concern has been at the foundation of African people's acceptance and practice of the principles and promise of Christianity, particularly the admonition to love thy neighbor as thy self. Unfortunately, the late comers who practiced and "brought Christianity to Africa" did not practice that fundamental tenet to love thy neighbor as thyself as the African had done in their sweet communion with deity!

Finally, if the Africans were rescued it was from an inhuman condition Europe had created called the Slave Trade and Slavery. If rescued from the frying pan of this condition, they were placed in the fire of colonialism that a century later the Africans are yet to recover "to enjoy the benefits Europe brought." Imperialism was replaced by Colonialism, and then independence was replaced by Neo-colonialism and the technological conundrum of challenges in the post-computer age manifest itself. So much so, Africa is only exploited for its mineral wealth albeit with the collusion of a gullible and greedy elite.

All this notwithstanding, in Egypt specifically, "Enlightened Imperialism" took the form of a "quid pro quo in the method of archaeological excavation to rescue the history of the past. This new form of historical inquiry complemented linguistic studies well underway for decades. Significant archaeological excavation was undertaken from 1870 onwards by the Egypt Exploration Fund, the British School in Egypt, the British School in Athens, and the French, Italians, Germans, Americans, etc. The work of the British in Egypt was particularly interesting for one man, William Matthew Flinders Petrie spearheaded the approach that brought along an untold number of colleagues and their wives who produced the superabundant body of work credited to the above groups. As excavation followed excavation, rapid publication of reports fueled a developing frenzy for knowledge of antiquity as well as artifacts of antiquity to hold and admire. Flinders Petrie established a scientific order in Egyptian archaeology.

EGYPT ESSAYS ON ANCIENT KEMET

The years 1870 to 1930 can be considered the "Golden Age" of British Archaeology in Egypt. Concessions to excavate were given freely since Egypt was under British colonial administration. Because a Frenchman, Champollion, had cracked the Code of Hieroglyphics, the tacit traditional acceptance held that the top antiquities position in Egypt should be held by a Frenchman. Rightly so, the French have maintained a distinguished tradition in Egypt from Champollion, through Mariette, Chabas, Maspero, Le Grain, Chevier, etc. While Mariette labored to excavate innumerable sites and establish a museum to house the recovered artifacts, Maspero emerged as a most prolific writer and authority on ancient Egypt, even though some of his calls were questionable.

Maspero collaborated well with the British Administrator Lord Cromer and this aided requests for British concessions to excavate. In addition, to organizational rights to dig, private individuals plied the Nile in their own boats and visited numerous sites and dispatched their observations to journals, newspapers, club meetings, and those therefore, supplemented the more extensive *Memoirs* published by such entities as the Egypt Exploration Fund and the British School in Egypt. Oftentimes, however, the observations of the private individuals though published in magazines, journals or newspapers never made it into the more established published works. As such then, these important tidbits are now "lost" from history and only the most resolute research inquiry could ferret out these gems that are caveats to the racist juggernaut that's' seeking to claim Egypt as Caucasian as opposed to African. This is why Dr. ben-Jochannan recommended his students, "when doing research on ancient Egypt, get the earliest materials available and work from there." This advice may very well be useful because modern books are so sanitized they have followed Hegel's dictum by removing Egypt from Africa and Africans from Egypt.

After the early ruthless methods of antiquities acquisition in the age of "Enlightened Imperialism" the cost to Egypt for systematic and scientific excavation was the right to pick some of the best pieces

FREDERICK MONDERSON

from recovered artifacts. Granted, much was recovered in excavation but when one views the displays mounted at museums throughout the world in Britain, France, Spain, Italy, Turkey, Australia, America, all with multiple cities housing Egyptian collections, one gets some idea of the great volume of the "Culture in Captivity." Fact is, only the best pieces were chosen for display in European public collections and with the suggestive nature of interior decoration enhanced by lighting, "Caucasian Egypt" has been achieved. However, it's sad that the general European and American public could be so misled by their own people, that all they know is based on a faulty foundation. This is not surprising since the Donation of Constantine, a forgery, remained undetected for nearly six centuries. What is, however, frightening, as critical Black scholarship such as the Afrocentrists unearth and expose the hypocrisy of "Race based Scholarship" they are attacked for seeking to set the record straight. I suppose people prefer the comfort of their ignorance rather than challenges of truth crushed to earth which shall rise to enlighten the ignorant and rightfully educate those searching for truth and meaning in historic scholarship.

Egypt Essays Photo 147. Karnak Temple of Amon-Ra. The "Red Chapel" of Hatshepsut. Whether kneeling or standing before the enthroned Ennead, Hatshepsut's image is erased.

EGYPT ESSAYS ON ANCIENT KEMET

25. EGYPT AS BLACK HISTORY

Egypt as Black history should be celebrated everyday, 365 days per year. Naturally this flies in the face of the falsity taught by those imperialists who colonized the intellectual and artifactual history of ancient Egypt. Dr. John Henrik Clarke taught, "the people who preached racism colonized history." To that end, the true history of Egypt is taught both from black and white perspectives. The European and American (white) dominated perspective teaches the intrinsic beauty of the art, architecture, science and mythology of Egypt which is underscored by the wonderful artifactual displays contained in Museums and private collections in cities across Europe and America. Interestingly enough, the displays are highlighted under wonderful lighting that obfuscates their true ethnological origins.

The perpetual fabrication began more than two centuries ago when Africa and Africans were prostrate in chains and justification was used to deny the humanity of Black Africans. In this age of "naked imperialism" the clash of empires led to a discovery of ancient Egypt.

Napoleon's soldiers and savants found the Rosetta Stone and began the study of ancient Egypt leading to Champollion's decipherment of hieroglyphics. In these early beginnings the African connection to Egypt was evident but Prof. Clarke's observation emerged in a divergent strand of scholarship. Just then the true history became distorted through pronouncements of individuals as Hegel, Samuel Cartwright's *Slavery and Ethnology* and theories as the "Hamitic Hypothesis." The movement to remove Africans from Egypt and Egypt from Africa began at this time.

Yet still, there were credible European scholars who decried the emerging falsification of the historical record. The first is Baron Vivant Denon who was part of Napoleon's expedition; Count Volney's *Ruins of Empires*; Godfrey Higgins' *Anacalypsis* in 2 volumes (1836); later Lenormant, etc. were some of those who

FREDERICK MONDERSON

sought very early to set the record straight. Unfortunately it was a terrible time for Africans who were victims of the piranha mentality of the age when men of Europe and America spoke of freedom, justice, humanity, brotherhood. But truth crushed to the earth shall rise and from mid-nineteenth century but practiced contradictions to such beliefs. Blacks became involved in the intellectual fray regarding Egypt. First Edward Wilmot Blyden, the West Indian who went to West Africa, began arguing of a Black Egypt from Biblical references. Then Martin Delaney and other religious Blacks, with very scant sources available to them began to question the incorrect portrayal of ancient Blacks in Egypt.

Egypt Essays Photo 148. Guide "Showgi" Abd el-Rady stands with friends before the First Pylon at Medinet Habu Temple of Rameses III.

From mid-19th Century onward a new impetus on Egypt emerged. Concomitant with the "whitening of Egypt," the search for antiquities for private and museum collections unleashed a "Rape of the Nile." This was all masked under the umbrella of ensuing "enlightened imperialism of the last half of the 19th Century. Under this masquerade, "intellectual imperialism" unleashed a multitude of ethnological, botanical, mineralogical, and zoological inquiries across wide areas of the world under colonization. In Egypt,

EGYPT ESSAYS ON ANCIENT KEMET

"intellectual imperialism," as a method utilized by explorers, archaeologists, writers, publishers and others whose efforts were fired by the "penny press" and rapid publication of any discovery.

The years from 1870 until around 1930 saw an unrelenting effort to excavate, analyze and publish the findings in the resurrection of Egypt and the Nile Valley. Here the "ancient records" of the "ancient records" were systematically retrieved and conventions established about how Egypt was to be interpreted. Naturally the role of Europe loomed paramount in this effort and the principal beneficiaries were Europe and America. In this, the role of Blacks diminished to a lowly status. Fortunately by the turn of the Twentieth Century Black scholarship was in the intellectual ascent and began to view Egypt as part of the African legacy.

Marcus Garvey, the great nationalist, met Duse Mohammed in London who impressed him on the role of Blacks in ancient Egypt. Then W.E.B. DuBois wrote *The Negro* (1915), yet with very little resources available to him, was able to produce a masterpiece that almost a century later much of his findings go unchallenged. His later work *The World and Africa* (1946) though dealing with the continent on a broader scale had significant information about Egypt.

Drusilla Dunjee wrote about the *Wonderful Ethiopians* in 1926 and Carter G. Woodson contributed his share about the role of Africans in the shaping of world history. Jackson and Huggins wrote their first *Introduction to African Civilizations* in the 1930 and this was followed by JA Rogers *Sex and Race* in 3 volumes then *The World Great Men of Color* in 2 volumes. From then on a whole litany of African scholars have dealt with the question and lack of credit given to Black people in this African civilization experience. There is no need to recount the names of the great Africans who have wrestled with this topic in the Twentieth Century. From ben-Jochannan to Ivan Van Sertima prodigious research was conducted on the topic of African intellectual redemption.

FREDERICK MONDERSON

An interesting observation can be made here. Certainly the Black scholar has as much credibility as his White counterpart. In the business of intellectual endeavor thirty years is a long time. Equally it must be granted that one can unearth a great deal of new information and this should sharpen and crystallize one's view of the pursued subject. However, while a Black scholar may spend thirty years of research and writing and solidify his position taken earlier in his research this cannot be said about his White counterpart. Seldom, if any, White scholars have corrected his earlier views about Blacks in Egypt even after some thirty years of researching the field.

The simple question reasonable enquiring minds must pose is this! How then should the evidence be viewed? Is critical Black scholarship as credible as their White counterparts? Thus, after some thirty years of research, writing and teaching Black scholars have reported that the historical record has been falsified to discredit Black achievement! This, then, is the correct view.

Egypt Essays Photo 149. Karnak Temple of Amon-Ra. The "Red Chapel" of Hatshepsut. In this instance, while the Ennead's image has been destroyed, Hatshepsut's has escaped the destructor's hands and she presents two vessels and a "Table of Offerings."

EGYPT ESSAYS ON ANCIENT KEMET

26. GREAT AFRICAN PHILOSOPHERS TEACH:

THE BOOK OF KAKIMNA. - A TREATISE ON MANNERS IN THE TIME OF THE KINGS HUNI AND SENOFERU OF THE THIRD DYNASTY.

"I am sure of being respected. A song that is right opens the stronghold of my silence; but the paths to the place of my repose are surrounded by words armed with knives against the intruder, no admittance except to those who come alright."

"As a glass of water quenches thirst, as a mouthful of vegetables strengthens the heart, as one good takes the place of another good, as a very little takes the place of much, he who is drawn away by his stomach when he is not on the watch is a worthless man. With such people the stomach is master. However, if thou sittest down to eat with a glutton, to keep up with him in eating will lead afar; and if thou drinkest with a great drinker, accept in order to please him. Do not reject the meats, even from a man repugnant to thee, take what he gives thee, and do not leave it; truly that is disagreeable."

THE PRECEPTS OF PTAH-HOTEP
I.
"The prefect Ptah-hotep says: 'O god over the two crocodiles,' my lord, the progress of time brings old age. Decay falls upon man and decline takes the place of novelty. A new misery weighs him down each day; the sight grows dim, the ears become deaf; the powers are constantly falling. The mouth is silent; speech is wanting, the mind flickers, not remembering yesterday. The whole body suffers. That which is good becomes bad, taste departs. Old age makes man miserable in every way; the nose is stopped, breathing no longer from exhaustion. In whatever position, this is a state (?) of.... (?)....Who will give me authority to speak that I may tell him the words of those who have heard the counsels of former times? The majesty of this god says: "Instruct him in the speech of former times. This it is that constitutes the worth of the children of the great.

FREDERICK MONDERSON

Whatever makes souls calm penetrates him who heeds, and what is thus told will not produce satiety."

II.
"Arrangement of good words," as a means of instructing the ignorant in the knowledge of the choice of good words. There is profit to him who will listen to this; there is loss to him who will transgress them. He says to his son: "Be not proud because of thy knowledge; converse with the ignorant as with the scholar; for the barriers of art are never closed, no artist ever possessing that perfection to which he should aspire. But wisdom is more difficult to find than the emerald; which is found by slaves among the rocks of pegmatite."

III.
"If thou hast to do with a disputer while he is in his heat, and if he is superior to thee in ability, lower the hands, bend the back, do not get into a passion with him. As he will not permit thee to spoil his speech, it is very wrong to interrupt him; that shows thou art not able to be quiet when thou art contradicted. If, then thou has to do with a disputer while he is in his heat, act as one not to be moved. Thou hast the advantage over him, if only in keeping silent, when his speech is bad. 'Better is he who refrains,' says the audience; and thou art right in the opinion of the great."

"Who will give me authority to speak that I may tell him the words of those who have heard the counsels of former times?"

"Instruct him in the speech of former times. This it is that constitutes the worth of the children of the great. Whatever makes souls calm penetrates him who heeds, and what is thus told will not produce saiety."

If thou hast to do with a disputer while he is in his heat, do not treat him with contempt, because thou art not of the same opinion. Do not be provoked with him when he is wrong; away with that! He is fighting against his very self; do not ask him to flatter thy views. Do not amuse thyself with the spectacle which thou hast before thee;

EGYPT ESSAYS ON ANCIENT KEMET

this is odious, small, and of a contemptible spirit. Struggle against this, as something condemned by the great, when on the point of giving thy views.

IX.
"If thou art a farmer, reap in the field which the great God has given thee. But do not surfeit they mouth among thy neighbors; it would be even better to make thyself feared by the possessor. As for him who, master of his own actions, all powerful, seizes like a crocodile in the midst even of the keepers, his children are by reason of that an object of cursing, of contempt, and of hatred; while his father is deep in trouble, and the mother who bore him, another is more happy than she. But a man becomes a god when he is chief of a tribe who has confidence in following him."

"If thou desirest that thy conduct be good and kept from all evil, beware of all fits of bad temper. This is a sad malady which leads to discord, and there is no more life at all for the one who falls into it. For it brings quarrels between fathers and mothers, as between brothers and sisters; it makes the wife and the husband abhor each other, it contains all wickedness, it encloses all injuries. When a man takes justice for his rule, walks in her ways, and dwells with her, there is no room left for bad temper."

"If thou art wise, take care of thy house, love thy wife purely. Fill her stomach, clothe her back; these are the cares (to give) to her body. Caress her, fulfill her desire, during the time of thine existence; it is a kindness which honors its master. Be not brutal; consideration will lead her better than force, this is her breath, her aim, her gaze. This establishes her in thy house; if thou repellest her, it is an abyss. Open thine arms to her for her arms; call her, show her thy love."

"Do not disturb a great man; do not distract the attention of the busy man. His care is to accomplish his task, and he strips his body for love of the work. Love for the work thy do brings men to god. Therefore compose thy face, even in the midst of trouble, so that

FREDERICK MONDERSON

peace may be with thee, when agitation is with...these are the people who succeed where they apply themselves."

XLIV
"Do that which thy master tells thee. Doubly good is the precept of our father, from whose flesh we come forth. May what he tells, be in our hearts; do for him more than he has said and satisfy him wholly. Surely a good son is one of the gifts of God, a son doing better than he has been told."

In his "Atlanta Compromise" speech, Booker T. Washington urged both Black and whites in the south, to "cast down your buckets."

Marcus Garvey said: "When I looked around for Africa's 'Men of Big Affairs' I could not find any. So, I created, titled nobility as "Duke of the Nile," "Count of the Congo," "Black Cross Nurses" and so on. W.E.B. DuBois insisted that a "talented Tenth" should lead the nation. While Martin Luther King, Jr., gave his "I have a Dream Speech" he also insisted, let me tell you, "Why we can't wait." The his often quoted, "The measure of a man is not where he stands in times of comfort and convenience, but where he stands in times of challenge and controversy."

Minister Louis Farrakhan in 1995 called for "one million Black men on the great lawn in Washington, D.C."

Even as Dr. Khalid Mohammed insisted, "The million youth will march down Lenox Avenue," Congressman Charles Rangel responded, "There will be no hate in my Harlem."

On October 24, 1997, on the Podium at the Million Women March in Philadelphia, one of the speakers uttered: "We are here, one million strong, in support of the brothers who marched in Washington, two years ago."

EGYPT ESSAYS ON ANCIENT KEMET

27. SENMUT, ARCHITECT OF QUEEN HATSHEPSUT

Senmut was an Egyptian nobleman who lived during the reign of Queen Hatshepsut in the XVIII Dynasty, about 1490-1470 BC. He came from a poor family but luck; intelligence, fortune and hard work helped him reach the top in Egyptian society. His lowly background is surmised from the poor tomb he built for his family. Some scholars believed that Senmut was a scribe. Others think he was a general in the army of the Queen's father Thutmose I. Hatshepsut loved her father. He made her co-regent with Thutmose II her half-brother. Still, the old king was aware that she would have political and social difficulties in the male dominated world of the pharaohs. Possibly Thutmose I may have advised her alliance with "strong males" in the kingdom. Thus, her fortune became intertwined with Senmut's

The Queen married Thutmose II. They had a girl child named Nefre-re. When Thutmose I died, Hatshepsut pushed aside young Thutmose III, her co-regent, and made herself ruler of all Egypt. Shortly after, she claimed to be the son of Amun and declared herself king of all Egypt. Senmut was well liked by Hatshepsut. Many people believed Senmut was behind all this, since, he headed a political party with powerful individuals in the country. William C. Hayes in *The Scepter of Egypt II* (Cambridge, Mass: Harvard University Press, 1959, p. 106 says: "He received some 80 titles from the Queen and became the most powerful man in the kingdom." In *Ancient Records of the Egypt*, J.H. Breasted informs: "He was the minister of Finance, Minister of Works, Hereditary Prince and Count, Wearer of the Royal Seal, and Sole Companion." Other titles were Great Father, Tutor of the Princess Nefru-re, Conductor of Festivals, Overseer of the Gardens of Amun, Chief Steward of the King, Overseer of the Prophet of Montu, Overseer of Administrative Officers, and Imy-Weret Priest, and so on.

Senmut was a famous architect, among others, of the Eighteenth Dynasty. He built two tombs for himself. The first was dug out of

FREDERICK MONDERSON

the hillside above the village of Abd el Qurna. Breasted's *History of Egypt* explained: "This elaborate tomb (No. 71) was built before he became powerful. It was decorated with a wonderful ceiling pattern and contained scenes of the Egyptian afterlife." Barbara Mertz in *Black Land, Red Land* notes Senmut: "Employed several bright colors such as yellow, blue, red, and green in its decoration. His family members and household helpers as well as his horse and a pet-ape were buried in and around the tomb. The horse, a mare, was twelve and a half hands high. Both animals were mummified."

From this site we know the names of Senmut's father Ramose, "the Worthy," and his mother, Hatnufer, "Lady of the House." His beloved sister was Ahotep "the Justified." Amenhotep, a younger brother and Harmose, a musician, with his lute lying beside his coffin, were all buried here. Also buried here were a young servant and an old woman Priestess of the God Amun. Senmut had another brother, Senmen, who was probably older. He too seems to have had royal children as protégées. His charge was Senenyah and probably Nefru-re. Senmen was also buried on a very steep slope of the hills at Sheikh Abu el-Qurna where Senmut was probably interred.

H. de Garis Davies in "The Tomb of Senmen, Brother of Senmut" in *Society of Biblical Archaeology* (1913: 382) wrote: "Higher upon, on the same hillside, is a feature unique in the necropolis, a group of man, woman and child, carved out of a great boulder, the back of which is still left in the rough." Interestingly enough, this is the prototype of the Mount Rushmore phenomenon in American political history.

Senmut had several close friends who helped the Queen rule the country. Their names were Nehsi, Chancellor, who led an expedition to Punt. Thutiy and Thutnofre were Treasurers. Puyemre was the Second Prophet of Amon. Hapuseneb was the Vizier or Prime Minister. Ineby was the Viceroy of Nubia. Dewaeben was the First Herald, and Tetenre, a scribe.

EGYPT ESSAYS ON ANCIENT KEMET

Senmut built the great Deir el-Bahari Funerary temple of Queen Hatshepsut, at Thebes. It is located on the West Bank of the Nile, near the XI Dynasty Temple of Mentuhotep II, which served as a model, built some five hundred years earlier. Here he had his second tomb, with a long sloping corridor, secretly dug under the Queen's temple. Herman Kees in *Egypt: A Cultural History* says of Senmut, he even "dared to have figures of himself carved behind the doors of the chapel shrines such as the rock-shrine of Hathor, and to have a new rock-tomb cut for himself under the forecourt of the temple so that he could rest within the sacred precinct." Hayes says further: "Senmut inscribed his name some 70 times in out-of-the-way places in the Queen's mortuary temple." His secret, unfinished, tomb was abandoned after his demise. Thutmose III's forces defaced and destroyed it.

Egypt Essays Photo 150. Karnak Temple of Amon-Ra. The "Red Chapel" of Hatshepsut. To the left, Hatshepsut (Cartouche *Ma'at-Ka-Ra* above) offers two plants to Amon-Ra, while to the right, now the now defaced Queen offers flowers to Amon as Min.

Hatshepsut's funerary temple is an architectural masterpiece with a platform and lower, middle and upper colonnades reached by two ramps. The sanctuary was located in the upper platform where the

FREDERICK MONDERSON

"Holy of Holies" resided. Thus, Deir el Bahari had columns, sandstone sphinxes, and Osiride states of the Queen. Some are still visible today as can be seen following the restoration by a Polish team that has worked there for decades.

W. Stephenson Smith in the *Art and Architecture of Ancient Egypt* (1959: 233) notes, the temple "combines a broad feeling of openness of space with a nicety of architectural detail which only gradually become apparent as one penetrates into the individual parts." On the south side of the temple, near the Anubis Shrine, the Queen recorded her "divine birth." Equally too, on the north side, the "expedition to Punt" is depicted.

The architect of the Deir el-Bahari structure employed square pillars and polygonal columns. "This variation between pillar and column is one of the reasons for Senmut's success in employing the polygonal channeled column, which had long been one of the happiest of Egyptian inventions."

Much has been said of the Indian Maharajah who built the Taj Mahal for the women he loved. Yet, not much has been said or written about the African named Senmut who built a temple at Deir el Bahari, Egypt, for the woman he loved and served. Unquestionably, Hatshepsut was an assertive, intelligent, beautiful and well-loved woman who ruled as pharaoh in early 18th Dynasty Egyptian history. In the unfolding drama of this cultural dynamic, Senmut was one of a group of influential men who served their queen and were rewarded.

Senmut it is said received more than forty titles, holding some of the most significant posts in the monarchical, administrative and religious domains of Egyptian culture. Nevertheless, he is remembered more for his skill as an architect in the queen's mortuary temple at Deir el Bahari, the worship temple of Mut in Asher and the two obelisks he quarried at Aswan, transported and had erected at Karnak. However, while time has taken its toll on the temple of Mut and one of the obelisks has fallen, the Deir el Bahari

EGYPT ESSAYS ON ANCIENT KEMET

structure has remained significantly intact. This is remarkable given the fact, supporters of Hatshepsut's successor, Thutmose III, have attacked, destroyed and defaced, even expropriated many of her monuments, and much of the temple. Abandoned, it was covered by the sands of time and essentially remained for modern explorers and archaeologists to discover and unearth the temple Senmut lovingly built for his queen. For decades Polish scholars have struggled to restore and preserve the upper terrace, the heart of the temple with its hypostyle hall, altar and sanctuary which suffered the most from the destroyer's wrath.

That much said; some more on Senmut should help identify this early lover who sat behind the throne of Egypt. According to some sources, Senmut was a general in the army of Hatshepsut's father Thutmose I. When the old king neared death he chose his daughter to succeed him. Yet, it was unthinkable for a woman to be pharaoh. Realizing the problems she would face in a male dominated society, he aligned her with strong, wise and experienced males. Besides being the tutor and guardian of Hatshepsut's daughter among his title, Senmut boasted of being custodian of the royal bedroom.

Such close proximity of commoner to royalty was unthinkable, but here is the assumed lover's connection. Equally too, perhaps, this is why he worked so assiduously to build religious and other structures to help justify the queen's rule. All this notwithstanding, history depicts Senmut as a gifted African lover, architect and administrator who built and enshrined the fame of his queen as a testimonial of his love. All this occurred at a time when Black men loved, respected and adored their women.

FREDERICK MONDERSON

Egypt Essays Photo 150a. Karnak Temple of Amon-Ra. The "Red Chapel" of Hatshepsut. While the Queen offers food with both hands to Amon as Min (left); she offers flowers with one hand (right) to Min balancing, not holding the flagellum.

28.   EGYPTOLOGY

From the earliest times scholars and travelers have been fascinated with the study of Egyptian culture, the beauty of it art and esoteric symbolism of the hieroglyphics, as well as the wonderful majesty of the experience. Evidence indicates New Kingdom visitors from Thebes were in Memphis and Sakkara, showing an intrinsic appreciation for the culture. Even Abu Simbel has inscriptional evidence of its visitors during later dynastic times. Many ancients wrote and made commentaries on the Greco-Egyptian priest Manetho. These included Diodorus Siculus, Josephus, Strabo and Pliny. Horapollo attempted to decipher the monuments and during the Middle Ages Athanasius Kircher also tried unsuccessful.

Nearly fifteen hundred years after the last Egyptian inscriptions were written on the Island of Philae interest in this antique culture was gain jolted by discovery of the Rosetta Stone, a block of black basalt in Greek, Demotic and hieroglyphics. In August 1799, during that age of antiquarian inquiry several scholars began attempts at decipherment of the trilingual inscription decree of Ptolemy

EGYPT ESSAYS ON ANCIENT KEMET

Epiphanes V. The principals were Sylvester De Sacy, Thomas Young and Jean Francois Champollion. The latter was most successful and by 1822 Champollion had deciphered the ancient script. He began working feverishly but within 10 years he was dead in 1832. Richard Lepsius visited Egypt in 1842-45 and began the German collection of Egyptian antiquities. Today Germany's collection is unrivaled.

After this many took up the study and for the next half century the field of Egyptology began to take shape. Garner Wilkinson, Bunsen, Birch, Chabas, Wiedemann, Goodwin, all began to study the history, culture and apply their linguistic skill in translating the language and writing books to move the study along.

In the next half century from 1880-1930 a new generation of scholars emerged and their successes in the discipline were aided by Europe's dominance in Egypt and elsewhere in Africa. These scholars now lent the study of Egyptology the disciplines of history, archaeology and anthropology. The field was further helped by even more new disciplines as anthropometry, biometrics, photography, architecture, medicine and art. The French led the field followed by the Germans, British and Swiss. Later Americans became involved. Flinders Petrie not only systematized Egyptian archaeology by his methods of Sequence Dating but also defined Egyptology as consisting of knowledge of Egyptian geography, language and history.

Auguste Mariette worked tirelessly to excavate, help restore and protect some of the existing structures in Egypt and to build the Cairo Museum. Gaston Maspero followed him in the post of Antiquities Curator and excavated and became a prolific writer on Egyptian culture. He inscribed many of the inscriptions in the display cases at the Cairo Museum. He was later succeeded by Legrain who particularly did restoration work at Karnak where he discovered the "Cachette Court" with its thousands of statuettes of numerous pharaohs spanning the entire history of Egypt. By the end of the second period the discipline of Egyptology had been set on firm footing with the tremendous assistance of archaeology that excavated from one end of the Nile Valley to the other.

F.C.H. Wendell in *Biblical World* (1889) wrote "The Value of Egyptological Study" and identified several forms of the Egyptian language with whose familiarity scholars must be aware. These are:

The "Pyramid Texts" were discovered by Maspero in Pyramids of kings of the IV, V, and VI Dynasties. The texts are much older that this period of about 2600 B.C., generally acknowledged to have been evolving in real form for millennia into the Prehistoric Period.

Texts of the Old Kingdom (2600-2200 B.C.) that and are mostly inscriptions.

Texts of the Middle Kingdom. These can be divided into two classes in which the language is quite different (a) the inscriptions which have a peculiarly heavy and often unintelligible style and (b) the language of some of papyri which differs grammatically and linguistically from the inscriptions.

The language of the Transition Period. (XVII-XVIII Dynasties) 1530-1320 B.C.

The New Empire Language (XIX-XX Dynasties) 1320-1000 B.C.

The Period of Decline. This is about 1000-800 B.C. In this period the language rapidly deteriorated.

Demotic. From about the VIIth Century. The language has reached its lowest ebb; the grammar is much the same as in Coptic.

Hieratic evolved as a common language and finally Coptic, though changing, retained structural and cultural elements of the wtiting.

EGYPT ESSAYS ON ANCIENT KEMET

Egypt Essays Photo 151. Karnak Temple of Amon-Ra. The "Red Chapel" of Hatshepsut. The ark at rest with victuals and unguents nearby.

29. BLACK EGYPT AND THE STRUGGLE FOR INCLUSION

Recently Hollywood has again imprinted upon the minds of young people with their films on Egypt which include *The Mummy, The Mummy Returns, The Scorpion King* as well as the Disney productions of *Prince of Egypt* and *Tarzan* which did not have any Africans in it. In olden times the Ten Commandments, The Mummy and several versions of Cleopatra, to name a few, have left indelible impressions on the mind's images regarding the people of Egypt. Equally too, National Geographic Magazine has done extensive writings on Egypt. More importantly, however, seeing these movies and reading *National Geographic Magazine* will not tell our people the ancient Egyptians were Black Africans. Many of the books, particularly those written by European and European-American writers today are so sanitized they give no inclination that the Egyptians were Black people in North-East Africa along the banks of the River Nile.

For this writer's Egyptian enlightenment I am indebted to Dr. ben-Jochannan, who in his admonition reminded me to "Get the oldest materials and work from there" when doing research on ancient

FREDERICK MONDERSON

Egypt. This is because of the need for a reference point, in view of modern Egyptological teaching, and interpretations of this critical branch of knowledge. Scholars must do so because a great many new books are devoid of constructive reference to the role of Black people in Egypt, therefore there is need for vigorous re-writing, or certainly critical analysis of their content. None of these books purposely propagate the fact of Queen Aahmes-Nefertari's blackness, despite her portrait in the British Museum that depicts a "coal-Black Ethiopian" wearing the fashion of the times, red, white and blue, 1500 years before Christ and some 3500 years ago. This Black queen is the ancestress of the 18th Dynasty. She was deified and worshipped along with her son Amenhotep I in their temple at Thebes, on the West Bank. Here they were regarded as patrons of the mortuary area. His son, Thutmose I is father of Queen Hatshepsut who ruled as pharaoh. When challenged for being an "uppity woman" who ruled as pharaoh, underscored her relationship to Aahmes-Nefertari, the Black Queen and Goddess.

The modern historical record is replete with distortions and omissions. In 1903 the temple and tomb of Mentuhotep II, founder of the 11th Dynasty and the Middle Kingdom, was found at Deir el Bahari, Thebes. In it they found King Mentuhotep dressed in Heb Sed festival garment wearing the Red Crown as symbolic of King of Lower Egypt. The assumption is there was a similar statue with the king wearing the White Crown as King of Upper Egypt. However, what was significant for the ethnicity of this monarch is he was painted Black. This surviving statue was then moved to the Museum of Egyptian Antiquities in Cairo, where it still rests. Importantly, this temple was described in the major archaeological and news media as being the most complete Middle Kingdom temple and the oldest temple at Thebes then discovered. No one said anything about the king's color. It was 1959 when W. Stephenson Smith of the Boston Museum of Fine Arts in his *Art and Architecture of Ancient Egypt* did say Mentuhotep had "Black flesh." It took decades before it was carried in this country. Ignorance is bliss.

EGYPT ESSAYS ON ANCIENT KEMET

In 1922, one hundred years after the decipherment of Hieroglyphics, Howard Carter discovered the intact tomb of King Tutankhamon, the boy king. There was such a great stir about this fabulous find, because of the wonderful treasures contained in his tomb. Still, two life-like wooden statues of the king were painted black and stood guard over the burial chamber. These are now at the entrance to the Hall of Tutankhamon in the Cairo Museum. People bypass them unnoticeably in their rush to view the wonderful treasures the young king carried to the next life. In 1978-79, the King Tut exhibition toured the United States and the symbol of that display was an alabaster bust of the boy king. Alabaster is a white marble-like material. How appropriate it was to show this picture or image of the young African Pharaoh. No one would suspect. All the major cultural institutions in the United States accepted the bust as symbolic of the king's representation. I don't think there was any objection, except perhaps by knowledgeable African Americans who understood the distortion and fraud being perpetuated. However and interestingly enough, it was a fraud also being perpetuated against the white public, forced to accept a distorted view.

It is my opinion and belief that the true color representation of kingly individuals can only be viewed in wooden statues. These statues are the only ones painted, while others of stone or metal reflect the color of the material being used. This is significant because inasmuch as so little artifacts have survived and then the need to understand what may possibly have been destroyed for their de-facto link to Black ethnicity of the Egyptians, everything is suspect. We must not forget that the remains of ancient Africa are scattered throughout the capitals of Western Europe, Canada, the United States and Australia. As such then, there is so much "culture in captivity."

In his *Destruction of Black Civilization: Great Issues of a Race 4500 B.C. to 2000 A.D.*, Chancellor Williams wrote about the record being distorting to show that despite Dynasties beginning with Black founders they end up being pictured as white. This is particularly true of the 18th Dynasty. There is a statue of Seti I in the British Museum that is made of wood. Even the untrained eye could detect this statue of the son of Rameses I, the founder of the 19th Dynasty, seemed willing to depict a Black pharaoh. There is a considered belief many such pieces are "doctored" in the "basement" of institutions willing to be in complicity with this historical distortion. Perpetuating such a fraud is to deny Rameses II, "the Great" would be Black and so too the 19th Dynasty. Which brings us to the 20th Dynasty and last but not least the 25th Dynasty.

There is talk that Egypt is building the world's largest museum to house some of its wonderful collection. Many things could be displaced, misplaced or certainly replaced. However, there is one case in the Cairo Museum, on the second floor where wooden statues are housed. Here there are small wooden statues of pharaohs painted black alongside a particular statue of a leopard also painted black. Now, if there is no connection between these wooden pieces it is hard to fathom. However, there is a question of whether they will be placed again in such close proximity when the new museum is opened.

In the 19th Century several European explorers visited and reported from all over Egypt and these appeared in some of the credible journals or newspapers of that age. An issue of the *Academy* in the 1880s mentions the discovery of a tomb of an official of King Thutmose I of the 18th Dynasty. Here the official is pictured in his tomb praying to a statue of Thutmose I, painted Black. This is lost to history and despite the numerous books being written today none contain any reference to this. Such a statue reinforces the Blackness of the 18th Dynasty. In this era another such tomb records a black image of Osiris. Cheikh Anta Diop in *The African Origin of Civilization: Myth or Reality* and *Civilization or Barbarism: An Authentic Anthropology* has shown how Egypt has been falsely represented. Underscoring the intellectual professionalism Diop brought to his studies, Cleggs' "Black Rulers of the Golden Age" in Van Sertima's *Nile Valley Civilizations* pointed out Dr. Diop relied on "anthropology, iconography, melanin dosage tests, osteological measurements, blood groupings, the testimony of classical writers, self-descriptive Egyptian hieroglyphs, divine epithets, Biblical eyewitnesses, linguistic and various cultural data in support of his opinion regarding the ethnicity of the ancient Egyptians." In fact,

EGYPT ESSAYS ON ANCIENT KEMET

Diop shows that the ancient gods and goddesses Apis, Min, Thoth, Isis, Hathor, Horus were all Black. So too was Amon the great god of Thebes during the Middle and New Empires. Equally too, in his African Origins, Diop quotes Herodotus that in Egypt the "Natives are black with the heat." Even further, regarding the Greek oracle at Adelphi, Herodotus said: "By calling the dove black they [the Dodonaceans] indicated that the woman was Egyptian." Diop further said Strabo wrote "Egypt founded Ethiopia" and that Diodorus noted "Ethiopia founded Egypt." Either way we are dealing with the same people, with the same cultural roots.

Even further, elsewhere in his *Physiognomonica*, Aristotle, in his search for the mean wrote: "Egyptians are cowards because they are black." So too were northern Europeans. The Greeks are the mean in between. Aristotle was wrong about their courage but right about their color.

If we start with the ancient scholars, historians and priests, Herodotus, Manetho, Diodorus Siculurus, Strabo, and even Aristotle and Lucian, all agree the ancient Egyptians were Black. Herodotus said the "Colchians, Ethiopians and Egyptians" were Negroes with "Broad noses, thick lips, wooly hair and had burnt" or Black skin.

Even more, when we look at the works of such brilliant scholars as Cheikh Anta Diop, the Senegalese "Pharaoh," *The African Origin of Civilization: Myth or Reality, Civilization or Barbarism: An Authentic Anthropology, The Cultural Unity of Black Africa* and Theophile Obenga's *Ancient Egypt and Black Africa*. Then Ivan Van Sertima's *Egypt Child of Africa, Egypt Revisited*, and Nile *Valley Civilizations*; then add Yosef ben-Jochannan's *Black Man of the Nile and His Family, Africa: Mother of Western Civilization, African Origins of the Major Western Religions*, and *Abu Simbel to Ghizeh: A Manual and Guide Book*. Equally too, Fred Monderson's *10 Poems Praising Great Blacks for Mike Tyson* and *Seven Letters to Mike Tyson on Egyptian Temples, Research Essays on Ancient Egypt, Egypt Essays on Ancient Kemet* and *Who were the Ancient Egyptians*, and the reader gets the full dimension of the issues, problems and solutions.

FREDERICK MONDERSON

Therefore, the work of reclamation and rectification of Africa and African roles in ancient Egypt must continually be stressed for the young should never allow their history to be systematically and continually distorted. They must continue to assert and defend Egypt as African. Not because the valuable antiquities of this wonderful heritage is in captivity in western collections and museums, must we acquiesce in the pernicious and false position that "there is no history of Africa, only a history of Europeans in Africa!" Africa has a long, rich and culturally diverse and enlightening history. She first spoke through Ethiopia, the Nile Valley and Egypt. We must continue to affirm that Egypt was a Black civilization. It was peopled by Black African for most of its duration and we must trust the work of redemptive Black scholars, researchers and historians who for many years in their careers have grappled with the questions of distortions and omissions. Now they have provided the tools to continue the fight for African historiographic reconstruction. Diop said the history of Africa couldn't be fully told without the inclusion of Egypt. As such, "The African scholar who refuses to deal with Egypt is either a neurotic or ill-educated." We must teach and defend Egypt as African and therefore Black. Egypt was a Black civilization!

Egypt Essays Photo 152. Karnak Temple of Amon-Ra. The "Red Chapel" of Hatshepsut. While Mut in Red Crown embraces Hatshepsut (left); an image of Hatshepsut, having escaped the destroyer, presents two plants to enthroned Amon-Ra (right).

EGYPT ESSAYS ON ANCIENT KEMET

30. WHO WAS MENTUHOTEP II?
BY
DR. FRED MONDERSON

Mentuhotep II's statue sits in the Cairo Museum and raises a multitude of questions about distortion, omission but even more important, who were the founders of the Middle Kingdom, the inhabitants of Thebes and Upper Egypt which goes to the heart of the question as to who were the ancient Egyptians. In 2005, this writer was told by a young female Guide in the Cairo Museum, "Mentuhotep II was painted black for the funeral ceremony." This is the "party-line" being fed visitors to the museum which is part of the grand strategy that misinforms at the root of setting the belief the ancient Egyptians were Caucasians. To this notion, any evidence that presents an individual as represented black is rationalized in a manner that purports otherwise. The most blatant example of this line of argument applies to the two lifelike statues of Tutankhamon and in his tomb discovered by Howard Carter in 1922.

In this particular case, the two life-like wooden statues of the boy king have been described as being painted black for the funerary ceremony. It has also been argued the two statues were simply guards designed to protect the king as he journeyed into the afterlife. The interesting thing about these straw-men prognosticators, and as more evidence reveal the lengths to which European and American scholarship on a racist, white supremacist bent, have gone to "paint the Egyptians white."

There are, however, many contradictions in this approach; for since, the moderns, caught in the vortex of racism, purport to know more about an ancient people, than their ancient counterparts, contemporary with these people visited, observed and lived among them and wrote about the ancient Egyptians.

Cheikh Anta Diop, in *The African Origin of Civilization*: *Myth or Reality* provides the names of several of these ancient commentators

FREDERICK MONDERSON

most notably Herodotus in his *Histories*, Book II, *Euterpe*, who wrote "The Egyptians, Ethiopians and Colchians have wooly hair, broad noses, thick lips, and are burnt of skin." A further contradiction regarding Tutankhamon's two wooden statues that are not only painted black to represent their true color but are kingly attired in gold and wearing royal insignia, viz., crowns, etc. Guards are certainly never so richly clothed! Even more, in the Hall where the statues are located, a plaque on the wall depicts other Africans colored black!

The same conundrum applies to Mentuhotep II. The young female Guide mentioned above in the Cairo Museum who described Mentuhotep as "painted black for the funerary ceremony," when asked who told you so, said, "My professors at the American University in Cairo did!" Thus, one has to wonder about the strange history being taught at this American University. After all, the American W. Stephenson Smith, in *The Art and Archaeology of Ancient Egypt* (1958) wrote Mentuhotep had "black flesh." Yet, as late as 2005, we get the above!

Now, on June 12, 1901 (291-293) the *Society of Biblical Archaeology* published, "The Tomb of Mentuhotep I at Der el Bahri, Thebes" by W.L Nash.

Accordingly, "This tomb was discovered in 1898 by Mr. Howard Carter, Inspector of Antiquities for Upper Egypt. The discovery was due to accident: Mr. Carter was returning at night to Der el Bahri when his horse stumbled into a depression in the sand which had not existed before. Hence the name Bab el Hosan, 'the tomb of the horse,' by which this tomb is commonly known among the Arabs."

In 1900 Mr. Carter commenced excavating, and at a depth of three feet from the surface came to the stone-lined sides of a passage sloping downwards from east to west, which extended close up to the south-east angle of the house; its floor, at the deepest part, being about 56 feet below the general surface of the ground. The passage was ended by the mud-brick sealing of a doorway, which was quite untouched. Beyond this doorway was a broad passage, cut in the

EGYPT ESSAYS ON ANCIENT KEMET

rock, sloping downwards, 164 yards in length, terminating in a domed chamber measuring 19 ft. 8 ins. X 26 ft. 3 ins. In this chamber was found a sandstone statue, seven feet high, of a seated figure, wearing the crown of Lower Egypt, the hands crossed over the breast, and clothed from the shoulders to the knees in a short tunic, the legs and feet left bare. The crown was painted red, the face and body black, the eyeballs white, and the tunic white. It was found lying on its side, wrapped in numerous folds of fine linen cloth. The head was broken off at the neck, no doubt whilst being lowered into the tomb, but the figure was otherwise perfect. There is no inscription, whatever on it. The other objects found in the chamber were : an empty XIth dynasty coffin, inscribed with the usual prayers for all good things to be given to the deceased, but without any name; the bones of portions of animals, including the complete skeletons of two ducks (no doubt funerary offerings); a number of red earthenware jars and shallow bowls; palm-fiber rope and wooden rollers, used for lowering the heavy statue into the tomb. In the center of the chamber the ground appeared to be hollow, and excavation revealed a shaft descending to a depth of over 100 feet below the ground level of the chamber, and therefore nearly 300 feet below the surface of the desert. The labor of clearing this shaft was very severed, the space being very confined, and the heat intense. From the bottom of this shaft opened a burial chamber, which had never been completed. Its door was closed. It contained only a few very roughly made wooden boats, and an earthenware pot.

So far nothing had been found that gave any clue to the identity of the person for whom this fine tomb was excavated; but further search revealed a shallow depression in the passage just outside the chamber – the commencement of a shaft which had never been completed – and in this was found a small wooden box made of sycamore wood, measuring about 8½ inches in length; 2 inches in width; and 5½ inches in depth, on which, very badly written in a pale blue color. Mr. Percy Newberry was the first to decipher the name of Mentuhotep.

Mr. Newberry suggests to me that the reading in the inscription on the lid of the box is very uncertain, and that the Mentuhotep whose name is given on one end of the box may be the well-known Neb Kheru-Ra, Mentuhotep; whose tomb is mentioned in the "Abbott" Papyrus as being in the neighborhood of Der el-Bahri.

In the finding of this box so inscribed may be taken as evidence that the tomb was made for Mentuhotep (whether the 1st or 3rd king of that name), the question arises, where is the king's body? It is true that tombs were often made for people who never occupied them, either they were far off when they died, or their successors adopted some other burial placed for them, etc.; but this tomb contains funerary offerings, and one can hardly suppose that such offerings have been made in the chamber of a tomb which did not contain, and never had contained, the body of the deceased. On the other hand, if the body had ever been placed in the burial chamber at the bottom of the shaft, it would surely be there now, for if it had at some time been removed, the robbers would never have taken the trouble to fill up the shaft, and to rebuild the door-sealing. It seems probable, or at all events possible, that if the rubbish was entirely cleared from the passage outside the doorway, that yet another shaft might be discovered, with, let us hope, more satisfactory results.

Today its generally acknowledged this is Mentuhotep II and as W. Stephenson Smith has affirmed, he had "Black flesh!"

Egypt Essays Photo 152a. Karnak Temple of Amon-Ra. The "Red Chapel" of Hatshepsut. Saluting Amon, Min and Amon again.

EGYPT ESSAYS ON ANCIENT KEMET

31. QUEEN OF SHEBA IN RACIAL PORTRAIT AS HISTORICAL DISTORTION
By
Fred Monderson

Standing in the line sometime ago for the cashier at a local supermarket, Met Foods, my eye caught one of the customary tabloids with headlines that read "World's Mysteries Solved." Like any enthusiastic of any such esoteric phenomenon, I purchased the paper and took it home. Such topics as a new "Discovery of Noah Ark" are re-occurring historical themes, and "Vatican Confirms the Existence of Angels," were some of the articles in this issue. Turning to the centerfold, my eyes caught the story, "Scientists Discover the Home of the Queen of Sheba." This was a short story, juxtaposed to a large picture of the Queen of Sheba. It was a picture of a beautiful woman, white! What's wrong with this picture?

Just then a friend, Rodolfo was visiting my home. When I brought this to his attention and having some familiarity with my work, he admonished: "You should write an article on this distortion." Finally I agreed. Looking at the Article again it read, "British Archaeologists have discovered the home of the Queen of Sheba, located in the southern Nigerian forest region." Often times the general reading public would overlook such a report.

Many times readers have questioned the veracity of the Tabloids to sensationalize their stories that in a number of instances are outright distortion of fact. Too often, Gary Byrd on WLIB New York radio has said, "The information you don't have cold kill you." Equally too Malcolm X has admonished his listeners to be skillful readers for newspapers have a tendency to put things in a manner that denigrates Blacks, and generally distorts the truth.

FREDERICK MONDERSON

At the beginning of the 21st Century and a new millennium Blacks in America and hence worldwide, must be concerned about the ever present problems of racism that distorts the image of Blacks whether politically, historically, culturally, psychologically or simply as human beings.

The fact is, in a general sense, the information presented to Blacks and Whites, pertaining to the same issue are colored differently. Blacks, who have been maligned for centuries, are presented with information by their scholarly researchers based on empirical inductive reasoning. Whereas, Whites are presented with the same information based on deductive reasoning. The end result is, Blacks in the know who trust the reports of serious Black researchers end up knowing the truth. Whereas, Whites who are either intentionally misinformed or are unconcerned about the nature of their sources, end up being mis-educated about a number of things. I say that to say, even in academia, you sometimes have two classes being taught down the hall from each other and the instructors teach two versions of the same issue.

I use ancient Egypt/Kemet as a good example but the distorted picture is not limited to that subject. Thus, to present my case, I will document a few examples to show that historical truths are perennially distorted and to set the record straight, men and women of objective scholarship must constantly challenge distortions.

As a student of Professor Ben-Jochannan, I have often listened to his debates and observed the ink spilled discussing a line in the Bible. Depending on the versions one consults, the question is always did the Queen of Sheba say, 'I am Black and comely.' Or, 'I am Black but comely.' In the first instance she is saying "I'm Black and Beautiful" and being proud of it. In the second instance, in saying "I'm Black but Beautiful" she is, if you will, "denigrating her Blackness but affirming her beauty." People on a pejorative bent towards Blacks flaunt the latter affirming she was not proud of her Blackness, though they would concede she was beautiful. Did the editor of the tabloid know this or was he simply uncaring and determined to distort in the belief it would go unnoticed. Of course,

EGYPT ESSAYS ON ANCIENT KEMET

if Solomon had married the Queen of Sheba and made an 'honest woman' out of her, this matter would probably have been solved. Now, in an extension of this argument, a more potent social issue is raised.

There is no need to dwell on the slavery issue in the master, slave, male-female, a la, Jefferson-Hemmings, relationship. Word on the street today is that "Black men marry white women to screw them. White men screw Black women but don't marry them." In most cases, a Black man marries a white woman for her beauty. Seldom, is she a professional. 'Guess who's coming to dinner', Michael Jackson, Clarence Thomas, Quincy Jones and O.J. Simpson. When they're out in public, more than the customary stares, questions, 'What is she doing?' and 'Why are they here?' When the relationship sours he is still the 'N' word! The White male, on the other hand, marries the Black female, primarily because of her professional standing, perhaps for her beauty. When they're out in public. 'Oh what a beautiful couple. If they're not married, it is not inconceivable that he would 'Roast her' as in the case with Whoopi Goldberg and the white actor she was seeing, who did just that on national TV. Now to move on!

Historical distortions like forgeries are nothing new. The "Donation of Constantine" is one such example of a forgery.

People with historical consciousness know that after the decline of Egyptian/Kemetic civilization, and the rise of Greece and Rome, Jesus the Christ came, was crucified, died, buried and rose again. In the centuries right after, early Christians were martyred through fear of the Roman rulers that the promised heavenly kingdom was a threat to the Roman Empire. After the games and the maulings by African lions, the martyrdoms, etc. Constantine the Great became Emperor of Rome. On the eve of a major military engagement he had a dream or vision that involved religious matters, priestly paraphernalia, the Bishop's Mitre, and insignia of his vestments. Succeeding in battle the next day, Constantine credited his dream with being part of his good fortune. He declared, "We killed enough Christians, Let's cage the lions, Stop Christians for lunch, end the crucifixion." He declared Christianity would be recognized as a legitimate religion in the Roman Empire. Church could get equal footing with state; Christians would be respected. He called the Council of Nicea in 325 A.D. and invited all the Bishops of the Christian church to hammer out the glitches in the fundamental tenets of Christianity. Constantine was hailed as the first Christian Emperor of the Roman Empire.

A document entitled "The Donation of Constantine" later surfaced and showed the Emperor had donated extensive tracts of land to the church that was tax-exempt, etc. A thousand years later, an Italian Pico Mirandella, a linguist, while doing research made a remarkable discovery. As anyone familiar with linguistics would know language constantly changes. New words are added and old words dropped. Remember, 'Where's the beef?" In this respect, Mirandella showed that the document contained words that did not come into the vernacular until centuries after Constantine; therefore, he declared the document 'Donation of Constantine' a forgery. Using the same "Where's the Beef" analogy, for example, we have a 1920s document purporting something of significance and the above line used, when the term was not yet "Born." Thus, it is considered historical fraud or misrepresentation.

The search for Prester John was one of those monumental failures that were a perennial success. Perhaps as equally important as the "riches of the east," the "search for Prester John" motivated Portuguese explorers for centuries. Since he was never found, it is not inconceivable that the thought of finding his kingdom is not a moot issue.

Following the decline of the Roman Empire and Rise of Islam, the Moors or Shakespeare's "Blackamoors" invaded Southern Europe. They occupied that land from 711 to 1485 providing the "Arab conduit" of ancient African intellectualism, developed in the Nile Valley. Perhaps in that age, the "Myth of Prester John" was born, yet it fueled particularly Portuguese aspirations of exploration and colonization. The notion of Prester John, a white king ruling a Black kingdom in Africa represented a phalanx of global White supremacy

EGYPT ESSAYS ON ANCIENT KEMET

on that continent. Everyone came, searching, yet to find this individual.

As Professor Clarke liked to say "The Africans invited Europeans for lunch and we became the meal." The result was "naked imperialism" "enlightened imperialism" and then "intellectual imperialism." Of course, the missionaries were a vanguard in colonial strategy. We can thank Jomo Kenyatta for his insightful assessment of this aftermath in *Facing Mount Kenya*. "When the missionaries came they gave us the Bible and taught us to close our eyes and pray. "When we opened our eyes, we were holding the Bible and the Europeans the land."

As a youngster growing up in Guyana, reading was an enjoyable past-time. There was no "Black History;" these were not yet "born." Even though such has been manifestly evolving from time immemorial. We were taught English History 1066-1485, from the Norman invasion to the war of the Roses and ascension of the Tudors. We read about the "Phantom" in Africa. He was a masked crusader who single-handedly subdued all comers in the heart of Africa. As if that was not enough, Edgar Rice Burroughs gave us Tarzan and Hollywood had field days in its systematic and well-choreographed denigration of the African persona. And, we all laughed heart-fully as one white man defeated and made fools of "tribes of Africans" portrayed and degraded as savages. A recent article indicated there were no Africans in 'Walt Disney's new movie, Tarzan.' That's taking it to the next level!

The Western literary traditions begin with Homer's Iliad and Odyssey. It is believed he visited Egypt/Kemet. The description of Thebes with its "palaces" and "hundred gates" refers to the City of Thebes in the time of Rameses III of the XXth Dynasty. The erudite Cheek Ana Diop argued: "If Homer visited Egypt and this fact is attested to by Greek tradition-it was probably during the time of the XXVth Sudanese Dynasty, under Piankhi or Shabaka, around 750 B.C." Then again, much controversy surrounds the Greeks in Egypt. Modern scholars have accepted some of these classical writers' views on the Egyptians but they reject salient parts particularly of an

FREDERICK MONDERSON

ethnological nature. Herodotus visited Egypt around 450 B.C. and in his *Histories* Book II, *Euterpe* is devoted to that land. Granted he traveled the land seeking information from priests who guarded their history and culture very well. Yet he secured information from them. He also observed much but he was right about their color which he observed!

In the era of the 18th Century, the American, French and Haitian Revolutions, when men aspired to the nobility of freedom, of spirit and body, Africans in American were enslaved. In that era of philosophes' and free thinking, Count Volney wrote his *Ruins of Empire*, he postulated the view, 'men and women of sable skin and frizzled hair, then enslaved, founded along the banks of the Nile River, the fundamental laws of science that governed the world, while much of humanity was still in a barbaric stage.'

In 1799, Napoleon's artillery officers discovered the now famous Black basalt tri-lingual inscription called the Rosetta Stone. In 1822, this became the basis of Champollion's decipherment of hieroglyphics, Medu Netcher. In 1836, Sir Godfrey Higgins published *Anacalypsis* in 2 vols. In this masterful work he identified the ancient races and military, political, spiritual, and religious luminaries who were Black. A powerful work of erudite scholarship, *Anacalypsis*, challenges all comers to contest its revelations.

In the age of political, military and economic imperialism intellectual advantage became an extension of that movement. Archaeological excavation in the Nile Valley got a significant boost in the years 1870-1930. Not only was that discipline placed on a systematic and scientific footing, a number of organs of literary expression were inaugurated to chronicle the constantly unfolding spectacular discoveries. The *American Journal of Archaeology* was a prominent publication among numerous others. In the 1903-04 Archaeological Season, the "Mortuary temple of Nebhepetra Mentuhotep II was discovered at Deir el-Bahari, Thebes. A statue of the king was found wearing his heb sed attire. The statue was removed and to this day resides in the Cairo Museum.

EGYPT ESSAYS ON ANCIENT KEMET

Egypt Essays Photo 153. Memphis Museum. The Memphis colossal lying in the prone position.

A phenomenon occurred which is not dissimilar by today's standards, "All the news printed to fit." All that AJA IX (1905: 98) could say of a physio-ethnological nature was the "thick lips with edges defaced by sharp ridges, the heavy chin and the muscles emphasized round the corners of the mouth and nose, are derived from the mannerisms of the late Sixth Dynasty." Again, Malcolm's admonition, "No matter what the man says, You better look into it."

For Black readers then, in an age of slavery, civil war, and aftermath reconstruction, Jim Crowism, Tenant Farming, Separate But Equal, discrimination, and racism, it was difficult for Black readers who could not analyze *AJA's* description, that it had no meaning! No major publishing vehicle in the United States carried it until W. Stephenson Smith in 1959 dared to say Mentuhotep II had "Black flesh." The statue is in the same place in the museum, but for more than half century Black readers did not know the Theban Mentuhotep II of the XIth Dynasty was a Black king. That is, until Dr. Ben Jochannan began carrying Afro-Americans to Egypt. That too, is why Prof. Monderson, a student of the august elder, intends to continue the tradition of research, writing and publication and

FREDERICK MONDERSON

carrying African people to Egypt to expose them to the ancient African heritage and legacy. Not simply Mentuhotep's statue in the Cairo Museum but the wonderful temples of Karnak, Luxor, Deir el-Bahari, Abydos, Dendera, Edfu, Esna, Kom Ombo, Philae, and Kalabsha and Beit Wali, and Abu Simbel, beckon all, with their wonderful architectural, spiritual and intellectual enlightenment, come view the wisdom of the ancients!

Tutankhamon, as Prof. Clarke likes to Say, "Was a minor king who got a major funeral." In 1922, Howard Carter discovered his tomb in the Valley of the Kings. Two life-like statues of the boy king stood at the entrance to the burial chamber. Comparative analysis is a potent tool or weapon in dismantling and destroying the myths of distortion. The French scholar Jean Yoyote in Georges Posener's *Dictionary of Egyptian Civilization* (p. 291) speaks of Tutankhamon's treasures: "Everything was there. Nests of sarcophagi, statues of the king, golden jewelry, magical and everyday furniture, golden shrines, and alabaster and faience vases, the whole comprising an unrivalled collection of objects for the study of the arts and ritual ceremonies." Elsewhere (p. 293) he says: "The everyday requirements of a prince were buried with him, including; weapons, chariots, vessels, embroidered garments, chests and other pieces of furniture. The funerary equipment of the glorified dead was always plentiful-canopic jars, ushabtis of every material and figures of gods, to which must be added portable shrines and the blackened wooden statues which had been used in the funeral rite. Everything was costly and worthy of a king. Again, elsewhere (p. 75) "The Red and Black Land." Red the desert, Black, the plain. Where the Nile "rose to flood the land and replenish it with new soil each year." Or, should I say, "Red equals Death and Black equals Life!

At the 1998, **ASCAC** Conference at City College, New York, in a taped interview, Prof. Diop says "Kemet" or "Black Land" referred to the indigenous people and not the land. He said the word does not appear with the derivative for land and that it is for the Black people. Even further, while this may not still be, owing to the reorganization of the Museum, "Blackened wooden statues" of the Kings

EGYPT ESSAYS ON ANCIENT KEMET

Amenhotep I and Amenhotep II, among others were observed by this writer. Interestingly enough, juxtaposed in the case was a black wooden statue of a panther. The placement of the panther in the case confronts and contradicts such claims those similar statues as the two from Tutankhamon's burial chamber only had ceremonial uses.

In 1985 as the nation approached the 50th Anniversary of the celebration of Columbus' discovery of America, this in itself a distortion, Dr. Cheek Ana Diop wrote a letter to the Journal of African Civilization. It discussed the finding of tobacco, a "New World strain," in the mummy of Rameses II. This mummy of the New Kingdom monarch, discovered in the late 19th Century, began to decay. It was rushed to Paris to undergo scientific surgery to arrest the decay. The Senegalese scholar Diop was qualified enough to be part of the examination team. He was only Black accorded that privilege. Perhaps had he not been there, the manifestation of the discovery and the tenacity to defend its meaning and significance would probably not been made manifest. Diop was mentioned in **UNESCO**'s final report on the "Peopling of the Nile Valley." They commended Cheikh Anta Diop and Theophile Obenga as being the best prepared of all the participants at the conference.

The esteemed multi-disciplinarian deduced that New World tobacco in Rameses' stomach meant he smoked the stuff or consumed some just before death. Even more important however, it meant his emissaries visited the New World and returned! This meant Africans were in the New World nearly 3000 years before Columbus! In addition, at the 1992 Temple University Diopian Conference, papers were presented showing the Malian king Abu Bekr and a fleet of ships left for the New World at the start of the fourteenth century nearly 200 years before Columbus. This being so, Africans should be celebrating the 700th year of that adventure. Much of this is not known, though we celebrate 500 years of the exploration, conquest and exploitation and extermination of New World peoples and cultures. Let's not forget, records in the logs of Magellan's ships indicate as they were crossing the Atlantic, 'Africans in long canoes' were observed returning from the New World. Dr. Charsee MacIntyre argued for the arrival of little

FREDERICK MONDERSON

Africans in the New World as early as 120,000 years ago. Prof. Betancourt cautioned those dates though he did affirm "firm dates" at "70,000 years" before our era.

Malcolm X looms so large in our history. A student at Temple University once submitted a dissertation request to show that the "Norse Epics" were those of Blacks! Also, that "Eric the Red" was not the white full red beard individual so often pictured. He was like say, Malcolm as "Detroit Red." The rather articulate and well-known Professor responded, "Well, without a lot more documentation, I can't sell this to the Graduate Board." It got the sort of "Let's kill it in Committee" treatment!

Finally, and cut this short, Dr. Cheek Ana Diop, also with an opportunity to examine the Cairo Mummies, in his Magnum Opus, *Civilization or Barbarism*: *An Authentic Anthropology*, informed us the mummies had their skins peeled like potatoes to hide their blackness! All this and so much more, distorted, omitted and hidden form Black readers. Thus, these bring us to the old adage: To be properly informed Blacks need critical Black researchers to ferret out the truth as well as the Black Press to keep them well informed.

Egypt Essays Photo 154. Memphis Museum. An offering table with the depression for blood to run out.

EGYPT ESSAYS ON ANCIENT KEMET

32. THE WISDOM OF THE ANCIENT EGYPTIANS

The wisdom of the ancient Egyptians is renowned for its originality and long lasting influence over time and geographical regions. From religious beginnings, through architectural and artistic experimentation, astronomy and other scientific observations, medical applications, creative literary recording and agricultural and navigational practices, the wisdom of the ancient peoples of Africa manifest through the Nile Valley region, has propelled humanity along the undulative march of civilization. Applying geographic, botanical and zoological themes to literary expression ushered in the earliest recorded writings. Exploiting the Nile River for agricultural and transportation standards and techniques, provided food, solved the problems of movement and allowed military strategy to support stable government, religious expression and patronizing of the arts. Thus, the wisdom of the ancient Egyptians can be seen in the realm of social love songs, wisdom sayings and educational teachings. It can be observed in imponderables of law, government and trade and travel. It can also be observed in divinely inspired religious ritual and royal and noble testimonials associated with their funerary practices.

Politically, centralized administration rested upon monarchical pronouncements, judicial rulings and bureaucratic and social practice. Military organization not only provided security but imperial daring helped spread cultural expression, adherence to civil order, imperialistic accumulation of wealth with patronage of the arts findings its fullest expression in statuary, painting and civil and religious architecture. So much more can be said for the renown of the wisdom of the ancient Egyptians. These Black men and women of ancient Africa who inhabited the Nile Valley spread their wisdom and influence down, up, and beyond the majestic Nile River in North-east Africa. Millennia later we celebrate their brilliance, wisdom and influence in all facets of knowledge, viz., building, science, religion, arts, literacy, transportation, measurement,

FREDERICK MONDERSON

agriculture and funerary practice. Truly the wisdom of these ancient Blacks of Africa is unparalleled.

Egypt Essays Photo 155. Native Guide "Showgi" Abd el-Rady and a friend in embrace while he does work on the cell-phone.

33. The Pyramids

The pyramids are synonymous with ancient and modern Egypt. Famous for their monumental nature, mathematical exactness, mystical wonderment and unquestioned durability, they defy the elapse of time. But what do these monuments truly represent? Some say tombs of the pharaohs. Others that these were national monuments with astronomical and religious implications. Still, others say they were designed to awe the pharaoh's contemporaries and to harness the unemployed labor force lying idle by the inundation of the Nile. All this notwithstanding, the pyramids represent early African man's conscious application of the principles of science, labor, geometry, religion, bureaucratic organizational application and a labor force willing to construct a national project in praise of their monarch and deity.

Nonetheless, careful perusal of the landscape exposes the phenomenon of natural pyramids. In a desert environment, wind and sand pounding the natural highlands creates erosion that forms a natural pyramid. Perhaps, this may be the origin of this house of

EGYPT ESSAYS ON ANCIENT KEMET

eternity. Whatever, it is difficult to argue against nature's influence against the man made creations. No matter, man's attempt to create the pyramids is a process begun in the Third Dynasty with Imhotep's Step-Pyramid at Sakkara for Pharaoh Zoser. In the first two dynasties, the kings were buried at Abydos, the nation's earliest religious capital, with cenotaphs or dummy tombs at Sakkara.

In his bold experiment, Imhotep made innovations in multi-storied building, engaged and freestanding columns, and the false-door façade. Whether end of the Third or beginning of the Fourth Dynasty, Snefru gets credit for the "Bent" and "True" Pyramids. The art advanced rapidly and within a generation before the end of the Fourth Dynasty Khufu, Khafre and Menkaure built the Great Pyramid Ghizeh group. By the Fifth Dynasty Unas had the Pyramid Texts inscribed in his structure. By the end of the Old Kingdom nearly 80 pyramids were built in Egypt. A few were built in the Middle Kingdom but by this period, the age of pyramids had passed.

The Ethiopians of the XXVth Dynasty built numerous pyramids at this later date in Nubia. These however were on a less grandiose scale.

Egypt Essays Photo 155a. Classic view of the Great Pyramid, devoid of its facings.

FREDERICK MONDERSON

34. THE CLERETORY

The Clerestory is a New Kingdom innovation in ancient Egyptian architecture that along with the colonnade beautified much of their buildings. Even more, this feature migrated and helped advance architecture in later Greece and Rome and further was significant in basilica architecture in Western Europe. Significantly however, in most post-native building in ancient Egypt, the clerestory was discontinued and cannot be found in the Graeco-Roman temples at Philae, Kom Ombo, Edfu and Esneh. This paradox raises questions as to why this feature developed and why was it discontinued.

We know it was a feature of both worship and mortuary temples. The first was developed at Thutmose's *Akh Menu* at Karnak and later in the Great Hypostyle Hall there. The last clerestory adorned the hypostyle hall of Rameses III's mortuary temple at Medinet Habu. Existing remains at the Ramesseum depict this feature. While most of the other mortuary temples littering the Theban plains have suffered at the hands of despoilers and time, the assumption is they probably followed this pattern of building feature. Nevertheless, the clerestory as an architectural feature will be explored to trace its evolution in the New Kingdom and further investigate why it was discontinued.

1.   Thutmose III Festival Temple, the Akh Menu, at Karnak

2.   Temple of Soleb of Amenhotep III represented a new form of architecture initiated by Amenhotep III utilizing the processional colonnade. The lateral extension of this structure enabled an expansion of the hall necessitating the use of a clerestory to light the building.

The possibility exists that Amenhotep's mortuary temple, destroyed in an earthquake may have had this feature particularly since his experimentation in a new form of architecture at Soleb and use of the processional Colonnade at both Karnak and Luxor.

3.   Karnak's Hypostyle Hall is a classic and visible example of the use of the clerestory particularly since some of its gratings have survived the vicissitudes of time, not necessarily the destructive acts of man since its height still posed a challenge to the long reach of "raiders of the Egyptian ark."

4.   The Ramesseum – In keeping with the tradition of the clerestory of mortuary temples, the Ramesseum found its most profound expression in use of this feature. All that has been said of Rameses II's building and expropriation of other's works, his final resting place represented some of his best work. It can be argued that with the clerestory feature of his predecessors and his involvement in finalizing Karnak's Hypostyle Hall, much of this influenced the planning and execution of his mortuary temple.

5.   Medinet Habu's Hypostyle Hall Temple of Rameses III – While the principal part of the Temple of Rameses III housed the Hypostyle Hall with a roof, this fell in some time ago. A village resided over it and this helped further in its deterioration. However, in as much as this temple was a carbon copy of Rameses' hero, Rameses II and Rameses III duplicated much of the Ramessseum in his mortuary structure, it is easy to argue, Medinet Habu had a hypostyle hall.

Nevertheless, since this structure was the last major building project of the New Kingdom, the hypostyle feature was discontinued after this time and the temples we know of the Graeco-Roman periods were devoid of this feature.

FREDERICK MONDERSON

35. WALLS IN ANCIENT EGYPTIAN TEMPLES AND TOMBS
By
Dr. Fred Monderson

Building walls in ancient Egypt is an art form that very early reached mastery levels. As a result, a number of types of walls were executed and while some were decorated others were not. This particular feature span the whole gamut of Egyptian architectural engineering and varied in size, placement, disposition, height, nature of the stone used and much more. The forms of this construction came to include the enclosure wall that surrounds any structure, whether religious, domestic or mortuary. While, however, not too many enclosure walls have remained intact in Egypt, there is equally a dearth of domestic buildings that have survived from ancient times simply because they were built of perishable materials. So we are therefore left mostly with religious and mortuary structures that were essentially built of stone to last for eternity. In such constructions then, the utility determined the expansion relating to size of area covered, height, thickness as well as the prevailing decorative feature that enhanced the outward appearance and equally what was encompassed within any such structure.

The earliest surviving example of this Enclosure Wall variety is found at Sakkara where Imhotep built his Step-Pyramid for the Pharaoh Zoser. The Third Dynasty, 2600 B.C., was a time of architectural innovation, motivated by genius elevating monarchy to divinity status. In this age of experimentation, the wall, as a convention, established standards of layout, decoration, durability and utility as the art form seemed guided by divine inspiration.

Praising his king, this multi-genius and architect built a wall some of which still stands that enclosed the parameters of the pyramid complex. Central to the mortuary complex was the pyramidal form of mastaba that rose several stories above ground with a sub-

EGYPT ESSAYS ON ANCIENT KEMET

structure that was very complex. In addition to his tomb, within the enclosure was found a Valley Temple along a Causeway, or roadway that led from the Nile River. Here the deceased was welcomed by priests who performed the ritual of reception. Along this path was found a Sacrificial Altar, and another, this time, Sun Temple. A Sphinx stood guard as customary and beside was an Obelisk. In a united land, the monarch was King of the Upper and Lower Kingdoms. Therefore, two "dummy buildings" represented the Upper and Lower Kingdoms and in the Heb Sed Festival he ran around them to signify encompassing the whole of Egypt over which he ruled. Of course, there was a Heb Sed Festival Pavilion from which he began the race. Beside these two were Magazines for Storage of necessaries the deceased hoped to utilize in the afterlife. On the other side of the King's Pyramid were smaller Pyramids for Queens and Princesses related to him. Beside these were Mastabas for Nobles who relished being buried in the shadow of their sovereign's final resting place. To be in close proximity of his immortality was beneficial to their everlastingness. In this vicinity there was another, this time, Temple for the God worshipped by the king. In a culture and nation served by a river, boats were the principal modes of transportation. Therefore, the king had a pit called a Solar Boat Pit dug to house his Solar Boat that would take him to the next world. By the time of the Great Pyramid's evolution, Zoser, its builder, had five such pits dug and equipped with Solar Boats. These then were the components Imhotep's Enclosure Wall encapsulated.

In the evolution of the building practice, religious worship and mortuary temples were not as varied in their components, though they were either single or multiple structures within the wall. Hence, from what we can tell, from the Middle Kingdom, down through the New Kingdom and into the Greek and Roman Periods, the Enclosure Wall came to serve a number of purposes. Sure they kept the secrets of the temple safe from prying eyes. They also kept others out. However, in times of danger, they also served as a refuge for which inhabitants hid within their seemingly impregnable or imposing dimensions.

FREDERICK MONDERSON

Within the Enclosure Wall the temple and ancillary buildings had walls that were decorated on the outside and within. Within the enclosure itself there was an Open or Great Court where celebrants were permitted to congregate yet prohibited from venturing further into the deeper recesses of the structure. Just as the outer enclosure wall was sometimes decorated, so too the inner wall beyond the Pylon was also decorated. Next, the temple structure itself was decorated on the outside and also on the inside that even fewer individuals were privy to their contents. So from historical events on the outside of the walls to more esoteric depictions of the temple ritual within, the walls were built to support the structure as well as to be a canvass on which a great deal of which we know today was inscribed.

Interestingly enough, from the earliest period of the Old Kingdom, temple and mortuary rituals were either handed down orally or reduced to scrolls as very little illustrations were found associated with the pyramids and early temples. This was not so with the mastaba tombs of great nobles who went to great lengths to graphically depict social existence with hopes of such having impacts on their future existence. By the Middle and New Kingdoms, temples began to be decorated, more or less, illustratively, with little text. However, by the Graeco-Roman Period there was a great deluge of illustrative and textual depictions on the walls of temples. Since such decoration simply continued the traditions of old, they helped, in their new form, to provide a great deal of the knowledge we now possess of the most ancient beliefs and practices.

EGYPT ESSAYS ON ANCIENT KEMET

36. THE BLESSING

The blessing, particularly at this time of year, is always a wonderful experience, in trying to reflect on the nature of courage in meeting challenges. My Uncle Lynton Lawrence has always made us aware, each obstacle that creates a challenge to be overcome, builds inner strength. How equally inspirational it seems when we remember some of our teachers' particularly wise sayings. I'm reminded of my greatest mentor, Dr. Leonard James, Emeritus of New York City Technical College of the City University of New York. Dr. James always admonished his students by telling us: "Granny always said, don't trust no shadows after dark," and even at noon, the shadows are there. Dr. James also said: "The more monkey climb up, the more monkey exposes himself."

Another favorite of his has been, "As a black-man in a racist society, I expect to be knocked down, but as long as I answer the bell, that all that matters."

Wilson (1901: 96) supplies the thoughts of the blessing. "Of Receiving Paths" from the *Papyrus of Nu* in the British Museum, No. 10,477, sheet 9:

THE CHAPTER OF RECEIVING PATHS [WHEREON TO WALK] IN RE-STAU.

"The chancellor-in-chief, Nu, triumphant, saith: "The paths which are above me [lead] to Re-stau. I am he who is girt about with his girdle and who cometh forth from the [goddess of] the Ureret crown. I have come, and I have stablished things in Abtu (Abydos), and I have opened out paths in Re-stau. The god Osiris hath eased my pains. I am he who maketh the waters to come into being, and who setteth his throne [thereon], and who maketh his path through the funeral valley and through the Great Lake. I have made my path, and indeed I am [Osiris].

FREDERICK MONDERSON

"[Osiris was victorious over his enemies, and the Osiris Nebqet is victorious over his enemies. He hath become as one of yourselves, [O ye gods], his protector in the Lord of eternity, he walketh even as ye walk, he standeth even as ye stand, he sitteth even as ye sit, and he talketh even as ye talk in the presence of the Great God, the Lord of Amentet.] [The words in brackets are from the Papyrus of Nebqet (sheet 3).]"

Wilson (1901: 96-97) "OF COMING FORTH FROM RE-STAU" from the *Papyrus of Nu* in the British Museum No. 10,477, sheet 9.

THE CHAPTER OF COMING FORTH FROM RE-STAU. The chancellor-in-chief, Nu,

Triumphant, saith: "I was born in Re-Satu, and splendor hath been given unto me by those who dwell in their spiritual bodies (sahu) in the habitation where libations are made unto Osiris. The divine ministers who are in Re-stau shall receive [me] when Osiris is led into the twofold funeral region of Osiris; oh, let me be a divine being whom they shall lead into the twofold funeral region of Osiris.

Wilson (1901: 97-98) "OF COMING FORTH FROM RE-STAU" from the *Papyrus of Nu* in the British Museum No. 10,477, sheet 9.

THE CHAPTER OF COMING FORTH FROM RE-STAU. [A fuller title of this chapter is: "The Chapter of knowing the name of Osiris, and of going into and of coming forth from Re-stau."] The chancellor-in-chief, Nu, triumphant, saith: "I am the Great God who maketh his light. I have come to thee, O Osiris, and I offer praise unto thee. [I am] pure from the issues which are carried away from thee. Thy name is made in Re-stau, and thy power is in Abtu (Abydos). Thou art raised up, then, O Osiris, and thou goest round about through heaven with Ra, and thou lookest upon the generations of men, O thou One who circlest, thou Ra. Behold, verily, I have said unto thee, O Osiris, 'I am the spiritual body of the God,' and I say, 'Let it come to pass that I shall never be repulsed before thee, O Osiris.'"

EGYPT ESSAYS ON ANCIENT KEMET

The following is the chapter in a fuller form. [For the text see Naville, op. cit. Bd. I. Bl. 130]. THE CHAPTER OF KNOWING THE NAME OF OSIRIS AND OF ENTERING AND OF GOING OUT FROM RE-STAU [IN ALL THE FORMS WHEREIN HE WILLETH TO COME FORTH.] The following is the chapter in a fuller form. [The words in the brackets are from the *Papyrus of Amen-em-heb*. See Naville, op. cit. Bd. II. p. 267.] The scribe Mes-em-neter, triumphant, saith: "I am the Great Name who maketh his light. I have come to thee, O Osiris, and I offer praise unto thee. I am pure from the issues, which are carried away from thee. [Thy] name hath been made in Re-stau when it hath fallen therein. Homage to thee, O Osiris, in thy strength and in thy powers, thou hast obtained the mastery in Re-stau, and thy power is in Abtu (Abydos). Thou goest round about through heaven, and thou sailest before Ra, and thou lookest upon the generations of men, O thou Being who circlest, thou Ra. Behold, verily, I have said unto thee, O Osiris, 'I am the spiritual body of the God', and I say, 'Let it come to pass that I shall never be repulsed before thee, O Osiris.'"

Wilson (1901: 98) "OF GOING ABOUT IN THE UNDERWORLD" from the *Papyrus of Nu* in the British Museum No. 10,477, sheet 9.

THE CHAPTER OF GOING IN AFTER COMING FORTH [FROM THE UNDERWORLD.] The overseer of the palace, the chancellor-in-chief, Nu, triumphant, saith:

"Open unto me? Who then art thou? Whither goest thou? What is thy name? I am one of you, 'Assembler of Souls' is the name of my boat; 'Making the hair to stand on end' is the name of the oars; 'Watchful one' is the name of its bows; 'Evil is it' is the name of the rudder; 'Steering straight for the middle' is the name of the Matchabet; so like-wise [the boat] is a type of my sailing onward to the pool. Let there be given me vessels of milk, together with cakes, and loaves of bread, and cups of drink, and pieces of meat in the Temple of Anpu," or (as others say), "Grant thou me [these things] wholly. Let it be so done unto me that I may enter in like a hawk, and that I may come forth like the Bennu Bird, [and like] the Morning Star. Let me make [my] path so that [I] may go in peace into the beautiful Amentet, and let the Lake of Osiris be mine. Let me make my path, and let me enter in, and let me adore Osiris, the Lord of life."

Wilson (101: 98-99) "ON ENTERING INTO THE GREAT HOUSE" from the *Papyrus of Nu* in the British Museum No. 10,477, sheet 10.

THE CHAPTER OF ENTERING INTO THE GREAT HOUSE. The overseer of the palace, the chancellor-in-chief, Nu, triumphant, saith: "Homage to thee, O Thoth. I am Thoth, who has weighed the two divine Fighters (i.e., Horus and Set), I have destroyed their warfare and I have diminished their wailings. I have delivered the Atu fish in his turning back, and I have performed that which thou didst order concerning him, and afterward I lay down within my eye. [I am he who hath been without opposition. I have come; do thou look upon me in the Temple of Nem-hra (or Uhem-hra).] I give commands in the words of the divine aged ones, and, moreover, I guide for thee the lesser deities."

Egypt Essays Photo 156. Partial view of greenery and the Cairo Skyline from the Mena House Garden Hotel.

EGYPT ESSAYS ON ANCIENT KEMET

38. REFERENCES

Armour, Robert A. *Gods and Myths of Ancient Egypt*. Cairo: The American University in Cairo Press, (1986) 1989.

Baines, John and Jaromir J. Malek. *Cultural Atlas of Ancient Egypt*. New York: Facts on File, 1980.

Ben-Jochannan, Yosef Antonio. *African Origins of the Major "Western" Religions: Judaism, Christianity, Islam*. New York: Alkebu-lan Book Publishing Company, (1970) 1973.

_____. *Africa: Mother of Western Civilization*. New York: Alkebu-lan Book Publishing Company, 1971.

_____. *Black Man of the Nile*. New York: Alkebu-Lan Book Publishing Company, 1972.

Bierbrier, Morris. *The Tomb-Builders of The Pharaohs*. Cairo: The American University in Cairo Press, (1982) 1989.

Breasted, J. H. *Ancient Records of Egypt*. Vol. I. Chicago: University of Chicago Press, 1905.

Budge, E. A. Wallis. *Osiris and the Egyptian Resurrection* Vol. II. New York: Dover Publishing Company, (1904) 1969.

_____. *Dwellers on the Nile*. New York: Benjamin Bloom, Inc., (1885) 1972.

Clarke, John Henrik. "African-Americans in Science and Invention: A Bibliographical Guide." *Journal of African Civilizations* Vol. 1, No. 2 (November 1979: 82-84).

Diop, Cheikh Anta. "Letter to the Editor." *Journal of African Civilizations* Vol. 1. No. 2. (November, 1979, 97).

_____. "Africa's Contribution to World Civilization: The Exact Sciences." *Nile Valley Civilizations*. Edited by Ivan Van Sertima. *Journal of African Civilizations* (1985) 1986: 69-83.

_____. *African Origins of Civilization: Myth or Reality*. New York: Lawrence Hill and Co., (1955) 1974.

_____. *Civilization or Barbarism: An Authentic Anthropology*. Brooklyn, New York: Lawrence Hill Books, (1981) 1991.

_____. *Pre-colonial Black Africa*. Westport, Connecticut: Lawrence Hill and Company, 1987.

FREDERICK MONDERSON

Erman, Adolf. *Handbook of Egyptian Religion*. London: Archibald Constable, and Company, 1907.
Finch, Charles. "The African Background of Medical Science" in *Blacks in Science: Ancient and Modern*. Edited by Ivan Van Sertima. New Brunswick, New Jersey: Transaction Books, (1983: 140-156).
George, R. D. "Mining and the Use of Metals in Ancient Egypt." *Popular Science* 67: 687.
Gillings, Richard J. *Mathematics in the time of the Pharaohs*. New York: Dover Publications, Inc., (1972) 1982.
Habachi, Labib. *The Obelisks of Egypt*. Cairo: The American University in Cairo Press, (1984) 1987.
Herodotus. *The Histories*. Trans. by Aubrey de Selincourt. Revised and with an Introduction and Notes by A. R. Burn. New York: Penguin Books, (1954) 1972.
How, W. W. and J. Wells. *A Commentary on Herodotus*. Vol. I (2 Vols.) Oxford at the Clarendon Press, 1912.
Hurry, Jamieson B. *Imhotep: The Egyptian God of Medicine*. Chicago: Ares Publishers, Inc., (1926) 1987.
Lucas, A. *Ancient Egyptian Materials and Industries*. London: Histories and Mysteries of Man, Ltd., (1926) 1989.
Lumpkin, Beatrice. "Africa in the Mainstream of Mathematics History" in Blacks *in Science: Ancient and Modern*. Edited by Ivan Van Sertima. New Brunswick, New Jersey: Transaction Books, (1983: 100-109).
_____. "Mathematics and Engineering in the Nile Valley" *Nile Valley Civilizations*. Edited by Ivan Van Sertima. *Journal of African Civilizations*: (1985) (1986: 102-119).
Magdi M. el-Kammash. "The Nile." *Encyclopedia Britannica* 15th Edition. Chicago: Encyclopedia Britannica, Inc., Vol. 13, 102-108.
Maspero, Gaston. *Manual of Egyptian Archaeology*. New York: G. Putnam and Sons, 1926.
Mertz, Barbara. *Red Land, Black Land*. New York: Dodd, Mead, and Company, (1966) 1978.
"Minerals." *Scientific American* 70 (July 26, 1913).
Murray, Margaret. *The Splendor That Was Egypt*. New York: Philosophical Society, 1949.

EGYPT ESSAYS ON ANCIENT KEMET

Newsome, Frederick. "Black Contributions to the Early History of Western Medicine." *Blacks in Science: Ancient and Modern*. Edited by Ivan Van Sertima. New Brunswick, New Jersey: Transaction Books, (1983: 127-139).

Pappademos, John. "An Outline of Africa's Role in the History of Physics" in *Blacks in Science: Ancient and Modern*. Edited by Ivan Van Sertima. New Brunswick, New Jersey: Transaction Books, (1983: 177-96).

Petrie, W. M. Flinders. *Religious Life in Ancient Egypt*. London: Constable and Co., (1924) 1932.

_____. *Social Life in Ancient Egypt*. New York: Houghton Mifflin Company, 1923.

_____. *Wisdom of the Egyptians*. London: Bernard Quaritch, 1940.

Reeve, Carole. *Egyptian Medicine*. Bucks: Shire Publications, 1992.

Rogers, J. A. *World's Great Men of Color*. Vol. I. New York: Macmillan, 1972.

Saber, Mohamed. *Pyramids and Mastabas*. Cairo: Lehnert and Landrock, Art Publishers, [ND].

Scheel, Bernard. *Egyptian Metalworking and Tools*. Bucks: Shire Publications Ltd., 1989.

Singer, Charles and E. J. Holymyard and A. R. Hall assisted by E. Jaffe, R. H. G. Thomson and M.M. Donaldson *A History of Technology Vol. I. From Early Times to the Fall of Ancient Empires*. Oxford at the Clarendon Press, (1954) 1956.

Steindorff, George and Keith C. Seele. *When Egypt Ruled The East*. Revised by Keith C. Seele. Chicago: University of Chicago Press, (1942) 1971.

Taylor, G. "Mediterranean Pilgrimage: Egypt in the Early Metal Age." *Canadian Journal* 22: 224.

Thomas, Angela P. *Akhenaten's Egypt*. Bucks: Shire Publications Ltd., 1988.

Uphill, Eric P. *Egyptian Towns and Cities*. Bucks: Shire Publications Ltd., 1988.

Watson, Philip. *Egyptian Pyramid and Mastaba Tombs*. Bucks: Shire Publications Ltd., 1987.

White, J. E. Manchip. *Everyday Life in Ancient Egypt*. New York: G. Putnam's Sons, (1963) 1980.

_____. *Ancient Egypt: Its Culture and History*. New York: Dover Publications, Inc., 1970.

Wilson, Epiphanus. *Egyptian Literature*. New York: The Colonial Press, 1901.

Wilson, J. A. *The Culture of Ancient Egypt*. Chicago: University of Chicago Press, (1951) 1975.

Egypt Essays Illustration 1b. In that familiar pose Goddess Isis kneels with outstretched arms exposing her winged prowess.

EGYPT ESSAYS ON ANCIENT KEMET

INDEX

Aahmose (Ahmose, Ahmosis, Amosis) 106-107
Abarry, Abu at Temple University 394-397
Abydos 69, 421-422
    Home of Osiris 405
    Royal Tombs at, 69
Abydos and Sakkara tombs 229
Adams, Barbara 66
    (1988) *Predynastic Egypt* 66
Adultery 428-430, 766-767
Aeschylus (525-456 B.C.) 55
African Art 365-393
African American intellectual nationalists 52
    African Religions 209-210, 259-260, 334-334, 361-362, 443-448, 452-456, 488, 494-496, 532-534, 551-552, 554-556, 575-576, 595-596, 624, 633-634, 661-662, 663-665, 679-680
    African scholars, great 210
Afrocentric Course of Study 281
Afrocentric scholarship 207-208
Afrocentricity 61, 77, 78
    Components of 353-359
    Challenge to 491-493
Age of Predynastic Period 767-768
Agricultural beginnings along the Nile 24
Akh Menu 133-134
Akhnaton with ear-holes 91
Akhnaton and knowledge 92
Aldred, Cyril 51, 85, 95, 105, 107
    (1967) 96
    (1987) *The Egyptians*
Alexandria 507-514
Alexandria, name of 740
Amenhotep (107)
Amon and Amon-Ra 272-273
Amon's Ennead 103
Amon in Nubia 774-775

FREDERICK MONDERSON

Amon's Second Home 145
Amarna Revolution 524-526
Ancestor Worship 769
Ancient History 234-235, 266-267, 268-269, 315-316, 331-332, 362, 397-398, 451-452, 534-536, 552-554, 556 571-572, 572-575, 594, 596, 615, 623, 624-626, 633-634, 666-667,
Annals of Thutmose III 134
Aristotle 40, 483
    Metaphysics 40
    Physiognomonica 50
Armour, Robert A 124
    (1989) *Gods and Myths of Ancient Egypt*
Art 460
Art in people's homes 622
Articles
    "Dr. Yosef A.A. Ben-Jochannan" 6-13
    "The Nile Valley" 23-39
    "Egypt, Kush, Ethiopia 49-53
    "Flow of the Nile" 62-63
    "Temple of Karnak: Majestic Architecture of Ancient Kemet" 79-145
    "Temple of Luxor" 145-164
    "The Ramesseum" 236-255
    "Technology in a Global Community" 309-313
    "Medinet Habu: Mortuary Temple of Rameses III" 335-337
    "The Dance, Music and Musical Instruments" 457-473
    "The Priesthood" 474-487
    "Abydos: Home of Osiris" 405
    "Temple of Dendera" 406-408
    "The Nile Valley in Antiquity History" 539-551
    "Fascination of Egyptian Archaeology" 578-591
    "Egypt and Africa" 627-631
    "Franklin Avenue Shuttle: Shuttle into the Millennium" 654-659
    "The Illustrious Queen Mother" 689-698
    "Black Egypt and the Struggle for Inclusion" 725-728
    "Queen of Sheba in Racial Portrait as Historical Distortion" 749-757

EGYPT ESSAYS ON ANCIENT KEMET

"Spreading the Knowledge" 783-784
Asante, Molefi 74, 256-257, 261-262 301-305, 399, 740
    Ancient Egyptian Philosophers 740
    (1991) "Afrocentricity and the Human Future" 317-326, 399-403
Asante's name 261
ASCAC 53, 88
Atone for transgressions 671
Authority 226-227
Avenue of Sphinxes 113, 152
Ba 227, 433
Bacon, Sir Francis (1561-1626) 40
    The Advancement of Learning 57
Badawy 81
    (1990)
Baikie, James 466-467
    (1917) "Egyptian Music"
Baines, J and J. Malek 65, 85, 86, 87123
    (1980) *Atlas of Ancient Egypt* 65
Balance 619
Baldwin, James 264
    Nobody Knows My Name
Barnett, Mary 93
    (1996) *Egypt: Gods and Myths of Ancient Egypt*
Battle of Kadesh 154
Bekenkhonsu 135
    Boast 151
Behaviors Egyptians frown upon 426
Belzoni 85
Ben-Jochannan, Dr. Yosef A.A. 6-13, 41. 120, 151, 463, 425
    (1970) *African Origins of the Major Western Religions* 59
    (1971) *Africa: Mother of Western Civilization* 59
    (1972) *Black man of the Nile and his Family* 59
    (1989) *Abu Simbel to Ghizeh* 59
Benjamin's, Dr. Lecture on Cairo Museum Visit 759-763
Bierbrier, Morris 92
    (1989) *The Tomb Builders of the Pharaohs*
Bishop Thomas Brigham 71

FREDERICK MONDERSON

Black Egyptians 219-220
Blacks removed from Egypt 201
Black History 393-394
    Importance of 203
Blacksmith, characteristics of 684
Blasphemy 619
Blessing, the 607-612
Bonechi 237
    (1994) *Art and History of Egypt*
Book of the Dead editions 223-225
Book of Thoth 277
Bovill, E.W. 391-392
    (1970) *Golden Trade of the Moors*
Bratton, Fred Gladstone 103, 119, 149, 238
    (1968) *A History of Egyptian Archaeology*
Breasted, James Henry 246-247, 248-249, 460
    (1923) *A History of Egypt*
Budge, E.A. Wallis 70, 114, 116, 125-127, 134, 249, 460-462
    (1904) *The Gods of the Egyptians*
    (1911) *Osiris and the Egyptian Resurrection*
    (1972) *Dwellers on the Nile*
Builders of Luxor Temple 147
Breasted, J.H. 135
    (1923) *A History of Egypt*
Brightness of Aton, the Great 92
Broderick, Matthew
    (1902) *Dictionary of Egyptian Archaeology* 32
Brown, John 55
Brugsch, H.
    Egypt Under the Pharaohs
Building materials 769-770
"Cachette Court" 102, 103
Cairo Museum 218
Calendars 32, 112, 528-530, 746-747
Campbell, David 238
    (1996) *Egypt: Everyman's Guide*
Canon of proportion 382-383
Carpiceci, Alberto Carlo 70

EGYPT ESSAYS ON ANCIENT KEMET

    (1994) *Art and History of Egypt*
Carruthers, Dr. Jacob on Hegel 214-215
Celestial cow 741
Centers of Civilization 24
Centers of Religious Worship 34, 111
Ceremonies 646
Champollion 85, 234
Chancellor 618
Change 618
Chappell 465
    (1874) *The History of Music*
Character, Egyptian 645
Chevier, H. 101
Childe, V. Gordon 24
    (1938) *New Light on the Most Ancient East* 24
Christianity and Christians in Egypt 569-570
Circumcision 748
Clarke, John H. Prof/Dr. 25, 51, 68, 202
Clarke and Engelbach 134
    (1930) (1990) *Ancient Egyptian Construction and Architecture*
Class in Egypt 569
Cleanliness of priests 747
Clemens of Alexandria (2nd Century A.D.) 86
Color of Egyptians 216
Columns, names or types of 642
"Coca Cola temple" 68
Command 617
Compte, Auguste (1798-1857) 41
    System of Positive Philosophy 41
Confucius (541-479) 57, 75
Conversation 617
Contributions of Africa 317
Council, the 617
Court of the Bubastites 115
Cottrell 136, 139
    (1965) *Egypt*
Covenant 617

Creator Gods 644
Creation myths 721
Criminal behavior 647
Criteria for Critical Reading 203
Critical African historians 52
Crowns of Egypt 741
Cubia, Teddy 78
    "Black is Light"78
    "The Game"61-62
    "Battle Cry" 232
    "Black Love" 283-284
    "Red, Black and Green" 360
    "Now's the Time to Kill the Swine" 497-498
    "What is a Brother" 537
Culture 330
Culture of ancient Egyptians 351-352
Damage to monuments 559-561
Danquah, J.B. 264
    (1924) *Africa at the Bar of Nations*
    (1928) *Akan Law and Customs*
David 150, 154, 157-158
    (1993)
Death, view of 427
Deir el Bahari 279-272, 631-632, 757-758
    Temples at 419-420
Dendera 69
Description of Egypt 100
Deity, supreme 523-524
Diodorus Siculus 50, 466
Diop, Cheikh Anta 42, 51, 59, 217, 265, 398
    (1974) *The African Origin of Civilization:*
        Myth or Reality 42
    (1991) *Civilization or Barbarism*
Divine lineage of kings 344
Dr. Monderson's schooling *620-621*
DuBois, W.E.B. 52, 115, 262,
    (1903) *The Souls of Black Folks*
    (1915) *The Negro* 52

EGYPT ESSAYS ON ANCIENT KEMET

    (1946) *The World and Africa* 52
    (1971)
Eames 82, 242
    (1990) (1992) *Insight Guides: The Nile*
Eastern Desert 25
Egyptian agriculture
Egyptian baptism 769
Egyptian books 619
Egyptian capitals 72
Egyptian chronology 347
Egyptian collections, most significant 530
Egyptian columns 73
Egyptian education
Egyptian family 668-670
Egyptian ideas of the future life 716
Egyptian magic 716-717
Egyptian marriage 719
Egyptian origin of Greek-Doric Column 74
Egyptian philosophy 490-491, 493
Egyptian myths 84
Egyptian sayings 514-516
Egyptian society 565
Egyptian symbolism 42, 84, 86
Egyptian Universe 435-441, 526-528, 556-559
Eliot, Charles William (1834-1926) 41
Eliot, Thomas Stearns (1888-1969) 75
Ellis, Havelock (1859-1939
    Dance of Life 74
Engel 470
    (1864) *History of Music*
Erman, Adolf 93, 118, 238
    (1907) *A Handbook of Egyptian Religion*
    (1995) *Ancient Egyptian Poetry and Prose*
Esneh, Edfu, Kom Ombo temples 499-507
Ethiopians, history 415-418
Ezekiel 40
Fagan, Brian 150
    (1975) *The Rape of the Nile*

FREDERICK MONDERSON

Fage, Bernard 388-389
    (1976) *History of West Africa*
Fairservis, Jr., Walter A. 39?
    (1962) *The Ancient Kingdoms of the Nile* 24
Fedden 122, 146
    (1986) Egypt: Land of the Valley
Festivals in Ancient Egypt 668
"Fighting Province" 90
First Intermediate Period 488
First Three Nomes 65
Foodstuff 34, 619
Fragner, Benjamin 83
    (1994) *The Illustrated History of Architecture*
Frankfort 58
    Before Philosophy 58Friendly, Alfred 370
Garvey's classic statement 690
Geography of the Gods 212
Geographical lists 128
Gladstone Atwell Middle School No. 61 298
Gods, animal forms 676-677
Gods, group of 676
Gods, sick 645
Gods, view of 675
Golden Section (phi) 84
Good-bye celebration 780-782
Good qualities 774
Goodwin 96
    (1876) *Records of the Past*
Great Hymn to Aton 92
Greek and Roman temples 722
"Grand Lodge" 147
Gregorian, Dr. Vartan 198
Grimal (1992) *A History of Egypt*
Gympel 83
    (1996) *The Story of Architecture*
Haag 151, 152, 242
    (1987) *Guide to Egypt*
    Josephine's brazen request of Napoleon 151

EGYPT ESSAYS ON ANCIENT KEMET

Habachi 86, 125, 127, 152
    (1987)
Hall of Ancestors 133
Hart 104, 113, 150
    (1990)
    (1996)
Hatshepsut 109, 123-129, 153, 694, 729-730
    Temple building foundation 153
    Punt 420
Heavenly existence 622-623
Heb Sed Festival 714
Helmholtz (1821) 1894) 76
    Academic Discourse 76
Herodotus 59, 465
    Histories
        Euterpe 50
Hieroglyphics 273
High Priest, function of 723
History, earliest fixed 348-349
Hobson 150
    (1987) *The World of the Pharaohs*
Youssef, Hisham and John Rodenbeck 406
    (1991) *Egypt: Insight Guides*
Horemhab (Horemheb) 136
Human sacrifice 673-674
Huxley, Thomas Henry (1825-1895) 70
Hyksos 105-106
Hymn to Amon 96-98
Hypostyle Hall 119-121
Ifa Divination 649-653
Imhotep 714
Imhotep's rise to divinity status 673
Imperial pharaohs 111
Inherited property 724
Inundation 431-432
James, T.G.H. 109
    (1984) (1985) *Pharaoh's People*
James, Leonard 203

Jewelry and tools 66
Job 71
Jordan, Paul 138
    (1976) *Egypt: The Black Land*
Joubert, Joseph (1754-1824) 41
Judges in the Hall 518
Justice administered 773
Ka 227, 433
Kamil 66, 115, 148, 149, 243, 406, 478, 481
    (1980) *Luxor: A Guide to Ancient Thebes*
    (1996 *Upper Egypt and Nubia*
Karnak temple 68-69
    Builders at 81
    "Most select of places" 68-69, 87
    Temples at 85
Kemetic pantheon 104
King list 349
King, names of 346-347
Kings, oldest name of 345
King and the Gods, relationship 347
Kiosk of Senwosret I (1970-1936) 65
King Lists 100
    Abydos 100
    Karnak 100
    Sakkara 100
    Second Abydos 100
King's Titles (Names) 65
    Horus 65
    Suten Bat 65
    Golden Horus 65
    Two ladies 65
    Son of Ra 65
Knopf, Alfred A. 87
    (1995) *Egypt*
Knowledge, possession 228
Kush, Indus Kamit 49
    (1983) *What They Never Taught You in History Class* 49
Langenscheidt 82, 239

EGYPT ESSAYS ON ANCIENT KEMET

    (1990) (1993) *Egypt: Self Guided*
Leakey, Mary and Louis 368-369
Legend of Osiris 644
Le Grain's work at Karnak 103
Lepsius 72-74
L'Hote, Henry 366-368
    (1938) "Tassili Frescoes"
Library of Congress 75, 263
Libraries in ancient Egypt 273-274
Locke, John (1632-1704) 75
    Second Treatise on Civil Government 75
Lord Burleigh (1592) 40
Love 275
Lumumba, Patrice 265
    Congo: My Country
Lurker, Manfred 84, 131, 151
    (1991) *The Gods and Symbols of Ancient Egypt*
Luxor Temple 433-434
    Pylon 154
    Visitors to 150-151
Ma'at, Goddess 227
Magic 33, 571
Manetho 276
Mann, A.T. 83, 84
    (1993) *Sacred Architecture*
Manners 276
Marriage 277
Maspero, Gaston 91, 92, 95, 121-122, 149, 150-151, 153, 236, 245-246, 249-250, 400
    407-408
    (1904) *History of Egypt, Assyria, Chaldea*
    (1926) *A Manual of Egyptian Archaeology*
Mastabas 277, 280
Materials for building 640-642
Maulana Karenga 260-261
Maxims 277
McGrath 103, 240
    (1982) *Frommer's Dollarwise Guide to Egypt*

FREDERICK MONDERSON

Medinet Habu: Mortuary Temple of Rameses III 335-337
Memphis 706-713
Milky Way 349-350
Merenptah (1221-1214 B.C.) 103
Messenger, the 278-279
Michalowski 124, 384-387
    (No Date)
Medinet Habu 96
Mentuhotep's temple at Deir el Bahari 279
Min 719
Mineral Resources 37
Mortuary temples of pharaohs 67
Mortuary temple, essential components 433-434
Moscati 58
    Faces of the Ancient Orient 58
Moses- Who was he? 350-351
Mother and child 431
Muller, Wolfgang 123, 129, 132
    (1963) "Egyptian Art" in *Encyclopedia of Art*
Mummy bandage 619
Mummies, color of 763
Mummy gods 646
Murder 430-431
Murnane, William C. 118, 128, 132
    (1983) *The Penguin Guide to Ancient Egypt*
Murray, Margaret 108, 109, 125, 138
    (1957) *The Splendor that was Egypt*
Murray, John 132
    (1888) *Handbook for Egypt* 132
Music 637-639
Myers 221, 423-425
    (1900) *Oldest Books in the World*
Myth of Isis and Osiris 691
Narmer 64
    Palette 64
    Macehead 64
Naumann, Emil 464, 468-469
    (1882) *The History of Music*

EGYPT ESSAYS ON ANCIENT KEMET

Nefertiti 343
Nefertiti and Nefertaris 343-344
Negative Confessions 774
New Kingdom 337-342
Newberry 93
    "An Egyptian Gardener: The Tomb of Nakht"
Nile River 592-593
Nkrumah, Kwame 207
Nomes 63
Nomarch responsibility 65
Nubian temples 441
Obenga, Theophile 92
    (1992) *Ancient Egypt and Black Africa*
Obelisk 622
Offerings 432
Open Middle Kingdom Court 129
Opet Festival 136, 157, 158
    Purpose of Luxor Temple 150
Osiris to Jesus, compares 672-673
Osiris cult 673
Osiris myth 523
Owens, Major 202
Palermo Stone 348-349
Panel Discussion 408-413
Parks, Gordon 42
    (1990) *Voices in the Mirror* 42
Payne, Elizabeth 92, 113
    (1964) *The Pharaohs of Ancient Egypt*
Pemberton, 238
    (1992) *Ancient Egypt: Architectural Guide for Travelers* 203
Period of Egyptian history
Petrie, W.M.F. 468, 478
    (1923) *Egyptian Religion*
    (1940) *Wisdom of the Egyptians*
    (1909) "Egyptian Art" 372-375
Pier, Garrett Chatfield 112, 129
    (1916) "The Great Temple of Amon-Ra at Karnak" in *Art and Architecture*

Plants 36
Plato (427-347) 55
    Republic 55
    Philosophers as Kings 55
Poem of Pentaurt 95
Polygamy 570
Polyglot 81, 462
    (1965) *Egypt Travel Guides*
Portman, Ian 103, 119, 123, 153
    (1989)
Precession, 26,000 years 25
    The Conquest of Peru 74
Priesthood 722-723
    Priesthood activities 770
Prisse D'Avennes 133
Proscription of Amon 92-93
Psalms 41
Psychology of the Egyptian 742
Purification of the king 747
Pylon, First 114
    Second 119
    Third 123
    Fourth 123-124
    Fifth 127
Pyramids of Gizeh 731-735
Pyramids with inscriptions (Pyramid Texts) 717-718
Queen 104
    Aahmes-Nefertari 106-107, 108, 694
    Aam (Mentuhotep's Mother) 693
        Achtothes (Intef's Mother) 693
    Hatshepsut
    Mother Moore 690
        Influences 690
    Nefertari 107
    Nzinga 695
    Neithhotep 693
    Teti-Sheri 104, 107
    Tiy 695

EGYPT ESSAYS ON ANCIENT KEMET

       Queen Mother 697
Queen Mother Crown 694
Question of truth 773
Quirke, Stephen 113, 125
       (1992) *Ancient Egyptian Religion*
Ra and Osiris conflict 778
Ra's popularity 771-772
Racist pseudo-scientific writers 202
Rameses II (1279-1213 B.C.) 83
       Temple of, 118
       Regiments 95
Rawlinson 213
       (1896) *The Story of Egypt*
"Records of the ancient records" 103
Religion of Egypt, message of 60
Religious (Books) inscriptions 718
Religious ritual in Book of the dead 522-523
Resurrection 432-433
Richards, Donna (Merimba Ani) 57
Richardson, Dan and Karen O'Brien 238, 241
       (1991) *Egypt: The Rough Guide*
       African Thought Systems 74
Riley, Dorothy Winbush 42
       (1995) *My Soul Looks Back* 42
Robbins, Gay 107
       (1993) *Women in Ancient Egypt*
Rogers, J.A. 464
       (1944) *Sex and Race*
Rohl, David 117
       (1995) *Pharaohs and Kings: A Biblical Quest*
Ruffle 121, 243
       (1977) *The Egyptians*
Sacrifice 514
Sacrifice, purpose of 768-769
Sacramental ideas and usages 764-766
Sacred Lake 134
Sakkara 257-259, 698-705
Salvation 6465-646

FREDERICK MONDERSON

Samkange, Stanlake 106
    (1971) *African Saga: A Brief Introduction to African History*
Sanctuary 129
    Approach to 677-678
Sauernon 85, 114
    (1962) *A Dictionary of Egyptian Civilization*
Scarab at the Sacred Lake 516-517
Scheel, Bernard 381
    (1989) *Egyptian Metalworking and Tools*
Scholz, Piotr 89
    (1997) *Ancient Egypt: An Illustrated Historical Overview*
Schwaller de Lubicz 149
Science 225-226
Scientific American Supplement 137
    (1899, Feb 25) 137
    (1899, Dec 30) 137
Second birth 517
Selden, John (1584-1654) 75
Senmut 109, 271-272
Serpent, role of 519-520
Shaw, Ian and Paul Nicholson 79, 82
    (1995) *The Dictionary of Ancient Egypt*
Shishak 115
Showker 102
    (1989)
Silence, notion of 520
Simpkins 114, 134
    (1982) *The Temple of Karnak*
Sister marriage 670-671
Sites for temple erection 637
Slander, laws against 521
Smith, Fay 82, 238
    (1991) *Egypt at Cost*
Sneferu 715-716
Soul, construction of the 520-521
Soul, parts of the 742-746
South African Iron Ore industry 25
Speech, pros and cons 521

EGYPT ESSAYS ON ANCIENT KEMET

Sphinx 732
Spirit world 672
Steindorff and Seele 89
    (1971) *When Egypt Ruled the East*
Strabo 466
Stratham 72
Summary of trip 775-779
Sun God cleanliness 736-739
Swearing 563-564
Syncretism 89
"Table of Offerings" 768
Taharka 115-117
    Column 116
Tarik es-Sudan 390
Tarik al-Fattah 390
Temple building foundation 153
Temple of Isis 597-607
Temple of Mut in Asher 147
Temple plans 642
"Tety the Handsome" 104
Theban Triad 79, 85
Thoth 564, 568-569
Thutmose I 123, 127
    Thutmose I and Valley of the Kings 280
Thutmose III 123, 127, 132-133
Time-Life Books 134
    (1997) *What Life Was Like on the Banks of the Nile*
Tithes 636
Tomb, the 565-566
    Purpose of 228-229
Tomb decoration 678
Tomb painting 432
Traunecker, Claude and Jean Claude Golvin 99
    (1992) *History and Archaeology*
Treachery 566
"Tree of Life" 566-568
Trees 37
Trigger, Et. Al. 136, 138

FREDERICK MONDERSON

Triumph over death 772
Types of temples 770
Unas' Pyramid 279
Uniters of Egypt 69
Unity of the Deity
Uraeus 569
Vercoutter, Jean 99-100, 101
    (1992) *The Search for Ancient Egypt*
Violence 569
Washington, D.C. Cultural Institutions 60
Watterson, Barbara 100
    (1997) *The Egyptians*
Wayne, Scott 238
    (1990) *Egypt and the Sudan*
Weigall, A.E.P. B. 80, 86, 145, 147, 151
    (1910) (1996) *A Guide to the Antiquities of Upper Egypt*
Weighing of the heart 621
Weights and measures 278
West, J.A. 148-149, 154
    (1987)
Western Desert – Nabta Playa 25
Western Necropolis 68
White, J.E Manchip 244
    (1970) *Ancient Egypt: Its Culture and History*
    (1980) *Everyday Life in Ancient Egypt*
Wilkinson, J. Gardner 55, 89
    (1850) (1996) *The Architecture of Egypt* 55
Wilkinson, Alix 91, 107
    (1971) *Ancient Egyptian Jewelry*
Williams, Bruce 51, 375-376
    (March 1, 1979) "World's Earliest Monarchy" 51
Williams, Chancellor 86, 244
    (1996) *The Destruction of Black Civilization*
Wilson, J.A. 58, 475, 476, 477l 484
    (1959?) *The Culture of Ancient Egypt* 58
Winnie Mandela 690
Wisdom of Ancient Egypt 487-488

www.ingramcontent.com/pod-product-compliance
Lightning Source LLC
Chambersburg PA
CBHW061946300426

44117CB00010B/1243